Penguin Books

THE

Time Out

LONDON

GUIDE

The *Time Out London Guide* is more than a book for tourists. We have covered the spectrum of London life, from the Changing of the Guard to the best of the street markets. All the information you need to find your way round the city is listed and we've added our own reviews of the best and worst that London has to offer. Every place listed in the guide has been visited and we are not afraid of giving an honest review – what it's like, what to see and what to avoid. By the time you've used the guide, you'll know London like a Londoner.

For 20 years, *Time Out* magazine has been covering what's happening in London, from museums, nightclubs and shopping to the theatre, pubs and cabaret clubs. If something is worth seeing (or avoiding) in the city, we know about it. During those two decades *Time Out* magazine has never lost its position as London's best-selling, most knowledgeable and best-written listings guide. It should be stressed that the information we give you is impartial. No organization or enterprise has been listed in this guide because its owner or manager has advertised in our publications. That's why our opinions carry weight in London. If you disagree with our views, we want to know. Readers' comments on places they have visited are welcomed. Let us know what you think of London.

Edited and designed by
Time Out Publications Limited,
134-146 Curtain Road, London
EC2A 3AR
(729 5959)

Publisher
Tony Elliott
Managing Director
Adele Carmichael
Financial Director
Kevin Ellis
Managing Editor
Hayden Williams

Art Director
Paul Carpenter
Art Editor
Ashleigh Vinall

Advertisement Director
Lesley Gill
Sales Director
Mark Phillips

Cover Illustration
Lo Cole

THE Time Out LONDON GUIDE

Penguin Books

PENGUIN BOOKS

Published by the Penguin Group
27 Wrights Lane, London W8 5TZ, England
Viking Penguin Inc., 40 West 23rd Street, New York, New York 10010, USA
Penguin Books Australia Ltd, Ringwood, Victoria, Australia
Penguin Books Canada Ltd, 2801 John Street, Markham, Ontario, Canada, L3R
1B4
Penguin Books (NZ) Ltd, 182–190 Wairau Road, Auckland 10, New Zealand

Penguin Books Ltd, Registered Offices: Harmondsworth, Middlesex, England

First published 1990
10 9 8 7 6 5 4 3 2 1

Made and printed in Great Britain by
Richard Clay Ltd, Bungay, Suffolk

Contents

Big Band Dancing
At The Ritz

Fridays and Saturdays are enchanted evenings in The Ritz Palm Court. Here, in a venue steeped in history, we turn the clock back to the authentic big band sounds of the 20's, 30's and 40's.

For sheer romance, there's nothing to compare in the whole of London. As you enjoy a delicious supper you can sense the presence of the rich and brilliant from the Palm Court's illustrious past: Tallulah Bankhead, Noel Coward, Nancy Astor, Evelyn Waugh, Charlie Chaplin and a host of others.

Join us. Dance the night nostalgically away. The big bands start at 10 pm and play on till 1 am to turn your theatre evening into an occasion to treasure.

Please phone for a reservation: 01-493 8181

THE RITZ
PICCADILLY·LONDON

IT'S BEEN AN OVERNIGHT SENSATION FOR OVER 80 YEARS.

Introduction

The **London Guide** is our third comprehensive handbook for visitors to London. Naturally, we cover all of the capital's famous attractions, but we also take a critical look at them. We're honest about both the sights worth seeing and the ones that are living on hype and reputation. In addition, we review hundreds of lesser-known, unusual and local places in the centre of town and out in the suburbs. What's more, we tell you what's happening in the capital – exhibitions, events and pageants – between April 1990 and March 1992.

We've taken a journalistic, not a passive approach to this Guide. The 2,000-plus detailed reviews are based on our recent experiences of London's attractions, restaurants, shops and places of entertainment. *Time Out* magazine has been London's main listings magazine for over 20 years. We've drawn on that experience and used our expertise from the *Time Out Guides* to Eating Out, Shopping & Services and Sport in London, to create a handbook with a depth and breadth that no other volume on London can match. Furthermore, most guide books are only reissued after several years. Because our information is being constantly updated, and since the Guide is completely re-written every two years, it includes details about what's happening in London before it happens.

Since 1989, we've produced not just one Guide, but two. Complementing the *London Guide*, the annual *Time Out Guide to London for Visitors* is a magazine specifically written with tourists in mind. It has features and previews of events and entertainments during the London summer season, and is available from newsagents between May and September.

PRACTICAL GUIDE

However interesting we've tried to make this Guide, we also want it to be usable. Addresses, telephone numbers, opening times, admission prices, discounts and credit are all printed in full. And, as far as possible, we've given details of facilities, services and events.

All the information we list was checked and correct when we went to press – but please bear in mind that owners and managers can change their arrangements at any time. We urge you to phone, before you set out, to check opening times, the dates of exhibitions, admission fees and other important details.

PRICES

The prices we've listed throughout the Guide should be used as guidelines. Fluctuating exchange rates and inflation can cause prices, in shops especially, to change rapidly. Occasionally, you may encounter a rip-off, so if prices or services somewhere vary greatly from those we've quoted, ask whether there's a good reason. If not, go elsewhere. Then, please let us know. We try to give the best and most up-to-date advice, so we always want to hear if you've been overcharged or badly treated.

TELEPHONES

On 6 May 1990 London's telephone numbers changed. The prefix is no longer 01 for London. Now it's 071 for Central London and 081 for the rest of Greater London. If you're in a 071 area you'll have to dial 081 and then the phone number to reach someone in the suburbs; in a 081 area dial 071 for Central London. If you're phoning to somewhere in the same band, no prefix is needed. All calls in Greater London are charged at the local rate. British Telecom define Central London as being within four miles/6.5km of Charing Cross, but the band veers out to include Docklands and Hampstead. Of course, all the telephone numbers we list are given with the appropriate prefix. If you don't know which area you're in, consult the operator on 100, quoting your number. BT will be making a fortune from wrong numbers – don't add to it. For an explanation of the British phone system, *see chapter* **Essential Information**.

CREDIT CARDS

In the listing entries marked **Credit**, we've used the following abbreviations: **A:** Access/Mastercard; **A/c:** Account customers; **AmEx:** American Express; **BT:** Book Tokens; **CB:** Carte Bleu; **DC:** Diners Club; **EC:** Eurocheque/card; **ER:** En Route; **GM:** Grand Metropolitan; **HP:** Hire Purchase; **JCB/JCT:** Japanese credit cards; **LV:** Luncheon Vouchers; **SC:** Store's own card; **TC:** Travellers' cheques in any currency; **£TC**, **$TC**, **frTC**, etc: Travellers' cheques in sterling, US dollars, French francs, or other specified currencies; **THF:** Trust House Forté Gold Card; **V:** Visa/Barclaycard.

Discover "the loveliest castle in the world."

A magnificent mediaeval castle set in a motionless lake and surrounded by acres of rolling parkland. For centuries Leeds Castle has been a secret jewel in the 'Garden of England'.

Now you can discover the enchanting woodland garden and Culpeper Flower Gardens. Wander through the aviaries with rare collections of exotic tropical birds. Explore the maze and secret grotto. Or visit the castle greenhouses. Even play our superb nine-hole golf course.

The castle itself dates from AD 857 and was converted into a royal palace by Henry VIII. It contains a wealth of fine paintings, antiques and mediaeval tapestries. The Gate Tower houses a unique museum of ornamental dog collars.

There's also a fine restaurant in a 17th century tithe barn. Here 'Kentish Evenings' are held every Saturday and private functions on other evenings, by arrangement.

**Come for the day, any day, from 1 April to 31 October (11 am to 5 pm*).
Or weekends between November and March (12 pm to 4 pm*).**

(Also daily in Christmas Week)

Leeds Castle, nr. Maidstone, Kent.   Tel: (0622) 765400

Nightmare on Tooley Street.

the London Dungeon

For a positively spine chilling day out, why not visit the worlds first medieval horror museum, just for the thrill of it.
OPEN 10 am every day (inc Sundays)
DISCOUNTS FOR GROUPS, STUDENTS & OAP

the London Dungeon

BENEATH LONDON BRIDGE STATION, TOOLEY STREET, SE1. 01-403 0606

Sightseeing

The insider's guide to the monuments, tourist traps and sights that every visitor to London comes to see.

London's big sights – the palaces, parks, museums and landmarks you've heard about before your visit – each attract between half a million and four million visitors a year. This can make sightseeing murder in high summer and at Christmas. We offer advice on the best times to go, and how to make the most of your time there. We've also taken a critical look at the tourist traps you'll find it hard to avoid. The **London Tourist Board** *(071 730 3488)* can help with any further enquiries.

One way of getting to grips with London is to take a bus tour of the main sights *(see below* **Bus Tours***).* But it has to be said that pre-packaged coach parties are the bane of the liberated tourist. Fortunately, fewer tours operate on Mondays and many follow a daily pattern. About 20 coach-loads invade Westminster Abbey at 9.30am, then crowd out Buckingham Palace's Changing of the Guard ceremony at 11.15am. After blitzing St Paul's Cathedral, they end up, like many an historical pariah, at the Tower of London. Come evening, they dine at the Cockney Pride before being forced to watch an Andrew Lloyd-Webber musical. So, now you can plan to avoid them.

If your stay in London falls during college term-time, sights that attract school parties are best visited after about 2.30pm. College vacations coincide with the main tourist seasons, so do your sightseeing as early in the day as possible, avoiding weekends, to miss the hordes of families and student groups.

Battersea Park
Albert Bridge Road, SW11 (081 871 7530). Sloane Square underground/Battersea Park or Queenstown Road BR/19, 39, 44, 45, 49, 130, 137, 170 bus. Open dawn to dusk daily. This riverside park was opened in 1858 by Queen Victoria and it's now one of London's liveliest open spaces. Its most famous feature, the Festival Gardens, were one of the main attractions of the 1951 Festival of Britain. There are excellent sports and children's facilities and many events take place through the year. The Easter Sunday Parade is held here, as are Bank Holiday fun-fairs (for both *see chapter* **London by Season**) and a Christmas circus (mid-December to mid-January). The graceful Buddhist Peace Pagoda overlooking the Thames was built by Japanese monks and nuns, and is the focus for an Anglo-Japanese Festival (8 July 1990) and for Hiroshima Day (8 August). *Boating lake. Garden for the disabled. Zoo.*

HMS Belfast
Morgan's Lane, Tooley Street, SE1 (071 407 6434). London Bridge underground/BR/river boat from Tower Pier (Feb-Oct daily, Nov-Jan Sat, Sun 30p adult,
20p under-16s). **Open** *Mar-Oct* 10am-6pm daily, *Nov-Mar* 10am-4.30pm daily. **Admission** £3.50 adults; £1.75 under-16s, OAPs, students, UB40s; free under-5s; £9 family ticket (2 adults and 2 children). **Credit** A, AmEx, DC, £TC, V.
The liberal parent's moral dilemma: should kids play with guns and visit a battleship? Well, the people who do go, love to pose on the prow before the 6in/152.4mm guns, or stand on the bridge and pretend that they're full-steaming ahead to sink the *Scharnhorst*. This 1938 cruiser is an uncompromisingly physical tourist attraction: there is effort – and hence fun, unless you're wheelchair-bound – involved in getting round it. To see the cabins, gun turrets, sick-bay, brig and boiler-room with its gleaming instruments (polished daily), you must negotiate gangways, airlocks and near-vertical stairways. It's interesting to see the domestic problems of living in a battleship and the technical inge-

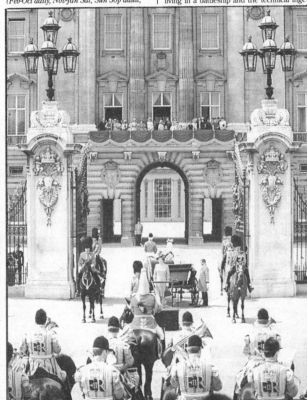

Buckingham Palace *is essential viewing and the* **Changing of the Guard** *ceremony is especially popular. The Palace was less palatial when Queen Victoria first took up residence in 1837: hundreds of windows wouldn't open, the servants' bells didn't work (bad luck, that) and the drains were faulty. John Nash had turned Buckingham House into a regal home for George IV, but unfortunately in 1913 his work was inelegantly refaced in the style of an insurance company (look at the Pearl Assurance building, Holborn). The most flattering view is from the bridge over St James's Park lake. The Royal Standard flies when the Queen is at home and there are regular opportunities to royalty spot (see chapter* **London by Season***). Thousands of guests attend Summer Garden Parties in the grounds.*

nuity involved – the pipes carrying oil, water, sewage and so on are colour-coded. The exhibition on D-Day (in which the *Belfast* took part) is a reminder of why the ship was built. *See also chapter* **The World Wars**. *Group discount. Shop. Wheelchair access on main deck only.*

British Museum

Great Russell Street, WC1 (071 636 1555; recorded information 071 580 1788). Holborn, Russell Square or Tottenham Court Road underground/7, 8, 14, 19, 22, 24, 25, 29, 38, 55, 68, 73, 77, 77A, 134, 188 bus. **Open** 10am-5pm Mon-Sat; 2.30-6.30pm Sun; 6-9pm first Tue every month. **Admission** free daily; £5 6-9pm first Tue every month; *exhibitions* £2 adults; £1 children, OAPs, students, UB40s. **Credit** (shop only) A, AmEx, DC, £STC, USA currency, V.
Perhaps the greatest museum of all – and the busiest. Four million visitors a year

traipse around to gaze at the Egyptian mummies and the Elgin Marbles (the Parthenon friezes that the Athenians want back). To see all the other treasures, from the dawn of civilization to the present, would take years and many people visit regularly. Just as well it's still free. For full details and advice on when best to visit, *see chapter* **Museums**.
Café & licensed restaurant (10.30am-4.15pm Mon-Sat; 3-5.15pm Sun).. Cassette tours of the library, Elgin marbles 60p. Guided tours (105 mins; £5 inclusive). Lectures. Shop. Toilets for the disabled. Wheelchair access by prior arrangement

Buckingham Palace

SW1 (071 930 4832). St James's Park or Victoria underground. **Only Queen's Gallery** (*see chapter* **Art Galleries**) and **Royal Mews** (*see below*) open to the public. *See* **picture and caption**.

When the **Palace of Westminster** *(including the* **Houses of Parliament***) was cleaned recently, its architectural beauty was fully revealed. In 1834 all of the old Palace except Westminster Hall burnt down, to be replaced by this neo-Gothic edifice, designed by Charles Barry and Augustus Pugin: it was completed in 1852. There are 1,000 rooms, yet our politicians are so cramped-up, most share an office. Despite the new televizing of the House of Commons, it's still best to see the politicians – often dozing off – from the Visitors' Galleries. If you haven't an advance ticket and don't want a long wait, go after 5pm. Don't take noisy children, since the fancy-dressed warders take their job very seriously. One even told off the then Governor of the Falkland Islands for resting on the balcony rail during a debate on the Falklands War.*

Changing the Guard

Buckingham Palace *SW1. St James's Park undergroundor Victoria underground/BR.* **Times** *Apr-Jul* 11.30am daily; *Aug-Mar* 11.30am alternate days.
Tower of London *Tower Hill, EC3. Tower Hill underground.* **Times** *Apr-Jul* 11.15am daily; *Aug-Mar* 11.30am alternate days.
Whitehall *SW1. Charing Cross underground/BR.* **Times** 11am, 4pm Mon-Sat; 10am, 4pm Sun.
Get in position very early to see London's most famous ceremony – it's invaded by coach parties. The gates of Buckingham Palace are the best spot, but you can see the regiment of foot guards, resplendent in scar-

let tunics, blue trousers and Bearskin hats, as they march along their routes. At 11am the St James's Palace Old Guard is inspected in Friary Court, setting off at 11.15am down The Mall to Buckingham Palace. Meanwhile, the Duty Guard is lined up in front of the Palace, and the New Guard leaves Wellington Barracks on Birdcage Walk at 11.27am and marches to the Buckingham Palace forecourt. There, the sentries are changed. In bad weather, or during major State events, the ceremony is called off. For the smaller and slightly less-crowded Whitehall ceremonies, mounted Life Guards ride from Hyde Park Barracks via Hyde Park Corner and The Mall to the Whitehall side of Horse Guards Road; the afternoon ceremony is an inspection only. There's a more modest guard change at the Tower of London.

Guinness World of Records

The Trocadero, Piccadilly Circus, W1 (071 439 7331). Piccadilly Circus underground. **Open** 10am-10pm daily. **Admission** £4.20 adults; £3.25 OAPs, students; £2.60 under-16s; under-4s free.. **Credit** A, AmEx, DC, £TC, V.
An exhibition of superlatives doesn't make a superlative exhibition, but the Guinness World of Records is reasonable as tourist-traps go; plus it's open (and quietest) in the evening. Trivia from the *Guinness Book of Records* (itself included as the best-selling copyright book) is well suited to this kind of display. The exhibits can often be effective – a popular one compares your vital statistics with the world's tallest and fattest people – but they're a bit tacky and tatty. We've received complaints about the lack of inter-active exhibits and about the hefty prices: young families can find it prohibitively expensive. There's also lots of reading to do, which is tiresome for children, who otherwise find it fun. Unsurprisingly, Guinness books are heavily promoted in the shop, and you can't avoid the whining voice of David Frost accompanying you around.
Group discounts. Shop. Toilets for the disabled. Tour by prior arrangement. Wheelchair access.

Hyde Park *is central London's largest park and its 340 acres/136 hectares of greenery are a wonderful place to relax. You can row a boat on the Serpentine lake, trot a horse down Rotten Row, gaze at paintings in the Serpentine Gallery (see chapter* **Art Galleries***) or simply collapse into a deckchair and, on summer Sundays, listen to military bands. But the cafés are poor value and the park should be avoided after dark. Marble Arch, at the north-east corner, was once the entrance gate to Buckingham Palace. On Sundays, at Speaker's Corner near the arch, ranting – and often hilarious – soapbox orators revive the flagging tradition of British free-speech.*

Hampstead Heath

NW3 (Parliament Hill 071 485 4491; Kenwood House 081 340 5303; Golder's Hill 081 455 5183). Belsize Park or Hampstead underground/Gospel Oak or Hampstead Heath BR/24 bus. **Open** *24 hours daily.*
A stroll through this huge semi-landscaped heath rejuvenates both the tired Londoner and the visitor. On weekends it's packed with everyone and their dog, granny, child and frisbee. The 800 acres/320 hectares of rolling, wooded hills have been popular with the literary set for close on 200 years – **Keats' House** (*see chapter* **Museums**) is near the southern end. Unfortunately it is also popular with less savoury characters after dark. There are woodland bathing ponds, the mansion **Kenwood House** (*see chapters* **Georgian London** and **Music: Classical & opera**), funfairs on Easter, May and August

Bank Holidays and remarkable views from Parliament Hill (*see below* **Bird's-Eye Views**). Bring a kite and catch the Hampstead air. *See also chapter* **Local London**.
Toilets for the disabled at the running track. Three swimming ponds.

Houses of Parliament

Parliament Square, SW1 (071 219 4272). Westminster underground. **Open** *when the Houses of Parliament are in session House of Commons Visitors' Gallery 2.30-10pm (or later) Mon-Thur; 9.30am-3pm Fri. House of Lords Visitors' Gallery 2.30pm until debating ends Mon-Wed; 3pm until debating ends (6-10pm) Thur; 11am (approx) until debating ends (about 4pm) Fri. Victoria Tower Gardens 7am-dusk daily.* **Admission** *free for both houses.*
See **picture and caption**.

See also chapters **The West End** and **Victorian Times**.
Educational facilities/worksheets. Post Office. Shop. Guided tour (Mon-Thur only) or a seat at Question Time (2.30pm Mon-Thur) by prior arrangement with your MP or embassy. Toilets for the disabled. Wheelchair access.

Hyde Park

W2 (071 262 5484). Hyde Park Corner, Knightsbridge, Lancaster Gate, Marble Arch or Queensway underground. **Open** *5am-midnight daily.*
See **picture and caption**.
See also chapter **Sport & Fitness**.
Playground. Toilets for the disabled.

Kensington Gardens

W8 (071 724 2826). Bayswater, High Street Kensington, Lancaster Gate or Queensway underground. **Open** *5am-dusk daily.*
These royal gardens merge into Hyde Park, but have a distinct, more formal character. Kensington Palace is the London home of Prince Charles and Princess Diana, and the State Apartments (*see chapter* **Tudors & Stuarts**) are a good fix for royalty addicts: the Court Dress Collection includes Princess Di's wedding outfit. In the grounds

you can wander through the sunken garden and the Orangery. The statue of Peter Pan, near the modest Italian fountains, is modelled on a girl not a boy, and was erected to delight children, which it does. There are daily puppet shows in the summer and a playground near Black Lion Gate.
Toilets for the disabled.

Kew Gardens

See **Royal Botanic Gardens**.

London Dungeon

28-34 Tooley Street, SE1 (071 403 0606). London Bridge underground/BR. **Open** *Apr-Sept 10am-6.30pm daily; Oct-Mar 10am-5.30pm daily (last admission 1 hour before closing).* **Admission** *£4.50 adults; £2.50 under-16s, OAPs; £3.50 students; free entry for disabled in wheelchairs.* **Credit** *£TC.*
Peer through corroded railings in a dank, dark, musty-smelling maze of towering arches and eerie nooks. You'll see medieval torture scenes and hear the screams as the rack tightens. But why do the tortured models possess all the realism of shop dummies? The location, artefacts, atmosphere and basic idea of presenting the grizliest moments of British history are brilliant and most people enjoy their visit. But the Dungeon is let down by dated effects, a lack of surprise-shocks, and robotic devices that are feeble, compared to **Rock Circus** (*see below*). The £250,000 Great Fire simulation was pathetically dull. Still, the coach parties pile through, overdosing on tat from the

shop. The Dungeon is least busy before noon, Monday to Wednesday. The tacky café is uncomfortable and the washrooms could also be greatly improved.
Café. Group discount. Shop.

London Planetarium & Laserium
Marylebone Road, NW1 (071 486 1121; Laserium 071 486 2242; credit card 071 379 4444). Baker Street underground. **Open** *Planetarium* 12.20-5pm daily; school holidays 10.20am-5pm. *Laserium* performance times vary. **Admission** *Planetarium* £2.95 adults; £1.90 under-16s; £2.30 OAPs; £2.65 students, UB40s. *Combined ticket with Madame Tussaud's* £6.65 adults; £4.25 under-16s; £5.25 OAPs. *Laserium* £3.95 adults; £2.95 under-16s; £3.45 students. **Credit** (telephone booking only) A, AmEx, DC, V; (shop) £TC.
Wallow in an inclined padded seat (very welcome after shuffling around in queues at Madame Tussaud's), gaze up into the large dome-ful of stars, and prepare for a lesson in astronomy. The audio-visuals are enjoyable but presume you know nothing about the universe, as do the know-it-all brats that comment loudly. The habits of planets, stars and time itself are demystified with sophisticated projections onto the inside of the dome. Sit on the immediate right as you enter. Before the show, you pass at your own speed through a substantial gallery on astronomy and space travel. In the evening the Planetarium reopens as the Laserium. Lasers are projected to a rock music soundtrack, but it's not as good as you might expect.
Café. Shop.

London Zoo
Regent's Park, NW1 (071 722 3333). Camden Town underground. **Open** *Apr-Oct* 9am-6pm daily; *Nov-Mar* 10am-dusk daily. **Admission** £4.30 adults; ; £3.50 students, OAPs; £2.60 under-16s; free under-4s. **Credit** A, £TC, V.
The British obsession with pets gets serious at London Zoo, where you can adopt an octopus for £15 or an elephant for £6,000. A hissing cockroach (£15) makes an eloquent gift. The money goes towards looking after the beast for a year and your name will go on a plaque by its enclosure. Try to get into position for one of the feeding times. Of the 8,000-plus animals, the koalas and Rosie the Rhino (the first to be hand-reared in Europe) are the current hits. It's a marvelous place for kids and there's even a Children's Zoo (*see chapter* **Children's London**). A big fuss is brewing about the Zoo enlarging into 7 acres/2.8 hectares of Regent's Park, provoking largely unfounded fears of it becoming a theme park. Zoo buildings include some gems of modern architecture; look for the 1934 Penguin Pool and the Aviary by Lord Snowden. Avoid the tacky shop and expensive café.
Education centre. Films. Group discount. Lectures. Restaurant. Shop. Toilets for the disabled. Wheelchair access.

Madame Tussaud's
Marylebone Road, NW1 (071 935 6861). Baker Street underground. **Open** *Jul, Aug* 9am-5.30pm daily; *Sept-Jun* 10am-5.30pm Mon-Fri; 9.30am-5.30pm Sat, Sun. **Admission** £5.20 adults; £3.45 under-16s; £3.95 OAPs. *Combined ticket with Planetarium* £6.65 adults; £5.25 OAPs; £4.25 under-16s. **Credit** £STC.

To be measured up for a wax model in **Madame Tussaud's** *is proof of fame. Ideas for new figures come from a poll of visitors. Public heroes are a mixed bag: Bob Geldof, Joan Collins, even Mrs Thatcher (now retouched four times, to catch up with her image changes). It emerges that British politician Edwina Currie is as hated as Charles Manson and that TV's Anneka Rice beats Jack the Ripper for inclusion in the Chamber of Horrors. While there are several eerie likenesses, George Bush and the royal family make convincing wax dummies. It's permanently crowded, attracting 2.7 million visitors a year, so there's a long wait to get in.*

See **picture and caption.**
Café. Group discount. Toilets for the disabled. Wheelchair access by prior arrangement.

National Theatre (NT)
South Bank, SE1 (071 928 2252). Waterloo underground/BR/Riverbus. **Open** 10am-11pm Mon-Sat. **Tickets** *Olivier and Lyttleton Theatres* £2-£15.50; *Cottesloe Theatre* £5-£8.50. **Credit** A, AmEx, DC, V.
Daringly unlike the classical edifices that most national theatres tend to be, Denys Lasdun's 'concrete bunker' (as Prince Charles calls it) has been controversial since it opened in 1976. But it is a dramatic sight, especially when floodlit. It's a visitor-friendly place, with open foyers, bars, restaurants, free music, exhibitions and riverside views. The fascinating, but too-restricted, backstage tour shows why actors bemoan the lack of character. Yet the place does foster many brilliant productions in its three well-designed theatres. *See chapter* **Theatre.** *Bookshop. Car park. Group discount (071 620 0741). Front seats for the partially sighted by prior arrangement. Infra red audio for the hard of hearing. Restaurants & cafés. Tour by prior arrangement (071 633 0880). Toilets for the disabled. Wheelchair access.*

Nelson's Column
Trafalgar Square, WC2. Charing Cross underground/BR.
This familiar landmark to Admiral Horatio Nelson has recently had a tonne of pigeon droppings cleaned off it. Consider the unintentional insult when you feed the birds that flock here. Erected in the 1840s, the 170-foot/51-metre Corinthian column dominates the Square (named after Nelson's naval defeat of Napoleon). Clambering over Landseer's sentinel lions at the base is a great

Piccadilly Circus *is a perennial meeting point for Londoners and the cliché place to be photographed to prove you've experienced London. Flower girls used to sell their blooms 'down Dilly' until World War II, but later it became identified with the swinging sixties and then with punks charging to be photographed. The Circus's big draws are the huge neon advertisements and Alfred Gilbert's fountain statue* **Eros** *(see chapter* **Victorian Times***). No longer isolated in Nash's traffic circus, the aluminium statue points its arrow at the tourists who are wondering quite what to do now they're there amid the uncollected rubbish.*

sport for children. The square is a focus for demonstrations (including a permanent anti-apartheid picket of South Africa House) and New Year celebrations around the Christmas Tree (*see chapter* **London By Season**).

Piccadilly Circus
SW1. Piccadilly Circus underground.
See **picture and caption**.

Regent's Park
NW1 (071 486 7905). Baker Street, Camden Town, Great Portland Street or Regent's Park underground. **Open** *park* 5am-dusk daily; *Queen Mary's Rose Garden, tennis courts* 7am to 30 mins before dusk daily; *playgrounds* 10.30am to 30 mins before dusk daily.
The strikingly beautiful Regent's Park is the centrepiece of John Nash's master street-plan for the Prince Regent. It's bordered by Regent's Crescent, Palladian mansions and

the Regent's Canal. A former hunting ground of Henry VIII, it's still a lively place in the summer with puppet shows, band-stand music, softball players and pantaloon-clad actors in the **Open Air Theatre** (*see chapter* **Theatre**). Controversially, London Zoo is planning to encroach further into the north of the park.
Car park. Running track. Softball and football at weekends. Toilets for the disabled.

Richmond Park
Surrey (081 948 3209). Richmond underground/BR. **Open** *pedestrians* 24 hours daily; *traffic Mar-Nov* 7am to 30mins before dusk daily, *Dec-Feb* 7.30am to 30mins before dusk daily.
The best countryside-substitute in London, Richmond Park is the largest city park in Europe, with 2,500 acres/820 hectares of land. It is ideal for rambling, cycling and rid-

ing, and is also a home to wildlife. You can spot foxes scurrying about at dusk, badgers barging through the undergrowth and herds of red and fallow deer in the enclosures. The Isabella Plantation is a particularly beautiful watery, woodland garden enclosed by Lord Sidmouth in 1831. A wide variety of birds can be seen among the azaleas and rhododendrons.
Two public golf courses by Roehampton Gate (081 878 8432) £5 Mon-Fri; £7 Sat, Sun. Horseriding facilities at Roehampton Riding Stable (081 876 7089).

Rock Circus
London Pavillion, Piccadilly Circus, W1 (071 734 7203). Piccadilly Circus underground. **Open** 10am-9pm Mon-Thur, Sun; 10am-10pm Fri, Sat. **Admission** £4.20 adults; £3.15 under-16s, OAPs, students, UB40s; free under-5s ; £11.60 family (2 adults, 2 children). **Credit** £STC.
Rock fans just love to get close to their heroes, so seeing a bionic wax model of Madonna or the Beatles in a revolving theatre must be far out, yeah? There's no denying the eerie sensation when the lips and singing synchronize, or when Bruce Springsteen thrashes at his guitar and a drugged-up Janis Joplin stands up to sing. But when a video backing was used it rather undermined the whole concept. The spectre of a robotic middle-aged Tim Rice as compère raises the biggest laugh. Before this half-hour 'concert' (there's no re-entry after the show), you're free to wander past static tableaux of wax pop stars. The cleverest bit is the headphones, which pick up infra-red signals and play the song from whichever display you're looking at. It's all good fun. Sadly there's only a tiny snippet of one song from each artist and the intrusive, patronizing commentary by DJ Paul Gambaccini is a big turn-off. The shop is stocked with books, T-shirts and the grossest souvenir we've come across: a £155 leather jacket bearing the pink Rock Circus logo.
Group discount. Shop. Toilets for the disabled. Wheelchair access.

Royal Botanic Gardens, Kew
Kew Road, Richmond, Surrey (081 940 1171). Kew Gardens underground/Kew Bridge BR/27, 65 bus. **Open** *Nov-Jan* 9.30am-4pm daily; *Feb* 9.30am-5pm daily; *Mar* 9.30am-6pm daily; *Apr-mid Sept* 9.30am-6.30pm Mon-Sat, 9.30am-8pm Sun and Bank Holidays; *mid Sept-Oct* 9.30am-6pm daily. **Admission** £1 adults; 50p under-16s, OAPs; under-5s; free for educational groups of students or school children; £8 season tickets. **Credit** (shop only) A, £TC, V.
See **picture and caption**.
See chapter **The River & Docklands**.
Café, restaurant. Shop. Toilets for the disabled. Tour by prior arrangement. Wheelchairs for loan. Wheelchair access.

Royal Mews
Buckingham Palace Road, SW1 (071 930 4832). St James's Park or Victoria underground/BR. **Open** 2-4pm Wed, Thur. **Admission** £1 adults; 50p under-16s, OAPs, students; free for disabled. **No credit cards**.
The best appointed garage in town, the Mews houses the royals' coaches, and pram-like carriages along with their livery. Unexpectedly, there's a new exhibit, the first since 1910. This is the Australian State Coach, donated on the Australian bicenten-

nial. The gilt palmwood of the Coronation Coach, the immaculately-groomed horses and the craftsmanship of the sleek black landaus make the Mews one of the capital's better value collections, but the exhibits are abysmally labelled, if at all.
Shop. Wheelchair access.

Royal Opera House
Bow Street, WC2 (071 240 1066). Covent Garden underground. **Open** *box office 10am-8pm Mon-Sat.* **Tickets** *ballet £8.50-£41; opera £12-£82.* **Credit** *A, AmEx, DC, V.*
This elaborate theatre was built in 1858 by Edward Barry and is home to the Royal Opera and Royal Ballet Companies. All operas are sung in their original languages. The redevelopment of Covent Garden (1993-96) will dramatically improve the Opera House's Victorian facilities and complete Covent Garden Piazza with colonades in Inigo Jones's original style. Public pressure has reduced the scale of office space and ensured that much of Barry's Floral Hall is saved. *See also chapters* **Dance** *and* **Music: Classical & Opera.**
Bar. Opera and ballet education officers. Shop. Toilets for the disabled. Wheelchair access.

St James's Park
The Mall, SW1 (071 930 1793). St James's Park underground. **Open** *dawn to dusk daily.*
Compact, beautiful and convenient for the West End, St James's also has the best vistas of any central park. The buildings of Westminster and Horse Guards Parade peep above the trees, and along The Mall are Admiralty Arch, Nash's Carlton Terrace, the Duke of York's column and two palaces: Buckingham and St James's. The Park is ideal for a civilized stroll, particularly on late afternoons in summer, to see the wildfowl (the famous pelicans have been imprisoned in London Zoo, because they kept eating the pigeons). It's also a good place to glimpse the Queen's guards passing through for the **Changing of the Guard** (*see chapter* **London By Season**). It's most special at night, when you can steal across to the bridge to see Buckingham Palace floodlit over the lake.
Playground. Restaurant. Toilet for the disabled at Marlborough Gate.

St Paul's Cathedral
EC4. (071 248 2705). St Paul's underground. **Open** *doors open 7.30am-6pm daily; galleries, crypt and ambulatory 10am-4.15pm Mon-Fri, 11am-4.15pm Sat.* **Admission** *cathedral free (donation requested; £1 adult, 60p under-16s); galleries £2 adult, £1 under-16s; crypt £1.10 adult, 55p under-16s; ambulatory 60p adults, under-16s free.* **Credit** *(shop only) A, £TC, V.*
See **picture and caption.**
See also chapters **The City** *and* **Tudors & Stuarts.**
Guided tours. Shop. Wheelchair access to main body and crypt.

Space Adventure
64-66 Tooley Street, SE1 (071 378 1405). London Bridge underground/BR/boat to London Bridge Pier. **Open** *May-Oct 10am-6pm daily; Nov-Apr 10.30am-6pm daily.* **Admission** *£3.95 adults; £2.50 under-16s, OAPs, students, UB40s.* **Credit** *A, £TC, V.*
The idea of experiencing space travel using Europe's largest flight simulator is brilliant. But tackling the asteroid belt in this abysmal

tourist-trap really is barely more exciting than being jolted about in a tube train. The movements rarely match the image on the screen, which follows a 20-minute 'storyline', narrated by a ludicrously camp pilot. Adding to the embarrassment, even adults get presented with a bravery certificate for 'rescuing' a stricken spaceship. The tiny display of weakly-animated monsters from the TV show *Dr Who*, has some kitsch appeal, but is very insubstantial. Although it's well positioned by *HMS Belfast* and London Dungeon, this is one to avoid for its expense, short length, and tackiness. We've yet to receive a positive opinion of it.
Group discount. Shop.

Tower of London
Tower Hill, EC3 (071 709 0765). Tower Hill underground/Fenchurch Street BR/15, 42, 78 bus. **Open** *Mar-Oct 9.30am-6pm Mon-Sat,*

2-6pm Sun; *Nov-Feb 9.30am-5pm Mon-Sat.* **Admission** *£4.80 adults; £2 under-15s; free under-5s ; £3 OAPs, students, UB40s, disabled.* **Credit** *(shop only) A, £TC, V.*
See **picture and caption.**
See also chapter **The Middle Ages.**
Gift shop. Group discount. Guided tours (free, every half hour for one hour). Restaurant. Wheelchair access with assistance (1 adult admitted free if assisting disabled person).

Trocadero
Piccadilly Circus, W1 (071 439 1791; Food Street 071 287 4224). Piccadilly Circus underground **Open** *10am-midnight daily; Food Street noon-midnight Mon-Sat, noon-11pm Sun.* **No credit cards.**
Most visitors end up in this tourist-trap because of where it is and because the **Guinness World of Records** (*see above*) is on the top floor. But apart from chainstores,

The **Royal Botanic Gardens** *is one of the most beautiful places in London and it attracts thousands of visitors, particularly on summer weekends. But it has a lot to offer in the winter, too. The climate is constant in Decimus Burton's glorious iron and glass Temperate House and Palm House (the latter reopens in late 1990). It's not a park, but a scientific institute and important horticultural research is carried out here (it has the world's largest collection of orchids, for instance). The gardens were first laid out in 1751 by William Chambers, also responsible for the famous Pagoda. Destruction by the storm of 1987 has offered a unique opportunity for modern landscapers. The Marianne North Gallery was designed by North to display her paintings of rare flora and this remains the Gardens' quietest corner.*

*Dominating London's skyline, **St Paul's Cathedral** is Christopher Wren's masterpiece. His epitaph on the floor below the dome states, 'If you seek his monument, look around you,' and looking up you'll spot people on the Whispering Gallery straining to hear reverberating voices above the muffled din of the crowds. Beyond that are the viewing galleries (see **Bird's-eye Views**). Happily, some of the tower blocks that mar the setting of St Paul's are to be demolished and Prince Charles has fought for the replacements to be classically inspired. Ironically, Wren's design was popularly hated when first built for being so modern.*

11.15am (choral), 3pm (choral), 5.45pm (organ recital), 6.30pm (free singing). **Admission** *Nave* free; *Royal Chapels* £2.20 adults; 50p under-16s; £1.10 OAPs, students, UB40s (except free 6-7.45pm Wed). *Abbey Museum* £1.60 adults; 40p under-16s; 80p OAPs, students, UB40s. **Credit** (shop only) A, AmEx, £STC, V.
See **picture and caption**.
See also chapter **The Middle Ages**.
Guided tour Mon-Sat, £6 (information 071 222 7110). Shop (9.30am-5pm Mon-Sat).
Wheelchair access.

BIRD'S-EYE VIEWS

The beautiful London riverscape Canaletto painted may have been destroyed, but the city's skyline and panoramas are still magnificent. The river views are good, but there's nothing like climbing up above the rooftops for the sights suddenly to become obvious above the maze-like confusion at street-level. Here's how to put London into perspective.

Alexandra Park
Muswell Hill, N22 (park 081 444 7696; general information 081 365 2121). Wood Green underground/Alexandra Park BR/144, 144A, W2, W3, W7 bus. **Open** 24 hours daily.
The 'Palace' (known universally as Ally Pally), at the top of this steep north London park, once housed the BBC's first television studio, but it's now a multi-purpose entertainments centre. The view over London is impressive and clear. Many events take place here; *see chapter* **London by Season** for the low-down on the funfairs on Easter, Whitsun and August Bank Holidays and for the free firework display on 5 November, Guy Fawkes Night.
Boating lake. Café. Pitch and putt golf course. Ski slope (dry). Zoo.

Cabair Helicopters
Elstree Aerodrome, Elstree, Herts (081 953 4411). Elstree Thameslink BR (will pick up free; phone from station/Edgware underground then taxi. **Open** by appointment only. **Fare** four people £460 inclusive. **Credit** A, AmEx, DC, £TC, V.
Get your own back on those damned pigeons by invading their airspace to sample an exclusive view of London. You can choose your own hour-long helicopter route, but most favour the loop past Heathrow, then along the Thames past Hampton Court, Kew Gardens, Westminster, the City and Greenwich to the Flood Barrier; going back via north-east London. At 1,000ft/305m the sights seem alarmingly close, and the ride's great for photography. You need to book a week or so ahead in summer and chance the weather (*see chapter* **Essential Information**), but there's only a refund if the flight's cancelled.

Constable Gallery, Victoria & Albert Museum
Henry Cole Wing, Victoria & Albert Museum, Exhibition Road, SW7 (071 938 8500/recorded information 071 938 8441). South Kensington

---

there's nothing here but **Food Street**. This pseudo-Eastern food mall is more imaginative than most fast food emporia – the dim sum and satay are palatable and inexpensive. But two minutes' walk away is the genuine Chinatown (*see chapter* **The West End**). Eat there instead.

Victoria & Albert Museum
Cromwell Road, SW7 (071 938 8500; recorded information 071 938 8441). South Kensington underground, 14, 30, 74, 503 or C1 bus. **Open** 10am-5.50pm Mon-Sat, 2.30-5.50pm Sun. **Admission** free (donation requested: £2 adults; 50p child, students, OAPs, UB40s). **Credit** (shop only) A, AmEx, £TC, V.
The V&A's seven miles/11.2km of galleries bulge with the world's greatest collection of decorative and applied arts. In addition to the treasures procured during the Empire are a popular dress collection, Raphael's cartoons and frequently-controversial exhibi-

tions. For full details *see chapter* **Museums**; *see also below* **Bird's-Eye Views**.
Gallery talks (2.30pm daily). Lectures. Restaurant (10am-5pm Mon-Sat; 2.30-5.30pm Sun). Shop. Touch sessions for the visually impaired. Wheelchair access.

Westminster Abbey
Dean's Yard, SW1 (071 222 5152). St James's Park or Westminster underground/3, 11, 12 bus. **Open** *Nave* 8am-6pm Mon, Tue, Thur-Sat; 8am-7.45pm Wed; between services on Sunday. *Royal Chapels* 9am-4pm Mon, Tue, Thur, Fri; 9am-4pm, 6-7.45pm Wed; 9am-2pm, 3.45-5pm Sat. *Chapter House, Pyx Chamber, Abbey Museum* 10.30am-4pm daily. *College Garden* Apr-Sept, 10am-6pm Thur; Oct-Mar, 10am-4pm Thur. *Brass Rubbing Centre* (071 222 2085) 9am-5pm Mon-Sat. **Services** *Mon-Fri* 7.30am, 8am, 12.30pm, 5pm (choral); *Sat* 8am, 9.20am, 3pm (choral); *Sun* 8am, 10am (choral),

underground/14, 30, 74, 503, C1 bus. **Open** 10am-5.50pm Mon-Sat; 2.30-5.50pm Sun. **Admission** free (donation requested: £2 adults; 50p child, OAPs, students, UB40s). **Credit** (shop only) A, AmEx, £TC, V.

A similar vantage point to Queen's Tower (*see below*), but at roof-top level, looking from Harrods to Westminster. Inside the gallery, you're surrounded by Constable's paintings of a more rustic landscape. *See above* **Victoria & Albert Museum** and *chapter* **Museums**. *Gallery talks (2.30pm daily). Guided tours. Lectures. Restaurant (10am-5pm Mon-Sat, 2.30-5.30pm Sun). Shop. Touch sessions for the visually impaired. Wheelchair access.*

Golden Gallery, St Paul's Cathedral

EC4 (071 248 2705). St Paul's underground. Open gallery 10am-4.15pm Mon-Fri; 11am-4.15pm Sat. Admission £2 adults; £1 under-16s.

The rickety steps up to the 281ft/85m Golden Gallery of St Paul's Cathedral (*see above*) are not for those with vertigo; it's crowded and you can't turn back. But you'll see why the view was used for spotting fires all over the City during the blitz in World War II (*see chapter* **The World Wars**).

Greenwich Hill

Greenwich Park, Charlton Way, SE10 (081 858 2608). Greenwich, Blackheath Village or Maze Hill BR/53, 177, 180, 286 bus/boat to Greenwich pier. Open pedestrians 5am-dusk daily; traffic 7am-dusk daily.

The symmetry of the view from the Wolfe Monument on top of this hill is stunning. East meets West at the Prime Meridian in the Old Royal Observatory, which bisects the two wings of Wren's Naval College and the Thames's loop around the Isle of Dogs. The tall Canary Wharf development will soon become centre (or rather, annoyingly off-centre) stage. *See also chapter* **The River & Docklands**.

Hungerford Foot Bridge

between Victoria Embankment, WC2, and the South Bank, SE1. Embankment, Charing Cross or Waterloo underground/BR.

Brave the thunderous noise of the trains on Hungerford Bridge for a river panorama from Cleopatra's Needle past the City to the Festival Hall. It's unforgettable at night. The next span downstream, **Waterloo Bridge**, offers a more all-round view, taking in both Westminster and the City.

London Hilton

Roof Restaurant and Bar, London Hilton, Park Lane, W1 (071 493 8000). Hyde Park underground. Open restaurant 7-10.30am, 12.30-2.30pm, 7pm-2am Mon-Sat; 7-10.30am, 11.30am-3pm, 6.30-11pm Sun; bar noon-3pm, 5.30pm-2am daily. Credit A, AmEx, DC, £TC, V.

Get vertigo on a full stomach 28 floors up in London's highest restaurant and bar. Sadly, it's the only high-rise restaurant in town. Sip one of the hotel's 70 cocktails as you wander round to see London fanning out below. It's spectacular at night. *See also chapter* **Accommodation**.

Jackets in restaurant (men); no denims. Wheelchair access.

Monument

Monument Street, EC2 (071 626 2717). Monument underground. Open Apr-Sept 9am-6pm Mon-Fri, 2-6pm Sat, Sun (last admission 20 mins before closing); Oct-Mar

9am-4pm Mon-Sat. **Admission** 50p adults; 25p under-16s, OAPs.
See **picture and caption.**
See also chapter **Tudors & Stuarts**.

Parliament Hill

Hampstead Heath, NW3 (071 485 4491). Kentish Town underground, then C2 bus/Hampstead Heath or Gospel Oak BR. Open 24 hours daily.

Dubbed Kite Hill because kite-fliers exploit its exposed position at the south end of Hampstead Heath, Parliament Hill offers a peach of a view. On a clear day you can take in the whole of central London (there are boards outlining landmarks), even to Crystal Palace in the south-east. The hill was to have had a beacon in 1605 to signal Guy Fawkes' attempt to blow up Parliament – hence the name.

Café. Toilet for the disabled at athletic track.

Primrose Hill

NW3 (071 486 7905). Chalk Farm or Camden Town underground/31, 74 bus. Open 24 hours daily.

Not a primrose in sight, but on a fine day a cluster of the central-London landmarks are visible from this hill, with London Zoo in the foreground and Crystal Palace in the distance. In winter, the wooded park is a venue for scudding toboggans; there are fireworks on Bonfire Night and druids conduct pagan rites at the Autumn Equinox (1pm, 23 Sept 1990 and 1991). *See chapter* **London by Season**.

Queen's Tower

Imperial College, Imperial Institute Road, SW7 (071 589 5111). South Kensington underground. Open Jul-Sept (college vacation) 10am-6pm daily. Admission 80p. **No credit cards.**

A trot up this Victorian tower makes a

The **Tower of London** *has been a castle, a palace and a prison during its long history and it remains one of the capital's most important sights. It's expensive, but it's not a rip-off. It takes several hours to see it all, from William the Conqueror's White Tower to the ravens and polite Beefeaters, who give free tours. Traitor's Gate and the Bloody Tower allow a glimpse into Britain's macabre history, but the Bowyer Tower's torture display could be bigger and less static. Of the many armour museums, the remarkable oriental display is the one your tired body won't regret exploring. When ogling the Crown Jewels, it's best to go round the no-stopping, close-up route first, then linger on the balcony – or go late on when its far quieter. Otherwise, Mondays and weekday mornings are the best time to visit.*

rewarding (but exhausting) diversion if you're visiting the South Ken museums: it's one of the best vantage points in town. Queen's Tower is the last remnant of the neo-Gothic Imperial Institute, demolished amid outrage in 1956. Recuperate from climbing up the 324 steps by gazing at an unimpaired view across Hyde Park to the West End.

St Edward's Tower, Westminster Cathedral

Victoria Street, SW1 (071 834 7452). St James' Park underground or Victoria underground/BR. **Open** *Apr-Oct* 9.30am-5pm daily. **Admission** 70p adult; 30p children, OAPs, students. **No credit cards.**

For a superb perspective of the Palace and Abbey of Westminster, take the lift up the 273ft/83m campanile (bell tower) of Westminster Cathedral. This striking, striped building is the headquarters of the British Catholic church (*see chapters* **Early 20th Century** and **Survival**). Unforgivably, Victoria Street's tower blocks obscure much of the West End and City, but the vistas south over the Thames and west across Kensington are impressive. Sadly, no signs show what is where.
Shop. Wheelchair access.

Tower Bridge

SE1 (071 407 0922). Tower Hill or London Bridge underground/BR. **Open** *Apr-Oct* 10am-6.30pm daily; *Nov-Mar* 10am-4.45 pm daily (last admission 45mins before closing). Closed Good Friday, Christmas Eve, Christmas Day, Boxing Day and New Year's Day. **Admission** £2.50 adults; £1 children, OAPs. **Credit** (shop only, but shop sells tickets) A, £TC, V.

The up- and down-stream panoramas from the overhead walkways give about the best of the many views of the City, and they are unique for viewing the Thames's bridges and Docklands. The only hazard in the safe, glazed walkways is the running about of kids. There are useful platforms and portholes for picture-taking and panels clearly indicate the landmarks. For the admission price, you also get interesting displays and a museum. *See also chapter* **The River & Docklands.**
Group discount. Shop. Wheelchair access.

BUS TOURS

Bus tours vary from 90-minute drives through the City of London and the West End, passing all the main sights; to full-day tours which include lunch and visits to places such as the Tower of London. Guides can make or break a tour. Below we've listed tours whose guides have the London Tourist Board qualification, the Blue Badge; phone for details of pick-up points. Pre-recorded commentaries are often inaudible and get out of synch when you're stuck in traffic. Live guides are better and can answer questions, but are more expensive.

Westminster Abbey *looks more French than English. But it's been the wedding, coronation and burial church of British royalty since the Saxon Edward the Confessor. He built the first church on this site before the Normans invaded and his tomb's still here. The jumble of statues and tombs of the great, the good and the rich have a unique charm. The ceiling stonework is breathtaking. Everyone heads for Poets' Corner, Statesman's Aisle, the chapels and the Coronation Chair, the graffitti on which is by Georgians who despised anything Gothic. Visit after late morning midweek to avoid a crush. On Wednesday evenings you can take photographs.*

Can-Be-Done

9-11 Kensington High Street, W8 (081 907 2400). Kensington High Street underground. **Open** 9am-8pm Mon-Fri. **Credit** AmEx, £STC. This flexible company can arrange anything within reason – from a tour of famous cemeteries to a visit to the Houses of Parliament. Tours are arranged and priced individually.

Cityrama

British Rail Yard, Silverthorne Road, SW8 (071 720 6663). **Open** 24 hours daily. **Journey time** 90 mins. **Fares** £7 adult, £3.50 4-14 years; free under-4s. **Credit** £TC. This is only satisfactory if you want a very basic tour. The individual headsets broadcast an uninformative general commentary on the most obvious sights. We decided to abandon the commentary and admire the spectacular vistas from the top deck. The

bus sets off from five different departure points every 30 minutes from 9am to 6pm daily in the summer and from 9am to 4.30pm in the winter.
Headsets with commentaries in eight languages.

Evan Evans

27 Cockspur Street, SW1 (24 hours 071 930 2377). Charing Cross underground/BR. **Open** 8am-6.30pm daily. **Fares** *half day* £11.50-£16 adults; £9.50-£14 3-17 years; *full day (including lunch)* £33 adults; £29 3-17 years; free under 3. **Credit** A, AmEx, DC, £TC, V.

This company picks up from over 30 hotels each morning. It offers seven tours around London including all the big attractions, for a full or a half day. Cruises on the Thames are also available. The air-conditioned coaches are new and comfortable. It's essential to book in advance.

Out on the town?

If anybody knew how to have a great time on the town, it was King Kong.

But the truth is, there never was a King-size Kong. Just a jointed steel model, eighteen inches high, with rubber muscles and a skin of rabbit fur.

Yet he was a monster at the box office. Why?

You can find out for yourself at MOMI, the Museum of the Moving Image.

Here, you can see how the camera has been tricking us for the best part of a century. See how special effects can make a superhero fly. Even take to the air yourself. Try your hand at animation. Or read the news. You can also trace the entire history of film and television.

And meet MOMI's professional actors in the shape of Hollywood directors, Soviet guards and 1930s cinema staff.

The Museum of the Moving Image, an epic adventure on both sides of the screen.

Open Tuesdays to Saturdays 10am–8pm. Sundays and Bank Holidays 10am–8pm June–September. Sundays and Bank Holidays 10am–6pm October–May. Closed Mondays and 24th–26th December.

At the South Bank, near Waterloo. Tel: 01-401 2636.

 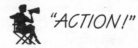

Frames Rickards

Offices and main pick-up: 11 Herbrand Street, WC1 (071 837 3111; night service: 071 951 8344). Russell Square underground. **Open** 7.30am-7.30pm daily. **Journey time** 2 hours 30 mins. **Fares** £8 adults; £6 under-16s. **Credit** A, AmEx, £TC, V.

The tours are run twice daily in summer, starting at 10am and 2.30pm; and once a day in winter (at 2.30pm). Coaches are air-conditioned single-deckers and the trips take in all the major sights, from the West End to Tower Bridge, but with taped commentaries.

London Tour Company

Offices: 618 Linen Hall, 162-168 Regent Street, W1 (enquiries 071 734 350, 8am-midnight daily). Oxford Circus or Piccadilly Circus underground. **Meeting point** Coventry Street, W1. Piccadilly Circus underground. 9am-8pm daily. **Journey time** 90 mins. **Fares** £6 adults; £2 children; £4 OAPs, students. **Credit** A, AmEx, DC, £TC, V.

This panoramic tour of the major sights in an open-top bus runs every 30 minutes. The bus travels nearly 20 miles/32km around the City of London and Westminster, with a taped blurb about the sights. It also runs full-day tours.

London Transport Sightseeing Tour

offices: Wilton Road Coach Station, Wilton Road, Victoria, SW1 (071 227 3456). **Open** *Oct-Mar* 8am-6pm daily; *Mar-Oct* 7.30am-8pm daily. **Meeting points** Victoria Station, SW1; Marble Arch, W1; Haymarket, SW1 (Piccadilly Circus underground); Baker Street, NW1. 10am-4pm daily. **Journey time** 90 mins. **Fares** £7 adult; £4 under-16s; £1 reduction if in advance from a Travel Information Centre (*see above* **London Regional Transport**). **Credit** A, AmEx, DC, £TC, V.

The tour sets off every 30 minutes and takes in all the main sights. Traditional red double-decker buses are used; in summer they're open-topped. The live commentary is full of interesting facts, but sit underneath one of the loud speakers if you want to hear it clearly. *Language buses in French and German.*

William Forrester

1 Belvedere Road, Guildford, Surrey (0483 575401).

William Forrester is a wheelchair user who in 1989 deservedly became the first ever winner of the London Tourist Board's award for the best London Guide of the year. Will's tours, booked in equal numbers by both 'able-bodied' and disabled people are informative, racy and always highly entertaining. Will's services include itinerary-planning, illustrated lectures on British Heritage, study tours, consultancy on access and mini-bus tours. For information and fees contact him on the above number.

WALKING

Walking in London is often the fastest way to travel around and certainly the best method of getting to know the city. From a central point such as Leicester Square, you can walk to Piccadilly, Soho, Covent Garden, or Trafalgar Square in less than ten minutes. But like most European cities, London is not very safe to walk around late at night.

Anecdotes about the hidden corners and lesser-known aspects of London are the speciality of the many walking tours available. The entertainment level depends upon the guide's personality and knowledge. Prepare yourself for a couple of hours' walking, and the likelihood of ending up in a pub. Tours are listed throughout this Guide, but for details consult the Around Town section of *Time Out* magazine, phone the London Tourist Board on *071 730 3488* or contact the following companies.

Citisights
(081 806 4325).

City Walks of London
(071 937 4281).

Historical Tours
(081 668 4019).

Londoner Pub Walks
(081 883 2656).

London Walks
(081 441 8906).

The **Monument** *is London's reminder of the Great Fire of 1666. The 202-foot/60.6-metre height of the Wren-designed column is equal to its distance from the Pudding Lane bakery where the five-day blaze apparently started. Sadly, it's become isolated amid faceless office blocks. Even St Paul's is slightly obscured, but the riverscape and bits you can see make the climb worthwhile.*

London by Season

It doesn't always rain. It's not always crowded. Its traditions are often odd. London's like that. It's just that time of year.

What have Londoners pencilled into their diaries for the year? Big occasions, such as the Lord Mayor's Show, Wimbledon, the Proms and the London to Brighton Rally spring instantly to mind. But most people who live in the city probably haven't even heard of the more obscure traditions. From the vicar who conducts a service on horseback to livery company officials counting swans, odd individuals are trying to keep the modern world at bay. It makes a great spectator sport. The **London Tourist Board (LTB)** book *Traditional London* has the low-down on British ceremonies from the bizarre to the familiar. Indeed, the LTB information service, *071 730 3488* (9am-6pm Mon-Fri), will help with enquiries on almost any event.

ROYALTY SPOTTING

Tabloid newspapers around the world make it their business, and so yours, to know every personal detail of the Windsor family. Despite all the purple prose on Prince Charles' inner-city crusades or Fergie's lack of dress sense, royalty fanatics are still not satisfied. They come to London to see the Princess Di kissing babies or the Queen riding side-saddle in fancy dress at Trooping the Colour. Royalty spotting is a fine art and the *court circular* columns of the *Times*, *Daily Telegraph* and *Independent* newspapers

list exactly where the 136th-in-line-to-the-throne is opening a supermarket. They also give warning of **State Visits**, when a carriage procession takes HMQ and the visiting supremo from Victoria Station, down Whitehall and the Mall to Buckingham Palace.

FESTIVAL TIME

London is a world city, so during your visit there's bound to be an international festival going on. The major multi-media bean feasts are held at the **Barbican** and **South Bank Arts Centres** (for both *see chapters* **Music: Classical & Opera**). The South Bank hosts the annual **Summerscope Festival of Performing Arts** (July-Aug), which includes film, theatre, dance, classical music and the International Festival of Street Music (in July). A huge, nationwide Japan festival will be colonizing lots of venues in late 1991, phone 071 603 4600 for details.

London's own multi-ethnic culture has spawned the **Notting Hill Carnival** and **Chinese New Year** celebrations. Smaller or more specialist festivals are usually spread over several venues: the **Greenwich Festival** in mid June (081 854 8888); the July **City of London Festival** (071 248 4260); the **Soho Jazz Festival** (late Sept-early Oct, 071 437 6437); the March **Camden Jazz Festival** (081 860 5866); and the **Capital Radio Music Festival** (mid June-mid July, 071 380 6100), which is Europe's biggest music festival.

London's authorities enjoy nothing more than banning buskers, but you can see jugglers, magicians and break-dancers doing their stuff legally. Weekday lunchtime shows (May-Oct, 12.30-2pm) liven up **Broadgate Arena**, EC2 (*071 588 6565*); *see chapter* **The City**. Every day, crowds mob performers at **Covent Garden Piazza**, WC2 (*071 836 9136*); *see chapter* **The West End**. The August **International Street Performers Festival** is held in the Covent Garden Piazza and 1990 (12-22 Sept) will see the first biannual **Covent Garden International Festival** (*071 497 8903*).

Trooping the Colour *(listed under* **Summer***) is the Queen's official birthday party – her real one is in April. The ceremony originates in the battlefield tradition of raising a regiment's colours for identification. If you can't get a ticket, there might be some left for the rehearsals, but after three decades' practice, the Queen does not rehearse. The royal party can be glimpsed during its procession down the Mall, leaving Buckingham Palace at 10.40am. The route to Horseguards Parade is always packed but you may find space on the Green Park side of the Mall. Back home in the palace by 12.30pm, the Queen takes to the balcony to watch an air force jet zoom past at about 1pm.*

FREQUENT EVENTS

Ceremony of the Keys
HM Tower of London, EC3 (071 709 0765). Tower Hill underground. **Date** daily (except

Christmas Day), 9.35-10.05pm. **Maximum** in party *Apr-Oct 7; Nov-Mar 15* . **Admission** free, by prior arrangement.
'Halt! Who comes there?' 'The keys.' 'Whose keys?' 'Queen Elizabeth II's keys' 'Pass the keys. All's well.' This laborious routine of locking-up the Tower of London has been going on every night for 700 years. Ticket holders should arrive by 9.35pm. The real business begins at 9.53pm exactly, when the Chief Warder leaves the Byward Tower and it's all over before the clock chimes 10 o'clock and the Last Post is sounded. Apply for tickets, giving alternative dates, at least two months in advance in writing with a stamped addressed envelope to: The Resident Governor, Queen's House, HM Tower of London, EC3.

Changing the Guard
Buckingham Palace *SW1. St James's Park or Victoria underground.* **Times** *Apr-Jul* 11.30am daily; *Aug-Mar* 11.30am alternate days.
Tower of London *Tower Hill, EC3. Tower Hill underground.* **Times** *Apr-Jul* 11.15am daily; *Aug-Mar* 11.30am alternate days.
Whitehall *SW1. Charing Cross underground/BR.* **Times** 11am, 4pm Mon-Sat; 10am, 4pm Sun.
These famous – and very photogenic – ceremonies derive from the days when the lifeguards directly protected the monarch's life. Now they entertain both tourists and British patriots, who just love the uniforms and royalist imagery. For full details *see chapter* **Sightseeing**. There's yet another ceremony at **Windsor Castle** (*see chapter* **Trips Out of Town**; phone *0753 868286* for details).

Druid Ceremonies
Summer Solstice *Stonehenge, A303, Wiltshire or White Horse Stone, A229, 2 miles east of Aylesford, Kent.* **Date** Dawn (about 4.30am), 21 June 1990, 1991.
Autumn Equinox *Primrose Hill, NW3.* **Date** noon 23 Sept 1990, 1991.
Spring Equinox *Tower Hill Terrace, EC3.* **Date** Noon 21 Mar 1991; 20 Mar 1992.
Admission free.
By day the druids are probably bank clerks, but come a solstice or equinox, they don white, hooded gowns and worship the seasons. You can witness their rites at these symbolic sites (Primrose Hill and Aylesford are allegedly the burial barrows of, respectively, Boudicca and Horsa); for details on Stonehenge *see chapter* **Trips out of Town**. Don't expect to see any bloody sacrifices – unless the hippies get set on by the police.

Funfairs
Alexandra Park, *Muswell Hill, N22 (081 365 2121).* Wood Green *underground/Alexandra Park BR/144, 144A, W2, W3, W7 bus.*
Battersea Park *Albert Bridge Road, SW11 (081 871 7530).* Sloane Square *underground/Battersea Park or Queenstown Road BR/19, 39, 44, 45, 49, 130, 137, 170 bus.* **Hampstead Heath** *NW3 (071 485 4491). Belsize Park or Hampstead underground/Gospel Oak or Hampstead Heath BR/24 bus.*
Dates *Spring Bank Holiday* Fri 25-Mon 28 May 1990; Fri 24-Mon 27 May 1991. *Aug Bank Holiday* Fri 24-Mon 27 Aug 1990; Fri 23-Mon 26 Aug 1991. *Easter* Fri 29 Mar-Mon 1 Apr 1991; Fri 17-Mon 20 April 1992.
Admission Free.
On the many rides at these fairgrounds you

can regurgitate your candyfloss and disorientate yourself you've just won. All the funfair works are here, from dodgems to merry-go-rounds.

Gun Salutes
Hyde Park, W2 and the Tower of London, EC3. **Dates** 2 Jun (Coronation Day); 10 Jun (Duke of Edinburgh's birthday); 16 Jun (Trooping the Colour, *see below* **Summer**); 4 Aug (Queen Mother's birthday); 6 Feb (Accession Day); 21 Apr (the Queen's birthday); the State Opening of Parliament (*see below* **Autumn**). If the date falls on Sun, salutes are fired on following Mon.
Admission free.
The cannons are primed on important royal occasions for gun salutes. What happens is the King's Troop of the Royal Horse Artillery make a mounted charge through Hyde Park, set up the guns and fire a 41-gun salute (noon, except for Opening of Parliament); then, not to be outdone, at the Tower of London, the Honourable Artillery Company fires a 62-gun salute at 1pm.

Swearing on the Horns
Ye Olde Wrestlers Tavern, 98 North Hill, N6 (081 340 1846). Highgate underground. **Dates** One day in May, Jul, Sept 1990, 1991, phone to confirm. **Starts** 8.30pm. **Admission** free.
Cattlemen of old on their way to market used to swear not to 'drink small beer when you can get strong' which seems sensible enough. Today you can make the same oath before a 'court'. Visitors are fined for looking too miserable.

Given London's litter problem, mention of a tradition of **Road Sweeping** *(listed under* **Summer***) would make you incredulous. After the swearing in of the new master of the Vintners' livery company, a procession goes from the Vintners' Hall to the church of St James Garlickhythe, Garlick Hill, EC4. It's headed by huge porters in white smocks who sweep the ground so the members of the company can pass untroubled by the inevitable fast-food cartons and tin cans. It's all over very quickly, so get on site early.*

SUMMER

Beating the Bounds
from All-Hallows-by-the-Tower to St Dunstan's, Idle Lane, EC3 (071 488 4772). Tower Hill underground. **Date** Ascension Day Thur 24 May 1990, Thur 9 May 1991; starts 3pm, service about 5pm, meet Tower of London Beaters 7pm. **Admission** free.
The boundaries of each London parish were once reaffirmed by an annual ceremony. Even today, the boys of St Dunstan's School march from All-Hallows, carrying sticks to beat the boundary marks around the Tower of London. One is in the Thames, so a poor lad is dangled outside the boat to beat the water, before they head back to St Dunstan's via Custom House. The Lord Mayor usually attends the 5pm service at All-Hallows. Every third year (1990), the Tower of London yeomen meet the beaters at about 7pm for some good-natured jeering. It's quite a spectacle.

Chelsea Flower Show
Royal Hospital, SW3 (071 834 4333). Sloane Square underground. **Dates** Tue 22-Fri 25 May 1990; Tue 21-Fri 24 May, 1991. **Open** 8am-8pm Tue-Thur; 8am-5pm Fri.
Admission (*RHS members only* Tue, Wed £10, after 3pm £7). *Members* Thur, Fri £6; *non-members* Thur £15, after 4pm £7; Fri £12. The world-famous gardening extravaganza, laid on by the Royal Horticultural Society, is a prime chance for the green fingered to turn the less able green with envy. The garden gnomes add an authentically British flavour.

Beating Retreat

Horse Guards Parade, Whitehall, SW1 (071 930 4466). Westminster underground or Charing Cross underground/BR. **Dates** Tue 5 Jun 6.30pm; Wed 6, Thur 7 Jun, 9.30pm; Tue 12-Thur 14 Jun 1990, 6.30pm. Similar dates for 1991, phone to confirm. **Admission** 5-7 June £3-£7; 12-14 June £4-£9 1990.

The 'retreat', beaten on drums with pomp by the Household Division, refers to the setting of the sun, not of the British Empire. The soldiers, on foot and on horseback, provide a great splash of colour and some rousing band playing. The floodlit evening performances are very atmospheric. The later 'Sounding Retreat' is similar, and each year is performed by a different regimental band. Ticket from *Premier Box Office (071 930 0292).* There are often tickets left on the day of performance.

Kenwood Lakeside Concerts

Kenwood House, Hampstead Lane, NW3 (071 734 1877). Archway, Golders Green or Hampstead underground/210 bus. **Dates** Every Sat from Jun to Aug. **Tickets** book on *071 379 4444,* or on the night two hours before the concert begins. **Admission** £3-£7.50.

A picnic at one of these outdoor concerts of popular classics can make an idyllic summer evening. For details, *see chapter* **Music: Classical & Opera**.

Derby Day

Epsom Racecourse, Epsom, Surrey (03727 26311). Epsom BR. **Date** Wed 6 Jun 1990; Wed 5 Jun 1991. **Open** 8am. **Race** 3.30pm. **Admission** £5-£40. **Credit** V.

This world-famous horse race over the flat is responsible for millions of bets and a few heart attacks. The poorer classes are herded into one enclosure; those with big wallets, stripey blazers and braying voices strut about in another.

Royal Academy Summer Exhibition

Royal Academy, Burlington House, Piccadilly, W1 (071 439 7438). Green Park or Piccadilly Circus underground. **Dates** 9 Jun-19 Aug 1990; 8 Jun-18 Aug 1991. **Open** 10am-6pm daily. **Admission** *1990* £3 adult; £1.50 under-18s; £2 OAPs, students, UB40s; *1991* £3.20 adults; £1.60 under-18s; £2.10 OAPs, students, UB40s.

Something of an artistic pick 'n' mix with loose criteria for determining what's exhibited. It's an amateur event, so would-be Bacons and Warhols rub canvasses with precise architectural elevations and tediously tasteful watercolour landscapes.

Trooping the Colour

Horse Guards Parade, Whitehall, SW1 (information 071 930 4466). Westminster or Charing Cross underground/BR. **Date** Sat 16 Jun 1990; 15 Jun or 22 Jun 1991. **Rehearsals** 2 Jun, 9 Jun 1990; 3 Jun, 10 Jun or 9 Jun, 16 Jun 1991. *Starts* from Buckingham Palace 10.40am. **Tickets** Write by end of Jan to *The Brigade Major (Trooping the Colour), Household Division, Horse Guards, SW1.* **Admission** about £7.50 – two per person. **No credit cards**.
See **picture and caption**.

Royal Ascot

Ascot Racecourse, Ascot, Berkshire (0990 22211). Ascot BR. **Dates** 19-22 Jun 1990;

similar period 1991, phone for details. **Open** 11am until last race. **Admission** £3-£17.

The Queen and assorted other royals travel down the racecourse in open pram-like carriages each day before the cup races are run. Ascot institution, Gertrude Shilling has retired from parading her ludicrously-designed hats, but like Frank Sinatra, she's bound to return for an encore one year.

Polesden Fair & Open-Air Theatre

Polesden Lacey, Dorking, Surrey (0372 57223). **Dates** *Theatre* 20 Jun-8 Jul 1990; 19 Jun-7 Jul 1991. *Fair* 8 Jul 1990; 7 Jul 1991. **Admission** £2-£6.

Bring a picnic and sit in the grounds of an elegant Regency mansion. The stunning view over the Downs makes a dramatic setting for this famous open air theatre. The 1990 programme includes *As You Like It* and Gilbert and Sullivan's *The Sorcerer*. Polesden Fair, held on the last day of the season, has old-fashioned stalls and attractions, from strong-man contests to veteran cars, with staff in Edwardian costume and fireworks at the end.

Lord's Test

Lord's Cricket Ground, NW8 (071 289 1611; recorded information on state of play 071 286 8011). St John's Wood underground. **Dates** *New Zealand* 21-26 Jun 1990 (excluding Sun); *India* 26-31 Jul 1990 (excluding Sun) 1990. **Open** 9am; *Play* 10.30am-6pm. **Admission** phone for details. **Credit** A, V.

England play at home each summer and the Lord's Test is a big party for the society mob in blazers. In 1990 England play New Zealand

in three five-day tests (the second is at Lord's) as a warm-up for defeat by India (the first of three tests is at Lord's). Bemusing to the uninitiated, cricket attracts enthusiasts who calculate the statistics. Do as they do and take a radio to hear the witty BBC Radio 3 commentary (*see chapter* **Media**).

Middlesex Show

Showground, Park Road, Uxbridge, Middlesex (0895 50472). Uxbridge underground. **Dates** Sat 23 Jun-Sun 24 Jun 1990; Sat 22 Jun-Sun 23 Jun 1991. **Open** 9am-7.30pm. **Admission** £4.50 adults; £1 under-16s, OAPs; free under-5s. £3 in advance. **No credit cards**.

County shows are a British institution, harking back to when ye olde British yeomen chewed straw at farm gates. This major show is a great family day out for fans of Morris dancing, falconry, farmyard animals and dog agility trials.

Wimbledon Lawn Tennis Championships

All England Club, PO Box 98, Church Road, SW19 (081 944 1066; recorded information 081 946 2244). Southfields underground/Wimbledon BR/39, 93, 200 bus. **Dates** Mon 25 Jun-8 Jul (excluding Sun 1 Jul) 1990; 24 Jun-7 Jul (excluding Sun 30 Jun) 1991. **Open** 11am; *Play on outside courts* 12.30pm; *Play on show courts* 2pm. **Admission** £3-£6 to all outside courts and standing room at show courts; £10-£39 for Centre Court; £9-£18 for Court 1. Tickets by ballot of entries between Sept and Dec previous year; send SAE to above address for application form. **No credit cards**.

Europe's biggest outdoor festival, the **Notting Hill Carnival** *(listed under* **Summer***) gets into seriously crucial party mood in 1990 for its 25th birthday. Special events include a multi-ethnic Carnival Village during August, probably at Wormwood Scrubbs park. As ever, there'll be live music (at Portobello Green), dancing in the street, a procession of floats and Caribbean food sold from front gardens. Sunday is best for children, but Monday is the main day. Sadly, calypso and reggae sounds get drowned out by harder rap rhythms, particularly in the volatile All Saints Road. The Carnival has been better organized and more trouble-free of late, but don't bring any valuables or linger into the evening.*

To Steffi Graf, Wimbledon is tennis' highest ranking tournament, but it's also a major date on the British social circuit. If you haven't ordered tickets or blagged free seats at a company marquee, you'll have to queue from early morning. Go early evening, when you can usually get a seat for an evening match.

Royal Tournament
Earl's Court Exhibition Centre, Warwick Road, SW5 (071 373 8141). Earl's Court underground. **Dates** Wed 11-Sat 28 Jul 1990; similar period 1991, phone to confirm. **Programme** 7.30pm Wed, Mon; 2.30pm; 2.30, 7.30pm Tue-Sat. **Admission** £6-£18; *Matinée, except Sat,* £3-£9 under-12s, OAPs; £2.50 disabled. **Credit** A, AmEx, V.
Presented by the armed forces, the Royal Tournament is a sanitized, family show with deafening military bands, pageantry and lots of running about with gun carriages. In the centenary show (1990) it's the turn of the Navy and the Royal Marines to host it; the theme is the story of the sea soldier. The 50th anniversary of the Battle of Britain will be marked by a re-enaction of the (aeroplane) dog fights which saved the country from German invasion.
Group discount. Wheelchair access.

Road Sweeping
Vintners' Hall, Upper Thames Street, EC4 (071 236 1863). Mansion House or Cannon Street underground. **Date** Wed 11 Jul 1990; Wed 10 Jul 1991; 11.55am. **Admission** free.
See **picture and caption.**

Swan Upping on the Thames
from Sunbury, Surrey to Pangbourne, Surrey, and back (071 236 1863). **Dates** Mon 16 Jul-Fri 20 Jul 1990; Mon 15 Jul-Fri 19 Jul 1991; 9.30am-5pm each day. **Admission** free.
Utterly eccentric, this tradition of marking swans is a tricky spectator event. All the swans on the Thames belong to either the Queen or to the Vintners' or Dyers' livery companies. For five days herdsmen paddle about attempting to record the birds by marking their beaks. The Dyers' swans get one nick, the Vintners' two and the Queen's remain unblemished. In theory, the fleet should reach Windsor, Marlow and Sonning Lock on respective nights, and then turn back at Pangbourne, but its exact whereabouts depends on how cooperative the swans are feeling.

Doggett's Coat & Badge Race
London Bridge, EC4, to Cadogan Pier, near Albert Bridge, SW3 (071 626 3531). **Date** 19 Jul 1990; similar date in 1991, phone to confirm. *Start* 6.45pm London Bridge; *Finish* 7.15pm Cadogan Pier. **Admission** free.
Thomas Doggett, a popular actor-manager, inaugurated this 4.5-mile/7-kilometre race from London Bridge to Chelsea in 1715 to commemorate the accession of George I. Doggett granted monies for a scarlet coat and a huge silver badge for the winners. It's a private race, which only boatmen up to two years out of apprenticeship can compete in.

The best views are from London Bridge, but upstream you can see the rowers grimace as they battle against the tide.

BBC Henry Wood Promenade Concerts
Various venues; Last Night at the Royal Albert Hall, Kensington Gore, SW7 (071 927 4296). South Kensington underground. **Dates** 20 Jul-15 Sept 1990; 19 Jul-14 Sept 1991. **Admission** varies. **Credit** A, AmEx, DC, V.
This is one of the world's greatest classical music festivals (*see chapter* **Music: Classical & Opera**). The Last Night of the Proms at the Albert Hall is famous for its overdose of patriotism, culminating in a tumultuous rendition of *Land of Hope and Glory.*

Cart Marking
Guildhall Yard, EC2 (071 480 7259 for details). Bank underground or Moorgate underground/BR. **Date** 1 Aug 1990; Similar date in 1991, phone to confirm. **Starts** 11am. **Admission** free.
Traffic jams in 1861 forced the city authorities to pass an act of common council limiting the number of carts on the road to 421. With traffic today back to horse and cart speeds, there's a lesson here for the authorities. Many superb vintage vehicles assemble for this revived ceremony, lasting about three hours. The participants are from the Worshipful Company of Car Men.

Notting Hill Carnival
Around North Kensington (081 964 0544/081 969 3603). Ladbroke Grove, Notting Hill or Westbourne Park underground. **Date** Sun 26-27 Aug 1990; Sun 25-26 1991. Noon-7pm Sun, Mon. **Admission** free.
See **picture and caption.**

AUTUMN

Thamesday
Jubilee Gardens, South Bank, SE1 (071 928 3002/071 921 0682). Embankment or Waterloo underground/BR. **Date** Sat 8 Sept 1990. **Admission** free.
This party to celebrate London's river has a mixed programme of events, many actually happening on the Thames. A funfair and craft stalls are set up in Jubilee Gardens and street performers jump and juggle in the area. Thamesday will go out with a bang; the early-evening fireworks – the best display in London – will signal the end of this festival, for good. Not only is the seat of London's abolished council, County Hall, disgracefully to become a luxury hotel, but Jubilee Gardens next door is to be landscaped to stop outdoor festivals at the South Bank – the fun would disturb the few precious hotel guests.

Chinatown Mid-Autumn Festival
Chinese Community Centre, Gerrard Street & Newport Place, WC1 (071 437 5256). Leicester Square or Piccadilly Circus underground. **Date** Sun 30 Sep 1990; Sun 22 Sep 1991 (phone to confirm). **Admission** free.
A smaller, but similar festival to the Chinese New Year (*see below* **Winter**). Colourful lanterns of every shape and size are made by and for children, and there's plenty of entertainments and stalls. A stage is set up in

Cockney clichés are for real at the **Costermonger's Pearly Harvest Festival** *(listed under* **Autumn***). Costermongers sell fruit and veg on the streets of London. Their representatives, the Pearly Kings and Queens, are gathered here for the harvest festival service. Over a hundred of this hardy breed will be wearing their pearl-button decorated garments, mouthing 'cor blimey' and cockney rhyming slang: 'boat race – face'; 'pork pies – lies'; 'dog and bone – phone'.*

The Tourist's Guide to Hiring a Car

While you're in London, you may want to hire a car for a more independent look at the city, or the rest of the country.

But be careful, there are many rental companies around, all claiming to offer the best cars at the best prices.

There is a company, however, that can justifiably claim to have the customers' interests at heart. **Central Rent-a-Car.**

No Hidden Extras

For a start, unlike the majority of rental companies, they don't surprise you with any hidden extras; so compared with the multinationals they really do offer excellent value for money. All the prices include VAT, insurance and unlimited mileage. There's no surcharge on overseas visitors, additional drivers or 21 to 25 year olds, and free AA membership is also available. On top of this, Central also offer free extras like roof racks and child seats. Hardly surprising then that Central Rent-a-Car enjoy regular and loyal custom.

Where To Find Them

Central Rent-a-Car have three London offices at **Victoria** (48-56 Ebury Bridge Road, SW1, Tel: 01-730 9130/ 6391), **Hyde Park** (28 Queensway, W2, Tel: 01-229 7211/2), and **Battersea** (41a Queenstown Road, SW8, Tel: 01-627 4681). There are two further offices in **Manchester** and **Glasgow**, plus Airport offices at **Heathrow, Gatwick, Glasgow, Prestwick** and **Manchester** (call Free 0800 833938). Visitors to the continent will also find Central Rent-a-Car offices in Paris and Nice. So whether you're after a Ford Fiesta, Mercedes, or a Minibus, you're never far from **Central Rent-a-Car** and the best hire package around.

Gerrard Street and dragons dance about outside Chinese restaurants and shops. Much of the food on sale is specially for this festival.

Horseman's Sunday
Church of St John & St Michael, Hyde Park Crescent, W2 071 262 3791). Marble Arch underground or Paddington underground/BR. **Dates** Sun 23 Sept 1990; Sun 22 Sept 1991. 11.30am. **Admission** Free.
At this weird 30-minute service, the vicar's pulpit is in fact a saddle. From horseback he blesses over 100 horses at this equine ceremony. Afterwards, the blessed animals trot around the surrounding streets and then through Hyde Park. Later (1.30-5.30pm) you can watch showjumping at nearby Kensington paddock, in the north of Kensington Gardens.

The Clog and Apron Race
Broad Walk, Kew Gardens, Richmond, Surrey (081 940 1171). Kew Gardens underground or Kew Bridge BR. **Date** late Sept (phone to confirm). **Admission** £1 adults; 50p 10-16 years; free under 10s.
A peculiar race held by the horticultural students of Kew Gardens. They don leather clogs and leather aprons with garden knives in the pockets and race along Broad Walk. Apparently this is the uniform of the original students. The course record for the 350 metre distance is 60 seconds. Watch the race, then amble about the stunning Royal Botanical Gardens (*see chapter* **Sightseeing**).

Costermonger's Pearly Harvest Festival
St Martin-in-the-Fields, Trafalgar Square, WC2 (071 930 0089). Leicester Square underground or Charing Cross underground/BR. **Dates** Sun 6 Oct 1990; Sun 5 Oct 1991. **Service** 3pm. **Admission** free.
See **picture and caption**.

Bonfire Night
All over England, Scotland and Wales (phone London Tourist Board 071 730 3488 9am-6pm Mon-Fri for major firework displays). **Date** 5 Nov; firework displays on nearest weekend.
In 1605 Guy Fawkes, one of the leaders of a group of Catholic conspirators, was caught beneath the Houses of Parliament with enough gunpowder to blow up James I and his Protestant Parliament. Since then Bonfire Night has been celebrated all over Britain. A bonfire is stacked high with the 'guy' (an effigy of Fawkes) on top and someone rushes about letting off fireworks. Organized firework displays are the best and the safest; check *Time Out* magazine or phone the LTB (*071 730 3488*) for details

London to Brighton Veteran Car Run
Starting point: Serpentine Road, Hyde Park, W2 (081 686 2525 for details). Hyde Park Corner underground. **Date** Sun 4 Nov 1990; Sun 3 Nov 1991. Start 8-9am. **Admission** free.
This colourful day out for cars over pension age may mean little to today's GTi drivers, but they owe a lot to those who first held the rally in 1896. The rally celebrated the abolition of the Act that forced cars to be heralded by a runner with a red flag at a 2mph/2.5kmh speed limit. The motors, now limited to an average of 20mph/32kmh, aim to reach Brighton before 4pm. Only cars

*The **Lord Mayor's Show** (listed under **Autumn**) banishes the usual severe, pin-striped face of the City of London for one day a year. The plume-hatted new Lord Mayor travels down river to Tower Pier from Westminster, leaving at 9am. From 11.10am at the Guildhall, a procession of the 1756 State Coach and around 140 floats, snake through the City to the Law Courts at 11.50am. There the new mayor swears solemn vows before heading off to the Embankment, turning back down Queen Victoria Street to the mayoral home, Mansion House, by 2.20pm. Fireworks are later launched from a barge moored on the Thames between Waterloo and Blackfriars bridges. Try to find a place 30 minutes before the procession starts.*

built before 1905 can be entered, so the sight of all the gleaming coachwork and distinctive radiator grilles is magnificent. The start at Hyde Park has a great sense of occasion, but crowds line the whole route (via Westminster Bridge and Croydon, along the A23), particularly outside pubs.

State Opening of Parliament
House of Lords, Palace of Westminster, SW1 (071 219 4272). Westminster underground. **Date** usually first week in Nov, phone for details. **Admission** free.
After their summer hols Members of Parliament are welcomed back by the Queen at the State Opening of Parliament, who then reads a speech outlining the government's legislative plans. Although it's a private (if televised) affair, the public do get a good chance to see the Queen. In either the Irish or Australian State Coach, she leaves Buckingham Palace at 10.37am and passes through the Mall and Horse Guards Parade; on her entry to the House of Lords at 11.15am, a gun salute (*see above* **Frequent Events**) goes off in Hyde Park. Spectators should get into position early: a good place to watch the event is at the north side of the Mall where the crowds are slightly less heavy.

Lord Mayor's Show
Various streets in the City of London (071 606 3030). **Date** Sat 10 Nov 1990; Sat 9 Nov 1991. 9am-5pm. **Admission** free.
See **picture and caption**.

Remembrance Sunday Ceremony
Cenotaph, Whitehall, SW1 (071 730 3488). Westminster underground or Charing Cross underground/BR. **Date** Sun 11 Nov 1990, Sun 10 Nov 1991; 10.30am-11.30am. **Admission** free.
For details of this ceremony to remember the dead of two world wars, *see chapter* **The World Wars**.

WINTER

Christmas Lights
Covent Garden, WC2 (071 836 9136); Oxford Street, W1 (071 580 9170); Regent Street, W1 (071 629 1682); Regent Street, W1 (071 629 1682); Trafalgar Square, SW1. **Date** *Lights on early Nov. Trafalgar Square Christmas Tree early Dec.*
Every year Norway thanks Britain for liberation from the Nazis by sending us a fir tree to put up in Trafalgar Square. But acid rain damage to Norwegian firs by British pollution has put the tradition in doubt. Regent Street has London's best illuminated decorations, putting Oxford Street's dreary effort to shame. Don't go to see them being switched on by a celebrity; the congestion is a nightmare, so go later. Other lights to gawp at are at St Christopher's Place, W1, Bond Street, W1, and Kensington High Street, W8, plus 'alternative' lights around

Carnaby Street, W1. Back in October, the shop windows will have been stuffed with angels, snowmen and, in the big stores, a Santa Claus in his grotto. Superior window displays include those at Hamleys, Harrods, Harvey Nichols, Liberty and Selfridges (*see* chapter **Shopping**).

New Year's Eve Celebrations
Trafalgar Square, W1. Leicester Square or Charing Cross underground/BR. **Date** 31 Dec 1990-1 Jan 1991; 31 Dec 1991-1 Jan 1992. **Admission** free.

To Scots, hogmanay is a major drunken festival; other Britons just get drunk. The national centre for ringing in the new year is Trafalgar Square, where thousands congregate to sway about, singing *Auld Lang Syne*. Apart from the discomfort, drunkenness, pickpocketing, occasional violence and absence of joy at this knees-up, the actual moment of midnight is infuriatingly unclear as Big Ben is drowned out by all the noise. Choose almost any pub or club and have a far better time there. In recent years, Fosters beers have done the one thing to stop drunk driving the Government won't admit works, by sponsoring free public transport all night.

January Sales
Liberty, Regent Street, W1 (071 734 1234). **Date** about 27 Dec 1991, phone to confirm. *Selfridges, Oxford Street, W1 (071 629 1234).* **Date** 27 Dec 1991. *Harrods, Knightsbridge (071 730 1234).* **Date** about 3 Jan 1991, phone to confirm.

It's become a traditional Christmas pastime to huddle on a pavement outside one of the big stores, waiting for a mega-bargain at the January Sales. It's easier to turn up on the day the sale starts armed with a baseball bat and a crash helmet. The discounts can be tremendous, but so are the crowds.

Chinese New Year Festival
Chinatown, around Gerrard Street (Chinatown Chinese Association 071 437 5256). Leicester Square, Piccadilly Circus or Tottenham Court Road underground. **Date** On a Sunday next to 15 Feb 1991 & 4 Feb 1992, phone to confirm. 11am-5pm. **Admission** free.

See **picture and caption**.

SPRING

Soho Pancake Day Race
Carnaby Street, W1 (071 287 0907). Oxford Circus underground. **Dates** Tue 12 Feb 1991; 3 Mar 1992. *Races start* from noon. **Admission** free.

Shrove Tuesday is the last day before the fasting of Lent begins. Traditionally, it was a day for scoffing all the stuff you weren't supposed to be eating for the following 40 days, hence the eggs, flour and milk of the pancakes. God knows how tradition decreed that races would be held of people tossing pancakes in a frying pan as they went. You can join them if you like; phone a few days in advance.

Ideal Home Exhibition
Earl's Court Exhibition Centre, SW5 (071 222 9341). Earl's Court underground. **Dates** 10 Mar-1 Apr 1990, 10am-8pm; 16 Mar-7 Apr 1991 (provisional), 10am-8pm. **Admission** phone for details.

Your dream, fitted kitchen, bathroom and colour-coordinated bedroom are all here. Stands offering anything from gold taps to hard-wearing doormats fill the Centre. It's best to go on weekdays, when it's quieter.

Oxford and Cambridge Boat Race
On the Thames from Putney to Mortlake (071 730 3488). **Date** 13 Apr 1991. **Admission** free.

Oxford and Cambridge universities clash on the Thames in this annual sporting battle and social shindig. Starting from Putney, SW6, it finishes at Mortlake, SW14. Bridges and pubs, like the Swan Inn at Mortlake, are good but crowded vantage points from which to see the race and the earlier reserves challenge between Goldie and Isis.

April Fool's Day
Daily newspapers. **Date** 1 April.

By tradition, practical jokes are performed *ad nauseam* before noon on April 1. The odd British sense of humour also invades the daily papers, most of which print bizarre, semi-believable, but false stories. The sober *Guardian* is usually inspired, but tabloid journalism is so debased that you often can't guess which is the April Fool story.

Easter Day Parade
Battersea Park, SW11 (081 871 6363). Sloane Square underground or Battersea BR. **Date** Sun 31 Mar 1991, Sun 19 Apr 1992; noon-6pm. **Admission** free.

The Easter parade of colourful floats around Battersea Park starts at about 3pm. There's also a funfair and plenty of sideshows.

London Harness Horse Parade
Regent's Park, NW1 (071 486 7905). Camden Town, Great Portland Street or Regent's Park underground. **Date** Mon 1 Apr 1991; Mon 20 Apr 1992; 9.30am-1.30pm. **Admission** free.

Before the parade around the Inner Circle of Regent's Park gets underway at noon, you're free to inspect the horses.

London Marathon
Greenwich Park, Blackheath to Westminster Bridge via the Isle of Dogs, Victoria Embankment and St James's Park (081 948 7935). **Date** 21 April 1991. **Admission** free to spectators.

The London Marathon rivals New York's as the world's biggest road race. Over 90 per cent of the 25,000-odd starters finish the route. It's a friendly spectacle, as the crowds lining the route urge on the more rubber-legged athletes. The racers are a mixed bunch of record breakers, celebrities, fancy dressers, joggers, club runners and wheelchair racers. The atmosphere and crowds are are greatest at the start and finish and at Tower Bridge.

The **Chinese New Year Festival** *(listed under* **Winter***) is a garish, exuberant affair. Spilling out of the main Gerrard Street/Newport Place area are stalls selling crafts and delicacies, surrounded by performers and big crowds. Lions and dragons wade through the streets to 'eat' cabbages and coins donated by the Chinese restaurants. There's a stage for performers in Leicester Square and early Chinese history is told to anyone who'll listen. The 1991 festival will start the Year of the Sheep; 1992 is the Year of the Monkey.*

Essential Information

Read this chapter for a happy, safe and trouble-free stay.

There are some things you need to know right at the start of your visit to London. We list the basics here, but more detailed information can be found in *chapter* **Survival.**

VISAS

You don't need a visa if you live in a Commonwealth country, unless you come from Nigeria, Ghana, India, Bangladesh, Sri Lanka or Pakistan. And if you're a resident of certain non-Commonwealth countries, including USA, Japan, Austria, Finland, Iceland, Mexico, Sweden and Switzerland, you'll be allowed to visit Britain without a visa. If you do need a visa, apply to the British Embassy, High Commission or Consulate in your own country before leaving. The visa allows you to stay for a maximum of six months. If you want a work permit, see *chapter* **Survival.**

Rapid Visa
15 Hogarth Road, SW5 (071 373 3026). Earl's Court underground. **Open** 9am-6pm Mon-Fri; 10am-2pm Sat. **Credit** £TC.
Avoid the aggro of sorting out visas and let RV take the strain. You needn't be British to use the service and it costs £10. Certain countries, including Italy, Canada, Guyana and Japan, require personal applications.

MONEY

The currency in Britain is **pounds sterling** (£). One pound equals 100 pence (p). One and 2p coins are copper; 5p, 10p, 20p and 50p coins are silver; and £1 is a yellow coin. Thereafter, money becomes paper notes: the blue £5 note, the brown £10 note, the purple £20 and the green £50 note.

You can exchange foreign currency at either **banks** or **bureaux de change.** But if you're here for a long stay, you may need to open a bank or building society account. You'll probably need to present a reference from your regular banker,

and certainly a passport as identification. **Barclays,** *68 Knightsbridge, SW1 (071 930 9020),* deals exclusively with non-residents.

Banks
Open usually 9.30am-3.30pm Mon-Fri; some 9.30am-noon Sat.
Banks generally offer the best exchange rates. Commission is sometimes charged for cashing travellers' cheques in foreign currencies, but not for sterling travellers' cheques, provided you cash the cheques at a bank affiliated to the issuing bank (obtain a list when you buy the travellers' cheques). Commission is charged if you change cash into another currency. You always need identification, such as a passport, when exchanging money.

Bureaux de change
At major rail and underground stations and in tourist areas. **Open** most 8am-9pm, many 24 hours.
If you cash travellers' cheques or buy and sell foreign currency here, you'll be charged for it. No consumer organization controls the practices of the bureaux so commission rates – which should be clearly displayed – do vary. **Deak International, Chequepoint** and **Lenlyn** are reputable bureaux.

INSURANCE

It's advisable to take out insurance for your personal belongings. Medical insurance is often included in travel insurance packages, and it's important to have it unless your country has a reciprocal medical treatment arrangement with Britain (*see chapter* **Survival**). Make sure you're insured before you leave home, since it's almost impossible to arrange in a foreign country.

TELEPHONES

Public call boxes are usually cheaper to use than the telephones in hotel rooms, the charges for which are added to your bill. All call boxes display instructions for use. The old-fashioned ones in the famous red cabins do not take your money until you're connected and give no

change. The newer, smoked-glass cubicles have digital displays and are cleaner. There are two types, one accepts money and the other only accepts a **Phonecard** (*see below*). The money type takes the money first and gives change. Scattered throughout London you will see blue and grey **Mercury** telephone booths. In emergencies, dial **999** for police, fire or ambulance services.

Here's a phonetic guide to British telephone sounds. A steady, deep *brrrrrr* when you lift the receiver means go ahead and dial. A higher *brrr-brrr* pause *brrr-brrr* pause, etc means that the number's ringing. Quick, evenly-spaced *boop-boop-boop* means it's engaged (busy); a solid *woooo* means unobtainable (dial the operator – *100* – and ask for help). Further operator and directory services are listed in *chapter* **Survival.**

Telecom Phonecards
Cards available from post offices and larger newsagents. **Cost** 10p per unit; cards available in units of £1 to £20. **Credit** *phones in some stations accept credit cards:* A, AmEx, DC, V.
Call boxes with the green Phonecard symbol take prepaid cards. A notice in the call box tells you where the nearest Phonecard stockist is. The phone's digital display shows how many units you have left. British Telecom are currently fitting all phonecard call boxes with credit card facilities.

Mercury Phonecards
(071 528 2000). *Cards available from British Rail stations and larger newsagents.* **Cost** 5p connection fee, then 1p per unit; cards available in units of £2, £4, £5 and £10. **Credit** *all phones accept cards* A, AmEx, DC, V.
British Telecom was privatized in November 1984, opening up the telecommunications market to competition. There will be 400 Mercury phone booths in London by 1990, located at most train stations and throughout the capital. They don't take cash and work on the same principles as the Telecom Phonecards. Mercury calls (including international) are up to 20 per cent cheaper than Telecom calls, partly because they're priced in 1p units: Telecom would charge 20p for an 11p call. Less people own Mercury cards, so the queues are usually shorter.

POST

Post Offices
Open *hours usually* 9am-5.30pm Mon-Fri; 9am-noon Sat, *can vary.*
You can buy stamps and have letters weighed at all post offices, but stamps are also widely available at newsagents. **Stamp** prices are, at time of writing, 15p for second-class letters (inland only) and 20p for first-class letters to all EC countries. Charges for other letters and parcels vary according to the weight and destination. Courier services are listed under *chapter* **Business;** packaging and shipping under *chapter* **Shopping & Services.**

PUBLIC HOLIDAYS

On public holidays, aka **bank holidays**, many shops remain open, but there is always a less frequent public transport service.

May Day Holiday Monday 7 May 1990; Monday 6 May 1991.
Spring Bank Holiday Monday 28 May 1990; Monday 27 May 1991.
Summer Bank Holiday Monday 27 August 1990; Monday 26 August 1991.
Christmas Day Tuesday 25 December 1990. Wednesday 25 December 1991.
Boxing Day Wednesday 26 December 1990; Thursday 26 December 1991.
New Year's Day Tuesday 1 January 1991; Wednesday 1 January 1992.
Good Friday Friday 13 April 1990; Friday 29 March 1991; Friday 17 April 1992.
Easter Monday Monday 16 April 1990; Monday 1 April 1991; Monday 20 April 1992.

TIME

Every year (31 Mar 1991) we put our clocks **forward by one hour** to give British Summer Time (BST). In autumn (28 Oct 1990; 27 Oct 1991) the clocks go **back by one hour** to Greenwich Mean Time (GMT).

INFORMATION

Tourist Information Centres can help on all aspects of your stay. They also supply a free map of Central London, as does the *Time Out* office, Tower House, Southampton Street, WC2. If you're venturing outside Central London, you'll need an *A-Z Atlas of London*, available from most newsagents and bookshops. The British press, radio and TV are reviewed in *chapter* **Media**. A list of foreign newspaper stockists is in *chapter* **Survival**.

City Of London
St Paul's Churchyard, EC4 (071 606 3030). St Paul's underground. **Open** 9.30am-5pm daily.

Harrods
Basement Banking Hall, Harrods, Knightsbridge, SW1 (071 730 1234). Knightsbridge underground. **Open** 9am-6pm Mon, Tue, Thur-Sat; 9.30am-7pm Wed.

Selfridges
Basement Services Arcade, Selfridges, Oxford Street, W1 (071 629 1234). Oxford Circus underground. **Open** 9.30am-6pm Mon-Wed, Fri, Sat; 10am-8pm Thur.

The red **telephone call box** *(listed under* **Telephones***) is a famous symbol of Britain, but you may be surprised to hear that they are now very rare. Always easy to find, Giles Gilbert Scott's much-loved red boxes have almost all been replaced by modern ones. These smoke-grey cubicles are cleaner but become invisible when you need to find one and are eyesores when you don't. Unfortunately, the average British male seems to be incapable of passing a public call box without either attacking it, or mistaking it for a public toilet.*

Tower of London
West Gate, EC3 (071 709 6765). Tower Hill underground. **Open** *Apr-Nov* 10am-6pm daily.

Victoria Station Forecourt
Victoria Station, SW1 (071 730 3488). **Open** *Nov-Mar* 9am-7pm Mon-Sat; 9am-5pm Sun. *Apr-Oct* 9am-8.30pm daily.

TIPPING

In Britain it's generally accepted that you tip in taxis, minicabs, restaurants, hairdressing salons, hotels and some bars. The amount can be anything up to 15 per cent.

WEATHER

Britain has one of the most changeable climates in the world. Perhaps that's why the British are obsessed with the weather – and why television weather forecasters are media personalities.

BBC1 & BBC2
Bulletins are broadcast at regular intervals throughout the day. There's also a more concentrated look at the weather on Weather View at 11.15pm Mon-Fri on BBC1, and at 3.15pm Sun on BBC2 (times may vary).

BBC Radio
All of BBC's radio stations have weather bulletins throughout the day after each news bulletin. The best station is Radio 4 (on LW 198kh, 1515m; VHF/FM 92.4-94.8), which also broadcasts shipping forecasts at 12.30am, 5.50am, 1.55pm and 5.50pm.

Capital Radio
194m/1548kHz (MW); 95.8mHz (FM). This local radio station has weather summaries every 20 minutes from 6.40am to 9pm, concentrating on London and the South East.

London Weather Centre
Penderel House, 284-286 High Holborn, WC1 (071 836 4311). Holborn underground. **Open** 10am-4pm Mon-Fri.
At the centre, part of the Met Office, your weather enquiries are answered and useful personal forecasts given for anywhere in Europe, for up to five days ahead. The shop sells a large selection of souvenirs and books.

Travel

Getting around London is like navigating a spider's web. But we give you the essentials to make meaning out of the mayhem.

London's transport system is the busiest in Western Europe: you'll be vying with millions of commuters and Londoners for that elusive seat on the underground. Yet compared to other European capitals, the level of subsidies for public transport is very low. Take time to get to know the system, work out your route carefully, and travelling on public transport can be an excellent insight into London life.

For information on breakdowns, car parks, 24-hour petrol stations, de-clamping, motorbike hire, hitch-hiking and so on, *see chapter* **Survival**. For bicycle hire *see chapter* **Sport & Fitness**.

PUBLIC TRANSPORT

The underground system, commonly referred to as the tube, is generally faster than buses, although it's not recommended if you don't like crowds, heat and standing up. If you have the time, travelling by bus is far less crowded or stressful and gives you a better understanding of the layout of the city.

The underground system and buses within the London area are both run by **London Regional Transport (LRT)**, which has a 24-hour, seven-day enquiry telephone service on *071 222 1234*. This provides information about routes, fares and times for buses, the underground and the London lines operated by **British Rail (BR)**. In addition, there is a constantly updated 24-hour recorded information service on *071 222 1200*.

LRT Travel Information Centres provide free maps and night-bus timetables. They also give information about the underground, the Docklands Light Railway and the day-time buses, plus some details on British Rail's London routes. You can find them in the following underground stations:

Euston (open 7.15am-6pm Mon-Thur; 7.15am-7.30pm Fri; 7.15am-6pm Sat; 8.15am-6pm Sun).
Heathrow station at terminals 1, 2 & 3 (**open** 7.15am-6.30pm Mon-Sat; 8.15am-6.30pm Sun).
King's Cross (open 8.15am-6pm Mon-Thur, Sat, Sun; 8.15am-7.30pm Fri).
Oxford Circus (open 8.15am-6pm Mon-Sat).
Piccadilly Circus (open 8.15am-6pm daily).
Victoria (open 8.15am-9.30pm daily).

There are also centres at the Heathrow Airport terminals:
Terminal 1 Arrivals (open 7.15am-10.15pm Mon-Fri; 7.15am-9pm Sat; 8.15am-10pm Sun).
Terminal 2 Arrivals (open 7.15am-9pm Mon-Sat; 8.15am-10pm Sun).
Terminal 3 Arrivals (open 7.15am-2pm Mon-Sat; 8.15am-3pm Sun).
Terminal 4 Arrivals (open 6.30am-6.30pm Mon-Sat; 8.15am-6.30pm Sun).

Look out for the orange help points and telephones situated on the platforms or in the corridors of the major underground stations.

For disabled people, LRT publishes a booklet called *Access to the Underground*, which gives information on lifts and ramps at individual underground stations. It costs £1 and is available from *London Regional Transport, Unit for Disabled Passengers, 55 Broadway, SW1H 0BD (071 227 3312)* and at Travel Information Centres *(see above)*. The unit also provides details on buses for the disabled and Braille maps for the visually impaired. The Docklands Light Railway has wheelchair access at all its stations.

LRT bus and underground fares are based on a zone system. There are five zones which stretch 12 miles/20 km out from the centre of London *(see* **Maps of London**). The most economical way to get about is to buy a **Travelcard** (usable on the underground, buses, British Rail's Network SouthEast, Docklands Light Railway, and some Green Line services *(see below)*. At the time of writing, the one-day Travelcard costs £2.60 for all zones and can be used from 9.30am Mondays to Fridays; all-day Saturdays, Sundays and public holidays. Passes are available in different combinations of zones (central only, one zone, two zones, and so on); the weekly (£19.70, all zones) and monthly (£75.70 all zones). Passes are valid at any time of day and can be purchased from various newsagents, underground stations, and Network SouthEast stations within the zones. You'll need a passport-sized photograph for weekly and monthly cards.

On all London buses, tubes and British Rail's Network SouthEast trains, children are classified as under 16 years of age. Under-fives travel free. Under-16s pay a child's fare until 10pm, but 14- and 15-year-olds must carry Child Rate Photocards (these are free and available from underground stations and post offices in the London area). The child's one-day travelcard costs 90p and covers all zones. The weekly card costs £5.50 and the monthly is £21.20 for all five zones.

It's advisable to get the correct ticket; in a draconian campaign to prosecute fare evaders, LRT threaten with relish to give you a criminal record as well as a hefty fine.

THE UNDERGROUND

London has the world's biggest underground train system, yet the service to some residential districts is shambolic. The lines were largely built unplanned by private companies. The routes of proposed new lines to north-east and south-east London are influenced less by the self-evident needs of the population, than by the businesses financing them. The government is as reluctant to fund such investment as it is to subsidize public transport. This is why travel is more expensive in London than it is in Europe.

If you haven't a Travelcard *(see above)*, tickets can be bought from a station ticket office or from the self-service machines, now in most stations. Put your ticket through the new automatic checking gates (in zone one only), or show it as you pass through the barriers. You must hold on to your ticket until you have passed the barriers at your destination.

Tube trains run daily, except for Christmas day, starting at around 5.30am Monday to Saturday, 7am

*The **Docklands Light Railway** is a hi-tech service that runs on a raised track from Tower Gateway (a short walk from Tower Hill underground) to the tip of the Isle of Dogs. It's a great way to see the Docklands developments. Designed to carry 22,000 people a day by 1991, it already had 30,000 users by 1989. Engineering work, on a major extension to Bank underground station, means that the service can be limited in the evenings or at weekends.*

Sunday. Last underground times vary according to lines and journeys: they're usually between 11.30pm and 1am on week nights, and 11.30pm on Sundays (but you can catch some trains after midnight). First and last train times are displayed in stations and timetables are issued free at Travel Information Centres (*see above*).

Smoking is illegal anywhere on the underground, including in the ticket halls, on stairs, escalators and platforms, as well as in the trains. This and other safety measures follow the King's Cross fire of 1987. The closure for cleaning and repair of so many escalators, even of whole stations, is a result of years of neglect and cuts in funding.

Crime on London's underground system is nowhere near as bad as on New York's subway. Minor harassment (mostly begging) goes on however and women are more frequently approached. Be careful about getting into an empty tube carriage on your own and beware of pickpockets in

crowded places. Some platforms in central London stations are equipped with closed-circuit television cameras and there is a small, but increasing number of police patrolling the underground. You may also encounter one of the Guardian Angel vigilante groups, a controversial import from New York.

The Docklands Light Railway (DLR) is administered as part of the underground system. The trains run overground from the end of the Isle of Dogs to Tower Gateway or Stratford. The nearest underground station to the DLR Tower Gateway entrance is Tower Hill. From Mondays to Fridays it runs from 5.40am to 9.30pm. For travel enquiries phone *071 222 1234. See also chapter* **The River & Docklands**.

BUSES

Buses are the best way to see London, but they are subject to endless delays in the rush hour. The famous open-backed, red double deckers were designed to fit

London's roads and many still work after 20 years. The new buses, bigger and more ungainly, are actually slower and block traffic. Even worse, most don't have conductors. This foolish cost-cutting measure means that not only passengers, but also other road users, have to wait until the last person has paid for their ticket. LRT also runs small single-decker buses, called Hoppas, for short trips in central London. Some of LRT's routes have been privatized, unthinkingly destroying that symbol of London: the red bus. These routes are: 24 from Pimlico to Hampstead (grey and green buses); and Route 188 from Euston to Greenwich (yellow and blue buses). LRT tickets and passes are valid on these buses.

If there's a conductor, he or she will come round and collect fares or check your pass; otherwise pay the driver as you enter (you should have the correct change). Hang on to your ticket until you get off, in case an inspector gets on.

Buses stop automatically at the stops marked with the LRT symbol (red horizontal line through red circle on a white background). They stop at the red request stops only if you hail the driver by raising your arm. To get off, ring the bell once as the bus approaches the stop.

Night buses run through central London from about 11pm to 6am, about once an hour on most routes. All pass through **Trafalgar Square**, which is the best place to head for if you're unsure which bus to get. Night buses have the letter 'N' before the number and their stops have blue and yellow route numbers. One-day Travelcards cannot be used on night buses, but period passes are valid. The Travel Information Centres (*see above*) can supply you with timetables and route maps. *See also* **Maps of London**.

GREEN LINE BUSES

Green Line buses serve the suburbs and towns within a 40-mile/64-kilometre radius of London. The main departure point is **Eccleston Bridge**, SW1 (near Victoria underground and BR station). For information on schedules and fares telephone *081 668 7261*.

BRITISH RAIL

Network SouthEast is run by British Rail and criss-crosses

AN

index

of

Possibilities

Art

Books

Cabaret

Children

Dance

Film

Gay

Music

Poetry

Politics

Sport

Theatre

Nightlife

Tv &

Broadcast

London's Weekly Guide

HAVE <u>YOU</u> PASSED THROUGH TOWER BRIDGE YET?

· MUSEUM · EXHIBITIONS ·
· FULLY ENCLOSED PANORAMIC WALKWAYS ·
· VICTORIAN STEAM ENGINES ·
· VIDEO · GIFT SHOP ·

Entrance Ticket £2.50 · Children and OAPs £1.00 · Open every day from 10 a.m.

 Tower Hill.

TOWER BRIDGE

Tel: 01-407 0922.

London and the suburbs. Most routes interchange with at least one main underground line and you don't have to buy a separate ticket if you have an LRT Travelcard.

British Rail Travel Enquiries
(24-hour information 071 928 5100).

British Travel Centre
12 Regent Street, SW1 (071 730 3400). **Open** *Oct-last Sat in May:* 9am-6.30pm Mon-Fri; 10am-4pm Sat, Sun. *Last Sat in May-Sept:* 9am-6.30pm Mon-Fri; 9am-5pm Sat; 10am-4pm Sun; closed Christmas Day & Boxing Day.
This office has maps, timetables and other details. Or go to one of the Transport Information Centres (*see above*).

RIVER TRANSPORT

Riverbus (formerly Thames Line), runs daily services between **Chelsea Harbour** and **Docklands**. The boats are fast, punctual and, usually, have no queues. If you're jetting off to Amsterdam or Paris there's the **London City Airport Express Service** (*see below* **Airports**) from Charing Cross Pier and Swan Lane Pier. For details, *see chapter* **The River & Docklands**.

TAXIS

The traditional London taxis are called black cabs even though they can now be red, blue, green or even white. All licensed black cabs should have a For Hire sign and a white plate on the back of the vehicle stating it is permitted to carry four or five people (depending on the model).

To get a licence, drivers of black cabs must pass a rigorous test (called 'The Knowledge') to prove they know where each street is and the shortest route to it. If you have any complaints, take a note of the cabbie's number (which s/he should wear on the left lapel) and the number of the cab (which should be displayed below the Fare Table inside the cab, and on the back plate). Complaints should be made to the **Public Carriage Office** (*071 278 1744*).

Charges are displayed on the Fare Table facing you on the back of the driver's seat, and, if you are within the London Metropolitan Police district, you can only be charged the amount shown on the meter. As soon as your journey has been accepted the meter will be set.

So if you have a lot of luggage, load it in quickly. The meter will automatically start at £1, plus 20p per person, 10p per large piece of luggage, and 40p if it's after midnight, a Sunday or a Public Holiday. Tips are usually between 10 and 15 per cent, but they're strictly voluntary.

A cab is available for **hire** when its yellow sign is lit. If the driver does stop and asks where you're going, s/he is then obliged to take you wherever you want to go, provided it is a journey of no more than six miles/9.6 kilometres. Many refuse to obey this rule and can face prosecution. If a driver agrees to take you outside the London Metropolitan Police district, you should negotiate the fare before you start off.

You can order a black cab by phone 24 hours a day, but expect to pay for being picked up, as well as for being driven to your destination. Order one on *071 286 0286, 071 272 0272, 071 272 3030* or *071 253 5000*. Each company has facilities for the disabled, but it's wise to book a day in advance.

If you leave anything in a cab, phone the **Metropolitan Police Lost Property Office** (*071 833 0996*), **open** 9am to 4pm, Monday to Friday. It sometimes takes a week to get property back as the driver is only obliged to hand it in to the nearest police station.

MINICABS

Any driver with an ordinary four-door car can set up in business as a minicab driver. No special qualifications are needed and the cars usually have no meters. Most companies have a minimum charge which is normally £3. Over long distances, minicabs are usually cheaper than black cabs, especially at night and weekends. Always ask the price when you book and confirm it with the driver before you set off.

Minicabs can't be hailed in the street; you should avoid drivers touting for business (common at night) as it's illegal, and they're probably not insured to carry a paying passenger. Below we have listed some reputable 24-hour services.

Atlas Cars
(071 602 1234).

Embassy Cars
(081 560 5346).

Greater London Hire
(081 340 2450).

Acton: ABC Cars
W3 (081 995 2244).

Battersea & Clapham: Addison Lee
SW8 (071 720 2161).

Clapton: Clapton Cars
E5 (081 985 1666).

Dalston: Essex Cars
E8 (071 241 3000).

Docklands: Smart Cars
E14 (071 987 1888).

Ealing: Radio Cars
W5 (081 567 4774).

Earls Court: Hogarth
SW5 (071 370 2020).

Finchley Road: Meadway
NW11 (081 458 5555).

Finsbury Park: Rainbow Cars
N4 (071 263 6433).

Fulham: Anderson Young
SW6 (071 602 0833).

Hammersmith: Clover Cars
W6 (081 741 1244).

Hither Green: DJ's
SE13 (081 318 9880).

Islington: Bartley Cars
N5 (071 226 7555).

Paddington: Abbey Car Hire
W2 (071 727 2637).

Shepherd's Bush: Sky Jump
W12 (081 749 3456).

CAR HIRE

To hire a car you must have at least one year's driving experience with a full current driving licence. If you are an overseas visitor your current driving licence is valid in Britain for a year. If you live in the European Community (EC), Australia or New Zealand, and want to drive for longer than one year, you must exchange your licence for a British one; it costs approximately £15, and the appropriate form is available at a post office. Otherwise, you must retake your test.

Throughout Britain you must drive on the left-hand side of the road. The law states that drivers and front-seat passengers must always wear safety belts. Get a copy of the *Highway Code* (60p from newsagents) for a

London Coaches

See the sights of London from a Traditional Double Decker London Bus.

London Coaches
Sightseeing
London and England
Winter 1989/90

London Transport

Day and half day sightseeing tours in and around London

London Coaches

ON THE ORIGINAL LONDON TRANSPORT SIGHTSEEING TOUR YOU SEE ALL THE FAMOUS SIGHTS . . . TOWER BRIDGE, BIG BEN AND THE HOUSES OF PARLIAMENT, TRAFALGAR SQUARE AND ST. PAUL'S CATHEDRAL, WITH LIVE COMMENTARIES BY OFFICIAL LONDON TOURIST BOARD GUIDES.

THERE ARE SPECIAL COMBINED TICKETS FOR THE SIGHTSEEING TOUR THAT ALLOW YOU INTO MADAM TUSSAUDS OR LONDON ZOO WITHOUT HAVING TO QUEUE.

LONDON COACHES FULL AND HALF DAY FULLY GUIDED TOURS IN LUXURY COACHES INCLUDE MANY HISTORIC SIGHTS IN AND AROUND LONDON SUCH AS . . . BATH, STONEHENGE, WINDSOR, LEEDS CASTLE, STRATFORD UPON AVON, RIVER THAMES CRUISES AND THEATRE DINNER EVENINGS.

Please contact:
London Coaches
Wilton Road Coach Station, Wilton Road,
Victoria SW1 1DE. England. Tel: 071 227 3456.

London Coaches. Jews Row, Wandsworth, London SW18 1TB. Tel: 081 877 1722. Fax: 081 877 1968.

London's **Taxi drivers** *are self-confessed experts on any subject you might care to mention; from the England football team to the intricacies of world politics. But however much you might doubt their wisdom on some subjects, the cabbie's understanding of London's streets is awesome. To get a licence for a black cab, drivers must pass a severe test called 'The Knowledge' to prove they know where every street is and the shortest route to it.*

complete rundown on motoring regulations. If you want to hire a car for the weekend, book during the week. If you leave it until Friday night you'll find little available.

The phrase 'unlimited mileage' in the following entries, means that you're not charged for wear and tear to the car for the distance you travel; it does not mean you get free petrol for an unlimited distance. 'All inclusive' prices include insurance costs and Value Added Tax (VAT). Most firms hire out cars that are categorized into three groups — A, B and C according to the car's engine power. Below we have listed the cheapest prices in group A (cars with up to 1,000cc engines).

Avis
(Central reservations 081 848 8733). **Open** 8.30am-6pm Mon-Fri; 9am-4pm Sat. **Credit** A, AmEx, DC, £TC, V.
It costs from £29.75 per day/£143.50 per week to hire a car; this includes unlimited mileage, insurance and VAT. Chauffeur-driven cars cost from £10 an hour — luxury models include Porsches and Rolls-Royces. Check the phone directory for the nearest Avis branch. You must be over 21.

Hertz
(Central reservations 081 679 1799). **Open** 8am-6pm Mon-Fri; 8am-5pm Sat. **Credit** A, AmEx, CB, DC, JCB, V.
Charges start at £32 per day. If you hire a car for a week the rate goes down to £25 per day. That's for unlimited mileage, and is all inclusive. You must be over 21.

Practical Used Car Rental
111 Bartholomew Road, NW5 (071 284 0199). Kentish Town underground/29, 253 bus. **Open** 8.30am-5.30pm Mon-Fri; 8.30am-noon Sat. **Credit** A, V.
This exciting franchise is the cheapest car hire in the the country (over 70 branches). Daily hire is from £6.84 per day plus 6p per mile. Weekend packages start from £42, including VAT, insurance and 400 free miles. The age limit is 23 with credit card ID, otherwise it's 24 years old. All cars have full AA cover and are, really, as good as new.
Branches *43 Gunnersbury Lane, W3 (081 992 8199); 249 Cambridge Heath Road, E2 (071 729 6276).*

Supercars
14 Warner Street, EC1 (071 278 6001). Chancery Lane or Farringdon underground. **Open** 8.30am-5.30pm Mon-Fri; 8.30am-1pm Sat. **Credit** A, £STC, V.
A tried, trusted and very cheap car hire firm. The rate for a Fiat Panda is £16.10 per day/£80 per week. No deposit is required, just three forms of identification. A 5p per mile/1.6km charge operates after the first 200 miles/320km.

Heathrow
Piccadilly Line underground. **Times** *from Heathrow 5.08am-11.49pm Mon-Sat; 6.01am-10.43pm Sun. From Piccadilly Circus to Heathrow 5.46am-12.21pm Mon-Sat; 7.05am-11.36pm Sun.* **Tickets** *from central London £1.90; 70p under-16s.*
Airbus *A1 from Grosvenor Gardens, SW1 (Victoria undergound/BR); A2 from Woburn Place, WC1 (Tottenham Court Road underground);* Euston Bus Station, Marylebone Road, NW1 *(Baker Street underground)* or Oxford Street, W1 *(Marble Arch underground).* **Times** 6am-10.15pm daily, every 20-30 mins. **Tickets** £4 single, £6 return; £2 single, £4 return under-16s.
Flightline 767 Victoria Bus Station *(081 668 7261). Victoria underground/BR.* **Times** 6.15am-6.30pm daily, every hour. **Tickets** £5 single, £6 return, £7 period return; half-price under-15s; free under-5s.
The Piccadilly Line underground is the fastest (50-60 minutes from Piccadilly Circus) and cheapest way to the airport. The Airbuses A1 and A2 are also recommended: the journey takes 60 to 80 minutes *(071 222 1234).* Flightline 767 buses take about 65 minutes. Taxi fares are high (£18 or more).

Gatwick
Gatwick Express *(071 928 5100). Victoria underground/BR.* **Times** *from Victoria railway station* 5.30am-10pm (every 15 mins), 10pm-midnight (every half hour), midnight-5am (every hour on the hour), daily. **Tickets** £5.50 adults; £2.75 under-17s.
Flightline 777 *(081 668 7261)* Victoria *underground/BR.* **Times** *from Victoria Bus Station* (approx once an hour) 6.35am-11.25pm daily. **Tickets** £5 single, £6 return, £7 period return; half-price under-15s; free under-5s.
The roads to Gatwick are always jammed; consequently, driving is a nightmare. The Gatwick Express is much the fastest service, taking approximately 30 minutes; trains run through the night. The regular Flightline 777 is cheaper but takes an average of 75 minutes.

London City Airport
King George V Docks, Silvertown, E16 (071 474 5555).
It takes about 45 minutes to get to this new airport in a taxi from the West End, costing approximately £11. The cheapest way to go is by rail; get the underground Central Line to Stratford and then a BR train to Silvertown; this takes about 45 minutes from the West End and costs approximately £3, but there is a five to ten minute walk from the station to the airport. The fastest and by far the most pleasant way to get there is to catch the **London City Airport Express Service** boat *(071 474 5555)* from Charing Cross Pier *(Hungerford Bridge, Victoria Embankment, WC2)* for £5 or from Swan Lane Pier *(Upper Thames Street, London Bridge, EC4)* for £4; it goes approximately every hour and takes about 35 minutes; *see also* chapter **The River & Docklands.**

Accommodation

You won't enjoy London unless you've got somewhere to stay. Whether you want a suite in the Savoy or a tent in the park, you'll find it here.

Although London is suffering from an accommodation crisis, visitors to the city shouldn't find it too difficult to find a room (or a tent) for the night. Unless you're from New York or Tokyo, you'll find the cost of staying here draining; but it's also surprising how (with some help) it's possible to find something clean and comfortable that'll suit your budget.

Hotel classification in Britain is complicated. There's a star system, or a crown system, administered by the various national and local tourist boards. For both systems, the highest score is five. Organizations such as the Automobile Association also have their own systems. We've listed the best (and most expensive) of London's hotels, such as the **Savoy** and the **Ritz** (*see below* **Hotels: Expensive**) because even if you're not going to be staying in one, they're still great places for drinks, afternoon tea and pottering about.

The mid-range hotels are often the best value. Those classified with three or four stars (or crowns) are usually friendly, clean and not too pre-packaged – although they're not necessarily that cheap. Hotels like **Edward Lear**, **Hazlitt's** or the **Fielding** (for all three, *see below* **Hotels: Medium**) will give you a taste of traditional London without tearing a hole in your holiday budget. Of course, it's hard to run a medium-priced hotel in the centre of London because of the cost of land – many of the cheaper hotels tend to lurk in the suburbs.

Hotels in the lower end of the market can be seedy, but we've tracked down a few that are cheap and clean. Some of these are listed in the bed and breakfast section. Don't expect great facilities in a cheap hotel but, as a rule, most visitors to this city comment on the friendliness of hotel keepers and their staff. This comes as something of a surprise to native Londoners. If you do have a complaint about a hotel, contact the London Tourist Board (*see below)* and, if we've included the culprit in our selection, let us know.

The London Tourist Board (*071 730 3488)* runs a number of Tourist Information Centres which have hotel booking services (*see chapter* **Essential Information**). You'll have to pay a deposit on booking and a fee of £4.50 for the service.

We've classified hotels according to the price of a single room for one night. 'Expensive' is over £120 (usually well over); 'Medium' is from £120 down to £30; Cheap is from £30 down to £2.50.

The information we've provided is correct as we go to press, but hotels, their facilities and prices can change very quickly. It's always sensible to ring in advance to check on what you'll be getting – and for how much.

HOTELS

EXPENSIVE

Athenaeum Hotel
116 Piccadilly, W1 (071 499 3464). Green Park or Hyde Park Corner underground. **Rates** *single* with bath from £140 per night; *double* with bath from £170 per night. **Credit** A, AmEx, CB, DC, TC, V.
Many of the 112 rooms at the Athenaeum command splendid views over Green Park, but all of them are plush, comfortable and obsessively clean. There are three private suites available for business meetings and a few apartments adjoining the hotel for longer visits. The bars and restaurant are elegantly international, although a rather painful attempt has been made to give tourists a glimpse of olde London. The staff are warmly welcoming, but tipping is not expected.
Hotel services *No-smoking rooms. Restaurant. Theatre & tour booking.* **Room services** *Air-conditioning. Telephone. TV & in-room films.*

Brown's
19-24 Dover Street, W1 (071 493 6020). Green Park underground. Rates *single* from £130 per night; *double* from £165 per night. Credit A, AmEx, CB, DC, JCB, TC, V.
James Brown, Lord Byron's valet, opened this richly traditional hotel in 1837. Recently, the hotel was bought by the giant chain, Trust House Forte. Nevertheless, Brown's has retained a homely, English country house atmosphere. The rambling (mildly oppressive) interior is stuffed with antiques, the food in the restaurant, L'Apéritif, is pretty good and Brown's afternoon tea is worth its hefty price tag. *See chapter* Eating & Drinking.
Hotel services *Barbers shop. Laundry. Restaurant. Valet.* **Room services** *Mini bar. Telephone. TV.*

Claridges
Brook Street, W1 (071 629 8860). Bond Street underground. **Rates** *single* from £160 per night; *double* from £200 per night. **Credit** A, AmEx, DC, TC, V.
A night at Claridges is not going to be cheap, but then you're paying for a degree of old-fashioned luxury that most other London hotels can only dream about. The walls won't cave in if you push them too hard; and you're not going to be kept awake by someone snoring five floors down. The bedrooms are elegantly decorated in an art deco style, the bathrooms are adorned with gold moustache cups (no tacky gold taps here).
Hotel services *Restaurants. Secretarial service.* **Room services** *Telephone. TV. Valet.*

Connaught
Carlos Place, W1 (071 499 7070). Green Park underground. **Rates** *single* from £131 per night; *double* from £163 per night. **Service** 15%. **Credit** A, £TC.
Rooms are booked months in advance at the Connaught, so if you were thinking of staying in 1990, reconsider and book for 1991. The 90 rooms are filled with people who come here for the service and hanker for a past when staff in morning dress would shimmy about attending to their every whim. The rooms are superbly decorated with antiques and mounds of fresh flowers. The restaurant is eye-catching, expensive and one of the few to serve great classical cooking.
Hotel services *Laundry. Restaurant. Valet.* **Room services** *Telephone. TV.*

Fortyseven Park Street
47 Park Street, W1 (071 491 7282). Marble Arch underground. **Rates** *single suite* with bath from £258 per night; *double suite* with bath from £414 per night. **Credit** A, AmEx, CB, DC, TC, V; no personal cheques.
A small, luxury, privately-owned hotel with 52 well-furnished suites. The suites have one or two bedrooms, a bathroom, a kitchen and a separate sitting-room. Gourmands take note: Le Gavroche, the first restaurant in the UK to gain three Michelin stars, is linked to the hotel. Albert Roux oversees the hotel cuisine and the restaurant. Fortyseven's own dining suite is run by Mr Roux, seats 20 and has an adjoining cocktail room.
Hotel services *French, German, Italian & Spanish spoken.* **Room services** *Telephone. TV.*

Inn on the Park
Hamilton Place, Park Lane, W1 (071 499 0888). Hyde Park Corner underground. **Rates** single from £184 per night; double £230 per night. **Credit** A, AmEx, DC, TC, V.
See **picture and caption**.
Hotel services *Business facilities. Laundry. Secretarial service. Shops. Valet.* **Room services** *Air-conditioning. Hair dryer. Mini bar. Telephone. Trouser press. TV & free movies. 24-hour room service.*

The Ritz
Piccadilly, W1 (071 493 8181). Green Park underground. **Rates** *single* with bath £165 per night; *double* with bath £195 per night. **Credit** A, AmEx, DC, V.
The Ritz offers the kind of deferential treatment that makes all the guests feel like they're worth a million dollars. Teas and breakfasts are popular with guests and ogling outsiders alike and they're surprisingly cheap. Surprisingly, because everything in the Ritz's décor suggests that a

great deal of money has been spent, and never mind the cost: marble pillars, gilt inlaid woodwork and mirrored extravagances at every corner. Bedrooms approach the acme of comfort and good taste, but are occasionally let down by tacky paintings on the walls. The view over Green Park from some bedrooms is glorious.
Hotel services *Babysitting. Currency exchange (open 24 hours). Restaurant. Shop. Spanish spoken. Theatre & tour booking.* **Room services** *Hair dryer. Mini bar. Radio. Telephone. TV.*

The Savoy
Strand, WC2 (071 836 4343). Charing Cross underground/BR. **Rates** *single* with bath £140 per night; *double* with bath from £165 per night. **Credit** A, AmEx, DC, V.
If you're arriving at the Savoy by car, try to remember that this is the only stretch of road in the UK on which you're expected to drive on the right. You wouldn't want to crush one of those Daimlers or Rolls Royces that are stacked three-deep outside the spectacular frontage. The Savoy is eccentric and impressive. Some of the rooms offer mouth-gaping views over the Thames, all of them are opulently tasteful and come with a dangerously-tempting mini bar. If you like to drink in company, the American cocktail bar won't disappoint. And the Savoy theatre is only a short stagger away (*see chapter* **Theatre**).
Hotel services *Car hire. Chauffeur service. Currency exchange (24 hours). French, German, Italian & Spanish spoken. Restaurant. Savoy Grill Shop. Theatre & tour booking.* **Room services** *Mini bar. Radio. Telephone. TV. Valet.*

MEDIUM

Alexander Hotel
9 Sumner Place, SW7 (071 581 1591). South Kensington underground. **Rates** *single* from £82 per night; *double* from £95 per night. **Credit** A, AmEx, CB, DC, TC, V.
Another well-renovated Victorian house, with a homely feel and a small garden. Prices are reasonable and room service is available from 7am-11pm. There's a restaurant, but the surrounding area has many alternatives. The hotel is well placed for the museums and the underground to Heathrow.
Hotel services *Garden. Laundry. Restaurant.* **Room services** *In-room films. Telephone. TV.*

Basil Street Hotel
8 Basil Street, SW3 (071 581 3311). Knightsbridge underground. **Rates** *single* with bath from £85 per night; *double* with bath from £110 per night. **Credit** A, AmEx, DC, EC, S£TC, V.

A uniformed doorman presides at the front of this traditional hotel, that's just over the road from Harrods. Antiques are scattered about the small sitting rooms and the comfortable bedrooms. There's a room for disabled people by the lift. The restaurant isn't great, but there's a wine bar and café; and this is restaurant-heavy Knightsbridge.
Hotel services *Café. Conference facilities. Restaurant. Wine bar. Women's club.* **Room services** *Radio. Telephone. TV.*

Ebury Court Hotel
26 Ebury Street, SW1 (071 730 8147). Victoria underground/BR. **Rates** *single* with bath £45 per night; *double* with bath £77 per night. **Credit** A, £STC, V.
There are many medium-priced hotels in the vicinity of Victoria Station, but this one has built up a reputation for friendly service, a calm, country house atmosphere, comfortable rooms and good, traditional British food. There's a pleasant bar in which to while away the hours.
Hotel services *Restaurant. TV room.* **Room services** *Radio. Telephone. TV hire.*

Edward Lear
30 Seymour Street, W1 (071 402 5401). Marble Arch underground. **Rates** *single* from £37 per night; *double* from £49.50 per night. **Credit** TC, V.

Although the **Inn on the Park** *(listed under* **Hotels: Expensive***) is part of an international chain, it's a relief to find that it hasn't succumbed to the usual, charmless, temptations. The 228 rooms are beautifully idiosyncratic (16 of them have conservatories attached) and tastefully furnished. There are more (well-attuned) staff than there are guests and the bars and restaurants are superb. The mention of the Four Seasons restaurant, for example, gets London gourmets drooling with ill-disguised lust.*

Edward Lear, the nonsense-poem writer and artist, used to live here, but you won't find any Jumblies, pea-green boats or birds nesting in beards. What you will find, however, is a charming, 30-room hotel, with friendly staff and a comfortable, home-from-home appeal. It's a well-preserved, Georgian house situated in the centre of town. Not all the bedrooms have en suite bathrooms and there's no bar or restaurant.
Hotel services *In-house films.* **Room services** *Tea & coffee-making facilities. Telephone. TV.*

Fielding Hotel
4 Broad Court, WC2 (071 836 8305). Covent Garden underground. **Closed** 24-26 December. **Rates** *single* with shower £46 per night; *double* with shower £57.50 per night. **Credit** A, AmEx, CB, DC, V.
Opposite the Royal Opera House and in a small pedestrian precinct off Drury Lane, this is one of the best of the cheaper hotels in central London. This year many of the rooms have been modernised and enlarged, without losing any of their eighteenth-century appeal.
Hotel services *Babysitting. French, German & Spanish spoken. Theatre & tour booking.* **Room services** *Telephone. TV.*

Hazlitt's Hotel
6 Frith Street, W1 (071 434 1771). Leicester Square or Tottenham Court Road under-

ground. **Closed** 24-26 December. **Rates** *single* from £75; *double* from £87 per night. **Credit** A, AmEx, DC, £TC, V.
See **picture and caption.**
Hotel services *Babysitting. French, German, Portuguese & Spanish spoken.* **Room services** *Telephone. TV.*

Hotel Ibis (Euston)
3 Cardington Street, NW1 (071 388 7777). Euston Square underground or Euston underground/BR. **Rates** *single* £48 per night; *double* £53 per night. **Credit** A, AmEx, DC, £STC, V.
The French Ibis chain continues to impress with its affordable new hotels in places that you want to be. Staff and facilities are good, and the bedrooms comfortable rather than luxurious. The bedrooms and the restaurant have been designed to accommodate disabled people; and children aged under 14 are admitted free if they're sharing a room with their parents. Some of London's finest Indian vegetarian restaurants are round the corner in Drummond Street. There are sister hotels at Heathrow and Greenwich.
Hotel services *Gift shop. Restaurant. Tour bookings. Wheelchair access.* **Room services** *Telephone. TV.*

Hotel Russell
Russell Square WC1 (071 837 6470). Russell Square underground. **Rates** *single* with bath £95 per night; *double*: with bath £115 per

night. **Credit** A, AmEx, CB, DC, V.
A huge, palace of a hotel offering every conceivable service and amenity. There's a shop, a brasserie, a 24-hour currency exchange and, that rarity in London hotels, disabled toilets. The interior is lined with marble and the food in the restaurants is good. The rooms are large and comfortable and the staff are eager to help.
Hotel services *Babysitting. Carvery & Brasserie. Currency exchange (open 24 hours). French, German, Italian & Spanish spoken. Shop. Theatre & tour booking. Toilets for the disabled. Wheelchair access.* **Room services** *Hairdryer. Mini bar. Telephone. Trouser press. TV.*

New Barbican Hotel
Central Street, EC1 (071 251 1565). Old Street underground or underground/BR with bath £62.50 per night; *double*: with bath from £75 per night. **Credit** A, AmEx, DC, TC, V.
There aren't many hotels in this part of town, so the large and modern New Barbican is a useful place to know about. Rooms are small and functional, although there are some larger executive rooms, and all are equipped with a bath and shower. The staff are friendly and helpful. The 170-seat restaurant is open for lunch and dinner and is fairly cheap.
Hotel services *Babysitting by prior arrangement. Currency exchange (open 24 hours). French, German, Italian & Spanish spoken. Restaurant: English carvery and a la carte cuisine. Theatre & tour bookings.* **Room services** *Hair dryer. In-house films. Tea & coffee-making facilities. Telephone. TV. Trouser press.*

The Portobello Hotel
22 Stanley Gardens, W11 (071 727 2777). Hammersmith underground. **Rates** *single* from £54.50 per night; *double* from £86.25 per night. **Credit** A, AmEx, DC, £STC, V.
Portobello is a lovely, relatively-unspoilt part of London, and this hotel is similar. It's a six-floor, terrace house round the corner from the market (*see chapter* **Shopping & Services**) and many of the rooms are delightful. Some of the top rooms are very small, but they get larger the lower down you go. All have en suite bathrooms and idiosyncratic décor. The restaurant's open 24 hours a day.
Hotel services *Restaurant.* **Room services** *Radio. Refrigerator. Tea-making facilities. Telephone. TV.*

South Kensington Guest House
13 Cranley Place, SW7 (071 589 0021). South Kensington underground. **Rates** *single* from £35 per night; *double* from £50 per night. **Credit** A, AmEx, £STC, V.
The South Kensington offers a mixture of modern facilities in a 150-year-old house in a preserved residential area. Some rooms have *en suite* bathrooms.
Room services *Tea & coffee-making facilities. TV.*

Strand Palace Hotel
Strand, WC2 (071 836 8080). Covent Garden underground or Charing Cross underground/BR. **Rates** *single* with bath £74 per night; *double* with bath £89 per night; *triple* with bath £97 per night. **Credit** A, AmEx, DC, £STC, V.
This international-style, modern block on the Strand has recently undergone refurbish-

Hazlitt's Hotel (*listed under* **Hotels: Medium**) *was once the home of the author and politicking pamphleteer, William Hazlitt. The house was built in the early eighteenth century and rooms are rather small, but they're charmingly decorated in period style. The service is effusive and friendly, straight out of another age. Hazlitt probably never expected his home to be turned into a hotel, so he negligently omitted to have enough rooms built - booking is essential. You'll be staying in the centre of Soho, so it's worth every penny.*

BERNERS RESTAURANT

Situated just off Oxford Street, the Berners Restaurant, with its listed ceiling, **must** be the most elegant dining room in London.

This magnificent Edwardian building offers its famous carvery and an excellent selection of 'a la carte' dishes.

In addition, traditional English Afternoon Teas, (sandwiches, scones and cream, etc . . .), are served at the fireside in the lounge, while a harpist plays in the background.

Ramada Hotel
10 Berners Street,
LONDON WI
01-636 1629
(Close to London's theatre land)

ment; the rooms remain spacious and clean and one of the three restaurants is a competently-run carvery. The service is calm but welcoming, even though the hotel can seem a little bland. It's cheap for the area.
Hotel services *Babysitting. Café. Currency exchange (open 24 hours). French, German, Spanish & Italian spoken. Restaurants. Shop.* **Room services** *Tea & coffee-making facilities. Telephone. TV.*

Tower Thistle Hotel
St Katharine's Way, E1 (071 481 2575) Tower Hill underground/DLR. **Rates** *single* with bath £96 per night; *double* with bath £111 per night. **Credit** A, AmEx, CB, DC, TC, V.
Although rooms are small at this modern hotel, they're extremely well equipped. The exterior is an ugly, modernist hulk that's designed to drive the sturdiest guest back to the West End; but press on past the foul muzak in the lobby, and you'll find a friendly, comfortable hotel. The service is of a very high quality. There's a superb view of Tower Bridge from some rooms. Breakfast costs the same in all dining-rooms, so try out the Princess Restaurant first thing in the morning for a tasty breakfast. A snazzy discotheque, Which Way West, is open from 10.30pm to 3am.
Hotel services *Babysitting. Café. Currency exchange (open 24 hours). French, German, Italian, Spanish & Arabic spoken. Restaurants. Shop. Theatre & tour bookings.* **Room services** *Hair dryer. Safe in executive rooms. Tea & coffee-making facilities. Telephone. Trouser press. TV. Video.*

Wilbraham
1 Wilbraham Place, SW1 (071 730 8296). Sloane Square underground. **Rates** *single* from £38 per night; *double* £55 per night, with bath £76 per night. **Credit** $ETC.
The 50 rooms of the Wilbraham are comfortable, old-fashioned, but furnished with all the modern conveniences. Not all the rooms have bathrooms *en suite*, but the hotel is cheap for the area. The service is efficient.
Hotel services *Baby-sitting service. TV room.* **Room services** *Telephone. TV.*

CHEAP

Boka Hotel
35 Eardley Crescent, SW5 (071 373 2844/370 1388). Earl's Court underground. **Rates** *single* £18 per night, £84 per week; *double* £24 per night, £120 per week; *family room* £10 per person per night. **Credit** V.
This is a basic hotel but it comes at a basic price. Most rooms are doubles/twins and some have an *en suite* bathroom. Groups of over 40 can enjoy a small discount.
Hotel services *TV room.*

Curzon House Hotel
58 Courtfield Gardens, SW5 (071 373 6745). Gloucester Road underground. **Rates** *dormitory* from £9 per night; *single* from £15 per night; *double* from £23 per night; weekly rates available. **Credit** £TC.
Guests get their own front door key, as well as access to the kitchen and dining facilities. A very low price to be close to the West End.
Hotel services *TV lounge.*

Flaxman House
104 Oakley Street, SW3 (071 352 0187). Sloane Square or South Kensington under-
ground. **Rates** *single* £22 per night; *double* from £35 per night. **Credit** A, AmEx, DC, £TC, V.
A cheap, calm haven in a busy part of London.

George Hotel
60 Cartwright Gardens, WC1 (071 387 6789). King's Cross or Euston underground/BR. **Rates** *single* from £25 per night; *double* from £39 per night. **Credit** A, £TC, V.
Stay in Bloomsbury which, although it's a bit shabby nowadays, is still very handy for the centre of town. Residents can use the private garden square and its tennis court. Some rooms have private bath or shower. A family of three can stay for £48 per night.
Hotel services *TV & video in lounge.* **Room services** *Radio alarm. Tea & coffee-making facilities.*

Kent House
325 Green Lanes, N4 (081 802 0800). Manor House underground. **Rates** *four-bed room* from £8.50 per night; *single* £14 per night; *double* £10 per person per night. **No credit cards.**
Restricted to those aged between 16 and 45, Kent House is mainly used by students. It's cheap and basic, and there are no rooms with anything more elaborate than hot and cold running water. There's a dining-room that's open to self-caterers.
Hotel services *Common room. Group discount. Kitchen for self-catering. TV.*

Sass House Hotel
11 Craven Terrace, W2 (071 262 2325). Lancaster Gate underground or Paddington underground/BR. **Rates** *single* £15-£18 per night; *double* £22-£26 per night. **Credit** A, AmEx, CB, DC, V.
The rooms are cheap, but then none of them have any facilities. Prices include a continental breakfast.
Hotel services *TV room.*

BED & BREAKFAST

Staying at a bed and breakfast can be a good way to become involved with a London family. Breakfasts are usually of the eggs, bacon and fat variety, prices are cheap, and the owner is often only too pleased to regale you at length about London and its sights. We've also included some moderately-priced hotels, which deliver breakfast to your room. If you want to find one yourself, there are lots in Paddington down to Lancaster Gate, Victoria and Pimlico, and around King's Cross station. Many advertise in the Evening Standard, others are listed in *Where to Stay in London* (published by the London Tourist Board, £2.50; available from the **Tourist Information Centres**; *see chapter* **Essential Information**.

Anne Elizabeth House
30 Collingham Place, SW5 (071 370 4821). Gloucester Road or Earl's Court underground. **Rates** £8-£11 per night. **No credit cards.**
Basic facilities. But only £8 for a room near the centre of London, and with breakfast included, is a bargain.
Hotel services *Cooking facilities. TV room.*

The Claverley
13-14 Beaufort Gardens, SW3 (071 589 8541). Knightsbridge underground. **Rates** *single* £55 per night; *double* £60 per night. **Credit** A, V.
The Claverley is possibly the best bed and breakfast in London, even though you have to pay a bit extra for the privilege of sleeping so close to Harrods. The rooms are clean, comfortable and welcoming, the staff are friendly and eager to help, and the place has a family atmosphere that'll please anyone who's finding the streets of London a struggle.
Hotel services *Baby-listening service. Refreshments.* **Room services** *Telephone. TV.*

Elizabeth Hotel
37 Eccleston Square, SW1 (071 828 6812). Victoria underground/BR. **Rates** *single* £28 per night; *double* with shower £48 per night, with bath £61 per night; *family room* £54 per night. **No credit cards.**
Julian Maslinski's hotel scooped a merit award from the British Tourist Authority in 1987, and was commended for its warm service and for the superb English breakfast. It's a tall, thin Victorian house in a very pretty square, with 22 rooms. Not all the rooms have a bathroom, but there are facilities on every floor and the rooms are decorated in period style. It's best to book.
Hotel services *German & French spoken.*

The Sandringham Hotel
3 Holford Road, NW3 (071 435 1569). Hampstead underground. **Rates** *single* £30 per night; *double* from £50 per night. **No credit cards.**
When this Victorian house was built, Hampstead was still a village with views over the rolling Heath to north London in the far distance. The Heath's still there (800 acres of heath and woodland), but Hampstead, despite its pretensions, is no longer a village. Still, it's much quieter than central London (which is only 20 minutes away by tube). This small hotel is a very pleasant place to stay, with a pretty garden, clean, period rooms and friendly staff. There's a car park at the front.
Hotel services *Garden. TV. Most rooms without facilities.*

The Willett
32 Sloane Gardens, SW1 (071 824 8415). Sloane Square underground. **Rates** *single* from £52 per night; *double* from £69 per night. **Credit** A, AmEx, DC, TC, V.
Sloane Gardens are convenient for the centre of London. Rooms are large, bright and well equipped. Staff are helpful. The Willett is part of a proficient chain of three hotels; if you can't get a room here, they can always refer you to another.
Hotel services *Currency exchange (open 24 hours). Spanish spoken. Theatre & tour booking.* **Room services** *Hair dryer. Tea & coffee-making facilities. Telephone. TV.*

SELF-CATERING

If you intend to stay longer than a fortnight, self-catering in a holiday let or service apartment can be a cheap alternative to a hotel. Service apartments may or may not offer services (maid, cleaner, porter) and are usually more expensive than holiday lets. The best way of finding such accommodation is through an agency (*see below*). A fee is usually payable on acceptance and some or all of the rent must be paid in advance, plus a deposit.

With service apartments, you can cut out the agency and approach the owners directly. Some blocks are privately owned and others are part of a group. **Draycott House** 10 Draycott Avenue, SW3 (contact Mrs Coulthard; 071 584 4659) and **Elvaston Lodge** 12 Elvaston Place, SW7 (contact Mrs Stoner; 071 589 9412) are centrally-located blocks of flats rented out to visitors. For further details look in *Where to Stay In London* (£2.50 from the Tourist Information Centres *listed under* **Booking Services**; *see above*).

ACCOMMODATION AGENCIES

Derek Collins Agency
Panton House, Panton Street, SW1 (071 930 7986). Leicester Square or Piccadilly Circus underground. **Open** 9.30am-2pm, 2.30-5.30pm, Mon-Fri.
No agency fees for finding holiday lets and long-term accommodation.

Flatsearch
68 Queensway, W2 (071 221 6335/071 229 0036/071 221 5918). Bayswater or Queensway underground. **Open** 9.30am-5.30pm Mon-Fri; 9am-3.30pm Sat.
This agency deals with long and short-term stays, but prefers a minimum stay of one month. A bedsit should cost about £50 per week. It also handles service apartments. The fee (which is payable on acceptance of accommodation) is one week's rent.

Jenny Jones Agency
40 South Molton Street, W1 (071 493 4801). Bond Street underground. **Open** 9.30am-2pm, 2.30-5.15pm Mon-Fri.
There are no agency fees. Holiday lets of two months minimum and long-term stays are available.

APARTMENTS

Crawford Holiday Flats
10 Wyndham Place, W1 (071 402 6165). Baker Street underground. **Open** 9.15am-5.15pm Mon-Fri. **No credit cards.**
Each flat is completely self-contained and fully furnished. The cheapest accommoda-tion costs £195 per week and flats can accommodate up to six adults. Three weeks' cancellation notice is needed to ensure a full refund; otherwise one week's rent is taken as a fee.

Number One Luxury Apartments
1 Harrington Gardens, SW7 (071 370 4044). Gloucester Road underground. **Open** 9am-6pm Mon-Fri; 9am-1pm Sat. **Credit** A, AmEx, DC, TC, V.
These luxury furnished and serviced suites are in South Kensington. Flats are cheaper in the winter, when a one-bedroom apartment (with kitchen) will cost £245 per week. Prices rise sharply after that and you'll have to be carrying a lot of traveller's cheques in order to snuggle into a flat in the summer. Apartments are available for a night, a week or a month; one week's rent is required as a deposit.

HALLS OF RESIDENCE

Most university halls of residence are cheap and basic, sometimes shabby, but usually close to the centre of town. All are attached to London colleges and they can only be let during the vacations (usually Easter and the long summer break, from June to September). The halls don't encourage short-term stays, preferring visitors to book for the entire period, but it's worth phoning to see if there have been any cancellations. Write months in advance as the halls get booked up very quickly. There are usually communal cooking facilities attached; and most halls have a television room and a café serving very cheap food. To book any of London University halls, contact the accommodation office at *Senate House* (071 636 2818).

Canterbury Hall
Cartright Gardens, WC1 (071 387 5526). Russell Square underground. **Reception open** 24 hours daily. **Rates** *single* with bath £23 per night, *single* without bath £21 per night. **Available** Mar-Apr, Jun-Sept, Dec.
Visitors can stay in this expensive hall during the Easter, summer and Christmas university vacations. It's popular with a slightly older clientèle and the price includes breakfast and dinner. Cheaper rooms (just bed and breakfast) are available: a single with a bath is £20.50; a single with a shared bath is £18.50.
Facilities *Baths. Squash court. Tennis court. TV room.*

Carr Saunders Hall
18-24 Fitzroy Street, W1 (071 580 6338). Warren Street underground. **Reception open** 8am-11.30pm daily. **Rates** *single* £18. **Available** Mar-Apr, Jul-Sept. **No credit cards.**
A central hall in an area with some fine pubs and restaurants. There's a common room and a TV room. The dining-room is open for dinner from 6-7.15pm daily.
Facilities *Baths. Games room. Kitchen. Laundry. Showers. TV room.*

Centre Français
61-69 Chepstow Place, W2 (071 221 8134). Notting Hill Gate underground. **Reception open** 7am-9pm daily. **Rates** *dormitory* £9.50 per person per night; *single* £17 per night; *double* £15 per person per night; *triple* £12 per person per night. **Credit** £TC, V.
A hostel offering accommodation to students and young people under 30 years. Rates for 1990 are not fixed at time of writing.

Imperial College
15 Prince's Gardens, SW7. Book through Summer Accomodation Centre, Linstead Hall, Watts Way, SW7 (071 589 5111, ext 3600). South Kensington underground. **Reception open** *Easter* 8am-5pm daily; *summer* 24 hours daily. **Rates** *single* £18 per night for stays of less than one week; £15.50 per night for stays of over one week. **Available** Easter, Jun-Sept. **Credit** £TC.
Bed and breakfast in single rooms is available in the summer, but for groups only in the Easter. No one aged under-16 is admitted. There are some basic self-catering apartments available, but the prices had not been fixed at time of writing; the minimum stay is one week.
Facilities *Baths. Games room. Kitchen. Showers. TV room.*

John Adams Hall
15-23 Endsleigh Street, WC1 (071 387 4086/071 387 4796). Euston Square underground or Euston underground/BR. **Reception open** 8am-10pm daily. **Rates** *single* £15.52 per night; *double* from £27 per night. **Available** Jun-Sept, Easter. **Credit** A, AmEx, £TC, V.
For students only. This is a Georgian building complete with original interiors. Over 100 single rooms and a few doubles are available; book ahead. Dinner costs £3.50.
Facilities *Baths. Games room. Group discount. Laundry. Library. Showers. Study. TV room.*

King's College
King's College Campus Vacation Bureaux, 552 King's Road, SW1 (071 351 6011/071 351 2488). Fulham Broadway underground. **Reception open** 24 hours daily. **Rates** *single* from £14 per night. **Available** Jul-Sept; Mar-Apr. **Credit** £TC.
King's College, part of the University of London, has seven halls of residence spread over London. Two of them are in Chelsea. Each hall has TV rooms, laundry facilities, baths and showers; some have basic cooking facilities. There's no curfew, and the receptions are open 24-hours. Children under 16 are allowed in with parents.

Passfield Hall
1 Endsleigh Place, WC1 (071 387 3584/071 387 7743). Euston Square underground. **Reception open** 8am-11pm daily. **Rates** Mar, Apr £13.80 per night; Jul-Sept £18 per night. **No credit cards.**
This is the hall of residence of the London School of Economics, providing bed and English breakfast in single, twin and triple rooms, all fitted with sinks. Facilities are basic and it's suitable for families.
Facilities *Baths & showers. Games room. Kitchen. Laundry. TV room.*

CAMPING & CARAVANNING

Sing ho! for the great outdoors. Yes, despite our notorious weather, and despite London's drab appearance, it is possible to camp here in the summer months. Big marquees are erected on Wormwood Scrubs every summer, which act as dormitories to create **Tent City**. You don't actually need a tent and every night there's a merry band of mixed nationalities, gathered round the camp fires, strumming their ol' guitars. For those with transport and their own tent or caravan, try **Caravan Harbour** or **Abbey Wood Caravan Club.** Pause to consider, however, how difficult it's going to be driving a caravan through London.

Abbey Wood Caravan Club
*Federation Road, SE2 (081 310 2233).
Charing Cross underground/BR.* **Open** office 8am-10pm daily. **Credit** A, £TC, V.
Arrivals after 10pm can stay the night and check in the next morning. Rates per night: summer (21 May-30 Aug) £2.40 per person; winter £2 per person. Pitch fee £3 per tent for walkers or cyclists; £3.50 for motorcyclists; £4.50 for cars; £5 for caravans. There's also an electricity charge:

in summer £1, the rest of the year £1.40. Facilities: toilets, hot showers, phone, shop. Maximum stay 14 nights in the summer; 21 nights in the winter. Advance booking necessary in July, August and Bank Holidays.

Caravan Harbour
Crystal Palace Parade, SE19 (081 778 7155). Crystal Palace BR. **Open** office 8am-10pm daily; site 24 hours daily. **Credit** A, £TC, V.
Arrivals after 10pm can stay the night and check in the following morning. No tents for hire. Rates per night are the same as at the **Abbey Wood Caravan Club** (*see above*). Hot showers, no on-site eating facilities, but there are cafés nearby. There's no shop. Maximum stay is two weeks.

Lee Valley Park
Pickett's Lock Centre, Pickett's Lock Lane, N9 (081 803 4756). Ponder's End or Lower Edmonton BR/W8 bus. **Rates** car with tent or caravan £5.30 for two people per night, £1.30 for each extra person; backpackers £1.50 per night. £1.50 per night electricity charge.
Pickett's Lock Sports Centre is a huge sports complex with many facilities and lots of room.

Tent City
Old Oak Common Lane, W3 (081 743 5708). East Acton underground/7, 12, 52A bus. **Open** 24 hours daily, May-Oct. **Rates** *per person per night* £4 adult; £2 age 5-14; free under - 5s..
In the summer, large dormitory tents are put up in Tent City to provide accommodation for visitors. You can pitch your own tent instead, for the same price, which includes showers and baggage store. There's a friendly, holiday

atmosphere and it's a good place to meet other low-buget travellers.

EMERGENCY ACCOMMODATION

We would not advise anyone to try sleeping out in the streets or parks of London. Of course, you will see people huddled in cardboard boxes around the South Bank Centre, but it's not warm, it's not pleasant and it's not safe. If you try sleeping in a sleeping bag in a park, you'll probably be moved on by the police. If there really is no alternative to sleeping out, always leave your rucksack/bags in a left luggage department at a railway station (*see chapter **Survival***).

Otherwise, if you've got a little bit of spare cash left, first contact **Housing Advice Switchboard** (*see below*), **Tent City** (*see above* **Camping & Caravanning**) or one of the cheap hotels. Despite the housing crisis, there are 128,000 empty properties in London at the moment. Squatting is legal and squatters do have legal rights, but

*Back-packers heading for **Holland House** (listed under **Youth Hostels**) will have the unexpected privilege of staying in what's left of a Jacobean mansion (see chapter **Local London**). The 190-bed hostel is not palatial, but has been recently refurbished, and it's situation in Holland Park is stunning. With easy access to the park amenities, public transport, Notting Hill and Kensington High Street, this is the best-located hostel in town. That is, until the YHA building at **Carter Lane**, EC2, under the shadow of St Paul's Cathedral, reopens in autumn 1991 after a major restoration.*

you may have problems with basic things like gas and electricity.

The following organizations also publish helpful leaflets. Bear in mind that travellers' housing problems are considered a low priority by overworked aid organizations.

Advisory Service for Squatters
2 St Paul's Road, N1 (071 359 8814). Highbury & Islington underground/BR. **Open** 2-6pm Mon-Fri.
Get *The Squatter's Handbook* (60p) here.

Housing Advice Switchboard
7A Fortess Road, NW5 (071 434 2522). Kentish Town or Tufnell Park underground. **Open** 24 hours daily.
Phone the Switchboard and you'll be put in touch with emergency, cheap accommodation. This is an advisory service for people who are short of money and desperate for a room; it's not for people who can't decide whether to stay in the Ritz or the Savoy.

International Traveller's Aid
Platform 16, Victoria Station, SW1 (071 834 3925/071 834 3901). **Open** times vary, phone for details.
A voluntary body connected to the YMCA, which helps foreign nationals arriving in London, particularly with accommodation.

London Council for the Welfare of Women & Girls/YWCA
Accommodation Services, 57 Great Russell Street, WC1 (071 430 1524). Tottenham Court Road underground. **Open** 10am-5pm Mon-Wed; 10am-7pm Thur; 1-5pm Fri for personal callers; 10am-5pm Mon-Fri for telephone enquiries.
This organization publishes two free leaflets entitled *Temporary Accommodation in London* and *Vacation Accommodation*.

Y HOTELS

There are 18 Y hotels around London offering both long- and short-term accommodation. You can write to, or ring, the **National Council for YMCAs** at 640 Forest Road, E17 (081 520 5599) for a list of their addresses. We list a few below.

YMCA (London Central) /St Giles Hotel
112 Great Russell Street, WC1 (071 636 8616). Tottenham Court Road underground. **Reception** open 24 hours daily. **No credit cards.**
At the time of going to press, the hotel was negotiating to buy out the hostel, which is currently closed. Hotel rates per night are: single room £42; double £63.50.

Barbican YMCA
2 Fann Street, EC2 (071 628 0697). Barbican underground or Moorgate under-

ground/BR. **Reception open** 24 hours daily. **Credit** £TC.
Accommodation for 240 people, all in single and double rooms. Rates: £15.50 per night including breakfast. Long term (over 12 weeks) per week £58 single, £49 per person sharing. Short term £80 single; £51 double. All includes breakfast and dinner during the week, three meals Saturday and Sunday. Book at least two months ahead.

Indian YMCA
41 Fitzroy Square, W1 (071 387 0411). Warren Street underground. **Reception open** 24 hours daily. **Credit** £TC.
This Y has 117 beds for longer stay students and trainees. A few beds are available for tourists. Preference is given to Indian citizens, but the hostel regularly has a few vacancies and welcomes people of any nationality. A single room costs £22.50 per day; a double costs £30 per day. Both include breakfast and dinner.

London City YMCA
8 Errol Street, EC1 (071 628 8832). Barbican or Moorgate underground/BR. **Reception open** 8.30am-10pm daily. **Credit** £TC.
Most of the year this Y is booked up with long-term student residents, but most rooms are vacated during July and August. Rooms are all singles, costing £20 per night including breakfast, or £91 per week including breakfast and dinner (no self-catering facilities). Longer term stays have to be applied for, and the waiting list is huge. Book in April if you want to stay in July.

Stockwell YMCA
40-46 Stockwell Road, SW9 (071 274 7861). Stockwell underground. **Reception open** 7.30am-10pm daily. **Credit** £TC.
This is a huge building, with accommodation for 330 people, mostly in rooms sleeping two to five (a few single rooms are available). Single rates are £16.10 per night including breakfast, £80.50 per week including breakfast and dinner (three meals during weekends). For shared rooms, these rates drop to £13.80 per person per night, £75.90 per week. Long-term stay is limited to students and people in employment under the age of 35, but all must be prepared to stay a mimimum of 12 weeks (the rates go down to £57.60 per week). Booking ahead is always a good idea.

YOUTH HOSTELS

The **YHA** (Youth Hostel Association) is part of the IYHF (International Youth Hostel Federation) and has five youth hostels in London. You should book at least two to three months in advance. You must become a member (you can join when you arrive at the hostel) and yearly membership is: £1.70 under-16s; £3.70 age 16-20; £7 over-21s; £7.50 international

guest card. Prices per person per night, including breakfast: £8.60 under-16s; £9.60 age 16-20; £11.10 over-21s. Unlimited stay unless otherwise stated. All the hostels have a cafeteria and all the accommodation is in dormitory form. Contact: YHA, 14 Southampton Street, WC2 (071 240 3158).

Holland House
Holland Park, Holland Walk, W8 (071 937 0748). South Kensington underground. **Reception open** 7am-midnight daily. **Credit** A, £STC, V.
See **picture and caption.**

Earl's Court Hostel
38 Bolton Gardens, SW5 (071 373 7083). Earl's Court underground. **Reception open** 7am-midnight daily. **Credit** A, V.
Maximum stay is four days.

Highgate Hostel
84 Highgate West Hill, N6 (081 340 1831). Highgate underground/210 or 271 bus. **Reception open** 8.45am-noon; 5pm-midnight daily. **Credit** A, V.

Hampstead Hostel
4 Wellgarth Road, NW11 (081 458 9054). Golders Green underground. **Reception open** 7am-11.30pm daily. **Credit** A, V.

BUDGET STAY

If you don't have the money for a holiday let or service apartment (*see above* **Self-Catering**) and are planning on staying longer than a month, you should try finding a bedsit, or a room in a flat. London accommodation prices are high and the competition is fierce. You'll usually have to pay a month's rent in advance, but this is returned when you leave. Look in *Time Out* magazine every Wednesday; *LAM*, a free Australian weekly; *Loot*, issued on Thursday; the 11am edition of the *London Evening Standard*; *Dalton's Weekly* and the *London Weekly Advertiser* on Thursday; and *Capital Gay*, a free weekly magazine from gay clubs and bookstores. The Capital Radio flatshare list is available at 11am every Tuesday from the foyer of *Capital Radio* at Euston Tower, Euston Road, NW1, Warren Street underground, or in *Midweek* magazine, free from major underground stations on Thursday.

London by Area

You've been sightseeing, visited the Tower of London and St Paul's Cathedral, and watched the Changing of the Guard. You're probably rather tired of being shunted around with herds of other visitors and you're eager to meet some Londoners. But where are they? We've divided the capital into areas to show where the natives of this vast city eat, drink and make merry.

The West End, the City of London and the River Thames are famous for their big sights. But in the following pages you'll also discover their day-to-day character and hidden corners. It's also worth venturing out, travel-card in hand, into London's diverse and fascinating hinterland. Places such as Hampstead and Clapham were once villages; engulfed by the city, they've kept their local qualities. Other districts – Brixton, Camden, the East End – have become cosmopolitan, multi-ethnic communities.

You can be sure that these local shops, pubs, parks and traditions are the true soul of London. More specialist information about the city's history, its shopping and services, where to drink and have a meal, and what entertainments are on offer, can be found throughout the Guide.

CONTENTS:

The West End

Long shot: Big Ben. Close up: Trafalgar Square. You've seen the movie; now visit the real West End.

The few square miles between **Park Lane** and **Charing Cross**, **Oxford Street** and **The Mall** make up the area that most Londoners and visitors agree upon as The West End. It's packed with celebrated sights, shops, streets and hotels that are internationally recognised as symbols of the capital, including **Big Ben**, **Buckingham Palace**, **Piccadilly Circus** and **Trafalgar Square**. Because of the frequent appearance of these highlights on picture postcards and in films, it's difficult not to treat the West End as if it were just a collection of photo opportunities. This can mean missing out on the more characterful spots and hidden parks that make the streets of central London such a pleasure to explore.

Contained within the geographical boundaries of the West End are five very individual neighbourhoods. **Mayfair** reeks of the rich smell of money, **Soho's** odour is of cosmopolitan cooking and smoky jazz clubs. By way of contrast are the squares of **Westminster**, home to parliamentary bureaucracy and political ritual. **Covent Garden** bustles with shoppers, while neighbouring **Piccadilly's** streets are more sedate, the stores more expensive and exclusive.

COVENT GARDEN

Medieval monks from **Westminster Abbey** once grew vegetables and buried bodies at the convent gardens where today shoppers peruse designer bric-à-brac. Following **Henry VIII's** confiscation of church property in the Reformation, this promising site just outside the City walls passed to the Russell family in 1533, and then to the Earl of Bedford. His enterprising descendant employed the architect **Inigo Jones** to create London's first planned square. Jones's elegant Palladian houses were much sought after by the seventeenth-century 'in' crowd. The spacious square around which they lived rapidly became the most convenient centre for fruit and vegetable traders from outlying villages. The Earl built permanent sheds for the makeshift market, and by 1671, **Charles II** had granted a charter and official market rights, which remained with the Bedford family until 1900.

The market was a pretty lively affair, with 'puppet shows, parrots and love birds' on sale to 'people of quality'. Coffee houses and taverns proliferated around the Piazza, and during the eighteenth century Covent Garden became the stamping ground for fashionable young ruffians known as Mohocks, who had a penchant for overturning coaches and their contents on to rubbish tips. Affronted aristocratic residents moved out, and market traders, publicans and pimps came to dominate the area. The streets around **Seven Dials**, once elegant and admired, sunk to the depths, becoming a nineteenth-century synonym for poverty and rowdiness.

Eventually, energetic Victorian developers cleared the slums, carved out the **Charing Cross Road** and built the iron and stone market buildings in the centre of the piazza in 1850. After centuries of residency the thriving fruit and veg trade became too cramped, and in 1974 moved south of the river to **Nine Elms**. After demolition plans were scuppered by popular protest (*see chapter* **To the Eighties**), the Greater London Council developed the area with an exemplary mix of conservation and innovation. The many cafés, boutiques, craft shops and market stalls make Covent Garden today one of the West End's most lively places to stroll, browse and shop. Sadly, astronomical rent rises are forcing out unique small shops, to be replaced by conformist chainstores and offices.

Famous as a theatre district, Covent Garden is known internationally as the home of the **Royal Opera House** (*see chapter* **Music: Classical & Opera**). At the Piazza is, appropriately, the **Theatre Museum** and, inappropriately because of its cramped conditions, the **London Transport Museum** (for both *see chapter* **Museums**).

Africa Centre
38 King Street, WC2 (071 836 1973; restaurant 071 836 1976; shop 071 240 6098). Covent Garden underground. **Open** *Kikapu shop* 10am-6.30pm Mon-Fri; 9am-7pm Sat; 10am-6pm Sun; *Calabash restaurant* noon-3pm Mon-Fri; 6-10.30pm Mon-Sat. **Admission** free; phone for ticket prices for special events. **Credit** (restaurant and shop only) A, AmEx, V.
The umbrella for London-based African organisations, this centre is an unbeatable resource for information about culture, politics and travel in that continent. The ground floor crafts shop sells hand-made jewellery, and the basement restaurant offers an imaginative, changing menu of pan-African food at reasonable prices.

Covent Garden Market
The Piazza, Covent Garden, WC2. Covent Garden underground. **Open** *Antiques*: 9am-5pm Mon; *Crafts*: 9am-5pm Tue-Sat.
See **picture and caption**.

Crown & Anchor
22 Neal Street, WC2 (071 836 5649). Covent Garden underground. **Open** 11am-11pm Mon-Sat; noon-3pm, 7-10.30pm, Sun. **No credit cards.**
A convenient and very popular meeting place, especially during the summer, when customers crowd the pavements on the corner of Shelton Street and Neal Street. Ideal for a post-theatre drink after an evening at the **Donmar Warehouse Theatre** (*see chapter* **Theatre**), when the audience mingles with the cast in a companionable crush.

Ecology Centre
45 Shelton Street, WC2 (information centre 071 379 4324; shop and café 071 497 2723). Covent Garden underground. **Open** 10am-6pm Mon-Fri; *shop and café* 10am-9pm Mon-Sat **Admission** free. **Credit** A, AmEx, V.
This multi-purpose building is London's best source of information on all things green. Its small, well-stocked shop sells environmentally-sound household products and a good range of T-shirts, cards and books. The exhibition space has changing displays of art, crafts and gifts, and the Yours Naturally Café is busy and friendly, although the quality of the food is variable. Stick to the spicy toasties and delicious cakes. Prices are low and portions are large.

Food for Thought
31 Neal Street, WC2 (071 836 0239). Covent Garden underground. **Open** noon-8pm Mon-Sat. **No credit cards.**
This popular vegetarian restaurant sells ample portions of imaginative and tasty food at reasonable prices. Both the take-away section (upstairs) and the eat-in basement are mobbed between 1pm and 2pm, but during the afternoons and evenings it's a lively place to meet and eat.

Jubilee Market
Jubilee Hall, The Piazza, Covent Garden, WC2 (071 836 2139). Covent Garden underground.

Open *Antiques* 7am-5pm Mon; *General* 9am-5pm Tue-Fri; *Crafts* 9am-5pm Sat, Sun.
Behind this uninspiring edifice is staged a useful weekend crafts market of high quality toys, clothes, gifts and pictures – you won't find any bargains here. Weekdays offer a more prosaic range of budget fashion, shoes and household goods, while Monday is antiques day. It's packed out on Sunday afternoons, but whatever the day, go well before lunchtime, when traders are good-tempered and crowds are thin.

Lamb & Flag
33 Rose Street, WC2. Covent Garden underground. **Open** 11am-11pm Mon-Sat; noon-3pm, 7-10.30pm, Sun. **No credit cards.**
Tucked away down a side street, this pub has been frequented by theatre and literary folk for centuries. The only timber building left in the West End, it's quaint and characterful – if only its hideous illuminated Fosters sign were disposed of. Wonky doors, low ceilings and a stream of appreciative regulars mean that it's often a struggle to reach the bar, particularly in the early evening. About the best ploughman's lunches in town are served here.

Neal's Yard Clock
above Neal's Yard Wholefood Warehouse, Shorts Gardens, WC2. Covent Garden underground. See **picture and caption.**

Penguin Bookshop
10 The Piazza, The Piazza, Covent Garden, WC2 (071 379 7650). Covent Garden underground. **Open** 10am-8pm Mon-Sat; noon-6pm Sun. **Credit** A, AmEx, DC, £TC, V.
Like an iceberg, most of this popular bookshop is hidden below the surface. Beneath the counter area, every spare inch of the cavern-like basement is stocked with the full range of Penguin titles and books on every subject. The shop is a frequent venue for author-signing sessions; dates are listed in *Time Out* magazine. At 1 The Market is the **Puffin Bookshop** (*see chapter* **Children's London**), which caters for younger readers.

Oasis Baths
32 Endell Street, WC2 (071 831 1804). Covent Garden, Holborn or Tottenham Court Road underground. **Open** 8am-7pm Mon-Fri; 10am-4pm Sat, Sun. **Admission** £2 adults; 40p under-16s.
Aptly named, this retreat from the crowds has central London's only public outdoor pool, where you can laze on the patio in the summer; it also has an Olympic-size indoor pool. There's a small café, saunas, aerobics classes and regular aromatherapy sessions. It gets very packed at lunchtimes, but you can have the place to yourself at around 11am.
Discount scheme by prior application.

St Paul's ('The Actors') Church
Bedford Street, WC2 (071 836 5221). Covent Garden underground. **Services** 1.10pm Wed; 8.30am Thur; 11am Sun.
See **picture and caption.**

Seven Dials Monument
Seven Dials, corner of Monmouth Street and Earlham Street, WC2. Covent Garden or Leicester Square underground. See **picture and caption.**

Covent Garden Market (*listed under* **Covent Garden**) *no longer stores fruit 'n' veg, but traders still sell their wares off carts in its refurbished arcades. Antiques, crafts, knitwear and jewellery are sold at inflated prices at what is tweely dubbed the Apple Market – but the quality is high. Browsing through the traffic-free area of stalls and specialist shops is enjoyable despite the huge crowds. This is one of the few places where Britain's prudish, kill-joy authorities allow street performers to entertain legally and where there's still a lively atmosphere on Sundays and into the evenings.*

MAYFAIR

The seventeenth-century May Fair, 'that most pestilent nursery of impiety and vice', gave this area its name – and a reputation for sinful excess and rioting. From 1686 until the 1750s, for a fortnight each spring, the streets of what is now London's most sophisticated 'village' seethed with drunken revellers, prostitutes and shrewd traders like Tiddy Dols, the gingerbread man, upon the site of whose stall the current restaurant at 55 **Shepherd's Market** was established (*see chapter* **Eating & Drinking**). Once the annual junketing of the Fair was shut down, Mayfair began its upward spiral to respectability. Yet even today, reminders of the area's risqué history still exist in the shape of the 'hostesses', who ply their trade around Shepherd Market.

A favourite address for the London homes of English aristocrats, the area remained essentially residential until quite recently. The balance between high class homes, hotels, shops and clubs was upset by an invasion of solicitors, financiers and media folk, who have converted an enormous number of properties into office space. The dwindling number of residents, and the small businesses which cater to their needs, has dramatically changed the character of Mayfair. The vociferous residents' association is currently battling with Westminster Council to ensure that offices revert to residential use, and that local shops and businesses are preserved.

Berkeley Square
W1. Green Park underground. **Open** 10am-4.30pm Mon-Fri. **Admission** free.
The extensive rebuilding and heavy traffic encircling this square make it difficult to imagine the peaceful elegance of its past, when, as the song goes, 'a nightingale sang in Berkeley Square'. For a quiet rest, try the I Am The Only Running Footman pub in

espite its noisy bor-
s still very popular
ociety.

nd.
3ond Streets link
y with a string of
stores. This is
its New York sister, but every bit as pricey.
It's a window-shopping experience, only the
darkened windows of Saint Laurent, 143
New Bond Street, conceal garments so
expensive that they carry no price tag. The
distinctive clothing at Chanel, 26 Old Bond
Street, is hidden behind the formidable perfume displays, protected from the gaze of
lesser mortals.

Brown's Hotel
Albermarle Street, W1 (071 493 6020).
Green Park underground. **Afternoon tea
served** 3-6pm daily. **Credit** A, AmEx, DC, V.
An investment of £10.50 per head secures
an afternoon tea experience of remarkable sophistication and elegance. Waiters
in tail-coats flutter round your armchair,
with constant supplies of delicious tea,
scones, pastries and sandwiches. You
leave feeling very pampered and too full
even to think about dinner. *See also chapter* **Acommodation**.

Church of the Immaculate Conception
*Farm Street, W1 (071 493 7811). Green
Park or Bond Street underground.* **Services**
7.30am, 8.30am, 12.05pm, 1.05pm, 6pm
Mon-Fri; 7.30am, 8.30am, 11am, 6pm Sat;
7.30am, 8.30am, 10am, 11am (sung Latin),
12.15pm, 4.15pm, 6.15pm Sun.
This splendid Gothic revival building, beside
the Mount Street Gardens *(see below)*, is the
London headquarters of the Jesuit Fathers. It's
one of the very few Catholic churches in the
city where a sung Latin mass is celebrated.

Cork Street
W1. Green Park or Piccadilly underground.
Dominated by Waddington's five separate
gallery spaces (at no's 2, 4, 5, 11 and 34 Cork
Street), this street behind the Royal
Academy is home to the most concentrated
collection of commercial art galleries in town.
Work on sale is at the very top end of the
market, with pieces by Miro, Matisse and
Picasso diplayed alongside exhibits from
well-established contemporary British and
foreign artists. The Nicola Jacobs Gallery (26
Cork Street) is the only space selling work by
relatively unknown young artists, for under
£1,500 *(see chapter* **Art Galleries**).

Grosvenor Square
W1. Green Park or Bond Street underground.
Open 10am-5pm Mon-Sat. **Admission** free.

Dominated by the monolithic US Embassy
building *(see chapters* **To the Eighties;
Survival**), Grosvenor Square is a spacious,
pleasant park in which to stroll or rest awhile.
Around lunchtime on fine days the steps of
the Roosevelt Memorial are crowded with
local office workers and visitors.

Hard Rock Café
*150 Old Park Lane, W1 (071 629 0382).
Hyde Park Corner underground.* **Open** 11.30-
12.30am Mon-Thur, Sun; 11.30am-1am Fri,
Sat. **Average** £10.50. **House wine** £7 bottle,
£1.90 glass. **Credit** £STC.
Avoid the lengthy queues by arriving at
11.30am and make lunch into brunch at this
food institution. The American-style generous portions of excellent steak and burgers
are served to a mainstream rock sound-
track. Musical memorabilia on the walls
changes periodically – check out Clapton's
old Fender and one of the Gibsons to survive the Jimi Hendrix Experience. If you
wear a Hard Rock Café T-shirt you are irrevocably branded a tourist. *See chapter*
Eating & Drinking.

The May Fair Hotel
*Stratton Street, W1 (071 629 7777). Green
Park underground.* **Open** *Coffee House* 7am-
10.30pm Mon-Sat, 7.30am-11pm Sun;
Mayfair Bar 11am-11pm Mon-Sat; *Le Château
restaurant and bar* 12.30-2.30pm, 6.30-
10.30pm, Mon-Fri. **Credit** *(Le Château and
Coffee House only)* A, AmEx, DC, £STC, V.
One of the district's plush hotels, the May
Fair was fashionable with thirties high society. But don't let the conspicuous luxury
deter you from using the hotel's services, all
of which are open to the non-resident public.
As well as a comfortable coffee house (afternoon tea 3-5pm daily), and a relaxed bar,
there's a business service, a health club with
sauna, a pool, a weights room, and a friendly
hair and beauty salon.

Mount Street Gardens
*between Farm Street, Mount Street and South
Audley Street, W1. Green Park underground.*
Open 7am-7pm daily.
Tucked behind the Church of the
Immaculate Conception *(see above)*, this is a
tranquil spot to sit, except during playtimes
at the neighbouring school. Handy for the
Mayfair Library in South Audley Street,
whose friendly and informative staff run a
series of talks by authors and broadcasters.

Shepherd Market
W1. Green Park underground.
This pedestrianized network of lanes
between White Horse Street and Curzon
Street is a delightful spot for a relaxed stroll.
Residents and visitors always pack-out the
coffee shop, The Village (corner of Trebeck
Street and Shepherd Market), at around
11am, so arrive earlier for a seat – or try the
Da Corradi deli and café for a quieter cuppa.
Among the antique dealers and ironmongers
is a good sprinkling of wine bars and restau-
rants catering for both tourists and locals.

Sotheby's
*34-35 New Bond Street, W1 (071 493 8080).
Bond Street, Green Park or Oxford Circus
underground.* **Open** 9am-4.30pm Mon-Fri
for buying and viewing. **Admission** free.
No credit cards.
The exhibition halls and sale rooms of this
famous auction house are a free source of

The eccentric **Neal's Yard Clock** *(listed under* **Covent Garden***) owes its
design to cartoonist, Tim Hunkin. The minute tube fills with water until on the
hour the water passes through the system, ringing bells and tipping watering cans
to nourish flowers, which appear to grow as they are mounted on floats.
Unsuspecting people underneath once got a soaking, but spoilsports have erected a
guttered awning. Inside the tiny Neal's Yard courtyard are health shops and cafés.
Here, another Hunkin device has wooden figures, which squirt water for just 10p.*

fascinating entertainment. Just walk in to view anything from vintage teddy bears to rock and roll memorabilia, or bring your own treasures for a free valuation by the experts. All items for sale are on show to the public for three days before auction (*see chapter* **Shopping & Services**).

South Molton Street & Avery Row

W1. Bond Street underground.
Chic designer-fashion stores line these streets, and the cosmopolitan shoppers they attract stray across Oxford Street into St Christopher's Place, and down to Maddox Street and Lancashire Court. The area is riddled with trendy cafés: The Widow Applebaum's Deli and Bagel Academy on South Molton Street is pricey, with coffee at £1 a cup, but the best spot in town for people-watching. The Vidal Sassoon Hairdressing School in Davies Mews offers cut-price styling by students for willing guinea-pigs; phone *071 499 5808* for an appointment.

PICCADILLY

Piccadilly Circus (*see chapter* **Sightseeing**) is not just an intersection on a street map – it's a national byword for any kind of overcrowded chaos. Currently besieged by builders, bags of rubbish and nightmarish traffic, London's famous meeting place is crazier than ever. Only the freshly restored **Eros** statue remains unperturbed above the pandemonium. The neon-lit Circus of today is a far cry from the elegant design envisaged by the Prince Regent. He commissioned John Nash to design a sweeping thoroughfare to link **Regent's Park** to his home at **Carlton House** on **Pall Mall**. The grandeur of the original plan, completed in 1812, lingers on in the high quality stores which line **Piccadilly** and **Regent Street**. No doubt Lady Hamilton, Lord Byron and other notable ex-residents of this area would still appreciate the windows of the gents' outfitters in **Jermyn Street**, which continue to exemplify old-fashioned refinement. Some exceptionally good taste is also on show at **The Royal Academy of Art** (*see chapter* **Art Galleries**) on **Piccadilly**. If all this is getting just too British for you, look in at the **Museum of Mankind** (*see chapter* **Museums**) for a glimpse of some treasures from around the world.

The ideal place for a quiet stroll away from the mêlée is the wonderfully deserted network of streets at the end of **Pall Mall,** between **Green Park** and **The Mall**. **Stable**

In 1633 the Earl of Bedford commissioned Inigo Jones to build **St Paul's ('The Actors')Church** *(listed under* **Covent Garden***) on the cheap, to be 'no better than a barn'. Jones called his work 'the handsomest barn in England'. Its splendid portico on the Piazza, famously featured in* My Fair Lady, *is in fact at the back. There's a secluded churchyard at the front where you can relax, reached through King Street, Henrietta Street or Inigo Place. Theatrical memorials, including the casket containing Ellen Terry's ashes, decorate the interior – this theatreland church is dedicated to actors.*

Yard, Cleveland Row and **Catherine Wheel Yard** are neglected by visitors and Londoners alike, but they still feel very much like Royal St James.

Built upon the site of a medieval leper hospital, only the gatehouse and clock of Henry VIII's original **St James's Palace** survive today, but the royal tone of the neighbourhood prevails: many of the houses contain grace-and-favour apartments occupied by people who have been granted the right to residence by the sovereign. **Carlton Gardens**, linked to the north side of the Mall by several flights of steps, is a charming spot to pause and take in the view over the park and Westminster. The lively and controversial **Institute of Contemporary Arts (ICA)** nearby will bring you right back up to date.

St James's Park is one of London's loveliest spots and is a good place to retreat to after seeing **The Changing of the Guard** at **Buckingham Palace** or after viewing the **Queen's Gallery** or the **Royal Mews** (*see chapters* **Sightseeing** and **London by Season**).

And of course every London visitor must see **Trafalgar Square** (*see chapter* **Sightseeing**), which boasts the **National Gallery** and the **National Portrait Gallery** next door to each other. *See chapter* **Art Galleries**.

All Souls Church

Langham Place, W1 (071 580 4357). Oxford Circus underground. **Services** 1.05pm Thur; 9.30am, 11am, 6.30pm Sun; 7pm prayer meeting alternate Tuesdays.
At the far north end of Regent Street, slap bang in front of the BBC building, this curious little round church is a calm spot for contemplation. It hosts a bi-annual 'prom prayer' festival and one-off series of organ recitals.

Burlington Arcade

off Piccadilly and Old Bond Street, W1. Green Park or Piccadilly Circus underground. See **picture and caption.**

The Design Centre

28 Haymarket, SW1 (071 839 8000). Leicester Square or Piccadilly Circus underground. **Open** 10am-6pm Mon, Tue; 10am-8pm Wed-Sat; 1-6pm Sun. **Admission** free.

Credit (bookshop only) A, AmEx, £TC, V.
The Design Council has been rather eclipsed by the arrival of the more ambitious Design Museum (*see chapter* **Museum**). But it does excellent educational work and holds some good temporary exhibitions on every aspect of design. The shop has a superb stock of books and magazines on art and design.

Fortnum & Mason
181 Piccadilly, W1 (071 734 8040). Green Park or Piccadilly Circus underground. **Open** 9am-5.30pm Mon-Fri; 9am-5pm Sat. **Credit** A, AmEx, CB, DC, JCB, £STC, V.
Fortnum's is the quintessentially English department store. Its quaintly chaotic air may make finding your way among the tasteful piles of goodies a bit confusing. The Fountain Restaurant is great value and open late (11.30pm), the lingerie department has a good range of reasonably priced tights and stockings and there are some bargains in stationery on the third floor, but most of the stock in the famed ground floor food hall is outrageously expensive. The staff are numerous and courteous, but rushed off their feet. The best time to beat the crowds is weekday mornings. *See chapter* **Shopping & Services.**
Christmas catalogue. Delivery. Export scheme. Restaurants.

Green Park
Green Park or Hyde Park Corner underground. **Open** 7am-dusk daily.
A pleasant spot to stroll, away from the stylish bustle of Piccadilly, Green Park was a favourite duelling site for eighteenth-century gents. Today, its most notorious visitors are the traders who flog gaudy pictures along the Piccadilly railings.

Leicester Square
WC2. Leicester Square and Piccadilly Circus underground.
'Lester' Square – as you'll need to pronounce it to get directions without a smirk – is London's epicentre of glitzy entertainment. In addition to the local clubs, pubs and restaurants, this is the home of four monster cinemas: the Warner, the Empire and the Odeons Leicester Square and West End (*see chapter* **Film**), and of the SWET cut-price theatre ticket booth (*see chapter* **Theatre**). But all you'll see of the square until late 1990 is a huge, muralled hoarding. An electricity sub-station is being built underground – giving an opportunity to rejuvenate what's become a slightly squalid place. It'll stay a garden square, but with an improved layout throughout the surrounding streets, so that events and street performers can entertain the thousands of people that flock here by day and night. The

statues of Shakespeare and Chaplin, and the busts of Hogarth, Newton, Hunter and Reynolds will also be spruced up.

St James's Church
*197 Piccadilly, W1 (071 734 4511).
Piccadilly Circus underground.* **Open** 8.30am-6.30pm daily. *Café* 8am-7pm Mon-Fri; 10am-7pm Sat; 10am-4pm Sun. **Services** 8.30am Tue-Fri; 8.30am, 11am, 5.45pm Sun.
St James's Church, designed by Sir Christopher Wren and officially designated 'the visitors' church', is much more than a beautiful place to worship. Regular concerts are performed here (*see chapter* **Music: Classical & Opera**); on Fridays and Saturdays there's a busy crafts market in its courtyard; the Wren Café has delicious snacks; and throughout the year the 'Alternatives Ministry' organises worthy lectures, workshops and support groups.

St James's Square
St James Square, SW1. Piccadilly Circus underground. **Open** 10am-4.30pm Mon-Fri.
The small formal garden in the centre of St James's Square, surrounded by hedges, is a restful and secluded spot to munch your sandwiches.

SOHO

'Soho is untidy, full of Greeks, cats, tomatoes, Italians, queer names, people looking out of upper windows; it dwells remote from the British body politic.' So commented novelist John Galsworthy in 1889, and Soho has remained central London's most cosmopolitan area over the past hundred years. The land from **Greek Street** to **Regent Street** was once a sporting ground, where the old hunting cry, 'So Ho!', to draw off the hounds, was frequently heard (hence the name). Since the seventeenth century it's been home to successive waves of immigrants and refugees, and each of them have left their distinctive cultural and gastronomic mark – this is London's major eating-out district. French Huguenots first arrived in 1685, followed by an influx of Germans and Italians, then Russians, Poles and Greeks in the 1860s. Since World War II, the Cantonese Chinese came to work in the hotel and catering trades and have made the area between **Leicester Square** and **Shaftesbury Avenue** the capital's **Chinatown** (*see below* and *chapter* **Ethnic London**).
Soho has always been London's hippest district. The former home of Mozart, Marx and Casanova, it's been in recent decades the epitome of fashion for both the artistic com-

Seven Dials *(listed under* **Covent Garden***) is London's newest ancient monument, although it's in fact nearly 300 years old. It was removed from the focus of the seven-street junction in 1773, reputedly because it was thought that there was treasure hidden beneath it. If you're wondering why it's called Seven Dials when there are only six sundials on the column, the answer is that the column itself is the seventh gnomon (the pillar showing the time by its shadow). Traffic careering round the base makes it a treacherous place to rest.*

munity, the film industry and the jazz and popular music scene (*see chapter* To the Eighties). Soho's drift into pornography during the seventies has been curtailed by a clean up campaign. Some strip joints and 'hostess' bars remain, but, typical of the trend, the stylish wholefood restaurant Mildred's occupies premises vacated by a gay sex cinema and illegal back room club.

The eighties influx of rich, trendier-than-thou advertising and design agencies, with attendant boutiques and eateries, has overwhelmed the old community. The former artistic elite of the private Colony Club, Dean Street – Francis Bacon, Peter Cook, Lucien Freud, Jeffrey Bernard – now seems of a different era. Unique specialist shops, delis, cafés are being forced out by rocketing rents. Soho's character comes from its scruffy individuality, so plans by the fanatically tidy council to make the Berwick Street Market stalls nice and neat and uniform are ominous. Chain stores might be appearing in Old Compton Street area, but this is still where you'll find London's best cappucino (at Bar Italia, *see chapter* Eating & Drinking) and most colourful streetlife.

Berwick Street
W1. Piccadilly Circus underground. **Open** *market only* 9am-5pm Mon-Sat.
Berwick Street has retained the noisy chaos lost by so many of the area's streets. The daily Market offers bargain fruit and veg, while Borovick's (Number 16; *071 437 2180*) is the best of the many fabric shops in the street. Its walls are crammed with extravagant materials and a gallery of signed photos from circus performers and thespians who've worn costumes made from Borovick's textiles. The staff are outrageously theatrical and exceptionally helpful. The café on the corner of Broadwick Street is a lively place for a cuppa.

Bunjie's Coffee House
27 Litchfield Street, WC2 (071 240 1796). *Leicester Square underground.* **Open** noon-llpm Mon-Sat. **No credit cards.**
Named after its founder's cousin's hamster, Bunjie's is a tiny, informal folk venue, with a time-warped, beatnik feel about it (it opened in 1954). Having excellent coffee and cheap and tasty vegetarian food, it's very popular with workers from the local bookshops.

Charing Cross Road
WC2. Leicester Square or Tottenham Court Road underground.
Soho's eastern boundary is paradise for bibliophiles, as recorded in Helene Hanff's book *84 Charing Cross Road* (now a classical music shop). Of the eighteen bookshops here, Foyle's (119) is the biggest and the most infuriating – its stock is chaotic and its

system of purchase ludicrously antiquated. The Waterstone's branch next door (121-125) is a contrasting exercise in logic and clarity. The small and friendly Silver Moon (68) has a superb range of feminist literature, while Henry Pordes (58-60) is the place to pick up good quality bargain books. Zwemmers, 26 Lichfield Street, WC2, is the Mecca for art book fans and Sportspages, by the Cambridge Circus shopping centre, speaks for itself. Cecil Court, off the main road, is lined with antiquarian bookshops.

Coach & Horses
29 Greek Street, W1 (071 437 5920). *Leicester Square underground.* **Open** 11am-11pm Mon-Sat; noon-3pm, 7-10.30pm, Sun. **No credit cards.**
Notorious both for its sozzled, artsy regulars like Jeffrey Bernard, and its rude landlord, this pub has stylish bar staff, good food, and an entertaining collection of cartoons by Michael Heath, which first appeared in *The Times* and *Private Eye* and now hang on the bar walls. It's crowded.

The French House
49 Dean Street, W1 (071 437 2799). *Picadilly Circus underground.* **Open** noon-11pm Mon-Sat; noon-3pm, 7-10.30pm, Sun. **Credit** (restaurant only) A, AmEx, £STC, V.
This basic pub was a meeting place for the French Resistance during World War II and

has several signed photographs of famous French people adorning its walls. Ignore the beer, which it only serves by the half pint, and go for the excellent selection of house wines. A unique atmosphere, more akin to a continental watering hole than a Soho boozer.

Golden Square Gardens
W1. Piccadilly Circus underground.
A remarkably peaceful and elegant little square, lined with publishing houses, which makes a useful bolt-hole from the crowds in nearby Regent Street. It's sometimes used for street entertainment events.

Govinda's
9 Soho Street, W1 (071 437 3662). *Tottenham Court Road underground.* **Open** 10am-7pm Mon-Sat. **Credit** A.
If you're handed a voucher for a free meal by one of the chanting Krishna devotees in Oxford Street, head to Govinda's for a tasty lunch. It's in the headquarters of the Radha Krishna organisation, but it's unlikely you'll be inveigled into a spiritual discussion over dinner.

Harry's
19 Kingly Street, W1 (071 734 3140). Oxford Circus underground. **Open** l0pm-9am Mon-Fri; l0pm-6am Sat. **No credit cards.**
This all-night café is a magnet for a weird and wonderful mixture of shift workers,

Burlington Arcade (*listed under* **Piccadilly**) *is the most celebrated of London's shopping arcades; a beautifully preserved monument to Regency refinement. The uniformed beadles help maintain the restrained atmosphere, ensuring that nobody runs, sings, whistles, carries large parcels, or opens an umbrella in the Arcade. The oldest shop in here is Lords, which has high-quality, British-made goods, including velvet smoking jackets.*

Chinatown *(listed under* Soho*) is the area around Gerrard Street and Newport Place. Not only is this London's greatest collection of Chinese restaurants and shops, the street names are sub-titled in Chinese and the tops of telephone boxes are decorated like pagodas. The restaurants offer varying levels of authenticity, comfort and price: try the tea in one of the cafés or the exotic vegetables from the many stalls. It's one of the liveliest areas of town on Sundays.*

The Soho Society
St Anne's Tower, 57 Dean Street, W1 (071 439 4303). Leicester Square underground. **Open** 2-4pm Mon-Fri.
Currently housed in a Portakabin in St Anne's Gardens, this information office is staffed by an eccentric and amiable band of volunteers, who seem to possess encyclopaedic knowledge about the area.

Soho Square Gardens
W1. Tottenham Court Road underground.
Tucked away behind Oxford Street and Charing Cross Road, these gardens are a favourite hang-out for weary couriers and shoppers – and the inevitable winos. The intiguing pseudo-Tudor shed in the centre is, disappointingly, a ventilation shaft for the underground. A restful spot for an insight into the self-contained sub-culture of London's despatch riders.

CHINATOWN

To make this Chinese district (*see chapter* **Ethnic London**) look like the popular image of a chinatown, the pedestrianized **Gerrard Street** has been given ornamental gateways and benches, even pagoda-style telephone boxes. This lurch into oriental clichés thankfully hasn't altered the chaotic, lively nature of this network of streets. The grocer's stores, supplying exotic provisions to residents and restaurateurs, are unusual attractions in themselves. The annual celebrations of the **Chinese New Year** and the Autumn **Moon Festival** remain community events, but are major dates in London's calendar (*see chapter* **London by Season**). A good tip if you're to eat here is to observe where the Chinese themselves eat.

Chinatown
around Gerrard Street, W1, Leicester Square or Piccadilly Circus underground.
See **picture and caption.**

Loon Fung's Supermarket
42-44 Gerrard Street, W1 (071 437 7332). Leicester Square underground. **Open** 10am-8.30pm daily. **No credit cards.**
The cheapest fresh tofu and beansprouts in town, as well as a bewildering selection of noodles, dried fish and strange sweets and spices. The stock is fascinating, the staff accommodating and the pretty dishes and unusual cookware make affordable gifts.

New Chan May Mai Restaurant
25 Lisle Street, WC2 (071 437 3602). Leicester Square or Piccadilly Circus underground. **Open** noon-11.30pm daily. **No credit cards.**
This noisy, brash and very busy restaurant, along with its next door neighbour (Man Lee Hong, 26 Lisle Street), is immensely popular with the local Chinese community. Not the spot for a romantic dinner, but unbeatable for tasty, cheap food. Prices and atmosphere are similar to the more famous Poon's (27 Lisle Street), but the menu is wider.

---

nightclubbers and lonely insomniacs. The demand for cholesterol-laden full English breakfasts, for a fiver, is so great that there's often a queue. *See chapter* **Late-Night London.**

Melati Restaurant
21 Great Windmill Street, W1 (071 437 2745). Piccadilly Circus underground. **Open** noon-11.30pm Mon-Thur, Sun; noon-12.30am Fri, Sat. **Credit** A, AmEx, DC, £TC, V.
Recommended by Malaysian Londoners, reasonably priced Malaysian food is served here in an informal atmosphere to a young and lively clientèle. There's extra seating upstairs, but the ground floor is pleasanter and gets very busy, so it's wise to book at weekends.

Maison Bertaux
28 Greek Street, W1 (071 437 6007). Leicester Square underground. **Open** 9am-6.30pm Mon-Sat; 9.30am-1pm, 3-6pm, Sun. **No credit cards.**
It takes an iron will to walk past the delicious temptations in the window display of this French patisserie. The upstairs tea room is a little too cosy during the crush for afternoon tea; arrive before 4pm to get a seat. The Mont Blancs are particularly irresistible.

Marshall Street Leisure Centre
Marshall Street, W1 (071 798 2007). Oxford Circus or Piccadilly Circus underground. **Open** 7.30am-7pm Mon; 7.30am-9pm Tue-Fri; 8.30am-7pm Sat. **Membership** £21.60. **Admission** (non-members) £1.50 (members) £1.25 adults; 55p under-16s; free for OAPs, UB40s resident in Westminster. **Credit** A, V.
Housed in a beautiful listed building, with an elegant glass, arched roof above the pool, Marshall Street baths are an unusual – and very convenient – place to swim. School parties crowd the pool out mid-morning, but the afternoons are peaceful.

Mildred's
58 Greek Street, W1 (071 494 1634). Tottenham Court Road underground. **Open** noon-10pm Mon-Sat. **Credit** £TC.
Mildred's has quickly established a reputation for reasonably priced, sophisticated wholefood. Fish, vegetarian and vegan dishes are served to a mixed Soho clientèle. It's always busy at lunchtimes and on Thursday and Friday evenings, so mid-afternoon is the best time. The home-made kiwi and passionfruit ice-cream is wonderfully good.

WESTMINSTER

The City of Westminster has had a long and chequered history. The Palace of Westminster, better known as **The Houses of Parliament** (*see chapter* **Sightseeing**), is where English governments have attempted to hold-back the tide since the days of King Canute (1016-35). **Whitehall** has been the principal corridor of power since medieval times, when Whitehall Palace stretched almost to Somerset House. All that remains of it today is **Banqueting House** (*see chapter* **Tudors & Stuarts**). Among the great concentration of government buildings here is, of course, **10 Downing Street**. You can now visit the less grand, but more intriguing **Cabinet War Rooms** (*see chapter* **The World Wars**) behind the Foreign Office.

Westminster hasn't always been a dignified place, however. Until the reign of Victoria, when massive slum clearance programmes established **Victoria Street** in 1851 and **Parliament Square** in 1868, much of the area was crowded with dangerous, filthy alleys. Aptly-named **Thieving Lane** ran from **Little Sanctuary** to **Tothill Street**, while modern-day **Abingdon Street** used to be referred to as **Dirty Lane**. The unusually high proportion of undesirables stemmed from the ancient practice of offering sanctuary to fugitives from justice in **Westminster Abbey**. Even the elegant eighteenth century-development of **Queen Anne's Gate** is adjacent to **Cockpit Steps**, a reminder of the local popularity of the bloody, brutal sport of cock-fighting, not outlawed until 1849.

St John's Smith Square
Smith Square, SW1 (071 222 1061).
Westminster underground. **Open** *box office:*
10am-6pm Mon-Fri. **Admission** £2-£20.
Credit A, AmEx, £TC, V.
In an attractive square off Millbank, this converted church offers an adventurous programme of classical and contemporary chamber music on most evenings, with plenty of cheap seats, if you don't object to listening from behind a pillar (*see chapter* **Music: Classical & Opera**). The lunchtime BBC concerts make an inexpensive treat. Try the interesting Footstool Restaurant in the crypt.

Downing Street
W1 Westminster underground.
See **picture and caption.**

Little Sanctuary
SW1. Westminster underground.
Across from the grounds of Westminster Abbey is a well-kept secret. The aptly-named Little Sanctuary, on the site of the old sanctuary of St Peter, is a grassed square secluded behind government buildings, including the offices of Hansard, the parliamentary record.

St Margaret's
Parliament Square, SW1 (071 222 6382).
Westminster underground. **Open** 9.30am-5.30pm daily. **Services** 12.30pm Wed; 11am (choral) first Sun of month.
Even Socialist politicians pray here to St Margaret (no, not that Conservative deity, Mrs Thatcher). This was adopted as the parish church of the House of Commons in 1614, when protestant MPs (wrongly) suspected that Westminster Abbey was about to go Catholic. Samuel Pepys, John Milton and Winston Churchill got married at St Margaret's and Sir Walter Raleigh was apparently interred here in 1618, after losing his head just over the road in Old Palace Yard. The head was buried decades later in Sussex and there are tasteless plans for a reunification. The stained glass is among the best in London. The impressive 1501 east window pre-dates the present church by some twenty years. The Caxton window celebrates Britain's first printer, William Caxton, buried here in 1491. The south windows are a subtle work from 1967 by John Piper.
Wheelchair access.

Victoria Tower Gardens
Millbank, SW1. Westminster underground.
Open 7am-dusk daily. **Admission** free.
Deckchairs 50p per day; 35p per session.
A charming, quiet riverside garden with a beautiful view across the Thames to Lambeth Palace – and plenty of deckchairs to laze in. There's a gothic-revival drinking fountain, a children's play area, a cast of Rodin's *Burghers of Calais* and a splendid bronze statue of the suffragette, Emmeline Pankhurst, poised as if to address a public meeting.

Whitehall
SW1. Charing Cross or Westminster underground.
This wide, elegant thoroughfare leads from Trafalgar Square to the Houses of Parliament. At the north end is the Admiralty and, behind Banqueting House (*see chapter* **Tudors & Stuarts**), the Ministry of Defence. At **Horse Guards Parade** (1753), adjoining the Victorian Treasury buildings, the mounted guard is changed (*see chapter* **London by Season**). Opposite Downing Street is the Cenotaph war memorial (*see chapter* **The World Wars**).

Downing Street (*listed under* **Westminster***) is named after a 'perfidious rogue' from Dublin, Sir George Downing, ambassador to The Hague, who constructed four 'well built houses, fit for persons of honour and quality' in 1681. No 10 has been at the centre of British political life ever since Sir Robert Walpole made it the Prime Ministerial residence in 1735. No 11, next door, is the home of the Chancellor of the Exchequer. You can't go down the street anyway, but in a fit of paranoia (or was it regal pretension?), Mrs Thatcher has commissioned protective gates for the Whitehall end.*

The City

Within the famous and seriously-rich square mile lies a hidden city which few visitors ever see. We give you the insider information on this eclectic part of London.

The City is Britain's financial nerve-centre. It's an area which dates back to Roman times, yet contains all the latest communications systems and intricate money markets. 'The City may be historically interesting, but who cares so long as it makes loadsamoney?' replied a trader on the London International Financial Futures Exchange floor when asked about the Square Mile. This is not the most commendable view of such a fascinating area of London, although it's understandable considering that the Stock Exchange alone has a £1 billion a day turnover and the City as a whole makes over £7 billion every year. That's the amount of money it would cost to cover the entire surface of Central London with 22k gold leaf.

The City is just one square mile/259 hectares big, but it rivals New York and Tokyo as a world financial centre, with over 500 foreign banks and security houses. Walk through the building site that it is today, where new sky-scrapers burgeon alongside Wren's churches, and you'll find a half-crazed world filled with tired workers, exhaust fumes and some impressive architecture.

Practically no-one now lives in this nightmarish, Orwellian world. Out of the 320,000 people who inhabit the square mile during the day, only 4,500 remain after twilight. The influx of City workers is a sight to behold at rush hour or during lunch times; in the evenings you'll find the occasional beery broker staggering home along wind-swept streets, not dissimilar to those on Wall Street or western ghost towns.

As the most ancient district of London (much of the Saxon street-plan premains), the City has much to offer the visitor. Apart from the obvious attractions (such as the **Bank of England** and **St Paul's Cathedral** *listed below*), there are some fascinating buildings hidden among the tightly squeezed streets and a large number of astounding architectural flights of fancy.

THE OLD CITY

Londinium was bordered by Roman walls (*see chapter* **Roman & Saxon London**) which contained the whole of London until the population explosion in the eighteenth century (the Roman ruins can be seen at their best around the Barbican Centre and the Tower of London).

The Lord Mayor of London still heads the **Corporation of London**, which governs the area within the City boundaries. Over the centuries, the Corporation's medieval privileges have been defended so successfully, that His Worshipfulness takes precedence over the Queen whenever she visits the City; a quaint gesture to the financiers who often helped the more impoverished of Her Majesty's ancestors. The annual **Lord Mayor's Show** (*see chapter* **London by Season**), when the new Lord Mayor is sworn in, is a great excuse for pageantry. Thousands of people line the parade route, flag-waving as the decorated floats and the gilt mayoral State Coach pass by.

College of Arms
Queen Victoria Street, EC4 (071 248 2762). Blackfriars underground/BR. **Open** 10am-4pm Mon-Fri. **Admission** free.
The College of Arms, in its recently restored seventeenth-century building, is the home of heraldry. It grants arms to those who think they are worth having and can afford them. If you want to trace your roots, write for an appointment to the Officer in Waiting, College of Arms, Queen Victoria Street, EC4. The College is linked with the **Heralds' Museum** at the Tower of London (*see chapter* **Sightseeing**). *Tour by prior arrangement.*

The Guildhall
off Gresham Street, EC2 (071 606 3030). Bank underground. **Open** 10am-5pm daily. **Admission** free.
See **picture and caption**.
Guided tours (free; write in advance to: The Keeper of Guildhall, Guildhall, EC2). Shop. Toilets for the disabled. Wheelchair access.

Leadenhall Market
Whittington Avenue, off Gracechurch Street, EC3. Bank underground. **Open** 7am-3pm Mon-Fri.

A wonderful Victorian setting, it's best to wander into this glass-covered, paved area either in the morning or at lunch time, when the stalls overflow with fish and vegetables and City workers unwind at the local bars and restaurants. You can buy exotic fruits, oysters, game, gulls' eggs, caviar and vintage champagne, as well as crabs, lobsters and other marine life. Originally the site of the Roman forum (*see chapter* **Roman London**), Leadenhall Market takes its name from a lead-roofed mansion that stood here in the fourteenth century. The outstanding Victorian iron and glass arcades were designed by Horace Jones in 1881.

Livery Companies' Halls
All over City. **Admission** free, by ticket only.
The forerunners of modern trade unions, the livery companies were guilds of craftsmen that were established in medieval times and acquired political strength, as well as amazing amounts of money and possessions. Nowadays, their trade connections are minimal and they function more as private clubs, with charitable and ceremonial duties. The largest livery building is the **Merchant Taylors' Hall** (at 30 Threadneedle Street EC2). Some halls hold open days, for example the **Fishmongers' Hall** (London Bridge, EC4), the **Ironmongers' Hall** (Barbican, EC2) and the **Vintners' Hall** (Kennet Wharf Lane, EC4). Information and tickets from: City of London Information Centre, St Paul's Churchyard, EC4 (071 260 1457).

Mansion House
EC4. Bank underground. **Open** by written application only, 11am and 2pm Tue-Thur. **Admission** free.
The Lord Mayor is annoyingly reluctant to share his comfortable home with the general public. The most impressive room is the Egyptian Hall, decorated in 23-carat gold and the scene of his Lordship's sumptuous feasts. Written applications only will be considered for a one-hour tour; apply well in advance. Applications to: The Principal Assistant, Mansion House, London, EC4N 8BH.

Museum of London
150 London Wall, EC2 (071 600 3699). Barbican or St Paul's underground/Moorgate underground/BR/4, 141, 279A, 502 bus. **Open** 10am-6pm Tue-Sat; 2-6pm Sun. **Admission** free. **Credit** (shop only) A, V.
The story of London from its Roman beginnings, through the plague, the Great Fire, Civil War, the Blitz to present day financial metropolis. It's right next to the Roman wall by the massive Barbican Centre (*see below* **The Arts**) and has some of the finest facilities of any of London's museums. *See chapter* **Museums**.
Braille guide and taped commentary for the visually impaired. Lectures and films with induction loop for the hard of hearing in the theatre. Restaurant (10am-5pm Tue-Sat; noon-5pm Sun). Shop. Toilets for the disabled. Wheelchair access. Workshops.

Royal Britain
Barbican, Aldersgate Street, EC2 (071 588 0588). Barbican underground (closed Sun) or Moorgate underground/BR/4, 6, 9, 11, 15, 509 buses. **Open** 9am-5.30pm daily. **Admission** £3.95 adults; £2.50 under 16s, OAPs; £2.95 students; £10 family ticket (2 adults plus 2 children). **Credit** A, AmEx, V.
The kind of place pedantic historians love to

hate; so it's perfect for anyone who wants royal history served up in a fun way (did you know Anne Boleyn had three breasts? and so forth). There are over 1,000 years of royal history, from Edgar (the first king) to Elizabeth II, told by way of 'feature environments'. Mary Queen of Scots is decapitated via audio-visual effects, Stuart England is seen in a puppet show and the Victorian era as one big iron foundry. Some scenes work better than others, although the overall effect is informative.
Educational packs for children. Group discount. Restaurant. Shop. Wheelchair access.

WALK

Historical Tours
(071 668 4019). **Meeting point** Monument underground (Fish Street Hill exit), Sat 2.15pm. **Duration** 2 hours. **Cost** £3.50 adults; £2.50 OAPs, students; under-14s free if accompanied by adult. **No credit cards.**
A comprehensive tour covering 2,000 years of City history, exploring the lesser known nooks and alleys, with plenty of juicy anecdotes.

BUSINESS

Bank of England Museum
Bartholomew Lane, EC2 (071 601 4444). Bank underground. **Open** *1 Oct-Good Friday:* 9am-5pm Mon-Fri: *Good Friday-30 Sept:* 10am-6pm Mon-Sat; 2-6pm Sun. **Admission** free.

In a side entrance through the Bank's windowless curtain security walls, designed by Sir John Soane, is this well thought-out museum. There's a faithful restoration of the Bank Stock Office designed by Soane and original artwork for banknotes, which are displayed inside closely monitored cabinets that check humidity and thieving hands. The Bank seems to be trying to shed the stuffy image of the Old Lady of Threadneedle Street (the Bank's nickname), by using the Museum to put on displays of twentieth-century communications and a computerized dealing desk illustrating how financial markets work.
Educational films. Lectures by prior arrangement. Shop. Tour and touch sessions for the visually impaired by prior arrangement. Wheelchair access by prior arrangement.

Broadgate Centre
Eldon Street, EC2 (071 588 6565). Liverpool Street underground/BR. **Open** 24 hours daily. *See* **picture and caption.**

Daily Express Building
121-128 Fleet Street, EC4. Blackfriars underground/BR. **Open** 24 hours daily. **Admission** free.
Owen Williams's Daily Express building, completed in 1932, has an innovative black glass curtain wall and a brash Art Deco foyer and staircase (*see chapter* **Early Twentieth Century**). While today's press barons have abandoned Fleet Street for the dubious attractions of Docklands, the

Express building stands as a monument to journalism's more respected days. The last national papers to leave the street, the Express group, handed over this listed landmark to new owners in 1989.

Lloyd's of London
Lime Street, EC3 (071 623 7100). Bank or Monument underground. **Open** 10am-2.30pm Mon-Fri (groups of more than six people can visit between 10am-3.45pm by prior arrangement). **Admission** free. *See* **picture and caption.**
Café (9am-5.30pm Mon-Fri). Exhibitions. Shop. Wheelchair access.

London International Financial Futures Exchange (LIFFE)
Royal Exchange, EC3 (071 623 0444). Bank underground. **Open** 11.30am-1.45pm Mon-Fri. **Admission** free.
The reason for visiting William Tite's splendid 1844 neo-classical **Royal Exchange** building (*see chapter* **Victorian Times**) is not, simply, to stare at yet another historical City building, but to see the City in action. Its dealers, trading face to face on the floor of the London International Financial Futures Exchange, haggling, shouting bids and frantically waving arms, is a colourful sight. Visitors to the public gallery can watch the floor, while nearby videos and boards explain how the markets work. Those in the know make sure they're around when the Chicago market opens (after 1.30pm) as it's then that the trading really starts to hot up. The building is undergoing renovation and is to gain a barrell roof to Tite's original design.

Telecom Technology Showcase
135 Queen Victoria Street, EC4 (071 248 7444). St Paul's underground or Blackfriars underground/BR. **Open** 10am-5pm Mon-Fri (including Saturday of Lord Mayor's Show). **Admission** free.
An interesting tour of telecommunications history. Visitors travel back 150 years through time by means of photos, relics of the Bell era, old films, videos and then fast forward to the future. There are lots of snazzy buttons to press and you even get to send a fax (via satellite) from one side of a room to another and watch your voice in the form of sound waves.
Lectures and films by prior arrangement. Parking. Shop. Wheelchair access by prior arrangement.

The Stock Exchange
Old Broad Street, EC2 (071 588 2355). Bank underground. **Open** 9.30am-3.30pm Mon-Fri. **Admission** free.
A rather sedate picture awaits those who step into the Stock Exchange's public gallery. Since the Big Bang back in 1987, when those-on-high decided that haggling by phone (as opposed to trading face to face on the floor of the Stock Exchange) was OK, most brokers and jobbers have withdrawn to their computerized offices, away from public scrutiny. Visitors will find the faithful few still trading on the floor, though lunchtimes – when the building is deserted – should be avoided. Databanks that explain the jargon as well as presentations (these should be pre-booked and last 45 minutes; phone 071 588 2355 ext 26818) help bring this institution to life.
Shop. Wheelchair access by prior arrangement.

A bizarre, geometric modern façade obscures the **Guildhall** *(listed under* **The Old City***), built in 1411 and restored after both the Great Fire of 1666 and the Blitz. Look out for the inscriptions of the names of criminals who were tried in the Guildhall and then executed in grizzly ways. The Guildhall is still the seat of the City's local government. You can even attend their meetings, presided over by the Lord Mayor, on every third Thursday (except during August; phone for dates), starting at 1pm.*

LEGAL LONDON

To the casual observer, a stroll through the legal enclave that are the **Inns of Court** can be a time-warp experience. Some buildings (such as the **Middle Temple Hall**) date back to medieval or Elizabethan times; others, for example King's Bench Walk in the Inner Temple, were built after the Great Fire in 1666. Furthermore, you'll not only see dark Jermyn Street suits topped with the occasional bowler hat, but lawyers donned in wigs and gowns carrying paperwork wrapped in the traditional red ribbon. The Courts, particularly the **Old Bailey**, can also provide a fascinating insight into how this old fashioned world deals with twentieth-century criminals.

The legal world has come in for some criticism of late, largely because of the public's outcry at the ever increasing cost of litigation and the time it takes to get a case to court. Changes are on the way (possibly) to fuse the two branches of the profession (solicitors and barristers). Whether these proposals will ever be implemented will depend on how long the powerful legal lobby drags its feet.

Lawyers have been in the Temple since 1320 when the land was leased by the Knights Hospitaller of St John to members of the profession who were working in Holborn. Prior to that, the area belonged to the Knights Templar (an order of monastic knights originally founded to protect pilgrims travelling to the Holy Land) who settled in the Temple in 1162. Such was their high standard of living and privileges that when King John was summoned by his barons to sign the Magna Carta he was living with the Knights Templar (*see* chapter **The Middle Ages**). The legal profession obtained the freehold (total ownership) of the land in 1608. Both the rich and famous have studied and passed through the Inns: Thomas More, Oliver Cromwell, Sir Francis Bacon and Margaret Thatcher to name but a few.

The Inns of Court
Lincoln's Inn, WC2 (071 405 1393); Gray's Inn, WC1 (071 405 8164); Inner Temple, EC4 (071 353 8462); Middle Temple, EC4 (071 353 4355). Temple, Holborn or Chancery Lane underground. **Open** dawn-dusk daily . (Lincolns Inn closed Sat,Sun). **Admission** free.
This is a part of London which few get to see and yet encapsulates everything that is tradi-

The spectacular **Broadgate Centre** *(listed under* **Business***) has risen out of the Liverpool Street station sidings. Vast glass atriums surround the Arena, a performance space on summer lunchtimes, an open air ice-skating rink by winter. It works not only because it was developed at the same time, so the buildings complement each other, but also because the rents here are low by City standards. Companies moved in even before building had finished. There are bars, shops, restaurants and sculptures to keep visitors and the resident bankers entertained.*

tional and eccentric about the British. Described as walking through an Oxford college by many a visitor and client, a stroll through the Inns of Court is a spellbinding and eye-opening experience. Anyone can enter the tranquil sanctity of these green oases, which date from the thirteenth century, and peer at the bewigged barristers. Each Inn (Honourable Society of barristers) is very different in style and atmosphere, though what is most notable is the fact that *all* London barristers work from within their walls. Students to the Bar not only have to pass the Bar exams, but must also join one of the four Inns and dine 24 times in the imposing halls before being eligible to be called to the Bar. Particularly worthy of mention are the immaculate lawns of **Lincoln's Inn** beside medieval and neo-classical buildings, and the **Middle Temple Hall** (*see chapter* **Tudors & Stuarts**), where Shakespeare acted in *Twelfth Night* in 1601 and which contains a wooden table reputedly made from the hatch of Sir Francis Drake's ship *The Golden Hind*. Also of interest is the only circular church in London, the **Temple Church**, constructed by the Knights Templar in 1185, as a model of either the Dome of the Rock or the Church of the Holy Sepulchre in Jerusalem. In August, during the summer recess, the Inns tend to be quieter than at other times of the year.

Old Bailey
on the corner of Newgate Street and Old Bailey, EC4 (071 248 3277). St Paul's underground.

Open 10.30am-1pm, 2-4pm, Mon-Fri; closed August. **Admission** free (no under 14s admitted, 14-16s accompanied by adults only). *See* **picture and caption.**

Royal Courts of Justice
Strand, WC2 (071 936 6470). Aldwych or Temple underground. **Open** 10.30am-4.30pm Mon-Fri; during August the building is open to the public, although court cases are suspended for the summer recess. **Admission** free.
The civil equivalent of the Old Bailey, where litigants battle it out, often for large sums of money. Cases are varied, ranging from divorce and libel hearings to company and bankruptcy actions. The neo-Gothic building, designed by G E Street, is a fine example of Victorian architecture, with its towers, pillars and great entrance hall. Visitors can walk into any of the public galleries at the back of the 58 courts to watch the proceedings. *Wheelchair access to main hall only.*

THE ARTS

The July **City of London Festival** is the Square Mile's biggest annual cultural event (for details, phone *071 377 0540*). Its classical and jazz concerts are not confined to the **Barbican Arts Centre** and **Broadgate Arena** (*see* *above* **Business**), but also test the acoustics of many City churches (*see below* **Churches**). The **Mermaid Theatre** (*see chapter* **Theatre**), founded by Bernard Miles, was the first new playhouse in the City for three centuries when it opened at Puddle Dock, Blackfriars, in 1959.

Barbican Centre

Silk Street, EC2 (general information 071 638 4141; 24-hour information 071 628 2295/071 628 9760). Barbican underground (closed Sun) or Moorgate underground/BR. **Open** *9am-11pm Mon-Sat; noon-11pm Sun.* **Admission** *free; tickets vary for exhibitions and performances, phone for details.* **Credit** *A, AmEx, DC, V.*
As far as initiative tests go, escaping from Alcatraz is kid's stuff compared to finding your way into the vast concrete world of the Barbican. But do perservere; this jungle of dispiriting architectural ego-trips contains a wonderful assortment of exhibition halls, concert auditoriums, an art gallery and three cinemas. It's the largest complex of its kind in Western Europe, and serves as home to the London Symphony Orchestra and the London base of the Royal Shakespeare Company, both of which stage regular events (box office 071 638 8891 open from 10am-8pm daily; tickets £5-£40). There's also an extensive library and various shops and refreshment areas, namely an à la carte restaurant, a waterside terrace café and various bars. A good way to spend a restful lunchtime is to hear the free jazz or classical concerts held in the foyer of Level 5 between noon and 2.30pm, and between 5.30pm and 7.20pm. There are also concerts on the sculpture terrace by the fountains. Lesser known is the level 8 conservatory, full of lush foliage (open 10am-4.30pm Sat; noon-4.30pm Sun, bank holidays, and most weekdays between 1 May-30 Sept). Should your eyes chance upon the incongruous shape of St Giles's Cripplegate (the church where Oliver Cromwell got married and the poet John Milton is buried), now stuck in the middle of the Barbican residential sector, you will not be alone in thinking that many of today's developers don't know their bricks from their mortar. For more information on the concerts, *see chapter* **Music: Classical & Opera**. *Car park (8am-midnight Mon-Fri). Cafés & bars. Conference halls. Guided tours (071 638 4141, ext 218). Information leaflets available. A la carte restaurant. Shops. Wheelchair access.*

CHURCHES

Hidden among the bustle and traffic-choked streets of the City are a fascinating collection of architectural masterpieces – the City churches. While stressed brokers take refuge in overcrowded pubs, many a visitor has discovered the beauty and tranquility of these centres of calm and meditation. The Great Fire of 1666 destroyed 84 out of a total of 109 churches; 54 were rebuilt (51 by Christopher Wren).

World War II saw almost all the churches bombed and 11 were totally destroyed. They number today only 48 and although a far cry from the huge number in Elizabethan times, it still means that there's a church virtually around every corner. Most are open between 10am and 4pm on weekdays, and on Sundays during Services. Admission to the City's churches is free unless otherwise stated.

St Bartholomew-the-Great

West Smithfield, EC1 (071 606 5171). Barbican (closed Sun) or Farringdon underground. **Open** *8.30am-4.30pm daily.* **Services** *12.30pm Wed, Fri; 9am, 11am (choral) and 6.30pm (choral) Sun.*
Built on the site of an enormous twelfth-century priory church, St Barts is the City's only surviving Norman church (*see chapter* **The Middle Ages**). The oldest bells in the City are rung here. Enter the churchyard through the thirteenth-century gateway (opposite the east corner of Smithfield Market).

St Bride

Fleet Street, EC4 (071 353 1301). Blackfriars underground/BR. **Open** *8.15am-5.30pm daily.* **Services** *Mon-Fri 8.30am, 5.15pm (recitals at 1.15pm); Sun 11am (choral) and 6.30pm (choral).*
Sunday is the best time to visit this church designed by Christopher Wren and finished in 1703: one of London's finest church choirs sings at 11am and 6.30pm. In the crypt, lying amid the foundations of seven churches and a Roman house, there is a museum and an exhibition of printing history. The spire – Wren's tallest at 226 feet/69 metres – became the model for English wedding cakes when it was copied by a local baker.
Wheelchair access to ground floor only.

St Etheldreda's

Ely Place, EC1 (071 405 1061). Chancery Lane underground. **Open** *8.30am-5.30pm daily.* **Services** *Mon-Fri 8am and 1pm; Sun 9am, 11am (choral) and 6pm.*
Considered to be one of the finest examples of Gothic architecture in Europe, St Etheldreda's is (with the exception of part of Westminster Abbey) the only surviving edifice from the reign of Edward I (1239-1307); *see chapter* **The Middle Ages**. It's also Britain's oldest catholic church, originating from the time when provincial bishops (in this case from the Cambridgeshire town of Ely) had their episcopal houses in London, so as to be able to sit in Parliament. At the height of the Tudor religious persecution, Catholic martyrs were paraded down Holborn to their place of execution at Tyburn (*see chapter* **Tudors & Stuarts**). The statues on the walls in the church commemorate the martyrs. Ely Place, with its wonderful Dickensian atmosphere (the Bleeding Heart Yard, where you can eat, was mentioned in *Little Dorrit*) is still famous for its strawberries (refered to in Shakespeare's *Richard III*) and hosts an annual Strawberrie Fayre.

Take the lift up the outside of **Lloyd's of London** *(listed under* **Business***) and see why this is the most embarrassingly impractical for its residents, the world's most famous building in London. Designed in the boilerhouse style by Richard Rodgers, it's proved society of underwriters. From the public gallery there's a bird's-eye view of the underwriters in their 'boxes', styled after the tables of seventeenth-century coffee houses in which Lloyd's originated. The bell of* HMS Lutine, *on the ground floor, is tolled once for bad news, twice for good news.*

St Mary-le-Bow

Cheapside, EC2 (071 248 5139). Bank, Mansion House or St Paul's underground. **Open** 9am-6pm Mon-Fri. **Services** Mon 8.15am and 5.45pm; Tue 7.30am and 5.45pm; Wed 8.15am, 12.30pm and 5.45pm; Thur 8.15am and 5.30pm (choral); Fri 8.15am.

The elegant white tower of this renovated church rises incongrously above busy and modern Cheapside. In the past, people only considered themselves a true Londoner, or 'cockney', if they had been born within the sound of Bow bells. The Great Fire of 1666 and the Blitz during World War II destroyed, in turn, the first two sets of bells; a small model inside the church gives you an impression of what was left after the Great Fire.

St Paul's Cathedral

EC4 (071 248 2705). St Paul's underground. **Open** 7.30am-6pm daily.; *galleries, crypt and ambulatory* 10am-4.15pm Mon-Fri; 11am-4.15pm Sat. **Admission** *cathedral*: free (donation requested; £1 adult, £1 under 16s); *galleries* £2 adult, £1 under 16s; *crypt* £1.10 adults, 55p under 16s; *ambulatory* 60p adults, free under 16s. **Services** Mon-Fri 8am, 12.30pm (not Fri), 5pm (choral); Sat 8am, 10am (choral), 12.30pm, 5pm (choral); Sun 8am, 10.30am (choral), 11.30am (choral), 3.15pm (choral). Times vary because of special events, phone first to check.

One of the most famous cathedrals in the world, this impressive edifice jostles for attention among sixties, carbuncle-like towerblocks which have already been earmarked for demolition. Prince Charles (who was married in the cathedral) has publicly criticized proposed radical architectural plans for Paternoster Square which have not met with his neo-classical vision of future buildings. Based on the classic Gothic long-naved plan, Wren topped the cathedral with a marvellous lead-covered dome. His tomb is in the crypt, where you'll also find the various models Wren made of the cathedral. Walk around the Whispering Gallery inside the dome, whisper something against the wall and you'll be heard 112 feet/34 metres away on the other side. Climb further up to the Golden Gallery for a magnificent view over London. Sundays are the quietest time for visiting the cathedral, but the galleries and crypt are closed. *See chapter* **Tudors & Stuarts**. *Guided tours. Shop. Wheelchair access to main hall and crypt.*

PUBS & WINE BARS

The City of London is famous for its wonderful watering holes which fill to bursting point at lunchtimes. Make sure you book if you're eating at a restaurant; if you just want to drink, you'll simply have to shove like all the rest. For restaurants and more wine bars, *see chapter* **Eating & Drinking**.

Bow Wine Vaults

10 Bow Church Yard, EC4 (071 248 1121). Mansion House or St Paul's underground. **Open** 11.30am-3pm, 5-7pm Mon-Fri. **Credit** A, AmEx, DC, £TC, V.

Socialise with City folk while watching the video screens blaring out the latest Stock Market figures. This large, rambling bar gets very full at lunchtimes; in the evenings the atmosphere is less hectic. The restaurant serves unpretentious food – booking is advisable.

El Vino

47 Fleet Street, EC4 (071 353 6786) Temple underground. **Open** 11.30am-3pm, 5-8pm Mon-Fri; 11.30am-3pm Sat. **Credit** A, £TC, V.

A legendary wine bar (with a fantastic wine list) in the middle of the legal area of London. It provides a sedate atmosphere for lovers of tradition, with bottles and barrels lining the walls and lawyers propping up the bar. It can get crowded, so expect to have to stand unless you book one of the small circular tables. Dress code is strictly enforced; women must wear skirts, men a jacket, collar and tie.

La Paquerette

Centre of Finsbury Square, EC2 (071 638 5134). Moorgate or Old Street underground/BR. **Open** 7.30-9.30am, noon-3pm. **Credit** A, AmEx, V.

In the middle of this imposing square sits a strange beast. Most passers-by remain ignorant of the fact that housed in the low, wooden buildings is a delightful restaurant overlooking a bowling green — a manicured monument to the more civilised things in life. City folk meet at the restaurant for breakfast, unwind at lunchtime and in the evenings bowl woods across the beautifully kept grass..

Ye Olde Cheshire Cheese

Wine Office Court, 145 Fleet Street, EC4. Temple underground. **Open** 11.30am-11pm Mon-Fri; 11.30am-3pm, 5-11pm Sat; noon-3pm Sun.

An old haunt of writers (notably Dickens, and Doctor Johnson), today it's the journalists and lawyers who stand on the sawdust-covered floorboards while drinking real ales. It's advisable to book for the popular restaurant (*see chapter* **Eating & Drinking**), where the specialities are steak 'n' kidney puddings and roast beef .

At the **Old Bailey** *(listed under* **Legal London***) you can watch real life court-room dramas unfold. The Old Bailey (its proper name is the Central Criminal Court) has dealt with the goriest and most publicized criminal cases in London's history. Past defendants include Oscar Wilde in 1895, the murderous Dr Crippen in 1910, and in 1987, Geoffrey Collier, the first insider dealer to be prosecuted in Britain. Built on the site of the notorious Newgate prison, the gilded figure of Justice, up on the dome roof, overlooks the area where convicts were once executed.*

The River & Docklands

The smart way to see London is still from the Thames. And out of the ruined docklands a futuristic new city is rising.

For centuries, the Thames was London's thoroughfare and the trade from the docks and canals its source of wealth. They were the busiest waterways in the world until the British Empire crumbled and they, too, sank into decline and neglect. Over the past decade the river and canals have again become lively places, busy with pleasure craft and commuter boats. If you want to explore London from water level *see below* **Water Transport**. The former docklands have been designated a development zone and a subsequent building free-for-all has produced dynamic schemes. The construction sites have become an unlikely tourist attraction.

DOCKLANDS DEVELOPMENT

In 1981 the government gave the **London Docklands Development Corporation (LDDC)** almost unrestricted powers to revive the vast area from the Tower to Beckton. It's easy to forget that few believed the old docks *could* be regenerated. Now vast, 50-storey towers are being erected at **Canary Wharf**. Huge amounts of money and an unparalleled amount of greed have been unleashed on the area, virtually unrestrained by any thought for the consequences. Londoners are renewing their call to have some say in what's happening, championed by the Prince of Wales.

With city workers moving into chic converted warehouses, the authorities pay lip-service to the original locals. The contrast between the high-rise slums and the post-modern blocks is most graphically seen from a ride on the **Docklands Light Railway (DLR)**. A raised track designed to carry 22,000 people a day by 1991, it already has 30,000 users.

DOWNSTREAM

TO THE TOWER

Starting at Westminster Pier, on your left is **Whitehall** with the red-striped **New Scotland Yard** and the monolithic copper-roofed **Ministry of Defence**. Opposite Charing Cross Pier is the gigantic façade of **County Hall**, home of local government for 64 years until 1986, but now with an uncertain future. The uncompromisingly concrete **South Bank Centre** (*see chapter* **Music: Classical & Opera**) follows on the same side. On the Victoria Embankment (left) is **Cleopatra's Needle** and, moored beyond that, the paddle-steamer **Tattershall Castle**, now a bar and club, and two former River Clyde ferries, the **RS Hispaniola** and the **TS Queen Mary** (another floating restaurant). Past Waterloo Bridge, the City's church steeples and office blocks come into view, dominated by the dome of **St Paul's Cathedral** and the bland **National Westminster Tower**. You get a brief glimpse of **Southwark Cathedral** *see chapter* **Middle Ages** to the right just before you go under London Bridge, emerging to a dramatic encounter with **HMS Belfast** (*see chapter* **War**), by **Hays Galleria**, once out the other side. London's oldest medieval fortress, the **Tower of London** (*see chapter* **Sightseeing**), is on the left.

Hay's Galleria

Tooley Street, SE1 (071 357 7770). London Bridge underground/BR/47, 70, 7A bus/boat to London Bridge Pier. **Open** 6am-11.30pm Mon-Sun.
A typical Docklands creation. Hay's Dock has been filled, given a Victorianesque barrel-vaulted glass roof and its warehouses have been refitted to form an elegant arcade. The ground floor is lined with chainstores and restaurants for the office workers from

the upper floors and the local area (dubbed London Bridge City). Much more fun is the fantastic fountain sculpture, *The Navigators*, by David Kemp.

Kathleen & May

St Mary Overie Dock, Clink Street, SE1 (071 730 0096). London Bridge underground/BR/47, 70 bus/boat to London Bridge City Pier. **Open** 10am-5pm Mon-Fri; 11am-4pm Sat, Sun. **Closed** Sat, Sun during winter (no set dates). **Admission** £1 adults, 50p children, OAPs, students, UB40s. **No credit cards.**
The last surviving three-masted, topsail, trading schooner, moored in the tiny St Mary Overie Dock, is now a floating museum. The **Old Thameside Inn** next door is a great place from which to view the river. *Group discount. Shop.*

Tower Bridge

SE1 (071 407 0922). Tower Hill underground or London Bridge underground/BR/boat to Tower Pier. **Open** *Mar-Oct*: 9.30am-5pm Mon-Sat; 2-5.30pm Sun; *Nov-Feb*: 9.30am-4pm Mon-Sat (last admission 30mins before closing). **Closed** Good Friday, Xmas Eve, Xmas Day, Boxing Day, New Year's Day. **Admission** £2.50 adults; £1 children, OAPs. **Credit** A, £TC, V. *See* **picture and caption**.
See also chapter **Victorian Times.**
Group discount. Shop. Wheelchair access.

DOCKLANDS: WAPPING & ROTHERHITHE

Immediately past the Tower on the left bank is **St Katherine's Dock** yacht haven. Facing it lies **Rotherhithe**, a maritime district retaining many of its Dickensian streets and the Georgian Nelson Dock House. Its first feature is **Butler's Wharf**, a very expensive mixed development. It includes the **Design Museum** (*see chapter* **Museums**) and the charming **St Saviour's Dock**. Further on, the **Angel** inn is the first of many riverside pubs. Over the water at Wapping are the **Town of Ramsgate** and **Prospect of Whitby**; for details *see chapter* **Eating & Drinking**.

On the left, behind a bright red iron bridge is **Shadwell Basin**, lined by classic examples of the new Docklands architecture: little Legoland houses with garish coloured balconies tacked on for decoration. Passing between the two ventilation towers for the **Rotherhithe Tunnel** and the new development of **Free Trade Wharf**, you reach **Limehouse Basin**. This was the business end of Britain's canal network, where cargo travelling down the **Regent's Canal** arrived for shipping abroad. The basin is to become a yacht marina lined with up-market shops and flats.

Some of the Georgian houses around **Newell Street** and **Narrow Street** survived the Luftwaffe, but little else remains of what was London's Victorian Chinatown.

Brunel Engine House Museum
St Marychurch Street, SE16 (081 318 2489). Rotherhithe underground/95 bus/boat to Cherry Garden Pier. **Open** 11am-4pm first Sunday in every month or by appointment. **Admission** £1.50.
This small museum is housed in a building originally constructed for the steam engines that pumped water from Brunel's Rotherhithe Tunnel, a great engineering feat of the 1800s that can be seen from Wapping tube station.
Guided tours. Shop. Wheelchair access.

St Anne's, Limehouse
Three Colt Street, E14 (071 987 1502). Westferry DLR. **Open** call in at rectory during office hours. **Services** 10.30am, 6pm, Sun.
A major landmark, St Anne's is one of six remarkable Baroque churches designed by Nicholas Hawksmoor (1661-1736), long-time assistant to Christopher Wren.

St George-in-the-East
The Highway, E1 (071 481 1345). Shadwell underground/DLR. **Open** 8am-5pm Tue-Sun. **Service** 10.15am Sun.
Hawksmoor's 'trademark' tower, broad-based and massive with pepperpot turrets, is visible from the river. World War II fire bombs put paid to the interior; the 1964 replacement was designed by Arthur Bailey.

St Katherine's Dock
E1 (071 488 2400). Tower Hill underground/Tower Gateway DLR/23, 42, 78 bus. **Open** 24 hours daily. **Admission** free.
See **picture and caption.**

Tobacco Dock
The Highway, E1 (071 702 9681). Wapping underground/Shadwell underground/DLR. **Open** *Shops* 10am-6pm daily; *restaurants* noon-11pm daily.
See **picture and caption.**
Wheelchair access.

DOCKLANDS: ISLE OF DOGS

As you skirt the horseshoe bend of the **Isle of Dogs**, evidence of the changing riverside now emerges with **Cascades**, an apartment block shaped like a ship's funnel. Further back there are a few impressive old structures such as **Warehouses 1 & 2**, by West India Quay station, and interesting new ones emerging, like the **Daily Telegraph Building** (*see chapter* **Media**) on South Quay. There's also a new, 12,000-seater music and sports venue, the **London Arena** (*see chapter* **Rock, Folk & Jazz**).

Billingsgate Fish Market
87 West India Dock Road, E14 (071 987 1118). West India Quay DLR/N95, N723 bus. **Open** 5.30-8.30am Tue-Sat. **Admission** free. **No credit cards.**
From shark to cod, this bustling wholesale market (recently decamped from the City) sells all things piscatory. Unless you're buying the more exotic and expensive varieties, the traders don't like to sell in small quantities. One of the market constables might show you round if asked.

Docklands Light Railway Visitor's Centre
3 Limeharbour, E14 (071 515 3000). Island Gardens DLR/Greenwich BR then foot tunnel to Island Gardens. **Open** 9am-6pm Mon-Sat; 10am-4pm Sat, Sun.
The staff here must spend most of their time explaining why the line's so often closed (to check times, phone 071 538 0311/071 22). The Visitor's Centre gives away free maps and other information and can book groups a three-hour tour (Isle of Dogs, two hours; Royal Docks and Surrey Quays, one hour).
Guided tours (up to 25 people £80.50 Mon-Fri, £115 Sat, Sun; 26-50 people £115 Mon-Fri, £184 Sat, Sun). Shop. Wheelchair access.

Mudchute City Farm
Pier Street, E14 (071 515 5901). Mudchute or Island Gardens DLR/277, D7 bus. **Open** Apr-Oct: 8am-6.30pm daily; Nov-Mar: 8am-5pm daily. **Admission** free. **Membership** £1 adults.
City farms are an unusual, but valuable British phenomenon, devised to offer inner-city children a taste of the rural life. On these 35 acres/14 hectares you can see all kinds of farm animals and an orchard. Children aged seven to 16 and the disabled can enjoy a 15-minute pony ride for 50p (except Mon); details on 071 515 5901.
Café (11am-4.30pm daily)

GREENWICH

Ever since the Vikings landed here to execute their hostage, the Archbishop of Canterbury, in 1011, Greenwich has been a maritime town. On landing by boat you'll first see the masts of the **Cutty Sark** and **Gipsy Moth IV**. When Britain ruled the waves, ship captains waived the rules by press-ganging men from the local inns to become 'jolly Jack Tars' on board ships sailing to the New World. Their problems navigating were made easier when the Prime Meridian was established in 1884 at the **Old Royal Observatory**. Particularly

The famous **Tower Bridge** (*listed under* **The Tower**) *is one of London's best value sights. The 1,000-tonne bascules (arms) open for large shipping up to five times a day in the summer. There's only 24 hours notice so phone first, or see the back page of* The Times *for a daily list of times. There are spectacular vistas from the glazed overhead walkways. In the towers are clear, interesting displays and models depicting the history of the Thames bridges, including unused designs for Tower Bridge. Fans of Victorian engineering will enjoy the gleaming engine room in the adjoining museum; animated diagrams make it easy to understand. Refreshingly, the staff are very helpful.*

popular with royalty, the area grew after Wren built the famous **Royal Naval Hospital.**

Cutty Sark
King William Walk, SE10 (081 853 3589). Greenwich or Maze Hill BR/Island Gardens DLR/177, 180, 286 bus/boat to Greenwich Pier. **Open** *Apr-Sept:* 10am-6pm Mon-Sat; noon-6pm Sun. *Oct-Mar:* 10am-5pm Mon-Sat; noon-5pm Sun. **Admission** £1.40 adults; 70p under-15s, OAPs. Children must be accompanied by an adult. **No credit cards.** *See* **picture and caption.**
English, French & German information point. Shop. Underground car park. Wheelchair access to one deck only.

Gipsy Moth IV
King William Walk, Greenwich, SE10 (081 853 3589). Greenwich or Maze Hill BR/1, 177, 188 bus/boat to Greenwich Pier. **Open** *Easter-Oct:* 10am-6pm daily. (Last admission 5.30pm). **Admission** 30p adults; 20p under-16s, OAPs.
Beside the *Cutty Sark, Gipsy Moth IV* looks like a toy, but it's a record-breaking boat. Francis Chichester deserved his knighthood just for staying on it for 226 days when aged 66, let alone for using the 54-foot/16-metre craft to make the first English solo circumnavigation of the world in 1966-67.
Shop (on Cutty Sark, see above).

Greenwich Park
Charlton Way, SE10 (081 858 2608). Greenwich or Maze Hill BR/177, 180, 286 bus/boat to Greenwich Pier. **Open** *Pedestrians:* 5am-dusk daily; *Traffic:* 7am-dusk daily.
One of the oldest royal parks in London, Greenwich Park was first enclosed by the Duke of Gloucester in 1433, then tastefully re-designed in the 1660s for Charles II by Le Nôtre, who landscaped Versailles. Crowning Greenwich Hill is the Old Royal Observatory and the Wolfe Monument. The view from here, over the Queen's House, Royal Hospital and the river is one of the best in London. Further back is a deer enclosure and Blackheath. In summer, brass bands perform (Whit Sunday-end September; 2-7pm Sun) and there are puppets shows (July and August).

Greenwich Theatre
Crooms Hill, SE10 (081 858 7755). Greenwich or Maze Hill BR/177, 180, 286 bus/boat to Greenwich Pier. **Credit** A, AmEx, DC, V.
An intimate 426-seat ex-Music Hall, Greenwich Theatre has an eclectic programme of good, solid drama, with occaional gems that transfer to the West End. It has a picture gallery and a restaurant, where there's live jazz on Sunday lunchtimes.

National Maritime Museum
Romney Road, SE10 (081 858 4422). Greenwich or Maze Hill BR/1, 177, 188 bus/boat to Greenwich Pier. **Open** *Mar-Oct:* 10am-6pm Mon-Sat; 2-6pm Sun; *Nov-Feb:* 10am-5pm Mon-Sat; 2-5pm Sun. **Admission** (includes entry to Old Royal Observatory) £3 adults; £1.50 age 7-16, OAPs, UB40s, students, disabled; free under-7s. **Credit** A, AmEx, £TC, V.
To see the world's most exhaustive collec-

tion of marine artefacts would take-up a lot of your time in Greenwich. There are many fine exhibits, in particular, the beautiful model ships. *See also chapter* **Museums.**
Educational department. Group discount. Library. Restaurant. Shop. Wheelchair access to ground floor only.

Old Royal Observatory
Greenwich Park, SE10 (081 858 1167). Same details as the **National Maritime Museum** *(above).*
Crowning Greenwich Hill is Wren's Old Royal Observatory of 1675. Since the 1880s people have climbed up to the home of the Prime Meridian and acted out the ritual of standing with one leg either side of the metal marker, proclaiming, 'Look, I'm straddling two time zones'. The site was chosen because almost three-quarters of the world's ships already had the Greenwich Meridian on their charts. The Meridian building is now a museum of optical instruments, but its telescope gallery is a bit baffling to non-aficionados. The house of John Flamsteed, the first Astronomer Royal, has some luxurious rooms and a fine collection of timepieces, including the first accurate visual one, the Timeball, which is hoisted and dropped at 1pm precisely.
Planetarium (regular programmes, phone for details). Shop.

DOCKLANDS: ROYAL DOCKS
With south-east England slowly sinking and global warming raising the sea level, the **Thames Flood Barrier** was built a few years ago to protect London from freak tides. But nobody expected a tidal wave of corporate offices to engulf the **Royal Docks.** Together, the **Victoria, Albert** and **George VI Docks,** covering seven miles of quay, were the largest in the world. Today, the central area has already become the **London City Airport** (*see below* **River Transport: Commuter Services).**

Museum in Docklands
Unit C14, Poplar Business Park, 10 Preston Road, E14 (071 515 1162). Coach departs from Museum of London, Aldersgate Street, EC2. Barbican, Moorgate or St. Paul's underground. **Times** 10.45am middle Sat of each month; advance bookings advisable. **Duration** 210 minutes. **Admission** £5 adults; £4 under-16s, OAPs, students, UB40s. **No credit cards.**
This bus tour takes you not only around Docklands, emphasizing the impact of

The first of the Docklands redevelopments, **St Katherine's Dock** *(listed under* **Docklands: Wapping & Rotherhithe***) was Thomas Telford's only complete London project (1828). Since 1973 the network of warehouse conversions has been an ideal place to relax and eat in once you've trudged round the Tower of London over the road. The dock is full of bobbing yachts and vessels, including a bright red lighthouse ship, the Nore, and barges that once worked around the London docks. The Dickens Inn pub is a popular refuelling stop.*

events on the local community, but also to a preview of exhibits for the Museum in Docklands at Victoria Dock, which opens in 1992. The entire Port of London Authority archives – photographs, documents – can be seen by appointment, but many of the artefacts explaining dockland trades are displayed at the visitors centre, including thirties diving equipment, a rigger's workshop and model ships.
Education department. Group discount. Shop.

Thames Barrier Visitors Centre
Unity Way, Woolwich, SE18 (081 854 1373). Charlton BR/boat to Thames Barrier Pier/180 bus. **Open** 10.30am-5pm Mon-Fri; 10.30am-5.30pm Sat, Sun. **Admission** £2 adults; £1.20 under-16s, OAPs; £5.50 family ticket (two adults plus three children). **Credit** (shop only) A, V.
See **picture and caption.**
Café. Cruises around the barrier (£1.10 adults, 80p under-16s, 20% discount for groups of 15 or more. Information 081 854 5555). Shop. Toilets for the disabled. Wheelchair access.

UPSTREAM

Embarking from Westminster Pier, you get a memorable perspective of the **Houses of Parliament**. Just before you pass under Lambeth Bridge you can catch sight of the brick tower of **Lambeth Palace**, home of the Archbishops of Canterbury since the twelfth century. After passing the **Tate Gallery**, the massive brick 'upturned table' of **Battersea Power Station** rises out of a gloomy industrial landscape. Plans for it to become Europe's biggest pleasure palace by the early 1990s are in some turmoil. Opposite is elegant **Pimlico** which blends into one of London's oldest riverside villages, **Chelsea**. Beyond Chelsea Suspension Bridge you'll see Christopher Wren's **Royal Hospital Chelsea**, facing the **London Peace Pagoda** on the Battersea Park riverside.

London's rowing clubs own most of the boathouses lining the riverbanks after the **Fulham** railway bridge. From **Putney**, you follow the course of the famous **Oxford and Cambridge University Boat Race** (*see chapter* **London By Season**) under **Hammersmith Bridge**, around the great **Barnes** river-bend to the finish at **Chiswick Bridge**. Shortly after the pretty converted fishermen's cottages of **Strand-on-the-Green** is **Kew Pier**. If you don't disembark for the **Royal Botanical Gardens**, you get the stunning vista

of the gardens from the water. On the Brentford side is the confluence of the **Grand Union Canal/River Brent** with the Thames.

KEW

You could spend the rest of the day in the Kew Gardens area, which includes **Kew Palace** and **Kew Green**, with its charming seventeenth- and eighteenth-century houses and summer cricket matches. After crossing **Kew Bridge**, an energetic walk in either direction will take you to **Syon House and Park** *(see chapter* **Georgian London**), or through **Strand-on-the-Green**, with its three old pubs, to **Chiswick Marina.**

Kew Palace
Kew Gardens, Richmond, Surrey (081 940 3321). Kew Gardens underground/Kew Gardens or Kew Bridge BR/boat to Kew Pier/7, 22, 65, 90B, 237, 267 bus. **Open** *Apr-Sept* 11am-5.30pm daily. **Admission** £1 adults; 50p under-16s; 75p OAPs. **Credit** £TC.
As the smallest and most intimate of the

royal homes, Kew Palace was used as a country retreat. Built in 1631, the Jacobean house was modernized several times by its Georgian residents.
Cafés in gardens. Group discount. Shop. Wheelchair access to ground floor only.

Maids of Honour
288 Kew Gardens, Surrey (081 940 2752). Kew Gardens underground/Kew Gardens or Kew Bridge BR/boat to Kew Pier/27, 65 bus. **Open** 10am-1pm Mon; 10am-5.30pm Tue-Sat. *Lunch* 12.30-2.15pm Tue-Sat. *Set tea* 2.30pm-5.30pm Tue-Sat. **Average** *Lunch:* £6; *Set tea* £2.65. **No credit cards.**
This famous tea room is named after the tarts that Henry VIII liked so much – they were baked by a Maid of Honour he imprisoned in Richmond Palace to keep him supplied with the pastries. This country cottage would be a charming place to sample a few home-baked Maids of Honour after a stroll in Kew Gardens, if only it weren't for the queues: more than 1,000 people are served per day on an average summer weekend.
Alcohol licence. Babies, children welcome; high chairs for babies; children's portions. Takeaway service.

Royal Botanic Gardens
Kew Road, Richmond, Surrey (081 940 1171). Kew Gardens underground/Kew Bridge BR/27 or 65 bus/boat to Kew Pier.

Tobacco Dock *(listed under* **Docklands: Wapping & Rotherhithe***) is an attractive new complex of shops, restaurants and street entertainment. It's proclaimed as a 'shopping village';estate agents' language for a blatant copy of Covent Garden which it does resemble, although it's three times the size. The prevalence of chainstores and gimmick shops however underline its tourist trap pretentions and the locals see it as a mixed blessing. The listed warehouses with their elegantly curved vaults date from 1814 and have been ingeniously adapted by Terry Farrell. Moored by the dockside are replicas of two ships of the type that once delivered tobacco and wine to the dock.*

*The **Cutty Sark** (listed under **Greenwich**) is the closest to perfection that a sailing ship could be. The only surviving tea and wool clipper, this 1869 vessel was a wonder of its times, smashing speed records. You're free to roam about the beautifully restored decks and crew's quarters and gaze up at the masts and rigging. Inside are collections of prints and naval relics, plus the world's largest collection of carved and painted figureheads; these embodiments of maritime superstition are great fun.*

Open *Nov-Jan*: 9.30am-4pm daily; *Feb*: 9.30am-5pm daily; *Mar, Sept, Oct*: 9.30am-6pm daily; *Apr-Sept*: 9.30am-6.30pm Mon-Sat, 9.30am-8pm Sun and Bank Holidays. **Admission** £1 adults; 50p under-16s, OAPs; free under-5s, educational groups; £5 season tickets. **Credit** (shop only) A, £TC, V.

Thousands of visitors descend on Kew Gardens on summer weekends. Luckily, it's vast and there are so many attractions that the numbers don't spoil one of the most pleasant sights around. The Royal Botanic Gardens is both park and scientific institution (*see also chapter* **Sightseeing**).

Cafés & restaurant. Shop (10am to one hour before gardens close). Tour by prior arrangement (£2 per person per hour). Wheelchairs available. Wheelchair access.

RICHMOND

Richmond has been a privileged town, patronized by monarchs since the twelfth century. It was the Anglo-Saxon manor of Shene until 1499, when Henry VII named his new palace (the remains are by the river) after his Yorkshire estate of Rychemonde. Up the steep hill is the nearest gate to **Richmond Park**, the largest park in Europe (*see chapter* **Sightseeing**).

Museum of Richmond

Old Town Hall, Whittaker Avenue, Richmond (081 332 1141). Richmond underground/BR/boat to Richmond Pier/27, 33, 37, 65, 71, 202, 270 bus. **Open** 1.30-5pm Tue; 1.30-8pm Wed; 1.30-6pm Thur, Fri; 10am-5pm Sat; 1.30am-4pm Sun (May-Sept only). **Admission** 80p adults; 40p under-16s, OAPs, students, UB40s. **No credit cards.**

The Old Victorian Town Hall is now one of London's best local museums. Naturally it dwells on Richmond's popularity as a royal resort, although it doesn't ignore its commuterland role today. An impressive gallery of famous inhabitants includes actor Edmund Kean, painters Gainsborough, Reynolds and Pissaro, and writers George Eliot, Virginia Woolf and Bertrand Russell (whose progressive school in nearby Petersham still exists).

Café (10am-5pm Mon-Sat). Shop. Wheelchair access.

HAMPTON COURT

The river goes on past **Marble Hill House** on the right (*see chapters* **Georgian London** and **Music: Classical & Opera**, and **Ham House** on the left (*see chapter* **Tudors & Stuarts**), both of which are an easy walk from Richmond. It then bends into Twickenham by Eel Pie Island. Around the island are cluttered architectural reminders of the days when the high and mighty built their country love nests along the banks of the Thames. Further upstream, past **Teddington Lock**, is **Kingston-upon-Thames**, where once the Saxon kings of England were crowned but where now people mostly go shopping. Another loop in the river brings you to **Hampton Court**, where the river cruisers terminate.

Hampton Court Palace

East Molesey, Surrey (081 977 8441). Hampton Court BR/boat to Hampton Court Pier (Apr-Oct)/111, 131, 216, 267, 461 bus. **Open** *Apr-Oct:* 9.30am-6pm daily; *Oct-Mar:* 9.30am-4.30pm daily (last admission half an hour before closing). **Park open** dawn to dusk daily. **Admission** *Inclusive ticket to palace, courtyard, cloister and maze:* £3.40 adults; £1.70 under-16s; free under-5s; £2.50 OAPs; *Maze only: Mar-Oct* £1 adults; 50p under-16s; 75p OAPs. **Credit** A, V. *See* **picture and caption.** *See also chapter* **Tudors & Stuarts.** *Car park. (free) Group discount. Guided tours (Mar-Sept; 11.15am & 2.15pm Mon-Sat; free with full price ticket). Shop. Toilet facilites for the disabled. Wheelchair access.*

THE CANALS

London's 54 miles/86.4km of canal are a peaceful place to relax. Stroll along the tow paths or chug by in a narrow boat (just six feet/2.4m wide, so three can pass at the same time). Before railways the **Grand Union Canal** was the artery carrying goods destined for London's Docks. It splits at Bull's Bridge, Middlesex, the southern branch connecting with the Thames at Brentford. The Paddington Arm flows to **Little Venice**, the pretty bit where million-pound stucco houses dip their toes into the picturesque, but murky waters. From here it's the **Regent's Canal** (opened in 1820), which cuts across Regent's Park, past **London Zoo** to **Camden Lock** (*see chapter* **Local London**). Emerging from the Islington Tunnel, the canal flows through the City Basin to the Thames at **Limehouse Basin.**

Tow paths are open from 9am until dusk; some areas are quite isolated, so it's best to go in groups.

There are no paths at Maida Hill and Islington Tunnels and at Limehouse Cut. Cyclists will need a permit from **British Waterways** (*see below*), but the nautically-minded should try one of the narrowboat companies still operating.

British Waterways Information Centre
Melbury House, Melbury Terrace, NW1 (071 262 6711). Marylebone underground/BR. **Open** 9.30am-5pm Mon-Thur; 9.30am-4.30pm Fri. **Credit** A, V.
British Waterways administers the canals. You can buy cycling permit forms (£3) and maps and information in the shop or by post. *Educational packs.*

Regent's Canal Information Centre
Camden Lock, NW1 (071 482 0523). Camden Town or Chalk Farm underground/Camden Road BR/24, 29, 168, 253 bus. **Open** daily from April 1990. Phone for details.
See **picture and caption.**
Shop. Wheelchair access.

WATER TRANSPORT

RIVER CRUISES

Services on cruisers vary between the different operators. Most boats have bars, some have restaurants. The crew give commentaries on a voluntary basis. Do ask for one as they can be a very entertaining, if you get a witty guide with a few irreverent tales to tell. You're most likely to hear one in the summer when the boat is full (a hat is passed round afterwards). On return trips the commentary is given on the way out only. Head for the seats at the front of the boat from where you can see landmarks on both riverbanks. You'll regret not taking a camera or a pair of binoculars; most of the boats are partly uncovered, so you can snap away on deck. Wrap up well as the wind can be sharp and the temperature is several degrees lower on the river. Some of the boats have wheelchair access, but do phone to check beforehand.

For recorded river trip information telephone 071 730 4812. **Westminster Passenger Services Association** *(071 930 4721/2062)* have more information on return services from the upstream piers. Upstream trips only run in the summer.

Charing Cross Pier
Victoria Embankment (opposite Embankment underground), WC2 (071 839

3572). Embankment underground or Charing Cross underground/BR.
To Greenwich *Apr-Sept:* 10.30am then every 30 mins until 4pm daily. **Duration** 45 mins. **Fares** *Single:* £2.60 adults, £1.30 under-16s; *Return:* £4.20 adults, £2.10 under-16s.
To Tower of London *Apr-Sept:* 10.30am then every 30 mins until 4pm daily. **Duration** 20 mins. **Fares** *Single:* £2 adults, £1 under-16s; *Return:* £3 adults, £1.50 under-16s.
Evening round trip: between Tate **Gallery & Tower Bridge** *Easter-Sept:* 7.30pm, 8.30pm. **Duration** 45 mins. **Fares** £3 adults, £1.50 age 5-16s.

Greenwich Pier
Cutty Sark Gardens, SE10 (071 858 0079). Greenwich BR/1, 108, 177, 185 or 188 bus.
To Tower Pier *(071 858 6722).* 11.30am then every 30 mins until 4pm. **Duration** 25 mins. **Fares** *Single:* £2.20 adults, £1.10 under-16s; *Return:* £3.50 adult, £1.80 under-16s
To Charing Cross *(071 858 3996).* 11.15am then every 30 mins until 4pm. **Duration** 45 mins. **Fares** *Single:* £2.60 adults, £1.30 under-16s; *Return:* £4.20 adults, £2.10 under-16s.
To Thames Barrier *(071 305 0300)* 11.15am, 12.30pm, 1.45pm, 3pm, 4.15pm. **Duration** 30 mins. **Fares** *Single:* £1.50 adults, £1 under-16s; *Return:* £2.50 adult, £1.50 under-16s.
To Westminster *(071 858 3996).* 11.30am

then every 30 mins until 3.45pm. **Duration** 45 mins. **Fares** *Single:* £2.50 adults, £2 OAPs, £1.20 under-16s; *Return:* £4 adults, £3 OAPs, £2 under-16s.

Tower Pier
Tower Hill (opposite main entrance to Tower of London), EC3 (071 488 0344). Tower Hill underground/Tower Gateway DLR.
To Butler's Wharf (Design Museum) *(071 403 6933/071 407 6261).* Feb-Nov: 11.30am then every 20 mins until 6.30pm Tue-Sun. *Nov-Feb:* 11.30am then every 20 mins until 6.30pm Sat, Sun. **Duration** 5 mins. **Fares** *Return only:* 80p adults; 60p child, OAPs, students, UB40s.
To Greenwich *(071 488 0344).* 11am then every 30 mins until 4.30pm. **Duration** 30 mins. **Fares** *Single:* £2.20 adults, £1.10 under-16s; *Return:* £3.50 adults, £1.80 under-16s.
To Westminster *(071 488 0344).* 11am then every 20 mins until 6pm. **Duration** 20 mins. **Fares** *Single:* £2 adults, £1 under-16s; *Return:* £3 adults, £1.50 under-16s.

Westminster Pier
Victoria Embankment (steps from Westminster Bridge), SW1. Westminster underground.
To Greenwich *(071 930 4097).* 10.30am then every 30 mins until 4pm. **Duration** 45 mins. **Fares** *Single:* £2.50 adults, £2 OAPs,

The **Thames Flood Barrier** *(listed under* **Docklands: Royal Docks***) is the largest of its type in the world. A prudent piece of architecture, it guards against the Thames flooding the capital, as it did in 1928, when 14 people drowned in waves of 20 feet/6 metres. Nine metal-capped concrete piers support the giant steel floodgates. The Visitors Centre has scale models and audio-displays plus an incongruous bonus exhibit of Roger Hallett's Panorama, a vast 1983 balloon-eyed painting of the city of Bath.*

Hampton Court *(listed under* Travelling Upstream*) is the grandest Tudor residence in Britain, so it's not surprising that Henry VIII appropriated it from his Lord Chancellor, Cardinal Wolsey. Christopher Wren did some home improvement in 1689. The King's apartments are presently closed, following a fire in 1986. If the state rooms get a bit wearing, the gardens and parkland are great for a picnic — or for getting lost in the famous maze. Beyond Wren's mile/1.6km-long Chestnut Avenue is a wilder expanse of plantations, ponds and herds of fallow deer, an area known as Bushy Park. The palace also boasts a rare 'real tennis' court, where Henry VIII once played.*

£1.20 under-16s; *Return*: £4 adults, £3 OAPs, £2 under-16s.
To Hampton Court *(071 930 2062/071 930 4721)*. *Apr-Oct*: 10.30am, 11.15am, noon, 12.30pm. **Duration** 180-240mins. **Fares** *Single*: £5.50 adults, £3.50 age 4-14; *Return*: £7 adults, £5 age 4-14.
To Kew *(071 930 2062/071 930 4721)*. *Apr-Oct*: 10.15am, 10.30am, 11am, 11.30am, noon, 12.30pm, 2pm, 2.30pm, 3pm, 3.30pm. **Duration** 90mins. **Fares** *Single*: £3.50 adults, £2.50 under-14s; *Return*: £5 adults, £3.50 under-14s.
To Putney *(071 930 2062/071 930 4721)*. *Apr-Oct*: 10.15am, 10.30am, 11am, 11.30am, noon, 12.30pm, 2pm, 2.30pm, 3pm, 3.30pm. **Duration** 40mins. **Fares** *Single*: £2.50 adults, £1.50 under-14s. *Return*: £4 adults, £2.50 under-14s.
To Richmond *(071 930 2062/071 930 4721)*. *Apr-Oct*: 10.30am, 11.15pm, noon, 12.30pm. **Duration** 150 mins. **Fares** *Single*: £5 adults, £3.50 under-14s; *Return*: £6.50 adults, £4.50 under-14s.
Round trip: between Tate Gallery & Tower Bridge *(071 237 1322/071 928 9009/081 467 6314)*. *Apr-Oct*: 11.15am, then every 30 mins until 4.45pm. Phone for details of winter trips. **Duration** 60 mins. **Fares** £2.40 adults, £1.10 under-16s, OAPs.
To Thames Barrier *(071 930 3373)*. *Apr-*

Oct: 10am, 11.15am, 12.30pm, 1.30pm, 2.45pm. *Nov-Mar*: 11.15am, 1.30pm, 2.45pm. **Duration** 75 mins. **Fares** *Single*: £2.40 adults, £1.30 under-16s, £1.80 OAPs; *Return*: £4 adults, £2.30 under-16s, £3 OAPs.
To Tower of London *(071 930 4097)*. 10.20am then every 20 mins until 5pm. **Duration** 30 mins. **Fares** *Single*: £2 adults, £1 under-16s; *Return*: £3 adults, £1.50 under-16s.

COMMUTER SERVICES

Since the watermen and lightermen (ferry workers) were put out of business by dastardly Victorian bridge builders, the Thames has been ignored as a means of daily transport – until recently. The bus and underground strikes of 1989 converted many a commuter to the new speedy riverboat services.

London City Airport Express Service
(071 474 5555).
From Charing Cross Pier *Victoria Embankment (opposite Embankment underground), WC2. Embankment underground or*

Charing Cross underground/BR. 7.10am, then 10 mins past the hour until 6.10pm (no service at 1.10pm) Mon-Fri. **Duration** 35 mins. **Fare** £5.
From Swan Lane Pier *Upper Thames Street (by London Bridge), EC4. Monument underground or London Bridge underground/BR.* 7.10am, then 15 mins past the hour until 6.10pm (no service at 1.10pm) Mon-Fri. **Duration** 30 mins. **Fare** £4.
The highly civilized staff on board this motor launch notify the airport that you are on the way and can order your duty free goods in advance. In a race from the West End, the boat would beat both taxi and train by at least ten minutes, taking just 35 minutes at half the price (about £5) of a taxi. A bus meets you at the pier for a six-minute ride to the airport.

Riverbus
(formerly Thames Line)
The Chambers, Chelsea Harbour, Lots Road, SW10 (071 376 3676). **From:** **Chelsea Harbour** off Lots Road, SW10; **Charing Cross Pier** Hungerford Bridge, WC2; **Festival Pier** South Bank Centre, SE1; **Swan Lane Pier** City, EC4; **London Bridge City Pier** Hays Galleria, SE1; **West India Pier** Canary Wharf, E14; **Greenland Pier** Greenland Dock, SE8; **Greenwich Pier**, SE10. **Services** 7-10am, 4-7pm Mon-Fri every 20 mins; 10am-4pm, 7-10pm Mon-Fri every 30 mins; 10am-6pm Sat, Sun every 30 mins. **Fares** £1-£4; *Season tickets*: £100-worth for £70; £26-worth for £21.25. **Credit** A, AmEx, V.
This exemplary daily service, running between Chelsea Harbour and Greenwich, is rapidly expanding. The eight motor launches (increasing to 20 by 1991) have comfortable aircraft-like seats, helpful crews and are easy to use. They're also surprisingly fast (travelling up to 25mph/40kmph): Charing Cross to the City in ten minutes for £1 is good going. Every pier has a floating waiting room with a ticket machine, so there's no delay upon entry.
No wheelchair access.

EVENING CRUISES

Capital Cruises
45A Heathfield Street, SW18 (071 350 1910). **Times** by appointment. **Fares** *Jan-Nov*: £8.95 Mon-Fri; £10.95 Sat, Sun. *Dec*: £12.95 daily. **Credit** A, AmEx, V.
Capital's boats are used for private functions; the higher December prices cover the vast expense of supplying Christmas balloons. Book in advance.

Disco Cruise
Westminster Pier, Victoria Embankment, SW1 (071 839 2164). *Westminster underground/12, 24, 29, 53 bus*. **Leaves pier** 7pm Mon-Fri; 8pm Sat. **Duration** 240 mins. **Fares** Mon-Thur £6 (£8 incl dinner); Fri, Sat £7.65 (£11 incl dinner). **Credit** £TC.
Dancing on deck is an art you can master all the way to the Thames Barrier and back. The nautical cuisine amounts to a few pieces of chicken, a jacket potato, salad and a roll. The trip must be booked and paid for in advance.

Floodlit & Supper Cruise
Westminster Pier, Victoria Embankment, SW1 (071 839 3572). *Westminster underground/12, 24, 29, 53, 77 bus*. **Leaves pier** *May-Sept*: 9pm Mon-Fri, Sun.

Duration 90mins. **Fares** £12 adult, £8 under-15s. **Credit** A, AmEx, V.
The conventional supper doesn't quite match the wonderful floodlit views between Tower Bridge and Westminster. You need to book in advance.
Wheelchair access on some boats.

Late-evening cruise
Charing Cross Pier, Victoria Embankment, SW1 (071 839 3572). Embankment underground or Charing Cross underground/BR.
Leaves pier *May-Oct*: 7.30pm, 8.30pm Mon-Fri, Sun. **Duration** 45mins. **Fares** £3 adult; £1.50 under-15s. **Credit** A, £TC, V.
A commentary spells out the sights on this floodlit jaunt to the Tower of London. You can buy your tickets on board.
Wheelchair access on some boats.

CANAL TRIPS

Jason's Trip
Little Venice (opposite 60 Blomfield Road), W9 (071 286 3428). Warwick Avenue underground/Paddington underground/BR/6 bus.
Little Venice/Camden Lock.
From Camden Lock *Easter-May*: 1.15pm, 3.15pm daily. *Jun-Aug*: (no commentary) 11.15am, 1.15pm, 3.15pm, 5.15pm daily. *Sept-Oct*: 1.15pm, 3.15pm daily. **Duration** 90 mins round trip; 45 mins one way. **Fares** *Single*: £2.50 adult; £1.25 under-14s, OAPs; *Return*: £3.25 adult; £2 under-14s, OAPs. **Credit** A, AmEx, V.
From Little Venice *Easter-May*: 10.30am, 12.30pm, 2.30pm daily; *Jun-Aug*: (with commentary) 10.30am, 12.30pm, 2.30pm, 4.30pm daily; *Sept-Oct*: 12.30pm, 2.30pm daily. **Duration** 90 mins round trip; 45 mins one way. **Fares** *Single*: £2.50 adult; £1.25 under-14s, OAPs; *Return*: £3.25 adult; £2 under-14s, OAPs. **Credit** A, AmEx, V.
Gaudily painted in a traditional fashion, *Jason* was the first narrow boat to pleasure-cruise on the Regent's Canal after a lifetime of carrying cargo. Buy tickets on board or at the office. A restaurant boat is also available for private hire in the evenings.
Group discount. Shop at mooring.

Jenny Wren
Office: 250 Camden High Street, NW1 (071 485 4433/071 485 6210). Camden Town underground/Camden Road BR/24, 29, 168, 253 bus.
Camden Lock/Little Venice.
From Camden Lock *Mar-Oct*: 10am, 11.30am, 2pm Mon-Fri; 2pm, 3.30pm, Sat; 11.30am, 2pm, 3.30pm Sun. **Duration** 90 mins. **Fares** *Return*: £2.40 adult, £1.20 children, OAPs; no single tickets. **Credit** A, V.
This traditional canal boat travels from Camden Lock to Little Venice without stopping. The Sunday Lunch Cruise (£12.75) on the sister boat *My Fair Lady* (*see chapter* Eating & Drinking) makes a pleasant family trip.
Wheelchair access.

London Waterbus Company
Little Venice (corner Warwick Crescent and Westbourne Terrace), W9. Warwick Avenue underground or Camden Lock, NW1 (071 482 2550, 24 hours). Camden Town underground/Camden Road BR.
From Little Venice *Apr-Oct*: on the hour 10am-5pm daily; *Oct-Mar*: 10.30am, noon, 1.30pm, 3pm, Sat, Sun. **Duration** *to Zoo*: 35 minutes; *to Camden Lock*: 50 mins; *Round trip*: 110 minutes. **Fares** *to Zoo: single (including admission to Zoo)*: £5.75 adults;

*For ideas on how to enjoy London's canals visit the **Regent's Canal Information Centre** (listed under Canals). The charming, castellated former lock-keeper's cottage of Camden Lock is a newly refurbished outlet for maps, books and things related to the canal. A floating information centre is planned for the lock in front of it. This is the ideal place to start a towpath walk or narrowboat trip, particularly if you want to get away from the trendy and crowded weekend markets by Camden Lock.*

£2.90 under-14s; *to Camden Lock: single* £2.20 adults, £1.20 under-14s.
From Camden Lock *Apr-Oct*: on the hour 10am-5pm daily; *Oct-Mar*: 11.15am, 12.45pm, 2.15pm, 3.45pm Sat, Sun. **Duration** *to Zoo*: 15 mins; *to Little Venice*: 50 minutes. *Round trip*: 110 minutes. **Fares** *to Zoo: single (includes admission to Zoo)*: £4.85 adult, £2.90 under-14s; *to Little Venice: single* £2.20 adults, £1.20 under-14s.
From London Zoo *Apr-Oct: to Camden Lock* 35 minutes past the hour 10am-5pm Mon-Sat; *to Little Venice* 15 minutes past the hour 10am-5pm Mon-Sat; *Oct-Mar: to Camden Lock* 11am, 12.30pm, 2pm, 3.30pm, Sat, Sun; *to Little Venice*: 11.30am, 1pm, 2.30pm, 4pm, Sat, Sun. **Fares** *to Zoo: single* £1.80 adults; £1.10 under-14s; *return* £2.55 adult, £1.40 child; *to Camden Lock: single* 90p adults, 55p under-14s; *return* £1.35 adult, 90p child.
Tickets are issued on board. Bookings are not required. The company will arrange lock demonstrations for groups; phone to arrange. From May, on certain Saturdays, there will be all-day trips to Limehouse, through north and east London (tickets are £7.25, £5.50 OAPs). Ticket prices will rise in 1990.

WALKS & TOURS

The Thames **tow paths** can make a lovely walk, but to go great distances you need to cross from one riverbank to the other. There is also the problem that ad hoc development over the centuries has created inconvenient pockets of private property. Unless a tow path is a designated bridle or cycle path, you can't travel down one on a horse or a bicycle.

Thameside Pub Walks
Perfect Pub Walks *PO Box 1708, NW6 (071 435 6413). Walkers meet at Blackfriars underground ticket barrier.* **Times** 7.30pm every Fri. **Duration** 150 minutes.
Admission £4 adults, £2 under-16s, students, OAPs, UB40s.

London's Historic Docklands
(071 739 4853). Walkers meet at Tower Hill underground exit. **Times** *Sept-Mar* 11.15am Sat. **Duration** 90-120 mins hours.
Admission £3.50 adults; £2.50 OAPs, students, UB40s; accompanied under-8s free.
No credit cards.
This guided walk through the London Docks ends with a lunchtime pint in either the Prospect of Whitby or Town of Ramsgate pub.

Local London

Two hundred years ago, you could walk cross-country from Highgate to Islington. London still has vestiges of villages, and natives with a fierce parochialism.

The massive metropolis of London is basically an odd collection of villages, swallowed up by a city which has been growing like a glutton since the seventeenth century. Some of these towns and villages are still recognizable – Samuel Taylor Coleridge would find himself quite at home in Highgate High Street 150 years ago (apart from the traffic, that is). Others have changed out of all recognition, but if you know where to look you can still find vestiges of the past.

BAYSWATER TO HOLLAND PARK

Do visitors to **Marble Arch** realize, we wonder, that this nineteenth-century monument was built right next to the site where highwaymen were once hanged? It wasn't until the public gallows were moved from Tyburn in 1783 that the area north of Hyde Park began to become respectable. You can see the exact spot where the infamous 'Tyburn Tree' stood, marked by a brass plaque, on a small traffic island at the junction of Bayswater Road and Edgware Road, next to the huge Odeon Cinema.

Bayswater's main street is **Queensway**, presided over by the first of the great department stores, **Whiteley's**, now refurbished as a shopping centre. Further down the road is the **Queen's Ice-Skating Club** (*see chapter* **Sport & Fitness**). On Sundays artists and artisans display their (mostly naff) wares on the park railings along the Bayswater Road.

Most of **Notting Hill Gate** village disappeared in the fifties, although a few old houses can be seen on the north side of the main road. The Gate Theatre (*see chapter* **Theatre**) and two cinemas, the Gate and the Coronet, are here, but it's primarily the stopping-off place for **Portobello Road Market**. In August this area is home to Europe's biggest street party, the **Notting Hill Carnival** (*see chapter* **London By Season**). At the northern end of Portobello Road is an expanding group of galleries selling contemporary art (*see chapter* **Art Galleries**).

West of Notting Hill is **Holland Park** — not an old village, but the result of speculative building in the early nineteenth century. The curving crescents that run down from the church to **Ladbroke Grove** are a reminder of the Hippodrome Racecourse, which was built here in 1837. It closed five years later because no horse could run on the waterlogged clay soil.

Further north, a brick kiln built into one of the houses at **Hippodrome Mews** is all that is left of the notorious Piggeries and Potteries, a Victorian slum, infamous for crime and cholera epidemics. To the south, **Holland Park Avenue** boasts a very grand row of large porticoed houses on its south side, backing on to the road. This and the road behind it are labelled 'Holland Park', but don't be deceived; the park proper is further up Abbotsbury Road.

Transport Bayswater, Queensway, Notting Hill Gate, Ladbroke Grove or Holland Park underground; 8, 12 or 27 bus.

Aubrey House

Aubrey Walk, SW12. Holland Park underground.
The last of the country houses which once stood around Notting Hill village. You can peer through the gates but cannot go in: Aubrey House is still privately owned. It's on the hill above Campden Hill Square (where the residents all light candles in their windows on Christmas Eve). Miss Cicely Alexander used to live here - she was the subject of Whistler's *An Arrangement in Grey and Green.*

Books for Cooks

4 Blenheim Crescent, W11 (071 221 1992). Notting Hill Gate or Ladbroke Grove underground. **Open** 9.30am-6pm Mon-Sat. **Credit** A, AmEx, £STC, V.
Every cuisine imaginable is dealt with in this shop. All the great cookery writers and chefs are represented among a selection of over 5,000 books in ten different languages.

Coronet Theatre

Notting Hill Gate, W11 (071 727 6705). Notting Hill Gate underground. **Admission** £3.50; £1.50 OAPs, under-16s. **No credit cards.**
Mrs Patrick Campbell, Sarah Bernhardt, Ellen Terry and Sybil Thorndike all appeared on the Coronet stage. It's now a relatively cheap and shabbily wonderful cinema.

Holland House & Park

Entrances in Holland Park, Abbotsbury Road, Holland Walk and Kensington High Street, W8. Holland Park or High Street Kensington underground. **Open** 7.30am-30minutes before dusk daily.
Everyone who was anyone in politics, literature or society met at Holland House in the eighteenth century. Built in 1606 as a gentleman's country house near the village of Kensington, it was heavily bombed in World War II and only one wing, now part of the Youth Hostel *(071 937 0748)*, remains. But the park, which was opened to the public in 1952, still has its woods and formal gardens. There is an open-air theatre here in the summer, and also the Belvedere restaurant *(071 602 1238)*, from which you can watch the peacocks going to roost. For children, there is a splendid adventure playground, with tree walks, rope-swings and other delights.

Plastic Passion

2 Blenheim Crescent, W11 (071 229 5424). Notting Hill Gate or Ladbroke Grove underground/7, 15, 52 bus. **Open** 10.30am-6.30pm Mon-Sat. **Credit** A, £TC.
Collectors of new wave, punk, American and British sixties' psychedelia, and eighties' hardcore, rare and re-issued records should head here.

Porchester Baths

Queensway, W2 (071 229 9950). Bayswater or Royal Oak underground. **Open** 7am-10pm daily. **Admission** *Swimming pool* £1.25; *Turkish baths* £10.50. **No credit cards.**
These baths have tubs-full of old world atmosphere and faded charm. Take a Turkish bath, have a body scrub, plunge into the ice-cold pool or just take a leisurely swim in the heated pool. There are steam rooms, a sauna, a weight-training room, and a squash court.

Portobello Road Market

Portobello Road, W11. Notting Hill Gate or Ladbroke Grove underground/12, 28, 31, 52 bus. **Open** *Fruit and vegetables* 8am-3pm Mon-Wed, Fri, Sat; 8am-1pm Thur; *General* 8am-3pm Fri; 8am-5pm Sat; *Antiques* 8am-5pm Sat. *See* picture and caption.

Rough Trade

130 Talbot Road, W11 (071 229 8541). Notting Hill Gate or Ladbroke Grove underground/12, 52 bus. **Open** 10am-6.30pm Mon-Sat. **Credit** A, £TC, V.
A record shop with a skateboard shop in the basement. Rough Trade (it's also a record label) is the best in London for independent and avant-garde pop releases. One of the few survivors from the punk era.

Travel Bookshop

13 Blenheim Crescent, W11 (071 229 5260). Ladbroke Grove or Notting Hill Gate underground/52, 15, 7 bus. **Open** 10am-6pm Mon-Wed, Fri; 10am-8pm Thur; 10am-5pm Sat. **Credit** AmEx, BT, £TC, V.
Take a break from the hurly-burly of Portobello

Road to visit this specialist bookshop. Every continent and country is covered in great depth, by books both ancient and modern.

Whiteley's
Queensway, W2 (071 229 8844). Queensway underground. **Open** 9am-8pm Mon-Sat.
Whiteley's was one of the first department stores. It's now lost some of its turn-of-the-century glory, but has been converted into a lively, cosmopolitan jumble of cafés, restaurants and shops of all sorts, retaining its wonderful staircase. Whiteley's also has an eight-screen cinema (*see chapter* **Film**).

CAMDEN TOWN

In the 1820s, the Prince Regent had a scheme for developing a whole new area of London. Regent Street was to lead north from his newly-acquired Carlton House in The Mall, to a great new park surrounded by crescents and terraces. A canal was built to bring transport and industry to the area north of the park and hot on its heels grew the working-class district of **Camden Town**.

Today, the streets around the canal's lock are filled with trendy weekend shoppers and browsers. They come to visit the **Camden Lock Markets** (*see chapter* **To the Eighties**), that are crammed with craft workshops and stalls stocking all manner of clothing, accessories and second-hand goods. Camden High Street has busy fruit and vegetable markets, splendid fish shops and Asian grocers.

Perhaps the most famous inhabitants near Camden Town are the 8,000 animals in London Zoo (*see chapter* **Sightseeing**), where you could easily spend a whole day walking around trying to see everything.

The area has some of the best venues in London for live music, including **Dingwalls** at Camden Lock, NW1 (*071 267 4967*) and the **Electric Ballroom** (*see chapter* **Music: Rock, Folk & Jazz**). The population has a strong Irish element (*see chapter* **Ethnic London**) and the music from the pub juke-box is as likely to be Irish folk as Top of the Pops.

Transport Camden Town or Chalk Farm underground; Primrose Hill or Camden Road BR; 3, 24, 27, 29, 31, 46, 53, 68, 134, 137, 214 or 253 bus; waterbus from Little Venice or the Zoo to Camden Lock.

Café Delancey
3 Delancey Street, NW1 (071 387 1985). Camden Town underground/24, 29, 137, 235, C2. **Open** 9.30am-midnight daily.
Credit A, £TC, V.
All the daily papers are provided at this agreeable brasserie, pleasantly removed from the hurly-burly of the main road. The atmosphere is authentically Gallic and the food is simple but good. Enjoy a leisurely snack, meal, or coffee and cakes; or restore your energy level with an alcoholic bevy or two.

Camden Brasserie
216 Camden High Street, NW1 (071 482 2114). Camden Town underground/29 bus. **Open** noon-3pm, 6.30-11.30pm Mon-Sat; noon-3pm, 6-10.30pm Sun. **No credit cards.**
This brasserie manages to be large and welcoming and at the same time intimate enough for romantic dinners. It's cool and airy in summer, with a cosy open fire in the winter.

Camden Markets
Chalk Farm Road, NW1. Camden Town or Chalk Farm underground. **Open** 8am-6pm Sat, Sun.
Thousands of Londoners and visitors converge on Camden every weekend, mainly for the markets. You need to spend at least a morning to see the clothes, ethnic goods, records and antiques stalls that cluster around Camden Lock, by the Chalk Farm Road and in the Electric Ballroom (*see chapters* **To The Eighties** and **Shopping**). When

you've spent most of your money, you can blow the rest on a boat trip on the Regent's Canal or walk along its towpath (*see chapters* **The River & Docklands** and **Sport**).

Compendium Books
234 Camden High Street, NW1 (071 485 8944/071 267 1525). Camden Town underground/24, 29, 31, 134, 253 bus. **Open** 10am-6pm Mon-Sat; noon-6pm Sun. **Credit** A, £TC, V.
The varied selection of titles in this excellent bookshop covers two floors. The staff are unusually knowledgeable, and it's one of the very few British bookshops stocking the latest North American imports.

Rock On
3 Kentish Town Road, NW1. Camden Town underground. **Open** 10.30am-6pm Mon-Sat; 11am-6pm Sun. **No credit cards.**
A small, scruffy, second-hand record shop. The speciality here is sixties' soul, blues, northern soul and rock. It's very popular with collectors.

St Pancras Old Church
St Pancras Way, NW1 (071 387 7301). Camden Town underground. **Services** 7pm Tue-Thur; 10pm Sat; 10am Sun.
You can reach this church by going east from Camden High Street. It has a marvellously gloomy churchyard. Shelley courted Mary Godwin, author of the gothic novel *Frankenstein*, over the grave of her mother,

Portobello Road Market (*listed under* **Bayswater to Holland Park**) *is one of London's best street markets and has been going since the 1890s. It gets very busy on Saturdays, but this is the best day to go. The antiques stalls are at the posher Notting Hill Gate end of the market, which leads on to the fruit and vegetable stalls, and then to the maze of second-hand stalls. A productive rummage will unearth period clothing, old records and books and obscure bric-a-brac. Street performers frequently entertain the market-goers.*

Mary Wollstonecraft. The church dates from the twelfth to thirteenth century (although it was rebuilt in 1848).

CHELSEA & KENSINGTON

Chelsea began life as a fishing village, but in Tudor times it became fashionable to have an out-of-town riverside residence here — Henry VIII and Sir Thomas More started the trend — and in the nineteenth century it gained fame as the home of an artists' colony.

Modern Chelsea begins at **Sloane Square**, close to the site of the Chelsea Bun House, which stood on Pimlico Road until 1839. This shop sold the original Chelsea bun, a rather delicious sticky and spicy confection filled with raisins. The district unfolds as you go down its artery, the **King's Road** – once part of the private royal route from Whitehall to Hampton Court. Nip down **Lower Sloane Street** for a sight of red-coated Chelsea pensioners and the **Royal Hospital** (*see chapter* **Tudors & Stuarts**).

Much of **Kensington** still exudes an air of studied affluence. It's a royal borough and was the birthplace of Queen Victoria. Royals still live in **Kensington Palace** (*see chapter* **Tudors & Stuarts**), but you're free to stroll in the delightful **Kensington Gardens** (*see chapter* **Sightseeing**). Here you can see the enormous Victorian mansions of 'Millionaires' Row'. Nearby Kensington Square is one of the more handsome eighteenth-century developments in the area and Melbury Road was the home to several Victorian artists. Kensington High Street is a bit of an intrusion: there has been an influx of chain stores, and the street is now like most major shopping areas. The exceptions are **Hyper Hyper**, a well-established showcase for young innovative designers, and **Kensington Market**, a three-floor maze of stalls selling unusual and second-hand clothes, shoes, and accessories (*see chapters* **Shopping & Services** and

To the Eighties). Down the road is the **Commonwealth Institute** (*see chapter* **Museums**). South Kensington, of course, is different. It grew up around the great complex of museums and colleges, planned by Prince Albert, Victoria's husband (*see chapter* **Victorian Times**).

Transport *Chelsea:* Knightsbridge or Sloane Square underground; 9, 10, 11, 14, 19, 22 or 503 bus. *Kensington:* High Street Kensington or South Kensington underground; 9, 33, 49, 52 or 73 bus.

Chelsea Old Church
Cheyne Walk, SW3 (071 352 5627). Sloane Square underground/19, 39, 45, 49, 219 bus.
Services 8am Thur; noon Fri; 8am, 10am, 11am (matins), noon, 6pm Sun.
The original church dates back to 1157, but it has been much restored. Henry VIII reputedly married his third wife Jane Seymour in Chelsea Old Church before their state wedding, and Sir Thomas More had a private chapel here. Look for the monuments to Henry James and the architect Sir Hans Sloane — after whom Sloane Square and Sloane Street are named.

Cheyne Walk
SW3. Sloane Square underground/19, 39, 45, 49, 219 bus.
As well as being home to the rich and famous, Cheyne Walk at one time housed the assorted pets of Pre-Raphaelite painter Dante Gabriel Rossetti, including peacocks, a kangaroo and a wombat. Another exotic resident was Rolling Stone Mick Jagger, who had a home here in the sixties. Nos 19 to 26 are on the site of Chelsea Manor, where Queen Elizabeth I lived as a child. The Walk was a riverside lane until the Embankment was built in the 1870s. **Crosby Hall** (*see chapter* **The Middle Ages**) was moved here in 1910 from Bishopsgate. There's a good pub, **The King's Head & Eight Bells** (*see chapter* **Eating & Drinking**) at No.50. **Carlyle's House** is in nearby Cheyne Row (*see chapter* **Museums**).

Edwardes Square
SW8. High Street Kensington underground.
See picture and caption.

Hyde Park Barracks
Knightsbridge, SW1. Knightsbridge underground.
Every day at 10.30am the Household Cavalry can be seen riding through Hyde Park from the barracks to Buckingham Palace. The Life Guards wear red tunics and white helmet plumes; the Blues and Royals blue tunics and red plumes. Basil Spence's brutal 1959 building design has been popularly barracked as an eyesore.

Kensington Square
SW8. High Street Kensington underground.
A square of handsome eighteenth-century houses, occupied at various times by such luminaries as William Thackeray, John Stuart Mill and Edward Burne-Jones.

King's Road
SW3. Sloane Square underground/11, 19, 22, 137, 219, C1 bus.
Mods and punks made the King's Road famous as the fashion centre of London (*see*

The original inhabitants of **Edwardes Square** *(listed under* **Chelsea & Kensington**) *had to promise not to beat carpets outside, exercise a horse in the garden or allow pigs to roam free — on pain of a fine, or three months' hard labour. This charming square of small, early nineteenth-century houses includes the Scarsdale pub. A variety of real ales are sold here and in summer, it's very popular with the young and affluent, who crowd into the outside terrace.*

chapter **To the Eighties**). In the sixties, the grocers, bakers and butchers that once served the locals gave way to fashion shops and antiques galleries. Yet now the small, characterful shops that made the road's reputation are being driven out by ludicrous rent rises. *See chapter* **Shopping & Services**.

Melbury Road
W14. High Street Kensington underground.
Many successful Victorian artists lived in this area. Leighton House Museum (*see chapter* **Victorian Times**) was Lord Leighton's extraordinary home. It had only one bedroom because he didn't like visitors. Also worth a look is the Tower House, designed by the architect William Burgess in neo-Gothic style in 1875.

CLAPHAM &
BATTERSEA

Clapham contains some of the best examples of London's Victorian houses. There are lots of different places to shop, eat, and drink, but Clapham High Street is less impressive than the **Northcote Road** which is a bustling mix of nationalities and classes: halal butchers, Italian delicatessens, and West Indian greengrocers. A fruit and vegetable market runs the length of the road every weekday.

Battersea has a different feel and there are fewer people on the streets. This is partly due to the influx of the upwardly mobile into previously working-class housing. The *nouveau arrivistes* pompously christened the area 'South Chelsea'. The skyline is dominated by **Battersea Power Station**, the largest brick building in Europe. Resembling an upturned table, Giles Gilbert Scott's 1926 art deco design is officially protected, yet this much-loved landmark now faces possible demolition. An incompetent attempt to turn it into a theme park has tragically left it a semi-ruin.

On the Thames border is **Battersea Park**, where the Duke of Wellington fought a duel in 1829. It's less dangerous territory now, and is a good place to watch the river go by. Nearby Lavender Hill is the main shopping and entertainment area, with **Jongleurs at the Cornet** (*see chapter* **New Comedy**) and **Battersea Arts Centre**.
Transport Battersea Park, Clapham Junction, Queenstown Road, Wandsworth Common or Wandsworth Town BR; Clapham

Common or Clapham South underground; 28, 37, 39, 44, 77A, 156, 170, 280 or G2 bus.

Arding &Hobbs
Lavender Hill, SW11 (071 228 8877). Clapham Junction BR/45, 77, 137 bus. **Open** 9am-5.30pm Mon-Wed; 9am-8pm Thur; 9am-6pm Sat. **Credit** A, AmEx, DC, V.
A large, old-fashioned department store, where you can buy household goods, clothing and furniture at fairly cheap prices. It doesn't have a food hall, but there is a restaurant.

Battersea Arts Centre
Old Town Hall, Lavender Hill, SW11 (box office: 071 223 8413). Clapham South underground/Clapham Junction BR/45, 77, 156 bus. **Membership** £1 for six months.
An adventurous South London venue for films, theatre (from mainstream to fringe) and folk music (every Friday night). Children's movies are shown on Saturday afternoons at 3.30pm — admission is only £1 for under-18s.

Battersea Park
Albert Bridge Road, SW11 (081 871 7530). Sloane Square underground/Battersea Park or Queenstown Road BR/19, 39, 44, 45, 49, 130, 131, 170 bus. **Open** dawn to dusk daily. *See* **picture and caption**.
Boating lake. Garden for the disabled. Zoo.

Bombay Bicycle Club
95 Nightingale Lane, SW12 (071 673 6217). Clapham South underground/Wandsworth Common BR. **Dinner served** 7-11.15pm Mon-Sat. **Credit** A, V.
An Indian restaurant, with a bright airy dining room (recently extended) and excellent Lahore machli (fish in a spicy batter). It's named after an incongruous penny-farthing bicycle which is displayed centre-stage.

Bridge Lane Theatre
Battersea Bridge Road, SW11 (071 228 5185). Battersea Park BR. **Open** *Box office* 10.30am-5.30pm Mon-Fri. **Credit** A, V.
Recently reopened, this small theatre stages an eclectic range of plays by both established and first-time playwrights.

Dub Vendor
274 Lavender Hill, SW11 (071 223 3757). Clapham Junction BR/45, 77, 137 bus. **Open** 9.30am-6.30pm Mon-Sat. **No credit cards**.
The best reggae record shop in London. It's chock-full of the latest imports from Jamaica.

Northcote Road Antiques Market
155A Northcote Road, SW11 (071 228 6850). Clapham Junction BR/49 bus. **Open** 10am-6pm Mon-Sat; noon-5pm Sun.
This small covered-market houses 30 traders selling a selection of antique jewellery, china and household fixtures with the emphasis very much on the 1930s. There is a café upstairs.

The Ship
41 Jews Row, SW18 (081 870 9667). Wandsworth Town BR/28, 95, 291 bus. **Open** 11am-11pm Mon-Sat.
A popular riverside pub with good food, although the barbecues in the summer are overpriced.

EARL'S COURT
& FULHAM

The posher residents of Fulham would recoil in horror at their borough being coupled with Earl's

Battersea Park (*listed under* **Clapham & Battersea**) *was opened by Queen Victoria in 1858, but is most famous for its Festival Gardens, a major attraction of the 1951 Festival of Britain (see chapter* **To The Eighties**). *Events held here vary from the colourfully exuberant Easter Sunday Parade (see chapter* **London By Season**) *to Buddhist contemplation on Hiroshima Day (8 Aug) at the ornate riverside pagoda. But if you're more the sporty type, there are 19 tennis courts to choose from.*

Feeling a need to stretch your legs? **Hampstead Heath** *(listed under* **Hampstead & Highgate***) is the place to go if you want a bit of exercise. You can walk, jog, run, swim, or fly your kite from the top of Parliament Hill (near South End Green). Or you can just sit still and admire the splendid views over London and count how many of the hundred or so resident species of birds you can spot. Funfairs are held here on the Easter, Whitsun and August Bank Holiday weekends (see chapter* **London by Season***).*

Court. Although the areas run side-by-side, they each have unmistakable and distinct characters.

Earl's Court originated in 1155 when Lord de Vere of the Manor of Kensington became Earl of Oxford. His manor court house once stood near the site of the underground station. More recently, Earl's Court has become a vibrant, multi-ethnic community, famously a magnet for Australasian back-packers. This antipodean community, sustained through free magazines such as *LAM* and *TNT*, is found on both sides of the bar in the local pubs.

This is very much a 24-hour zone – shops and cafés open round the clock – but luckily it remains fairly free of the undesirable debris common to many late-night hotspots. In the seventies, Earl's Court was the centre of London's gay community, which congregated in pubs like **The Coleherne** and **Brompton's** *(see chapter* **Lesbian & Gay***)*. **The Troubador** *(see chapter* **To The Eighties***)* is a coffee shop that still attracts poets, beatniks and leather-clad gentlemen.

At the intersection of Earl's Court Road and Old Brompton Road is a cluster of restaurants to suit most tastes, although some of them are a little pricey. The area's also home to two of London's largest exhibition halls, the **Earl's Court Exhibition Centre**, SW10 and the **Olympia Exhibition Centre**, W14.

Parts of **Fulham** have been inhabited by the affluent for years; particularly around Parsons Green, where many original Georgian houses remain intact. This may be a largely residential borough, but it has fine amenities. The Brompton Cross end of Fulham Road forms a tight-knit community of high-fashion shops and restaurants, dominated by **Michelin House** *(see chapter* **Early Twentieth Century***)*.

The area's strong on sport. It's home to two football clubs, **Chelsea FC** and **Fulham FC**, and the **Queen's Club** hosts the annual *Stella Artois Grass Court Championships* in mid June (for all *see chapter* **Sport & Fitness***)*. For a more peaceful time, take a stroll through **Brompton Cemetery** *(see chapter* **Victorian Times***)*. For further details contact Earl's Court Information Centre *(071*

373 7837) or Fulham Information Centre *(071 748 3020)*.

Transport *Earl's Court* Earl's Court underground; 31, 74 or C3 bus; N97 nightbus. *Fulham* Fulham Broadway underground; 11, 14, 28, 91 or 295 bus.

BJ Atkins
140 Wandsworth Bridge Road, SW6 (071 731 1232). Fulham Broadway or Parsons Green underground/28, 44, 295 bus. **Open** 11.45am-6pm Tue, Wed, Sat; 11am-2pm Thur; 11am-5pm Fri. **No credit cards.**
Stop off for a cheap lunch at this traditional pie and mash shop with beautiful original tiled walls and bench seating.

The Boltons
SW10. Earl's Court underground/30 bus.
Purpose-built between 1850-60, the Boltons (allegedly taking its name from the family who owned the land) is two picturesque crescents, designed by architect George Godwin, with a gothic church (St Mary's) in the central gardens.

Fulham Palace
Bishop's Park, Fulham Palace Road, SW6 (081 741 3535). Putney Bridge underground/220 bus. **Open** ring to check.
Admission phone to check.
As we went to press, Hammersmith & Fulham Council disclosed that plans are underway to re-open Fulham Palace as a museum in spring 1990. The building was the official residence of the Bishops of London from the eighth century right up to 1973. The Fulham Palace museum will follow the history of the building, with relics and furniture from the centuries of clerical occupancy. There is no charge for walking through the surrounding Bishop's Park which contains many plants that were brought back from the Americas in the seventeenth century and has pleasant river views.

North End Road Market
SW6. Fulham Broadway or West Kensington underground/11, 14, 28, 91, 283 bus. **Open** 8.30am-6pm Mon-Wed, Fri, Sat; 8.30am-1pm Thur.
A popular, thriving market notable for the sheer diversity of goods on sale. Among the highlights are exotic fruit, fresh salmon and eels, an excellent plant stall, cheap clothes and hardware.

HAMPSTEAD & HIGHGATE

Despite the urban sprawl which has engulfed them, **Hampstead** and **Highgate** are both still very much villages, each with its own character, history and celebrities. They're separated by Hampstead Heath, 800 acres/320 hectares of wonderful, wild parkland.

Hampstead, west of the Heath, was a health resort in the eighteenth century and ever since has been the chosen home of writers, artists (although it is some time since impoverished ones could afford to live here) and politicians. General de Gaulle lived at **No 99 Frognal** during World War II. You can also visit the houses of **Keats** and **Freud** *(see chapter* **Museums**). Hampstead has grand mansions such as **Fenton House** *(see chapter* **Tudors & Stuarts**), streets of Georgian houses like **Church Row**, and innumerable small, pretty houses and cottages in the narrow streets that wind around the hill to the Heath. There are restaurants of almost every kind, and pleasant old pubs, such as the **Flask** and **Spaniard's Inn.** And if you want celluloid entertainment, Hampstead has one of London's best cinemas, the **Everyman** *(see chapter* **Film**).

If it weren't for the views of London from Highgate Hill you could mistake **Highgate** for a small country town, complete with its high street lined with local shops (not a chain store or supermarket in sight) and dignified Georgian houses. You'll see **Highgate Woods**, a charming, peaceful spot, as soon as you emerge from Highgate underground station. The local stately home is **Kenwood House**, set on the edge of Hampstead Heath *(see chapter* **Georgian London**), and there's also the early seventeenth-century **Lauderdale House**, where Nell Gwynne is said to have lived for a time. It's open to the public, and has frequent recitals and exhibitions *(see chapter* **Music**: **Classical & Opera**). One of Highgate's most famous former residents is Karl Marx. You can visit his grave at **Highgate Cemetery** *(see chapter* **Victorian Times**).

Transport *Hampstead* Hampstead underground; Hampstead Heath BR; 24 or 46 bus. *Highgate* Highgate or Archway underground; Hampstead Heath BR; 4, 27 or 135 bus.

Burgh House (Hampstead Museum)
New End Square, NW3 (071 431 0144). Hampstead underground/Hampstead Heath BR/24, 46, 168, 210, 268 bus. **Open** noon-5pm Wed-Sun; 2-5pm Bank Holidays. **Admission** free.
One of the early inhabitants of Burgh House, a Queen Anne building constructed in 1703, was a Dr William Gibbons, who grew rich prescribing the foul-tasting waters of Hampstead Wells to his gullible patients. It's now a local history museum and a centre for classical concerts and exhibitions.

There's a display of prints (but no paintings) of John Constable, who was a local resident. *Café (11am-5.30pm). Shop.*

The Flask
77 Highgate West Hill, N6 (081 340 7260). Highgate underground/43, 271 bus. **Open** 11am-3pm, 5.30-11pm, Mon-Fri; 11am-11pm Sat, Bank Holidays; noon-3pm, 7-10.30pm Sun. **Credit** A, AmEx, TC, V.
A very pleasant pub with an open fire in winter and a beer garden for the summer. The eighteenth-century chronicler of low life, William Hogarth, used to sketch scenes of drunken revelry here. Good, traditional pub food is served in the restaurant at lunch-times.

The Grove
N6. Highgate or Archway underground/210, 271 bus.
This handsome avenue is lined with seventeenth- and eighteenth-centry houses. Those on the north side have spectacular gardens with views over Hampstead Heath. Some are open to the public in the summer. The nineteenth-century poet, Samuel Taylor Coleridge, lived at No.3 from 1823 to 1824.

Hampstead Heath
NW3 (Parliament Hill 071 485 4491; Kenwood 081 340 5303; Golder's Hill 081 455 5183). Belsize Park or Hampstead underground/Gospel Oak or Hampstead Heath BR. **Open** 24 hours daily.
See **picture and caption**.
See also chapter **Sport & Fitness**.
Fishing. Three swimming ponds. Toilets for the disabled.

Hampstead & Highgate Bathing Ponds
Hampstead Mixed Bathing Pond *East Heath Road, NW3 (071 435 2366). Hampstead underground.* **Open** May-Sept 10am-6pm daily.
Highgate Pond *Millfield Lane, N6 (081 340 4044). Kentish Town underground/210, C2 bus.* **Open** 6am-8pm daily.
Competent male swimmers only.
Kenwood Pond *Millfield Lane, N6 (081 340 4044). Kentish Town underground/210, C2 bus.* **Open** 7am-7pm daily.
Females must be over eight years only.
Admission all free
Free, fresh-water bathing can be shivered through at these three ponds. The Hampstead mixed bathing pond is rather more seedy than the single-sex ponds but pleasant nonetheless, and it has an indomitably British feel. The Highgate men-only pond is close to the shops, and the wooded setting is delightful. And the Kenwood women-only pond has few facilities, but is in a beautiful secluded spot surrounded by trees and banks for sunbathing. Take along a picnic for those after-swim hunger pangs *(see chapter* **Sport & Fitness**).

The **Spaniard's Inn** *(listed under* **Hampstead & Highgate***) is famous as the watering-hole of highwayman Dick Turpin. It is also one of the many pubs that Charles Dickens supped in. The building dates from 1585, making it one of the oldest pubs in London. In the winter, you can huddle around an open fire; in the summer there's a classic English garden. The restaurant has a hot and cold buffet and traditional pub food.*

Jack Straw's Castle

North End Way, NW3 (071 435 8374/071 435 8885). Hampstead underground. **Open** noon-2pm, 6-10pm Mon-Sat; noon-2pm, 7-9.30pm Sun.

Charles Dickens certainly got about: he drank here as well as at the **Spaniard's Inn** (*see below*). This pub was built on the site of an old coaching inn and named after one of the leaders of the Peasant Revolt of 1381. It was rebuilt in the 1960s. There's an excellent view of Hampstead Heath from here and a restaurant upstairs.

Spaniard's Inn

Spaniard's End, NW3 (081 455 3276). Hampstead underground/210 bus. **Open** 11am-11pm Mon-Sat; noon-3pm, 7-10.30pm Sun. **Credit** A, £TC, V.
See **picture and caption.**

Waterlow Park

Highgate Hill, N19. Highgate or Archway underground. **Open** dawn to dusk daily.
This leafy park on the west side of Highgate Hill has an aviary and lakes with water-birds, a putting green and tennis courts.

Whitestone Pond Open Air Art Exhibition

Whitestone Pond, Heath Street, NW3. Hampstead underground. **Open** May-Aug 11am-7pm Sat, Sun, Bank Holidays.
Pottery, paintings, prints and jewellery are on sale around the pond at the top of Heath Street on summer weekends.

Whittington Stone

Highgate Hill. Archway underground.
Dick Whittington was the boy who came to London to seek his fortune and became the city's mayor four times between 1397 and 1419; he served one interim term (on the death of the previous incumbent) and three full terms. This block of stone was placed here in 1821 to mark the spot where he is said to have heard the bells of London summoning him: 'Turn again Whittington, thrice Mayor of London'. The charming cat which sits on the stone was added in 1964 to commemorate the animal whose skill in rat-catching was the foundation of Whittington's fortune. Alas, in all probability it never existed.

ISLINGTON

North of the low-lying City of London are the two hill-top villages of Clerkenwell and Islington. Until the eighteenth century, these districts were famous for their spas and quantities of running water which were much favoured by London's nobility.

The growth of Islington was not entirely due to the spas. As the first village to the north out of the City, it was the final stopping off point for all trade coming down from the north of the country, in particular farmers and their cattle. Today the only evidence of Islington's agricultural past are the clocktower of Caledonian Market and the **Business Design Centre** (*see chapter* **Business**) which was formerly the Agricultural Hall. Note also the raised pavement on Upper Street which was built to stop pedestrians being splashed by the animals and carts.

The best way to see Islington is to walk through its streets and squares, so often described in Charles Dickens' works and those of other writers. Worth visiting are Thornhill, Canonbury, Barnsbury, Cloudesley, Londale, Milner and Gibson Squares. Much of the village atmosphere remains; there are Chapel, Exmouth and Whitecross street markets, schools, local shops and a small village green. But modern Islington also has 11 theatres, a cinema, four swimming pools, two sports centres and a city farm.

Unfortunately Islington is having to pay for its central location; business developers and road planners are beginning to encroach on this residential area and parts of the district have been earmarked for demolition.

In the eighteenth century there was an established community of Italians living in Clerkenwell, giving rise to the name of Little Italy by which the area is still known. Every July a festival and procession are held around **St Peter's Italian Church** in honour of Our Lady of Carmel (*see chapter* **Ethnic London**).

In the past, residents of Islington and Clerkenwell have included a varied mix of artists, writers, philosophers and political leaders: Tom Paine wrote the first section of *The Rights of Man*, Lenin edited the journal *Iskra* and Trotsky studied books in what is now the **Marx Memorial Library** (*see chapter* **Museums**). Literary residents have included Evelyn Waugh, George Orwell, Joe Orton, Mary Lamb and Kate Greenaway. For information on the area, contact Angel information at Islington Green (*071 226 3640*).

Transport *Clerkenwell* Farringdon underground/BR; 4, 19, 30, 38, 153, 171, 214, 279 or 279A bus. *Islington* Angel underground or Highbury & Islington underground/BR; 4, 19, 30, 38, 43, 73, 153, 171, 171A, 196, 214, 263A, 277, 279 or 279A bus.

There's a wonderful, Dickensian setting for **Camden Passage** *(listed under* Islington*), one of the more interesting antiques markets in London. The street was originally built around 1776, although it wasn't until 1960 that antiques stalls began to appear, initially grouped on two bomb sites. Don't expect bargains, but it is possible to pick up some interesting buys or trinkets. Most visitors just like to browse.*

Camden Passage
off Upper Street, N1. Angel underground. **Open**
shops vary; market 8.30am-3pm Wed, Sat.
See **picture and caption**.

Chapel Market
Chapel Street, N1. Angel underground. **Open**
8.30am-5pm Mon-Sat.
A typical fruit and veg market. The stalls display all manner of food and wares, from pota-
toes and cauliflowers to records and T-shirts.

Crown and Woolpack Pub
*St John Street (071 837 2159). Angel under-
ground.* **Open** 11am-3pm, 5.30-11pm, Mon-Thur,
Sat; 11am-11pm Fri; noon-3pm, 7-10.30pm Sun.
Many a revolutionary plot has been hatched
at this pub. One story tells how a secret
agent, sent out to spy on Trotsky and Lenin,
was forced to listen to the Russian conspirators here without understanding a word.

King's Head
*115 Upper Street, N1 (071 226 1916). Angel
underground.* **Open** 11am-midnight Mon-
Sat; noon-3pm, 7-11.30pm Sun.
See **picture and caption**.
See also chapter **Theatre**.

Tower Theatre
*Canonbury Place, N1 (071 226 5111).
Highbury & Islington underground/4, 19, 30,
43, 271, 279 bus.* **Open** *Booking hall* 10am-
5pm Mon-Fri; *Shows* 7.30pm Mon-Sat
(closed August); *Matinées* 3pm every second Sat. **Admission** £5; £3 OAPs; £3
(standby) students, UB40s. **Credit** A, V.
Home of the Tavistock Repertory Company
which has been in residence for 36 years.
Productions vary from Shakespeare to musicals such as *Cabaret*. The Theatre adjoins
what remains of the sixteenth-century
Canonbury Manor, once the home of Sir
Francis Bacon. Information is given on
what's showing at all of Islington's Theatres.

Union Chapel
*Compton Terrace, N1 (071 354 3631).
Highbury & Islington underground/4, 19, 30,
279 bus.* **Open** by appointment only.
Services 11am Sun.
Built by a group of Nonconformists and
Anglicans, the Union Chapel is an impres-
sive edifice designed by Cubitt, who was
inspired by the church of Santa Fosca,
Torcello, near Venice. It houses a piece of
the Plymouth Rock (upon which the Pilgrim
Fathers first landed in 1620) donated by the
Pilgrim Society in 1883.

Upper Street Fish Bar
*324 Upper Street, N1 (071 359 1401). Angel
underground/19, 30, 43 bus.* **Open** 5.30-
10pm Mon; noon-2pm, 5.30-10pm Tue-Fri;
noon-3pm, 5.30-10pm Sat. **No credit cards.**
An institution among Islington's residents.
Come here for the best fish and chips this
side of town. Olga, the small and energetic
proprietor, is on first-name terms with her
diners and seems to know all the local gossip.

PIMLICO

With the major exception of the
Tate Gallery (*see chapter* **Art
Galleries**), Pimlico is one of the

The olde worlde atmosphere at the **King's Head** *(listed under* **Islington***)
charges in shillings and pence for drinks. A cosmopolitan crowd sits in the
polished Victorian surroundings and listens to free performances of jazz, rock
or pop (at lunchtimes and evenings). The back-room theatre puts on enterprising plays, which often move on to the West End. Alcohol can be served
after 11pm to customers who have bought food.*

best-kept secrets in London, and
that's the way the locals like it.
Although it's within walking distance of most of the great sights of
the city, Pimlico is a quiet district
with a one-way traffic system
which deters all but the most
determined motorists.

Residents have included Winston
Churchill, among a host of past and
present politicians (many of whom
have lived in Dolphin Square, SW1),
and the artist Aubrey Beardsley.

The stretch of river between Chelsea
and Westminster was little but an
unhealthy swamp-land, and a refuge
for criminals and the poor, before
Thomas Cubitt — who had already
built Belgravia, SW1 — started erecting the lovely white stucco squares and
terraces of Pimlico. Three great
squares — **St George's**, **Warwick** and
Ecclestone — are linked by terraces
with pillared porticoes, friendly shopping streets and mews.

Now the area has antique shops
(in **Pimlico Road**); a lively street
market for fruit, vegetables, fish and
household goods (in Tachbrook

Street) and a number of very good
restaurants.

Pimlico is now full of hotels, from
bed 'n' breakfasts to the lavish
Grosvenor, because one of the
great Victorian rail terminals,
Victoria Station, was opened in
the north of Pimlico in 1862.
Victoria Street's now clogged with
huge offices and government
departments, but it has shops, such
as the Army and Navy Store, and
the Catholic **Westminster
Cathedral** (*see chapter* **Early
Twentieth Century**). Two major
theatres are here: the **Apollo
Victoria** and the **Victoria Palace
Theatre** (*see chapter* **Theatres**).
Transport Victoria BR/under-
ground or Pimlico underground;
Victoria National Express Coach
Station; 24 or 29 bus.

Chimes of Pimlico
*26 Churton Street, SW1 (071 821 7456).
Pimlico underground or Victoria under-
ground/BR/2, 36, 70, 73 bus.* **Open** 11.30am-
4pm, 5.30-10pm Mon-Sat; noon-2.30pm, 7-
10pm Sun. **Credit** A, AmEx, £TC, V.
This wine bar and restaurant is terribly
English, so of course you can drink tea

instead of coffee. Chimes serves traditional British food — pies, roasts, and so on — with English country wines and ciders.

Cornucopia
12 Upper Tachbrook Street, SW1 (071 828 5752). Victoria underground/BR. **Open** 11am-6pm Mon-Sat. **Credit** A, £TC, V.
Hundreds of pieces of extravagant costume jewellery are kept at Cornucopia. Lavish evening gowns in chiffon, velvet, satin and crêpe are suspended from the ceiling in this wonderful den of elaborate period clothes.

Mekong
46 Churton Street, SW1 (071 630 9568). Pimlico underground/Victoria underground/BR. **Open** noon-2.30pm, 6-11.30pm daily. **Credit** A, £TC, V.
Arguably the best Vietnamese food in town and always beautifully presented and not too expensive. This is still the Vietnamese restaurant to see and be seen in.

Pimlico Gardens
Grosvenor Road, SW1. Pimlico underground .
A bizarre monument enlivens this little park on the riverbank: a statue in memory of William Huskisson, an unpopular statesman who was run over by the *Rocket* in 1830, becoming the first person to be killed in a railway accident. Osbert Sitwell described the statue, by John Gibson, as 'Boredom Rising From The Bath'.

Queen Mother Sports Centre
23 Vauxhall Bridge Road, SW1 (071 798 2122). Victoria underground/BR. **Open** 8am-10pm Mon-Fri; 8am-5pm Sat; 9am-4pm Sun.
A pleasant sports centre which has the added advantage of not requiring membership. Sports catered for include tennis, squash and badminton, and there's a good swimming pool. *See also chapter* **Sports & Fitness**.

Villa dei Cesari
135 Grosvenor Road, SW1 (071 828 7453/071 834 9872). Pimlico underground/24 bus. **Credit** A, AmEx, DC, V.
A Roman-theme restaurant where the menu is in Latin. But there's nothing old-fashioned about the prices – the average cost per person for a three-course meal —without wine — works out at £50. You can dance, listen to music, or just sit and look at the river while you worry about how you're going to pay the bill.

WIMBLEDON

Say the word 'Wimbledon' and most people think immediately of tennis, but there's more to this quiet, suburban area than the All-England Lawn Tennis Club. Wimbledon Village has a high street, a duck pond, and 110 acres/44 hectares of **Wimbledon Common**. There's not a Womble in sight, but it does boast a Windmill Museum (*see chapter* **Children's London**). It was also, reputedly, the site of Julius Caesar's camp in about 55 BC. If you don't manage to get tickets for the Centre Court, you could always visit the

Wimbledon Lawn Tennis Museum (*see chapter* Museums).
Transport Wimbledon BR; Wimbledon or Southfields underground; 57, 77A, 77C, 93, 131, 155, 200 or 293 bus.

Cannizaro House
West Side, Wimbledon Common, SW19 (081 879 1464). Wimbledon underground/BR, then 80 bus. **Open** *Restaurant* 12.30-2.30pm; 7.30-10.30pm daily; *Park* dawn-dusk daily. **Credit** A, AmEx, DC, £TC, V.
This Georgian mansion on the Common is establishing a reputation for its restaurant, where you have to be a German tennis player to afford the bill. The park is open to the public and is one of London's little known jewels. Its rolling downs contain an amazing collection of rare trees, an Italian garden, one or two follys, a jungle of heather and bracken and a tea house (May-Sept) run by the Brownies (the Girl Guides).

Fox & Grapes
Camp Road, SW19 (081 946 5599). Wimbledon underground/BR. **Open** 11am-3pm, 5.30-11pm Mon-Sat; noon-3pm 7-10.30pm Sun.
Set in the middle of the Common, this lovely quiet old pub has a low-ceilinged bar that dates from the seventeenth century. *Wheelchair access.*

Rose & Crown
55 High Street, SW19. Wimbledon underground/BR.
This old ivy-covered inn is a perfect place to sit in front of an open fire, play cribbage, pretend you're a poet or have a ploughman's lunch in the courtyard.

Wimbledon Society Museum
26 Lingfield Road, SW19. Wimbledon underground/BR. **Open** 2.30pm-5pm Sat. **Admission** free.
A collection of maps, old photographs, prints and paintings chart the local history. There are also archaeological and natural history exhibits.

Wimbledon Village Stables
24A & B High Street, SW19 (081 946 8579). Wimbledon underground/BR/93 bus. **Rides** 10.15am, 2pm, 5.15pm, Tue-Thur; 10.15am, 2pm, 3.15pm Fri; 9am, 10.15am, 11.30am, 2pm, 3.15pm Sat, Sun. **Courses** £120 per week. *See* **picture and caption**.

Windmill Museum
Windmill Road, SW19 (081 788 7655). Wimbledon underground/BR. **Open** Easter-Oct 2-5pm Sat, Sun, Bank Holidays. **Admission** 30p adults; 15p under-16s.
The only example of a 'hollow post' mill in Britain provides an original setting for a museum that illustrates the history and developmnet of windmills. There are working models and examples of tools and machinery.

The busy, friendly **Wimbledon Village Stables** *(listed under* **Wimbledon***) is tucked away behind the Dog and Fox pub. A morning's canter on the Common can be an exhilarating experience. An hour's lesson will cost you £21 during the week and £23 at weekends. The rides are extremely popular, so it's as well to book in advance. Regular jumping and dressage competitions are held to give riders a taste of competitive riding. Extra rides set off at 6.30pm from Tuesday to Thursday during the summer.*

Ethnic London

If you're tired of the English way of life, come to London. Within the city's boundaries a clutch of cultures, from Asian to Italian, add an extra zest to the capital's life.

Throughout the centuries, London has provided a haven for refugees of diverse nationalities. Although some managed to arrive with plenty of money, the majority of these people, escaping political, religious or economic upheavals, have been poor. The East End of London has been the first resting place of many groups. It provided shelter for the French Huguenots of the seventeenth century before becoming home to the Jews of the early twentieth century. These, in turn, have mostly departed to affluent north London and have left the area to newer immigrants from Bangladesh. Each of the capital's ethnic communities brings with them shops, restaurants and festivals that help to enrich the London scene.

AFRO-CARIBBEAN

Although Africans came to Britain as soldiers in the Roman Army, large-scale black settlement didn't begin until the mid-seventeenth century, when Britain was involved in the slave trade.

By the nineteenth century, the black population, mostly male sailors, had assimilated with the locals. It wasn't until the nineteen fifties, when Britain needed workers and advertised throughout the Commonwealth for people to come, that a substantial black community developed. Many Jamaicans took up the offer, and most settled where housing was cheap. There are four main areas to visit for Afro-Caribbean culture today. **Brixton**, SW9, is the best place in the capital for Caribbean and African food, but there are also many vibrant shops and markets. In 1990 the **Black Cultural Archives Museum** is due to re-open in Brixton at 378 Coldharbour Lane, SW9 (081 969 3452). This collection will document the accomplishments of black people from Roman times to the present day.

Hackney, E8, residents have a sense of community spirit that's evident in everything from the community bookshops to the housing co-operatives. Although in recent years Hackney has been gentrified, the black community is still strong and evident.

Technically, **Brent** is an outer London Borough but it has inner-city characteristics: industry, high unemployment and lots of local authority housing. The mix of the Afro-Caribbean and Irish (*see below* **Irish**) communities means great restaurants and superb pubs.

Most visitors to the capital will have heard of the **Notting Hill Carnival** (*see chapter* **London by Season**), held every August Bank Holiday weekend since 1964. This event is organized by the local Afro-Caribbean community and is visited by up to a quarter of a million people. The streets of west London are given over to floats, processions and steel bands.

All Nations
4 Martello Street, E8 (071 249 2168/071 254 2674/071 254 4168). Bethnal Green underground, then 253, 106 bus/6, 35, 55, 277 bus. **Open** 9pm-4am Fri; 9pm-6am Sat. **Admission** £5. **Membership** free. **No credit cards.**
A nightclub in a massive building with reggae in the basement, soul on the middle floor and soca and calypso on the top. Patties, rice 'n' peas and curried goat provide the nourishment. Habitués are young and dressed to impress. It can get packed, especially at Christmas. Not a place for the fainthearted, but good value.

Brixton Artists' Collective
Unit 134, Brixton Enterprise Centre, 444 Brixton Road, SW9 (071 274 4000 ext 292). Brixton underground/BR. **Open** 9.30am-5.30pm Mon-Wed, Fri, Sat; 9.30am-6.30pm Thur.
A mixed black and white collective that publishes postcards by Afro-Caribbean and Afro-American artists. Exhibitions are often on show.

Brixton Market
Brixton Station Road and Electric Avenue, SW9. Brixton underground/BR. **Open** 8am-6pm Mon, Tue, Thur; 8am-1pm Wed; 8am-7pm Fri; 8am-6pm Sat.
See picture and caption.

Index Book Centre
10-12 Atlantic Road, SW9 (071 274 8342). Brixton underground/BR. **Open** 10am-6pm Mon-Sat. **No credit cards.**
A general bookshop which specializes in politics. There's a good selection of Afro-Caribbean literature, including works by Maya Angelou, June Jordan and June Riley.

Red Records
500 Brixton Road, SW9 (071 274 4476). Brixton underground/BR. **Open** 9.30am-6pm Mon-Thur; 9.30am-7pm Fri, Sat. **Credit** A, AmEx, £TC, V.
Vendors of African, soul, funk, hip-hop, house, jazz, cut-outs and rare groove records. They're particularly good for 12-inch imports.

A Taste of Africa
50 Brixton Road, SW9 (071 587 0343). Oval underground/3, 95, 109, 133, 159, 196 bus. **Meals served** noon-midnight Mon-Sat; 5pm-midnight Sun. **Average** £10. **House wine** £5 bottle, £1.50 glass. **Credit** A, AmEx, DC, V.
A busy African restaurant where you'll find Nigerian and Ghanaian specialities. Egusi stew, served with a variety of meats (£2.95-£3.70) is recommended. Booking is advisable for dinner and at weekends.
Dress: smart casual. Vegetarian dishes available.

A Taste of Paradise
Bridge Park, Brentfield, Harrow Road, NW10 (081 963 0718). Harlesden or Stonebridge Park underground/18 bus. **Dinner served** 6.30-11pm Mon-Sat. **Average** £10. **House wine** £5.60 bottle, 90p glass. **No credit cards.**
This renovated bus garage contains one of the most chic Caribbean restaurants around. Deep azure carpets and green wooden furniture reflect the colours of the Caribbean. In such a delightful place you can't help but relax. The chicken fricassee is deservedly popular, but we recommend the fish dishes.

CHINESE

London's Chinatown is neither Britain's oldest (that's in Liverpool) or the largest (Manchester) but it is still the cultural and financial centre for Britain's Chinese community. The first settlers here were sailors, traditionally employed on British ships as cooks. Because of the maritime connection, the original Chinatown in London was in the docklands. **Limehouse**, E14, was for a century the centre, and traces can still be found there in street names (Ming Street, Canton Street, Mandarin Street).

Today's Chinatown, based around **Gerrard Street**, W1, began in the early fifties with the last great influx of Cantonese from Hong Kong. It is now a thriving and growing community; a self-contained home-from-home with restaurants, supermarkets, doctors, cultural and sports associations, discos, cinemas and schools. The Chinese community can be caught at it's most hospitable and visible during the celebrations for Spring Festival (during the first moon of the lunar new year) and the Mid-Autumn Festival (on the 15th day of the eighth lunar month); for details *see chapter* **London by Season**. At these times, the streets of Chinatown come alive with lion and dragon dancers, traditional and modern Chinese musicians, martial arts demonstrations, plus many other cultural events.

Chinese Film Society
27 Old Gloucester Street, WC1 (071 633 9878).
Russell Square underground. **Open** 9am-5pm Mon-Fri. **Membership** £10 per year.
Screenings: Metro Cinema *Rupert Street, W1 (071 437 0757). Piccadilly Circus underground.* **Programme** 2pm Sun. **Admission** £2 members, £3 non-members.
Contact Susie Wong at the Chinese Film Society, to find out about future programmes. Chinese art movies are the favourites. Also, the **Odeon Leicester Square** (*see chapter* **Film**) screens Chinese double-bills (11.30pm Sundays), a popular meeting point for young Chinese.

Eastern Art Gallery
40 Great Russell Street, WC1 (071 631 4868).
Tottenham Court Road underground. **Open** 10.30am-5.30pm. Mon-Sat. **Credit** A, V.
Not a tourist shop, but a discreet Chinese-style scroll gallery. The staff specialize in modern and contemporary Chinese paintings; the woodblock prints start at £40, original paintings and calligraphy are £100 upwards.

Guang Hua
7-9 Newport Place, WC2 (071 437 3737).
Leicester Square underground. **Open** 10.30am-7pm Mon-Sat; 11am-7pm Sun. **Credit** A, V.
One of the oldest bookshops in Chinatown, with a collection of mainly technical, scientific and cultural journals. Classical and contemporary literature is also stocked, including the works of famous novelists Gu Hua and Zhang Xin Xin. There are daily copies of *Renmin Ribao* (China's version of the *Sun* newspaper, but even less truthful) and the English-language paper *China Daily*.

Mr Kong
21 Lisle Street, WC2 (071 437 7341).
Leicester Square underground. **Meals served** noon-2am daily. **Average** £13. **Minimum** £7.
House wine £5 40 bottle, £1.50 glass.
Service 10%. **Credit** A, AmEx, DC, £TC, V.
Generally considered the best Cantonese restaurant in London. All three floors are usually packed, from early evening right through to the small hours. Booking is essential, especially during festival time.

Shaftesbury's
24 Shaftesbury Avenue, W1 (071 734 2017). Piccadilly Circus underground.
Open 9pm-3.30am Tue. **Admission** £5-£8.
Credit A, AmEx, V.
This Tuesday-night club for fashionable young Hong Kongers and British Chinese has found a home amid the chrome and shiny-black of Shaftesbury's. All the latest disco hits from Hong Kong and Taiwan are played, and dress is *very* smart.

Shaolin Way
10 Little Newport Street, WC2 (071 734 6391). Leicester Square underground. **Open** 11am-7pm daily. **Credit** A, AmEx, V.
A tiny, but very popular, martial arts shop on the fringes of Chinatown. Authentic equipment and clothes are sold at knock-down prices and they also stock martial arts magazines from around the world.

The Sound of China
6 Gerrard Street, W1 (071 734 1970).
Leicester Square underground. **Open** noon-8pm daily. **No credit cards.**
This music shop has a large selection of tapes by pop stars from Hong Kong and Taiwan. There's also a section of fashionable magazines including HK's major rival to *The Face*, called *Fresh*.

CYPRIOT

The Cypriot community in London is about 200,000 strong. During the violent decade that led up to independence in 1960, and continuing through the bloody clashes between Turkish and Greek Cypriots that began in 1963, over 100,000 immigrants sought a new life in London. However, Cypriots in London are quick to emphasize that no such division exists between the two groups here.

Initially the Greek Cypriot community was based in central areas of London such as Soho and Camden, but as it became more established its members moved further out to Hackney, E8; Islington, N1, and Haringey, N6, in north London; and Peckham, SE15 in the south. Over the years a community that started off running barber shops and groceries has expanded, and Cypriots are now found in every walk of life. The main Greek Cypriot newspaper, published in England in the Greek language is *Parikiaki (071 272 6777)*. It has a circulation of 8,000 and comes out weekly. The main social organization for the community is the **Greek Cypriot Association** *(071 381 3272)*.

Unlike the Hellenic immigrants, many of London's Turkish community come from the mainland and not from Cyprus. Apart from fully-fledged restaurants, many of those handy late-night kebab takeaways are provided by Turkish Cypriots. The **Turkish Cypriot Community Association** *(071 359 5231)* provides a meeting place and organizes social events for the community.

Brixton Market (*listed under* **Afro-Caribbean**) *has livened up the district since the end of the last century. Visit Electric Avenue for the best selection of Afro-Caribbean fruit and veg in Europe. Wander up Brixton Station Road for second-hand clothes and bric-a-brac stalls. In the background there's always reggae or calypso pounding from one of the music stalls.*

Mandy's Irish Shop (listed under Irish) may be a small place, but it's crowded with the best the Irish nation has to offer. It specializes in tea, Irish soup, cheese, marmalade, breads, sausages and cakes (including black and white pudding). Music is another highlight: sounds range from traditional or medieval harp tunes, through John McCormack, the famous tenor, to The Dubliners. Mandy's also stocks Claddagh rings, Irish crystal, linen and tin whistles.

T Adamou
124 Chiswick High Road, W4 (081 994 0752). Turnham Green underground. **Open** 8.30am-6.30pm Mon-Sat; 10am-1pm Sun. **No credit cards.**
Established 30 years, this grocer's is notable for a wide range of fresh, bottled and canned foods from Greece and the Middle East.

Hodja Nasreddin
53 Newington Green Road, N1 (071 226 7757). 30, 38, 73, 141, 171 bus. **Meals served** noon-1.30am Mon-Thur; noon-3.30am Fri-Sun. **Average** £10. **Credit** A, AmEx, DC, £STC, V.
Run by Turkish Cypriots, this is one of the capital's oldest Middle Eastern restaurants, having been here for over 20 years. Delicious pastries stuffed with cheese can precede your choice of meaty main courses. Book weekends.

Jimmy's
23 Frith Street, W1 (071 437 9521). Leicester Square underground. **Lunch served** 12.30-3pm. **Dinner served** 5.30-10.45pm, Mon-Sat. **Average** £5.50. **House wine** £4.60 bottle, 95p glass. **Credit** £TC.
The guarantee of a cheap and cheerful meal keeps Jimmy's constantly busy. Greek Cypriot staples such as kleftiko, stifado and moussaka come with chips and salad. Lamb, pork chops and steak are available for the unadventurous.

St Sophia
Moscow Road, W2 (071 229 7260). Bayswater underground. **Services** 5.30-6.30pm Sat (vespers); 9.30-11am (matins), 11am-12.30pm (high mass), Sun.
Designed by John Oldrid Scott, son of Gilbert Scott, this church is considered to be the architect's masterpiece. It is Greek Orthodox and is well-attended by Cypriots.

Sheik Nazim Mosque
9-15 Shacklewell Lane, E8 (071 249 4723). Dalston Kingsland BR/67, 76, 243 bus. **Services** 12.30pm Mon-Thur, Sat, Sun; 1.30pm Fri.
The most important Turkish Cypriot mosque. About 400 people, most of them Cypriots, attend the main Friday service.

Theatro Technis.
26 Crowndale Road, NW1 (071 387 6617). Mornington Crescent underground. **Open** 10am-4pm Mon-Fri. **No credit cards.**
Theatro Technis, the main Greek Cypriot Theatre in London, was set up to provide a cultural base for the immigrant community in the fifties. It provides an advisory service (10am-5pm weekdays) and a lunchtime social group (noon-1pm weekdays) primarily for elderly people. Theatre schemes are provided for children, women, and young people.

Yassar Halim Patisserie
495 Green Lanes, N4 (081 340 8090). Manor House or Turnpike Lane underground/29 bus. **Open** 8am-10pm daily except Christmas Day. **No credit cards.**
An excellent and huge baker's selling fresh bread, sweets and pastries. Try the real Turkish delight.

London is the third largest Irish city after New York and Dublin, and the Irish community here is continuing to grow. It's likely that there are now more Irish cultural events in London than in the whole of Ireland, including Dublin.

Ireland has had a long and complicated relationship with Britain since the country was first invaded by the English in 1169. The first Irish settlement in Bristol dates from soon after this date. By the seventeenth century, **St Giles**, WC1 had a large Irish community which was drawn there by the cheap lodgings and available work.

The Great Famine in Ireland in 1846-1847 caused the death of one million people and the emigration of two thirds of its total population — the largest recorded mass movement of a nation in history. A second mass exodus occurred in the 1950s when the Irish were recruited to fill mainly manual jobs in labour-starved Britain.

Many Irish settled in the cheaper areas of London or traditional Irish areas close to railway termini, including **Camden**, NW1; **Kilburn**, NW6; **Paddington**, W2; and **Hammersmith**, W6. Although Kilburn is still the focal point of the community, the Irish have now spread across Greater London, and constitute about ten per cent of the total population.

There are more than a hundred recognizably Irish pubs in London offering a reasonable range of Irish beers, including the ubiquitous Guinness, and often providing traditional Irish music. **St Patrick's night** (17 March) is the excuse for a London-wide party, usually with major shindigs at the **Mean Fiddler**, the **National Club** and the **Sir George Robey** (*see chapter* **Music: Rock, Folk & Jazz**).

The Irish community is served by three weekly newspapers. The *Irish Post*, The *London Irish News* and The *Irish World*. These are available from all large newsagents and from virtually all newsagents in Irish areas.

Archway Tavern
Archway Roundabout, N6 (071 272 2840). Archway underground. **Open** 11am-3pm, 5.30-11pm Mon-Sat; noon-3pm, 7-11pm, Sun. **Admission** £1 Thur, Fri, Sun; £1.50 Sat.
Irish bands play here every night of the week.

Biddy Mulligan's

205 Kilburn High Road, NW6 (071 624 2066). Kilburn underground/8 bus. **Open** 11am-midnight Mon-Sat; noon-3pm, 7-10.30pm, Sun.

Biddy's is a famous example of the archetypal Irish pub. Guinness flows like a Texan oil blow-out, especially on St Patrick's night which is a rowdy riot. There's no charge to watch the bands that play here every night of the week: music is usually traditional Irish folk and U2 covers.

Green Ink Books

8 Archway Mall, N19 (071 263 4748). Archway underground. **Open** 10am-6pm Mon-Sat. **Credit** A, AmEx, V.

The extensive selection of publications includes drama, poetry, history, Irish language and children's books.

Mandy's Irish Shop

161 High Road, NW10 (081 459 2842). Willesden Green or Dollis Hill underground. **Open** 7.30am-7.30pm daily. **No credit cards.** *See* **picture and caption.**

Pyms Gallery

13 Motcomb Street, SW1 (071 235 3050/071 245 9114). Knightsbridge underground. **Open** 9.30am-6pm Mon-Fri; 10.30am-1pm Sat during exhibitions. **No credit cards.**

This is an important gallery for Irish art of the nineteenth and twentieth century showing the work of artists such as Dermot O'Brien and Mary Swansea.

St Gabriel's

Holloway Road, N19 (071 272 8195). Archway underground. **Service** third Sun of the month 6.45pm

The only church in London to hold a Gaelic mass.

ITALIAN

The focus of activity for Anglo-Italians is the annual **Procession of Our Lady of Mount Carmel** on 22 July 1990 and 21 July 1991 (*see* **picture and caption***)*. It's held in **Clerkenwell**, EC1, which was London's equivalent of Little Italy during the twenties. Since those times, Italians have spread across the city in all directions. Today, the Italian influence on London is diffuse and most obvious in the proliferation of restaurants and delicatessens (**Soho**, W1, is the best place to visit for these; *see chapter* **Eating & Drinking**).

Britain's best-known and best-loved clown was the Anglo-Italian Joey Grimaldi. His first London stage appearance was in 1780 when he was barely a toddler. Grimaldi is commemorated in stained glass at **Holy Trinity Church**, E8 *(071 254 5062)*. There is an annual Clowns' Service at the church which takes place on 3 February 1991. After the ceremony, the clowns do a show in the church hall.

For current events within the Italian community buy a copy of the monthly *Back Hill* (half English, half Italian) or the fortnightlies *La Voce degli Italiani* and *Londra Sera* (all Italian). **George & Graham** stocks them all. The **Italian Institute of Culture,** 39 Belgrave Square, SW1 *(071 235 1461)* also publishes a monthly list of events of Italian interest.

Bar Italia

22 Frith Street, W1 (071 437 4520). Tottenham Court Road underground. **Open** 7am-9pm daily. **No credit cards**

An Italian snack bar with excellent coffee. It can get noisy during screenings of Italian football matches on the video screen at the back of the bar. Expensive but authentic. *See also chapter* **Eating & Drinking**.

Cantina Augusto

91 Clerkenwell Road, EC1 (071 242 3246). Farringdon underground. **Open** *Shop* 9am-6pm Mon-Fri; *Wine bar* 11.30am-4pm Mon-Fri. **Credit** A, V.

A wine business with a shop that stocks spirits as well as wines. The wine bar in the basement has a menu which usually includes three hot dishes a day ranging from pasta to curries.

Cinecitta Discotheque

74 Welbeck Street, W1 (071 935 2371). Bond Street underground. **Open** 9pm-3am Thur-Sun. **Admission** free Thur, £5 Fri; £6 Sat; £4 Sun. **Credit** A, AmEx, DC, V.

A discotheque popular with young Italians, but you'll probably feel old if you're past 20.

Fratelli Camisa

1A Berwick Street, W1 (071 437 7120). Piccadilly Circus or Tottenham Court Road underground. **Open** 9am-6pm Mon-Wed, Fri, Sat; 9am-2pm Thur. **Credit** A.

This delicatessen sells a wide variety of cheeses. You can also buy a copy of *The Fratelli Camisa Cookery Book* which tells you how Italians really cook.

George & Graham

3 Back Hill, EC1 (071 278 1770). Farringdon underground. **Open** 7am-6pm Mon-Fri; 7am-2.30pm Sat, Sun. **No credit cards.**

This newsagent stocks *Back Hill*, *Londra Sera* and *La Voce degli Italiani* as well as Italian daily newspapers.

St Peter's Italian Church

136 Clerkenwell Road, EC1. **Office** *4 Back Hill, EC1 (071 837 1528; ansaphone 071 837 9071). Farringdon underground.* **Services** 10am, 7pm Mon-Sat; 9am, 10am, 11am, 12.15pm, 7pm Sun.

Opened in 1863, St Peter's is modelled on the Basilica of St Crisogona in Rome. On the Sunday following 16 July, the streets around

The Procession of Our Lady of Mount Carmel *brings dozens of groups out onto the streets around* **St Peter's Italian Church** *(listed under* **Italian***) to celebrate the feast day. The procession starts at the church and moves along Clerkenwell Road, Back Hill, Baker's Row, Farringdon Road, St Cross Street and Leather Lane. Thousands of people watch. After the parade there is a sagra (fête). In 1990 the procession will be held on 22 July at 3pm; in 1991 it will be on 21 July.*

the church are used for the **Procession of Our Lady of Mount Carmel** (*see* **picture and caption**). It is usually locked between services because of problems with vandals, so telephone first if you want to see inside.

JEWISH

About three-quarters of Britain's Jewish population lives in Greater London; the latest estimate is that 241,600 Jews inhabit the capital. The areas most associated with Jewish life – **Golders Green**, NW11 and **Stamford Hill**, N15 – still account for many of these people.

The affluence of many Jewish people today is a far cry from 700 years ago when Edward I expelled the Jews from Britain, in 1290. The Christian Church had decided to allow its own people to charge interest on loans and the Jews' function as money lenders was no longer needed. Jews were not permitted into Britain again until 1656 when Sephardic Jews of Spanish and Portuguese origin arrived to escape the Spanish inquisitions. When the pogroms in Russia and Poland erupted in the mid nineteenth century, there was a mass exodus to Britain and America. A barely altered deconsecrated Polish synagogue of the 1860s can be seen in the back of the **Spitalfields Heritage Centre**, 19 Princelet Street, E1 (*071 377 6901;* Mon, Tue 10am-5pm). By now life in the East End of London was thriving and many Jews chose to settle there. Finally, the Nazi period brought another, smaller influx of German and Austrian Jews. The home of one of the most famous of these is now the **Freud Museum** (*see chapter* **Museums**) and can be visited.

To most Jews, the East End is of only historical interest now. It has very few Jewish residents and a steadily decreasing number of Jewish businesses. However, weekly walking tours are organized which show the rich Jewish culture the area once had (phone **Historical Tours** *081 668 4019*).

Today, Jewish life in London is very varied: from the Chassidic (ultra-orthodox) Jews that can be seen on the streets of Stamford Hill, to the cosmopolitan bustle of Sunday shopping in Golders Green. The *Jewish Chronicle (071 405 9252)* provides the definitive voice on everything that's happening in Jewish London.

Ben Uri Art Gallery
21 Dean Street, W1 (071 437 2852). Tottenham Court Road underground. **Open** 10am-5pm Mon, Wed; 10am-7pm Thur. **Admission** free.
An art gallery that displays works of Jewish interest from both Jewish and non-Jewish artists. Highlights include several works by Chagall.

Bevis Marks Synagogue
Bevis Marks, EC3 (071 289 2573). Liverpool Street underground/BR. **Services** 7am Mon, Thur; 9am Sat.
Britain's oldest surviving Synagogue – purpose built in 1701.
Tour by prior arrangement.

Bloom's Restaurant
90 Whitechapel High Street, E1 (071 247 6001). Aldgate East underground. **Meals served** 11am-10pm Mon-Thur, Sun; 11am-2pm Fri. **Average** £10. **House wine** (kosher) £6.50 bottle. **Credit** A, V.
See **picture and caption**.
See also chapter **Eating & Drinking**.
Supervised: Beth Din.

Crisis Line counselling service
(24-hour answering machine 081 203 6211). **Open** 6pm-midnight Thur; noon-midnight Sun and Bank Holidays.
Jewish counselling service.

Golders Green Crematorium
Hoop Lane, NW11 (081 455 2374). Golders Green underground. **Open** 9am-5pm Mon-Fri. **Admission** free.
The ashes of Sigmund Freud are housed here, as well as those of Marks and Spencer founder Israel Sieff, and Marc Bolan, whose fans come annually to pay homage.

Jerusalem the Golden
146A Golders Green Road, NW11 (081 455 4960/081 458 7011). **Open** 9.30am-6pm Mon-Thur; 9.30am-2pm Fri; 10am-2pm Sun. **Credit** A, V.
Many goods of Jewish interest are stocked in this shop, from arts and crafts to skullcaps, records and books.

London Museum of Jewish Life
The Sternberg Centre, 80 East End Road, N3 (081 346 2288/081 349 1143). Finchley Central underground. **Open** 10am-4pm Mon-Thur; 10.30am-4.30pm Sun; closed Jewish holidays. **Admission** free.
Documents and displays of Jewish social history are kept in this museum on the third floor of the Sternberg Centre. Permanent exhibitions include a reconstruction of a Jewish tailor's workshop and there are regular photo-displays of social life in the nineteenth and twentieth centuries. The **Jewish Museum** (*see chapter* **Museums**) also contains artefacts relating to Jewish life.
Jewish vegetarian restaurant; noon-2pm Mon-Thur. Walks around East End by prior arrangement.

Bloom's *(listed under* **Jewish***) is the most famous of London's Jewish restaurants, although not necessarily the best. Booking is essential for Sunday lunch when it is noisy, energetic and packed with Jewish families. It's a good place for hot chicken soup and a salt beef sandwich after walking around Petticoat Lane market (see chapter* **Shopping & Services***).*

SOUTH ASIAN

Asians have been settling in London since the late thirties. Most of these early arrivals were doctors, lawyers or seamen who scattered themselves around the major cities of Britain. After World War II, and the independence of India and Pakistan, mass immigration changed these small groups into the larger communities of today.

The three major religions of South Asia are all represented in London. The Hindu community is more scattered than the other sects because many of them run shops and so move to areas where businesses already exist. The **Spitalfields/East End** area has become densely populated with Bangladeshis who are mostly Islamic; and the Sikh religion plays a large role in the life of **Southall**, Middlesex.

Notable South Asian Londoners include Britain's first Asian Member of Parliament, **Dadabhai Naoroji**, who was born in Bombay and elected by his constituency, Finsbury Central, in 1892. He was a Liberal, and wrote on sensitive issues of the day, such as reforms for India and home rule for Ireland.

One of the brightest and loudest festivals on the Indian calendar is **Diwali**, the festival of light. It starts at the end of October when dance and musical performances are held all over London. Earlier in the month, Hindus celebrate **Navratri**, which commemorates the nine days and nights that the goddess Ambaa Mataa took to conquer evil forces. They celebrate by dancing through the night. **Holi**, is another colourful festival and is held in spring in public parks. For current events within the Indian community obtain a copy of the monthly, *Bizarre*, on sale at good Indian newsagents.

East London Mosque
*84-86 Whitechapel Road, E1 (071 247 1357).
Aldgate East or Whitechapel underground.*
Open 9am-9pm daily. **Service** 1.15pm Fri.
See **picture and caption**.

Guru Granth Gurdwara
45 Villiers Road, Southall, Middlesex (081 574 7700). Southall BR. **Open** 6am-9pm daily.
Services hourly between 6am-8pm daily.
This reasonably small Sikh temple is conservatively decorated and the atmosphere is very friendly. The temple has its own network of OAP and youth clubs.

Milans Enterprises
6-8 High Street, Southall, Middlesex (081 571 5697). Southall BR/207 bus. **Open** 10am-6.30pm Mon-Sat. **Credit** A, £$TC, USA currency, V.
One of the nine outlets this traditional store has around the country. It has established a reputation for exclusive ranges of saris and a host of other garments. There's no opportunity to haggle over prices, as there is in various other sari emporiums.

New Taj Stores
112 Brick Lane, E1 (071 377 0061). Aldgate East underground. **Credit** A, AmEx, DC, V.
A huge food supermarket, packed almost from floor to ceiling with every imaginable South Asian ingredient. There's a wide selection of fruits and vegetables, together with a meat counter. Prices are very cheap, because you must buy in bulk. It is open on most Bank Holidays.

The Shampan
79 Brick Lane, E1 (071375 0475). Aldgate East underground. **Lunch served** noon-3pm daily. **Dinner served** 6pm-midnight, daily. **Average** £11. **House wine** £4.95 bottle, £1.25 glass. **Credit** A, A/c, AmEx, DC, LV, TC, V.

This newly-established restaurant may lack sufficient seating, but it makes up for it in the quality and quantity of its food. An elaborately thought-out menu and a famous chef are promising signs.

Shree Nathji Sanatan Hindu Mandir
159-161 Whipps Cross Road, Leytonstone, E11 (081 989 7539). Leytonstone underground/257 bus. **Open** 8.15am-8pm Mon-Fri; 8.15am-1pm, 4-8pm Sat, Sun. **Services** 8.15am, noon, 7.15pm daily.
One of the largest Hindu temples in London. It has two main halls and four shrines (to Rama, Durga, Shiva and Krishna). There are plans to start OAP and youth clubs.

The Veeraswamy
99-101 Regent's Street, W1 (071 734 1401). Piccadilly Circus underground. **Lunch served** noon-2.30pm daily. **Dinner served** 6-11.30pm Mon-Sat. **Average** £17. **Set lunch** £10.50. **Set dinner** £15. **House wine** £9.50 bottle, £2.50 glass. **Service** 15%. **Credit** A, AmEx, DC, £$TC, V.
The oldest South Asian restaurant in London has acquired a reputation over the years for above-average food. Interesting dishes are served in luxurious surroundings.

The **East London Mosque** *(listed under* South Asian*) marks a watershed in the growth of Islamic London. Previous mosques have largely been housed in existing buildings, often disused churches — the mosque at Brick Lane, E1, was originally a French Huguenot chapel, then a synagogue. This mosque is brand new. Traditional themes have been incorporated into the design and it is now used for daily prayers. Some 3,000 Bengalis congregate here for Friday's jumma ceremony.*

Old London

London's past is more alive than the history books and television costume dramas would have you believe. Two thousand years of history have shaped this city. Roman gladiators, Queen Boudicca's avenging hordes, the Black Death, the Plague and Great Fire, the Civil War and the Blitz have all stormed through and left their mark. Of course, not every street corner will bear Roman graffiti or Great Fire scorch marks, but once we've told you where to look, you'll soon get to know London's colourful and bloody past.

You're most likely to discover history when you're doing something else. Having a pint in Ye Olde Cheshire Cheese or a dinner party in a Huguenot house give unusual insights into Georgian life. But you must also see London's splendid musuems, which have long shaken off their fusty, establishment image. Make the excellent Museum of London your first stop, but keep your eyes open *en route*. If you see nothing else there are two sections of Roman Wall a spear's throw away.

CONTENTS:

Roman & Saxon London

From Romans to Vikings; how it all began.

Although it was Julius Caesar who, in 54 BC, first cast an expansionist eye over Britain, no lasting Roman imprint was left on London until AD 43, when a second wave of Roman invaders crossed the channel. Roman London (Londinium) was founded at this time.

With its potential as a deep-water port and good defensive location, Londinium soon ousted Colchester as the capital of Rome's new province. A bridge was built across the Thames and a settlement quickly grew up around what is now the City, stretching from Leadenhall in the east to St Paul's in the west.

Rome was never able to completely subdue the troublesome natives, although for some time, Londinium was a significant part of the empire.Now, despite centuries of neglect, we have a fairly accurate idea of how Londinium developed. Most of the excavated material can be seen in the **Museum of London** and the **British Museum**.

British Museum
Great Russell Street, WC1 (071 636 1555; recorded information 071 580 1788).
Holborn, Russell Square or Tottenham Court Road underground. **Open** 10am-5pm Mon-Sat; 2.30-6pm Sun; 6-9pm first Tue every month. **Admission** free daily; £5 first Tue every month; *exhibitions.* £2 adults, £1 children OAPs, students, UB40s. **Credit** (shop only) A, AmEx, DC, £STC, USA currency, V.
The British Museum houses a varied selection of artefacts collected from throughout the Roman Empire, including the decorative tomb of Julius Classicianus, Procurator of London in AD 61. *See chapter* **Museums**. *Café & licensed restaurant (10.30am-4.15pm Mon-Sat; 3-5.15pm Sun). Cassette tours of Library, Elgin Marbles 60p. Lectures. Shop. Tour (105 mins; £5 inclusive). Toilets for the disabled. Wheelchair access by prior arrangement.*

Museum of London
150 London Wall, EC2 (071 600 3699).
Barbican, St Paul's underground or Moorgate underground./BR. **Open** 10am-6pm Tue-Sat; 2-6pm Sun. **Admission** free. **Credit** (shop only) A, S£TC, V.
The Museum of London contains the most treasured artefacts to have been recovered from the remains of Londinium, including the celebrated sculptures discovered in the **Temple of Mithras** (*see* **picture and caption**). A public gallery overlooks a section of the famed Roman wall. Visitors can also view the West gate of the **Cripplegate Fort** on the first Tuesday and the third Friday of every month. *See also chapter* **Museums**. *Braille guide and taped commentary for the visually impaired. Lectures and films with induction loop for the hard of hearing in the theatre. Restaurant (10am-5pm Tue-Sat; noon-5pm Sun). Shop. Toilets for the disabled. Wheelchair access. Workshops.*

Although the architectural development of Londinium up to AD 60 is unclear, evidence suggests a street plan in accordance with the strict grid patterns typical of Roman towns. Excavations have revealed that **Fenchurch Street** and the east end of **Lombard Street**, EC3, lie more or less above Londinium's first main road.

However, despite Londinium's auspicious birth, the excesses of imperial machismo soon surfaced. A public flogging of Boudicca (the Queen of the Iceni, a tribe from East Anglia), the confiscation of her client kingdom and the rape of her daughters initiated the Iceni unrest which led to Londinium's sacking in AD 60.

Statue of Boudicca & Daughters
Victoria Embankment, SW1.
The statue depicts Boudicca and her daughters in their chariot ominously poised to wreak vengeance on the Roman despots who had defiled their honour. It was sculpted in the 1850s by Thomas Thorneycroft.

After the Iceni revolt, Londinium was rebuilt on a grander scale. At one point, the site achieved sufficient prominence to be graced with the largest Basilica north of the Alps, located where **Leadenhall Market**, EC3, now stands.

An amphitheatre, which would have hosted the full range of *de rigueur* blood sports and which could seat 35,000 baying spectators, was discovered at the **Guildhall**, EC3, in 1987. The remnants of changing-rooms have also been unearthed. The site is closed to the public, although many of the finds are currently displayed at the **Museum of London**.

The Governor's Palace, which is buried somewhere under **Cannon Street Station**, EC4, had private baths, lavish state rooms and ornamental gardens, and showed all the signs of a provincial residence basking in the full patronage of Rome. The enigmatic **London Stone**, set behind an iron grille in the outside wall of the Overseas-Chinese Banking Corporation at 111 **Cannon Street**, EC4, may have been placed at the Palace entrance. A viewing gallery is planned for the **Fleet Valley** excavation, between Holborn and Blackfriars. For details contact the **Department of Urban Archaeology, Museum of London** (*see above*).

Bank of England Museum
Threadneedle Street, (071 601 5793). Bank underground. **Open** *Easter-Sept* 10am-5pm Mon-Fri; 25pm Sun; *Oct-Easter* 10am-5pm Mon-Fri.* **Admission** free.
The Museum has a limited selection of antiquities relating to Roman London, including elaborate mosaics discovered on Threadneedle Street. *See also chapter* **The City**. *Educational films. Lectures by prior arrangement. Shop. Tour and touch sessions for the visually impaired by prior arrangement. Wheelchair access by prior arrangement.*

Once Rome had consolidated her position, she set about introducing her new citizens to the creature comforts enjoyed elsewhere in the empire. By AD 100 Londinium had at least two public baths, located at **Cheapside**, EC2 (close to where St Mary Le Bow now stands), and at **Huggin Hill**, EC4, where the populace could enjoy stripping and steaming before braving the *frigidarium*. These baths have been completely destroyed, but remains of a Roman baths can be found at *Aqua Sulis* (**Bath**); *see below*. For enduring the gloomy conditions of provincial life, a touring dignitary or client prince would expect to be housed in a stately villa. The Roman palace at **Fishbourne** (*see below*), styled in the opulence of the first century AD, is an architectural tribute to the golden age of Roman occupation.

Roman Baths and Museum

Stall Street, Bath, BA1 (0225 461111 ext 2785). **Getting there** *by train* from Paddington 80 minutes (longer on Sun); *by bus* National Express from Victoria 3 hours; *by car* M4 to exit 18. **Open** *Nov-Feb* 9am-4.30pm Mon-Sat; 10am-5pm Sun; *Mar-Oct* 9am-5.30pm daily; *Jul, Aug* 9am-6.30pm Mon-Sun. **Admission** £2.70 adults; £1.40 5-16 year olds; free under-fives. **Credit** A, V.

The museum houses the celebrated Roman baths, created around AD 60 under Flavian rule, and in use until the fourth century. Though neglected for 1,400 years, the famous watering hole of Aqua Sulis has been the subject of numerous excavations since the eighteenth century, the most recent exposing the temple precinct. Artefacts displayed in the museum, include the Gorgon's head, an icon created specifically for Bath and which would have squatted menacingly on the temple roof. *See also chapter* **Trips out of Town**.

Group discount by prior arrangement. Guided tour. Restaurant (The Pump Room). Shop. Toilets for the disabled. Wheelchair access to balcony (free).

Fishbourne Palace and Museum

Salthill Road, Fishbourne, Chichester, West Sussex (0243 785859). **Getting there** *by train* from Victoria (change at Chichester), 2 hours; *by bus* National Express from Victoria, 3 hours then bus 266 or 700 Coastliner, 10 minutes; *by car* A3 to Portsmouth then A27 (or take the pretty A286 route via Midhurst). **Open** *Mar, Apr, Oct* 10am-5pm daily; *May-Sept* 10am-6pm daily; *Nov* 10am-4pm daily; *Dec-Feb* 10am-4pm Sun only. **Admission** £2 adults; £1 under-fives; £1.60 OAPs, students. **Credit** A, £TC.

The provincial villa, which was unearthed in Fishbourne in 1960, is the largest Roman building of its type found in Britain. It's thought to have been built for Cogidubnus, a Celtic prince who became a client king, or *legate*, and who would have governed the region on behalf of Rome. The building was found to have an unparalleled series of geometric mosaic floors, dating from the first century AD. The tessellated corridors have survived the ravages of time virtually intact and give a unique insight into the creative excesses of Roman interior design.

DECLINE & FALL

Londinium, in its heyday, exported pottery from Highgate, iron from Kent, tin from Cornwall and slaves.

It also dispersed imports from other parts of the Roman empire throughout Britannia. Rubbish tips dating from AD 60 to 120 reveal wine amphoraes from Rhodes and Palestine alongside cooking earthenware from Brockley Hill.

Roman cities, with so many of their buildings made of daub, wattle and other inflammable materials, were especially vulnerable to fire. The great fire which swept the city in AD 125 marked the decline of Londinium. Other towns had become less dependent on it for trade and there was little real effort to rebuild the settlement. A wall was built around the capital in AD 200, marking a shift in imperial policy away from integrating the local population and towards defending Roman Londoners (*see above*). Barbarian raids upset the equilibrium in other areas of her empire and Rome didn't have the resources to garrison such a distant province effectively. They left Britain around AD 410 and the stage was cleared for the Saxon ascendancy.

MARAUDING VIKINGS

After the Romans deserted the city, latin, literacy and personal hygiene disappeared from eastern Britain. London wasn't rehabited until King Alfred moved in from Ludenswic to confront the marauding Vikings in AD 886. The Saxons, who had previously gained control of south eastern Britain, had no real administrative system and little need for a centralised seat of government. One Saxon poet, on first entering Londinium, was so unprepared for the mass of crumbling masonry and disused warehouses that he referred to it as 'the work of giants'. London began to re-establish itself under Saxon rule and though it never regained its position as either an administrative or trading centre, a few remains have been unearthed indicating some growth.

In 1065 the last Saxon king, Harold, Earl of Wessex, came to the throne. One year later he lost it to the Norman bastard, William the Conqueror, at the Battle of Hastings. English culture was altered for ever and the Middle Ages had begun.

The Syrian god, **Mithras,** *(listed under* **Museum of London**) *held dear by the Roman legions for his qualities of virility, strength and light, would have been worshipped in secret. Several treasures have been recovered, including a marble head of Mithras and busts of other less eminent deities such as Serapis and Minerva. The marbles were hidden in the fourth century to escape the Christian purges which were sweeping the Empire. The foundations of the temple, built in about AD 240-50, have been restored and can be seen on Queen Victoria Street, EC4.*

Middle Ages

Dirty, noisy and smelly, London hasn't changed much in the last thousand years. Political intrigue, back-stabbing royalty and corrupt monks; it all happened back in the Middle Ages.

Modern London's politics, religion and trade, all have their roots in developments that took place during the Middle Ages. **The Guildhall** and **Westminster Abbey** are the most outstanding remnants of that age. Throughout medieval times (lasting roughly from the eleventh to the fifteenth century) fires were a constant hazard. Most buildings were made from wood and the city burned merrily. Stone buildings were the privilege of the rich and the church.

Another serious health hazard was the rubbish and excrement thrown onto the streets by uncaring householders. Although water was provided in cisterns at Cheapside, EC2, and elsewhere, the supply was limited and polluted. Most of the rivers that provided London's water were also the sewers. **Houndsditch**, EC3, was so called because London residents threw their dead livestock into the ditch that formed one of the city's boundaries. Matters were brought to a head by the Black Death in 1348, which killed approximately 35,000 people out of a population of around 50,000.

Outside the City walls, the areas which were developed most were Southwark and Westminster. Because much of London was marshland, Westminster was based on Thorney Island (an area surrounded by ditches, where **Westminster Abbey** now stands). The importance of Westminster was confirmed when William the Conqueror chose it as the venue for his coronation in 1066. Meanwhile Southwark gained notoriety as the centre for prostitution, drinking and gambling.

British Museum
Great Russell Street, WC1 (071 636 1555; recorded information 071 580 1788). Holborn, Russell Square or Tottenham Court Road underground. **Open** *10am-5pm Mon-Sat; 2.30-6pm Sun; 6-9pm first Tue every month.* **Admission** *free daily; £5 6-9pm first Tue every month; exhibitions £2 adults; £1 children, OAPs, students, UB40s.* **Credit** *(shop only) A, AmEx, DC, £STC, USA currency, V.*
A permanent display of medieval crafts is kept here. Gold and silver work, jewellery,

glass, carved ivory, and late medieval icons are some of the more valuable treasures on view. *See also chapter* **Museums**.
Café & licensed restaurant (10.30am-4.15pm Mon-Sat; 3-5.15pm Sun). Cassette tours of Library 60p. Lectures. Shop. Tour (105 mins; £5 inclusive). Toilets for the disabled. Wheelchair access by prior arrangement.

London Dungeon
28-34 Tooley Street SE1 (071 403 0606). London Bridge underground. **Open** *10am-4.30pm daily.* **Admission** *adults £4.50; under 15s £2.50; free disabled.* **No credit cards.**
The darker side of medieval London is the blood-curdling speciality here (*see chapter* **Sightseeing**).
Café. Gift shop. Group discount. Toilets for the disabled. Wheelchair access.

ROYALTY

For much of the early Middle Ages, London suffered from Danish raiders. Ironically, it was a successful Danish invader, King Canute, who established London as the capital of England. **St Clement Danes**, WC2, was named after the Danes who settled between Westminster, SW1 and Ludgate, EC4.

Richard II had a tough time, being only ten years of age when he came to the throne in 1377 and then having to deal with the Peasants Revolt of 1381 (a mass protestation against the Poll Tax, the effects of which fell disproportionately on the poor). Faced with an angry mob, Richard reputedly cried out 'I will be your chief and captain'. Believing that they had won the battle, the crowd dispersed and peace was restored. Part of Richard II's legacy included the rebuilding of the royal Palace of Westminster. Hugh Herland was responsible for the famous hammerbeam roof, a surviving masterpiece of medieval carpentry and the largest of its kind in the world. The Jewel Tower also still stands with all of its original architecture.

When Edward IV died suddenly in 1483, his brother Richard decided to grab the throne for himself. He quickly had Edward's two young sons imprisoned in the **Tower of London**, which was then used as a royal residence. They were never seen again. Popular belief is that Richard III, as he was to become, had them murdered, but there's no hard evidence to support this.

Tower of London
Tower Hill, EC3 (071 709 0765). Tower Hill underground/Fenchurch Street BR/15, 42, 78 bus. **Open** *Mar-Oct 9.30am-5.30pm Mon-Sat; 2-5pm Sun; Nov-Feb 9.30am-4pm Mon-Sat; closed Sun.* **Admission** *£4.80 adults; £3 OAPs, disabled, student; £2 under-15s; free under-5s.* **Credit** *(shop only) A, £TC, V.*
Begun by William I, this medieval fortress houses the Crown Jewels and the Royal Armouries. A longish wait is normally necessary so go during the week *See also chapter* **Sightseeing**.
Gift shop. Group discount. Guided tours (free every half hour for one hour). Restaurant. Wheelchair access with help (one adult admitted free if assisting disabled person).

GOVERNMENT

By the fourteenth century Westminster Hall was established as the centre of administration for royalty.

In 1215 at Runnymede near Windsor, King John was forced by his rebellious barons to sign the Magna Charta, a document which redefined the limits of royal power and effectively determined the fate of democratic parliament. John, who was trying to steal the throne from his brother Richard the Lionheart, also confirmed the right of the City to elect its own mayor. He granted this in return for support against his own brother. King John eventually did become regent in his brother's absence.

Westminster Hall
Parliament Square, SW1 (071 219 4273). Westminster underground. **Open** *by appointment only; contact your local MP or the Information Officer (071 219 3000) eight weeks in advance.* **Admission** *free.*
See **picture and caption.**

TOWN & TRADE

London was superbly placed for trade. The River Thames allowed for ships to pass along bringing wares – including cloth, wine and linen – from foreign parts, and in turn exporting whatever England had to offer: fur, wool and skins were common commodities.

King Alfred would grant blocks of land to those who were capable of restoring them to their former importance and glory. Such land always had access to the river and access to one of the two market places. Eastcheap (now known as Cheapside) was patronized mainly by ordinary citizens, and divided into sections according to the goods sold, as is apparent by street names – Fish Street Hill, Sea Coal Lane, Milk Street, Ironmonger Lane – that still exist 1,000 years later.

Each trade developed its own organization, able to defend their interests and dependents. These associations were early versions of the City guilds and livery companies, who today are responsible for administering charitable funds and property. The best surviving medieval livery companies' hall is the Merchant Taylors' on Threadneedle Street.

Crosby Hall
Cheyne Walk, SW3 (071 352 9663). Sloane Square underground. **Open** 10am-noon, 2-4pm, daily, but functions are held regularly so phone first. **Admission** free.
The only surviving part of a medieval merchant's house in London, Crosby Hall is referred to by Shakespeare on three occasions. It was removed to Chelsea, from the City, in 1910 under threat of demolition. Sir Thomas More leased the Hall and Richard III is known to have stayed here.

Guildhall
off Gresham Street, EC2 (071 606 3030). Bank underground. **Open** 10am-5pm Mon-Fri. **Admission** free.
The Gothic porch, finished in 1430, is still the entrance to the hall from Guildhall Yard. The Great Hall can be freely visited but the interior of the building can be seen by guided tour only: contact the Keeper of the Guildhall (address above).
Bookshop. Guided tours (free). Wheelchair access.

Museum of London
150 London Wall, EC2 (071 600 3699). Barbican (closed Sun), St Paul's underground or Moorgate underground/BR. **Open** 10am-6pm Tue-Sat; 2-6pm Sun. **Admission** free. **Credit** (shop only) A, V.
The whole of London's past is on show here. Medieval artefacts, discovered during excavation work, are stored alongside maps and models of buildings from the period. *See also chapter* **Museums.**
Braille guide and taped commentary for the visually impaired. Lectures and films with induction loop for the hard of hearing in theatre. Restaurant. Shop. Toilets for the disabled. Wheelchair access. Workshops.

MUSIC

Medieval music falls into two categories: sacred and secular. Only sacred music was written down for it was generally only men of the cloth who were literate. Both Westminster Abbey and St Paul's Cathedral have choirs that date back to the twelfth and thirteenth centuries and sometimes sing authentic sacred music at evensong service, a tradition which dates back to medieval times.

Early Music Shop
48 Great Marlborough Street, W1 (071 439 8282). Oxford Circus underground. **Open** 9am-5pm Mon-Fri. **Credit** A, £TC, V.
Tucked away in the basement of Schott, the music publishers, the Early Music Shop stocks replicas of crumhorns, percussion, keyboards and many more early wind and string instruments. Recorders cost from £20 to £800.

Tiddy Dols
55 Shepherd Market, W1 (071 499 2357). Green Park underground. **Dinner served** 6-11.30pm daily. **Average** £20. **House wine** £8.50 bottle, £1.85 glass. **Credit** A, AmEx, EC, TC, V.
All the recipes used at this restaurant are adapted from a collection of ancient cookbooks: dishes include Venison pevorat (a medieval pepper sauce) and Woodeford's Cornish chicken pasty. Period music is played by a troupe of strolling players, who perform on reproduction Renaissance instruments. At 8pm and 9.30pm a town crier announces the day's news.
Vegetarian meals. Wheelchair access.

CHURCH

The Catholic Church had its heyday in the Middle Ages. The church buildings in London are probably the few remaining examples of medieval architecture that exist intact in the capital. In 604 King Ethelbert had the first (Old) **St Paul's Cathedral** built. All that remains of St Paul's today, from

Westminster Hall *(listed under* **Government***) was built in 1097 and is the only surviving part of the original Palace of Westminster, where early parliaments were held until 1307. It was built for William the Conqueror's son, William Rufus; but he was obviously a difficult customer to satisfy, and called the massive 72 metres/79 yards long and 12 metres/13 yards high hall 'a mere bedchamber'.*

medieval times, are the ruined cloisters and the chapter house in the gardens on the south side.

Edward the Confessor instigated the replacement of the little timber church of St Peter's with **Westminster Abbey** around 1050-65. Extensive rebuilding took place in the thirteenth and fourteenth centuries and almost nothing of the original structure remains.

During the Middle Ages the construction of churches went into overdrive and it wasn't long before London had hundreds of churches. Initially, designs were simple, then Gothic influences began to take effect, and aisles and towers were added. St Ethelburga's at Bishopsgate, EC2 is a typical example of the local city churches, once found in great numbers.

By the end of the twelfth century there were several important monastic institutions in London, supposedly practising a life of self-denial and chastity. Such moral restrictions were, however, undermined by an undercurrent of church corruption, prevalent until Tudor times. In April 1303 a travelling merchant carried out a robbery at Westminster Abbey with the aid of ten monks. Found with the King's jewellery amounting to £75,000 on his person he was executed but his ten partners in crime were merely imprisoned.

St Bartholomew-the-Great (listed under **Church**) was built by Henry I's court jester, Rahere. During a journey of penance to Rome he fell very ill and had a vision of St Bartholomew. Rahere promised to build a hospital for the poor if his life could be saved. Built adjacent to the hospital the oldest remaining part of the church is the nave, dating from 1225.

Brass Rubbing Centre
St Martin-in the Fields, Trafalgar Square, WC2 (071 437 6023). Charing Cross underground/BR. **Open** 10am-6pm Mon-Sat; noon-6pm Sun. **Admission** free. **Brass rubbings** according to size 50p-£10.50. **Credit** A, V.
Rub replicas of medieval church brasses here, and continue a long-standing British hobby. *Gift shop. Wheelchair access.*

St Etheldreda
Ely Place, EC1 (071 405 1061). Chancery Lane underground. **Open** 7.30am-7pm daily.
Services 8am, 1pm Mon-Fri; 8am Sat; 9am, 11am, 6pm Sun.
The only pre-Reformation Catholic church in London, its crypt, which has original carpentry, dates from about 1251.

Southwark Cathedral
Montague Close, SE1 (071 407 2939). London Bridge underground/BR/Riverbus to London Bridge City Pier. **Open** 8am-6pm daily. Closing times vary on religious holidays. **Services** 12.45pm, 1.10pm, 5.30pm, Mon-Fri; noon, 5.30pm, Sat; 11am, 3pm, Sun. **Admission** free. **Credit** (café & shop only) A, AmEx, £TC, V.
The oldest Gothic church in London, Southwark Cathedral, dates back to 1220, when it was known as St Mary Overie. It possesses a delightful mixture of architecture and, as it's little known, makes a quiet retreat.

Café (10am-4.30pm Mon-Fri). Crèche (Sun 11 am service only). Shop. Tour by prior arrangement. Wheelchair access.

Westminster Abbey
Dean's Yard, SW1 (071 222 5152). St James's Park or Westminster underground/3, 11, 12 bus. **Open** *Nave* 8am-6pm Mon, Tue, Thur-Sat; 8am-7.45pm Wed; between services on Sunday. *Royal Chapels* 9am-4.45pm Mon, Tue, Thur, Fri; 9am-4pm, 6-7.45pm Wed; 9am-2pm, 3.45-5.45pm Sat. *Chapter House, Pyx Chamber, Abbey Museum* 10am-4pm daily. *College Garden Apr-Sept,* 10am-6pm Thur; *Oct-Mar,* 10am-4pm Thur. Brass Rubbing Centre (071 222 2085) 9am-5pm Mon-Sat. **Services** *Mon-Fri* 7.30am, 8am, 12.30pm (choral), 5pm (choral); *Sat* 8am, 9.20am, 3pm (choral); *Sun* 8am, 10am (choral), 11.15am (choral), 3pm (choral), 5.45pm (organ recital), 6.30pm (free singing). **Admission** *Nave* free; *Royal Chapels* £2.20 adults; 50p under-16s; £1.10 OAPs, students, UB40s (except free 6-7.45pm Wed). *Abbey Museum* £1.60 adult; 40p under-16s; 80p OAPs, students, UB40s. **Credit** (shop only) A, AmEx, £STC, V.
A superb example of medieval architecture, many medieval kings, including Edward the

Confessor, are buried here. Adjacent to the Chapter House there's the Pyx chamber. Once used to standardize coinage, it is now fitted out as a treasury with displays of coins. *See also chapter* **Sightseeing**.
Guided tour Mon-Sat, £6 (information 071 222 7110). Shop: 9.30am-5pm Mon-Sat. Wheelchair access.

St Bartholomew-the-Great
57 West Smithfield, EC1 (071 606 5171). Barbican (closed Sun) or St Paul's underground. **Open** 8am-4.30pm daily. **Services** 9am, 11am, 6.30pm Sun. **Admission** free.
See picture and caption.
Bookshop. Tour by prior arrangement. Toilets for the disabled. Wheelchair access.

Temple Church
Inner Temple, King's Bench Walk, EC4 (071 353 1736). Temple underground. **Open** 10am-4pm Mon-Sat; 1-4pm Sun. **Services** 8.30am Holy Communion, 11.15am morning service, Sun. **Admission** free.
Built by the Knights Templars between 1170 and 1240, the beautiful Temple Church is based on the Church of the Holy Sepulchre in Jerusalem.
Wheelchair access.

Tudors & Stuarts

The Golden Age of Elizabethan London preceded a century of civil war, plague, fire, and finally, a glorious revolution.

Early Tudor London was a long way behind the great cities of Renaissance Europe in size (population 37,000), wealth and culture. However, the sixteenth century saw an explosion in commerce throughout the world and as overseas trade expanded, so did London, rapidly becoming a huge, dirty, overcrowded city. By 1600 there were 200,000 people living in the capital.

The walled City of London was separated from the City of Westminster by fields and from Southwark by London Bridge. The Thames was much wider than it is today (about 1,900 feet/579 metres) and much more important in terms of transportation. It was also used for both sewage disposal and drinking water, which did nothing to improve the short life expectancy.

Tudor London was much nearer the countryside. Beef cattle and sheep were pastured in Islington then herded to Smithfield Market, and there were windmills on high ground in Finsbury, Islington, Lambeth and Greenwich.

Museum of London
150 London Wall, EC2 (071 600 3699). Barbican, St Paul's or Moorgate underground/BR/4, 141, 279A, 502 bus. **Open** 10am-6pm Tue-Sat; 2-6pm Sun. **Admission** free. **Credit** (shop only) A, V.
The Tudor and Stuart collections reflect London life through the Reformation, the English Civil War, the Great Plague of 1665, the Great Fire of 1666 and the subsequent rebuilding of London. Perhaps the most colourful Tudor find on display is the Cheapside jewellery hoard, a typical goldsmith's stock-in-trade. *See also chapter* **Museums**.
Braille guide and taped commentary for the visually impaired. Lectures (with induction loop for the hard of hearing in theatre) and films. Restaurant (10am-5pm Tue-Sat; noon-5pm Sun). Shop. Toilets for the disabled. Wheelchair access. Workshops.

National Portrait Gallery
2 St Martin's Place, WC2 (071 930 1552). Charing Cross underground/BR. **Open** 10am-5pm Mon-Fri; 10am-6pm Sat; 2-6pm Sun. **Admission** free.
The National Portrait Gallery's first acquisition was a picture of William Shakespeare in 1856. Portraits of every Tudor and Stuart monarch hang in the gallery, together with pictures of those who attempted to rival them in power and influence. Gaze too upon the faces of Sir Walter Raleigh, the sailor-explorer; Thomas Cranmer, the Protestant martyr; Sir Francis Drake, the state-sponsored pirate; poet John Milton; diarist Samuel Pepys, and Nell Gwynn, the most renowned of King Charles II's mistresses. *See also chapter* **Art Galleries**.
Shop. Tour by prior arrangement. Wheelchair access by prior arrangement.

Citysights of London
(081 806 4325). **Cost** £3.50 adults; £2.50 OAPs, students, UB40s; free under-14s. **Meet** 2.30pm at the Museum of London (*see above*). **Walks** once a month; *London Churches* Fridays; *The Architecture of Christopher Wren* Fridays; *Tudor London; Shakespeare's City* Saturdays; *The Great Fire, Plague and the Civil War* Saturdays; *John Stow's Tudor London* Sundays; *The London Diaries of Pepys and Evelyn* Sundays.

THE TUDORS

The Wars of the Roses, from 1455 to 1487, were so named by nineteenth-century historians after the emblems of the warring factions, a white rose for York and a red rose for Lancaster. This bloody affair was sparked off by Yorkist opposition to the weak Henry VI. The wars provided lots of juicy material for Shakespeare – his Henry VI parts I and II and Richard III are all many of us know of the history of the period. It was finally ended by the strong rule of the Lancastrian Henry VII after the death of the Yorkist king, Richard III, at Bosworth Field in 1485.

Henry VII, the first Tudor monarch, prevented any further dispute over the succession by marrying one of his enemies.

Henry VII's son, Henry VIII, is one of England's more colourful historical figures. His desperate longing for a son and heir led him to work his way through six wives, execute two of them, row with the Pope and create the new Church of England.

Henry's financial situation wasn't much happier, as wars against France and Scotland drained the coffers. However, as the Church was now his, he could claim all its wealth and sell most of its land, which was considerable. Between 1535 and 1540 he ordered the seizure of churches and monasteries, making great areas of land available for building.

The split from Rome made the two great European powers of France and Spain (both staunchly Catholic) religious, as well as political enemies of England. Henry therefore decided he needed to develop a full-time professional navy, leading to the foundation of the royal dockyards at Woolwich and Deptford.

Chapel of Henry VII
Westminster Abbey, SW1 (071 222 5152). Westminster or St James's Park underground. **Open** 9am-4pm Mon-Fri; 9am-2pm, 3.45-5pm, Sat. **Admission** £2 adults; 50p children; £1 OAPs, students. **No credit cards.**
The tombs of Henry VII and his mother are among the earliest examples of Renaissance art in England. Other inhabitants of this royal necropolis are Mary Queen of Scots, Elizabeth I and Mary Tudor. Look up at the early sixteenth century pendant-vaulted roof and also admire the remarkable collection of sculptured saints. The chapel is also open on Wednesday evenings (6-7.45pm) when admission is free and you're allowed to take photographs.
Guided tour. Shop.

Hampton Court Palace
East Molesey, Surrey (081 977 8441). Hampton Court BR/boat to Hampton Court Pier (Apr-Oct). **Open** Apr-Oct 9.30am-6pm daily; Oct-Mar 9.30am-4.30pm daily (last admission half an hour before closing). **Park open** dawn to dusk daily. **Admission** Inclusive ticket to palace, courtyard, cloister and maze £3.40 adults; £1.70 under 16s; free under-5s. £2.50 OAPs. *Maze only Mar-Oct* £1 adults; 50p under-16s; 75p OAPs. **Credit** A, V.
The grandest Tudor residence in England, Hampton Court Palace was built as a country residence by Cardinal Wolsey in 1514. Wolsey 'presented' the Palace to Henry in 1525 in an attempt to retain the King's favour after he'd failed to secure the longed-for divorce. It didn't work – Wolsey was arrested for high treason and died on his way to imprisonment in the Tower of London. Henry's additions to the Palace include the magnificent roof of the Chapel Royal, which took 100 men nine months to complete. The State Apartments, added by William and Mary, were designed by Sir Christopher Wren in the late seventeenth century; the famous Maze is fun to get lost in (*see chapter* **The River & Docklands**).
Car park (free). Group discount. Guided tours (Mar-Sept; 11.15am & 2.15 pm Mon-Sat; free with full price ticket). Shop. Toilets for the disabled. Wheelchair access.

Historic Barts & Smithfield
(071 837 0546). Farringdon underground.
Meet Henry VIII Gateway,.West Smithfield,
EC1. **Tour** *Apr-Oct* 2pm Sun. **Cost** £3
adults, children free.
The tours last between one and a half and
two hours, taking in St Bartholomew the
Less, the Hogarth murals in St Bart's
Hospital, Smithfield Market, Cloth Fair and
St Bartholomew the Great. The cost of the
tour goes to Bart's Heritage Fund.

The Royal Armouries
HM Tower of London, EC3 (071 480 6358).
Tower Hill underground. **Open** *Mar-Oct*
9.30am-5.45pm Mon-Sat; 2-5.30pm Sun; *Nov-
Feb* 9.30am-4.30pm Mon-Sat. **Admission**
£4.80 adults; £2 children, £3 disabled, OAPs,
students, UB40s. **Credit** (shop only) A, V.
See **picture and caption.**
For **Tower of London** *see chapter*
Sightseeing.
Group discount. Wheelchair access..

NEW AGE

Although Henry's son, Edward VI,
died young, even Henry would have
been proud of his daughter,
Elizabeth I. During her 45-year
reign, London became a major port
for America, Africa and the Far East
– 90 per cent of England's overseas
trade went through it. British explor-
ers sailed far and wide claiming continents, lands and lumps of rock in
the name of Queen and country.

In 1581 Elizabeth I knighted Sir
Francis Drake at Woolwich Dockyard
on his return from a three year hit-
and-run raiding trip round the world
(also known as the first British circumnavigation of the globe).

The Spanish attempted to invade
England in 1588, but the Armada
sent to carry the invasion force was
defeated by Drake, with a some help
from bad weather in the Channel.

Few buildings survive from this
period in central London. Most were
consumed in either the Great Fire or
the Blitz, or have fallen prey to redevelopment schemes. Two splendid
examples however are **Staple Inn**
and **Middle Temple Hall.**

Hatfield House
Hatfield, Hertfordshire. (07072 62823).
Hatfield BR. **Open** *Mar-Oct* noon-4pm Tue-
Fri; noon-4.30pm Sat; 1.30-5pm Sun; 11am-
5pm Bank Holidays. **Admission** £3.50
adults; £2.40 children; £3 OAPs. **Credit**
(shop only) A, £STC, V.
A splendid, fully-furnished Jacobean house
with paintings (including the Rainbow
Portrait of Elizabeth I), tapestries and
armour. Look round the late fifteenth century gardens and see the ruins of the Royal
Palace of Hatfield where Elizabeth I spent
much of her childhood.

*Café. Children's playground. Elizabethan ban-
quets (07072 62055). Garden festival
(June). Group discount. Guided tours. Multi-
lingual tours by prior arrangement.
Restaurant. Shop. Toilets for the disabled.
Wheelchair access.*

Middle Temple Hall
Middle Temple Lane, EC4 (071 353 4355).
Temple underground. **Open** 10am-noon, 3-
4.30pm, Mon-Fri (the Hall is often in use in the
afternoon so phone first). **Admission** free.
The most impressive feature of the Hall, completed in 1573, is its oak, double hammerbeam roof. The 29 foot/9 metre Bench Table,
given to the Temple by Elizabeth I, was made
from a single Windsor Park oak. The smaller
table in front of the Bench Table, known as
'the Cupboard', was made from a piece of
wood from Sir Francis Drake's *Golden Hind.*
Take time to wander around the courtyards
which are also open to the public.

Staple Inn
Holborn, WC1. Chancery Lane Underground.
Open *Courtyard only* 8am-8pm Mon-Fri.
Admission free.
See **picture and caption.**

SHAKESPEARE

Tudor theatre was performed for
the common people and regarded
with disdain by the authorities.

Actors were often treated as little
more than itinerant, workshy beg-
gars. The Corporation of the City of
London banned theatres in 1575
and expelled the actors, so they
moved themselves and their theatres to Bankside at the south end
of London Bridge, outside the juris-
diction of the City.

The Rose, the first theatre on the
South Bank, was built next to the
Rose brothel. Bear and bull baiting
also attracted the crowds to the
area. Law and order was enforced
by the Bishop of Winchester, who
owned many of the brothels.
Unspeakable things were done to
religious dissenters, political prison-
ers and criminals in the Clink
Prison, also run by the good Bishop
(*see below* **The Clink Exhibition**).

Today Bankside is rediscovering
its history and you can visit a thriving area tucked away behind
Southwark Cathedral, SE1: the
Globe Theatre Museum, the site of
the Rose Theatre (until it's buried
under a large office block for a couple of years, then re-excavated), the
Clink Museum and the nineteenth-
century Kathleen & May ship in St

London's oldest museum, **The Royal Armouries** *(listed under* **The Tudors**)
*contains exhibits from the Dark Ages to the present day. Major attractions
include a Tudor and Stuart gallery with the armours of Henry VIII and
Charles I. There's an Oriental armoury with the world's largest suit of armour,
designed for an Indian elephant, plus a collection of eighteenth- and nineteenth-
century British military weapons.*

Staple Inn (*listed under* **New Age**) *is the only surviving half-timbered Elizabethan terrace in central London. It was founded in 1378 as an Inn of Chancery, a type of prep school undertaken before the serious business of joining one of the Inns of Court to train to become a barrister, and it became part of Gray's Inn (on the opposite side of Holborn) in 1529. The present splendid building dates from 1586. A silver dragon on a plinth in front of Staple Inn marks the boundary of the City of London.*

Marie Overie's Dock, outside the Old Thameside Inn. From the Dock, take a walk along the River under Southwark Bridge to Blackfriars Bridge and admire the view of St Paul's and the City.

All's Well That Ends Well

Scotney Castle, Lamberhurst, Kent (0892 890651). Wadhurst BR. **Dates** *29 Aug-1 Sept,1990, 7.30pm; matinées 2pm 31 Aug, 1 Sept.* **Admission** *ring for details, booking from May.* **No credit cards.**
Open-air Shakespeare in sight of the ruins of a fourteenth century castle. If it rains it goes ahead anyway, so bring suitable English summer-wear. Book early as tickets sell quickly. *Wheelchair access by prior arrangement.*

The Clink Exhibition

1 Clink Street, SE1 (071 403 6515). London Bridge underground/BR. **Open** *Apr-Sept* 10am-6pm Mon-Wed, 10am-10pm Thur-Sun; *Oct-Mar* 10am-6pm daily. **Admission** £2.50 adults, £1.50 under-16s, OAPs, UB40s. Under-16s must be accompanied by an adult. **No credit cards.**
In the fifteenth century, the Bishop of Winchester ran 22 brothels, and any prostitutes he wasn't pimping he incarcerated in his private prison. Thus 'Clink' became a byword for jail. It later held debtors and their families in degrading conditions. The displays, in a warehouse on the site of the prison (which was destroyed in the Gordon Riots of 1780), has recreations of cells and torture implements, but few real artefacts from Southwark's ribald past. Many visitors head straight for the 'adults only' exhibition – a display of low life, including anti-masturbation devices.
Café. Dramatised tours (1pm, 5pm, 8pm Thur-Sun no extra charge; 10pm-12.30am Fri, Sun, £10 for two, including wine and buffet. Shop.

George Inn

77 Borough High Street, SE1 (071 407 2506). Borough or London Bridge underground/BR. **Open** 11am-11pm Mon-Fri; noon-3pm, 6-11pm, Sat; noon-3pm, 7-10.30pm, Sun. **Credit** A, AmEx, DC, V.
This large, half-timbered pub is the only galleried coaching inn left in London. The present building dates from 1676 but the pub was mentioned by John Stow in his 1598 *Survey of London.* During the summer there are occasional Shakespeare productions in the yard – the way plays were performed before 1576, when the first purpose-built theatres appeared. We recommend the beer and the ambience, but try the food at your peril.

Shakespeare Globe Museum

1 Bear Gardens, Bankside, SE1 (071 928 6342). Mansion House or London Bridge underground/BR. **Open** 10am-5.30pm Mon-Sat; 1.30-5pm Sun. **Admission** £1 adults; 50p under-16s, OAPs, students, UB40s, Southwark residents. **No credit cards.**
Built on the site of the Hope Theatre, this is the only record of the world's first theatre area. Plays by Shakespeare and his contemporaries are presented on a replica 1616 stage (phone for details). The Museum is home to the Globe project which will include a full-scale reconstruction of Shakespeare's theatre, an indoor Jacobean theatre, shops, a pub, a restaurant, a cinema and a study centre, all due to open in 1992. *See chapter* **Museums.** *Café. Lectures. Walks around local area. Workshops.*

Historical Walks

(081 668 4019). **Admission** £3.50 adults; £2.50 OAPs, students, UB40s; free under-14s if accompanied by an adult. **No credit cards.**
The Inns of Court: 11am Thursdays; meet at Temple underground. Takes in the Middle and Inner Temples, Lincoln's Inn and Sir John Soane's Museum (*see chapter* **Georgian London**).
The London of Dickens and Shakespeare: 11am Sundays; meet at Blackfriars underground. This walk round Bankside includes the site of the Globe theatre, Southwark Cathedral, and a couple of historic pubs.
Royal and Aristocratic Stuarts: 2.30pm Sundays; meet at Green Park underground for this tour of Mayfair and St James's.

SCOTTISH TAKEOVER

Elizabeth I died the 'Virgin Queen' in 1603 and the Tudor dynasty died with her. James VI of Scotland, also James I of England and Wales, united the two kingdoms for the first time.

On 5 November 1605, James narrowly escaped death when Guy Fawkes and his gunpowder were discovered in a cellar underneath the Palace of Westminster. The Gunpowder Plot to blow up the king and Parliament was in protest at the failure to improve conditions for the persecuted Catholics.

The early Stuart period saw the first real flowering of Renaissance architecture in London. Inigo Jones, stage designer and architect, designed Covent Garden (completed in 1639) as the first planned square in London and initially financial killings were made by the developer, the Earl of Bedford, by selling 31-year leases.

Banqueting House

Whitehall, SW1 (071 930 4179). Westminster underground or Charing Cross underground/BR. **Open** 10am-5pm Tue-Sat; 2-5pm Sun (can be shut at short notice for Government receptions). **Admission** £1.60 adults; 80p children; £1.20 OAPs, students, UB40s. **No credit cards.**
The Banqueting House is the only surviving part of Whitehall Palace. It was designed by Inigo Jones, completed in 1622, and was the first purely Renaissance building in London. Charles I commissioned Rubens to celebrate the divine right of the Stuarts. The 12 can-

vasses were put on the ceiling of the saloon room of the Banqueting House where they have remained for over 350 years. This is the only room open to the public and, unless you want to study the paintings in detail, can be seen in five minutes.
Shop. Group discount.

Forty Hall Museum
Forty Hill, Enfield, EN2 (081 363 8196). Enfield Chase or Enfield Town BR/191, 231 bus. Open Easter-Sept 10am–6pm Tue-Sun; Oct-Easter 10am–5pm Tue-Sun. Admission free.
Forty Hall is a magnificent Caroline mansion built in 1629. On the ground floor are displays of seventeenth and eighteenth-century furniture. Upstairs is devoted to a bizarre exhibition of the history of advertising and packaging and a childhood gallery (*see chapter* **Museums**).
Café (11am–5pm). Tour by prior arrangement. Shop. Wheelchair access to ground floor.

Ham House
Ham, Richmond, Surrey (081 940 1950). Richmond underground/BR then 71 bus. Open 11am-5pm Tue-Sun (last admission 4.30pm). Admission £2 adults; £1 under-16s, students. No credit cards.
Ham House is a brilliantly-restored Stuart mansion, with all the original furniture. The decorative taste of the resident Dysart dynasty certainly reveals what seventeenth-century social climbers lived like. The ostentation is an eloquent political statement by Royalists who bounced back into favour during the Restoration. Surrounded by water

meadows, the formal garden looks much as it did 300 years ago.
Café (Easter-Oct). Guided tour (3pm Thur). Shop (Easter-Oct). Wheelchair access by prior arrangement.

CIVIL WAR

Hobbes, the philosopher, writing in 1651, described the condition of man as 'solitary, poore, nasty, brutish, and short'. And so it was for the vast majority of London's population, which numbered 400,000 by 1650. Life was also short for Charles I, who was tried and executed as a tyrant at Whitehall in January 1649, a momentous act which made Britain a republic.

Commemoration of Charles I
Citysights of London (081 806 4325). **Meet** Westminster underground. **Date** last Sunday in January, 10.30 am. **Admission** *ceremony* free; *walk* £3.50 adults; £2.50 OAPs, students, UB40s; free. under 14.
See the King's Army of the English Civil War Society march in period costume from St James's Palace and lay a wreath at

Banqueting House (*see above* **Scottish Takeover**) in commemoration of Charles's execution. You will then be guided round the sites of early Stuart London and the trial and execution of the king.

PLAGUE & FIRE

Between 1660 and 1690 a property development boom swept Piccadilly, The Strand and Soho. Either side of Tottenham Court Road remained fields while the satellite villages of Kensington, Camberwell, Hackney, Islington and Hampstead grew.

The boom continued despite the Great Plague of 1665 (which killed at least 69,000 Londoners) and was fuelled by the Great Fire of 1666 which destroyed four-fifths of the City. By 1673 most houses had been rebuilt, mostly in brick and stone, and in 1686 some bright spark came up with the idea of fire insurance.

Up until the mid-seventeenth century banking was in the hands of foreigners, mainly the Italians who had centuries of pecuniary experience from dealing with the Papal finances. The commercial development of London however encouraged the evolution of native banks from brokers, scriveners and goldsmiths. By the time the Bank of England was established in 1694 there were about 40 banks in London, with those in the West End catering for the aristocracy and gentry and those in the City dealing with businesses.

The increased use of private coaches, sedan chairs and hackney carriages led to traffic congestion. Modern London had been born.

Monument
Monument Street, EC2 (071 626 2717). Monument underground. Open Apr-Sept 9am-6pm Mon-Fri; 2-6pm Sat, Sun; Oct-Mar 9am-4pm Mon-Sat. Admission 50p adults; 25p under-16s, OAPs. See picture and caption.

Prince Henry's Room
17 Fleet Street, EC4 (071 353 7323). Temple underground. Open 1.45-5pm Mon-Fri; 1.45-4.30pm Sat. Admission free.
Built in 1611 and named in honour of James I's eldest son, this is one of the few City buildings to survive the Great Fire, with oak panelling and plaster ceiling intact. It now houses a collection of Samuel Pepys' memorabilia, which seems apt as much of what we know about the Fire was vividly described in his diary.

Queen's House
Romney Road, SE10 (081 858 4422). Greenwich or Maze Hill BR/Island

The Monument (*listed under* **Plague & Fire**), *London's reminder of the Great Fire of 1666, is 202 feet/60.6 metres high; equal to its distance from where the five-day blaze started in a Pudding Lane bakery. When built, it was the world's tallest isolated stone column. And isolated it is, amid faceless office blocks, from Wren's other rebuilding works. Even St Paul's is obscured, but the riverscape and bits you can see make the climb worthwhile (see chapter* **Sightseeing**).

Gardens DLR/53, 54, 75, 89, 108, 177,
180, 188 bus; then Greenwich foot tunnel.
Open May-Sept 10am-6pm Mon-Sat; noon-
6pm Sun. **Admission** see below **National
Maritime Museum.**
After six years of restoration and refurbishment, Queen Henrietta Maria's Palace at
Greenwich reopens in May 1990. Inigo Jones
designed the house in 1616 as the first truly
classical Palladian building in Britain and it is
the architectural ancestor of the White House
in Washington DC. The royal apartments
have been restored as they were in 1660,
when Charles II's dowager queen moved in.

The National Maritime Museum & Old Royal Observatory

Romney Road, SE10 (081 858 4422).
Greenwich or Maze Hill BR/Island Gardens
DLR/53, 54, 75, 89, 108, 177, 180, 188 bus;
then Greenwich foot tunnel. **Open** summer
10am-6pm Mon-Sat; 2-6pm Sun; winter
10am-5pm Mon-Sat; 2-5pm Sun. **Admission**
(for both museums) £3 adults; £1.50 children, OAPs, students, UB40s; £7.50 family
(2 adults and up to 5 children). **Credit** A,
AmEx, £TC, V.
See **picture and caption.**
See also chapter **River & Docklands.**
Shop. Café. Group discount.

Royal Hospital

Chelsea Royal Hospital Road, SW3 (071 730
5282). Sloane Square underground 11, 19,
22, 137 bus. **Open** Museum, Chapel and
Great Hall 10am-noon, 2-4pm Mon-Fri; 2-
4pm Sat, Sun. **Services** (in Chapel)

Communion 8.30am Sun; Parade Service
11am Sun. **Admission** free.
This 1682 Wren building was founded by
Charles II for veteran soldiers and is still
home for 420 Chelsea Pensioners. See the
famous painting of Charles II on horseback by Antonio Verrio and Van Dyck's
Charles I and family.

Royal Naval College

King William Walk, SE10 (081 858 2154).
Greenwich or Maze Hill BR. **Open** 2.30-5pm
Fri-Wed. **Admission** free.
Walk through the Greenwich foot tunnel to
Island Gardens for a superb view of the
College (possibly the least altered view in
London). It was founded by William III as a
naval hospital, designed by Wren, and built
on the site of Greenwich Palace. The
College (which is a working naval college) is
split in two because Queen Mary didn't want
the view of the River obscured from the
Queen's House. Inside, the Chapel ceiling is
classically ornate and the Hall lavishly
painted by Sir James Thornhill.
Shop. Wheelchair access by prior arrangement.

St Paul's Cathedral

EC4 (071 248 2705). St Paul's underground.
Open 7.30am-6pm daily; galleries, crypt and
ambulatory 10am-4.15pm Mon-Fri, 11am-
4.15pm Sat. **Admission** cathedral free (donation requested; £1 adult, 60p under-16s); galleries £2 adult, £1 under-16s; crypt £1.10 adult,
55p under-16s; ambulatory 60p adults, under-
16s free. **Credit** (shop only) A, £TC, V.
Just as today's architectural plans for the St
Paul's area come under fierce scrutiny and

provoke national debate, so too did Wren's
ideas which were seen as revolutionary back
in the late 1660s. The great designer actually
had his first three St Paul's models rejected
but in the end still got his own way by taking
'designer's licence' to include large elements
of his favourite plans in the final breathtaking masterpiece. See chapter **The City.**
Guided tours (£3.60 adults, £1.60 under-16s;
at 11am, 11.30am, 2pm and 2.30pm). Shop.
Wheelchair access to main body and crypt.

GLORIOUS REVOLUTION

James II laid the basis for the Royal
Navy to become a modern department of state, with Samuel Pepys
(sometimes described as 'the first civil
servant') as secretary to the admiralty.
He also introduced fox hunting as a
sport. However, James's religious affil-
iations aroused fears of a return to
state-Catholicism and led to support
for William of Orange's invasion and
the Glorious Revolution of 1688.

Political parties were the Whigs,
who stood for a limited monarchy,
and the Tories, who supported the
Stuarts and believed in the divine
right of kings.

In the meantime the majority of
people got on with their everyday
lives. By 1700 London's population
stood at 500,000, by now the
biggest city in Western Europe and
the fourth largest city in the world.
One in four Londoners were
directly dependent on the port for
their livelihoods and they provided
ancillary work for another 25 per
cent of Londoners.

Fenton House

Hampstead Grove, NW3 (071 435 3471).
Hampstead underground. **Open** May- Oct
11am-5pm Sat-Wed. **Admission** £2.50
adults; £1.25 children. **No credit cards.**
Built in 1693, Fenton House is one of the earliest William and Mary style houses, set in a
walled garden. It boasts a collection of pictures, porcelain, furniture and keyboard
instruments, including a 1612 harpsichord.
Wheelchair access to ground floor only.

Kensington Palace

Kensington Gardens, W8 (071 937 9561).
Queensway or High Street Kensington underground. **Open** 9am-5pm Mon-Sat; 1-5pm Sun.
Admission £3 adults; £1.50 children; £2
OAPs, students, UB40s. **No credit cards.**
William and Mary came here in 1689 to
escape from Whitehall Palace. The State
Apartments have been open to the public
since 1899 and the Court Dress Collection is
a unique collection dating from the mid-eigh-
teenth century onward.
Café. Group discount. Shop. Wheelchair
access to ground floor only.

The **Old Royal Observatory** (listed under **Plague and Fire**) commands
a fine view across Greenwich Park to the **National Maritime Museum**, the
Queen's House and beyond. The National Maritime Museum is the world's
largest maritime collection, and tells the story of Britain and the sea. The
Observatory was founded by Charles II in 1675 to find a solution to the problem
of determining longitude at sea. It's the home of Greenwich Mean Time and the
zero meridian line, dividing the globe into East and West.

Georgian London

The Georgian period gave us: Nash terraces; gin palaces; the first stock market crash; and the name George.

The vogue for calling Englishmen George began less than 300 years ago, when a succession of German fathers and sons, sharing the same name, became Kings of England for more than a hundred years.

George I (1660-1727). An unpopular man who spoke no English and made no effort to learn. He divorced and imprisoned his wife for 32 years for infidelity, left government to his fawning ministers and all but ended the monarchy by being implicated in the infamous South Sea Bubble stock market collapse of 1720. Building legacies: all the Hawksmoor churches; much of Spitalfields; Hanover Square; Cavendish Square; St Martin-in-the-Fields; Church Row, NW3.

George II (1683-1760). Famous both for his patronage of Handel and for being the last English king to take part in a battle. He relied heavily on Britain's first prime minister, Robert Walpole, for government and paved the way for constitutional monarchy. Building legacies: St Bartholomew's Hospital; Berkeley Square; Mansion House; Horse Guards; Marylebone Road; Euston Road.

George III (1738-1820). The king who is remembered for having lost Britain the American colonies. His mental health deteriorated in the 1780s, and by 1811 he was completely insane. Building legacies: Bedford Square; Portland Place; Lord North Street; Somerset House; Baker Street; Russell Square; The Docks; Dulwich Art Gallery.

George IV (1762-1830). Because of his father's insanity, he ruled as Regent from 1811-1820, and in his own right from 1820-1830. The duration of his reign was called The Regency. His first marriage – to a Catholic – was declared invalid, while his second to a Protestant ended in separation after only a few years. He was clever, even artistic, but given to such bouts of dissipa-

tion and extravagance that his behaviour seriously discredited the monarchy. His intimate friendship with the architect John Nash gave rise to many of London's more spectacular edifices, including Regent Street, Regent's Park Terraces and Buckingham Palace. Other building legacies: Eaton Square; British Museum; Belgrave Square.

William IV (1765-1837). 'Silly Billy' was little more than an idle philanderer, siring ten illegitimate children by an Irish actress (paid for as always by the long suffering Georgian tax payer) before marrying someone more suitable and siring none. He was succeeded by his niece Victoria. Building legacy: the National Gallery.

Museum of London
*150 London Wall, EC2 (071 600 3699). Barbican (closed Sun), St Paul's underground or Moorgate underground/BR/4, 141, 279A.. **Open** 10am-6pm Tue-Sat; 2-6pm Sun, Bank Holidays. **Admission** free. **Credit** (shop only) A, £TC, V.*
The museum's new eighteenth-century gallery provides a good general synopsis of life in Georgian London. Exhibits have been collated mainly from the lives and homes of the well-to-do classes; there's George III's writing desk, a magnificent doll's house, a silver ceremonial trumpet, and a mahogany mousetrap. Period music accompanies the show: extracts from Handel's *Messiah*, one of Haydn's *London Symphonies*, and songs. *See also chapter* **Museums**.
Braille guide and taped commentary for the visually impaired. Lectures and films with induction loop for the hard of hearing. Restaurant (10am-5pm Tue-Sat; noon-5pm Sun). Shop. Toilets for the diasabled. Wheelchair access.

ARCHITECTURE

The design of the Georgian house emerged from a coincidence of constraints: money, space and building regulations. The inventiveness necessary to unite and subdue these impediments, produced what many consider to be peerless in terms of efficient building design.

The Great Fire of 1666 may have been an unmitigated disaster in terms of damage, but it provided Londoners with an unprecedented opportunity to radically rebuild their city.

By the time the area of **Spitalfields** (*see* **picture and caption**) in East London had been built in the first quarter of the eighteenth century, the Georgian town house had already achieved a more or less standard design. A stroll around here is the quickest way of getting to know early Georgian architecture. A leaflet entitled *A Walk Through Spitalfields* is available from the **Tower Hamlets Environment Trust** (*071 377 0481*).

Spitalfields enjoyed a boom period as a silk-weaving centre in the eighteenth century but the area was subsequently neglected by the authorities and became the home of a succession of impoverished immigrant communities. After the silk weavers came East European Jews, and latterly a community of Bengalis which has perpetuated the textile tradition with large numbers of synthetic fabric warehouses and sweat-shops. A substantial square building at the end of **Fournier Street**, E1 is a paradigm for the changing community: built in 1743 as a French Protestant church, it has subsequently seen service as a Methodist chapel, a synagogue, and now a mosque.

INTERIORS

Strictly speaking, the definition of an antique is an artefact manufactured before the year 1830, the presumed date of the industrial revolution. In our modern day view, the Georgian era was one when the greatest handicraft skills were widely practised. Certainly there can have been few finer furniture makers than **Thomas Chippendale** or **Thomas Sheraton** and a tour of those antique furniture shops specializing in Georgian items will do nothing to dislodge the opinion.

Genuine Georgian shop fronts in London are extremely rare. One of the finest is at **56 Artillery Lane**, E1, although the computer company behind its period panes appears not to recognize the pricelessness of its façade.

The interior of a Georgian town house conformed to certain patterns. Pairs of oak- or pine-panelled rooms were situated at the front of each floor. A smaller room shared the rear of the house with a dog-leg staircase running up through the house. Attics and basement kitchens were for servants.

Dennis Severs' House
18 Folgate Street, E1 (071 247 4013). Liverpool Street underground/BR. **Open** three times per week for theatrical performances, played to an audience of eight people. Phone for details **Performance** 7.30pm.. **Admission** *Performance* £25; *tour* £5. **No credit cards.**
In a performance lasting three hours, Mr Severs' eight paying guests become ghosts of an imaginary family, who inhabit the various rooms of the house (built 1724) between the years 1685 and 1919. It's a great introduction to the flavours and feelings of eighteenth-century life. The house is also open occasionally for tours – phone for details. You should book about three weeks in advance for the shows; although it's always worth phoning to see if there's been a cancellation. The house is marked by a canary (a popular eighteenth-century pet) in a wicker cage, hanging outside the front door next to a gas lantern.

NEO-CLASSICISM
As the century wore on, new architectural ideas served to modify the Georgian terraced house, though none managed to change its basic, straightforward shape. Palladian and neo-classical styles (which widely influenced the architecture of larger mansions and country houses) added door arches, stucco façades, elegant interior plasterwork, reproduction carvings of figures and motifs from antiquity, and a mathematical precision and regularity of design that was readily associated with the ancients. Many Georgian terraces still stand in London but few have been left untouched by the intervening years. Only **Bedford Square**, WC1 and **Lord North Street**, SW1, off Smith Square, remain untarnished.

GREAT ARCHITECTS
If buildings in the earlier part of the century had been erected largely by anonymous builders, in the latter half it became a matter of some social cachet to have a house built by a well-known architect. Property owners, speculators and the state all vied with each other to commission the likes of John Adam (Portland Place); his brother Robert Adam (the Courtauld Institute at 20 Portman Square); William Kent (Horse Guards; 44 Berkeley Square and its marvellous interior); John Soane (Dulwich Picture Gallery); William Chambers (Somerset House); Robert Smirke (British Museum); William Wilkins (National Gallery); and Decimus Burton (the Athenaeum).

And then there was John Nash, whose work is the apotheosis of late-Georgian architecture; his extravagant plans for London, including Regent Street and Buckingham Palace, were heartily supported by the Prince Regent, the future George IV.

Yet it is to the eternal discredit of the Victorians and later commercially-motivated twentieth century entrepreneurs that almost all of Nash's Regent Street has been pulled down. Only Suffolk Place and the eccentric church of All Soul's, Langham Place remain to tell the tale. Even the present façade of Buckingham Palace is a later, Victorian addition. The Marble Arch too, was moved in 1847 to its present site, at the north east corner of Hyde Park, as a result of the redevelopment of the Palace.

Sir John Soane's Museum
13 Lincoln's Inn Fields, WC2 (071 405 2107). Holborn underground. **Open** 10am-5pm Tue-Sat. **Admission** free.
See **picture and caption**.
Guided tour (2.30pm Sat).

COUNTRY SEATS
Elegant uniformity that eventually became overpowering may have characterised Georgian urban architecture, but the country seats of the period were remarkable in how much they differed from each other. London today has grown so large that many of the estates, once considered so charmingly rural and far from the madness of the city, are well within its boundaries.

Chiswick House
Burlington Lane, W4 (081 995 0508). Turnham Green underground/Chiswick BR. **Open** *Apr-Sept* 10am-6pm daily; *Oct-Mar* 10am-4pm daily. **Admission** £1.65 adults; £1.05 OAPs, students, UB40s; 70p children. **No credit cards.**
The Italian architect Andrea Palladio's architectural studies of ancient buildings influenced designers more than any other in the eighteenth century. Lord Burlington's 1729 design for this exquisite mansion is based on Palladio's Villa Rotunda in Vicenza and was realized the architect William Kent (also responsible for Horse Guards Parade). The furniture and decoration include many fine period examples.
Group discount.

Spitalfields *(listed under* **Architecture***) was a haven for French protestant Huguenots fleeing persecution in Catholic France. Many of them were silk weavers and Spitalfields quickly became the European centre of the silk trade. Weaver's houses are distinguished by the large-windowed lofts where the looms were kept. The silk worms fed on mulberry leaves in the basement and the ground floor shops sold the silk cloth (examples of which can be seen at the* **Victoria & Albert Museum***; see chapter* **Museums***).*

Kenwood House

*Hampstead Lane, NW3 (081 348 1286).
Highgate, Archway or Golders Green underground/210 bus.* **Open** *Apr-Sept* 10am-6pm
daily; *Nov-Jan* 10am-4pm daily; *Oct, Feb,
Mar* 10am-5pm daily. **Admission** free.

The Gainsboroughs and Rembrandts
(including one of his famous Self Portraits)
displayed here are worth visiting for their
own sake, quite apart from the house. The
latter's present shabbiness is rather appealing and should not be renovated: no lived-in
house was ever pristine. Georgian painting
and furniture are of the highest quality.
There is no more life-enhancing way of
accounting for a warm summer Saturday
than a visit to the house and gardens followed by evening attendance at one of
Kenwood's lakeside concerts (*see chapter*
London by Season).
Café. Gift shop. Wheelchair access.

Marble Hill House

*Richmond Road, Twickenham, Middlesex
(081 892 5115). Richmond
underground/BR/33, 90B, 202, 270, 290
bus.* **Open** 10am-6pm *Apr-Sept* 10am-4pm
Oct-Mar **Admission** free.
See **picture and caption**.
See also chapter **Music: Classical & Opera**.
*Café (Apr-Sept). Wheelchair access to
ground floor only.*

Osterley Park

*Osterley, Isleworth, Middlesex (081 560 3918).
Osterley underground.* **Open** 11am-4.30pm
Tue-Sun. **Admission** £2 adults; £1 children,
OAPs, students, UB40s. **No credit cards.**

There are only so many state rooms you can
see before boredom sets in. The fascinating
parts of Osterley are the rooms 'below
stairs', the kitchens, the housekeeper's
rooms and the head butler's offices. This
was where real life happened. The well-worn
sideboards and work surfaces seem to summon ghosts and the list of wage payments
on the wall only encourages the pretence.
The gardens are extensive and magnificent
with huge cedars, spreading oaks, and a
very old mulberry tree, its trunk enclosed in
a wooden frame to ward off young, would-be
climbers. The artificial lake is restful and the
small floating pagoda, a gift from an oriental
financial corporation, is a mild visual joke.
*Café (Apr-Oct). Group discount. Tour by
prior arrangement.*

Syon House

*Syon Park, Brentford, Middlesex (081 560
0881). Gunnersbury underground/Syon Lane
BR/237, 267 bus.* **Open** *Apr-Oct* noon-
4.15pm Sun-Thur; *Gardens* 10am-dusk daily.
Admission £1.75 adults; £1.25 children,
OAPs; *Gardens* £1.50 adults; £1 children,
OAPs. *Combined ticket* £3 adults; £2 children. **No credit cards.**

This house is arguably Robert Adam's masterpiece and was achieved when the architect was at the height of his fame as the
nation's greatest architect. His task was to
remodel an existing house that had been the
home of the Percy family (the Earls of
Northumberland) since 1594. Nowadays all
rooms on the ground floor (except the toilet) are accessible to both men and women,
but in the eighteenth century the gender of
the rooms was clearly defined and they were
decorated accordingly. The long gallery
leading to the circular bird-cage room was
designed for use by the ladies and reaches

Sir John Soane's Museum (*listed under* **Architecture: Great Architects**)
*is Britain's smallest and most unusual national museum. Sir John (1753-1837),
a contemporary rival of John Nash, was not only a superb architect but also an
avid collector of sublimely beautiful objects, from Hogarth's* The Rake's Progress
*to the sarcophagus of Seti I, pharaoh of Egypt 1303-1290 BC. He had the good
sense to leave his house and its contents for later generations to explore, sketch and
gaze at in awe. The lanterned room, bristling with statues, is quite an experience.*

the very height of camp with its pastel purples, greens, delicate light grey, sickly-sweet
pinks and relieving white. The dining room,
ante-room, and hall, on the other hand, were
bastions of male superiority and are fittingly
adorned with the serious figures of classical
heroism. The grounds were landscaped by
Capability Brown.
*Car Park. National Trust shop. Wheelchair
access to gardens only.*

WHAT'S UP DOCK?

The River Thames had always been
one of the focal points of London life,
one of its principal thoroughfares
and one of its most accessible public
stages. A picture by Canaletto hanging in the entrance of the **Museum
of London** (*see above*) depicts the
Lord Mayor's procession of 1775
when it went by river in a giant
flotilla of disparate boats from
Mansion House to Westminster.
Even then overcrowding was a problem, and even if the event in the picture was a special occasion, it's easy
to imagine how congestion would
soon become a serious problem.

From 1802, the docks were built.

They revolutionized London's river
life and in many ways were the key
to London's (and by extension, the
nation's) greater prosperity.

Because Britain's trans-global
empire was based on trade, there
were few exotic goods destined for
the West, that did not first go through
London's docks. All the coffee drunk
in Europe in the eighteenth and nineteenth centuries passed first through
Britain's capital. London became the
greatest and richest middle man in
the history of world trade (*see chapter*
River & Docklands).

THE POOR

Just as today, London is roughly
divided into the wealthy West End
and the poorer East End, so the
eighteenth century knew the same
distinction between port and court.
The docks and associated industries
thrived on a surfeit of cheap labour,
which became even cheaper as
more and more people from the
provinces came in search of work.

Poverty in Georgian London was

on a par with the conditions in some third-world countries today. Dr Johnson's splendid four-storey house off Fleet Street (*see below* **Home Sweet Home**) was within a stone's throw (literally) of slums where 20 people a week died of starvation.

The usual picture of life during this period is not tainted with such unsavoury facts, inherited as it is from the sanitized world of Hollywood, or jolly anecdotes about Dr Johnson and his cronies. We think of hearty, red-faced squires and generous, buxom tarts. The reality was very different, with areas such as Covent Garden becoming one huge, dangerous whore-house.

Worse still, the well-off seemed completely impervious to compassion, for they not only found the squalid surroundings that bred prostitution a source of comedy, they also regularly amused themselves with organized trips to Bedlam (Bethlehem Hospital, since become the Imperial War Museum) to mock the mental patients. It goes without saying that the eight-times yearly executions at Tyburn (close to where Marble Arch now stands) were among the most popular events on the social calendar.

A LOOTIN' & A SHOOTIN'

Where poverty is, crime thrives and the lack of any cohesive law-keeping force only exacerbated the situation. In the decade from 1770 to 1780, the Prince of Wales, the Prime Minister, and the Lord Chancellor were all robbed in broad daylight in the West End, and the Lord Mayor was held up at pistol point on Turnham Green.

In 1780, London was hit by the Gordon Riots, the worst in its violent history. They started when Lord George Gordon, an MP, led a crowd of 50,000 to Parliament with a petition against the repeal of anti-Roman Catholic legislation. Gordon soon lost control of his mob which, apparently forgetting why it had assembled, spent the next five days looting and pillaging the capital. Prisons were burnt down and the inmates set free; a distillery was broken into; Downing Street and the Bank of England were unsuccessfully stormed. The riots were eventually suppressed with the loss of 850 lives.

Spaniard's Inn
Spaniards Road, NW3 (081 455 3276). Hampstead underground/210, 268 bus. **Open** 11am-11pm Mon-Sat; noon-3pm, 7-10.30pm, Sun.
The registered ghost of a grey lady inhabits this low-ceilinged, oak-panelled pub, built 1585 when it was the home of the Spanish ambassador to James I. The Gordon rioters (1780) refuelled here but the landlord managed to keep them drinking for so long that the King's Guards were able to catch up with and apprehend them.
Children admitted. Garden.

A PINT OF GIN, PLEASE

Drink was both the catalyst that turned misery into crime and the anaesthetic that distanced poverty's problems. Cheap gin was the ruin of many. The average per capita consumption (children very much included) was two pints a week. This resulted in an appalling death rate: in the years 1725 to 1750, three out of four children aged one to five died.

The problem was that society was still relatively new to mass-produced booze and had not thought to regulate its availability or price. And even when the government did try to pass legislation, the breweries, unwilling to see their sources of revenue restricted, resisted change with the help of powerful parliamentary allies. It was not until Victoria was on the throne that the licensed public house came into being.

Nowadays, of course, the imbibing of alcohol is a comparatively civilized activity pursued on legal premises all over the country. Many of them are original eighteenth-century buildings. All the pubs listed serve food.

Assembly House
292 Kentish Town Road, NW5 (071 485 2031). Kentish Town underground. **Open** 11am-11pm Mon-Sat; noon-3pm, 7-10.30pm, Sun.
This was once the assembly point for travellers who believed that safety in numbers would thwart highwaymen, like Dick Turpin, who also drank here. It's now a cavernous Irish pub.

Dog & Duck
34 Bateman Street, W1 (071 437 3478). Leicester Square or Tottenham Court Road underground. **Open** noon-11pm Mon-Sat; noon-3pm, 7-10.30pm, Sun.
Nothing's changed since 1773 except the customers. Varnished oak, Georgian tiles and frosted glass in the smallest pub in Soho.

In line with contemporary three-dimensional architectural experiments, **Marble Hill House** *(listed under* **Architecture: Country Seats***) has the proportions of a cube – it's in fact wider at the top than at the bottom. This fine example of the Palladian style was commissioned by Henrietta Howard, the mistress of George II, and designed by Lord Herbert and the builder Roger Morris. The interior Cube Hall contains fine moulded decoration. Those interested in Georgian furniture and fine art could do worse than start here.*

Dirty Dicks

202 Bishopsgate, EC2 (071 283 5888).
Liverpool Street underground/BR. **Open**
11am-9pm Mon-Fri; noon-3pm Sun. **Lunch
served** Mon-Fri, Sun.
In 1787, when Nathaniel Bentley's fiancée
died on the eve of their wedding, he lost his
mind and never washed again, saying,
'what's the point? If I wash today, I will be
dirty again tomorrow'. Cobwebs, skeletal
mice and a mummified cat remind drinkers
of the former proprietor, in an original cellar
bar (built 1745).
Restaurant.

The Owl & The Pussycat

34 Redchurch Street, E2 (071 739 2808).
Shoreditch underground. **Open** 11am-3pm, 5-
11pm, Mon-Thur; 11am-11pm Fri; 11am-
3pm, 7-11pm, Sat; noon-3pm, 7-10.30pm, Sun.
A fine Georgian edifice, built 1720, with a
pleasant garden.
Children admitted.

Ye Olde Windmill

*Clapham Common South Side, SW4 (081
673 4578). Clapham Common or Clapham
South underground.* **Open** 11am-11pm Mon-
Sat; noon-3pm, 7-10.30pm, Sun.
An eighteenth-century coaching inn and
meeting point for local hearties before athletic challenges on the Common, where outdoor drinking still takes place.
*Accommodation. Children admitted to garden
patio. Summer barbecues.*

REFORM

For the most part, the poor stayed
poor, and the drunk stayed drunk in
the eighteenth century. Reformers
were few and far between, though
there were some notable exceptions.
Henry Fielding, the satirical writer,
critic of society's ills, and author of
the picaresque novel *Tom Jones* was
also an enlightened magistrate at
Bow Street Court. In 1751, he established, with his brother John, a volunteer force of 'thief-takers' to back
up the often ineffective efforts of the
parish constables and watchmen
who were the only law-keepers in
the city. This freelance group of
early cops later became known as
the Bow Street Runners, to whom
the present day Metropolitan police
force may trace its origins.

Perhaps surprisingly, many of
London's great hospitals were
founded in this uncaring century. St
Thomas's and St Bartholomew's
had already been established as

monastic institutions for the care of
the sick, but Westminster (1720),
Guy's (1725), St George's (1734),
London (1740), and Middlesex
(1745) Hospitals were all instituted
in the eighteenth century.

Fortunately, few eighteenth-century surgical techniques are practised today, though there is one
magnificent reminder of what it was
like to visit the doctor then:

St Thomas's Old
Operating Theatre

*9A St Thomas Street, SE1 (081 806
4325/071 955 5000 ext 3182). London
Bridge underground/BR.* **Open** 12.30-4pm
Mon, Wed, Fri. **Admission** £1 adults; 60p
children. **No credit cards.**
Vistors climb a narrow, winding flight of 37
stairs to the belfry of an old church. In a
well-lit adjoining room, ancient banks of
viewing stands rise in semi-circles round a
crude wooden bed (really no more than an
adapted kitchen table). Close your eyes and
you can almost hear the screams from an
unanaesthetised, blindfolded patient, as the
blood-stained surgeon carefully saws
through his leg. This is one of the most vivid
museums in London and it was discovered
only by accident some 20 years ago. Many
exhibits are labelled and explained with lov-
ing care; pictures show all too graphically
how far the world has progressed.

GOD
ALMIGHTY

One body that should have known
better and didn't was the established church, which reached
superlative heights of self-satisfied
complacency in the eighteenth century. Having seen off the last of all
Catholic attempts for equality in the
kingdom with George I's accession,
there was for a while no other religious organization to challenge the
supremacy of the Church of
England. Parsons grew plump and
smug while the poor increased in
numbers outside their vestries. For,
while the eighteenth century witnessed the building of some of
London's most attractive churches,
there is little evidence to suggest
that the poor took part in the services and everything to suggest that
they would have been shooed away
had they tried. Well they must have
smelt terrible, mustn't they?

Christchurch, Spitalfields

Commercial Street, E1 (071 247 7202). **Open**
for concerts, otherwise apply at the crypt door.
This is the largest of Hawksmoor's
churches, currently undergoing restoration
work which should be finished by early

There's no better way to enjoy the soaring magnificence of **St Martin-in-the-
Fields** *(listed under* **God Almighty**) *than to attend one of the midday
lunchtime concerts on Mondays and Tuesdays throughout the year. James
Gibbs's beautiful church must have been one of the most influential of its time.
The wide portico is topped with a spire built on a tower; the interior is plain,
but embellished with dark woodwork and ornate Italian platerwork.*

1990. Its neat, triangular spire towers above the splendid Georgian houses in Spitalfields like a beacon. The crypt has been turned into a rehabilitation centre for alcoholics.

St Alfege with St Peter & St Paul
Greenwich High Road, SE10 (081 858 3458). Greenwich BR. **Open** 11am-3pm Mon, Wed-Fri; 2-4pm Sat, Sun.
The greatest Georgian churchbuilder was Nicholas Hawksmoor, who won a state contract to erect 50 new churches in and around the capital. In fact, only 11 were ever realized, but they rank among London's finest and his Greenwich church is perhaps the best of all. Sadly, especially as the woodwork was by one of the century's finest craftsmen (Grinling Gibbons), the interior decoration was thrown out and destroyed by the Victorians, but it is still a restful place to sit and think in the middle of Greenwich town. General Wolfe of Quebec is buried in the crypt.

St George
Bloomsbury Way, WC1 (071 405 3044). Holborn or Tottenham Court Road underground. **Open** 10am-3pm Mon-Fri. **Services** 1.10pm Wed, Fri; 10am, 6.30pm, Sun.
Another of Hawksmoor's churches and the only one he sited west of the City. With a nod to antiquity, the spire is obelisk-shaped. With another to royalty, the statue on top is of George I, masquerading as St George. The unpopular king's effigy was the target of some cruel practical jokes at the time.

St Martin-in-the-Fields
Trafalgar Square, WC2 (071 930 1862). Charing Cross underground/BR. **Open** 7.30am-7.30pm daily. **Services** 8am, 8.30am, 5.30pm, 6pm Mon-Fri; 1.05pm Wed; 12.30pm Fri; 8am, 9.45am (choral), 11.30am, 12.30pm, 2.45pm (service in Cantonese), 6.30pm, 7.30pm Sun.
See **picture and caption.**

JOHN WESLEY
One disgruntled member of the public who did not believe the church was doing all it could for the world was the great John Wesley, founder of Methodism. An account of the conversion of this eighteenth century Savanarola is written in stone outside the entrance to the **Museum of London** (*see above*). While he never missed an opportunity to preach, there is also no record of his ever having bored anybody. He gave his life to a methodical god and his money to the unmethodical poor.

Museum of Methodism
Wesley Chapel, 49 City Road, EC1 (071 253 2262). Old Street underground. **Open** 10am-4pm Mon-Sat. **Service** followed by lunch and guided tour,11am Sun. **Admission** *Museum or house* 75p adults; 40p children, OAPs, UB40s. *Joint ticket* £1.20 adults; 60p children, OAPs, UB40s. **No credit cards.**
In both Chapel and house all artefacts and memorials of the great philanthrope's life are original. The crypt houses a museum containing the most curious collection of

oddments pertaining to the growth of the religion. The wardens of the premises still maintain traditions that Wesley started. For a mere £1.50, worshippers may partake of simple lunches after midday services on Thursdays and Sundays.
Films. Shop. Tour by prior arrangement.

HOME, SWEET HOME

The Georgian era had its fair share of Very Important People. A few of them left their houses behind so that admirers from future epochs might come and pay them tribute.

Hogarth's House
Hogarth Lane, Great West Road, W4 (081 994 6757). Turnham Green underground/Chiswick BR. **Open** *Apr-Aug* 11am-6pm Mon, Wed-Sat; 2-6pm Sun; *Sept-Mar* 11am-4pm Mon, Wed-Sat; 2-4pm Sun (closed first two weeks in Sept and last three weeks in Dec). **Admission** free.
Hogarth's modest domicile has been restored more or less faithfully to its eighteenth-century condition and now provides

wall-space for some 200 of the great social commentator's prints, though his most famous work, the Rake's Progress, is present only in the form of photographic copies. The original is in **Sir John Soane's Museum** (*see above*).
Car Park. Gift shop. Tour by prior arrangement. Wheelchair access.

Dr Johnson's House
17 Gough Square, Fleet Street, EC4 (071 353 3745). Temple, Blackfriars or Chancery Lane underground. **Open** *May-Sept* 11am-5.30pm Mon-Sat; *Oct-Apr* 11am-5pm Mon-Sat. **Admission** £1.70 adults, £1 children, OAPs, students. **No credit cards.**
See **picture and caption.**
Shop.

Keats' House
Keats Grove, NW3 (071 435 2062). Hampstead underground/Hampstead Heath BR. **Open** *Apr-Oct* 2-6pm Mon-Fri; 10am-5pm Sat; 2-5pm Sun. *Nov-Mar* 1-5pm Mon-Fri; 10am-5pm Sat; 2-5pm Sun. **Admission** free.
The tragic Romantic poet penned many of his most inspired compositions here. Relics of the consumptive versifier's life tell a fascinating, if poignant, story. The library is much visited by students and connoisseurs of his works. *See chapter* **Museums.**
Tour and access to library by prior arrangement.

Dr Johnson's House (*listed under* **Home Sweet Home***) is a splendid example of a grand Georgian town house. The dog-leg staircase running up the rear of the building gives onto successive landings and pairs of rooms at the front of the house. The long top room is where he compiled his famous dictionary, which includes the definition: 'Dull: To make dictionaries is dull work'. Furnishings are few and visitors who go to see the great man's possessions will be disappointed. Those who go for the atmosphere won't be.*

Victorian Times

The Victorians built dark satanic mills and charted the last days of greatness for the first industrial nation.

London in Victorian times (strictly speaking 1837-1901) was a city of uncomfortable extremes. It was the capital of an empire that spanned one fifth of the globe and yet it was a city of squalor, poverty and prostitution. The dramatic increase in the inner-city population could only be dealt with by more effective government, more housing (particularly south of the river), a national education system, police, prisons, railways, cleaner water supplies, bigger docks, and safer factories.

CLEAN WATER

In an age famed for its engineering miracles, it took a surprisingly long time before the link between disease and drinking water was established. Before Edwin Chadwick managed to carry the Public Health Act through Parliament, cholera was claiming the lives of over 2,000 people a week at its height in 1849. The problem was simply that independent suppliers pumped unfiltered water direct from the Thames to communal street fonts. But it wasn't until 1860 that Sir Joseph Bazalgette devised a system to direct sewage to the Thames estuary via the Victoria and Albert Embankments.

Kew Bridge Steam Museum
Kew Bridge Pumping Station, Green Dragon Lane, Brentford, Middlesex (081 568 4757). Gunnersbury underground/Kew Bridge BR/27, 65, 237, 267 bus. **Open** 11am-5pm daily. **Admission** £1 adults; 50p under-16s, OAPs, students, £2.75 family ticket (2 adults, 3 children) Mon-Fri; £1.80 adults; 90p under-16s, OAPs, students; £5 family ticket Sat, Sun, Bank Holidays. **No credit cards.** *Group discount. Guided tour. Shop. Wheelchair access.*
See **picture and caption.**

HOME & HEARTH

In Victorian times the type of houses built varied as widely as the division between rich and poor. The success or failure of an area depended to a large extent on whether the railway ran through or near it. At the bottom of the pile were humble tenements, in line after line of bleak terraced houses adjacent to the tracks. The areas intended for the rich, such as **Belgravia**, SW1, were the most carefully planned, with generous-sized houses and elegant frontages, often built around squares.

Brixton
SW9. Brixton underground/BR.
Row after row of typical Victorian workers' terraces are found in the streets to the south and north of the Brixton Road. Many of the houses have been gentrified in the last few years as Brixton increasingly becomes colonized by the wealthy young.

Leighton House Museum
12 Holland Park Road, W14 (071 602 3316). High Street Kensington underground. **Open** 11am-5pm Mon-Sat. **Admission** free. Leighton House, designed by Lord Leighton in 1866 in collaboration with George Aitchison, derives its inspiration directly from the East. Its most striking feature is the exotic Arab Hall added in 1879. This domed structure, with its elaborate Persian tiles, mosaic floor and square fountain, has a startling cupola of stained glass. The unusual tiles were collected by Leighton and friends from frequent trips to Damascus, Rhodes and Cairo. Leighton, himself an artist of no mean repute, has a permanent collection of works on display.

Linley Sambourne House
18 Stafford Terrace, W8 (Victorian Society 081 994 1019). High Street Kensington underground. **Open** Mar-Oct 10am-4pm Wed; 2-5pm Sun. **Admission** £1.50. **No credit cards.**
Edward Linley Sambourne was a leading *Punch* cartoonist and political illustrator of the late Victorian and Edwardian period. His eccentric town house retains its original fittings and decorations (the wallpaper, carpet and textile designs are by William Morris). There is a magnificent clutter of period furniture, prints, photographs and ceramics.

Apsley House
149 Piccadilly, W1 (071 499 5676). Hyde Park Corner underground. **Open** 11am-5pm Tue-Sun. **Admission** £2 adults, £1 OAPs, students, under 16s. **No credit cards.**
The extensive collection of paintings and memorabilia belonging to the Duke of Wellington pays tribute to his enormous military and social stature. The victor at Waterloo and later Prime Minister, the Iron Duke referred to his home as 'No 1 London'. Works of art abound, and there's a portrait of Wellington by Goya. One of the more eccentric touches is an 11 ft/3.3m statue of the diminutive Napoleon.

BASTIONS OF EMPIRE

There are several examples in the city that demonstrate the lavish potential of Victorian design. Neo-Gothic, inspired by the medieval architecture of Europe, was the fashion at the beginning of Victoria's reign. One of the best examples is Pugin and Barry's **Houses of Parliament** (1837). **The Royal Exchange** is typical of the other favoured style, classical, and dominates Mansion House Place opposite the Bank of England.

The Gothic influence re-emerged in the substantial shape of the **Royal Courts of Justice**, designed by GE Street in the 1870s. and the glass-domed sheds in **St Pancras** railway station (*see below*).

A significant development for retailing was the abolition of the tax on glass which enabled ornate glass-fronted shopping arcades to flourish (notably in the vicinity of the **Royal Arcade** and **Leadenhall Market**). It also allowed Joseph Paxton to build the Crystal Palace (*see below* **The Great Exhibition**).

Athenaeum
107 Pall Mall, SW1. Piccadilly Circus underground.
Named after Emperor Hadrian's university in Rome, the classically-styled Athenaeum was designed by Decimus Burton and frequented by government ministers, bishops and writers. Although not open to the public, a visit may be arranged by writing to the Club Secretary.

Houses of Parliament
Westminster, SW1 (071 219 4273). Westminster underground. **Open** 2.30pm-10pm (or later) Mon-Thur; 9.30am-3pm Fri. **Admission** free.
Charles Barry and Augustus Pugin's magnificent building epitomized the aspirations

of a nation confident of her future. Admission to the visitors' galleries of both Houses is free, but you'll need a ticket for Question Times (Monday to Thursday 2.30-3.30pm, with Prime Minister's Question Time on Tuesday and Thursday). Tours can be obtained only by writing to your MP or embassy in London. *See chapter* **Sightseeing**.

Leadenhall Market
Whittington Avenue, EC3. Bank underground. Open 7am-3pm Mon-Fri.
Horace Jones's curved arcades of iron and glass (1881), house a market that was and still is a splendid place to buy both exotic and mundane foodstuffs. The market remains one of the few surviving bastions of the cockney barrow boy. *See chapter* **The City**.

Royal Arcade
connects Albemarle Street with Old Bond Street, W1. Green Park or Piccadilly Circus underground.
This fashionable shopping promenade, built in 1879, used to count Queen Victoria amongst its regular customers. The Royal Arcade is similar in style to the nearby Piccadilly and Burlington Arcades.

Royal Courts of Justice
Strand, WC2 (071 936 6000). Aldwych or Temple underground. Open 9.30am-4.30pm Mon-Fri. **Admission** free.
The last great Gothic building of the Victorian Age, the Law Courts are a cloistered and tur-

reted stone counterpart to the brick work of St Pancras (*see chapter* **The City**). *Wheelchair access to main hall only.*

Royal Exchange
Threadneedle Street & Cornhill, EC3 (071 623 0444). Bank underground. Open 11.30am-2pm Mon-Fri. **Admission** free.
Officially opened in 1844, the Royal Exchange was built as a meeting place for merchants and tradesmen. Now it's home to the London International Financial Futures Exchange (*see chapter* **The City**).

Smithfield Market
London Central Markets, West Smithfield, EC1. Farringdon underground/N21, N76, N89, N85, N98 bus. Open 5-10.30am Mon-Fri.
Smithfield has been the largest meat market in London since the Middle Ages. The present huge trading halls are covered by a domed and turreted roof designed by Henry Jones during the 1860s.

RAILWAYS

One of the greatest influences of the Industrial Revolution on Victorian London was the introduction of the railway and eventually the underground network. By the 1860s traffic congestion in the capital had

reached a point where people were prepared to accept any schemes that relieved the situation. The railway companies spent enormous sums of money designing ostentatious train stations to impress the cynical public. Euston Station's classical portico (destroyed by British Rail in 1963 in order to expand the station) cost nearly £40,000, but it fronted some very unspectacular railway sheds and platforms.

In 1863, the first underground line, between Paddington and Farringdon Street, proved an instant success, attracting over 30,000 travellers on the first day. The Metropolitan and Circle lines at Baker Street, NW1, and Great Portland Street, W1, are almost intact examples of mid-Victorian stations. The world's first electric track followed in 1890, opened between King William Street, EC4, and Stockwell, SW9.

In spite of the general enthusiasm for more underground railways, it was an American, Charles Tyson Yerkes, who exploited the idea and started building the Bakerloo, Piccadilly and Northern lines, which form the basis of today's system. Examples of the early underground trains are on view at the **Science Museum** (*see below* **The Great Exhibition**).

For a comprehensive view of Victorian travel, from horse-drawn trams and hackney carriages to the underground system, go to the **London Transport Museum**, 39 Wellington Street, WC2 (*see chapter* **Museums**).

St Pancras Station
Euston Road, NW1. King's Cross underground/BR.
See **picture and caption**.

BRIDGES

London's bridges, the majority of which were constructed during the Victorian era, are alternately ornate, functional, durable and historical. The housing boom south of the river made it expedient to provide a link for these new inhabitants with the business interests on the northern side. And these arteries cemented the two halves of London into a homogeneous, albeit sprawling, whole.

Incidentally, the **London Bridge**

At **Kew Bridge Steam Museum** *(listed under* **Clean Water***) you can see the huge beam engines that pumped most of west London's water until 1944. It's home to the world's largest of these steam-powered monsters; 40 foot/12 metres high, weighing 150 tons/152 tonnes. You can see the engines 'in steam' most weekends and bank holidays. The buildings, dominated by a campanile-style chimney, have a garage-like ambience, perfect for engineering enthusiasts.*

of the nursery rhyme, originally a wooden medieval structure, was replaced several times, penultimately in 1831 by a stone arched bridge. This was what, in 1967, was sold to an American millionaire, who re-erected it in the Arizona desert.

Albert Bridge
SW11. Sloane Square underground/19, 22 bus.
Built during the 1870s, this triple-arched, cast iron bridge is lit like a Christmas tree at night. Traditionally soldiers crossing Albert Bridge must break step because of the fear that their marching rhythm will weaken the structure.

Hammersmith Bridge
W6. Hammersmith underground.
The original Hammersmith Bridge, built in the 1820s, was the first suspension bridge across the Thames. It was replaced in 1887 by the present decorative structure.

Tower Bridge
SE1 (071 407 0922). Tower Hill underground or London Bridge underground/BR/Tower Gateway DLR.
Open *Apr-Oct* 10am-6.30pm daily; *Nov-Mar* 10am-4.45pm daily . **Admission** £2.50 adults; £1 children, OAPs. **Credit** (shop only) A, V .
London's most spectacular and famous bridge, built by Horace Jones and John Wolfe Barry in 1894. The two huge towers rising from the Thames are connected by a high-level footbridge, which offers great views of the city. The drawbridges, raised and lowered to allow large ships to pass through, weigh 1,000 tons/1,016 tonnes apiece. Inside the towers are exhibitions tracing the history, structure and engineering of the bridge. The times when the bascules (drawbridges) are raised are displayed by the ticket office.
Shop. Wheelchair access.

Westminster Bridge
SW1. Westminster underground.
The present bridge, built by Thomas Page and Charles Barry in 1862, measures over 80 ft/24m wide. It has the best views of Parliament, the Victoria and Albert Embankments and the beautiful Edwardian façade of County Hall.

CHURCHES

The Victorians were famous for their moralistic — and hypocritical — standards. A staggering 1,500 churches, of disparate spiritual aspirations and physical appearance, were built in London during this time. The following churches are worth comparing for opulence, innovation and size.

All Saints
7 Margaret Street, W1 (071 636 1788). Oxford Circus underground. **Open** 7.15am-7pm daily. **Services** 7.30am, 8am, 1.10pm, 5.30pm, 6.15pm, Mon-Fri; 7.30am, 8am, 5.30pm, 6.15pm Sat; 8am, 10.20am, 11am, 5.15pm, 6pm Sun.

The decorative exuberance of **St Pancras Station** *(listed under* **Railways***) symbolized the way Victorians justified the disruptive building of railways; they made catching a train an event. Giles Gilbert Scott's 1870s design for the luxury hotel frontage is inspired by late Medieval High Gothic. But the train shed is pure engineering. A lofty 100 feet/30 metres high, with a 240 feet/72 metres span, the glass arch is supported solely by its huge iron ribs. Many times threatened, St Pancras is to be restored in the King's Cross redevelopment.*

Designed by William Butterfield in the 1850s, this masterpiece of Victorian building was the first to use coloured bricks to decorative effect. The neo-Gothic exterior is complemented by an ornate interior, heavy with marble, alabaster and granite.

Brompton Oratory
Thurloe Place, Brompton Road, SW3 (071 589 4811). South Kensington underground.
Open 6.30am-8pm daily. **Services** six masses daily Mon-Sat (phone to check); 7am, 8am, 9am, 10am, 11am (Latin mass), 12.30pm, 4.30pm, 7pm Sun.
Brompton Oratory, built in 1884 by Herbert Gribble, was the leading Catholic church in London until Westminster Cathedral opened its doors in 1903. The most striking feature about this wonderful church, apart from its ornate, heavy Baroque exterior, is the dark, *chiaroscuro* atmosphere of the interior, ribbed with marble and festooned with statues.,

DISCOVERING THE WORLD

When the Victorians were not colonizing the world by brute strength, they had the foresight to combine their conquests with scientific developments. **The Royal Geographical Society** sent navigators to chart unknown waters, botanists to bring back new species, and geologists to study the earth. Many of these specimens ended up in the **Royal Botanic Gardens** at Kew (*see chapters* **Sightseeing** *and* **The River & Docklands**); others found a home in the South Kensington museums (*see below*). The most influential RGS expedition was **Charles Darwin's** voyage on *HMS Beagle*. The very foundations of science and religion were rocked when the naturalist published his theory of evolution.

Charles Darwin Memorial
Down House, Luxted Road, Downe, Orpington, Kent (0689 59119). Bromley South BR, then 146 bus. **Open** 1-6pm Wed-Sun. **Admission** £1.50 adults; £1 OAPs. students; 50p under-15s. **No credit cards.**
Charles Darwin's radical theory of evolution was partly thought-out and written in Down House, where he lived for 40 years. The large house has been restored as closely as possible to its state in Darwin's lifetime and contains the original drawing room and study where he wrote his *Origin of the Species*. A permanent Darwin exhibition is on display in the Western Gallery on the first floor of the **Natural History Museum** and some of the original manuscripts can be

perused in the library of the **British Museum** (*see chapter* **Museums**).
Shop. Wheelchair access.

Royal Geographical Society
Lowther Lane, Kensington Gore, SW7 (071 589 5466). South Kensington underground then 9, 33, 49, 52, 73 bus. **Open** *Main hall and map room* 10am-1pm, 2-5pm Mon-Fri. **Admission** free.
Lowther Lodge is the splendid red brick headquarters of this society dedicated to the exploration of the unknown. The map room has over 800,000 maps, including Livingstone's manuscript maps, his cap and the redoubtable Stanley's boots. There is a fine collection of paintings and nineteenth-century travel photography by fellows of the society.

THE GREAT EXHIBITION

The Great Exhibition of 1851 was the largest single arts and sciences event that had ever been staged. It was held in what Londoners nicknamed the Crystal Palace, a massive iron and glass structure built in Hyde Park.

About 100,000 exhibits from all parts of the globe were assembled. These ranged from stuffed animals to recent technical discoveries such as a steam-driven combine harvester. A staggering total of six million people visited the exhibition during the five months that it was open

When the exhibition finally closed, the Crystal Palace was taken apart and re-assembled at Sydenham where it served as an amusement park until destroyed by fire in 1936. You can learn about it and see the remains at the Crystal Palace Museum (*see chapter* **Museums**).

The profit made from the Great Exhibition of 1851 inspired the ambitious Prince Consort to establish a permanent centre, where the arts and sciences could be studied and applied. Though he never lived to see his vision fulfilled, he sowed the seeds for some of London's most famous museums and institutes.

The **Natural History Museum**, opened its impressive portals in 1881. Designed by Alfred Waterhouse in the style of a medieval cathedral, the building itself is just as awe-inspiring as its formidable collection of dinosaurs.

The **Victoria and Albert Museum** was redesigned by Aston Webb in 1890 so that it could house the congested collections of trea-

sures that had outgrown its original old corrugated structure. Of all London museums, it is undoubtedly the most ornate and lavish.

The **National Portrait Gallery** was erected in the 1890s to glorify those men and women who advanced the cause of Empire and 'civilization'. The gallery now has over 8,000 portraits, sketches and photographs of various heroes and villains from the late fifteenth century to the present day.

A prominent philanthropist, the sugar baron Sir Henry Tate, was the benefactor of the **Tate Gallery**, paying for the building and donating his collection of Victorian art to its wide-ranging collection.

The museum that was most strongly influenced by the Great Exhibition, however, is the **Science Museum**. Its collection of nineteenth-century machine tools, steam engines and mechanical instruments is the most comprehensive explanation of why Britain was once the foremost industrial nation

in the world. On the fourth floor, the excellent **Wellcome Museum** illustrates the history of medicine from pre-Roman times to the present day.

Natural History Museum
Cromwell Road, SW7 (071 938 9123; recorded information 071 725 7866). South Kensington underground. **Open** 10am-6pm Mon-Sat; 1-6pm Sun. **Admission** £2 adults; £1 under-15s, OAPs, students, UB40s; free 4.30-6pm Mon-Fri; 5-6pm Sat, Sun, Bank Holidays. **Credit** (shop only) A, AmEx, £TC, V.
A Diplodocus may have replaced the stuffed elephants that inhabited the Victorian Central Hall, but the museum has lost little of its period character. Many of the original mahogany display cases and stuffed exhibits are still in use (*see chapter* **Museums**). *Café. Discovery room for children (Easter and summer holidays). Films. Lectures. Wheelchair access.*

Royal Albert Hall
Kensington Gore, SW7 (071 589 8212). Knightsbridge or High Street Kensington underground, then 9, 33, 49, 52, 73 bus. **Guided tour** 5 June-mid Sept 10am, noon, 2pm, 3.30pm daily. **Tickets** £2.50 adults; £2 OAPs; £1.50 students, under-15s.
The famous oval concert hall was planned by Prince Albert and built as his memorial after his early death. The full guided tour lasts 60 minutes, and includes the Royal Box

Dickens's House (*listed under* **Writers & Thinkers**) *is a shrine to London's most famous novelist. The house holds an enormous collection of Dickens memorabilia, including portraits of the novelist and his family, personal effects and a comprehensive Dickens library. Although the novelist lived here for just two and a half years, this is where he wrote* Oliver Twist, Nicholas Nickleby *and the last five chapters of* The Pickwick Papers.

Kensal Green Cemetery (listed under **Cemeteries**) was very much an in-place to be buried during Victoria's reign. Famous bodies interred here include the novelists Anthony Trollope and William Thackeray, and engineer Sir Isambard Kingdom Brunel.

plus, if you're lucky, a rehearsal. The half hour tour is just as entertaining, but leaves you breathless (see chapter **Music: Classical & Opera**).

Science Museum
Exhibition Road, SW7 (071 938 8000; recorded information 071 938 8123). South Kensington underground. **Open** 10am-6pm Mon-Sat; 11am-6pm Sun. **Admission** £2 adult; £1 children, OAPs, UB40s. **Credit** (shop only) A, £TC, V.
The museum of the Industrial Age contains a collection of nineteenth-century steam engines, machines and several vital inventions (see chapter **Museums**).
Café. Dillons Bookshop. Dramatized galley talks. Films and lectures by prior arrangement. Group discount. Library. Wheelchair access.

Tate Gallery
Millbank, SW1 (071 821 1313; recorded information 071 821 7128). Pimlico underground. **Open** 10am-5.50pm Mon-Sat; 2-5.50pm Sun. **Admission** free. **Special exhibitions** £3 adults; £1.50 under-16s, OAPs, students, UB40s. **Credit** A, V.
The Tate records an almost definitive story of Victorian painting. The new Clore Gallery chronicles the development of the great JMW Turner with a first-class selection of his work. There are fine examples of nineteenth-century landscape and subject painting; some good Constables, and a superb collection of Pre-Raphaelites, including Millais's fetching Ophelia (see chapter **Art Galleries**).
Café. Shop. Wheelchair access.

Victoria & Albert Museum
Cromwell Road, SW7 (071 938 8500; recorded information; general 071 938 8441; exhibitions 071 938 8349). South Kensington underground/14, 30, 74, 503, C1 bus. **Open** 10am-5.50pm Mon-Sat; 1-5.50pm Sun. **Admission** free (£2 donation requested). **Credit** (shop only) A, AmEx, £TC, V.
The V&A has built up a magnificent collection of commercial art and design. There is an excellent selection of Victorian plate, glass, porcelain, silver, costumes and furniture. The cast courts display life-sized plaster casts of classical and renaissance sculptures and monuments. (see chapter **Museums**.)
Gallery talks (2.30pm). Guided tour. Lectures. Restaurant. Shop. Touch sessions for the visually impaired. Wheelchair access.

WRITERS & THINKERS

The Victorian age had more than its fair share of intellectuals and artists and the closing years of the century witnessed a reaction against the Victorian moral certitude. Uppermost among the writers and thinkers of the period was **Charles Dickens**, much of whose work was concerned with social injustice. The designer, novelist and poet **William Morris** was also moved to write about the conditions of the working class. At the same time, **Karl Marx** was beavering away in the British Library Reading Room writing Das Kapital, the work that would change political thinking irrevocably.

Café Royale
68 Regent's Street, W1 (071 437 9090). Piccadilly Circus underground. **Open** Brasserie noon-11.30pm Mon-Sat; noon-10.30pm Sun; Grill Room noon-2.30pm, 6-11pmMon-Fri; 6-11pm Sat. Cocktail Bar noon-3pm, 5.30-11pm Mon-Sat; noon-6pm Sun; Daniels: food noon-2.30pm Mon-Fri; bar noon-3.30pm Mon-Sat. **Credit** A, AmEx, DC, V.
This fashionable café-restaurant, decorated with huge mirrors and gilded caryatids, was founded by a Parisian wine merchant on a borrowed capital of £5. There will always be a faint taste of scandal and decadence in the air here, a lingering memory from the days when Oscar Wilde and Aubrey Beardsley frequented the café.
Wheelchair access.

Dickens's House
49 Doughty Street, WC1 (071 405 2127). Russell Square or Chancery Lane underground. **Open** 10am-5pm Mon-Sat. **Admission** £1.50 adults, students, UB40s; 75p under-16s; £3 family ticket (2 adults, 3 children). **Credit** (shop only) A, V.
Bookshop (sells first and early editions of Dickens). Research facilities.
See **picture and caption**.

Marx Memorial Library
37-38 Clerkenwell Green, EC1 (071 253 1485). Farringdon underground. **Open** 2-6pm Mon, Fri; 2-9pm Tues-Thur; 11am-1pm Sat (visitors are requested to come before 6pm Tue-Thur, phone on Sat). **Admission** free.
The Marx Memorial Library has an exceptional collection of political, social and philosophic literature. Lenin, the architect of the 1917 Russian Revolution, used an office in the building between 1901 and 1902. Only members may use the library. Marx is buried in **Highgate Cemetery** (see below **Cemeteries**).

William Morris Gallery
Lloyd Park, Forest Road, E17 (081 527 5544, ext 4390). Walthamstow Central underground/BR/34, 48, 69, 123 bus. **Open** 10am-1pm, 2-5pm, Tue-Sat; 10am-noon, 2-5pm 1st Sun every month. **Admission** free. **No credit cards.**
Morris was one of the most influential designers of his time – many of his wallpaper and textile patterns are still in production. The museum shop has tiles hand-painted to an original Morris design at £12.50 each. His wallpaper designs can be bought from Sanderson, 52 Berners Street, W1 (071 636 7800).
See chapter **Museums**.

CEMETERIES

Because of the massive increase in population, and subsequent problems of finding ground to bury bodies, the government was forced to rethink its approach to burials. Public graveyards were hazardous and extremely unhealthy. After a public inquiry into the matter, seven enormous cemeteries were laid out, providing much more agreeable surroundings for the dearly departed who could afford it. The cemeteries were operated by private companies, and one, **Kensal Green**, is still run by the original firm.

Brompton Cemetery
Finborough Road, SW10 (071 352 1201).
West Brompton underground. **Open** dawn-dusk daily.
The main entrance to this graceful cemetery is surrounded by catacombs and is crowned by a triumphal arch. It holds some eminent corpses, including those of Emmeline Pankhurst, the suffragette (died 1928), and Frederick Leyland, patron of the pre-Raphaelites.

Highgate Cemetery
Swain's Lane, N6 (081 340 1834). Archway underground/271 bus. **Open** *Apr-Sept* 10am-5pm daily *Oct-Mar* 10am-4pm daily.
Opened in 1839, this is London's most famous and exotic graveyard. The latest addition, east of Swain's Lane, is the resting place of Karl Marx. But apart from this, the east side is rather crowded and drab. The west side is a romantic wilderness of tombs, catacombs and gravestones covered in ivy and ornate stonework. Usually, this section can only be visited as part of a guided tour (which starts on the hour every hour), but on open days (held on three Sundays a year, phone to check) you can wander around by yourself. Eminent Victorians now residing here include Mrs Henry Wood, wife of the composer, and George Eliot, the female novelist.

Kensal Green Cemetery
Harrow Road, W10 (081 969 0152). **Open** 9am-4.30pm Mon-Sat; 2-4.30pm Sun.
See **picture and caption.**

MONUMENTS

Victorians wanted their heroic monuments to last. Huge, elaborate edifices, frequently dressed in marble, gilt and bronze, they were certainly not to be ignored. However when **Nelson's Column** was erected, many complained that Nelson's features were too crude and his column too high. The **Albert Memorial** in Kensington Gardens was tenuously acclaimed when first unveiled but universally snubbed ten years later.

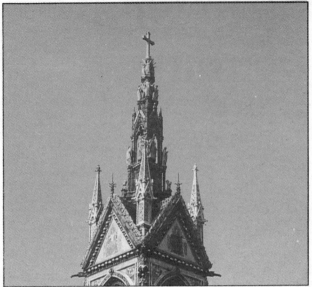

*The **Albert Memorial** (listed under* **Monuments***) is probably the most ostentatious memorial to an individual in Britain. This elaborate folly was built in the early 1870s to mourn the early death of the Prince Consort. A mere 175 feet/5.2 metres high, it's festooned with life-size marble friezes of artists, and crowned by an ornate Gothic canopy. The brooding, bronze figure of a much romanticized Albert sits in contemplation of his brainchild, the museums, institutes and educational faculties of South Kensington.*

Albert Memorial
Kensington Gardens, SW7. Knightsbridge or Kensington High Street underground, then 9, 33, 49, 52, 73 bus.
See **picture and caption.**

Cleopatra's Needle
Victoria Embankment, WC2. Embankment underground.
This 3,500-year-old monument was presented to the British in 1819 by the Turkish Viceroy in Egypt and was finally erected in 1878. One of the many intriguing fact abouts the Needle is that several Victorian items including a copy of *The Times*, a portrait of Queen Victoria and a railway timetable are buried under it in a time capsule.

Eros
Piccadilly Circus, W1. Piccadilly Circus underground.
London's unofficial mascot, this fountain statue is the memorial to the philanthropy of the 7th Earl of Shaftesbury. In fact it's not the God of Love, Eros, at all, but the Angel of Christian Charity. Erected in 1893, it was London's first aluminium statue.

Nelson's Column
Trafalgar Square, WC2. Charing Cross underground.
London's best-known landmark, the 16-ton/tonne statue by Baily, the 168-ft/50m pedestal by Railton and the enormous lions by Landseer were constructed to commemorate the famous admiral who defeated Napoleon in 1805. Today it's a rallying point for political demonstrations and New Year revellers.

Victoria Memorial
Queen's Gardens, Buckingham Palace, SW1. St James's Park underground.
This huge memorial is an unashamed glorification of Victoria's 60-year reign. Standing in front of Buckingham Palace, the 13-ft/3.9m-high Victoria stares implacably down The Mall like a figurine on a heavily iced cake.

WALKS

Victorian Walk
from Tower Hill underground,EC3 to St Thomas's Old Operating Theatre, SE1 (081 806 4325). **Time** *Apr-Nov.* For days and times call the above number. Tickets £3 adults; £2 OAPs, students, UB40s; free accompanied under-14s; includes admission to Operating Theatre Museum.
Organized by Citisights, this walk takes you through the London of Dickens and Florence Nightingale, ending at the **Old Operating Theatre** (*see chapter* **Georgian London**).

INFORMATION

The Victorian Society
(081 994 1019).
A very helpful lot who will try to answer enquiries about period architecture and interiors.

Early 20th Century

As revolution hit the modern world, Londoners danced the night away.

The old order broke up in the early part of the twentieth century. New thinking, new inventions and modernist buildings all transformed ways of living. The Russian Revolution, two major wars, the Depression and, for Britain, the loss of the Empire, opened the floodgates for political and social change. For many, the best way to cope was to live for the day and have a good time.

Modern politics – left versus right – emerged in Edwardian Britain with the rise of the Labour Party. Meanwhile the suffragettes, led by **Emmeline Pankhurst** (*see below*), put up spirited resistance for their rights and equal votes for women, finally achieved in 1928. Lloyd George's government averted revolution in 1918–19 by promising (but not delivering) 'homes for heroes' for the embittered returning soldiers. But socialism did get a brief opportunity in 1924 when the first Labour government was formed by Ramsay MacDonald, who as a pacifist had been disgraced in wartime.

Civil disturbances made the headlines with rising unemployment and increased cost of living. As a result of the 1926 General Strike, when the working classes downed tools en masse, the streets were teeming with army-escorted food convoys, aristocrats running soup kitchens and office workers cycling to work. After nine days of chaos the *Daily Mail* demanded 'Clear out the Soviets', but events evaporated into a surprising normality.

Modernism was the intellectual driving force of the time; experimental literature flourished. Aldous Huxley and George Orwell were writing angry novels about poverty and society's dismal future. The Bloomsbury Group was a renowned intellectual clique, boasting that important novelist Virginia Woolf and the influential economist JM Keynes.

Bloomsbury Workshop
12 Galen Place, WC1 (071 405 0632). Holborn underground/19, 22, 25 bus. **Open** 10am-5.30pm Mon-Fri. **Admission** free. **Credit** V.
This small, fascinating bookshop-cum-gallery sells works by, and relating to, the Bloomsbury Group, including first editions, biographies, prints, drawings and paintings. They can supply details of organized walks around the Bloomsbury landmarks. *Wheelchair access.*

Emmeline Pankhurst Statue
Victoria Tower Gardens, SW1. Westminster underground.
'Nothing has ever been got out of the British government without something approaching a revolution,' claimed Ms Pankhurst. After repeated imprisonment for her (successful) protests for women's rights, she is now commemorated in the grounds of Parliament.

IN VOGUE

Edwardian fashion took Victorian values to an extreme. Corsetted women pinned enormous hats to their long hair and were swathed in long, bustled dresses, even when playing tennis – showing even a little ankle was considered racy. Inevitably there was a reaction. The 'roaring' twenties saw the arrival of the 'flapper', with her bobbed hair, skin-tight boyish shimmy dress and cloche hat. The Charleston became the rage and Schiaparelli, Coco Chanel, *Vogue*, *Vanity Fair* and *Harper's Bazaar* set the trends. For men, plus fours and diamond-patterned sweaters were casual-chic and a tuxedo *de rigueur*.

The Dress Collection, Victoria & Albert Museum
Cromwell Road, SW7 (071 938 8500; recorded information: general 071 938 8441; exhibitions 071 938 8349). South Kensington underground/4, 9, 10, 45, 74, 264 bus. **Open** 10am-5.50pm Mon-Sat; 2.30-5.50pm Sun. **Admission** free (*donation requested £2 adult, £1 under-16s, OAPs, students, UB40s*). **Credit** (shop only) A, AmEx, V, £TC.
This period is well represented at the V&A's gallery of fashion. The array of gear includes flapper dresses, Edward VIII's checked suits and George Bernard Shaw's stetson. See the Twentieth Century Primary Galleries on the second floor for an interesting display of furniture, sculpture and Art Deco frippery. *See chapter* **Museums**.
Café. Shop. Wheelchair access.

Geffrye Museum
Kingsland Road, E2 (071 739 9893; recorded information 071 739 8543). Old Street underground/Dalston Kingsland BR/22B, 48, 67, 149, 243 bus. **Open** 10am-5pm Tue-Sat, Bank Holidays; 2-5pm Sun. **Admission** Free. **No credit cards.**
One of the most popular rooms here is the thirties living room where you can see a period three piece suite, bakelite wireless, tiled fireplace and other modest art deco features. *See chapter* **Museums**.
Café; 10am-12.30pm; 1.30-5pm. Gardens. Library. Shop. Wheelchair access to ground floor. Worksheets. Workshop.

FUN & DANCING

The horrors of World War I shattered moral codes and a whole new social life opened up, particularly for women. 'Flappers' would gather in cocktail bars to drink, smoke and swap comments about sex, Freud and the latest jazz music and dances. The revellers expected dancing as accompaniment to their food and gossip. Thus evening and tea dances became all the rage at the luxurious hotels, particularly the **Ritz**, W1 and the **Savoy**, WC2.

Café de Paris
3 Coventry Street, WC1 (071 437 2036). Piccadilly Circus or Leicester Square underground. **Open** *Tea dances* 3-5.45pm Wed, Thur, Sat Sun. *Nightclub* 7.30pm-1am Mon, 10.30pm-3.15am Wed, 7.30pm-1am Thur, 7.30pm-3am Fri, Sat; 7.30pm-midnight Sun. **Admission** *Tea dances* £2.50 Wed, £2.80 Thu, £3 Sat, Sun. *Nightclub* £6 Mon, Thur; £7 Wed; £5 Fri; £5-£7 Sat.
The fashionable, the rich and the royal – the Duke of Windsor was a regular – made this plush club the hub of twenties and thirties café society. It opened in 1924, designed as a replica of the Palm Court of the liner *Lusitania*; the *Herald Tribune* described it as 'a cross between a Victorian brothel and a bedouin tent'. Today the clientèle is the older and wealthier among the club crowd. And they still do that twenties fad – tea dances (with a live band, except on Wednesdays).

The Ritz
Piccadilly, W1 (071 493 8181). Green Park underground. **Tea served** 3pm, 4.30pm, daily. **Set tea** £11. **Credit** A, AmEx, DC, V.
The more refined can drink a leisurely tea in the afternoon (booking advised), then slip into a sequinned ball gown or a dapper dinner suit and tango in the Palm Court during the dinner dance (10pm-3am Fri, Sat). *Wheelchair access.*

ENTERTAINMENT

To the Edwardians, mass entertainment meant a night out at the music hall. Audiences cheered and jeered at the wittily filthy songs and jokes of Max Miller and Marie Lloyd right into the thirties. But, one by one, the variety shows fell victim to cinema, radio and television. Most music halls were converted into movie theatres. About the only variety venues remaining are the **Hackney Empire** and the **London Palladium**, Argyll Street, W1.

A night at the cinema became a fixture in everyone's lives, and cinemagoing was turned into an event with the advent of the thirties' art deco picture palace. The **Odeon Leicester Square** (*see chapter* **Film**) retains its dramatic geometric black frontage and tower, but is not unusual in having lost its elaborate interior; one of the few still intact is at the **Odeon Muswell Hill** (*see below*).

Radio also took off in a big way. Families gathered round enormous bakelite wireless sets, decorated with stylized sunbursts, to hear the latest sounds from the British Broadcasting Company (BBC). Television sets weren't available widely enough to make the masses square-eyed until after World War II, but the first BBC telecast went out live from the **Alexandra Palace** studios on 26 August 1936. At the **Museum of the Moving Image** (*see chapter* **Museums**) you can learn all about the early days of film and TV.

Broadcasting House

Langham Place, Regent Street, WC1. Oxford Circus underground.
Daily BBC radio programmes first emanated from Savoy Hill (next to the Savoy Hotel) on 14 November 1922, but by 1932 Broadcasting House was ready, complete with 22 sound-proofed studios. Vaguely reminiscent of an old bakelite radio, it was designed by G Val Myers and is decorated with a sculpture of Shakespeare's Ariel (as the symbol of broadcasting) by Eric Gill.

Hackney Empire

291 Mare Street, E8 (081 985 2424).
Hackney Central BR/22B, 38, 55 bus.
When this theatre was built in 1901, the architects evidently had in mind a Turkish bazaar. The turreted exterior and heavily ornate proscenium arch have been beautifully restored. It was originally a variety theatre, where Marie Lloyd, local girl turned famous bawdy singer, made her name. It's now a venue for both mainstream and alternative performers. *See chapter* **New Comedy**. *Bar. Wheelchair access.*

Odeon Muswell Hill

Fortis Green Road, N10 (081 883 1001). 43, 102, 134, W7, W9 bus. **Tickets** £2.90-£3.50 adult; £1.60-£2 under-15s, OAPs, students (UB40s on Mon only). **Credit** A, V.
This listed cinema from 1936 has one of the few remaining art deco interiors in London. The geometrically decorated orange foyer has a double staircase and was the model for the mock-up in **MOMI** (*see chapter* **Museums**). The auditorium continues the theme and has two clocks shaped like the octagonal Odeon logo. The foyer and stalls area have displays of old cameras and projection equipment. It shows mainstream first and second run films and is admirably cheap.

METROLAND

London became Greater London between 1900 and World War II, as suburbs and villages were swallowed up by the metropolis. Its population rose from four and a half million to a peak of eight and a half million in 1939. Commuter towns which benefitted from the new Metropolitan Line were romanticized by poet laureate, Sir John Betjeman, as 'Metroland'.

Road transport was revolutionized, too. By the mid thirties, motor buses started to replace electric trams, which had since 1901 made redundant the horse-drawn varieties. Also from Edwardian times, motorcars started to 'put-put' around ever congested streets. Cars of the time can be seen at the **Heritage Motor Museum** (*see chapter* **Museums**).

London Transport Museum

39 Wellington Street, WC2 (071 379 6344).
Covent Garden underground/6, 9, 11, 15 bus.
Open 10am-6pm daily. **Admission** £2.60 adults; £1.20 under-16s, OAPs, students, UB40s; free under-5s; £6 family (2 adults, 2 under-16s). **Credit** (shop only) A, V.
Models of the trams, trolleybuses and trains – and some examples of the real thing – can be seen in this museum. Wonderful art deco posters were commissioned by London Transport and are so popular that they sell

Owen Williams's **Daily Express Building** *(listed under* **Modernism***) is the most dramatic piece of art deco in central London. Completed in 1932, the building is sheathed in a chrome and black glass curtain wall. Behind this stark exterior is an art deco foyer and staircase. This is all that the public can see of Robert Atkinson's interior of zig-zag geometry and stylized images in black marble, figured ebony, travertine and chrome. Now under new owners, thankfully the building is to be preserved.*

The **Michelin Building** (*listed under* **Modernism**), *designed as an advertisement for the French tyre manufacturers, has often been threatened with demolition. Saved in 1985, the frontage has been restored, with tiles depicting motorcars, as has the exquisite mosaic Bibendum (tyre man) floor in the foyer. Lost original features, notably the glass cupolas, and Bibendum stained glass have been replaced. It's now home to a publishing company, the Conran Shop, the Bibendum restaurant and an oyster bar.*

by the thousand in the museum shop. *See chapter* **Museums**.
Group discount. Lectures. Shop. Toilets for the disabled. Wheelchair access. Worksheets.

MODERNISM

Although architecture was on the threshold of Modernism during this period the British were slow to adopt the geometric styles of le Corbusier, or the Bauhaus. Grand-scale buildings continued to go up, but with cleaner forms and invariably in Portland stone. **County Hall**, SE1 (1905–33) is a good example. The main British contribution to the modern movement was the use of local materials and a calmer, more domestic feel. Significant Arts and Crafts buildings include Richard Norman Shaw's **New Scotland Yard** (*see chapter* **The West End**) and **Hampstead Garden Suburb**, NW11. Two rare examples of art nouveau are the **Horniman Museum** (*see chapter* **Museums**) and the **Whitechapel Art Gallery** (*see chapter* **Art Galleries**). The neo-Byzantine **Westminster Cathedral** is simply in a style of its own.

Transport is a fitting symbol of the age, and the motorcar was the inspiration for two exuberant buildings of the period. **Michelin House** (*see below*) and the **Royal Automobile Club** (RAC) Pall Mall, SW1 (1911). Of the many underground stations built before World War II, many were modernist gems. Charles

Holden designed over 30, notably **Bounds Green** station (1930).

Modernism did have its moments, most impressively with the **Daily Express building**. The same architect, Owen Williams, was responsible for **Wembley Arena** (*see chapter* **Music: Rock, Folk & Jazz**). The **Penguin Pool** in **London Zoo** (*see chapter* **Sightseeing**) is a playful construction of interlocking concrete spirals, designed in 1934.

Londoners never seem happy without an architectural controversy. **Freemasons' Hall**, WC2, was loathed by half the population when it was opened in 1933 and kept the *Times* letters page filled for months (*see chapter* **Museums**). The bold University of London's **Senate House**, Malet Street, WC1, opened a year earlier as the tallest building in London at the time. Buildings of the thirties were built to be noticed and the massive **Battersea Power Station**, Kirtling Street, SW11 looks as if it's a left-over from the film set of Fritz Lang's *Metropolis*.

Daily Express Building
121–128 Fleet Street, EC4. Blackfriars underground/BR. **Open** 24 hours daily.
See picture and caption.

Hampstead Garden Suburb
Hampstead, NW11. Golders Green underground, then H2 bus.
Begun in 1907, this tree-lined domestic development was a fine, but fairly dull exercise in the vernacular style. Possibly the last successful suburban scheme in London, it's a good place for a pleasant stroll. The layout incorporates apartment buildings to the north, villas in the west and larger houses in the south. The central square is by Lutyens.

Michelin Building
Michelin House, Fulham Road, SW3 (071 581 9393; Bibendum restaurant 071 581 5817). South Kensington underground **Open** 9.30am-6pm Mon, Wed-Sat; 10am-6pm Tue.
See picture and caption.
Wheelchair access.

Westminster Cathedral
Victoria Street, SW1 (071 834 7452). Victoria underground/BR. **Open** 7am-8pm daily.
Services 7am, 8am, 8.30am, 9am, 10.30am, 12.30pm, 1.05pm, 5.30pm (sung Mass) Mon-Fri; 7am, 8am, 8.30am, 9am, 10.30am (sung Mass), 12.30pm, 6pm Sat; 7am, 8am, 9am, 10.30am (sung Mass), noon, 5.30pm, 7pm Sun.
Candy-like bands of red brick and stone in Christian Byzantine style make this 1903 cathedral an imposing sight. The view from the campanile is superb. It had taken Anglicans a long time to accept Catholicism in this country, but this is now the British headquarters of the Catholic church. Inside, the nave is the widest in Britain. The magnificent columns and mosaics are made of over a hundred kinds of marble, but the undecorated ceiling creates a mysterious ancient atmosphere.

The World Wars

Much of London was lost through bombing in the 1940s. But the city is still littered with memorials and museums to both World Wars.

Hitler's bombs did more to change modern London than anything since the Great Fire. But architects since 1945 don't seem to have measured up to the task of reconstruction. London has become a fractured city and few streets are completely in their original style. And then there was the human cost. Thousands of Londoners died in their homes, at factories, in offices or in defence of the city. Their memorials are everywhere. There are plenty of places, listed below, where you can find out what happened.

WORLD WAR I MEMORIALS

It's easy to overlook the fact that the capital was bombed in World War I. You need to look even harder to find the traces. Evidence of air-raids by German Zeppelin airships has been largely destroyed by the saturation bombing of World War II. But at **Cleopatra's Needle** on the Victoria Embankment, WC2, you can see where the first aircraft raid (17 December 1917) damaged the obelisk's plinth and one of its sphinxes.

The biggest impact of this war was at the human level, particularly in the trenches. Contemporaries reacted with revulsion at trench warfare; you can see why at the new World War I gallery of the **Imperial War Museum.** The Trench Experience is a multi-sensory display of the horrors of Flanders' field.

In response to the carnage, people in virtually every British town and village mourned the loss of a generation of young men by erecting war memorials. Sadly, World War I was not the 'war to end all wars' and the names of the dead of the 1939-45 conflict were subsequently added to the 1914-18 memorials. The national ceremony of Remembrance, for the

dead of both wars, takes place on the nearest Sunday to the World War I armistice anniversary (11 November 1918), at the **Cenotaph** in Whitehall. This geometric monolith was a bold piece of architecture in 1919-20. Timeless and devoid of religious symbolism, it's one of the best works by Edwin Lutyens.

There are many other memorials in the capital which are also important or unusual pieces of sculpture. Hyde Park Corner, SW1, has the **Royal Artillery Regiment** statue, the best of many such pieces by C Sergeant Jagger; and a bronze **Boy David** (by Francis Derwent Wood, 1925) bizarrely representing the Machine Gun Corps. Ironically, this muscular figure is a proven traffic hazard, distracting drivers so that they prang the vehicle in front. The statues are not all heroic; many reflect the way that ordinary men become cannon-fodder. Witness the ordinary **Tommy** (slang for a British soldier) at Paddington Station, W2, unarmed and reading a letter from home. You can also find oddities such as the **Submariners** (by Hatch and Tension, 1922), Victoria Embankment opposite Temple Gardens, WC2 and the small, but perfectly formed **Imperial Camel Corps** bronze (by Cecil Brown, 1920), in Embankment Gardens, SW1, topped by a soldier astride a dromedary.

Remembrances of a more personal nature can be seen at institutions from churches to colleges to businesses. Typical is the stone bench memorial in Lincoln's Inn, WC2, devoted to soldiers who had trained as barristers there. The ugliest war statue is dedicated to the Belgian heroine, Edith Cavell, at St Martin's Place, WC2 (by George Frampton, 1920). She never succumbed to German interrogation and was executed; her dying words, inscribed here, being 'Patriotism isn't enough'.

WORLD WAR II

Londoners were in the front line for much of World War II. Ordinary Londoners were now as exposed to mechanized mass-killing as the armed forces. Following the surrender of France in June 1940 and the rescue of the beleaguered British forces at Dunkirk, the German Forces were just 100 miles/160 kilometres from London. In September 1940 the bombs started falling on the capital to soften up the population ready for invasion. The Blitz had begun.

War had been declared on 3 September 1939, but at first the only fighting of this 'Phoney War' was in far-away Poland and people reassured themselves that it would be over by Christmas. The government didn't take any chances, though, and gave itself dictatorial powers to implement precautionary measures. Kitted out with just a change of clothes and a gas mask, some 750,000 children became evacuees when they were sent away to families in the remote countryside. Some were even shipped off to Canada. Battalions of Home Guard (dubbed Dad's Army) were prepared to fight the invasion, and London's factories stepped up weapon production. Of course, Britain took advantage of its Empire and soldiers from New Zealand and Australia flooded in. But it wasn't much fun being a German or Italian ex-patriate: thousands were victimized and the males were interned, even if they were shopkeepers who had lived here for years. As the months drew on, however, Londoners became used to rationing and night-time black-outs. They also started digging air-raid shelters and carrying their gas masks everywhere.

BLITZ

The much-feared gas attacks never came, but the bombing did. On 7 September 1940, a hot, sunny Saturday afternoon, several hundred German bombers dumped their load on east London and the docks. Whole streets were left burning and the dead and injured numbered over 2,000. There was no relief; the Germans returned on 56 consecutive nights before picking on the car-manufacturing city of Coventry.

As the dreaded air-raid klaxon sounded and giant searchlights scoured the skies above the blackened city, Londoners poured underground. Huge but cramped communal shelters were built; the largest, by Tilbury docks, held 16,000 people. Underground stations proved to be ideal shelters. The sketches by war-artist Henry Moore of warweary Londoners huddled on the platforms can be seen in the Imperial War Museum. Also displayed there is an Anderson shelter. These tiny, damp, concrete boxes were installed in back yards and suburban gardens all over Britain. Many still remain, grassed over. The Imperial War Museum's **Blitz Experience** (*see* **picture and caption**) brilliantly recreates the fearful atmosphere.

Londoners reacted with tremendous bravery and, because of the way communities pulled together, you'll still hear the nostalgic refer to the period as 'Britain's finest hour'. Most of them attempted to work as normally as possible, often covered in burns and sores, after interrupted sleep in a shelter. Others, like the poet Louis MacNeice, spent their nights up in the dome of St Paul's Cathedral fire-spotting, so the wardens could assist the injured and so the firemen – popular heroes of the time – could fight the continous blazes.

The government had to dodge Hitler's bombs, too. Prime Minister Winston Churchill, the War Cabinet and the Defence Committee planned the Allies' moves from an underground warren near Whitehall known as the **Cabinet War Rooms**. Their secretaries got so little day-light that they needed sun-lamp treatment. You can visit the Cabinet War Rooms, which were so spartan that Churchill preferred to kip at the Savoy Hotel, WC2. The hotel was often bombed; but nowhere was safe. Buckingham Palace, Westminster Abbey and St Paul's were all hit. BBC Radio's Broadcasting House – a prime target because of its propaganda role – was painted grey to elude the bombers' sight. It was eventually hit on 15 October 1940, during the Nine O' Clock News. Newscaster Bruce Belfrage continued to read the day's headlines.

Cabinet War Rooms

Clive Steps, King Charles Street, SW1 (071 930 6961). Westminster or St James's Park underground/24, 29, 53, 88 bus. **Open** 10am–6pm. **Admission** £3 adults; £1.50 under-16s, OAPs, students, UB40s. **Credit** (shop only) A, V.

The British Government's wartime headquarters lies underground near Downing Street and has been restored to its 1940 state. It must have been a grim life in this bunker: behind the heavy security doors are tiny rooms with spartan utility furniture. The appeal of the place lies in how realistic it is, but there's not much you can actually do but look at the room sets. Most interesting are the map rooms and Winston Churchill's bedroom. As there were no toilets, you also have the privilege of viewing the Prime Ministerial chamber pot.

Cassette-guided tour (£1.50). Group discount. Shop. Toilets for the disabled. Wheelchair access.

Imperial War Museum

Lambeth Road, SE1 (071 735 8922). Elephant & Castle, Lambeth North or Waterloo underground/BR. **Open** 10am–6pm daily. **Admission** £2.50 adult; £1.25 under-16s, OAPs, students, UB40s Sat-Thur; free

Fri. **Credit** (shop only) A, V.
See **picture and caption**.
See chapter **Museums**.
Films. Group discount. Lectures. Library. Nursing mother facilities. Research facilities. Restaurant. Shop. Toilets for the disabled. Wheelchair access.

Museum of London

150 London Wall, EC2 (071 600 3699). Barbican, St Paul's or Moorgate underground/BR/4, 141, 279A, 502 bus. **Open** 10am-6pm Tue-Sat; 2-6pm Sun. **Admission** free. **Credit** (shop only) A, V.

London was transformed by World War II, so it's appropriate that this museum, dedicated to the history of the city and its people, has a 50th anniversary exhibition on the Blitz. Special exhibits on all aspects of life at the time are on show from 4 September 1990 to early 1991. *See chapter* **Museums**.

Braille guide and taped commentary for the visually impaired. Lectures and films with induction loop for the hard of hearing. Restaurant (10am-5pm Tue-Sat; noon-5pm Sun). Shop. Toilets for the disabled. Wheelchair access. Workshops.

The **Cenotaph** *(listed under* **Victory at Last***) is the scene of the annual Remembrance Day Service. The Queen, Prime Minister and other dignitaries lay wreaths and observe one minute's silence to commemorate the British and Commonwealth citizens who died in both World Wars. It's held here on the nearest Sunday to the anniversary of the World War I armistice. Unless you're in the front row at dawn all you'll get to see is the parade of old soldiers as they go through Parliament Square at the end.*

*The **Imperial War Museum** (listed under **Blitz**) has recently been completely redesigned. Huddled up in a damp underground shelter you can experience the sounds, smells and even rumblings caused by an air-raid. You emerge from the bunker to a scene of devastation. In the Trench Experience, visitors will be able to discover something of what the British soldiers went through in Flanders. There are remarkable film and sound archive clips from both World Wars and lovingly polished aircraft, submarines and weapons are all explained by superb video displays. Go off-peak (Mondays or late afternoon weekdays) to avoid the queues.*

BATTLE OF BRITAIN

The threat of invasion was very real and London's defences were sorely stretched. Pillboxes (machine gun emplacements) sprang up everywhere. Some of them still survive: there's one by Putney Bridge underground station, overlooking the river. The last hope was the greatly-outnumbered Royal Air Force (RAF). But the pilots of the Hurricane and Spitfire fighters won out. You can see some of the planes which defended the capital – as well as some of the bombs that fell – in the Imperial War Museum, at **Duxford Airfield** near Cambridge and at the **Royal Air Force Museum**, Hendon. In 1990, the latter has an extended display on the Battle of Britain. Many of the visitors are former pilots reminiscing about their days in the cockpit.

Duxford Airfield

Duxford, Cambridgeshire (0223 833963; recorded information 0223 835000). **Getting there** *by car* M11 to Junction 10, then A505/Cambridge; *by train* to Whittlesford, Royston BR, then taxi; *by bus* daily from Victoria Station. **Open** *Mar-Oct* 10am-6pm daily. *Oct-Mar* 10am-4pm daily. **Admission** £4.50 adults; £2.25 under-16s, OAPs, students, UB40s. **Credit** (shop only) A, V.
Duxford aerodrome, a wartime RAF base, now has a large collection of civil and wartime aircraft from bi-planes to Concorde. The museum is currently exhibiting a renovated Battle of Britain operations' room, replete with table, maps and markers. There's also a forties' prefab house furnished with original utility (streamlined wartime) furniture.
Café. Group discount. Tour by prior arrangement (0223 322640). Shop. Toilets for the disabled. Wheelchair access .

Royal Air Force Museum

Grahame Park Way, NW9 (081 205 2266; recorded information 081 205 9191). Colindale underground/Mill Hill Broadway BR (Thameslink)/32, 226, 292 bus. **Open** 10am-6pm daily. **Admission** £3.30 adults; £1.65 under-15s, disabled, OAPs, students, UB40s. **Credit** (shop only) A, £TC, V.

World War II aircraft from both sides are on display here, including Messerschmitts, Lancasters, Spitfires and Hurricanes. It is one of the largest collections of aeroplanes in Europe. There are some reasonable audiovisuals depicting the Battle of Britain and the exploits of Bomber Command: the eradication of Dresden meant that there was no campaign medal for the bomber squadrons. *See chapter* **Museums**.
Classroom. Educational films. Restaurant (10am-5pm daily). Shop. Tour by prior arrangement. Wheelchair access. Worksheets.

THE HOME FRONT

The Blitz quietened a little after the Battle of Britain, and from 1942 the tide of the war slowly began to turn. By 1944 the Allies were preparing for the D-Day invasion of Europe, which began on 6 June. The London Underground workers in Acton had discovered a method of waterproofing tanks, invaluable during the D-Day beach landings, and in Walthamstow, factories stopped making furniture and started building Mosquito aeroplanes out of balsa and plywood. Even in the Houses of Parliament, a cellar was converted into a submarine factory. In preparation for the invasion, General de Gaulle and other members of the French government-in-exile met at the French House pub (*see chapter* **West End**) to coordinate the French resistance.

Meanwhile, life on the Home Front had taken on a completely different character to that of peacetime. Rationing was tight because German U-boats were sinking so many ships in the Atlantic. People were allowed just four ounces/100 grammes of bacon and cheese a week and a packet of dried eggs. The make-do-and-mend philosophy extended to wartime clothes, which were also strictly rationed, and you can see an example of a 'utility' dress in the **Victoria & Albert Museum**. Slogans such as 'Dig for Victory' were taken to heart: even the swimming pool of the prestigious Ladies' Carlton Club in Pall Mall was turned into a pigsty.

Dress Collection at the Victoria & Albert Museum

Cromwell Road, SW7 (071 938 8500; recorded information: general 071 938 8441; exhibitions 071 938 8349). South Kensington underground/4, 9, 30, 45, 74, 264 bus. **Open** 10am-5.50pm Mon-Sat; 2.30-5.50pm Sun. **Admission** free (*donation requested £2 adult,*

£1 under-16s, OAPs, students, UB40s).
Credit (shop only) A, AmEx, £TC, V.
The coarse fabrics of utility clothing are unlikely to make a comeback, but ironically the cut of the women's suits and day dresses now seems stylish.
Gallery talks (2.30pm daily). Guided tours. Lectures. Restaurant (10am-5pm Mon-Sat; 2.30–5.30pm Sun). Shop. Touch sessions for the visually impaired. Wheelchair access.

National Army Museum
Royal Hospital Road, SW3 (071 730 0717). Sloane Square underground/39, 11 bus.
Open 10am-5.30pm Mon-Sat; 2-5.30pm Sun. **Admission** free. **No credit cards.**
The life of British soldiers since Tudor times is presented here in a refreshingly matter-of-fact way, with no bombast or inappropriate patriotism. The full low-down on the British Army's role in World War II is given, with displays of uniform, weapons and armoury.
See also chapter **Museums.**
Café (10.30am-4.15pm Mon-Sat). Reading room. Tour by prior arrangement. Shop. Wheelchair access. Worksheets.

DEADLY DOODLEBUGS

As the Germans retreated, they unleashed the war's deadliest pre-atomic weapon. The V-1 was a pilotless plane, packed with explosives and with an engine programmed to shut down over London, crashing into the city. You can see some examples in the Imperial War Museum. After D-Day these 'Doodlebugs' fell at the rate of 73 a day, demoralizing Londoners even more than the Blitz, because there was so little defence against them. Even worse was the huge V-2, a rocket missile that arrived without warning and which could destroy a row of houses with an explosion you could hear ten miles/sixteen kilometres away.

VICTORY AT LAST

London was the scene of one big party on 8 May 1945 – V-E Day. Hundreds of thousands of people took to the streets after victory was announced. They went wild, dancing in the Trafalgar Square fountains, doing the conga in Leicester Square and making love in Green Park (hundreds of babies were conceived that night). In Piccadilly, a naked sailor climbed on to Eros's pedastal and draped himself in a Union Jack. The people of London were reclaiming their city. Unfortunately, much of their city was in ruins – two out of every five houses in Stepney, east London, were lost. Today, the majority have not had the experience of war, but every year, in the week before Remembrance Sunday, millions of people don red poppies and donate to soldiers' charities. Perhaps the most dramatic reminder of World War II is **HMS Belfast**. This landmark in the Thames is the last of Britain's great cruisers that protected the vital convoys in the Atlantic, and took part in D-Day. Less dramatic and cerainly less well known are the rare surviving public air-raid shelter signs on house numbers 7-10 and 13-17 Lord North Street, Westminster, SW1 (just behind Westminster Abbey).

Blunderbuss Antiques
29 Thayer Street, W1 (071 486 2444). Bond Street underground. **Open** 9.30am-4.30pm Mon-Fri; 9.30am-4pm Sat. **Credit** A, AmEx, £TC, V.
Militaria and wartime memorabilia is big business and Blunderbuss has a rapidly changing stock. You could spend anything from 50p for a badge, up to several thousands of pounds for a suit of armour.
Mail order. Wheelchair access.

Christ Church, Greyfriars
Newgate Street, EC1. St Paul's underground.
Wren's Christ Church (1691) was a victim of the incendiary devices that missed St Paul's Cathedral, but which destroyed many of the great City churches. The tower and vestry have been restored, but the bare walls are left to commemorate the destruction.

HMS Belfast
Morgan's Lane, Tooley Street, SE1 (071 407 6434). London Bridge underground/BR/10, 42, 44, 47, 48, 70 , 78 bus/boat from Tower Pier (Feb-Oct daily, Nov-Jan weekends; 30p adult, 20p under-16s). **Open** *Mar-Oct* 10am-6pm daily, *Nov-Mar* 10am-4.30pm daily. **Admission** £3.50 adults; £1.75 under-16s, OAPs, students and UB40s; free under-5s; £9 family ticket (2 adults and 2 children).
Credit A, AmEx, DC, £TC, V.
See **picture and caption.**
See chapters **Sightseeing** and **The River & Docklands.**
Group discount. Shop. Wheelchair access on main deck only.

Remembrance Service at the Cenotaph
Whitehall, SW1. Westminster underground.
Date *1990* 11 Nov , 11am;l *1991* 10 Nov , 11am. **Admission** free.
See **picture and caption.**

HMS Belfast (*listed under* **Victory at Last**), *the last of World War II's big gun ships, is moored opposite the Tower of London. It's now a floating museum, and you can explore its seven decks to see what it was like to live and fight at sea. A permanent exhibition details the D-Day landings, in which the ship took part.*

To the Eighties

Tower blocks and consumer culture made modern London. The rock 'n' roll fifties, permissive sixties, tasteless seventies and designer eighties live on in buildings, clothes and clubs.

World War II left Britain almost as shattered as Germany. A better Britain, it was promised by the politicians, would be built from the rubble. New towns would be created and the environment would be beautified. Planners were seen as the people who would construct a better life for everyone in the country. This included removing London's slums, free health care for everyone and a better education system available to all. For all the planned social changes, life was drab, regimented and austere. The rationing of food continued until the early fifties. Visitors to London in 1950 were appalled to find that they couldn't buy a steak in the better hotels; and it was only in February of 1953 that Londoners could buy unlimited supplies of chocolate. The only spark of colour and life came from the Festival of Britain in 1951, when London decided to party.

THE FIFTIES

'Let's be frank about it; most of our people have never had it so good' proclaimed Prime Minister Harold Macmillan in 1957. He'd nicked the 'never so good' bit from the Americans and was attempting to avoid outrage over the Suez Canal fiasco when imperial Britain had tried (and failed) to intimidate the Egyptians. The coronation of Queen Elizabeth II in 1953 was the biggest television broadcast in history and there was the feeling of a new age dawning. Trade with the Commonwealth countries reached its height in 1956, when the London docks handled a record 70 million tonnes of goods; ships arrived at the rate of 1,000 per week. DeHavilland of

Colindale produced the world's first jet airliner, the Comet, and the motor industry was the biggest exporter of all. Today, cars constitute Britain's greatest single import.

Royal Festival Hall
South Bank, SE1 (information 071 921 0682; box office 071 928 8800). Waterloo underground/BR. **Open** 10am-11pm daily; *box office* 10am-9pm daily. **Tickets** £3-£20. **Credit** A, AmEx, DC, £$TC, V.
See **picture and caption.**
See also chapter **Music: Classical & Opera.**

Stevenage
Hertfordshire (Tourist information 0438 369441). Stevenage BR.
When the village of Stevenage was designated London's first new town in 1946, its residents poured out their bile on planning minister, Lewis Silkin. 'Silkingrad' signs were strung out along the village boundaries and residents put sand in the petrol tank of Silkin's car. Local objections were overruled, and Stevenage became a new town in the fifties.

Trades Union Congress House
23-28 Great Russell Street, WC1 (071 636 4030). Tottenham Court Road underground. **Open** 9.15am-5.15pm Mon-Fri.
TUC House is a classic version of the light, curtain-walled block, so favoured in the fifties. A fad of the time was to tack a modernist sculpture by Barbara Hepworth or one of her peers onto anonymous concrete blocks. Bernard Meadows's bronze, *The Spirit of Trade Unionism*, on the TUC House frontage is a great example. Although visitors aren't really welcome, a kind word to reception will enable you to view Jacob Epstein's memorial to trade unionists who died in the two world wars, that rests in the courtyard.

United States Embassy
24 Grosvenor Square, W1 (071 499 9000). Bond Street or Marble Arch underground. **Open** 8.30am-5.30pm Mon-Fri.
Britain's reliance on the US in the new political atmosphere of the Cold War was symbolized by this 600-room embassy. Eero Saarinen's design (1957-60) is both massive and elegant. The gilded aluminium eagle (wingspan 35 feet/10.7 metres) is by Theodor Roszak and ironically faces away from America. The square saw massive demonstrations against the US involvement in Vietnam in 1968.

THE AFFLUENT SOCIETY

The fitted kitchen had been invented in Germany in the twenties. It took 30 years before the British housewife (never the husband) felt the benefit of a wipe-clean Formica worktop with integrated sink. The craze for consumer durables and labour-saving devices came via the USA and many were British made, like Belling fridges and New World cookers. The annual **Ideal Home Exhibition** (*see chapter* **London by Season**) displayed what people had to buy to 'keep up with the Jones's'.

Design Museum
Butlers Wharf, Shad Thames, SE1 (071 403 6933; recorded information 071 407 6261). Tower Hill underground/Tower Gateway DLR then Riverbus from Tower Pier/15, 42, 47, 70, 70A, 78 bus. **Open** 11.30am-6.30pm Tue-Sun, Mon Bank Holidays. **Admission** £2 adult; £1 under-16s, OAPs, students, UB40s. **Credit** A, V.
The fifties saw a revolution in the design of household items. Although many of the ideas came from before the war, most of the Design Museum's Study Collection is postwar. The themed displays of televisions, cars, chairs, office equipment and labour-saving devices date from the earliest models.
See chapter **Museums.**
Bar. Café. Cassette tour (free; £2 deposit). Education department. Films. Lectures. Reference library. Restaurant. Shop. Tour by prior arrangement. Toilets for the disabled. Wheelchair access.

Geffrye Museum
Kingsland Road, E2 (071 739 9893; recorded information 071 739 8543). Old Street underground/Dalston Kingsland BR/22B, 48, 67, 149, 243 bus. **Open** 10am-5pm Tue-Sat, Bank Holidays; 2-5pm Sun. **Admission** free. **No credit cards.**
The Geffrye's wonderful room-sets will from April 1990 include a fifties room. Opening with it is an exhibition on life in the fifties, with mock-ups of prefabs and council houses. *See chapter* **Museums.**
Café (10am-12.30pm; 1.30-5pm). Education department (worksheets, workshops). Gardens. Library. Shop (closed 12.30-1.30pm). Wheelchair access to ground floor.

Victoria & Albert Museum
Cromwell Road, SW7 (071 938 8500; recorded information 071 938 8441; exhibitions 071 938 8349). South Kensington underground/4, 9, 30, 45, 74, 264 bus. **Open** 10am-5.50pm Mon-Sat; 2.30-5.50pm Sun. **Admission** free (donation requested £2 adult; £1 under-16s, OAPs, students, UB40s). **Credit** (shop only) A, AmEx, £TC, V.
Choice items in the museum's Dress Collection include a Digby Morton tweed suit of 1954 and a flared mini-dress. Sadly, the seventies couture examples don't include downmarket improvization in fashion or the female trouser suit with penny-round collars, elephant cuffs and bell-bottom baggies.
Gallery talks (2.30pm daily). Lectures. Restaurant (10am-5pm Mon-Sat; 2.30-5.30pm Sun). Shop. Touch sessions for the visually impaired. Tour. Wheelchair access.

TEENAGE CULTURE

Fashion-conscious, youthful rebellion arrived in 1953 with rock 'n' roll. Elvis Presley replaced sentimental crooners, working class lads adopted gravity-defying quiffs and fashionable neo-Edwardian clothes. They were sneered at as 'Teddy boys'. Teenage girls copied the American high-school look: skimpy polkadot dresses, pony-tails and bizarrely framed sunglasses. The Saturday night 'hop' became a teen institution. Today the dance halls are barn-like discos like the **Hammersmith Palais** (now **Le Palais disco**, *see chapter* **Nightlife**) or closed like the Lyceum Ballroom in the Strand.

London's hippest district, Soho, was dominated by Bohemians, beatniks and jazz. By the mid fifties, international attention focused on Soho's jazz clubs. The ancestor of today's **Soho Jazz Festival** (*see chapter* **London by Season**) was the week-long Soho Fair that ran annually from 1955 till 1959. The Fair was a celebration of the area's musical and artistic life, but the media portrayal of Soho as a den of vice stopped the event.

Flip
125 Long Acre, WC2 (071 836 7044). Covent Garden or Leicester Square underground. **Open** 11am-7pm Mon-Wed, Sat; 11am-8pm Thur, Fri; noon-6pm Sun. **Credit** A, AmEx, DC, £TC, V.
Fifties Americana is the forté of this jam-packed two-floor emporium. Denims (about £20), jackets (£10-£40) and check flannel shirts (£3-£5) are so tightly racked that it's hard to extract them. You may find what you want, but make up your mind quickly if you do – it'll go fast.

Ronnie Scott's
47 Frith Street, W1 (071 439 0747). Leicester Square or Piccadilly Circus underground. **Open** 8.30pm-3am Mon-Sat. Music from 9.30pm Mon-Sat. **Admission** £12. **Credit** A, AmEx, DC, £TC, V.
Outliving the Soho jazz scene of the fifties, Ronnie Scott's (founded 1959) has become the Mecca of British jazz. The club bills jazz super-stars like Miles Davis, Branford Marsalis and Courtney Pine, but Scott's has always been open to wider influences, recently including 'world music'. A daring venture was the Who's première of their rock opera *Tommy* in May 1969. *See chapter* **Music: Rock, Folk & Jazz**.

Ted's Corner
Victoria Market, 3 Wilton Road, SW1 (071 834 1701). Victoria underground/BR. **Open** 10am-8pm daily. **Credit** £TC.
Latter-day Teddy boys (and girls) mustn't miss this rockers' emporium, where they can pick up crêpe soles, drape jackets and enough gel to quiff a lion's mane.

Enthusiasm to improve society led to the sweeping away not only of slums but also of Georgian squares. Nothing was sacred and there were plans to rebuild Whitehall and the Houses of Parliament. London councils erected more than 400 'streets in the sky' tower blocks and vast City office developments were of the same insensitive, uniform style. Yet many Londoners express affection for Centre Point, St Giles Circus, WC2, calling for the tower to be listed. But quality standards succumbed to corruption and an orgy of property speculation. When Ronan Point, a new block in Newham, East London, partially collapsed in 1968, so did the boom. By then, logistical problems – lifts not working, nowhere for children to play, lack of neighbourhood focus – had turned the high-rise dream into a nightmare for the residents. Conversely, immigrant communities (*see chapter* **Ethnic London**) rejuvenated many remaining slums and ran enterprises such as late-opening corner shops.

Chelsea College of Art & Design
Manresa Road, SW3 (071 351 3844). Sloane Square or South Kensington underground/11, 19, 22 bus.
Art colleges encouraged people to realize creative potential and had a massive impact on popular culture from rock music (Keith Richards, Pete Townsend) to fashion, design and advertising. Chelsea Art College (1965) is a typical, functional building of the time; a Henry Moore sculpture *Two-piece Reclining Figure* (1959) adorns the forecourt. Its students were a major influence on the Chelsea scene.
Toilets for the disabled. Wheelchair access.

Commonwealth Institute
Kensington High Street, W8 (071 603 4535). High Street Kensington, Holland Park, Earl's Court or Olympia underground/9, 10, 27, 28, 31, 49 bus/701, 704 Green line coach. **Open** 10am-5pm Mon-Sat; 2-5pm Sun. **Admission** free. **Credit** A, V.
See **picture and caption.**
See also chapter **Museums.**
Activity room with induction loop for hearing aids. Concerts and performances. Conference facilities. Educational programme. Festivals. Library. Restaurant. Shop. Wheelchair access.

South Bank Arts Centre
South Bank, SE1 (071 928 3002). Waterloo underground/BR/1, 4, 68, X68, 70, 70A, 76, 171, 171A, 176, 501, 502, 513 bus. **Open** 10am-8pm Mon-Sat. **Credit** A, AmEx, DC, V.
The neo-brutalist architect's love affair with concrete is now considered so perverted that there are plans to clothe much of the

The elegant **Royal Festival Hall** *(listed under* **The Fifties***) is all that remains of the Festival of Britain. Designed by Robert Matthew and JL Martin (1949-51), it's probably Londoners' favourite post-war building. Sadly, the other notable Festival structures have been lost. The Dome of Discovery exhibition space, the largest dome in the world, resembled the fifties idea of a UFO. The equally futuristic Skylon was a slinky, aluminium double-ended spike, seemingly suspended in mid air. There have been recent suggestions to re-erect the Skylon.*

*The bizarre **Commonwealth Institute** building (listed under* **The Sixties**) *was only the second sixties building to be listed (given official protection). The hyperboloid roof of Zambian copper and multi-level galleries are the work of Robert Matthew and Johnson-Marshall (1962). The centre started out as the Imperial Institute in 1887 in South Kensington. The proselytizing displays on national and cultural themes reflect official attempts to integrate Commonwealth immigrants into a multi-racial society.*

South Bank Centre with post-modern cladding by Terry Farrell. Creating a state-subsidized arts centre – the world's biggest – was a very sixties thing. Sadly the designs of the **Hayward Gallery**, **National Film Theatre**, **Queen Elizabeth II Hall** and **Purcell Room** (1967) are ugly and often impractical. Try finding the entrances. Yet even the nostalgic then-Poet Laureate, John Betjeman, enjoyed the confident presence of Denys Lasdun's **National Theatre** (completed 1977). *See chapter* **Theatre**.
Bar, restaurant and café. Bookshop. Car park (£1.50-£2.50). Group discount (071 620 0741). Front seats for the partially sighted by prior arrangement. Infra red audio for the hard of hearing. Tour by prior arrangement (071 633 0880). Toilets for the disabled. Wheelchair access.

British Telecom Tower
Maple Street, W1 (phone 100 & ask operator to connect you). Goodge Street or Warren Street underground.
A classic example of hi-tech architecture, the then Post Office Tower (by architect Eric Bedford) was completed in 1964 to transmit and receive radio, telephone and television signals and is the only building in London to look like a prop from *Thunderbirds*. At 580ft/177 metres, (excluding its 40-ft/12-metre-high radar mast) it became Britain's tallest building (now overtaken by the NatWest Tower, *see chapter* **The City**).

HIP, GROOVY, FAB MAN
Liberation was the buzzword of the sixties. The post-war baby boomers had money in their pockets and time to spend it. Life in the home and in the office became less formal and less moralistic. The decade started with the censorship trial of DH Lawrence's *Lady Chatterley's Lover*. Banned for 32 years as too erotic 'for your wife or servants to read', it sold two million copies in six weeks after Penguin were allowed to publish it. Another taboo collapsed when homosexuality was legalized in 1968. But women's lib was the main breakthrough. Feminism gained ground and the contraceptive pill (1961) transformed women's lives. Sexual liberty was a palliative though. Women's early-sixties freedom to wear sexy clothes transmogrified into the submissive sex object role.

Fashion achieved vast importance and innovative mod designs by people like Mary Quant broke the leadership of Parisian couture. Boutiques along the King's Road in Chelsea and Soho's Carnaby Street sold an ever wider range of clothes. Trends were influenced through fashion magazines by style gurus – cockney photographer David Bailey, models Jean Shrimpton and Twiggy, hairdresser Vidal Sassoon, designer Terence Conran and innu-

merable rock stars. Early sixties London was seen as the fashion and music capital of the world. Style pilgrims flocked to the city and one-in-ten workers ended up employed in tourist-related industries.

Carnaby Street
W1. Oxford Circus underground.
See **picture and caption.**

Habitat
Heal's Building, 196 Tottenham Court Road, W1 (071 631 3880). Goodge Street underground. **Open** 10am-6pm Mon; 9.30am-6pm Tue, Wed, Fri; 9.30am-7.30pm Thur; 9am-6pm Sat. **Credit** A, AmEx, V.
Terence Conran lamented the deplorable standard of design in British households. He set about persuading the influential new 'young adult' market that they should cook with Provençal pottery and sit on tubular steel chairs. The first Habitat shop opened on the Fulham Road in 1964 and stocked timelessly-styled variations on classic principles that still look modern.

Mary Quant
21 Carnaby Street, W1 (071 494 3277). Oxford Circus underground. **Open** 10am-6.30pm Mon-Sat. **Credit** A, AmEx, V.
The look of the Swinging Sixties is synonymous with Mary Quant – she invented the mini-skirt. Opened in 1955, her King's Road shop, Bazaar, was London's first boutique. It flouted conventions, stocking only Quant clothes with simple, geometric designs, and customers were encouraged to browse and use the shop as a meeting place (there was a café in the basement). In Quant's wake, the King's Road became the centre of mod fashion in the sixties; the middle-class 'Chelsea Set' frequenting its stylish boutiques, bistros, clubs and bars. Quant has started opening shops again, retaining the familiar stylized daisy logo, but now stocking down-market, skimpy Lycra wear and gaudy accessories aimed at teenagers and tourists.

Vidal Sassoon
60 South Molton Street, W1 (071 491 8848). Bond Street underground. **Open** 9am-5pm Mon-Wed; 8.30am-7pm Thur; 8.30am-6.30pm Fri; 8.30am-5pm Sat. **Credit** A, £TC, V.
Innovation and precise cutting are still the trademarks of this trail-blazing salon (this branch is women-only, prices from £27). Vidal Sassoon, an East Ender who trained under hairdresser-to-the-stars Mr Teasie-Weasie, founded his first salon in Bond Street. Sassoon dustbinned the old, elaborate styles and initiated the 'geometric cut', complementing Mary Quant's clothes and dominating mod fashion. Even more revolutionary was the effect of hairdressing for men, who no longer had to get shorn at barbers .

POP CULTURE
Pillorying the Establishment became one of the great occupations of the sixties. TV shows such as *That Was the Week That Was* and satirical magazines like *Private Eye* (60p, available from most newsagents unless it's facing a court injunction for libel) led the way in

Carnaby Street *(listed under* **The Sixties: Hip, Groovy, Fab Man***) was the heart of Swinging Sixties London. The boutiques that sprung up along the street became the place to buy the latest street fashions – and to be seen buying them; especially for pop stars. A focus for the modernists (mods) to hang out, it became more mainstream and commercialized by the mid-sixties. Today, despite grotesque signs proclaiming 'Carnaby Street welcomes the world', its decline is being reversed with the arrival of designer boutiques and street fashion outlets including Boy and Mary Quant.*

highlighting hypocrisy and cant in the British ruling classes. In 1964 off-shore 'pirate radio' stations revolutionized the music scene. The most famous was Radio Caroline, which played hits considered too racy for the BBC's mainstream radio stations and (still-running) *Top of the Pops* TV programme. Concurrently, the club-like show *Ready Steady Go!*, broadcast by commercial Independent Television, became required viewing for trendies wanting to see new bands like the ones playing the **Marquee** club. By 1967 the pirates were outlawed, *RSG!* had finished and the BBC had at last launched Radio London. But youth culture had by then gone 'underground'.

Discotheques without live music had been an innovation of the mod era, but were modest compared to post-1966 psychedelic clubs (UFO, Middle Earth, the Flamingo) with light shows, drugs and concept album music. A seminal event was the October 1966 launch party for the underground paper *International Times* (*IT*) at the **Roundhouse.** LSD-coated sugarcubes were distributed to the bacchanalian throng

that included Paul McCartney in Arab costume and Marianne Faithfull, award-winningly dressed as a nun. The Establishment was undecided about the new generation; pop music appeared to be a dangerous thing. Music, however, prevailed. The 1969 Rolling Stones gig in Hyde Park attracted half a million young people.

Events and entertainments in London were now so diverse that the capital's first listings magazine was an automatic success. Tony Elliot's *Time Out* magazine tapped a massive demand for information about the city's entertainment scene. It's been providing up-to-the-minute information about what's happening in London since its launch in 1968.

Marquee
105 Charing Cross Road, WC2 (071 437 6603). Leicester Square or Tottenham Court Road underground. **Open** 7-11pm daily. **Music** from 7.30pm. **Admission** £3.50-£6. **Credit** (shop & ticket agency) A, £TC, V.
To showcase new bands has always been the philosophy of the Marquee. Music of mixed quality is the result, but having nurtured The Who, Manfred Mann, Spencer Davis, Jethro Tull and the Police is a more than modest contribution. Originally opened on Oxford Street in 1958, new premises on Wardour Street were christened by the

Yardbirds in March 1964. It's temporarily moved again and the bands are more in the gothic, thrash and heavy metal mould. But it remains an essential rock institution. *See chapter* **Music: Rock, Folk & Jazz.**

Roundhouse
99 Chalk Farm Road, NW1 (071 482 5245). Chalk Farm underground.
This ex-engine house, a peculiar building with a circular balcony, achieved a legendary status in the sixties and seventies. Underground all-nighters such as the *IT* party and 'Psychodelphia Versus Ian Smith' (sic), run by Pink Floyd, were held here. These psychedelic happenings were the public's first introduction to sophisticated light-shows and demonstrate just what copyists the current Acid House party organizers are. The legendary Friday all-nighter, UFO, moved here in August 1967. An essential club and music venue right into the punk era, it's currently closed, but is likely to reopen in 1991/92 as an international multi-ethnic arts centre.

Troubadour Coffee House
265 Old Brompton Road, SW5. Earl's Court or West Brompton underground. **Open** 10.30am-11pm daily. **Breakfast served** 10.30am-12.30pm daily. **Lunch served** 12.30-2.25pm daily. **Dinner served** 5.30-10pm daily. **Average** £3.50. **Unlicensed.** **Credit** LV, £TC.
Remarkably little changed, the Troubadour was the site of one of the first 'contemporary style' clubs. It put on all styles of music and poetry, but by 1963 – the year Bob Dylan emerged from the audience to play some tunes – it had become predominantly a folk venue.

THE SEVENTIES

People don't like this decade; it's when everything went wrong. Strikes and international debt finally flushed the economy down the toilet. Too many Londoners remember it as a decade when rubbish was piled in the streets, electricity power-cuts blacked-out televisions and a three-day working week brought down the government when it lost its battles to control the trades unions. Britain's idiosyncratic past was finally relegated to history when its currency was replaced on 15 February 1971 with an eminently sensible decimal system (that worked on units of ten rather than the traditional 12). What's more, Britain decided (by a massive majority) to join the European Community in 1973. Chauvinists despaired. To make matters worse for them, oil prices shot through the ceiling and Arab businessmen started buying up tracts of London. For much of the decade, the country appeared to be out of control.

Against this background of strife and disunity, several important social changes took place. Racial discrimination was outlawed, as were practises that discriminated against women in the work-place. After more than ten years, these laws still have a long way to go before they prove effective. And the planners, the people who had been entrusted (almost unthinkingly) with Britain's safe passage through life after the war, faced their most major setback. When **Covent Garden** was to be redeveloped, the local residents fought back. The developers lost and the area retained much of its historical tradition as London's centre for arts and entertainments.

Covent Garden Market
The Piazza, WC2 (071 836 9136). Covent Garden or Charing Cross underground/BR.
In the mid-seventies the Covent Garden vegetable and flower market moved to Nine Elms, SW11. It's hard to believe that in 1971 the GLC wanted the handsome buildings replaced with a major road and office blocks. The local community – a motley band of actors, craftsmen, printers and traders – wanted to stay put. Vast meetings and candle-lit demonstrations finally achieved the preservation of many buildings and the council backed down. With the property boom and small scale development – specialist shops, design studios, restaurants and street entertainment – made it one of London's most interesting districts. Depressingly, soaring rents are forcing out unique establishments, vast offices are planned and the market's been bought by an insurance company. The British never learn. *See chapter* **The West End.**

THE DECADE THAT TASTE FORGOT
Excess was the by-word of seventies fashion. Unisex clothing moved from practicality to androgyny. Music veered between over-produced pap-pop and anarchic punk. Gold lamé was rife – either as a fashion accessory in jackets or as a rebellious statement in the form of fetishistic bondage gear. The decade served as a salutory lesson to Britain. People were not sure what they wanted, but were willing to do almost anything to show that they didn't like what there was. London of the eighties was shaped by a determination to avoid the horrors of the seventies.

Crazy Larry's
533 King's Road, SW10 (071 376 5555). Fulham Broadway or Sloane Square underground/N11, N14, 22 bus. **Open** 9.30pm-1am Tue, Wed; 9.30pm-2am Thur; 8pm-2am Fri,

Sat; 11am-5pm Sun. **Admission** £5 Tue-Thur; £6 Fri, Sat; £2.50 Sun. **Credit** A, AmEx, V.
The late eighties obsession with kitsch made Crazy Larry's, with its tacky seventies décor, hip once more. Clubbers even regressed into wearing suede waistcoats, flares and brown leather berets during what was dubbed the 'second summer of love', 20 years after the Woodstock era.

Metropolis
3 D'Arblay Street, W1 (071 494 2531). Oxford Circus or Tottenham Court Road underground. **Open** 10am-7pm Mon-Fri; 11am-6pm Sat. **Credit** A, AmEx, DC, V.
This new store is a treasure trove of kitsch items from the thirties to the seventies. The latter decade is particularly well represented thanks to the prevalence of such repulsive items as wave-making executive toys and 'globule' lamps.

Jubilee Gardens & Jubilee Walk
Jubilee Gardens, South Bank, SE1 (071 928 3002). Waterloo underground/BR/1, 4, 68, X68, 70 70A, 76, 171, 171A, 176, 188, 501, 502, 513 bus.
The old British remedy for runaway wage-inflation, unemployment and strikes is to wheel out the royal family and invent a bit of tradition. The silver jubilee (25 years' reign) of Queen Elizabeth II in 1977 upped the tourist trade with all its attendant pageantry and was an excuse for a nation-wide street party. Jubilee Gardens (a park on the South Bank used for major events) and the Jubilee Walk through London's landmarks, marked by pavement plaques, commemorate the happy event.

Kensington Market
49-53 Kensington High Street, W8 (071 937 1572/071 937 7508). High Street Kensington underground. **Open** 10am-6pm Mon-Sat. **Credit** varies between shops.
See **picture and caption.**

World's End
430 King's Road, SW10 (071 352 6551). Sloane Square underground/11, 19, 22, bus. **Open** 11am-6pm Mon-Sat. **Credit** A, AmEx, DC, V.
Let it Rock, Too Young To Live; Too Fast To Die, Sex and Seditionaries were previous incarnations of this shop run by Malcolm McLaren (manager of the Sex Pistols) and Vivienne Westwood. Whatever the name, it showcased their inspired punk designs – the Pirate outfit, for example – and remains the touchstone of King's Road couture. Today, only Westwood's uncompromising collection of clothing design is on sale. The Hansel and Gretel style décor is bizarre.
Postal delivery.

THE EIGHTIES
History will regard the eighties as the Thatcher era. Britain's first woman prime minister – the embodiment of consumer idealism and little Englander morality – set out to expunge socialism and the influence of the sixties and seventies. Unemployment soared in the early

Kensington Market *(listed under* **The Seventies: The Decade That Taste Forgot)** *is a rabbit warren of trendy stalls and shops that has been a major supplier of cultish accoutrements from punk to goth to Levi 501s. There are also outlets – Marvelette and Rock-a-Cha – for retro and second hand stuff from the fifties and sixties; Johnson's stocks high quality rock 'n' roll gear. You can still kit yourself out here in an original punk outfit. The dope-shrouded corridors remain a popular hang-out for safety-pinned purists with the obligatory mohican topping.*

eighties, but we now have a shortage of skilled workers in the capital, whilst in the north of England, many still live below the breadline. A monetarist policy and cuts in public services have neatly exacerbated the north-south divide.

Cash dispensers and wallets full of credit cards heralded the consumer-goods orgy of the eighties. In the money decade your bank account could now be a status symbol. Property prices – the biggest, and in the end the most boring, talking point of dinner parties in the eighties – rocketed.

'Lifestyle' became a buzz word. If you weren't in a social category, you didn't belong. Style magazines – *The Face, i-D, Blitz, Arena* – dictated distinct social types: yuppies, dinkies, Sloanes; of course no one actually admitted to being one.

The eighties trendy was obsessed with designer labels. Essential accoutrements included a mobile phone, a Porsche, a CD player and, of course, a warehouse in the London Docklands decked out in matt-black trinkets from **American Retro** (*see chapter* **Shopping & Services**). Imported

lager suddenly acquired unbelievable status and every new restaurant which opened was not a restaurant but a brasserie.

Next
54-60 Kensington High Street, W8 (071 938 4211). Kensington High Street underground. **Open** 10am-6pm Mon; 9.30am-6pm Tue, Wed; 9.30am-8pm Thur; 9.30am-6.45pm Fri; 9.30am-7pm Sat. **Credit** A, AmEx, DC, £TC, V.
George Davies has a lot to answer for. At the begining of the eighties he grabbed the dowdy, unimaginative British retailing industry by the balls by applying design ethics to both the garments and the shops. Initially concerned with women's clothing, Davies saw the proverbial gap in the market. Clothes for men, women and children, interior design, jewellery, hair salons, food, flowers, make-up and luggage were all launched on an unsuspecting public. Whilst many of us are sick to the back teeth with Next, it has to be admitted that the face-lift it brought to British fashion was long overdue.
Café. Baby-changing facilities. Export scheme. Toilets for the disabled. Wheelchair access.

The Filofax Centre
21 Conduit Street, W1 (071 499 0457). Oxford Circus underground. **Open** 9.30am-6pm Mon-Fri; 10am-6pm Sat. **Credit** A, AmEx, DC, EC, £TC, V.
Although it had been around since the 1930s, it wasn't until the eighties that the Filofax really came into its own as one of the more affordable designer trappings. In this palatial shop you can stock up on refills for

your Iguana-skin binder, the most useful of which will be the *Time Out* Filofax guides to eating, shopping, cities and so on (£3.25).

Café Freud
198 Shaftesbury Avenue, WC2 (071 240 9933). Covent Garden or Tottenham Court Road underground. **Open** 11am-11pm Mon-Sat; 11am-10.30pm Sun. **Average** £5. **No credit cards.**
The ultimate designer café, name-dropped by the trendiest of Londoners. Down in the basement of a chic furniture shop, the small bar has a tasteful but uncomfy concrete and beaten-steel interior design, with temporary art displays. The visually pleasing staff (often brusquely) dispense the latest imported lagers and light meals at stratospheric prices.

Camden Markets
Camden High Street to Chalk Farm Road, NW1 (071 485 4457). Camden Town or Chalk Farm underground/Camden Road BR. **Open** 8am-6pm Sat, Sun. **No credit cards.** *See* **picture and caption.**

ARCHITECTURE

In 1986, Prince Charles described the proposed **National Gallery** extension as 'A monstrous carbuncle on the face of a much-loved friend'. This remark sparked off more than just heated discussion amongst architects and the general public. With whole areas of London being redeveloped – Broadgate, King's Cross, Docklands – Charles has become a major influence on what gets built. Both the National Gallery plan and the development of Paternoster Square near St Paul's Cathedral have been redesigned according to the Prince's populist, classical tastes.

Richmond Riverside
Richmond Bridge, Richmond, Surrey. Richmond underground/BR/boat to Richmond Pier/27, 33, 37, 65, 71, 202, 270 bus.
Designed by architect Quinlan Terry, this classical edifice certainly pleases the eye, fits in with the surroundings and is on a human scale, but it's a brazen piece of façadism. It's dishonest because there's no classical structure behind the porticos, only an ugly iron-framed office space. Still, Terry's scheme is popular and works; significantly, the Tourist Information Centre is located here.

Sainsbury's
17-21 Camden Road, NW1 (071 482 3828). Camden Town underground/Camden Road BR. **Open** 8.30am-8pm Mon-Thur; 8.30am-9pm Fri; 8am-8pm Sat. **No credit cards.**
Sainsbury's supermarkets may look reassuringly identical inside, but the outsides are causing controversy. Nick Grimshaw's cantilevered metal design looks like a spare part for an engine. It has presence, but somehow deftly fits into the building line of the Victorian street. Behind it and overlooking Regent's Canal is a terrace of ten houses by Grimshaw. Resembling sections of an aeroplane, this terrace is so arrogantly daring that history will see it as a visionary highlight of the current era.

The trendy, canalside **Camden Markets** *(listed under* **The Eighties***) are packed with young Londoners and visitors every weekend. The current redevelopment of Camden Lock makes visits a bit frustrating and cramped. By late 1992 it will have gained about 20 more craft workshops, a pub, design studios and a covered market hall. Much of its rough-and-ready character will be lost, but its role as an outlet for artists and craftspeople will be boosted. All forms of post-war street fashion can be found on sale and, indeed, are worn by the market-goers.*

Eating and Drinking

London is experiencing a culinary renaissance and now ranks among the food capitals of the world. Thousands of restaurants offering dozens of cuisines, from New Wave British to Burmese, cater to every taste and budget. Visitors who arrive expecting braised beef and over-cooked cabbage will most likely depart pleasantly surprised

This chapter will guide you around some of the best restaurants, bars, pubs and cafés in town, but for a fuller selection of nearly 2,000 eating and drinking spots, we publish the annual *Time Out Guide to Eating Out in London* (£4.95 from newsagents; also available in Filofax format, £3.65 from stationer's and Filofax stockists).

CONTENTS:

Eating & Drinking

The best culinary moves these days are being made by British chefs. But if you still don't like the idea, then London is stuffed with cuisines.

London is one of the world's top culinary capitals. There are over 30 different cuisines offered by over 8,000 restaurants in Greater London; and that doesn't include the hybrids like Tex-Mex, vegetarian and modern European. On the following pages we list some of the best places to eat and drink in London. Some are grand and expensive, but many are the good, value-for-money places that Londoners like to keep to themselves.

OLD TRADITIONS, NEW IDEAS

At the moment the eyes of London gourmands are focused on British cooking and the new wave of young, talented chefs who are changing people's conception of British food as stodgy rubbish. Shaun Thomson at **Jason's Court Restaurant** cooks light traditional-with-a-twist dishes; **Alastair Little,** who has been at the forefront of modern British cooking for over four years, has a far more eclectic repertoire that includes Japanese and European influences.

RESTAURANT RULES

Like most businesses, the majority of restaurants are run fairly and well. However, just in case you have cause for complaint, it's best to know your rights.

Restaurants must display a copy of the current menu at the door. The prices on the menu must, by law, include value-added tax (VAT — Britain's equivalent of a sales tax). Some restaurants may add a cover charge of 50p to £2 (supposedly to pay for the bread, clean table-cloths, fresh flowers and so on). If entertainment is provided this charge could be higher. If any of these are automatically added to the bill, this must be stated on the menu.

Some places also include a service charge, usually from 10 to 15 per cent. If this is automatically added and the service was satisfactory you must pay it. If you have complaints about the service, you should withhold some or all of this charge, but you must call the manager/ess and explain why you are dissatisfied. If your service charge is not included, a tip of 10 per cent (preferably in cash) is normal.

EATING OUT IN LONDON

If you want to seriously explore the diverse range of cuisines and styles of cooking in London, you will find the *Time Out Guide to Eating Out in London* an invaluable dining companion. Published every Autumn, costing £5.75 it lists almost 2,000 of the best eating and drinking places in London; from British to Burmese, East End pubs to Soho style bars.

For the personally organized there is also a condensed Filofax version and a separate guide to London's watering holes, the *Time Out/Filofax Guide to Drinking Places in London,* both priced at £3.25. All these publications are available from good newsagents, bookshops and Filofax stockists.

The services offered by London's restaurants can change suddenly. Many of them welcome children, but are unable to cater for babies; wheelchair access may be available but not toilet facilities for the disabled; dress codes vary from 'tie and jacket' to 'no jeans'; some of the most unlikely places serve vegetarian and vegan foods. Phone for details and prevent a fruitless journey by booking in advance.

EATING

CELEBRATED CHEFS

Bibendum
Michelin Building, 81 Fulham Road, SW3 (071 581 5817). South Kensington underground. **Lunch served** 12.30-2.30pm Mon-Fri; 12.30-3pm Sat, Sun. **Dinner served** 7-11pm daily. **Oyster bar** open noon-11pm

daily (no alcohol served on Sunday afternoon). **Average** £38. **Set lunch** £19.50. **House wine** £9.95 bottle, £1.75 glass. **Service** 15%. **Credit** A, TC, V.
Simon Hopkinson serves a fairly unchanging menu of traditional French café favourites and robust regional dishes. The place has been packed since the day it opened and you must now book for dinner at least a fortnight in advance. If you want to sample the food, but not the prices, the downstairs oyster bar serves a shortened, seafood-orientated menu.

Chez Nico
35 Great Portland Street, W1 (071 436 8846). Oxford Street underground. **Lunch served** 12.15-2pm Mon-Fri. **Dinner served** 7-11.15pm Mon-Fri. **Average** £40. **Set lunch** two course: £25; three course: £34. **Set dinner** £34. **House wine** £13 bottle, £3.50 glass. **Credit** A, AmEx, DC, V.
Nico Ladenis is a notoriously tyrannical self-taught chef, whose knowledge and skill are his vindication. This year he's moved his restaurant to more comfortable premises near Oxford Circus. His inspiration is Provence and, despite the hype, dinner is a great experience.

Clarke's
124 Kensington Church Street, W8 (071 221 9225). High Street Kensington or Notting Hill Gate underground. **Lunch served** 12.30-2pm Mon-Fri. **Dinner served** 7.30-11pm Mon-Fri. **Supper served** 10-11pm Mon-Fri. **Set lunch** two course: £14; three course: £16. **Set dinner** £25. **Set supper** £19. **House wine** £7 bottle, £1.75 glass. **Credit** A, £TC, V.
Sally Clarke's cooking has been described as Californian because of the time she spent with Alice Waters at Chez Panisse in Berkeley, reputedly the best restaurant on the West Coast. The menu is short, and the flavours are robust.

The Connaught Hotel Grill Room
Carlos Place, W1 (071 499 7070). Green Park underground. **Lunch served** 12.30-2pm Mon-Fri. **Dinner served** 6-10.15pm Mon-Fri. **Average** £40. **Minimum** £20. **House wine** £9.50 carafe, £2.25 glass. **Service** 15%. **Credit** A, V.
The Connaught is perhaps the poshest hotel in town, discreet and very exclusive. The chef is Michel Bourdin, who's also chairman of the British branch of the Academie Culinaire (the 'top chefs' club), and he specializes in the highest standards of traditional cuisine. You may have to book more than two weeks ahead.

Le Gavroche
43 Upper Brook Street, W1 (071 408 0881/071 499 1826). Marble Arch underground. **Lunch served** noon-2pm Mon-Fri. **Dinner served** 7-11pm, Mon-Fri. **Average** *Lunch:* £35; *Dinner:* £70. **Minimum Dinner:** £40. **Set lunch** £19.50. **Set dinner** £45. **House wine** £14 bottle, £4 glass. **Credit** A, AmEx, CB, DC, TC, V.
Albert Roux is the godfather figure of haute cuisine in the UK. He was the first chef in Britain to gain three Michelin stars, and his restaurant is rightly acclaimed for its excellence and consistency. The set lunch is good value and in the evening there's a Menu Exceptional (£45 each for a minimum of two people).

Harvey's

2 Bellevue Road, SW17 (071 672 0114).
Wandsworth Common BR/49 bus. **Lunch**
served 12.30-2pm Mon-Fri. **Dinner served**
7.30-11.15pm Mon-Sat. **Average** Lunch: £15;
Dinner: £26. **House wine** £7.50 bottle, £1.75
glass. **Credit** A, £STC, V.
Marco Pierre White is the rock 'n' roule star
of the British restaurant scene; an outspo-
ken and successful chef, he's so far the
youngest to be awarded a Michelin star.
Marco has received a lot of flak for everything from shouting at his staff to having
long hair and tasting sauces with his fingers.
However, there's probably no better chef in
Britain today.

Alastair Little

49 Frith Street, W1 (071 734 5183).
Piccadilly Circus or Tottenham Court Road
underground. **Lunch served** 12.30-2.30pm
Mon-Fri. **Dinner served** 7.30-11.30 pm
Mon-Sat. **Average** £30. **House wine** £8 bot-
tle, £1.75 glass. **No credit cards.**
See **picture and caption.**

La Tante Claire

68 Royal Hospital Road, SW3 (071 352
6045/071 351 0227). Sloane Square
underground. **Lunch served** 12.30-2pm
Mon-Fri. **Dinner served** 7-11pm Mon-Fri.
Average £40. **Set lunch** £19. **House wine**
£11.50 bottle, £3 glass. **Credit** A, AmEx,
DC, TC, V.
Pierre Koffmann's pretty, light and airy
restaurant is one of the most respected in
the UK – and deservedly so. He spends little
time outside his kitchen, from which

emerges truly excellent modern French
cooking. The set lunch and dinner menus
keep the bill down.

BRITISH

Auntie's

126 Cleveland Street. W1 (071 387
1548/071 387 3226). Great Portland Street
or Warren Street underground. **Lunch**
served noon-2.45pm Mon-Fri. **Dinner**
served 6-10.30pm Mon-Sat. **Set**
lunch/dinner £16.50. **House wine** £7.50
bottle, £1.70 glass. **Service** 12½%. **Credit**
A, AmEx, DC, £TC, V.
This Edwardian-style tea-room serves a mixture of traditional and modern English
dishes. One of our favourite restaurants.

Chapter House Restaurant

Southwark Cathedral, Montague Close, SE1
(071 378 6446). London Bridge under-
ground/BR. **Lunch served** noon-2.30pm
Mon-Fri. **Dinner served** bookings only.
Average £13. **House wine** £5.50 bottle, £1
glass. **Credit** A, AmEx, DC, V.
Chapter House is a large, open-plan
space, with a stone floor, wooden furniture and high ceilings. The food is light,
traditional British food, with plenty of
chunky pies and even a couple of imaginative vegetarian dishes.

Jason's Court Restaurant

Jason Court, 76 Wigmore Street, W1 (071
224 2992). Bond Street underground. **Lunch**
served noon-2.30pm Mon-Fri. **Dinner**

served 7-10.30pm Mon-Sat. **Average** £25.
Set lunch £14.95. **House wine** £7.95 bottle,
£1.50 glass. **Credit** A, AmEx, DC, V.
See **picture and caption.**

Ye Olde Cheshire Cheese

145 Fleet Street, EC4 (071 353 6170).
Blackfriars or St Paul's underground. **Lunch**
served noon-2.30pm Mon-Sat. **Dinner**
served 6-9pm Mon-Sat. **Average** £14.
House wine £6.50 bottle, £1.05 glass.
Credit A, AmEx, DC, £TC, V.
Apart from the sawdust on the floor (which
changes every day), little has altered over
the last 200 years. The atmosphere and the
food are as close as you can now get to real
Old London. Pass over the starters in favour
of the roast beef or good, honest steak and
kidney pies and puddings. The seats once
favoured by Charles Dickens and Dr
Johnson are marked by two brass plaques.

Porters

17 Henrietta Street, WC2 (071 836 6466).
Covent Garden underground. **Open** noon-
11.30pm Mon-Sat; noon-10.30pm Sun.
Alcoholic drinks served noon-3pm,
5.30pm-midnight, Mon-Sat; noon-2.30pm, 7-
10.30pm Sun. **Average** £9. **House wine**
£5.85 bottle, £1.50 glass. **Service** 10% for parties of five and over. **Credit** A, £TC, V.
Porters is a modern version of the traditional
English pie shop. There are no starters, just
a short menu of seven pies (including fish
and vegetarian versions), and a selection of
good, but extremely calorific, steamed and
baked puddings.

Rules

35 Maiden Lane, WC2 (071 836 5314/071
836 2559). Covent Garden underground or
Charing Cross underground/BR. **Meals**
served noon-midnight Mon-Sat. **Alcoholic**
drinks served noon-midnight Mon-Sat.
Average £23. **House wine** £6.50 bottle,
£1.85 glass. **Credit** A, AmEx, £TC, V.
Almost 200 years old, Rules is one of
London's finest restaurants, serving British
food to Royalty and assorted thespians.
Guinness casserole, game and oysters in
season and Aberdeen Angus beef are typical
dishes. Dress smartly but informally and
always book.

Veronica's

3 Hereford Road, W2 (071 229 5079).
Bayswater, Notting Hill Gate or Queensway
underground. **Lunch served** noon-3pm
Mon-Fri. **Dinner served** 7pm-midnight
Mon-Sat. **Alcoholic drinks served** noon-
midnight. **Average** £14. **House wine** £6.50
bottle, £2 glass. **Service** 10%. **Credit** A,
AmEx, DC, V.
Even the most jaded gourmand will find
something exciting here. Each month the
changing menu has a different focus: traditional Scottish recipes; food from the North
East; Victorian food and so on.

BRITISH: FISH

Rudland & Stubbs

35-37 Greenhill Rents, Cowcross Street, EC1
(071 253 0148/071 253 1534). Farringdon
underground/BR. **Lunch served** noon-
2.45pm Mon-Fri. **Dinner served** 6-11pm
Mon-Sat. **Average** £15. **House wine** £6.75
bottle, £1.50 glass. **Credit** A, £STC, V.
This complex of bars and a fish restaurant

Alastair Little *(listed under* **Celebrated Chefs***) has been at the forefront of*
modern British food since his restaurant opened, four years ago; constantly
innovating and always retaining remarkably high standards. The décor of his restau-
rant, like the food, is unpretentious, with no embellishments. There's also a cheaper
bar area downstairs but remember to take cash — they don't accept any plastic.

CAFE PACIFICO
Mexican Restaurant-Cantina
5 Langley Street London WC2
Tel. 01-379-7728

Established in Europe since 1976

Jason's Court Restaurant *(listed under* **British***) is the best of the Modern British restaurants to open this year. Classic dishes are subtly reworked by the chef, Shaun Thompson. Service is professional but relaxed and the little touches (home-made herb bread served in ramekins, vegetables in individual silver saucepans) are fun without being too twee.*

has a stylish informality, with sawdust-strewn floors. You can pop in to a bar for a quick dozen oysters. The steak, kidney and oyster pie is excellent.

BRITISH: FISH AND CHIPS

Grahame's Seafare
38 Poland Street, W1 (071 437 3788/071 437 0975). Oxford Circus underground. **Open** noon-2.45pm Mon; noon-2.45pm, 5.30-8.45pm, Tue-Thur; noon-2.45pm, 5.30-7.45pm, Fri; noon-2.45pm, 5.30-6pm, Sat. **Average** £14. **House wine** £6 bottle, £1.10 glass. **Credit** AmEx, £TC, V.
London's only kosher fish restaurant, which gives it some interesting differences, in the starters particularly. You can have your batter made in the usual way with flour or, more deliciously, with matzo meal. There's a short list of wines.

Seafresh Fish Restaurant
80-81 Wilton Road, SW1 (071 828 0747). Victoria underground/BR. **Open** noon-11pm Mon-Sat. **Average** £9. **House wine** £5.25 bottle, £1.30 glass. **Credit** LV, £TC.
A favourite cabbie haunt where there are constant queues and you often have to wait for a table. The seafood plate is enough to feed a family for a week, all for £7.95.

BRITISH: PIE AND MASH

F Cooke & Sons
41 Kingsland High Street, E8 (071 254 2878). Dalston Kingsland BR/5, 6, 22, 48, 67, 149 bus. **Open** 10am-8pm Mon, Thur; 10am-6pm

Tue, Wed; 10am-10pm Fri, Sat. **Average** £2.50. **Unlicensed. No corkage. Credit** DC.
See **picture and caption.**

BRITISH: ROAST BEEF

Baron of Beef
Gutter Lane, EC2 (071 606 6961/071 606 9415). St Paul's underground. **Lunch** served noon-3pm Mon-Fri. **Dinner served** 5.30-9pm Mon-Fri. **Average** £26. **House wine** £8.50 bottle, £1.95 glass. **Service** 12½%. **Credit** A, AmEx, DC, GM, £TC, V.
In the basement of a hideous sixties' tower block is this restaurant decorated in the plush, British style of a Baronial dining-room or a gentlemen's club. The roast sirloin of beef makes a visit worthwhile. The desserts are very English: pear charlotte, English strawberries.

Simpson's in-the-Strand Grand Divan Tavern
100 Strand, WC2 (071 836 9112). Charing Cross underground/BR. **Lunch served** noon-3pm Mon-Sat. **Dinner served** 6-10pm Mon-Sat. Pre-theatre 6-7pm Sat. **Average** *Lunch:* £13; *Dinner:* £22; *Pre-theatre:* £13. **House wine** £6.75 carafe. **Corkage** £8 table wines; £9 champagne and fortified wines; £10 spirits and deluxe products. **Credit** A, AmEx, DC, TC, V.
See **picture and caption.**

MODERN EUROPEAN

Le Caprice
Arlington House, Arlington Street, St James, SW1 (071 629 2239). Green Park underground. **Lunch served** noon-3pm. **Dinner**

served 6pm-midnight, daily. **Average** £21. **House wine** £5.75 bottle, £1.75 glass. **Credit** A, AmEx, DC, £TC, V.
On Sunday the place is awash with the local bread-heads and wealthy Italians dressed in casual Armani numbers who roll in at about 1pm looking stylishly wasted. The food is imaginative, well-cooked and not as expensive as you might expect.

Langan's Brasserie
Stratton Street, W1 (071 493 6437/071 491 8822). Green Park underground. **Open** 12.30pm-1am Mon-Fri; 8pm-1am Sat. **Lunch served** 12.30-2.45pm Mon-Fri. **Dinner served** 7.30-11.45pm Mon-Fri; 8pm-12.45am Sat. **Average** £20. **House wine** £5.95 bottle, £1.75 glass. **Service** 12½%. Credit A, AmEx, DC, LV, £TC, V.
There are cheaper places to eat at, offering better food, better wine and better service, but Langan's remains as popular as ever. The menu is an eclectic European mix, and choosing is pot luck. The seating has a code: the incognito or the cognoscenti upstairs; downstairs for the life and glamour.

Leith's
92 Kensington Park Road, W11 (071 229 4481). Notting Hill Gate underground/12, 27, 28, 31, 52, 88 bus. **Dinner served** 7.30-11.30pm daily. **Alcoholic drinks served** 7.30-midnight. **Average:** *two course:* £26; *three course:* £32.50; *four course:* £36. **House wine** £9.75 bottle. **Credit** A, AmEx, DC, TC, V.
An elegant, stylish restaurant which, although it's been something of an institution since the late sixties, is not content to rest on its laurels. Trolleys laden with desserts and starters are shunted about the rooms, sparking off gluttony in the wealthy clientele. Pricey but excellent.

Mélange
59 Endell Street, WC2 (071 240 8077). Covent Garden underground.
Bar. **Alcoholic drinks and snacks served:** noon-11.30pm Mon-Sat.
Restaurant: **Lunch served** noon-3pm Mon-Fri. **Dinner served** 6-11.30pm Mon-Sat. **Average** £16. *Both:* **House wine** £6.50 bottle, £1.30 glass. **Service** 12½% for five or more. **Credit** A, AmEx, DC, TC, V.
A small, comfortable if somewhat surreal restaurant, with good food and friendly staff. The food is a mix of European and Oriental influences, which defies attempts to pigeonhole. With fame the service has gone from trendily chaotic to chaotically trendy.

FRENCH: BRASSERIES

La Brasserie
272 Brompton Road, SW3 (071 584 1668). South Kensington underground. **Open** 8am-midnight daily. **Average** £15. **House wine** £6.80 bottle, £1.30 glass. **Service** 15%. **Credit** A, AmEx, DC, £TC, V.
London's first approximation of a real French brasserie is authentic in every detail, down to the harassed expression on the face of the waiter. If the sun appears the french windows are folded back and the densely-packed seats spill into Brompton Road. It gets busy, so book at peak periods.

Café Delancey
3 Delancey Street, NW1 (071 387 1985).
Camden Town underground. **Open** 9.30am-
midnight daily. **Meals served** 9.30am-
11.30pm daily. **Alcoholic drinks served**
11am-midnight daily. **Average** £11.50.
House wine £5.70 bottle, £1.20 glass.
Credit A, £TC, V.
Delancey is atmospheric, community-based
and authentically free of formality and pretensions. The food is interesting without
being over-complicated.

Café Rouge
19 High Street, NW3 (071 433 3404).
Hampstead underground/BR. **Open** 10am-
11.15pm daily. **Meals served** noon-11.15pm
Mon-Sat; noon-10.30pm Sun. **Average** £15.
House wine £7.50 litre, £1.95 glass. **Service**
12½%. **Credit** A, AmEx, £TC, V.
See **picture and caption.**

FRENCH RESTAURANTS

Gavvers
*61-63 Lower Sloane Street, SW1 (071 730
5983). Sloane Square underground.* **Lunch**
served noon-2.30pm. **Dinner served** 7-
11pm, daily. **Average** *Lunch*: £15.50; *Dinner*:
£27. **House wine** £7 bottle, £2.10 glass.
Credit A, AmEx, DC, £TC, V.
This small, elegant restaurant, once the
home of Le Gavroche, now offers a good
line in modern French food. The set price
menus represent remarkable value, but the
operation is tightly run and they like to
have two sittings in the evening, so book
well in advance and turn up on time. For
the money you get a glass of kir, three
courses with a half bottle of wine. Coffee
and service is included.

Mon Plaisir
*21 Monmouth Street, WC2 (071 836
7243/071 240 3757). Covent Garden or
Leicester Square underground.* **Lunch**
served noon-2.15pm Mon-Fri. **Dinner**
served 6-11.15pm Mon-Sat. Pre-theatre 6-
7.15pm Mon-Sat. **Average** *Dinner*: £25;
Lunch: £11.95; *Pre-theatre*: £11.95. **House**
wine £6.95 bottle, £1.85 glass. **Service**
12½%. **Credit** A, AmEx, DC, £TC, V.
The atmosphere at this popular pre-theatre
haunt is quintessentially French with a
touch of showbiz thrown in. The menu features familar dishes, competently prepared,
and the food is never dull.
Branch: Mon Petit Plasir, *33 Holland Street,
W8 (071 937 3224).*

La Poule au Pot
231 Ebury Street, SW1 (071 730 7763).
Sloane Square underground. **Lunch served**
12.30-2.30pm Mon-Fri. **Dinner served** 7-
11.15pm Mon-Sat. **Average** *Lunch*: £10.95;
Dinner: £25. **House wine** £14.30 magnum,
£1.30 glass. **Service** 12½%. **Credit** A,
AmEx, DC, £TC, V.
One of London's most idiosyncratic French
restaurants. The walls are bare brick, hung
with brass and copper saucepans, and the
room is furnished with old oak tables. The
food is robust, tasty and served in ample,
bourgeois portions. House wine is poured
from magnums and you're charged according to consumption.
Branch: Maggie Jones, *6 Old Court
Place, Kensington Church Street, W8
(071 937 6462).*

GREEK

Rodos
*59 St Giles High Street, WC2 (071 836
3177). Tottenham Court Road underground.*
Lunch served noon-2.30pm Mon-Fri.
Dinner served 5.30-11.30pm Mon-Sat.
Average £13. Meze £13.75 per person.
House wine £5.70 bottle, £1.40 glass.
Service 10%. **Credit** A, AmEx, DC, £TC, V.
From the outside it looks a bit down-at-heel
and inside it's rather homely; it doesn't look
like one of London's finest Greek restau-
rants. Familiar dishes are a revelation here.

ITALIAN

Bertorelli's
*44A Floral Street, WC2 (071 836 1868/071
836 3969). Covent Garden underground.*
Lunch served *Restaurant*: noon-3pm Mon-
Sat; *Wine bar*: noon-3pm Mon-Fri; **Dinner**
served *Restaurant*: 5.45-11.30pm; *Wine bar*:
5.45-11.30pm Mon-Sat., Mon-Sat. **Average**
Restaurant: £15; *Wine bar*: £8 **House wine**
Restaurant: £6.75 bottle, £1.50 glass; *Wine
bar*: £5.50 bottle, £1.15 glass. *Both*: **Service**
12½%. **Credit** A, AmEx, DC, £TC, V.
A stylish restaurant decorated in art deco
revival style. The menu is simple and inexpensive, with various pastas, pizzas and meat
and fish dishes.

Como Lario
22 Holbein Place, SW1 (071 730 2954).
Sloane Square underground. **Lunch served**
12.15-2.30pm. **Dinner served** 6.30-11.30pm,
Mon-Sat. **Average** £15. **House wine** £6 bottle, £1.50 glass. **Credit** LV, £TC.
Hidden down a side-street that leads to the
Royal Court Theatre, this is a favourite
après-theatre venue. Queues often form after
10pm, so book for late suppers. The waiters
are very cheerful and maintain a light-
hearted atmosphere. The gnocchi is superb.

Orso
27 Wellington Street, WC2 (071 240 5269).
Covent Garden underground. **Meals served**
noon-midnight daily. **Average** £20. **House**
wine £7.50 carafe. **Credit** £STC.
This elegant, well cared-for restaurant has
pioneered good, modern Italian food in
London. Since it opened four years ago it
has become incredibly fashionable. The full
menu is served from noon to midnight
every day, so this is a great place for early
or late business lunches, pre-theatre dinners and after-theatre suppers. The atmosphere is soothing and immense care is
taken with the food.

PIZZA

La Delizia
*Chelsea Farmers Market, Sydney Street,
SW3 (071 351 6701). Sloane Square
underground/11, 19, 22, 49 bus.* **Meals**
served 10am-10.30pm daily. **Average** £9.
House wine £6 bottle, £1.50 glass. **No**
credit cards.
The gardens of the Chelsea Farmers
Market make this one of the nicest places in
town to eat pizza al fresco. But you may

Simpson's-in-the-Strand *(listed under* **British: Roast Beef***) has been
serving the British establishment with superlative roasts for over 150 years. The
quality is excellent and it's fair to say that nowhere in London serves better roast
beef. The hot sweets such as bread and butter pudding, spotted dick and
Simpson's treacle roll are simply delicious.*

have to wait for a table as La Delizia seems to be permanently busy. Claimed by some to make the best Italian pizza in town, Delizia turn out 27 varieties.
Branch: *63-65 Chelsea Manor Street, SW3 (071 376 4111).*

Pappagalli's Pizza Inc
7-9 Swallow Street, W1 (071 734 5182). Piccadilly Circus underground. **Lunch served** noon-3pm. **Dinner served** 5.15-11.15pm, Mon-Sat. **Average** £10. **House wine** £5.95 bottle, £1.75 glass. **Service** 10%. **Credit** A, £TC, V.
Pappagalli's is one of London's best US-style pizzerias. It's professionally run by keen, polite staff and a good place to bring the family. The menu lists salads, pasta and stuffed garlic bread loaves in addition to the pizzas. These are expensive; the regular size pizza is enough to feed two people with some left over for the dog (bag provided).

EASTERN EUROPEAN

The Gay Hussar
2 Greek Street, W1 (071 437 0973). Tottenham Court Road underground. **Lunch served** 12.30-2.30pm. **Dinner served** 5.30-11pm, Mon-Sat. **Average** £21. **Set lunch** £12. **House wine** £6.50 bottle, £2 glass. **No credit cards.**
An old-fashioned and comfortable Hungarian restaurant. The menu is authentic and the food is wonderful. The restaurant has recently won a *Harpers & Queen* award for its chilled, wild cherry soup (£2.75).

Wodka
12 St Albans Grove, W8 (071 937 6513). High Street Kensington underground. **Lunch served** noon-2.30pm Mon-Fri. **Dinner served** 7.15-11.15pm daily. **Average** £15. **House wine** £6.95 bottle, £1.75 glass. **Credit** A, A/c, AmEx, DC, £STC, V.
The modern Polish food at this pleasingly minimalist restaurant is well-prepared and authentic. Most people come here for the home-flavoured vodka; of the 13 kinds served we remember tasting those flavoured with plum, pepper and bison grass.

SPANISH AND PORTUGUESE

Casa Santana
44 Goldbourne Road, W10 (081 968 8764). Ladbroke Grove underground. **Lunch served** noon-3pm. **Dinner served** 6-11pm, daily. **Average** £9. **House wine** £4.75 carafe, £1.10 glass. **No credit cards.**
This café-cum-restaurant is an immensely enjoyable place and is the nearest you'll get to Portugal in London. The food is wholly authentic and incorporates the best qualities of peasant cuisine: large portions, tasty stews, cheap ingredients. Splendid.

Guernica
21a, Foley Street, W1 (071 580 0623). Oxford Circus or Great Portland Street underground. **Lunch served** noon-3pm Mon-Fri. **Dinner served** 7-11pm Mon-Sat. **Average** £18. **Set lunch** £12. **House wine** £6.30. **Credit** A, AmEx, DC, £TC, V.
This is the first serious Spanish restaurant in London. The chef is Basque and the cooking

F Cooke and Sons *(listed under* **British: Pie and Mash***) is the most magnificent of all the pie and mash establishments in London. It is still run by the original family and is unique for its decorative tiling, bench seating and marble tables. Honest fare at honest prices, and very popular with the locals.*

reflects a new, lighter Basque style which is currently sweeping Spain. The food is extremely good value.

Rebato's
169 South Lambeth Road, SW8 (071 735 6388/071 582 8089). Vauxhall or Stockwell underground/2A, 2B, 88 bus. **Lunch served** noon-2.30pm Mon-Fri. **Dinner served** 7-11.15pm Mon-Sat. **Average** £15. **Set meal** £9.75. **House wine** £4.95 bottle, £1 glass. **Credit** A, Air Plus, AmEx, DC, £TC, V.
The tapas bar at the front of this lovely restaurant must be the most comprehensively stocked in London. The long counter groans under the weight of dishes filled with traditional Spanish tapas, from callos (tripe), to fried livers of small songbirds in sauce. The restaurant at the back is expensive.

AFRICAN AND CARIBBEAN

Brixtonian: The Rhum Shop, Café and Restaurant
11 Dorrell Place, SW9 (071 978 8870/Fax 071 737 5521). Brixton underground/BR/2, 3, 109, 159 bus. **Meals served** 10.30am-11.30pm Tue-Sun. **Set dinner** £16.95. **House wine** £5.95 bottle, £1.50 glass. **Service** 12½%. **Credit** A, V.
The proprietors claim to have over 100 rums in stock, some over 25 years old. The décor is both subtle and striking; the atmosphere is as laid back as you could want.

Calabash
The Africa Centre, 38 King Street, WC2 (071 836 1976). Covent Garden underground. **Lunch served** 12.30-3pm Mon-Sat. **Dinner served** 6-10.30pm Mon-Sat. **Average** £12. **House wine** £5.75 bottle, £1 glass. **Service** 10%. **Credit** A, AmEx, DC, £TC, V.
As you would expect from the restaurant in the Africa Centre, the menu here does a good job of representing the food of that continent. Ever popular are the egusi (melon-shaped white seeds used to thicken stews or served with vegetables) from Nigeria and the dorowot from East Africa (chicken cooked in hot pepper sauce).

THE AMERICAS

Joe Allen
13 Exeter Street, WC2 (071 836 0651). Aldwych or Covent Garden underground. **Meals served** noon-12.45am Mon-Sat; noon-11.45pm Sun. **Average** £13. **House wine** £5.50 bottle, £1.20 glass. **Credit** £STC.
Food is of secondary importance to the preening and prancing of the diners and staff at this ever-popular basement restaurant. There are some pretty decent burgers (often not mentioned on the menu) which have earned a loyal following. There are some delicious, hugely fattening desserts like 'Death by Chocolate'.

Down Mexico Way
25 Swallow Street, W1 (071 437 9895). Piccadilly Circus underground. **Meals served** noon-11.45pm Mon-Sat. **Average**

*The décor of the new **Café Rouge** (listed under **French: Brasseries**) is remarkably authentic — right down to the French muzak that occasionally cuts its way through the lively atmosphere. The two-tier menu is composed of mainly traditional French fast food, all delivered to the table with a friendly, unintimidating smile. A perfect place for a hot, summer's evening.*

£14. **House wine** £6.50 bottle, £1.45 glass. **Service** 15%. **Credit** A, AmEx, V.
One of the most atmospheric places in which to eat in London. Originally a Spanish restaurant; wrought iron gates, greenery and a gushing fountain make you feel anywhere but Piccadilly.

Fifty One Fifty One
Chelsea Cloisters, Sloane Avenue, SW7 (071 730 5151). South Kensington underground. **Lunch served** noon-3pm Mon-Sat; noon-3pm Sun. **Dinner served** 6.30-11.30pm Mon-Sat; 7-10.30pm Sun. **Average** £19. **Set Sunday Brunch** £17.95. **House wine** £9.75 bottle, £2.25 glass. **Service** 15%. **Credit** A, AmEx, DC, LV, £TC, V.
It's the small touches at this restaurant that make it special: you're given fresh rolls and three types of butter (strawberry, pesto and normal) before the food arrives. The prettified Cajun food is good, particularly the blackened and mesquite-grilled meats and fish. The wine list claims to hold the most extensive collection of North American wines in the country.

Hard Rock Café
150 Old Park Lane, W1 (071 629 0382). Hyde Park Corner underground. **Meals served** noon-12.30am Mon-Thur, Sun; noon-1am Fri, Sat. **Average** £10.50. **House wine** £7 bottle, £1.90 glass. **Service** 12½%. **Credit** £STC.
What is there left to say about this institution and mecca for thousands of tourists? Part of its popularity is undoubtedly due to the excellent burgers and steaks available on a menu that's refreshingly devoid of the puns normally associated with fast food. Don't forget to buy your Hard Rock Café sweatshirt (black £14.95; white £13.95) on the way out.

Mitchell & O'Brien
2 St Anne's Court, W1 (071 434 9941). Tottenham Court Road or Leicester Square underground. **Meals served** noon-11pm daily. **Average** £14. **House wine** £7.95 bottle, £1.95 glass. **Credit** A, AmEx, V.
An immaculate and tasteful reproduction of a thirties' New York diner. The staff are as charming as ever, but the quality of the food has slipped a little. The cocktails are suitably potent.

Paulo's
30 Greyhound Road, W6 (071 385 9264). Barons Court or Hammersmith underground/11, 30, 74, 220 bus. **Dinner served** 7.30-10.30pm Mon-Sat. **Average** £11. **House wine** £6.95 bottle, £1.55 glass. **Corkage** £1. **Credit** £TC.
At this family-run Brazilian restaurant you can eat as much as you can pile on to your plate for £8.40. The choice is between about 20 traditional Brazilian dishes (lots of seafood with beef-flavoured palm oil). Drink Portuguese or Brazilian wine and enjoy the jolly atmosphere.

JEWISH

Bloom's
90 Whitechapel High Street, E1 (071 247 6001). Aldgate East underground. **Meals served** 11am-10pm Mon-Thur, Sun; 11am-2pm Fri. **Average** £10. **House wine** *Kosher.* £6.50 bottle. **Credit** A, V.
The best time to go to this branch of Bloom's is on Sunday. Then it's noisy, energetic, packed with Jewish families and you can get a tasty, filling lunch with the choice of practically every Jewish speciality you've ever heard of. It's rabbinically supervised, of course. The service is frenetic on Sundays, but rarely curt at this branch.
Branch: *130 Golders Green Road, NW11 (071 455 1338/071 455 3033).*

Hodari's Catering at B'Nai B'Rith Hillel House
1-2 Endsleigh Street, WC1 (071 388 0801). Euston Square underground. **Lunch served** noon-2.30pm Mon-Fri, Sun. **Dinner served** 6-8pm Mon-Fri. **Average** £4.50. **House wine** £6 bottle, £1 glass. **Credit** A, AmEx, LV, £TC, V.
Hillel House is the HQ of the Union of Jewish Students and its dining hall/restaurant is open to the public. Naturally the food is strictly Kosher and the kitchens rabbinically supervised. There are plenty of vegetarian dishes on the menu.

MIDDLE EASTERN

Fakhreldine
85 Piccadilly, W1 (071 493 3424). Green Park underground. **Meals served** noon-1am Mon-Sat; noon-midnight Sun. **Average** £20. **Set meal** £15. **House wine** £7 bottle, £2 glass. **Credit** A, AmEx, DC, £STC, V.
The grandest of London's Middle Eastern restaurants has a justifiably high reputation. It attracts the smartest of London's Middle Eastern residents and expense-account diners. There's a spectacular range of 55 different meze which start at £2, but save space for some of the best and freshest pastries we have ever tasted.

The Olive Tree
11 Wardour Street, W1 (071 734 0808). Leicester Square or Piccadilly Circus underground. **Meals served** 11am-11pm Mon-Sat; 11am-9pm Sun. **Average** £8. **Set lunch** £4.50. **House wine** £7.75 litre, £1.30 glass. **Service** 10%. **Credit** A, LV, £TC, V.
The Olive Tree has two menus: one for vegetarians, another for meat eaters. The food here is inexpensive and wholesome and the soups are particularly good.

VEGETARIAN

The Cherry Orchard
241-245 Globe Road, E2 (071 980 6678). Bethnal Green underground/8 bus. **Lunch served** noon-3pm. **Dinner served** 6-10.30pm Tue-Fri; noon-10.30pm Sat. **Average lunch**: £5; **dinner**: £9. **Unlicensed**. **Corkage** £1. **Service** 10% for six or more. **Credit** A, LV, V.
Light, airy and stylish, resplendent in tasteful shades of cream and soft blue, the restaurant is as delightful as the food. This is a home of new-wave vegetarianism. Drinks include elderflower cordial and a vast range of unusual teas, such as lavender, nettle and marigold.

TimeOut
GUIDES

EATING
OUT
IN LONDON

THE FULL RANGE
OF TIME OUT
GUIDES ARE ON
SALE NOW AT
ALL GOOD
NEWSAGENTS
AND BOOKSHOPS

SHOPPING
AND SERVICES
IN LONDON

SPAGHETTI HOUSE

A Group of Individuals

Jermyn Street
Well suited to everyone
16-17 Jermyn Street SW1. Tel: 734 7334

Haymarket
Opposite Burberry's
66 Haymarket SW1. Tel: 839 3642

♦ TRATT ♦
Close to the British Museum
4 Victoria House, Southampton Row WC1.
Tel: 405 6658

Vecchia Milano
Elegant Old Milan
74 Welbeck Street W1. Tel: 935 2371

Zia Teresa
Neighbour to Harrods
6 Hans Road SW3. Tel: 589 7634

Villa Carlotta
The freshness of a garden setting
Private banqueting suite for
120 people is available Tel: 637 9941
33/37 Charlotte Street W1. Tel: 636 6011

Head Office: 39 Charlotte Street, London W1.
Tel: 637 9941

East/West
188 Old Street, EC1 (071 608 0300). Old Street underground/BR. **Open** 11am-9.30pm Mon-Fri; 11am-3pm Sat, Sun. **Average** £6. **House wine** £4.60 bottle, 95p glass. **Credit** A, LV, £TC, V
East/West has evolved from being a hard-core macrobiotic restaurant into an alternative café with a buzzing atmosphere and art exhibitions, without losing the commitment to macrobiotic and vegan food. City workers, students and hippies are happy to eat together. Dishes are adventurous, inventive and usually successful.

Mildred's
58 Greek Street, W1 (071 494 1634). Tottenham Court Road underground/7, 8, 10, 25, 73 bus. **Open** noon-10pm Mon-Sat. **Average** £5.50. **Unlicensed. Corkage** £1 per bottle. **Credit** LV, £TC.
Mildred's is the latest designer-veggie venture in Soho. The food contains no preservatives or additives, and as much organic produce as possible is used; otherwise the dishes are as far removed from those of other vegetarian cafés as they can be. Certain dishes even contain fish. The menu changes daily and always features several vegan options.

CHINESE

Fung Shing
15 Lisle Street, WC2 (071 437 1539). Leicester Square underground. **Meals served** noon-11.30pm daily. **Average** £17.

Minimum charge £8. **Set lunches/set dinners** £9.50. **House wine** £7.50 bottle, £2 glass. **Service** 10%. **Credit** A, AmEx, DC, £TC, V.
Fung Shing is firmly established as one of Chinatown's best Cantonese restaurants and is always busy. Head chef Mr Wu offers a broad cross-section of traditional and newish Cantonese cuisine, plus a selection of seasonal specials. The standard of cooking and presentation is consistently high and the service is pleasant and helpful.

Mr Kong
21 Lisle Street, WC2 (071 437 7341). Leicester Square underground. **Meals served** noon-2am daily. **Average** £13. **House wine** £5. 40 bottle, £1.50 glass. **Service** 10%. **Credit** A, AmEx, DC, £TC, V.
Mr Kong's is a Chinatown legend, having introduced Cantonese approaches to traditional English game meats. The basic menu is solidly reliable, but the real delights can be found on the supplementary card of specialities.

Memories of China
67-69 Ebury Street, SW1 (071 730 7734/071 730 4276). Victoria underground/BR. **Lunch served** noon-2.15pm. **Dinner served** 7-10.45pm Mon-Sat. **Average** £30. **House wine** £7.90 bottle, £2 glass. **Service** 15%. **Credit** A, AmEx, DC, £TC, V.
This opulent restaurant is run by Ken Lo, food writer and tennis champion, his cookery-teacher wife and his Chinese chef, Kam-Po. The aim is to introduce Westerners to the variety of Chinese regional cuisines. If

you want a 'gastronomic tour of China' in one meal, try the £22-per-head set menu or the eleven-course banquet at £24.50. The wine list is spectacular. The prices are high. **Branch:** *Harbour Yard, Chelsea Harbour, SW10 (071 352 4953).*

The New Diamond
23 Lisle Street, WC2 (071 437 2517/071 437 7221). Leicester Square underground. **Meals served** noon-3am daily. **Average** £15. **House wine** £6.50 bottle, £1.50 glass. **Service** 10%. **Credit** A, DC, JCB, £STC, V.
Owner-manager Harry Lee has re-established the restaurant as one of Chinatown's best, with reliable food, comfortable seating on two floors, and a calm atmosphere. The menu delivers everything the setting promises, from exemplary seafood to ethnic Cantonese specialities.

Poons
50 Woburn Place, WC1 (071 580 1188). Russell Square underground. **Lunch served** noon-3pm. **Dinner served** 6-11.30pm, daily. **Average** £15. **Set lunches/set dinners** £7-£16 per person (minimum two). **House wine** £5.50 bottle, £1.50 glass. **Service** 12½%. **Credit** A, AmEx, DC, £TC, V.
This is the most modern of the Poons chain with its spacious, brightly-lit, and stylish split-level interior. Of the other branches, King Street is more opulent, tiny Lisle Street more atmospheric and the Leicester Street branch is the busiest. Poon's wind-dried rice specialities are available at all branches. **Branch:** *41 King Street ,WC2 (071 240 1743). 4 Leicester Street, WC2 (071 437 1528). 27 Lisle Street, WC2 (071 437 4549).*

SOUTH ASIAN

Anwar's
64 Grafton Way, W1 (071 387 6664). Warren Street underground. **Meals served** 10am-10pm daily. **Average** £6. **Unlicensed. Credit** LV, £TC.
See *picture and caption.*

Bombay Brasserie
Courtfield Close, Courtfield Road, SW7 (071 370 4040). Gloucester Road underground. **Lunch served** 12.30-2.45pm daily. **Dinner served** 7pm-midnight daily. **Average** £22.50. **Set lunch** £11.95. **Buffet lunch** £8.95. **House wine** £7.25 bottle, £1.65 glass. **Service** 12½%. **Credit** A, AmEx, DC, EC, £STC, V.
Decorated in sumptuous colonial style, the Bombay Brasserie set the pace for many Indian restaurants both in décor and menu. The menu is imaginative, with influences from the Moghul Empire, the ubiquitous tandoor, the Punjab, Goan fish specialities, fiery central Indian and of course Bombay's own hybrid street dishes. It's expensive.

Chutneys
124 Drummond Street, NW1 (071 388 0604/071 387 6077). Warren Street underground or Euston underground/BR. **Lunch served** noon-2.40pm. **Dinner served** 6-11.25pm, daily. **Average** £7. **Set buffet lunch** £3.50. **House wine** £4.95 bottle, £1.20 glass. **Service** 10%. **Credit** A, AmEx, DC, LV, £TC.
A clean, relaxed place, Chutneys is the latest addition to this street of superlative Indian restaurants. It is smartly done out in

Anwar's (*listed under* **South Asian***) rotis are so puffy and fresh and the spicing so authentic in this excellent counter-service café that we return again and again. The food is great value, with most dishes costing £2.50. There are specials of the day from all over India, catering for a wide range of dietary rules. Seating is at formica tables and the atmosphere is pleasant and informal.*

chrome, black and white. A great treat is the buffet lunch, giving a choice of seven vegetables, three desserts, rice, nans, pickles and dips, and you eat as much as you like for £3.50.

India Club
143 Strand, WC2 (071 836 0650/071 836 9270). Holborn or Aldwych underground. **Lunch served** noon-2.30pm daily. **Dinner served** 6-10pm Mon-Sat; 6-8pm Sun. **Average** £8. **Unlicensed. Corkage no charge. Credit** LV, £TC.
This spartan but warm restaurant with its canteen-style tables and friendly, if occasionally eccentric, service has a loyal following of Indians and non-Indians alike. The food is simple, excellent and mainly North Indian with a leavening of South Indian food. The prices are extremely reasonable.

Mandeer
21 Hanway Place, W1 (071 323 0660). Tottenham Court Road underground. **Lunch served** noon-3pm Mon-Sat. **Dinner served** 6-10.30pm Mon-Sat. **Average** £10. **Set meal** £8.50. **House wine** £5.25 bottle, £1.15 glass. **Credit** A, AmEx, DC, LV, £TC, V.
One of London's oldest and most atmospheric Indian vegetarian eating-places, the Mandeer is dark and atmospheric. Special diets are catered for, and special thalis, dishes without spices and meals without garlic or onion are cooked on separate stoves.

JAPANESE

Kitchen Yakitori
12 Lancashire Court, off New Bond Street, W1 (071 629 9984). Bond Street underground. **Lunch served** noon-2.30pm Mon-Sat. **Dinner served** 6-9.30pm Mon-Fri. **Average Lunch:** £7; *Dinner:* £14. **House wine** £5.95 bottle, £1.60 glass. **Saké** £2.20 tokkuri. **Service** 10%. **Credit** LV (lunch only), £TC.
This small place is very cheap by comparison with other Japanese restaurants in the area and does a good trade in take-away lunchboxes. A long menu of lunch dishes, all served with appetizers, soup, rice, pickles and fruit, range from £5.50 for yakitori and salad to £11 for barbecued eel fillet. Dinner is slightly more expensive.

Yoshino
Basement, Japan Centre, 66-68 Brewer Street, W1 (071 287 5947). Piccadilly Circus underground. **Meals served** 11am-7.30pm Mon-Fri, Sun; 11am-6pm Sat. **Average** £3.80. **Unlicensed. Credit** LV, V.
This small bar-like restaurant serves the cheapest Japanese food in London. The menu is short and includes tonkatsu, sushi and Japanese curry. The most expensive set meal on the menu is the tonkatsu at £4.80, which includes, salad, rice, pickles and miso soup. The sushi is £3.80.

BURMESE

Mandalay
100 Greenwich South Street, SE10 (081 691 0443). Greenwich BR. **Lunch served** noon-3.30pm Sun. **Dinner served** 7-10.30pm daily. **Average** £14. **Set Sunday lunch** £7.50. **House wine** £6 bottle, £1.50 glass. **Credit** A, AmEx, V.

Busan *(listed under* **Korean***) is by far the friendliest Korean restaurant. Not only is the service excellent, but the food is presented beautifully in a style seldom seen outside ritzier and vastly more expensive West End Japanese establishments. Fellow Koreans and ex-pat Japanese feature strongly amongst the growing band of local regulars.*

This is Britain's only Burmese restaurant. All the dishes are explained with care on the handwritten menu and they all sound equally tempting. The staff are helpful. There are no Burmese drinks on the wine list, but a choice of European wines that go well with the food.

KOREAN

Busan
43 Holloway Road, N7 (071 607 8264). Highbury & Islington underground/BR. **Lunch served** noon-3.30pm Mon-Sat. **Dinner served** 5.30-11pm daily. **Average** £20. **Set lunch** £4.90. **Set dinner** £12. **Unlicensed. Corkage** no charge. **Credit** A, AmEx.
See **picture and caption.**

Kaya Korean
22-25 Dean Street, W1 (071 437 6630/071 734 2720). Tottenham Court Road underground. **Lunch served** noon-3pm Mon-Sat. **Dinner served** 6-11.30pm Mon-Sat; 6-10pm Sun. **Average** £20. **Set lunches** £12. **Set dinner** £26. **House wine** £9.20 bottle. **Service** 15%. **Credit** A, A/c, AmEx, DC, £TC, V.
The most luxurious and tastefully decorated Korean restaurant in Soho, the tranquil Kaya Korean is furnished in a traditional manner: heavy carved wooden beams; waitresses in full national costume; and the sound of a flute from behind ornate screens. You could get away with spending less than £15 for a selection of

small starters, but for £10 more you can enjoy a slow banquet in exquisite and peaceful surroundings.

MALAYSIAN AND INDONESIAN

Garuda
150 Shaftesbury Avenue, WC2 (071 836 2644). Leicester Square or Tottenham Court Road underground. **Lunch served** noon-2.45pm Mon-Sat. **Dinner served** 6-11.30pm Mon-Sat; 5-10.30pm Sun. **Average** £13. **House wine** £5.80 bottle, £1.20 glass. **Service** 10% for five or more. **Credit** A, AmEx, £TC, V.
One of the most respected Indonesian restaurants in town. The clientele is mainly young and includes many Malaysian students. Most popular is the rijstafel, a seven- or ten-course meal, served one course at a time to a minimum of two people. Helpings are generous and the spicing is fresh and distinctive.

Melati
30-31 Peter Street, W1 (071 437 2011). Leicester Square or Piccadilly Circus underground. **Lunch served** noon-2.30pm Mon-Sat. **Dinner served** 6-11.30pm Mon-Sat. **Average** £14. **House wine** £5.50 bottle, £1.20 glass. **Service** 10% for five or more. **Credit** A, £TC, V.
By the time you read this, Soho's little Peter Street Melati will have extended into the next-door premises and will have been given a new look. Since it opened in the early

eighties it has gained a reputation for serving some of the best Malaysian food in London. The menu is long but easy to understand and lists plenty for vegetarians. **Branch**: *21 Great Windmill Street, W1 (071 437 2745)*.

THAI

Bahn Thai
21A Frith Street, W1 (071 437 8504). Leicester Square or Tottenham Court Road underground/29, 38, 55 bus. **Lunch served** noon-2.45pm Mon-Sat; 12.30-2.30pm Sun. **Dinner served** 6-11.15pm Mon-Sat; 6.30-10.30pm Sun. **Average** £15. **House wine** £6.45 bottle, £1.55 glass. **Credit** A, AmEx, £TC, V.
Colourful parasols hang upside-down from the ceiling of the Bahn Thai's pretty downstairs room, which is convenient to nip into for a quick lunch of dim sum or noodles. Upstairs is a serene green and the calm atmosphere makes for relaxing dinners. The owner has always taken pains to serve genuine Thai food, and the chef will obligingly spice any dish mildly or authentically.

Chiang Mai
48 Frith Street, W1 (071 437 7444). Tottenham Court Road or Piccadilly Circus underground. **Lunch served** noon-3pm Mon-Sat. **Dinner served** 6-11pm Mon-Sat. **Average** £9. **House wine** £6.25 bottle, £1.50 glass. **Service** 10%. **Credit** A, AmEx, £TC, V.
Our Thai reviewers have no complaints about any of a dozen or so dishes they ordered from the à la carte menu and the set meals are good value for people who are new to Thai food. If you're lucky you'll get a seat upstairs where you can see and be seen by the Soho glitterati.

VIETNAMESE

Pho
2 Lisle Street, W1 (071 437 8265). Leicester Square underground. **Meals served** noon-11pm daily. **Average** £5.50. **Service** 10%. **Unlicensed**. **No credit cards**.
Pho (pronounced 'far') has become so popular that it has opened another branch just around the corner in Wardour Street. Both places are busy, lively, café-style restaurants. Pho, the traditional Vietnamese soup, is sold on the streets of Vietnam and the pho sold here cannot be beaten. The choice on the menu is wide and prices are reasonable for central London. **Branch**: *34 Wardour Street (071 494 2592)*.

IN STORE

Heal's
196 Tottenham Court Road, W1 (071 636 1666). Goodge Street underground. **Tea served** 3-5.30pm Mon-Sat. **Set tea** £6.75. **Credit** A, AmEx, DC, £TC, V.
With dark, bent-wood chairs and black and white tessellated tiling, the Conran design signature has been writ large at this immaculate, in-store restaurant. The set tea is a lavish, help-yourself affair consisting of unlimited quantities of cheesecake, fruitcake, shortbread, sandwiches, fruit salad, several kinds of cream cake and a choice of six teas.

Justin de Blank
in The General Trading Co, 141 Sloane Street, SW1 (071 730 6400). Sloane Square underground. **Open** 9am-10.15pm Mon-Fri; 9am-2pm Sat. **Breakfast served** 9-11am Mon-Sat. **Afternoon tea served** 3-5.15pm Mon-Fri. **Average** *Lunch*: £9. **Service** 10%. **Credit** LV, £TC.
A delightful basement restaurant with a well-lit conservatory and a garden to breakfast in. It rapidly fills up and, as they don't take bookings, you may have to wait. If you come for tea, there are cakes, pastries, biscuits and scones - all freshly made.

St James's Restaurant
4th floor, Fortnum & Mason, 181 Piccadilly, W1 (071 734 8040). Green Park underground. **Open** 9am-5pm Mon-Sat. **English breakfast served** 9-11am Mon-Sat. **Tea served** 3-5pm Mon-Sat. **Breakfast** £6.50. **Afternoon tea** £5.50. **High tea** £7.50. **Credit** A, AmEx, DC, F&M, £TC, V.
In the elegant setting of Fortnum and Mason, English breakfasts and high teas are regarded as the most civilized meals of the day. A pianist accompanies you through your high tea. No bookings are taken for tea, so arrive before 4pm if you want a good table.

Terrace Bar
Harrods, Knightsbridge, SW1 (071 730 1234). Knightsbridge underground. **Afternoon tea served** 3.30-5.30pm Mon, Tue, Thur-Sat; 3.30-6pm Wed. **Set tea** £7.95. **Credit** A, AmEx, DC, EC, £STC, $US, V.
See picture and caption.

BREAKFAST, COFFEE AND TEA

Brown's Hotel
Albemarle Street/Dover Street, W1 (071 493 6020). Green Park underground. **Afternoon tea served** 3-6pm daily. **Set tea** £9.75. **Credit** A, AmEx, CB, DC, En Route, JCB, £STC, THF, V.
Afternoon teas at Brown's are civilized occasions. Waiters in tail coats bearing silver-tiered cake-stands with cucumber, tomato, potted meat and cream cheese sandwiches. The best time to be assured of a table (no bookings taken) is between 3pm and 4pm. *See chapter* **Accommodation**.

Gambarti
38 Lamb's Conduit Street, WC1 (071 405 7950). Holborn underground/19, 38, 171 bus. **Open** 7am-5pm Mon-Fri. **Average** £2.25. **Minimum** £2 (noon-2pm). **Unlicensed**. **Credit** LV.
The fresh, Italian coffee at Gambarti is regarded as some of the best in London and the English and continental breakfasts are reasonably priced at £2.25 each. The afternoon tea, which consists of scones, jam and cream and the obligatory pot of tea - with a choice of five flavours - costs £1.65.

Harry's
19 Kingly Street, W1 (071 734 8708). Oxford Circus or Piccadilly underground/6, 12, 15 or 88 bus. **Open** 10pm-9am Mon-Fri; 10pm-6am Sat. **Average** £6. **Service** 10%. **Credit** LV.
See picture and caption.

The attractive conservatory at the **Terrace Bar, Harrods** *(listed under* **In Store***), is a suitable place in which to recuperate from emptying your wallet in the famous store. The set price for afternoon tea (£7.95 per person) may seem steep, but everything is freshly cooked on the premises from ingredients shipped up from the formidable food hall. The quality, presentation and choice are as excellent as you would expect. The conservatory is popular, so arrive early for a seat.*

Bar Italia
22 Frith Street, W1 (071 437 4520).
Tottenham Court Road underground.
Open 7-1am daily. **Average** £5.
Unlicensed. Credit LV.
Bar Italia is small, noisy, thoroughly Italian and one of London's liveliest places to drink real cappuccino or espresso (80p). The simple, mirrors-and-formica décor has hardly changed since it opened and it's always been a rendezvous for Italians working around Soho. Sadly, Bar Italia has latterly become too fashionable for its own good and is in danger of imminent media suffocation.

Maison Sagne
105 Marylebone High Street, W1 (071 935 6240). Baker Street or Bond Street underground. **Open** 9am-5pm Mon-Fri; 9am-1pm Sat. **Breakfast served** 9am-noon Mon-Fri. **Afternoon tea served** 3-5pm Mon-Fri. **Average** £5. **Unlicensed. No credit cards.**
Little has changed at London's most elegant patisserie since it was established in 1921. Breakfast is a particularly civilized affair; customers are seated by uniformed, but not overly formal, waiters and provided with strong coffee and a selection of croissants, brioches and Danish pastries, paying only for what is eaten. The atmosphere is friendly, relaxed and unique.

Patisserie Valerie
44 Old Compton Street, W1 (071 437 3466). Piccadilly Circus or Tottenham Court Road underground. **Open** 8am-7pm Mon-Sat;

10am-6pm Sun. **Average** £3. **Unlicensed. Credit** £TC.
A long-established French patisserie, rightly famed for its cakes and pastries. Though it gets terminally crowded with fashion victims, thespians and people from the film world, it's still one of the most attractive cafés around. The best time to come is for breakfast when the atmosphere is at its most relaxed and you might actually find a seat.

DRINKING

It's been a couple of years since Britain's archaic drinking laws were modified to allow all-day drinking. However, even Londoners are still confused by the new laws, so here's a resumé of what's what on the drinking scene. All-day drinking in Britain only means a maximum of twelve hours a day, usually 11am-11pm. At the end of the licensed period (known colloquially as 'time') you have just ten minutes to finish your drinks, after which time the landlord is obliged to remove them.
Drinking with a meal: The daytime restrictions on drinking with a meal in a restaurant have simply

been removed. Whereas a year or so ago you could only drink until 3pm and then were forced to stop for the afternoon break because of the licensing restrictions, you can now drink through the afternoon on any day except Sunday, as long as you're eating a meal as well (a meal is defined as 'food that will satisfy hunger for at least two hours'). You must also eat and drink sitting down, although you can be seated at a counter instead of a table.
Drinking without eating: If you want to drink but not eat in an establishment which has a restaurant licence or certificate, the licensing laws remain unchanged. This means you have to stop drinking after 3pm. In Public Houses ('pubs'), wine bars and some brasseries, you can drink all day, apart from Sunday afternoon — the one time when you may want to.
Pubs: These have a licence which allows a publican to sell intoxicating liquors of all descriptions for consumption on or off the premises. Drinking-up time on this licence is no more than ten minutes after its expiry. Pubs can open for 12 hours a day between Monday and Saturday and 11 hours on a Sunday (noon-2 or 3pm and 7-10.30 or 11pm).

PUBS

When visitors to London think of drinking, their first thoughts are of warm beer and the British pub. What is commonly known in Europe and America as beer, the British call lager. British lagers generally tend to be a pale imitation of German lagers. If you want something with that stronger bite, ask for export lager or pilsner. However, Britain's national drink (the warm stuff) is beer, bitter or ale. The range available in London is extremely wide. If you like fruity beers ask for Fullers London Pride, Youngs Special or something similar. If you want your ale strong and full-bodied Abbot Ale, Ruddles County or Owd Roger will fit the bill better. Beware — the stronger darker beers have an alcohol content of 5%-8%, well over twice that of the weaker ones.

Hen & Chickens
Highbury Corner, N1 (pub 071 359 1030/theatre 071 226 3724). Highbury and Islington underground/BR. **Open** 11am-11pm Mon-Sat; noon-3pm, 7-10.30pm Sun. **No credit cards.**
Dick Turpin spent his ill-gotten gains in this

London's only all-night breakfast restaurant **Harry's** (*listed under* **Breakfast, Coffee and Tea**) *is the haunt of night clubbers with 3am munchies. The fry-ups are large, the atmosphere good, the staff are friendly and the service is better than in many other restaurants in this area.*

famous theatre pub featuring wooden tip-up seats taken from Brighton Pier. Refurbishment, however is imminent.

Kings Head and Eight Bells
50 Cheyne Walk, SW3 (071 352 1820). Sloane Square underground. **Open** 11am-3.30pm, 5.30-11pm Mon-Fri; 11am-11pm Sat; noon-3pm, 7-10.30pm Sun. **Credit** A, AmEx, DC, V. *See* **picture and caption.**

Lamb and Flag
33 Rose Street, WC2 (071 836 4108). Covent Garden underground. **Open** 11am-11pm Mon-Sat; noon-3pm, 7-10.30pm Sun. **No credit cards.**
Wonky doors and low ceilings. This famous pub once hosted bare-fisted boxing matches. You still have to fight to get to the bar.

Museum Tavern
Museum Street, WC1 (071 242 8987). Holborn underground. **Open** 11am-11pm Mon-Sat; noon-3pm, 7-10.30pm Sun. **Credit** A, AmEx, DC, V.
Karl Marx and Virginia Woolf drank in this mirrored black mahogany bar. Now tourists do. Good pub food.

Ship
Ship Lane, SW14 (081 876 1439). Mortlake BR. **Open** 11am-11pm, 5.30-11pm Mon-Sat; noon-3pm, 7-10.30pm Sun. **No credit cards.**
Sturdy riverside building next to Watneys brewery that rocks to the cheers of a partisan crowd at the finish of the annual Oxbridge boat race.

The Ship and Blue Ball
13 Boundary Street, E2 (071 729 1192). Old Street underground. **Open** 11.30am-11pm Mon-Sat; noon-3pm, 7-10.30pm Sun. **No credit cards.**
Small, friendly pub serving the excellent beers of the small Pitfield Brewery. Particularly recommended is Dark Star, an organic, additive-free beer that won the Supreme Champion Beer title last year.

The Sun
63 Lamb's Conduit Street, WC1 (071 405 8278). Holborn underground. **Open** 11am-11pm Mon-Sat; noon-3pm, 7-10.30pm Sun. **No credit cards.**
Hunched drinkers at the light, wooden bar enjoy a generous selection of 16 real ales. Join the cellar tour and meet the incorporeal draymen.

Waterside Inn
82 York Way, N1 (071 837 7118). King's Cross underground. **Open** *winter.* 11am-11pm Mon-Fri; noon-3pm, 7-11pm Sat; noon-3pm, 7-10.30pm Sun; *summer.* 11am-11pm Mon-Sat; noon-3pm, 7-10.30pm Sun. **Credit** A, V.
Real timbers, real spinning wheels, real canal, real ales. Good restaurant on canal boat behind pub.

The White Cross Hotel
Riverside, Richmond (081 940 6844). Richmond underground/BR. **Open** 11am-11pm Mon-Sat; noon-3pm, 7-10.30pm Sun. **No credit cards.**
High tides have been known to turn this 150-year old pub into an island - whereupon its unfortunate captives get cosy around the rare real fires to await rescue. Good food.

RIVER/DOCKLANDS PUBS

The Angel
101 Bermondsey Wall East, SE16 (071 237 3608). Rotherhithe underground/1, 77, 188, D13 bus. **Open** *May-Aug:* 11am-11pm Mon-Fri; noon-11pm Sat; noon-3pm, 7-10.30pm Sun. *Sept-Apr:* 11am-3pm, 5.30-11pm Mon-Sat; noon-3pm, 7-10.30pm Sun. **No credit cards.**
The eighteenth-century explorer Captain Cook had several tots of rum at this very naval inn. It has a ship's wheel, captains' chairs, a smugglers' trapdoor in the kitchen, and a balcony overlooking Tower Bridge.

The Gun
27 Coldharbour, E14 (071 987 1692). South Quay DLR/D5, D7 bus. **Open** 11am-2.30pm, 5.15-11pm Mon-Thur; 11am-3pm, 5.15-11pm Fri; 11am-2.30pm, 5.15-11pm Sat; noon-3pm, 7-10.30pm Sun. **No credit cards.**
Lord Nelson pursued his illicit love affair with Lady Hamilton at this old inn. You can sup real ale on the riverside veranda.

Mayflower
117 Rotherhithe Street, SE16 (071 237 4088). Rotherhithe underground. **Open** 11am-11pm, Mon-Fri; 11am-4pm, 7-11pm, Sat; noon-3pm, 7-10.30pm Sun. **No credit cards.**
The Pilgrim Fathers left on their historic voyage to the New World from this inn in 1620, when it was called The Shippe. The bar is small, dark and panelled, but you can take your drink out on to the long jetty. There are great bar snacks and a restaurant upstairs with enviable views, but not so great food. American and British stamps are sold at the bar.

Prospect of Whitby
57 Wapping Wall, E1 (071 481 1095). Wapping underground. **Open** 11.30am-3pm, 5.30-11pm, Mon-Thur; 11am-11pm Fri, Sat; noon-3pm, 7-10.30pm Sun. **Credit** A, AmEx, DC, V.
One of the oldest surviving drinking houses in London. The terrace and restaurant have superb views, but the pub is overpriced and overcrowded.

Town of Ramsgate
62 Wapping High Street, E1 (071 488 2685). Wapping underground. **Open** 11am-3pm, 5.30-11pm, Mon-Sat; noon-3pm, 7-10.30pm, Sun. **No credit cards.**
This unpretentious pub was where Judge Jeffreys, who was fond of hanging all and sundry, was saved from a lynch-mob in 1688. Australians might flinch on discovering that convicts were jailed in the basement before

In 1580 when the **Kings Head and Eight Bells** *(listed under* **Pubs***) was built, eight peals from the nearby church bell warned of royalty on the river. Whistler and Dylan Thomas got tight here. View of Battersea Peace Pagoda across river.*

Le Shaker *(listed under* **Cocktail Bars***) is run by Marc Boccart-Schuster, the darling of the cocktail-drinking public. There's no spinning of bottles, just a quiet clinking of glass against glass as Marc practises his craft, mixing flavours and colours from a palette of bottles ranked so tidily he can work with his eyes shut.*

deportation. Although a little dingy, the riverside garden gives a relaxing view. At low tide you can see the post to which smugglers and pirates (including Captain Kidd in 1701) were condemned to hang in chains until three tides washed over them.

Trafalgar Tavern
Park Row, SE10 (081 858 2437). Greenwich or Maze Hill BR/180 bus/boat to Greenwich Pier. **Open** 11am-3pm, 5.30-11pm Mon-Thur; 11am-11pm Fri, Sat; noon-3pm, 7-10.30pm Sun. **Credit** A, AmEx, DC, £TC, V.
Restored in 1965, this riverside inn was built in 1837. Its Whitebait Dinners, once attended by cabinet ministers and the likes of Dickens, Thackeray and Cruikshank, were a famous institution until river pollution robbed them of the main course in 1914. Today you can again eat whitebait with your pint of ale. *See chapter* **Lesbian & Gay**.

WINE BARS
The Actor's Retreat
326 St John Street, EC1 (071 837 0722). Angel underground/19, 38, 171, 171A bus. **Open** noon-2.30pm, 5.30-11pm, Mon-Fri; 6-11pm Sat. **Average** £18. **House wine** £5.50 bottle, £1.25 glass. **Service** 10%. **Credit** A, AmEx, DC, V.
The Sicilian-run Actor's Retreat, opposite Sadler's Wells, is a wonderful wine bar. From the film star photos on the walls to the excellent food and wine on the tables, everything conspires to make this one of the most relaxed, characterful venues around. A meal can be expensive, but is worth every penny.

The Archduke
Concert Hall Approach, South Bank, SE1 (071 928 9370). Waterloo BR/underground. **Open** 11am-11pm Mon-Sat. **Average** £10.50. **House wine** £5.45 bottle, £1.35 glass. **Service** 10% for eight or more. **Credit** A, AmEx, DC, £TC, V.
The bar itself is in typical South Bank style with several levels of arches, staircases and tables. The trappings are functional without being tasteless and it's a popular pre- and après-theatre retreat.

Bar des Amis
11-13 Hanover Place, WC2 (071 379 3444). Covent Garden underground. **Open** 11.30am-4.30pm, 5.30-11pm, Mon-Sat. **Average** £7. **House wine** £5.45 bottle, £1.20 glass. **Credit** A, AmEx, DC, £TC, V.
A popular basement wine bar. The atmosphere is buzzy and the service has, if anything, improved recently. The bar is low-ceilinged and smoky, with lots of bar-stools, but few tables and chairs; be prepared to eat or drink standing up at lunch-times and early evenings.

Julie's Bar
137 Portland Road, W11 (071 727 7985). Holland Park underground. **Open** 11am-11pm Mon-Sat; noon-10.30pm Sun. **Average** £16. **House wine** £5.95 bottle, £1.50 glass. **No credit cards.**
This labyrinthine establishment in Clarendon Cross is a firm favourite. Large and rangy with many levels and rooms furnished in Gothick style, Julie's inspires a fierce loyalty amongst Holland Park's conservative bohemians. The food, which comes from the downstairs restaurant, is generally very good.

CHAMPAGNE BARS
Brinkleys Champagne Bar
17C Curzon Street, W1 (071 493 4490). Green Park or Hyde Park Corner underground. **Open** 11.30am-11.30pm Mon-Fri. **Average** £16. **House champagne** £16 bottle, £3.50 glass. **Service** 12½%. **Credit** A, V.
Smoked glass mirrors, avant-garde prints and friendly, discreet service are the classic trappings of this chic champagne bar. The clientele are in the 35+ age bracket, but in the evenings you'll find a younger, yuppier crowd propping up the marble-slabbed bar.

COCKTAIL BARS
Athenaeum Bar
Athenaeum Hotel, 116 Piccadilly, W1 (071 499 3464). Green Park or Hyde Park Corner underground. **Drinks served** 11am-11pm Mon-Fri; 11am-3pm, 5.30-11pm, Sat; noon-3pm, 7-10pm, Sun. **Credit** A, AmEx, DC, £TC, V.
Drinks are taken seriously at this quiet, wood-panelled bar, renowned for its selection of 54 malt whiskies (one of the largest outside Scotland). Both the short cocktail list and the atmosphere are old-fashioned and civilized.

The Old Rangoon
201 Castelnau, SW13 (081 741 9655). Hammersmith underground/9, 33, 72 bus. **Drinks served** 11am-11pm Mon-Sat; noon-3pm, 7-10.30pm, Sun. **Credit** A, AmEx, DC, £TC, THF, V.
This squeaky-clean restaurant/bar, housed in a converted pub, has become a key meeting place for London yuppies. The saving grace of the Old Rangoon is the wonderful garden, which many consider to be the best spot for summer drinking in London.

Le Shaker
159 Old Brompton Road, SW5 (071 373 1926). Gloucester Road underground. **Drinks served** with food only: 12.30-3pm Mon-Fri; 6-11.45pm Mon-Sat. **Credit** A, AmEx, TC, V. *See* **picture and caption**.

Trader Vic's
Basement, London Hilton, Park Lane, W1 (071 493 7586). Green Park or Hyde Park Corner underground. **Drinks served** noon-3pm, 5.30-11pm, Mon-Fri; 5.30-11.30pm Sat; noon-3pm, 7-10.30pm, Sun. **Credit** A, AmEx, CB, DC, £STC, V.
The oldest cocktail bar in Europe, Trader Vic's has always been popular with cocktail connoisseurs, stars and beautiful people. There's no happy hour and cocktails cost about a fiver. Bar snacks, such as spare ribs, burgers and fried prawns, are served.

Shopping and Services

For many tourists, London *is* shopping. For those people with a more balanced approach it can still be a London highlight – if you know what you want and the right area in which to get it. But it can also be hell if you're in the middle of Oxford Street looking for a quiet, small shop selling genuine English craft-goods. Fortunately, shops of a kind cluster together, thus saving the shopper both shoe leather and time. If you aren't shopping for anything in particular, or if the very idea of shopping is anathema to you, pay a visit to some of London's excellent street markets. You'll not only pick up the best bargains here, you'll be treated to the best free show in town – Londoners going about their daily business.

The British have never won awards for the volume or the efficiency of services available to the average visitor, and London is no exception. However, of late there's been a mini-boom in services. If your taste is for sushi delivered to your bed, it can be arranged. You can get your old works of Shakespeare completely rebound or have orthopaedic footwear made to measure. We tell you where to look.

For an even wider selection of retailers and really useful people, buy the *Time Out Guide to Shopping & Services in London* (£5.75 from newsagents; £3.25 in Filofax format, available from stationers and Filofax stockists).

CONTENTS:

Shopping & Services

Sightseeing can show you the city but nothing beats a shopping expedition for a taste of London life.

Whether you're soaking up the atmosphere and picking up a few bargains in a street market or strolling down the trendy streets of the West End, you'll find London is one of the world's great shopping cities. On the whole, Londoners are friendly folk, but if you're unfamiliar with the currency or prices, avoid being conned and stick to reputable shops.

Forget souvenir shops: instead try scouring some of the many antique and junk shops for inexpensive, good quality, real British bargains. London has a rich and varied ethnic mix, so once you've bought that Aquascutum raincoat get down to Chinatown, in Soho, for a taste of the Orient, and don't leave town without making a trip to Brixton or another of the multi-cultural areas in South London.

This selection of shops is not comprehensive, so if you're looking for, and cannot find, something specific, try our *Time Out Guide to Shopping and Services* (£5.75); you'll find detailed descriptions of shops and services throughout London.

SHOPPING BY AREA

Shopping in London is made somewhat easier by the fact that certain types of shop tend to be grouped together in small areas. Most of the large bookstores, for example, are gathered on and around Charing Cross Road. Clothes shops cluster together depending on type of fashion and price range. South Molton Street, Sloane Street, Knightsbridge, Soho and St Christopher's Place are known for costly designer gear, whereas Oxford Street is the home of the chainstore, offering a wide selection of middle-of-the-road, inexpensive fashion. However, due to escalating rents in Central London, shops are closing down faster than you can count them; in the King's Road for example, over a quarter of the 200-or-so retail outlets are standing empty. We have grouped fashion shops according to the kind of clothes they are known for, rather than by area.

EXPORT SCHEME

Foreign visitors to London can sometimes claim back the 13 per cent net VAT charged on most goods in Britain: the catch is that you'll probably have to spend over £100 first. The procedure is simple: fill in a form at the shop, which the assistant will stamp, then hand the completed document to the customs office at the airport or port. There's normally a six week wait before you get the money back. Not all shops offer this scheme, so it's best to check first before spending any cash, in case you won't be getting any of it back.

FAULTY GOODS

As the law stands, you're entitled to a full refund if a purchase turns out to be faulty in some way; notices such as 'No refunds given' are misleading, so don't be put off. If, however, you have a change of heart after buying something in perfect condition, then legally you won't have a leg to stand on if you demand an exchange or money back. Always keep the receipt after every purchase just in case there's cause to return the goods.

SAFETY

Be careful when buying electrical goods as faulty wiring can be extremely dangerous. Appliances bearing the British Institute kitemark have passed rigorous safety tests and won't cause injury if used properly. Some toys can also prove to be lethal weapons with spikes, loose buttons and leaded paint, any of which could

There are more than 60 fashion departments with clothes for all occasions (but not all pockets) at **Harrods** *(listed under* **The Stores***). It's also an excellent stopping-off place for silverware, home accessories, glassware, kitchenware and cutlery. See also* **Food Halls***.*

seriously harm a child. The British Toy and Hobby Manufacturers Association has started to label items, which meet certain safety standards, with the symbol of a lion's head.

THE STORES

Burberrys
18-22 Haymarket, SW1 (071 930 3343).
Piccadilly Circus underground. **Open** 9am-
5.30pm Mon-Wed, Fri, Sat; 9am-7pm Thur.
Credit A, A/c, AmEx, DC, JCB, V.
The famous trench coats cost between £230
and £425. You'll also find golfing brollies,
hats, gloves, shoes and children's wear. Your
best bet is to wait for the sales.
Catalogue. Delivery. Export scheme. Mail order.

Debenhams
334-338 Oxford Street, W1 (071 580 3000).
Oxford Circus underground. **Open** 9.30am-
6pm Mon, Tue, Sat; 9.30am-8pm Wed-Fri.
Credit A, AmEx, DC, SC, £STC, V.
The layout in the men's department is confusing and the selection poor although the
women's department is quite extensive.
Clothes are staid but well-priced, and
there's a reasonable selection of household
goods and gifts.
Café. Delivery (£5 charge). Export scheme.

Harrods
Knightsbridge, SW1 (071 730 1234).
Knightsbridge underground. **Open** 9am-6pm
Mon, Tue, Thur-Sat; 9.30am-7pm Wed.
Credit A, A/c, AmEx, DC, SC, £STC, V,
most foreign currencies.
See picture and caption.
Baby-changing facilities. Bureau de change.
Cafés and restaurant. Car park. Export
bureau. Delivery. Mail and telephone credit
order (magazine £1.50). Many services. Store
map from Customer Services, 4th floor.

Harvey Nichols
109 Knightsbridge, SW1 (071 235 5000).
Knightsbridge underground. **Open** 10am-
8pm Mon-Fri; 10am-6pm Sat. **Credit** A,
AmEx, DC, SC, £STC, V.
Go to Harvey Nichols if you've seen what
you want in a glossy magazine but don't
know where to buy it. A mind-boggling selec-
tion of high fashion names like Helen Storey,
Byblos and Nichole Farhi all under one roof.
Cafés. Car park. Delivery. Export scheme.
Magazine. Mail order. Toilets for the disabled.

John Lewis
Oxford Street, W1 (071 629 7711). Oxford
Circus underground. **Open** 9am-5.30pm Mon-
Wed, Fri, Sat; 9.30am-8pm Thur. **Credit** SC.
John Lewis excels in reasonably-priced and
attractive household goods. The fashion is
aimed more at mature men and women so
don't expect innovation.
Alterations to own goods. Café. Delivery.
Toilets for the disabled. Wheelchair access.
Export scheme.

Liberty
Regent Street, W1 (071 734 1234). Oxford
Circus underground. **Open** 9.30am-6pm
Mon-Wed, Fri, Sat; 9.30am-7.30pm Thur.
Credit A, AmEx, DC, JCB, SC, £STC, V.

A former aeroplane factory strewn with wrought-iron railings, gates, crown-top
chimney pots and roof tiles is the home of **The House Hospital** *(listed under*
Architectural Salvage*). Radiators cost from £90; the ornate or heavy hospital*
styles are around the £225 mark. Antique, wooden fire-surrounds are mainly
Victorian and Edwardian.

Walk into Liberty at any time and it will be
full of shoppers snapping up clothes and soft
furnishings in distinctive prints. Oriental
goods, fine crystal and quirky accessories
are just as popular.
Café. Delivery. Export scheme. Mail order.
Toilets and lifts for the disabled.

Marks & Spencer
458 Oxford Street, W1 (071 935 7954).
Marble Arch underground/25, 30, 74 bus.
Open 9am-8pm Mon-Fri; 9am-6pm Sat.
Credit SC, £STC.
M&S clothes may not be the height of fash-
ion but they're inexpensive and reliable.
There are no fitting rooms, but goods can be
exchanged. Home accessories and small
gifts are of the same good quality. Don't miss
the excellent food hall.
Wheelchair access. Export scheme.

Selfridges
Oxford Street, W1 (071 629 1234). Bond
Street underground. **Open** 9.30am-6pm Mon-
Wed, Fri, Sat; 10am-8pm Thur. **Credit** A,
AmEx, DC, EC, JCB, Sears, V.
A massive department store worth braving
simply for the quantity and variety of household and fashion goods. The food hall on the
ground floor is impressive. Selfridges will
refund the difference if you find the same
item cheaper elsewhere.
Baby-changing facilities. Café. Disabled
facilities. Wheelchair access. Export scheme.
Free catalogue. Delivery . Mail and tele-
phone credit order. Restaurant. Services
arcade (in basement).

Simpson
203 Piccadilly, W1 (071 734 2002).
Piccadilly Circus underground. **Open** 9am-

5.30pm Mon-Wed, Fri, Sat; 9am-7pm Thur.
Credit A, AmEx, DC, JCB, SC, £STC, V.
Seven floors of mainly classic British fashion
goods for men and women, including the
DAKS label (Simpson's own). Accessories
are also worth a scan. On the whole high
quality is matched by high prices.
Export scheme. Mail order. Restaurant.
Wine bar/café.

ANTIQUES AND SECOND-HAND

ACCESSORIES

Mansfield
30-35 Drury Lane, WC2 (071 240 7780).
Covent Garden underground. **Open** 10am-
6pm Mon-Fri; 10am-4pm Sat. **Credit** A,
AmEx, DC, £STC, V.
Antique pens and travel goods are the specialities here. Splash out on a snappy
crocodile suitcase for £495 or a plain leather
briefcase from £85. Gold fountain pens retail
at between £45-£450.
Delivery. Export scheme.

ARCHITECTURAL SALVAGE

The Antique Fireplace Warehouse
194-196 Battersea Park Road, SW11 4ND
(071 627 1410). Battersea Park or
Queenstown Road BR/44,137, 170 bus.
Open 10am-6pm Mon-Sat. **Credit** A.V.
Around 90 per cent of the fireplaces here are

from 'El Abrazo' by J.M. Ferrater

TAKE A CLOSER LOOK
INTO POSTER ART

THE POSTER SHOP

fully restored English antiques. Prices
match the high quality: a finely-carved
Regency model costs £5,000, but there's also
a limited range of inexpensive original reproduction and pine surrounds.
*Brochure. Delivery. Export scheme. Installation
service. Mantelpieces made to order.*

The House Hospital
*68 Battersea High Street, SW11 (071 223
3179). Bus 19, 39, 44, 45, 49, 170.* **Open**
10am-5pm Mon-Sat. **Credit** A, V.
See **picture and caption.**
*Delivery. Export scheme. Fitting, restoration
and stripping services.*

The House of Steel
*400 Caledonian Road, N1 (071 607 5889).
Caledonian Road underground.* **Open** 10am-
5.30pm Mon-Fri; by appointment Sat.
Credit £TC.
The House of Steel is a massive warehouse
chock-a-block with eighteenth- to - nineteenth-century British ornamental and architectural metalwork. Judy Cole also designs
and makes steel furniture which she treats
with a verdigris finish, giving it a turquoise
bloom similar to weathered brass or bronze;
chairs start at £150, lamp tables at £50. If
you've got space in your hallway, an
18ft/5½m antique lamp post with four swans
at the base costs £3,000.
Delivery. Restoration service.

BUTTONS

Button Queen
*19 Marylebone Lane, W1 (071 935 1505).
Bond Street underground.* **Open** 10am-6pm
Mon-Fri; 10am-1.30pm Sat. **No credit cards.**
Thousands of antique and modern buttons
are crowded into this shop. Prices start at a
few pence but rise to around £200 for eighteenth-century Wedgwood buttons.
Export scheme. Postal delivery.

CLOCKS & WATCHES

Aubrey Brocklehurst
*124 Cromwell Road, SW7 (071 373
0319). Gloucester Road underground.*
Open 9am-1pm, 2-6pm, Mon-Fri; 10am-
1pm Sat. **No credit cards.**
Antique clocks and barometers are the speciality of the house. Restored Georgian,
Regency and Victorian carriage clocks cost
from £200 and barometers start at £600.
Delivery. Export scheme. Repair and restoration.

Strike One
*51 Camden Passage, N1 (071 226 9709).
Angel underground.* **Open** 9am-5pm Mon-
Sat. **Credit** A, AmEx, DC, £TC.
Some exquisite examples of European
clockmaking are gathered here in a somewhat reverential atmosphere. Don't expect
any bargains; a fine French carriage clock
costs £750 but each piece comes complete
with a one-year guarantee.
Catalogue. Delivery. Export scheme.

COSTUME

Gallery of Antique Costume
& Textiles
*2 Church Street, NW8 (071 723 9981).
Edgware Road or Marylebone underground.*
Open 10am-5.30pm Mon-Sat. **Credit** A,
AmEx, £TC, V.
Two floors overflow with antique clothing,

One of London's more unlikely institutions, the **Thimble Society of
London** *(listed under* **Thimbles***) stocks hundreds of thimbles dating from the
twelfth century to the present day. Silver, gold, steel, china and enamel pieces
cost from £3 and soar to £3,000. A silver model commemorating the birth of
Princess Beatrice is a newcomer to the collection and costs £24. Finger-protec-
tors have never been so fascinating.*

textiles and accessories from all over the
world. Original items date from the 1830s to
the 1930s, with a few exceptional earlier
pieces. Prices are reasonable and start from
£3 rising to £50,000.

JEWELLERY

Beau Gems
*26 Royal Exchange, EC3 (071 623 7634).
Bank underground.* **Open** 8.30am-5.30pm
Mon-Fri. **Credit** A, AmEx, DC, £TC, V.
Specialists in antique and modern jewellery,
Beau Gems stocks mainly Victorian and art
deco pieces although it also holds pieces
from other periods. You can buy a Victorian
brooch from £45 or an emerald and diamond
cluster ring for £7,000.
Export scheme.
Branch *418 The Strand, WC2 (071 836 7356).*

Benjamins
*124 New Bond Street, W1 (071 408 0173).
Bond Street underground.* **Open** 10am-
5.30pm Mon-Fri; 10am-3.30pm Sat. **Credit**
A, AmEx, £TC, V.
Antique and second-hand jewellery, including
genuine Victorian, Georgian, art deco and art
nouveau baubles, glisten here. A small
Victorian brooch costs £250 but £50,000 will
get you a sizeable gem-set necklace.
Export scheme.

MARKETS

Alfies Antique Market
*13-25 Church Street, NW8 (071 723 6066).
Edgware Road underground/Marylebone*

underground/BR/ 6, 8, 16, 16A, 159 bus.
Open 10am-6pm Tue-Sat. **Credit** stalls vary.
With 370 stalls, Alfies claims to be the
largest covered antique market in Britain.
Almost every antique field is covered includ-
ing gramophones and records, furniture,
pewter and porcelain, silver, postcards, toys
and cheap bric-à-brac.
*Bureau de Change. Café. Insurance scheme.
Removal.*

Antiquarius
*135-141 King's Road, SW3 (071 351 5353).
Sloane Square underground/11, 19, 22 bus.*
Open 10am-6pm Mon-Sat. **Credit** stalls vary.
With over 150 stalls, London's best-known
indoor antiques market offers a great diversity of goods. Among the goodies you'll find
costume jewellery, china, glass, antiquarian
books and prints.
Café.

Bermondsey Antiques
Market
*Corner of Long Lane and Bermondsey
Street, SE1. London Bridge
underground/BR.* **Open** 5am-noon Fri.
No credit cards.
Formerly known as the New Caledonian
Market, Europe's largest antique centre is
usually teeming with eager dealers at the
crack of dawn. Traders sell every conceivable form of objet d'art but get ready to
haggle if you want a fair price.

Bond Street Antiques Centre
*124 New Bond Street W1 (071 351 5353).
Bond Street underground/25 bus.* **Open** 10am-

THE ULTIMATE COMICS, SCIENCE FICTION, FANTASY AND HORROR BOOKSHOP

FORBIDDEN PLANET

Forbidden Planet is the world's largest comics, fantasy and science fiction store.
We have a massive selection of new and old comics plus t-shirts, toys and other comic paraphanalia.
We also have the fullest range available of British and American horror and fantasy books as well as a dazzling range of film and television fantasy matereial.

71 NEW OXFORD STREET, LONDON WC1A 1DG.
01-836 4179 AND 01-379 6042

PLEASE SEND SAE FOR OUR COMICS, TITAN GRAPHIC NOVELS,
JUDGE DREDD, FREDDY KRUEGER, BATMAN™, GERRY ANDERSON
AND STAR TREK™ PRODUCT LISTS.
MAIL ORDER. C/O 71 NEW OXFORD STREET, LONDON WC1A 1DG. 01-497 2150

Recent expansion at the **Cornflake Shop** *(listed under* **Audio & Hi-Fi***) has meant a considerable increase in the high quality stock. A basic Rega 2 system costs less than £400 and for £450 you can buy a compact disc system. Helpful staff give a full demonstration of the equipment, so you know what you're getting.*

6pm Mon-Fri. **Credit** A, AmEx, DC, £$TC, V. One of London's finest antique centres in terms of quality, BSAC is renowned for its rare examples of antique jewellery, watches, silver, porcelain and paintings.

Chelsea Antique Market
245-253 King's Road, SW3 (071 352 5689).
Sloane Square underground/11, 19, 22 bus.
Open 10am-6pm Mon-Sat. **Credit** stalls vary.
The oldest indoor antique market in London, this is also one of the friendliest, cheapest and scruffiest. You'll find period men's clothing, antiquarian books, theatre and cinema ephemera, old clocks, watches, phonographs, prints, scientific instruments and bric-à-brac.
Café.

Chenil Galleries
181-183 King's Road, SW3 (071 351 5353).
Sloane Square underground/11, 19, 22 bus.
Open 10am-6pm Mon-Sat. **Credit** stalls vary.
Fine, elegant antiques are in abundance at Chenil Galleries. Dealers come here for seventeenth- and eighteenth-century paintings and prints, long-case clocks, jewellery, art nouveau and art deco objets, porcelain and silverware, and antique toys.
Café.

Grays Antique Market
58 Davies Street/Grays Mews , 1-7 Davies Mews, W1 (071 629 7034). Bond Street

underground. **Open** 10am-6pm Mon-Fri. **Credit** stalls vary.
Over 200 dealers are housed here in two enormous Victorian buildings. Rummage through the antique luggage and leather goods, toys, games, militaria and jewellery. *Bureau de change. Cafés.*

MEMORABILIA

Hope & Glory
131A Kensington Church Street, W8 (071 727 8424). Notting Hill Gate underground.
Open 10am-5pm Tue-Fri; 10am-2pm Sat.
No credit cards.
All forms of commemorative china and glass are sold here. Around half of the mugs, plates, glasses and plaques are pre-1940 and some date back even further.
Export scheme. Postal delivery.

Mint & Boxed
110 High Street, HA8 (081 952 2002).
Edgware underground. **Open** 9.30am-5.30pm Mon,Tue,Thur-Sat. **Credit** A, AmEx, £$TC, V.
Mint & Boxed is so named because of the pristine condition of all its antique and collectable models. Most of the trains, planes, automobiles and boats date from between 1890 and 1980. Prices start at £5.
Local delivery. Export scheme. Catalogue (£5). Mail Order service. Wheelchair access.

MIRRORS

House of Mirrors
597 Kings Road, SW6 (071 736 5885).
Fulham Broadway underground/11 bus.
Open 9am-6pm Mon-Sat. **No credit cards.**
This family-run business boasts the largest shop collection of nineteenth-century English mirrors in London. They include Victorian Gothic, rococo, Adam, Chippendale, Kent and baroque examples. Prices start at about £350 and climb through the ceiling to around £20,000, although most pieces cost between £800 and £1,500.
Delivery. Export scheme.

Through The Looking Glass
563 King's Road, SW6 (071 736 7799).
Fulham Broadway underground/11 bus. **Open** 10am-5.30pm Mon-Sat. **No credit cards.**
Almost every type of mirror, from all over eighteenth- and nineteenth-century Europe, hangs here. Prices are between £500 and £20,000.
Delivery.
Branch *137 Kensington Church Street, W8 (071 221 4026).*

MUSICAL

Jack Donovan
93 Portobello Road, W11 (071 727 1485).
Notting Hill Gate underground. **Open** noon-5.30pm Tue-Fri; 11am-6pm Sat.
Credit £$TC.
Mr D deals exclusively in clockwork musical automata dating from 1840 to 1930. Prices range from £50 for a small music novelty to £13,000 for a lavish German music box.
Delivery. Export scheme.

QUILTS & CUSHIONS

Patchwork Dog & Calico Cat
21 Chalk Farm Road, NW1 (071 485 1239).
Camden Town underground. **Open** 10am-6pm Mon-Sat. **Credit** A, AmEx, DC, V.
Needlework enthusiasts will be impressed by the range of early twentieth-century English and American hand-made quilts at PD&CC. Prices start from £150 to £900.
Catalogue (25p). Delivery. Export scheme.

Pillows of London
48 Church Street, NW8 (071 723 3171).
Edgware Road underground. **Open** 10am-5.30pm Mon-Sat. **Credit** AmEx, £TC, V.
A delightful little shop crammed with antique cushions from the seventeenth century up to about 1940. Fork out £40 for a chintzy Victorian example or up to £1,000 for a seventeenth-century needlework cushion.
Postal delivery. Export scheme.

POSTERS

Dodo
286 Westbourne Grove, W11 (071 229 3132). Notting Hill Gate underground. **Open** 7am-4pm Sat; otherwise by appointment.
No credit cards.
Definitely the place to go to for vintage American, British and Continental advertising posters and signs. Everything on sale dates from about 1880 to 1945 and costs between £8 and £500.
Delivery. Export scheme.

POTTERY

Constance Stobo
31 Holland Street, W8 (071 937 6282). High Street Kensington underground. **Open** 11am-5pm Mon-Fri; 10am-2pm Sat. **Credit** £STC.
You will find mainly Staffordshire pottery in this immaculate corner shop with a particular emphasis on cottage and animal miniatures. *Export scheme.*

PRINTS & MAPS

Grosvenor Prints
28-32 Shelton Street, WC2 (071 836 1979). Covent Garden underground. **Open** 10am-6pm Mon-Fri; 10am-4pm Sat. **Credit** A, AmEx, £STC, V.
Grosvenor's claim London's largest selection of antique prints and engravings gathered under one roof. Prices vary from £5 to £2,000. *Export scheme. Postal delivery.*

Robert Douwma
4 Henrietta Street, WC2 (071 836 0771). Covent Garden underground. **Open** 10am-6pm Mon-Fri; 10am-5pm Sat. **Credit** A, AmEx, DC, £TC, V.
This collection of prints includes nineteenth-century satire, topography, natural history and contemporary colour editions. Prices start at £10 and rise to about £3,000. *Catalogues (£3 each). Export scheme. Postal delivery.*

THIMBLES

Thimble Society of London
Gray's Antique Market, 58 Davies Street, W1 (071 493 0560). Bond Street underground. **Open** 10am-6pm Mon-Fri. **Credit** A, DC, £STC, V.
See **picture and caption.**
Catalogue. Postal delivery.

WOODWORK

Simon Castle/Michael German
38B Kensington Church Street, W8 (S Castle 071 937 2268/M German 071 937 2771). High Street Kensington underground. **Open** 10am-5pm Mon-Fri; 10am-3pm Sat. **Credit** A, AmEx, DC, £STC, V.
Treen (small, domestic, wooden objects) and decorative carvings are Mr Castle's forté as you can tell by looking at his beautiful mahogany candlesticks and tobacco jars. Choose from Mr German's stock of over 500 walking-sticks, starting at £50 and rising to £2,000. *Export scheme. Postal delivery.*

Circus Circus *(listed under* **Children***) is one of the better kids' shops in London. There's a carnival atmosphere to the shop and the prices won't drive you to distraction. Osh kosh dungarees cost around £25 and shirt prices start at £2.99. There's also a department for nursery equipment and a collection of second-hand goods.*

AUDIO & HI-FI

Cornflake Shop
37 Windmill Street, W1 (071 631 0472). Goodge Street or Tottenham Court Road underground. **Open** 10am-7pm Mon-Sat. **Credit** A, HP, £TC, V.
See **picture and caption.**
Catalogue. Delivery and installation. Demonstration facilities. Export scheme. Mail order.

Doug Brady Hi-Fi
18 Monmouth Street, WC2 (071 379 4010). Covent Garden underground. **Open** 10am-6pm Mon-Sat; 11am-5pm Sun. **Credit** A, AmEx, DC, HP. V.
Choosing from the vast stock of quality British goods, the staff at DB can put together a system consisting of turn-table, amp and speakers costing a mere £350 or a mammoth £100,000. They offer a two-year parts and labour guarantee on all equipment. *Catalogue and brochures. Delivery and installation. Demonstration facilities. Export scheme. Mail order.*

Hi-Fi Care
245 Tottenham Court Road, W1 (071 637 8911). Goodge Street or Tottenham Court Road underground. **Open** 9am-6pm Mon-Sat. **Credit** A, AmEx, DC, £TC, V.
The stock of over 4,000 hi-fi accessories here includes headphones, tapes, microphones, cartridges and cables, video accessories and photographic lighting equipment. Speaker wall brackets start from £20 and a Target hi-fi table from around £50.
Export scheme. Postal delivery.

BOOKS

Bell, Book and Radmall
4 Cecil Court, WC2 (071 240 2161). Leicester Square underground. **Open** 10am-5.30pm Mon-Fri. **Credit** A, AmEx, DC, JCB, £STC, V.
Antiquarian books don't come cheap so it's not surprising that prices are high at this bibliophiles' paradise. However, the range of first editions is excellent, the staff are knowledgeable and the atmosphere cosy.
Free catalogue twice a year. Mail order.

Dillons The Bookstore
82 Gower Street, WC1 (071 636 1577). Goodge Street underground. **Open** 9am-5.30pm Mon, Wed-Fri; 9.30am-5.30pm Tue, Sat. **Credit** A, BT, £TC, V.
This is, just possibly, London's ultimate bookstore. Each category is listed on the enormous notice-board by the main door. Fortunately, the vast stock is computerized, so information is instant.
Disabled facilities. New books catalogues (phone for details). Mail order.

Foyles
119 Charing Cross Road, WC2 (071 437 5660). Leicester Square or Tottenham Court

Road underground. **Open** 9am-6pm Mon-Wed, Fri, Sat; 9am-7pm Thur. **Credit** AmEx, S£TC, V.
Surprisingly, stock at London's biggest and most confusing bookstore isn't listed on computer and it gets frustrating when staff can't find the book you want. However, Foyles has nearly every book imaginable so keep scanning the shelves patiently.
Export scheme on records and tapes. Mail order. Magazine (monthly). Postal delivery.

Hatchards
187-188 Piccadilly, W1 (071 437 3924/439 9921). Green Park or Piccadilly Circus underground/9, 14, 19, 22, 25, 38, 55 bus. **Open** 9am-6pm Mon-Fri; 9am-5pm Sat. **Credit** A, AmEx, BT, £STC, V.
The classiest of the bookstore chains has efficient, helpful staff and well-organized stock. You can order any book from Hatchards whether or not it's in print.
Catalogues. Delivery. Mail order. Monthly reviews of new titles (free).

CHILDREN

Children's World
317 Cricklewood Broadway, NW2 (081 208 1088). Kilburn underground/BR/16, 32 bus. **Open** 10am-8pm Mon-Fri; 9am-6pm Sat. **Credit** A, SC, V.
Children can enter this little 'world' via a giant slide if they're so inclined. Once inside, little Johnny can watch cartoons in the play area or gorge himself in the café. The clothes, for children up to 12 years old, are good value and well-styled. Babygros start at £4.50.
Café. Catalogue. Children's toilets. Father and baby room. Mother and baby room. Play area.

Circus Circus
176 Wandsworth Bridge Road, SW6 (071 731 4128). Fulham Broadway underground/28, 91, 295 bus. **Open** 10am-6pm Mon-Fri. **Credit** A, ILEA vouchers, £TC, V.
See **picture and caption.**
Baby-changing facilities. Delivery. Postal delivery.

Early Learning Centre
225 Kensington High Street, W8 (071 937 0419). High Street Kensington underground. **Open** 9am-6pm Mon, Wed-Sat; 9.30am-6pm Tue. **Credit** A, £TC, V.
A chain of shops where you can buy stimulating toys that are neither racist nor sexist. There's also plenty of choice for under £5.

Hamleys
188 Regent Street, W1 (071 734 3161). Oxford Circus underground. **Open** 9.30am-6pm Mon-Wed, Fri; 9.30am-8pm Thur; 9.30am-6pm Sat. **Credit** A, AmEx, DC, £STC, V.
The biggest toy shop in the world has all the latest trends packed into six floors. You'll find electronic and computer games, models, dolls, cuddly toys, trains and more.
Baby-changing facilities.

Kidstore
43-47 New Broadway, W5 (071 286 8670). Ealing Broadway underground/BR. **Open** 9am-5.30pm Mon-Sat. **Credit** A, TC, V.
See **picture and caption.**
Mother and baby room. Play area.

Kidstore *(listed under* **Children***) is a cheery department store stocking inexpensive toys and stylish clothes for fashion-conscious youngsters: snazzy denim bomber jackets (£24.99) and matching dungarees (£12.99). Be warned, the packaging of goods is so slick that you risk the constant 'Can I have that? Please, please, puhleeeze.' from your little loved one.*

Joanna's Tent
289B King's Road, SW3 (071 352 1151). Sloane Square underground/19, 22 bus. **Open** 9.30am-6.30pm Mon-Sat. **Credit** A, AmEx, DC, JCB, £STC, V.
Joanna's Tent isn't the most exciting name for a shop but there's compensation in the children's section packed full of colourful gear with designer labels. Kenzo dresses start at £47 while leather jackets begin at £73. Alison Robson's range of hand-knitted sweaters and dresses begins at £80 and goes up to around £96. JT also has its own range of toiletries for kids called Oilily which includes perfume, soaps and hair gel.
Postal delivery.

Mothercare
461 Oxford Street, W1 (071 622 6621). Marble Arch underground. **Open** 9.30am-6pm Mon-Sat. **Credit** A, £STC, SC, V.
Mothercare stocks everything from christening robes to swimming costumes. Kids enjoy motifs such as Docker Bear and brightly-coloured monsters which pop up on T-shirts, sweatshirts, hats and dresses.
Baby-changing facilities. Catalogue (30p). Delivery. Mail order from Mothercare, Cherry Tree Road, Watford, Herts WD2.

Peek-a-Boo
42 Chiltern Street, W1 (071 486 2800). Baker Street underground. **Open** 10am-5.30pm Mon-Fri; 10am-1pm Sat. **Credit** A, AmEx, £TC, V.

Exquisite babywear and hand-embroidered children's separates are the specialities here. Cardigans, rompers and shirts start at £10.95 while silk christening gowns cost from £200.

FASHION

CLASSIC

Aquascutum
100 Regent Street, W1 (071 734 6090). Piccadilly Circus underground. **Open** 9am-6pm Mon-Wed, Fri, Sat; 9am-7pm Thur. **Credit** A, AmEx, DC, JCB, £STC, V.
The most British fashion shop this side of Savile Row. Three floors hold every type of timeless classic; ladies raincoats retail between £225 and £1,000, men's are only slightly less expensive rising to £850. Gentlemen's cashmere scarves are a relative snip at around £69.
Catalogue. Dry-cleaning and alterations. Delivery. Export scheme.

Gieves & Hawkes
1 Savile Row, W1 (071 434 2001). Piccadilly Circus underground. **Open** 9am-5.30p6m Mon-Sat. **Credit** A, A/c, AmEx, DC, £TC, V.
The fact that HRH the Prince of Wales is on their client list is an indication that the tailors at G&H excel at their craft. They offer superb gentlemen's clothes at prices that are not unreasonable by Savile Row standards.

Ready to wear suits start at £275 and bespoke fit from £1,000.
Alterations to own goods. Bespoke tailoring. Catalogue. Export scheme. Mail order.

Tommy Nutter
19 Savile Row, W1 (071 734 0831). Oxford Circus underground. **Open** 9am-6pm Mon-Sat. **Credit** A, AmEx, DC, JCB, £STC, V.
Tommy Nutter was responsible for much of Elton John's wardrobe but many fashionable ladies also number amongst his clients. Impeccably made, natty, double-breasted suits start from £385 off the peg; a two piece made to order will set you back £920.
Delivery. Export scheme. Postal delivery. Fitting trips to USA customers.

Turnbull & Asser
69, 71 & 72 Jermyn Street, SW1 (No 69: 071 839 5133/Nos 71 & 72: 071 930 0502). Piccadilly Circus underground. **Open** 9am-5.30pm Mon-Fri; 9am-4.30pm Sat. **Credit** A, AmEx, DC, £STC, V.
T&A is famous for its Classic-cut shirts which cost from £45 for poplin and £85 for Sea Island cotton. Scarves come in brilliantly-coloured reversible silk (£125) and cashmere (£95); silk ties start at £25.
Delivery. Export scheme.

DANCEWEAR
Pineapple
7 Langley Street, WC2 (071 836 4006). Covent Garden underground. **Open** 10am-7pm Mon-Fri; 10am-6pm Sat; 11am-5pm

Sun. **Credit** A, AmEx, £TC, V.
Pineapple has veered away from the leotard and tutu dance image with the emphasis now on fitness and fashion. Cotton Lycra cycling shorts at £16.99 and skirts for £19.99 should be avoided if your figure is less than perfect.
Catalogue (£2). Export scheme. Mail order.

DESIGNER
A La Mode
36 Hans Crescent, SW1 (071 584 2133). Knightsbridge underground. **Open** 10am-6pm Mon, Tue, Thur-Sat; 10am-7pm Wed. **Credit** A, AmEx, DC, £TC, V.
Junior Gaultier, Antony Price and Rifat Ozbek, are some of the names here. The Liza Bruce collection in clingy Lycra presents the up-and-coming catsuit at £235. Paupers beware, most customers spend at least £150.
Export scheme. Free alterations to own goods. Mail order. Postal delivery. Wheelchair access.

Bazaar
1 & 4 South Molton Street, W1 (071 499 3127/629 1708). Bond Street underground. **Open** 10.30am-6.30pm Mon-Wed, Fri; 10.30am-7pm Thur; 10.30am-5.30pm Sat. **Credit** A, AmEx, DC, £STC, V.
Jean-Paul Gaultier, Giuliano, Fujiwara and Matsuda are some of the heavy-duty menswear labels carried by Bazaar. John Richmond is one of the few Brits to get a look in. Suits cost between £400 and £800.
Alterations to own goods. Delivery. Export scheme for goods over £50. Postal delivery.

The Beauchamp Place Shop
55 Beauchamp Place, SW3 (071 589 4155). Knightsbridge underground. **Open** 10am-6pm Mon, Tue, Thur, Fri; 10am-6.30pm Wed; 11am-6pm Sat. **Credit** A, AmEx, DC, £STC, V.
The Beauchamp Place Shop holds sophisticated and dressy women's fashion with a host of impressive names: Workers For Freedom; Cerruti; Edina Ronay; beautiful shoes by Robert Clergerie; jewellery by Pellini. A Cerruti suit will deprive you of about £400.
Alterations to own goods. Brochure. Export scheme. Mail order.

Boyd and Storey
12 Newburgh Street, W1 (071 494 3188/9). Oxford Circus or Piccadilly Circus underground. **Open** 10.30am-6.30pm Mon-Fri; 11.30am-5.30pm Sat. **Credit** A, AmEx, V.
Chain-mail comes to town at Boyd and Storey. Buy a jacket for £750 if you like your clothes heavy. If not there's always the ubiquitous Lycra; tops cost around £50 and a cat suit is ideal to show off a streamline figure. Embroidery, beading and luxurious silk combine to give an exotic, sensual feel to the clothes.
Export scheme.

Browns
23-27 South Molton Street, W1 (071 491 7833). Bond Street underground. **Open** 10am-6pm Mon-Wed, Fri, Sat; 10am-7pm Thur. **Credit** A, AmEx, DC, JCB, £STC, V.
For high fashion, Browns must be the first stop. Top names such as Gaultier, Conran, Hamnett, Christian Lacroix and Rifat Ozbek preside. Not surprisingly, prices are high so if money's tight, wait for the sales or shop elsewhere.
Alterations to own goods. Catalogue. Delivery. Export scheme for goods over £100. Postal delivery (£2 postage).

Christopher New
52 Dean Street, W1 (071 734 5363). Tottenham Court Road underground/14, 24, 29 bus. **Open** 10am-7pm Mon-Fri; 10am-6.30pm Sat. **Credit** A, AmEx, DC, £TC, V.
Classic-cut menswear with unusual trimmings set Christopher New apart from the Brit designer set. Coins, buttons, stars and medals decorate waistcoats and sweaters while shirts are jazzed up with some rather tasty embroidery. Keep an eye out for the sweet little sailor jackets at £145.
Delivery. Export scheme.

Crolla
35 Dover Street, W1 (071 629 5931). Green Park underground. **Open** 11am-6pm Mon-Sat. **Credit** A, AmEx, DC, £STC, V.
Scott Crolla's opulent clothes reflect the baroque splendour of his shop. Velvet waistcoats start at £180, in brocade they begin at £250 as do the exquisite cocktail dresses. Accessories include shorts (£15-£40) and boxers (£15-£28).
Export scheme. Postal delivery.

Designers Sale Studio
24 King's Road, SW3 (071 351 4171). Sloane Square underground/11, 19, 22 bus. **Open** 10am-7pm Mon-Fri; 10am-6pm Sat. **Credit** A, AmEx, DC, £STC, V.
End-of-lines and cancelled orders are up for grabs at the Designers Sale Studio. You'll find womenswear with labels like Byblos, Krizia and Ralph Lauren. However, cash-

*Bomber, duffle and flying jackets cost from £195 at **Natural Leather** (listed under **Leather**). This well-established shop stocks the range of Turner jackets, including parka styles (padded and hooded), costing from £450. Luggage, wallets, belts and bags are among a comprehensive selection of accessories.*

An exceedingly upmarket deli, **Hobbs & Co** *(listed under* **Delicatessens***) sells mainly English food but you'll also find French and Italian goods. Swiss chocolates, fresh foie gras and varieties of truffle rub shoulders with a fine collection of preserves and condiments. The shop has a certain rustic charm.*

mere jumpers cost £225 and silk blouses retail for around £75, so the clothes aren't cheap. But they're reasonable enough, considering the names they carry.
Delivery. Export scheme.

Issey Miyake
21 Sloane Street, SW1 (071 245 9891). Knightsbridge underground. **Open** 10am-6pm Mon, Tue, Thur-Sat; 10am-7pm Wed. **Credit** A, AmEx, DC, £STC, V.
Issey Miyake's ability to surprise with unusual garments seems never-ending; inflatable rubber jackets was one of his earlier ideas. The emphasis is on women's fashion although there's a small amount of men's clobber.
Export scheme.

John Richmond
2 Newburgh Street, W1 (071 734 5782). Oxford Circus underground. **Open** 10.30am-6pm Mon-Sat. **Credit** A, AmEx, V.
Religion is the theme for JR's latest collection. Crucifixes appear on jackets; T-shirts and sweatshirts are adorned with prayers. Long, tapered drape-coats with a slightly Gothic feel cost from £299. Jewellery and hats continue the ecclesial theme that will probably meet with your vicar's disapproval.
Export scheme.

Jones
13 Floral Street, WC2 (071 240 8312). Covent Garden underground. **Open** 10am-6.30pm Mon-Sat. **Credit** A, AmEx, DC, JCB, TC, V.
Junior Gaultier, John Richmond, Giuliano, Fujiwara and Issey Miyake crop up on the roll-call of high fashion names at Jones. Men will need to fork out anything from £45 to £300 for a shirt and £70 to £80 for a pair of trousers. Dresses can cost from £70 up to £600.
Alterations to own goods. Export scheme. Postal delivery.

Joseph Tricot
16 Sloane Street, SW1 (071 235 9868). Knightsbridge underground. **Open** 9.30am-6pm Mon, Tue, Thur-Sat; 10am-7pm Wed. **Credit** A, AmEx, DC, V.
The British knitwear at Joseph Tricot is much sought after with some great machine-knitted sweaters and skirts. Hand-knitted jumpers with tiger motifs hover around the £300 mark.
Café. Export scheme for goods over £100.

Katharine Hamnett
20 Sloane Street, SW1 (071 823 1002). Knightsbridge underground. **Open** 9.30am-6pm Mon, Tue, Thur-Sat; 10am-7pm Wed. **Credit** A, AmEx, DC, £TC, V.
Being a woman of extremes, Katharine

Hamnett's men's and women's clothes go from quiet, understated jackets to studded leather creations. Velvet bomber jackets for men (£220) look a treat with a pair of classic trousers.
Alterations to own goods. Catalogue. Delivery. Mailing list.

Pam Hogg
5 Newburgh Street, W1 (071 287 2185). Oxford Circus underground. **Open** 10am-6pm Mon-Sat. **Credit** A, AmEx, £TC, V.
Clothes for the bold, brash and daring tend to make up most of Ms Hogg's collection. Past collections have included Lycra battle dresses with acessoried studs and set off to perfection with a matching bra. Not recommended for the faint-hearted.

Paul Smith
41-44 Floral Street, WC2 (071 379 7133). Covent Garden underground. **Open** 10.30am-6.30pm Mon-Wed, Fri; 10.30am-7pm Thur; 10am-6.30pm Sat. **Credit** A, AmEx, DC, JCB, £TC, V.
Classic menswear, enlivened by witty details, ranges from sportswear to formal clothing. Clothes and accessories at No.43 are divided into the flamboyant, such as jazzy silk ties, and the timeless wool cardigans and linen shirts. At Nos. 41-42 there are cashmere blazers and beautifully-cut suits from £320.
Alteration to own goods. Embroidery service for own shirts. Export scheme. Catalogue. Postal delivery.

Whistles
12-14 St Christopher's Place, W1 (071 487 4484). Bond Street underground. **Open** 10am-6pm Mon-Wed, Fri; 10am-7pm Thur. **Credit** A, AmEx, DC, £STC, V.
Whistles caters for everyone; there's a combination of inexpensive and designer womenswear. The labels are fairly safe with names like Ghost, Lolita Lempica and knitwear by Artwork. Slinky catsuits at £30 form part of the maternity wear.
Export scheme. Postal delivery.

Workers For Freedom
4 Lower John Street, W1 (071 734 3767). Piccadilly underground. **Open** 10.30am-6pm Mon-Sat. **Credit** A, AmEx, DC, V.
Innovative and successful, Workers For Freedom are the bright boys of British fashion. Past themes have included 'Eskimo Summer' — raffia skirts and sequined lace trousers; silk tie-dyed evening wear in indigo and orange. Jackets cost from £230 and skirts start at £160.
Export scheme.

World's End
430 King's Road, SW3 (071 352 6551). Sloane Square underground/11, 19, 22 bus. **Open** 11am-6pm Mon-Sat. **Credit** A, AmEx, DC, V.
Hordes of fashion victims converge on Vivienne Westwood's eccentric shop for her unpredictable, humorous fashion. Tweed jackets (£240), Galaxy shirts (£65) and Time-machine T-shirts (£40) are some of the most popular items.
Postal delivery.

World Service
68 Neal Street, WC2 (071 836 0809). Covent Garden underground. **Open** 11am-7pm Mon-Fri; 11am-6.30 Sat. **Credit** A, AmEx, £TC, V.
Traditional clothes with a twist are the order of the day at World Service. Double-

breasted gaberdine suits come in aqua-marine green or canary yellow (£299). Printed bomber jackets start at £65. The selection of hats, ties, belts and shoes complements outfits perfectly.
Alterations to own goods. Postal delivery.

KNITWEAR

Patricia Roberts
31 James Street, WC2 (071 379 6660).
Covent Garden underground. **Open** 10.30am-7pm Mon-Sat; noon-5pm Sun. **Credit** A, AmEx, DC, £TC, V.
Hand-made women's knitted sweaters and cardigans cost from £250; soft cashmere and angora sweaters, plain and patterned, can cost up to £600. The cheapest item in the shop is a pair of angora gloves for £25.
Export scheme. Mail order to 60 Kinnerton Street, SW1.

The Scotch House
2 Brompton Road, SW1 (071 581 2151).
Knightsbridge underground. **Open** 9am-6pm Mon, Tue, Thur-Sat; 9am-7pm Wed. **Credit** A, AmEx, DC, V.
Arans, Argyll socks, cashmeres, kilts and sporrans are Scotch House specialities. Cashmere sweaters cost around £177 for a Pringle slipover and between £85 and £105 for a woman's heavy-knit cardigan.
Catalogue. Export scheme. Mail order. Postal delivery.

LEATHER

Lewis Leathers
122 Great Portland Street, W1 (071 636 4314). Great Portland Street or Oxford Circus underground. **Open** 9am-5.30pm Mon-Sat. **Credit** A, £TC, V.
LL carries masses of own-label leather wear at reasonable prices. Men's leather biking jackets cost from £134, women's from £129. A one-piece suit can be made to order but if you're buying off-the-peg the price is £289.
Export scheme. Mail order.

Natural Leather
62 Neal Street, WC2 (071 240 7748).
Covent Garden underground. **Open** 11am-7pm Mon-Sat; noon-6pm Sun. **Credit** A, AmEx, DC, £TC, V.
See **picture and caption.**
Export scheme. Mail order.

MARKETS

Hyper-Hyper
26-40 Kensington High Street, W8 (071 937 6964). High Street Kensington underground. **Open** 10am-6pm Mon-Wed, Fri, Sat; 10am-7pm Mon-Sat.
Over 70 young British designers are given first exposure in Hyper-Hyper and together they present the sharp and the rough edges of street fashion. Indoor stalls sell original clothes, shoes, hats, jewellery, belts and other essential items for fashion followers. You'll never be as trendy as the staff.
Café. Export scheme.

Kensington Market
49-53 Kensington High Street, W8 (071 937 1572). High Street Kensington underground. **Open** 10am-6pm Mon-Sat.
Cheap denim, second-hand clothes and leather are things to look out for in Kensington Market. Marvelette sells good

With more than 30 original and blended coffees, a fine selection of teas and knowledgeable service, it's easy to see why the Queen gets her supplies from **Higgins** *(listed under* **Tea & Coffee***). Wood panelling and the aroma of roast coffee (the Chagga is particularly good) combine to give the shop the ambience of a refined gentlemen's club. This place has class.*

quality forties' and fifties' clothing, either the real McCoy or reproduction. Upstairs, Western Styling stocks original gear for urban cowfolk along with fifties' Brando-style biker boots (£68-£95).

MEDIUM-RANGE

Boy
153 King's Road, SW3 (071 351 1115).
Sloane Square underground/11, 19, 22 bus. **Open** 10am-6pm Mon-Sat. **Credit** A, AmEx, DC, £TC, V.
Poseurs come from miles around for the trendy cycling shorts (£20), T-shirts (£10-£15) and gold lamé bomber jackets (£80). The new range of children's clothes, catering for mites aged between one and ten, is a scaled down version of the adult selection.
Catalogue (£2.50). Export scheme. Mail order from Unit 24, Chelsea Wharf, 15 Lots Road, SW10.

Esprit
6 Sloane Street, SW1 (071 245 9139).
Knightsbridge underground. **Open** 10am-6pm Mon,Tues, Thur-Sat; 10.30am-7pm.Wed. **Credit** A, AmEx, DC, £TC,V.
Casual clothes for men and women all have the Esprit tag and attractive prices. The cropped, checked jackets in the Italian collection come in autumnal colours and have matching waistcoats at £28. Treat yourself to a pure wool, Aran-style jumper from the men's department for a mere £56.
Export scheme for goods over £100.

Fenwick of Bond Street
63 New Bond Street, W1 (071 629 9161).
Bond Street underground/25 bus. **Open** 9.30am-6pm Mon-Wed, Fri, Sat; 9.30am-7.30pm Thur. **Credit** A, AmEx, SC, £STC, V.
The selection of womenswear is impressive, with prices from mid-range to designer. Equally extensive is the lingerie department which will suit most tastes and pockets. Goods are attractively displayed in the menswear department although stock is rather limited.
Alterations. Cafés (close 30 mins before store). Toilets for the disabled. Wheelchair access. Export scheme. Hairdressing salon.

Kodo
115 King's Road, SW3 (071 376 5082).
Sloane Square underground/11,19, 22 bus. **Open** 10am-6.30pm Mon-Sat. **Credit** A, AmEx, DC, £TC,V.
Kodo must be the ultimate in trendy, as Bobby Brown and the cast from Neighbours would tell you. An impressive range of accessories includes some of the

most original watches we've seen and some are displayed in glass-covered pot-holes in the floor. A Union Jack number will set you back £20 and £200 is the asking price for an elaborate silver, sculpted watch. As far as the clothes are concerned, Kodo is a disappointment but the bags, hats, belts and afore-mentioned watches more than make up for the lapse.

Marks and Spencer
(071 437 7722). 173 Oxford Street, W1 Oxford Circus underground. **Open** 9.30am-6pm Mon,Tue; 9.30am-7pm Wed, Fri; 9.30am-8pm Thur; 9am-6pm Sat. **Credit** SC, £$TC.
Four floors selling every possible item of moderately fashionable clothing you can think of. The women's departments offer sober dresses, skirts, coats, lingerie and hosiery. The ever popular tie-neck blouse retails at £19.99; most blouses hover around the £20 mark with a £35 silk effort being the most expensive.
Take away food.

Soldier Blue
184A King's Road, SW3 (071 352 7556). Sloane Square underground/11, 19, 22 bus. **Open** 9am-6pm Mon-Sat, Bank Holidays. **Credit** A, AmEx, DC, £TC, V.
If the label says Levi's, Soldier Blue stocks it. Jackets, shirts and, of course, jeans come in blue, beige, brown and black. Jeans start at £39 and are guaranteed good quality. You'll find all the right tags and an easy atmosphere.
Export scheme.

Warehouse
27 Duke Street, W1 (071 486 5270). Bond Street underground. **Open** 9.30am-5.30pm Mon-Wed, Fri; 10am-8pm Thur; 9am-6pm Sat. **Credit** A, AmEx, SC, £TC, V.
Renowned for stocking an affordable reflection of current trends, Warehouse always has a good selection of stylish clothes. A figure-hugging, jersey all-in-one costs £39.99 and silk blouses start at £44.95. Flannel jackets with matching trousers come in sulphur yellow, pink and red.
Export scheme.

PSYCHEDELIA

Planet Alice
284 Portobello Road, W10 (081 968 9646). Ladbroke Grove underground. **Open** 10am-6pm Mon-Sat. **Credit** £TC, V.
Christian Paris's Planet Alice supplies groovy fashions to the loyal crowd of nouveau-psychedelics. Patchwork leather trousers at £86 and £29 multi-coloured minis are all the rage, as are the brightly coloured, fake fur jackets at £48. Like wow.
Alterations. Brochure. Mail order. Postal delivery.

PERIOD REPRODUCTIONS

American Classics
400-404 King's Road, SW10 (071 351 5229/071 352 2853). Sloane Square underground/11, 19, 22 bus. **Open** 10am-6.30pm Mon-Sat. **Credit** A, £TC, V.
As the name suggests, AC sells Stateside cast-offs. Hawaiian shirts cost around £17, Western shirts start at £15 and baseball jackets retail at £35.

Blax
8 Sicilian Avenue, WC1 (071 404 0125). Holborn underground. **Open** 11am-7pm Mon-Fri; noon-7pm Sat. **Credit** A, £TC.
Most of the clothes in Blax are original and reproduction garments from the thirties, forties and fifties. Almost all the clothes, shoes and accessories are unworn and excellent quality.

Rebecca
66 Neal Street, WC2 (071 379 4958). Covent Garden underground. **Open** 10am-7.30pm Mon-Sat; 11am-6pm Sun, incl Bank Holidays. **Credit** A, AmEx, DC, £TC, V.
Here you'll find original womenswear dating from the twenties, thirties and forties. Cashmere and mohair classics in all colours cost from £15 and Capital E original Levis are a bargain at £39.
Export scheme.

T-SHIRTS

Daniel James
352 King's Road, SW3 (071 352 2933). Sloane Square underground/11, 19, 22 bus. **Open** 10.30 am-6.30pm Mon-Sat. **Credit** A, £TC, V.
DJ sells nothing but printed T-shirts with long or short sleeves. Look out for the Chris Perry collection of six shirts with ozone- and wildlife-friendly motifs. A percentage sale of these goes to the charity concerned, which softens the blow of paying between £13.50 and £29.50.
Branches *19A Jerdan Place, SW6; 57 Neal Street, WC2.*

Lynx
79 Long Acre, WC2 (071 836 9702). Covent Garden underground. **Open** 10am-6pm Mon-Wed, Sat; 10am-8pm Thur, Fri. **Credit** A, AmEx, V.
The campaign against the fur trade continues with slogans such as 'YUCK! Your Disgusting Fur Coat' emblazoned across T-shirts (£9.99) on sale at Lynx's shop-cum-information centre. All goods have an animal theme with leopard-print boxers costing £6.50.

FOOD

FOOD HALLS

Harrods
Knightsbridge, SW1 (071 730 1234). Knightsbridge underground. **Open** 9am-6pm Mon, Tue, Thur-Sat; 9.30am-7pm Wed. **Credit** A, A/c, DC, SC, £$TC, V, most foreign currencies.

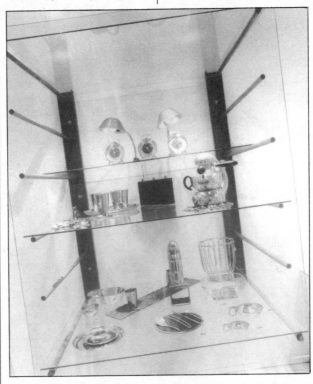

F. Fwd (Fast Forward) *(listed under* **Gifts and Accessories***) is the perfect place to come for inexpensive, classic and sometimes twee designer gifts. A leather-lined Filofax, designed to look like an old antique book, retails at £69.95; cigarette lighters that double as calculators cost £12.95.*

The spectacular food halls at Harrods offer a comprehensive range of goodies. The Halls are divided into Grocery, Fruit, Flowers, Meat, Poultry, Bakery, Confectionery and Wines and Spirits. If you can't find that special ingredient somewhere among all that, the staff might be able to order it for you (at a price).

Fortnum & Mason

181 Piccadilly, W1 (071 734 8040). Green Park or Piccadilly Circus underground. **Open** 9am-5.30pm Mon-Fri; 9am-5pm Sat. **Credit** A, AmEx, CB, DC, JCB, £$TC, V.
Fortnum & Mason is renowned for its stock of exotic and dubious culinary wonders. In 1886 it ordered Mr Heinz's entire stock of new-fangled canned food. Today, Fortnum's no longer sells chocolate-covered ants, but any true (and rich) connoisseur will advise you to buy your provisions from Harrods and your indulgences from Fortnum's. *Christmas catalogue. Delivery. Export scheme. Restaurants.*

BREAD & CAKES

Brick Lane Beigel Bake

159 Brick Lane, E1 (071 729 0616). Shoreditch or Whitechapel underground. **Open** noon-6am Mon-Thur; 24 hours Fri-Sun. **No credit cards.**
The popularity of this shop means that the food is always fresh and very cheap. The range of filled beigels includes *the* classic: smoked salmon and cream cheese for 85p.

John Forrest Bakers

401 King's Road, SW10 (071 352 5848). Sloane Square or Fulham Broadway underground. **Open** 7am-5.30pm Mon-Sat. **No credit cards.**
Although cakes and pastries are made in this small English bakery, the main speciality is bread. There are more than a dozen varieties including rye and muesli.

Patisserie Valerie

44 Old Compton Street, W1 (071 437 3466). Leicester Square or Tottenham Court Road underground. **Open** 8am-7pm Mon-Sat; 10am-6pm Sun. **Credit** £TC.
Despite the fact that Soho's most self-consciously trendy patisserie is often packed with fashion victims and office workers, it's still worth a visit just to sample the heavenly chocolate truffle cake.

CHEESE

Neal's Yard Dairy

9 Neal's Yard, WC2 (071 379 7646). Covent Garden underground. **Open** 9.30am-5.30pm Mon, Tue, Wed, Sat; 9:30am-6pm Thur, Fri. **Credit** £TC.
Randolph Hodgson buys immature cheeses from farms in Britain and Ireland, then brings them to peak condition in the shop's store rooms. He lists over 50 cheeses, 25 to 30 of which are in stock at any time. *Delivery. Mail order. Price list.*

Paxton & Whitfield

93 Jermyn Street, SW1 (071 930 0259). Green Park or Piccadilly underground. **Open** 8.30am-6pm Mon-Fri; 9am-4pm Sat. **Credit** A, AmEx, £TC, V.
Paxton & Whitfield is one of the best cheese merchants in London with over 250 different types of British and continental cheese. The

You'll find only natural products in **Neal's Yard Apothecary and Therapy Rooms** *(listed under* Health and Beauty/Herbalists*). Organically grown herbs are used in medicines and toiletries, like the geranium and orange massage oil that costs £4.25. The range of essential oils includes aniseed and marjoram for £1.95. The Therapy Rooms offer such treatments as reflexology, acupuncture and the Alexander Technique. Call first for an appointment.*

level of hygiene is impressive; the sense of genteel tradition is a peculiarly British joy. *Mail order. Price list.*

DELICATESSENS

Hobbs & Co

29 South Audley Street, W1 (071 409 1058). Bond Street or Green Park underground. **Open** 9am-8pm Mon-Fri; 9am-5pm Sat. **Credit** A, AmEx, V.
See **picture and caption.**
Delivery. Hamper catalogue.

HEALTH FOODS

Neal's Yard

off Short's Gardens, WC2. Covent Garden underground. **Open** 10am-6pm Mon-Sat. **No credit cards.**
Neal's Yard is a peaceful, little courtyard surrounded by health food cafés and shops: visit the tea-room in the Bakery (071 836 5199); try out the Farm Shop (071 836 1066) for fruit juices and take-away curries; buy your health food from the reasonably priced Wholefood Warehouse (071 836 5151) and sample some British cheese from the Dairy (*see above* **Cheese**).

TEA & COFFEE

Algerian Coffee Stores

52 Old Compton Street, W1 (071 437 2480).

Piccadilly Circus underground/9, 19, 24, 29, 55 bus. **Open** 9am-5.30pm Mon-Sat. **Credit** A, A/c, AmEx, DC, £TC, V.
Despite being called coffee stores, the teas now outnumber coffees by about 130 to 30. With mouth-watering names like Japanese Cherry and Mocha Parfait they'll make a change from your usual cuppa.
Delivery. Mail order. Price list.

H R Higgins

79 Duke Street, W1 (071 629 3913/071 491 8819). Bond Street underground. **Open** 8.45am-5.30pm Mon, Tue, Wed; 8:45am-6.30pm Thur; 8.45-6pm Fri; 10am-5pm Sat. **Credit** A, A/c.
See **picture and caption.**
Disabled access (ramp). Mail order from 10 Lea Road Industrial Park, Waltham Abbey, EN9 (0992 768254). Postal delivery.

GIFTS & ACCESSORIES

Coleridge

192 Piccadilly, W1 (071 437 0106). Green Park or Piccadilly Circus underground. **Open** 10.30am-6pm Mon-Sat. **Credit** A, AmEx, DC, £TC, V.
Being the largest glass gallery in England makes Coleridge the perfect show-case for

up-and-coming glass designers. Prices are surprisingly low considering each piece is handmade and unique: marbles are £4.50, paper weights £19.50 and glass jewellery costs from £12.50.
Export scheme. Postal delivery.

The Crafts Council Shop
Victoria & Albert Museum, Cromwell Road, SW7 (071 589 5070). South Kensington underground/14, 45 bus. **Open** 10am-5.30pm Mon-Sat; 2.30-5.30pm Sun. **Credit** A, AmEx, EC, £TC, V.
The excellent selection of gifts range in price from a few pounds for traditional wooden toys, to £90 for a silk scarf featuring a Henry Moore design. Replicas from museum exhibits, glass, ceramics, art books and jewellery make up the rest of the stock.

Endell Street Place
27-29 Endell Street, WC2 (071 240 1060). Covent Garden underground. **Open** 10am-6pm Mon-Sat. **Credit** A, DC, V.
A restored, covered courtyard packed with British handicrafts begging to be bought, or you can just watch the artisans at work. There are portrait painters, toy makers, scriveners, woodturners, ceramicists, potters and jewellery makers.

Fans
24 Frith Street, W1 (071 439 1294). Leicester Square or Tottenham Court Road

underground. **Open** 10am-7pm Mon-Sat. **Credit** A, AmEx, £TC, V.
Fans stock all the latest accessories for trendy kids. Unusually printed T-Shirts will set you back between £7 and £20 but if money's tight you can decorate your body with a packet of temporary tattoos costing £2.99.
Catalogue. Mail order.

F. Fwd (Fast Forward)
14A Newburgh Street, W1 (071 439 0091). Oxford Circus underground. **Open** 10am-6.30pm Mon-Sat. **Credit** A, AmEx, DC, JCB, £STC, V.
See **picture and caption**.
Catalogue. Export scheme. Mail order.

Gallery Of London
1 Duke Of York Street, SW1 (071 925 2082). Piccadilly Circus underground. **Open** 9am-6pm Mon-Sat. **Credit** A, AmEx, DC, EC, £STC, V.
All the British hand-embroidered crests, enamelled tie-clips, reproduction Victorian buttons and other gentlemen's accessories are handmade. Most items cost between £10.50 and £15.50.
Free catalogue. Export scheme. Mail order..

The General Trading Company
144 Sloane Street, SW1 (071 730 0411). Sloane Square underground. **Open** 9am-5.30pm Mon, Tue, Thur, Fri; 9am-7pm Wed;

9am-2pm Sat. **Credit** A, AmEx, DC, £TC, V.
The 12 departments sell kitchenware, oriental goods, pottery, toiletries and much else. Although most of the items are pricey and rather twee, there are some cheaper objects worth examining like silver teaspoons or brass boxes costing approximately £5.
Café. Catalogue. Delivery. Export scheme. Mail order. Postal delivery.

Gered Wedgwood & Spode
173 Piccadilly, W1 (071 629 2614). Green Park or Piccadilly underground. **Open** 9am-6pm Mon-Fri; 9am-4pm Sat. **Credit** A, AmEx, DC, EC, JCB, £STC, V.
Although Wedgwood is better known for its traditional china, the company is constantly updating ranges. Prices are as diverse as the designs: a five place setting from the Candlelight range costs £22 whereas the Black Astbury collection is an eyewatering £1,014.
Catalogue. Delivery service. Disabled access. Export scheme. Mail order. Postal delivery.

James Smith & Sons
53 New Oxford Street, WC1 (071 836 4731). Tottenham Court Road underground. **Open** *Jan-Mar* 9am-5.25pm Mon-Fri; *Apr-Dec* 9am-5.25pm Mon-Fri; 10am-4pm Sat. **Credit** A, £STC, V.
Being near the British Museum and having retained its original Victorian front makes JS&S extremely popular with the tourists. Inside you'll find a forest of umbrellas, sticks and canes in mostly traditional styles.
Export scheme for goods over £100. Postal delivery. Repairs to own goods.

Knutz
1 Russell Street,WC2 (071 836 3117). Covent Garden underground. **Open** 11am-8pm Mon-Sat. **Credit** A, V.
Knutz has supplies for practical jokers and perverts alike. Novelties, inflatables, games and cards are either amusing, sick or downright disgusting. The essentially juvenile might like Bum Care Kits at £3.99 consisting of a mirror, razor, creams and full instructions or they might want to go green with a can of ozone-friendly fart spray at 99p. Try the ultimate midnight snack: a packet of four edible condoms at £4.99.

The London Weather Centre Shop
284 High Holborn, WC1 (071 836 4311). Holborn underground. **Open** 9am-5pm Mon-Fri. **Credit** A, V.
Climatic charts and measuring instruments number among the goods in (what must be) the only weather shop in the world. Meteorological symbols and slogans are emblazoned on T-shirts (£4.95), mugs (£1.35) and scarves (£8.65). Too, too British for words.

Mappin & Webb
170 Regent Street, W1 (071 734 3801). Oxford Circus or Piccadilly Circus underground. **Open** 9am-5.30pm Mon-Fri; 9am-5pm Sat. **Credit** A, AmEx, DC, £STC, V.
Virtually everyone in London has heard of, or been to, Mappin and Webb. It's renowned for extremely expensive, luxury goods from Waterford crystal to silverware. The many showrooms hold seemingly endless displays of giftware and accessories including a massive selection of classic jewellery.
Delivery. Export scheme. Mail order. Postal delivery. Wheelchair access.

Traders at **Greenwich Open Air Market** *(listed under* **Markets***) offer second-hand clothes, books and bric-à-brac. Antique jewellery and small collectables are particularly prominent among the goods. Like every other open-air market in London, the earlier you come, the better the bargains. We've seen some lovely pieces of furniture (look out for the sea-chests) at ridiculously low prices, first thing in the morning. If you are interested in that kind of thing, the collection of poetry books in the book-market is a particular delight for collectors. Simply great.*

Naturally British

13 New Row, WC2 (071 240 0551). Covent Garden or Leicester Square underground. **Open** *Jan-Jul, Sept-Nov* 10.30am-7pm Mon-Sat; *Aug-Dec* 10.30am-7.30pm Mon-Sat; 1-6pm Sun. **Credit** A, AmEx, DC, £$TC, V.
Crafts and clothing all made in the UK. Chunky knitware, jewellery and traditional kitchenware are for sale but prices are rather high.
Catalogue. Delivery. Export scheme.

Richard Kihl

164 Regent's Park Road, NW1 (071 586 3838). Chalk Farm underground. **Open** 9.30am-5pm Mon-Fri; 11am-5pm Sat. **Credit** A, AmEx, EC, V.
A unique shop where you'll find wine accessories to gladden any connoisseur's heart. Delights, such as antique and new decanters, corkscrews, claret jugs and glasses, cost from £5 up to £3,000.

Royal Academy of Arts Gift Shop

Burlington House, Piccadilly, W1 (071 734 9052). Green Park or Piccadilly Circus underground. **Open** 9.45am-5.45pm daily, incl Bank Holidays. **Credit** A, AmEx, DC, V.
Royal Academy champagne (£13.50) nestles among the art books, posters, postcards and ceramics you'd expect to find in a gallery shop. Stock changes subtly to reflect current exhibitions.

LATE—OPENING CHEMISTS

Bliss Chemist

5 Marble Arch, W1 (071 723 6116). Marble Arch underground. **Open** 9am-midnight daily. Open Bank Holidays, incl Christmas Day. **Credit** A, AmEx, DC, £$TC, V.
The only chemist's in Central London that opens late seven days a week. Bliss Chemist in Willesden is open until 2am daily. (*See chapter* **Survival**.)
Branch *50 Willesden Lane, NW6 (624 8000).*

HERBALISTS

Crabtree & Evelyn

6 Kensington Church Street, W8 (071 937 9335). High Street Kensington underground. **Open** 9.30am-6pm Mon, Wed, Fri, Sat; 10am-6pm Tues; 9.30am-7pm Thur. **Credit** A, £$TC, V.
None of the products are tested on animals. Everything is packaged with the kind of grandiosity that suggests Duchesses shop here regularly. Not surprisingly, prices are on the high side; vetiver bath cream costs £5.95, but the juicy avocado and peach scents, body

Hire charges at **Leeds Film and Hire** *(listed under* **Camera and Video Hire***) are slightly cheaper than elsewhere, however, the stock available is less extensive. A 35mm Nikon F3 body (without a lens) costs £6.50 for the day minus VAT and insurance. A standard lens costs £4 per day to hire. The knowledgeable and friendly staff attempt to undertake all camera repairs in-house. All repairs carry a three-month guarantee.*

lotions, and bath gels make lovely gifts.
Catalogue. Export scheme. Gift-wrapping. Mail order from 36 Milton Park, Abingdon, Oxfordshire, OX14. Postal delivery.

Culpeper Herbalists

8 The Market, Covent Garden Piazza, WC2 (071 379 6698). Covent Garden underground. **Open** 10am-8pm Mon-Sat; 11am-6pm Sun. **Credit** A, AmEx, £TC, V.
Drawers of herbs and spices, (from 45p) and scented pot-pourri sachets (from 85p) fill the shop with a delightful smell. Most of the oils, creams, bath salts and soaps are made with Culpeper's own herbs grown in Suffolk.
Baskets made to order. Catalogue. Export scheme. Gift-wrapping. Mail order from Culpeper, Hadstock Road, Linton, Cambridge CB1.

Neal's Yard Apothecary and Therapy Rooms

2 Neal's Yard, WC2 (apothecary 071 379 7222/therapy rooms 071 379 7662). Covent Garden underground. **Open** 10am-6pm Mon, Tue, Thur-Sat; 10am-5.30pm Wed; 11am-4pm Sun. **No credit cards.**
See **picture and caption.**
Catalogues of herbs and cosmetics. Mail order. Postal delivery.

A Nelson & Co

73 Duke Street, W1 (071 629 3118). Bond Street underground. **Open** 9am-5.30pm Mon-Fri; 9.30am-4.30pm Sat. **Credit** A, £TC, V.
A homoeopathic pharmacy with over 4,000 remedies derived from herbs, minerals and other natural substances. Granules, pills and powders can be recommended for anything from bruising to flu.
Mail order from Nelson & Co Ltd, 5 Endeavour Way, SW19 Postal delivery. Price list.

PERFUMERIES

Floris

89 Jermyn Street, SW1 (071 930 2885). Piccadilly Circus underground. **Open** 9.30am-5.30pm Mon-Fri; 9.30am-4pm Sat. **Credit** A, A/c, AmEx, DC, £$TC, V.
Treat yourself to some traditional toiletries like rose mouthwash (£7.25) or Lily of the Valley toilet water. Toothbrushes with mother-of-pearl handles retail at a breathtaking £95.
Catalogue. Delivery. Gift-wrapping.

Penhaligon's

41 Wellington Street, WC2 (071 836 2150). Covent Garden underground. **Open** 10am-6pm Mon-Fri; 10am-5.30pm Sat. **Credit** A, AmEx, V.
Penhaligon's Eau de Toilette for dashing young blades costs £13 for the spray and £19 for a bottle. The gals will adore the fresh fragrance of Bluebell from £16. Winter Garden room spray at £12 imparts a fresh, non-sticky fragrance to your home.
Catalogue. Gift-wrapping. Mail order.

Blanks

271-281 Kilburn High Road, NW6 (071 624 1260/071 624 7777). Kilburn underground /Brondesbury BR. **Open** 10am-5.30pm Mon-

*At **Robe Noire** (listed under **Dress Hire**) each of Izabel Burton's designs is unique. Full-length gowns and cocktail dresses are made from luxurious fabrics such as silk, taffeta, chiffon and georgette. It costs from £69 to hire a dress and matching bag for three days, with a returnable £300 deposit. Rentable jewellery and evening gloves start at £5.75. Robe Noire's evening dresses can be made to order.*

Sat. **Credit** A, AmEx, HP, £STC, V.
Blanks is the biggest music shop in London and carries virtually every instrument ever invented. African talking drums (£25 to £75) mingle with authentic Scottish bagpipes costing £49.
Delivery. Export scheme.

RECORDS & TAPES

HMV
150 Oxford Street, W1 (071 631 3423). Oxford Circus or Tottenham Court Road underground. **Open** 9.30am-7pm Mon, Wed, Fri, Sat; 10am-7pm Tue; 9.30am-8pm Thur. **Credit** A, AmEx, Connect, DC, £TC, V.
The awesome collection of records, tapes and CDs makes it difficult to resist buying a recording of some description from HMV. The tight-fisted or hard-up will be content just to listen to the music.

Tower Records
1 Piccadilly Circus, W1 (071 439 2500). Piccadilly Circus underground. **Open** 9am-midnight Mon-Sat, incl Bank Holidays. **Credit** A, AmEx, Connect, £TC, V.
The comprehensive range of tunes almost guarantees against musical disappointment. Most impressive is the collection of international music; there are records from any country you might care to name.
Export scheme. Mail order. Wheelchair access.

Virgin Megastore
14-30 Oxford Street, W1 (071 631 1234).
Oxford Circus or Tottenham Court Road underground. **Open** 9.30-8pm Mon, Wed-Sat; 10am-8pm Tue; 9.30am-6pm Bank Holidays. **Credit** A, AmEx, Connect, DC, £TC, V.
Of the megastores, Virgin is the strongest on new releases, chart sounds and rock ephemera. The basement CD collection is well-presented and extensive, although the jazz and classical sections are slightly weaker.
Café. Export scheme. Listening facilities. Mail order. Wheelchair access.

STAMPS

Stanley Gibbons International
399 Strand, WC2 (071 836 8444). Charing Cross underground/BR. **Open** 9am-6pm Mon-Fri; 10am-4pm Sat. **Credit** A, AmEx, DC, £TC, V.
For more than 120 years, SGI has collected and sold stamps from all over the world. The depth of stock is impressive so it's worth a look if you have philatelic leanings.
Catalogues. Export scheme. Mail order. Wheelchair access.

STATIONERY

Get Organized
9 Avery Row, W1 (071 493 4485). Bond Street underground. **Open** 9am-6pm Mon-Fri; 10am-4pm Sat. **Credit** A, AmEx, £TC, V.
As the name suggests, Get Organized has everything you could slot into a personal organizer. You'll find loose leaf systems such as Filofax and PMS, but they wouldn't be complete without a *Time Out Filofax Guide* (£3.25). *Filofax mail order.*

Green and Stone
259 King's Road, SW3 (071 352 0837). Bus 11, 19, 22, 49. **Open** 9am-5.30pm Mon-Fri; 9.30am-5.30pm Sat. **Credit** A, £STC, V.
Artists have been buying their materials from G&S for more than 60 years. Together with modern equipment there's a collection of Victorian materials such as easels, pens and 1894 watercolour paper.

Smythson of Bond Street
44 New Bond Street, W1 (071 629 8558). Bond Street or Oxford Circus underground. **Open** 9.15am-5.30pm (stationery room closes 5.15pm) Mon-Fri; 9.15am-12.30pm Sat. **Credit** A, A/c, AmEx, DC, TC, V.
Since being established in 1887, Smythson of Bond Street, a firm of high-class stationers, has supplied specially-milled paper bearing the Smythson watermark. The zodiac range of papers, die-stamped with your sun-sign, costs £14 for 50 sheets and 50 plain envelopes; there's a variety of tantalizing colours. Leather-bound address books and diaries cost from £28.
Catalogue. Export scheme. Postal delivery.

MARKETS

GENERAL

Brixton Market
Brixton Station Road and Electric Avenue, SW9. Brixton underground/BR. **Open** 8am-5.30pm Mon, Tue, Thur-Sat; 8am-1pm Wed.
Stalls are piled high with every kind of exotic fish, meat, fruit and veg in South London's most exciting market. A wig shop, a cheap shoe stall and cafés help to make the streets groove and swing.

East Street Market
East Street, SE17. Elephant & Castle underground/BR/12, 35, 40, 45, 68, 171, 176 bus. **Open** 9am-noon Tue-Thur; 9am-5pm Fri, Sat; 9am-3pm Sun.
The friendly hustle and bustle make this one of London's best markets. Buy goodies such as fruit and veg, clothes, toys and fabrics or simply stroll along for an hour or two watching the traders.

Ridley Road Market
Ridley Road, E8. Dalston Kingsland BR/22, 30, 38, 149 bus. **Open** 9am-3pm Mon-Wed; 9am-noon Thur; 9am-5pm Fri, Sat.
Eastenders converge on this lively market to snap up the quality fruit and veg. You'll be tempted by the stalls packed with meat, fish and fabrics. The streets pound to reggae beat.

CRAFTS

The Courtyard
St Martin's Church Yard, St Martin's Place, WC2. Charing Cross underground/BR. **Open** 11am-6.30pm Mon-Sat.
The traders here offer high quality handmade goods. Fashion accessories, jewellery, pottery and leather-work are for sale at very reasonable prices.

WEEK-END

Brick Lane Market
Brick Lane, E1. Aldgate East underground.
Open 5am-2pm Sun.
If you don't mind the chaos, there's no better place to go bargain-hunting early on a Sunday morning. Traders sell everything from reject frozen food to Ronco toothpaste dispensers.

Camden Markets
Camden High Street to Chalk Farm Road, NW1. Camden Town underground/24, 28, 31, 68 bus. **Open** 8am-6pm Sat, Sun;
There are about eight weekend markets in Camden. Between them they sell everything from banana chutney to leather luggage.

Greenwich Open-Air Market
Greenwich High Road, SE10. Greenwich BR/108, 177, 188 bus. **Open** 7am-5.30pm Sat, Sun.
See **picture and caption.**

Petticoat Lane Market
Middlesex Street, E1. Aldgate or Aldgate East underground or Liverpool Street underground/BR. **Open** 9am-2pm Sun.
The most famous Sunday market in London has a fine selection of fashion and household goods and knick-knacks, although prices tend to be higher here than at other markets. Look out for the impressive array of leather goods.

Portobello Market
Portobello Road, W11. Ladbroke Grove or Notting Hill Gate underground/12, 28, 31, 52, 88 bus. **Open** *fruit and vegetables* 8am-5pm Mon-Wed, Fri, Sat; 8am-1pm Thur; *general* 8am-3pm Fri; 8am-5pm Sat; *antiques* 8am-5pm Sat.
Tourists cluster at the Notting Hill Gate end, which is crammed with antiques, dodgy foreign exchange booths and 'real London market stalls'. Fruit and veg stalls fill the street beyond Elgin Crescent; by the Westway, there's second-hand everything.

CONSUMER SERVICES

Want to hire a glamorous dress for the night ? Have your tennis racquet restrung ? Find a childminder ? Virtually anything you want can be made, mended or delivered in London. To make life easy we've compiled a list of some of the most essential services around. You'll discover where to go for the snazziest haircuts, who to see about hiring a glamorous sequined number and how to find a trustworthy childminder before hitting the town in a rented car.

The services mentioned below are just the tip of the iceberg: There are hundreds more in London. Scan the pages of the new *Time Out Guide to Shopping and Services* (£5.75) for a massive selection of the capital's shops and services. We've also listed services in other chapters of this guide. For police, fire, ambulance and other emergency services *see chapter* **Survival.** As you might expect, **Travelling Around London** contains details of transport services and services for business people are listed under **Business.** Large department stores also offer many services so look under **West End** and **Shopping**.
At the time of going to press, all details given for each review are accurate to the best of our knowledge. However, London is a constantly changing city, so it is always wise to phone in advance to confirm details before ordering a service that we have listed.

ANTIQUES
For packing and shipping of antiques *see below* **Packing and Removals.**

The London and Provincial Antique Dealers Association (LAPADA)
Unit 2, 14, 535 King's Road, SW10 (071 835 3511). Sloane Square underground/11,19,22 bus. **Open** 9am-1pm, 2-5.30pm Mon-Fri.
If you've ever wondered how to find your way around the antiques world, make LAPADA your first stop. The 225 members in the London area are committed to the Association's strict code of practice and any complaints that can't be resolved directly with the trader should be reported to the body. It also publishes a 192 page directory, *Buying Antiques in Britain* (£3 + 50p postage and packing), which gives details of all members as well as good advice on buying antiques, customers protection, antique markets, export services and more.

ANTIQUES VALUATIONS
Christies
85 Old Brompton Road, SW7 (071 581 7611). South Kensington underground.
Open 9am-7.30pm Mon; 9am-5pm Tue-Fri.
When it comes to Fine Art, Christie, Manson & Woods are the specialists. Their expert valuers will give free estimates on anything from toys to textiles. Vintage wine and most collectables are sold at more than 350 auctions every year but go to the South Kensington branch if you are looking for furniture, jewellery and silver.
Branch *8 King Street, SW1Y (071 839 9060).*

With a name like **Cuts** *(listed under* **Hairdressers***) it's no surprise that haircuts are the only service on offer here. A quick crop is a mere £5 but the standard cuts for men and women start at £15. Geometry in action has never looked so good on the head. Take the chance.*

Phillips

*101 New Bond Street/7 Blenheim Street W1
(071 629 6602). Bond Street underground.*
Open 8.30am-5pm Mon-Fri; 8.30am-noon
Sat; 2pm-5pm Sun (viewing only).
Valuations are mostly free, the exception
being home visits, in which case there's a
minimum call-out fee of £100. Each branch
has its own specialist knowledge: the
Hayes Place branch is strong on Fine Art;
Glendining's at the Bond Street branch
are the coin experts and at Salem Road
valuers have the gen on textiles, pianos
and furniture. Sales at all branches are
open to the public.
Branches *10 Salem Road, W2 (071 229
9090); Lisson Grove, NW1 (071 723 2647).*

Sotheby's

34-35 New Bond Street, W1 (071 493 8080).
Open 9am-4.30pm Mon-Fri; Viewing only
on Sunday, phone to check first.
Sotheby's is the biggest and the oldest
antique dealer in the world and covers all
aspects of art . Bring your antiques in for a
valuation or for larger pieces call out one of
their experts to your home; either way the
service is free. There are up to three sales a
day with everything from Islamic Art to vintage wine going under the hammer. All sale
goods are put on view three days prior to the
auction and there is an Auction Line (071
409 2686) to find out roughly when each
item will be sold.

BADGE/LABEL MAKER

Gallery

*1 Duke of York Street, SW1 (071 930 5974).
Green Park or Piccadilly Circus under*ground.
Open 9am- 5.30pm Mon-Sat. **Credit** A,
AmEx, DC, £STC, V, most foreign currency.
Gallery provides accessories to complete
the look for well-heeled gentlemen. Cuff-
links, metal buttons, tie-pins and badges
come in standard styles with names like
'Horse Artillery' or even 'Tally Ho'. For
one-off blazer button designs, there is a pattern charge of £20, then £4 per button; oval
and chain cuff-links can be engraved with
initials from £16.
*Catalogues. Postal delivery. Export scheme for
goods over £100.*

BEAUTY SALONS

Steiner

*25a Lowndes Street, SW1 (071 235 3154)
Knightsbridge or Sloane Square underground.*
Open 9.30am-8.30pm Mon-Fri. **Credit**
A,AmEx,DC,V.
Treatments *Bio peel, electrolysis, eye care, facials
make-up, manicure, pedicure and waxing.*
Each of the four rooms are completely private and luxurious, albeit lacking natural
light. The service is impeccable: thera-
pists are both polite and attentive, and top
therapist Arsho Grimwood is completely
dedicated to her art. Records are kept of
your skin type for reference on subsequent visits.

Tao Clinic

*5 Sloane Street, SW1 (071 235 9333).
Knightsbridge underground.* **Open** 9am-
8pm Mon-Thur; 9am-6pm Fri 9am-4pm
Sat. **Credit** A.
Treatments *Body peeling, ear piercing, elec-*

*Here, you'll find imaginative gifts covering the spectrum (from the twee to the
sublime).* **Prezzies** *(listed under* **Luxury Deliveries***) has everything. There
are teddy bears, champagne, gift baskets, flowers and chocolates, all of which
can be delivered by car or post. Delivery charges start at £3 and rise according
to the type of gift to be delivered.*

*trolysis, eye care, facials, make-up, manicure,
massage, pedicure, Slendertone and waxing.*
Original pioneers in the field of electrolysis, TC has expanded to include lots of
other body treatments. A ten minute electrolysis session costs £6.80 and an hour
£21.55. The six tiny cubicles are well-lit,
though a bit untidy. Treat yourself to a leg
wax, costing from £22.50.

MEN'S SALON

Daniel Rouah

*7 Station Approach, Baker Street, NW1 (071
935 4362). Baker Street underground.* **Open**
9am-6pm Mon-Wed, Fri, Sat; 9am-8pm Thur.
No credit cards.
Treatments *Aromatherapy, ear-piercing,
electrolysis, eye care, facials, haircare, laser
treatments, manicure, massage, pedicure,
shaving, waxing,*
Men who sport over-furry backs or cyclists
who need last-minute shearing can come
clean at Daniel Rouah's newly decorated
establishment, one of the few men's salons
in town. Friendly advice on hair care, shaving, acne and skin problems, is dished out as

a matter of course, as are copious quantities
of tea and coffee. Frequent visitors are
placed on the firm's mailing list and receive
lots of special offers.

BOOK SEARCH

Hatchards

*187 Piccadilly, W1 (071 439 99921/071 437
3924). Piccadilly Circus underground.* **Open**
9am-5.30pm Mon-Fri.
Don't despair if the book you've set your
heart on is out of print; Hatchards' book-find-
ing service has an excellent success rate and
isn't expensive (£1 per title). There's also a
book-binding service, the cost of which
depends on the book: a minor repair could
cost £15; major work can run into hundreds
of pounds.

CAMERA AND VIDEO HIRE

Keith Johnson and Pelling

*11 Great Marlborough Street, W1 (071 439
8811). Oxford Circus underground.* **Open**

VERY BRITISH FOREIGN EXCHANGE

When you have arrived in Britain, Thomas Cook can provide you with an excellent Bureau de Change service at all their branches in London and throughout Britain.

✳ All major currencies are accepted and sold.

✳ Travellers cheques and Eurocheques exchanged and sold.

✳ Travel insurance arranged.

✳ Open even when the banks are closed.

✳ Excursions and sight-seeing tours arranged.

✳ Car hire.

We're here to offer advice and to help make your visit more enjoyable.

So call into Thomas Cook – it's the Bureau de Change with the real difference.

9am-5.30pm Mon-Fri. **Credit** A, AmEx, DC, Kodak, Nikon, V.

KJP customers enjoy a choice of stock ranging from the large format 10in x 8in Sinar all the way down in size and price to Tamron zoom lenses. If you decide to buy a new camera within 28 days of having hired a similar model from here, the company's 'try before you buy' policy provides for a 50% refund on the hire charge. Technicians undertake repair jobs on the premises.

Leeds Film and Hire
20-22 Brunswick Centre, WC1 (071 833 1661). Russell Square underground. **Open** 9am-5pm Mon-Fri. **Credit** A, £TC, V.
See **picture and caption.**

CLAMP RESCUE

See chapter **Survival** *for information on parking charges, car recovery procedures and police fines.*

CAR VALETING

Kensington Car Wash
55 Russell Road, W14 (071 603 7191). **Open** 9am-7pm daily. **No credit cards.**
This while-you-wait beauty treatment for cars involves an exterior steam-clean and a good shampoo and leathering for £5; an inside clean up and vacuuming for £4, or a steam cleaned engine for £12. A full valet starts at £65 for an average-sized car.

CHILDMINDING

Childminders
9 Paddington Street, W1 (071 935 2049/9763). Baker Street underground. **Open** 9.15am-1pm, 2-5.15pm, Mon-Fri; 9.30am-1pm, 2-4.30pm, Sat. Membership £28.75 per year or £4 visitors' booking fee. Fees £3.50 per hour day-time; £2.20-£2.90 per hour evenings (minimum 4 hours), plus travel expenses.
A 23-year-old, reputable, licensed agency with hundreds of carefully chosen, experienced baby-sitters for central London and many suburban areas. It finds baby-sitters at short notice, and can provide staff for light domestic work and parties.

CLOTHING CARE/DRY CLEANING

For minor clothing repairs, ask your nearest dry-cleaners if they offer a mending service.

British Invisible Mending Service
32 Thayer Street, W1 (071 935 2487). Bond Street or Baker Street underground. **Open** 8.30am- 5.45pm Mon-Fri; 10am-1pm Sat. **No credit cards.**
Any woven fabric can be carefully repaired with the most minute care, by cunningly removing small pieces of material from unseen hems and weaving them into the required place. This takes about three days, and prices vary according to the delicacy of the work.

General Leather Company
56 Chiltern Street, W1 (071 935 1041). Baker Street underground. **Open** 10am-6pm

Mon-Fri; 10am-5pm Sat. **Credit** A, AmEx, DC, £STC, V.
Staff at this leatherwear shop specialize in bespoke work but can also alter and repair suede, leather and sheepskin. They cannot, however, clean, oil or re-colour garments. Re-lining a jacket costs around £60-£80, while tear repairs start from £10. New panels can be fitted where damage is severe.

Tuxedo Express
40 Drury Lane, WC2 (071 836 7193). Covent Garden underground. **Open** 8.30am-6pm Mon-Fri. 10am-1pm Sat. **No credit cards.**
Although primarily a rapid-return dry-cleaner, Tuxedo Express is extremely good at minor alterations and repairs. We took them an expensive silk jacket with a big ugly tear across the back - the repair was virtually invisible. Cost? £6.50. There is a price list for standard repairs; a new zip in your trousers costs £5.60. Most kinds of alteration can be done. *Wheelchair access.*
Branch 23-25 John Adam Street, WC2 (071 839 1039).

DRESS HIRE

C.W. May
1st Floor, Exchange House, 24 Maiden Lane, WC2 (071 836 5993). Covent Garden or

Leicester Square underground. **Open** 11am-7pm Mon-Fri. **Credit** A, AmEx, DC, £TC, V.
Sprawled over four floors, CW May has been involved in costume making since 1895, and it's the first place to head for good reproductions of period clothing. We saw a wonderful peach taffeta wrap with stiffened panels at the chest and a huge skirt draped over a full petticoat. Expensive.

Moss Bros
88 Regent Street, W1 (071 494 0666). Oxford Circus or Piccadilly Circus underground. **Open** 8.30am-7pm Mon; 9am-7pm Tue, Wed, Fri; 9am-8pm Thur; 9am-6pm Sat. **Credit** A, AmEx, DC, SC, V.
The hire departments here and in Covent Garden hold over 5,000 suits between them. A £50 deposit has been introduced to deter naughty gents from decamping with the suits. Prices are reasonable: most outfits cost between £28 and £38 to hire, although a classic morning suit complete with top hat, wing-collar shirt, cravat, pin and handkerchief is £54.
Branch 27 King Street, WC2 (071 497 9354).

Robe Noire
66-69 Great Queen Street, WC2 (071 831 9839). Holborn underground. **Open** 10am-6pm Mon-Wed, Fri; 10am-7pm Thur. **Credit** A, V.
See **picture and caption.**

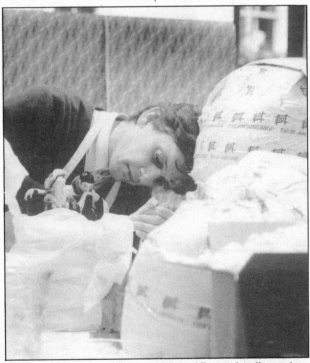

The Packing Shop *(listed under* **Packing and Removals***) offers a unique service. It specializes in the custom-packing and delivery of small and fragile items. However, the shop is more than capable of organizing the delivery of larger objects too. Same-day delivery is guaranteed in Britain. Elsewhere is less fast: there's a guaranteed 48-hour delivery to Europe and America. To send a Royal Doulton tea service to New York costs £95.*

*Basic colour-copying here, costs from £1.80 for an A4 sheet, but there are lots of other services at **Printronics** (listed under **Photocopying**). You can have slide or negative enlargements, up to A4 or A3, for £3.50 and £4.50 respectively, or you can have invitation cards printed at a cost of £48 per 200.*

FLORIST

Joan Palmer
31 Palmer Street, SW1 (071 222 4364). St James's Park underground. **Open** 8.30am-5.30pm Mon-Fri; 9am-12.30pm Sat. **Credit** A,AmEx, DC,£TC, V.
The speedy delivery service at JP ensures that flowers reach their destination as fresh and fragrant as the moment they were picked. Same-day delivery is guaranteed in the London area, if orders are placed in the morning, but loved ones elsewhere in the UK will have to wait 24 hours. The minimum delivery charge in London is £4.50. Bouquets start at £15.

GENERAL AND DOMESTIC

Cinderella Agency
323 Kirkdale, SE26 (081 676 0917/081 659 1689/7175). Sydenham BR. **Open** 9am-5.30pm Mon-Fri. Membership £100 per year plus VAT. **No credit cards.**
Cat-sitters, dog-walkers and plant-waterers cost £4 per visit from Cinderella, who has been providing staff for all occasions for six years. The hourly rate for cleaning staff is £3.50, party staff (waitresses, cooks, people to wash up the dishes) cost £4 and baby-sitters £2 Monday to Thursday, £2.50 weekends, and £2.50 after midnight any day. *Brochure.*

Domesticated
6 Rossiter Road, SW12 (081 673 4773). Balham underground. **Open** 9am-5.30pm Mon-Fri. **No credit cards.**
If you're not domestically-minded, help is at hand. This eight-strong team can do your cleaning, ironing, laundry, shopping, gardening, house sitting and dog walking. Charges are £6 per hour, although a shop at Sainsburys will cost £12 for £50 worth of goods bought.

HAIRDRESSERS

Antenna
27A Kensington Church Street, W8 (071 938 1866). High Street Kensington underground. **Open** 11am-8pm Mon-Fri; 11am-6pm Sat. **Credit** A, V.
Antenna has become synonymous with hair extensions, although the stylists also cut, colour and perm. A quarter head extension at £50 takes about 30 minutes and a whole head can take up to three hours and costs £160. The 'hair' used is actually an acrylic fibre that can look good for months, if taken care of.

Cuts Barbers Shop
23A Frith Street, W1 (071 734 2171) Leicester Square or Tottenham Court Road underground. **Open** 10am-7pm Mon-Sat. **No credit cards.**
See **picture and caption.**

Fish Hairdressing Company
30 D'Arblay Street, W1 (071 494 2398). Tottenham Court Road underground. **Open** 10am-8pm Mon-Fri; 10am-6pm Sat. **Credit** A, V.
Formerly a fishmongers, hence the name, Fish is now one of the trendiest salons in town. Streetwise kids groove to the latest house and hip-hop while their locks are permed, coloured and clipped. A basic cut and blow dry is £12 for men and £17 for women.

Toni & Guy
49 Sloane Street, SW1 (071 730 8113). Sloane Square underground. **Open** 9am-5.30pm Mon-Wed, Fri; 10am-6.30pm Wed; 9am-5pm Sat. **Credit** A, AmEx, DC, V.
A high-fashion profile and frighteningly trendy staff might terrify most of us, but it hasn't deterred clients such as comedienne Pamela Stephenson and singer Dusty Springfield. A cut and blow-dry starts at £24 for women (£18 for men); henna treatments start at £16 and perms begin at £30.

Trevor Sorbie
10 Russell Street, WC2 (071 379 6901/071 240 3816). Covent Garden underground. **Open** 9am-7pm Mon-Wed; 9am-7.30pm Thur, Fri; 9am- 4pm Sat. **Credit** A, AmEx, DC, £TC,V.
Trevor Sorbie is justly renowned for his colouring and perming, which take place on the lower floor of the comfortable, unintimidating salon. Highlights cost from £63.50 for short hair and £77 for long hair. A cut by a top stylist will cost about £27.50 but for a mere £7.50 you can have a refreshing deep-conditioner complete with head massage.

Truefitt & Hill
23 Old Bond Street, W1 (071 493 2961). Bond Street or Green Park underground. **Open** 9am-5pm (last appointment) Mon-Fri; 9am-noon Sat. **Credit** A, AmEx, £TC, V.
The aristocrat among barbers, T&F has been shaving gentlemen since 1805. This relaxing ritual, performed with large quantities of creamy soap and hot towels, costs £8.50 or you can have a beard trim for £7.50. A haircut at £11 and a manicure at £7 completes the look of distinction.

Vidal Sassoon
60 South Molton Street, W1 (071 491 8848). Bond Street underground. **Open** 9am-5pm Mon-Wed; 8.30am-7pm Thur; 8.30am-6.30pm Fri; 8.30am-5.15pm Sat. **Credit** A, AmEx, DC, £TC, V.
Vidal Sassoon has become synonymous with sharp precision cuts and innovation. Free consultations are offered for perms and prices vary considerably. Cuts for women start at £27 and £20 for men.

HATTERS

Kirsten Woodward
26 Portobello Green, W10 (081 960 0090). Ladbroke Grove underground. **Open** 10am-6pm Mon-Sat. **No credit cards.**
Kirsten will design you a fashionable hat, listen to your own design suggestions, and even work with a customer's material if it's possible. She has a small range of mass-produced, ready-made hats (£30) that she will trim to a customer's design; made-to-order hats cost from £60.

Stephen Jones
29 Heddon Street, W1 (071 734 9666). Oxford Circus underground. **Open** by

Possibly the finest shoe-making business in the world. **Lobb's** *(listed under* **Shoe-Makers***) has been making shoes and boots for more than 200 years. The current clientele includes members of the royal family, but records of past customers could provide an intriguing history of foot-wear for the rich and famous. Unfortunately, if you want to join the illustrious list of past purchasers, you may face a long wait for a pair of shoes: up to eight months is the norm, and prices start from £804+VAT.*

appointment. **Credit** AmEx, £TC.
Stephen's silk toppers and more extravagant creations have been seen on the pages of glossy magazines and in House of Fraser stores. Customers can supply their own material if the hat is to match an outfit. Prices begin at around £40, though the most popular are between £100 and £200, and take at least three weeks and two fittings to make. *Postal delivery. Export scheme.*

LUGGAGE REPAIRS

Barnards
10 Old Brompton Road, SW7 (071 584 4084). South Kensington underground. **Open** 9am-6.30pm Mon-Sat. **Credit** A, AmEx, DC, £TC, V.
In the past year, Mr Justin and his staff have improved their luggage-repair service, and will now undertake repairs on backpacks, holdalls, trunks and handbags as well as suitcases.
Delivery.

Leather Guild
111 Kingsway, WC2 (071 831 8718). Holborn underground. **Open** 9am-6pm Mon-Fri. **Credit** A, AmEx, DC, £STC, V.
The staff will replace zips and locks as well as relining or restitching goods in disrepair. There's a minimum fee of £10, and most

repair work costs upwards of £20. Be prepared to wait up to one month for the work to be completed, as this is one of the only firms which specializes in the repair of leather goods.

Mayfair Trunks
3 Shepherd Street, W1 (071 499 2620). Green Park underground. **Open** 9am-5pm Mon-Fri; 9am-1pm Sat. **Credit** A, AmEx, DC, V.
Mayfair Trunks supplies luggage to members of the Royal Family, and will repair damaged bags and cases. It's certainly not the cheapest luggage-repair workshop, but it's worthwhile getting a quote if you want a good quality suitcase or bag mended.

LUXURY DELIVERIES

Basket Express
4 Vale Close, W9 (071 289 2636). **Open** 9am-5pm Mon-Fri. **Credit** A, V.
Lingerie, champagne, picnics, toiletries, chocolates or flowers in a basket. Gift baskets cost from £10 and hampers from £25, excluding delivery charge.

Country Baskets
64 Besley Street, SW16 (081 769 0300). **Open** 9.30am-6pm Mon-Fri. **Credit** A, AmEx, DC, V.
Dried flowers, teddies, champagne and

gourmet food can all be attractively packaged in baskets. You can have a basket made up to a theme, or to celebrate an occasion. Prices range from £15 to £200. Free delivery within Central London.

The Green Delivery Company
34 Dukes Avenue W4 (081 994 0855). **Open** 9.30am-5.30pm, 24-hour answerphone at other times. **Credit** A/c.
The GDC concentrates on sensible, biodegradable Ecover cleaning products, recycled paper goods, organic pesticides and Granose baby foods, all guaranteed to be as environment-friendly as possible.

Prezzies
10 Sicilian Avenue, WC1 (24 hour answer phone 071 831 8098). **Open** 10am-6pm Mon-Sat. Credit A, AmEx, DC, V.
See **picture and caption.**

Telefruit
(071 403 0555). **Open** 24 hour answer phone. **Credit** A, AmEx, DC, V.
Get those enzymes going with the pick of exotic or seasonal fruits packed into a wicker basket and displayed to their best advantage. Prices start at £15 for 22 pieces of fruit. Delivery is free within Central London.

PACKING AND REMOVALS

The Packing Shop
19 George Street, W1 (071 486 0102). Baker Street underground. **Open** 9am-6pm Mon-Fri; 9.30am-3.30pm Sat. **Credit** A, AmEx, DC, V.
See **picture and caption.**
Brochure.

L.J. Roberton
Marlborough House, Cook's Road, E15 (081 519 2020). Stratford underground/BR. **Open** 9am-5pm Mon-Fri. **No credit cards.**
Specialists in overseas removals and the packing and transporting of antiques, Roberton also does removals in this country. Free estimates and storage facilities are available.

SBS Freight Agencies
Unit 2, Staples Corner Business Park, 1000 North Circular Road, NW2 (081 208 1677/081 554 8333). **Open** 8.30am-6pm Mon-Fri; 8.30am-noon Sat; 10am-2pm Sun. **Credit** A, AmEx, V, DC.
The minimum shipment that SBS will pack and ship to anywhere in the world is a suitcase. There's substantial storage facilities in NW2, and effects will be collected from London postal districts (free of charge), and also from anywhere in the UK (on a sliding scale of charges). Cars can be shipped with insurance arranged. Free estimates.
AIR member. Brochures.

PHOTOCOPYING

Printronics
24 Shelton Street, WC2 (071 836 2229/071 240 8301). Leicester Square underground. **Open** 9am-8pm Mon- Sat. **Credit** £TC, V.
See **picture and caption.**

PHOTOGRAPHY

Passport Photo Service
449 Oxford Street W1 (071 629 8540). Bond Street underground. **Open** 9am-6pm Mon

Fri; 9am-2pm Sat. **No credit cards.**
There's a ten minute wait and a £4 charge for three passport-sized photographs at PPS. Old photographs can also be copied or you can have them enlarged to post-card size (two prints for £6). You can get your portrait taken here.

Snappy Snaps
59 Shaftesbury Avenue, W1 (071 439 2092). Piccadilly Circus underground. **Open** 8.30am-6.30pm Mon-Fri; 11am-6pm Sat. **Credit** £TC.
Four passport photos, printed while you wait, cost £3. Copying old photographs is cheaper at £2 plus 30p for each additional copy, but takes 24 hours. Bring in your negatives for enlarging at £1.29 each (8in/20.32cm by 6in/15,24cm).

SHOE-MAKERS

John Lobb
9 St James's Street, SW1 (071 930 3664). Green Park underground. **Open** 9am-5.30pm Mon-Fri; 9am-1pm Sat. **Credit** A, AmEx, £STC, V
See **picture and caption.**
Export scheme. Delivery service.

James Taylor & Son; The Orthopaedic Footwear Co
4 Paddington Street, W1 (071 935 4149). Baker Street underground. **Open** 9am-5.30pm Mon-Fri; 10am- 1pm first Sat in the month. **Credit** A, AmEx, DC, £STC, V.
The speciality here is problem feet, and styles are predominantly traditional English. Leathers used include calf, kid, goat, lizard and sheep, notable for their suppleness and durability. Both men and women are catered for with prices starting at £495+VAT for shoes and £620+VAT for knee-length boots. Expect to wait eight to ten weeks.

Tricker's
67 Jermyn Street, SW1 (071 930 6395). Green Park or Piccadilly Circus underground. **Open** 9am-5pm Mon-Fri; 9am-4.30pm Sat. **Credit** A, AmEx, DC, EC, JCB, £TC, V.
Shoemakers since 1831, Tricker's turn out classic, prestigious shoes for both men and women. The shoes are made from individual casts and take six or seven months to be cobbled together, so you can expect to pay upwards of £585, or from £600 for riding boots.

SHOE REPAIRS

The Crispins Cobbler
5 Chiltern Street, W1 (071 935 7984). Baker Street underground. **Open** 10am-6pm Mon-Wed, Fri; 10am-7pm Thur; 10am- 4.30pm Sat. **Credit** A, AmEx, DC, £TC, V.
Crispins repairs, valets and renovates any kind of leatherwear. We brought in a pair of women's loafers with practically no soles left and asked for an overhaul including leather half soles; they were returned to us in almost mint condition. The bill came to £23. Rubber soles are cheaper at around £20.
Postal service.

SPORTS EQUIPMENT MAKERS

Alf Gover Cricket School Shop
172-174 East Hill, SW18 (081 874 1796). Wandsworth Town BR/44 bus. **Open** 9.30am-1pm, 2-5pm, Mon-Fri; 9am-1pm Sat. **Credit** £TC.
Amongst the cricket bats here you'll find the Graham Gooch Turbo Grand Prix (signed by the England international himself) at £115 and the Duncan Fearnley Extra Cover at £34.65. There's also a selection of youths' and boys' bats that can be modified, bat covers, balls, wickets, clothing and rubber grips. A repair service operates from the shop, so you can have a new handle (£24.50) or your bat re-covered.

Giddens
112-122 Tabernacle Street, EC2 (071 253 2888). Old Street underground. **Open** 9am-5pm Mon-Fri. **Credit** A, AmEx, DC, £TC, V.
See **picture and caption.**
Catalogue. Delivery. Export scheme.

Harry Busson
Walton Heath Golf Club, Tadworth, Surrey (073781 2927). Tadworth BR. **Open** 8am-7pm daily. **Credit** A, AmEx, DC, V.
Telephone for an appointment; Harry is much in demand, as he is one of the few craftsmen around who still carves golf clubs to order. A hand-crafted club will cost about £140, depending on the wood and time involved in making it.

Wigmore Sports
81 Wigmore Street, W1 (071 486 7761). Bond Street underground. **Open** 10am-6pm Mon-Wed, Fri; 10am-6.30pm Thur; 10am-5.30pm Sat. **Credit** A, AmEx, DC, V.
The stringer here offers a 24-hour restringing service for tennis racquets, which costs between £10 and £30, depending on the gut used. An electronic contraption on site sets the string tension. Racquets can also be regripped and adjusted for balance

TRAVELLING COMPANIONS/LIFT SERVICE

Odyssey
21 Cambridge Road, Waterbeach, Cambridge, CB5 (0223 861079). **Open** 9am-5pm Mon-Fri; answering machine all other times. **No credit cards.**
Anne Hemming will endeavour to find you a travelling companion or someone to split petrol bills with. If you're setting off to find work in another country she'll put you in touch with someone who's been there and can give you advice. All this will cost you £15 a year.

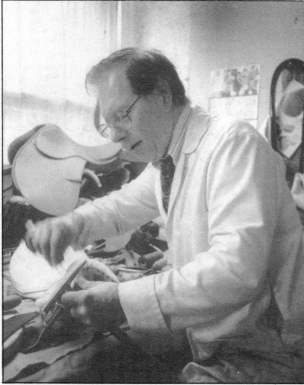

At **Giddens** *(listed under* **Sports Equipment Makers***), craftsmen make tack, driving harnesses and boots from high quality leather. This can all be made to a customer's order. Even the fussiest horse won't balk at the quality of workmanship. Saddle prices start at around £600, but a side saddle will cost up to £2,000. Ready-made tack is on sale at Giddens' shop in Clifford Street, W1.*

Arts and Entertainment

You could happily spend all your time in London sightseeing and watching uniformed men stomp up and down. But London has more to offer than its past. Each day there are hundreds of films and plays showing all over the capital; folk, jazz and rock bands strum their stuff; and alternative comedians insult anyone within shouting distance. As night falls, you can watch an elegant ballet, or stamp your feet to the acid beat; then, when you're back on the streets again, we show you where to recuperate with a black coffee, or where to find a large vodka at 6am. We throw a lifeline to despairing parents and whisk their kids into a fun-filled city. We'll even tell you what newspapers not to read. Mind you, London's rapacious past has been useful for something: it's given us some of the best-stocked museums and art galleries in the world.

CONTENTS:

Art Galleries

Whether you want to gaze at a Matisse or buy a pile of bricks, there's enough art in London to keep avid viewers and collectors happy. *Heather Waddell* **puts you in the picture.**

London has an astonishing 600 art galleries, plus over 150 museums. You shouldn't leave London without having visited either the **Tate Gallery** or the **National Gallery**. But with 4.2 million visitors to these two every year, you might prefer lesser-known gems, such as the **Courtauld Institute**This gallery, newly installed in Somerset House in the Strand, has many important Post-Impressionist paintings. More art collections can be found in *chapter* **Museums**. Some of these now ask for a donation, but most are still free.

You can see temporary exhibitions at three types of gallery . The **public galleries**, funded by both the state and commercial sponsorship, host the major, international exhibitions. The **commercial galleries** range from the expensively-stocked **Marlborough Fine Art** to smaller, more approachable galleries such as those in the Portobello Road area. Alternative, **fringe** spaces such as the **Young Unknowns Gallery** (*listed under* **Commercial Galleries**) are usually run by artists and often show avant garde work and performance art installations. Temporary exhibitions can also be seen in art schools, theatres (**National Theatre**, SE1, and **Royal Festival Hall**, SE1), and libraries such as **Swiss Cottage**, NW3. *Time Out* magazine lists and reviews exhibitions and *20/20* magazine covers the arts in more depth.

The quality of work shown in London galleries is very high, and young and established British artists are well received internationally. For the last ten years New British Sculpture has been in vogue internationally and the **Lisson Gallery** (*listed under* **Commercial Galleries**) is the place to find out more about sculptors such as Richard Deacon (a 1987 Turner prize winner) or Tony Cragg (1988 Turner prize winner). Other galleries that show new sculpture are **Anthony Reynolds** (*listed under* **Commercial Galleries**) now with an East End and central London gallery, and also **Karsten Schubert** (*listed under* **Commercial Galleries**).

For an overview of established British and international artists it's worthwhile visiting **Waddington's** six galleries in Cork Street, **Marlborough Fine Art** in Albermarle Street and **Anthony d'Offay's** three galleries in Dering Street (all *listed under* **Commercial Galleries**).

However, if you want to see what recent graduates of the best British art schools are up to, visit **Berkeley Square Gallery**, where colour is all-important; **Salama-Caro**, where photography in large-scale format and sculpture are experimental; **Edward Totah**, showing both British and international young artists; and **Paton Gallery**, where the gallery owner has a good eye for up-and-coming artists (*all listed under* **Commercial Galleries**).

If you'd like to know more about established British painters and what's currently going on, read *The School of London* by Alistair Hicks (*Phaidon Press*; published July 1989; £30). Those interested in buying contemporary art should get the *Time Out Guide to Shopping & Services in London* (£5.95, available from newsagents).

COLLECTIONS

Last tickets are usually issued 30 minutes before closing time. Most museums and galleries are closed over the Christmas holiday (24-26 Dec), New Year's Day (1 Jan), Easter bank holidays and the May bank holiday, and some during August. Phone if in doubt.

Courtauld Institute Galleries
Somerset House, The Strand, WC2 (081 872 0220). Temple underground. **Open** 10am-5pm Mon-Sat; 2-6pm Sun. **Admission** £1.50 adults; 50p children under 16, OAPs, students. **No credit cards.**
The Courtauld Collection has moved from Woburn Place to Somerset House, reopening in June 1990 with a major exhibition of drawings. The permanent collection was assembled by textile baron Samuel Courtauld. It features some fine baroque furniture, paintings by Cranach and Rubens, and the best collection of French Post-Impressionists in London: Cézanne, Gauguin and Van Gogh.

Dulwich Picture Gallery
College Road, SE21 (081 693 5254). North or West Dulwich BR/P4, 12, 37, 78, 176 bus. **Open** 11am-5pm Tue-Sat; 2-5pm Sun. **Admission** £1.50 adults; free children under 16; 50p OAPs, students. **No credit cards.**
Opened in 1814, the Dulwich is the oldest gallery in the country and one of the most beautiful; it's well worth a visit just to gaze at Sir John Soane's architecture. The Gallery is celebrated for its permanent collection of works by Rubens, Rembrandt, Poussin, Gainsborough and Canaletto. In September 1990 there's an exhibition to commemorate the 300th anniversary of the death of Le Brun (Louis XIV's court painter), called *Courage and Cruelty.*
Guided tours. Lectures. Shop.

Iveagh Bequest, Kenwood
Hampstead Lane, NW3 (081 348 1286). Archway, Golders Green or Hampstead underground/210 bus. **Open** 1 Oct-Maundy Thursday 10am-4pm; Good Friday-1 Oct 10am-6pm. **Admission** free. **Credit** A, DC, V.
This country villa north of Hampstead Heath is an attractive place to visit for the fine collection of paintings. There are paintings by Vermeer, Gainsborough and Reynolds, and a splendid Rembrandt self-portrait. The house is the setting for the Kenwood summer open air concerts. *See chapter* **London by Season**.
Café. Restaurant. Shop. Toilets for the disabled. Wheelchair access.

Leighton House
12 Holland Park Road, W14 (071 602 3316). Kensington High Street underground. **Open** 11am-5pm Mon-Sat. **Admission** free.
This is a fascinating place, both for its architecture and its collection of Pre-Raphaelite and High Victorian paintings. Located in the magnificent house of Lord Leighton, a wealthy and celebrated Victorian artist, there's a permanent collection of works by Leighton, Millais, Burne-Jones, Alma-Tadema and Watts. There are regular monthly exhibitions by young contemporary artists. *See chapter* **Victorian Times**.

National Gallery
Trafalgar Square, WC2 (071 839 3321). Leicester Square or Charing Cross underground/BR. **Open** 10am-6pm Mon-Sat; 2-6pm Sun. **Admission** free. **Credit** A, AmEx, £ETC, V.
The UK's major collection of historical paintings covers all the leading European schools of painting from the thirteenth to the twentieth centuries. A list of the Gallery's 16 most famous paintings is given at the entrance. Otherwise, it's best to choose what you want to see – perhaps Italian Renaissance, the Medieval rooms or the Post-Impressionists – and spend all your available time there. It's busiest weekends and noon-3pm weekdays. Between July and September 1990 there's an exhibition of works selected by artists, *The Artists' Eye*.
Baby-changing facilities. Café. Films. Guided tours. Lectures. Shop. Toilets for the disabled. Wheelchair access.

National Portrait Gallery
St Martin's Place, WC2 (071 930 1552). Leicester Square underground or Charing Cross underground/BR. **Open** 10am-5pm Mon-Fri; 10am-6pm Sat; 2-6pm Sun. **Admission** free; *temporary exhibitions* £1-£3. **Credit** (shop only) A, AmEx, V.
The Gallery's paintings, photographs and

sculptures make up the most comprehensive survey of historical personalities through portraits anywhere in the world. The collection ranges from medieval to contemporary portraits and the modern collection includes portraits of Warhol, Jagger and Geldof, and a painting of the Princess of Wales by Bryan Organ. In addition to the permanent collection there are temporary exhibitions of paintings and photographs. The BP Portrait Awards exhibition from the 8 June to 3 September 1990 displays the work of young professional artists.
Baby changing facilities. Bookshop. Lectures. Toilets for the disabled. Wheelchair access. Workshops.

Queen's Gallery
Buckingham Palace, Buckingham Palace Road, SW1 (071 930 4832). St James's Park underground or Victoria underground/BR. **Open** 10.30am-5pm Tue-Sat; 2-5pm Sun. **Admission** £1.50 adults; 60p under-16s, OAPs, students, UB40s, disabled. **Credit** (shop only) A, AmEx, £TC, V.
Treasures from the Royal Collection at Windsor Castle are on display until late summer 1990, including works by Rembrandt, Vermeer, De Hooch, Rubens, Holbein and Canaletto. The gallery is attached to Buckingham Palace.
Shop. Wheelchair access.

Tate Gallery
Millbank, SW11 (071 821 1313). Pimlico underground. **Open** 10am-5.50pm Mon-Sat; 2-5.50pm Sun. **Admission** free; *temporary*

exhibitions £3 adults; £1.50 under-16s, OAPs, students, UB40s; free under-9s. **Credit** (shop only) A, V.
The Tate has a dual role as the museum of British art and the holder of the national collection of contemporary paintings. Don't miss the post-modern Clore Gallery, designed by James Stirling (famous for his Stuttgart Staatsgallerei) to house the JM Turner collection. The museum has an especially good collection of Cubist work and has a room devoted to recent developments. Artists such as Picasso, Lagen and de Chevico are among those to be featured in the *Classicism 1910-1930* exhibition (6 June-3 September 1990). Weekends are packed, so visit on weekday mornings.
Baby changing facilities. Coffeeshop. Films. Guided tours. Lectures. Restaurant. Shop. Toilets for the disabled. Wheelchair access. Workshops

Wallace Collection
Hertford House, Manchester Square, W1 (071 935 0687). Bond Street underground. **Open** 10am-5pm Mon-Sat; 2-5pm Sun. **Admission** free (donations box in main hallway). **Credit** (shop only) A, £TC, V.
Located in a large house behind Oxford Street, this excellent museum has a superb collection of Canalettos, Joshua Reynolds and Bouchers, as well as antique furniture and an armoury. The grandfather clocks are particularly fascinating.
Lectures. Shop. Tour by prior arrangement. Wheelchair access.

Barbican Art Gallery
Level 8, Barbican Centre, Silk Street, EC2 (071 638 4141 ext 306; recorded information 071 588 9023). Barbican underground or Morrgate underground/BR. **Open** 10am-6.45pm Mon-Sat; noon-5.45pm Sun. **Admission** £3 adults; £1.50 under-16s, OAPs, students, UB40s, disabled; free under-6s. **Credit** (shop only) A, AmEx, DC, £TC, V.
The Gallery at the Barbican is on level 8, takes up two floors and holds a variety of thematic, international, contemporary and historical exhibitions. There are two exhibitions on Japan; one on photography and video (25 Jul-13 Oct 1991); the other on links with Britain 7 Nov 1991-2 Feb 1992). The Gallery is closed in August and September 1990.
Shop. Lectures. Toilets for the disabled. Tour by prior arrangement. Wheelchair access. Workshops.

Hayward Gallery
Belvedere Road, South Bank Centre, SE1 (071 928 3144; recorded information 071 261 0127). Waterloo underground/BR. **Open** Tues, Wed 10pm-8pm; Thur-Mon 10am-6pm. **Admission** £4.50 adults (£2.50 10am-2pm Sun); £2.50 OAPs, students, UB40s. **Credit** A.V.
Part of the South Bank Centre, the Hayward is one of London's main venues for large-scale temporary exhibitions of both historical and contemporary art. It's an uncomfortable exhibition space, particularly on weekends when the crowds make it unbearable. Many of the shows are of major importance and not to be missed.
Bookshop. Café. Guided tour.

ICA Gallery
The Mall, SW1 (071 930 3647; membership enquiries 071 930 0493; recorded information 071 930 6393). Piccadilly Circus underground or Charing Cross underground/BR. **Open** noon-8pm daily. **Admission** £1 adults; free under-15s accompanied by adult. **Membership** £15 per year; £7.50 students. **Credit** A, AmEx, DC, £TC, V.
A variety of dynamic contemporary art exhibitions and major shows are held here. The Institute of Contemporary Arts (ICA) is held to be one of the most innovative venues in town. There are two galleries showing work by the British and foreign avant garde.
Bar. Bookshop. Café.. Group discount. Lectures. Workshops.

Matt's Gallery
10 Martello Street, E8 (071 249 3799). Bethnal Green underground/Hackney Central or London Fields BR/6, 22, 30, 35, 38, 55, 106, 253, 277 bus. **Open** 2-6pm daily. **Admission** free.
There are not always exhibitions here, so check *Time Out* magazine for details of shows. Artists are invited to make work specifically for this fine space in a block of artists' studios.
Educational seminars. Workshops.

Riverside Studios
Crisp Road, W6 (081 741 2251 ext 230). Hammersmith underground. **Open** 1-8pm Tue-Sun. **Admission** free. **Credit** (restaurant only) A, V.

*The cream of British art students study at the **Royal College of Art** (listed under **Public Galleries**) in every branch of art, craft and design. The Henry Moore galleries host a variety of exhibitions, and the annual postgraduate degree shows: painting, printmaking and sculpture are in June and the rest are held in July. Past students have included David Hockney, John Bellany, Francis Bacon, Howard Hodgkin, Frank Auerbach, Kitaj and Paul Nash, so take your chequebook. The Mingei exhibition (Dec 1991 to Jan 1992) celebrates traditional Japanese crafts.*

Some of the best and liveliest new art has been seen here in recent years, including work by Bruce McLean and Kate Whiteford. The spectrum of contemporary art is covered. *See chapter* **Theatre**.
Bar. Bookshop. Café. Restaurant. Wheelchair access.

Royal Academy of Arts

Burlington House, Piccadilly, W1 (071 439 7438). Green Park or Piccadilly Circus underground. **Open** 10am-6pm daily. **Admission** £2.50-£5 adults; £1 under-11s. **Credit** (shop only) A, AmEx, DC, V.
The country's oldest and most venerable artistic institution. Since 1768 many of the great British artists – Gainsborough, Sir Joshua Reynolds, Constable, Turner – have exhibited and studied at the Academy. There have been major public exhibitions here for the last 200 years; the most famous of these is the annual **Summer Exhibition**, when thousands of works are on sale (*see chapter* **London by Season**). In 1990 it's on from 9 June to 19 August; and from 7 September to 9 December there's a major show of Monet in the 1890s. The crowds on weekends are huge and oppresive. *Wheelchair access. Toilets for the disabled. Restaurant. Shop. Export scheme. Lectures.*

Royal College of Art

Kensington Gore, SW7 (071 584 5020). High Street Kensington or South Kensington underground. **Open** 10am-6pm

Mon-Fri (occasional late openings for exhibitions). **Admission** free.
See **picture and caption**.
Shop. Student canteen. Toilets for the disabled. Wheelchair access.

Saatchi Collection

98A Boundary Road, NW8 (071 624 8299). St John's Wood underground/159 bus. **Open** noon-6pm Fri, Sat. **Admission** free.
Charles and Doris Saatchi are the major private art collectors in Britain. Several years ago they financed the building of this important new gallery space. It's well worth making a special visit to see the current exhibition (the display changes once every six months). Work includes sixties Pop Art by Warhol, plus European expressionist painters.
Lectures.

Serpentine Gallery

Kensington Gardens, Hyde Park, W2 (071 402 6075). Lancaster Gate or South Kensington underground. **Open** Apr-Sept 11am-6pm daily; Oct-May 11am-4pm daily (phone to check). **Admission** free. **Credit** (bookshop only) A, £TC, V.
Fine recent shows in the public gallery in Hyde Park have included a variety of British and foreign artists, continuing the high standard of art shown here over the years.
Bookshop. Lectures. Toilet for the disabled. Wheelchair access.

Whitechapel Gallery

Whitechapel High Street, E1 (071 377 0107). Aldgate East underground. **Open** 11am-5pm Tue, Thur-Sun; 11am-8pm Wed. **Admission** free. **Credit** (bookshop only) A, V.
Under the previous director, Nick Serota, the Whitechapel Gallery went from strength to strength, showing the London public a variety of major exhibitions. Catherine Lampert, the current director, is continuing this excellent trend. The *Whitechapel Open* show, in September and October 1990, is an good way to see work by some of our best contemporary artists. Studio visits are organized to coincide with this show .
Bookshop. Licensed café. Lunchtime talks. Toilets for the disabled. Tour by prior arrangement. Wheelchair access.

COMMERCIAL GALLERIES

CENTRAL

Albemarle Gallery

18 Albemarle Street, W1 (071 355 1880). Bond Street or Green Park underground. **Open** 10am-5pm Mon-Fri; 11am-1pm Sat (closed on Sat per month). **Credit**. £STC.
See **picture and caption**.
Wheelchair access to the groundfloor..

Anne Berthoud Gallery

First Floor, 10 Clifford Street, W1 (071 437 1645). Oxford Circus or Green Park underground. **Open** 10am-5.30pm Mon-Fri; 10am-1pm Sat. **Credit** £STC.
Anne Berthoud's small, friendly upstairs gallery has been open for ten years. She's taken on some exciting new works. On sale are colourful Kenyan ceramics by Magdalen Odundo. Peruvian ceramics (from £35) make ideal presents.
Delivery service. Export scheme.

Anthony d'Offay

9, 21 & 23 Dering Street, W1 (071 499 4100). Bond Street underground. **Open** 10am-5.30pm Mon-Fri; 10am-1pm Sat. **Credit** £STC.
Anthony D'Offay opened his third gallery at 21 Dering Street in 1989. No 9 is a small space on two floors where he shows British Post-Impressionists of the Camden Town school and pictures by Duncan Grant and Vanessa Bell. No 23 is a wonderful gallery in which established British artists – including Gilbert and George and Bruce McLean – alternate with foreigners such as Clemente and Anselm Kiefer. This is the place to see work by artists with major international reputations.

Austin/Desmond Fine Art

Pied Bull Yard, 15A Bloomsbury Square, WC1 (071 242 4443). Holborn underground. **Open** 10.30am-6.30pm Mon-Fri; 10.30am-2.30pm Sat. **Credit** £STC.
The ebullient Willie and John Desmond and John Austin specialize in modern British painting and produce excellent catalogues. They stock contemporary prints and also show contemporary paintings, many for under £2,000.
Wheelchair access.

The **Albemarle Gallery** *(listed under* **Commercial Galleries***) is run by the hugely informative Mark Glazebrook, Rodney Capstick-Dale and Celia Lyttleton. They specialize in showing young British and overseas artists, all of whom sell work for well under £2,000. The lesser-known artists are shown at the small back gallery while major artists hold exhibitions in the larger front and upstairs galleries.*

Benjamin Rhodes Gallery
4 New Burlington Place, W1 (071 434 1768). Oxford Circus underground. **Open** 10am-6pm Mon-Fri; 10.30am-1.30pm Sat. **Credit** £STC.
See **picture and caption.**
Export scheme.

Berkeley Square Gallery
23A Bruton Street, W1 (071 493 7939). Green Park or Piccadilly Circus underground. **Open** 10am-6pm Mon-Fri; 10am-2pm Sat. **Credit** A, AmEx, £STC, V.
A lively gallery which concentrates on new painters, some straight from college, others better established.
Export scheme. Wheelchair access.

Bernard Jacobson Gallery
14A Clifford Street, W1 (071 495 8575). Green Park or Piccadilly Circus underground. **Open** 10am-6pm Mon-Fri; 10am-1pm Sat. **Credit** £STC.
This small gallery, now with a new space at 14 Clifford Street, has a good selection of prints by established contemporary British artists such as Leon Kossoff, David Hockney and Bruce McLean. Barry Flanagan's linocuts, strange images by Victor Willing, Richard Smith's abstractions and Frank Auerbach's energetic portrait etchings are also on sale.
Wheelchair access.

Edward Totah
First Floor, 13 Old Burlington Street, W1 (071 734 0343). Green Park or Piccadilly Circus underground. **Open** 2-6pm Mon; 11am-6pm Tue-Fri; 11am-1pm Sat (closed August). **No credit cards.**
On the two floors above a tailor's, this gallery mainly shows figurative artists such as Stephen McKenna, whose work has a neo-classical flavour, and Graham Crowley, who covers wild domestic scenes.

Fabian Carlsson Gallery
160 New Bond Street, W1 (071 409 0619). Bond Street or Green Park underground. **Open** 10am-6pm Mon-Fri; 10am-1pm Sat (closed August). **No credit cards.**
Work by young British painters has supplanted European and American art as the gallery's focus. Andy Goldworthy's unique natural sculptures are shown at the gallery and large, dark drawings of Hughie O'Donoghue are on sale.
Delivery service. Export scheme. Wheelchair access limited.

Gimpel Fils
30 Davies Street, W1 (071 493 2488). Bond Street underground. **Open** 9.30am-5.30pm Mon-Fri; 10am-1pm Sat. **Credit** £STC.
Gimpel Fils displays large, colourful abstracts by Albert Irvin, William Scott and Alan Davie, and works by younger artists. Art in Ruins are a couple of sculptors who make ironic installations, photo-pieces, drawings and witty combines of found objects and painted images.
Delivery service. Export scheme. Wheelchair access to ground floor.

Horizon Gallery
70 Marchmont Street, WC1 (071 837 1431). Russell Square underground. **Open** 11am-6pm Mon-Fri. **Credit** £STC.
Horizon specializes in showing work by Indian artists. There's no permanent stable

The **Benjamin Rhodes Gallery** *(listed under* **Commercial Galleries***) has two large gallery spaces, which are usually filled with colourful and lively abstract and figurative exhibitions. The gallery stocks paintings and watercolours by Tricia Gillman and Sylvia Guirey; narrative landscapes by Christopher Cook; and some starkly-coloured, mother and child images by Eileen Spence. Sculpture fans should take a look at the work by the Israeli, Zadok Ben David. The staff are extremely helpful and informative.*

of artists, but work is always for sale and prices are very reasonable. A recent collection of traditional paintings in rice paint on paper by the Warli tribe cost from £100 each.
Lectures.

Karsten Schubert
85 Charlotte Street, W1 (071 631 0031). Goodge Street underground. **Open** 10am-6pm Tue-Sat. **Credit** £STC.
Mainly contemporary German, American and British art is shown on the two floors of this gallery. A visit is essential if you want to keep up with the latest developments.
Delivery service.

Marlborough
6 Albemarle Street, W1 (071 629 5161). Green Park underground. **Open** 10am-5.30pm Mon-Fri; 10am-12.30pm Sat. **No credit cards.**
The Marlborough shows many of Britain's best-known artists, including Frank Auerbach and Francis Bacon. But recently it has taken on some younger painters such as Thérèse Oulton, Stephan Conroy and Paula Rego. Prices here are high but a visit is recommended to keep abreast of British art.
Delivery service. Wheelchair access.

Nicola Jacobs Gallery
9 Cork Street, W1 (071 437 3868). Green Park or Piccadilly Circus underground. **Open** 10am-5.30pm Mon-Fri; 10am-1pm Sat. **No credit cards.**

The artists shown at this lovely, two-tiered space are becoming established here and abroad, with works on sale below £2,000.
Delivery service.

Paton Gallery
2 Langley Court, WC2 (071 379 7854). Covent Garden underground. **Open** 11am-6pm Tue-Sat. **Credit** £TC.
Covent Garden once had several notable galleries, but now Graham Paton battles on alone, mainly with exhibitions of young British artists, including Sally Heywood, Eithne Jordan and Mary Mabbutt.
Wheelchair access to ground floor.

Raab Gallery
29 Chapel Street, SW1 (071 823 1393). Hyde Park Corner underground. **Open** 10.30am-7pm Mon-Fri; 11am-5pm Sat. **No credit cards.**
See **picture and caption.**
Delivery service. Export scheme.
Branch *6 Vauxhall Bridge Road, SW1 (071 828 2588).*

Salama-Caro Gallery
5-6 Cork Street, W1 (071 734 9179/071 581 1078). Green Park or Piccadilly Circus underground. **Open** 10am-6pm Mon-Fri; 10am-1pm Sat. **Credit** £STC.
This gallery specializes in young British artists, and prices are still reasonable. One of the most interesting is Calum Colvin, who paints images across elaborate sets and then

makes large cibachrome photographs that contrast the real and the imagined.
Delivery service. Export scheme. Wheelchair access.

The Scottish Gallery
28 Cork Street, W1 (071 287 2121). Green Park or Piccadilly underground. **Open** 10am-6pm Mon-Fri; 10am-1pm Sat. **Credit** A, AmEx, DC, £STC, V.
See **picture and caption**.
Branch *94 George Street, Edinburgh, Scotland (031 225 5955).*
Delivery service.

Smith's Galleries
54-56 Earlham Streeet, WC2 (071 836 6252). Covent Garden underground. **Open** 11am-7pm Mon-Sat. **No credit cards.**
The three galleries for hire have high fees and so attract successful artists, who exhibit in various media. The Contemporary Art Society exhibition is held here in November. *Café. Restaurant. Wheelchair access to Gallery 1. Wine bar.*

Waddington's
5, 11, 12 & 34 Cork Street, W1 (071 437 8611). Green Park, Oxford Circus or Piccadilly Circus underground. **Open** 10am-5.30pm Mon-Fri; 10am-1pm Sat. **No credit cards.**
Leslie Waddington now has six spaces in Cork Street. At No 11 he shows a superb collection of modern masters, including Picasso and Miro, juxtaposed with living artists of

international standing, such as Hoyland and Paladino. No 4 is the Print Gallery, where you can see a similar range of graphics from Picasso to Ben Nicholson, pop artists such as Jim Dine, Hockney and Hamilton, and favourites like Elizabeth Frink. Over the road, the corner gallery is where changing exhibitions of international names are staged.
Wheelchair access to ground floor.
Branch *16 Clifford Street, W1 (071 439 1866).*

EAST END

Anthony Reynolds Gallery
37 Cowper Street, EC2 (071 608 1516). Old Street underground/BR. **Open** 11am-6pm Wed-Sun. **Credit** £STC.
A five-year-old gallery in a marvellous warehouse space, showing the likes of Tim Heald and Andrew Maresfield. Work sells from £250 to £7,000.
Delivery service.
Branch *5 Dering Street, W1 (071 253 5575).*

Flowers East
199-205 Richmond Road, E8 (081 985 3333). Bethnal Green underground/6, 35, 55, 106, 253 bus. **Open** 10am-6pm Tue-Sun. **Credit** A, £STC, V.
This magnificent space has three gallery spaces, including a graphics gallery. The Flowers stable includes Jonathan Waller, Amanda Faulkner and Nicola Hicks.
Bookshop. Export scheme. Postal delivery.

Interim Art
21 Beck Road, E8 (071 254 9607). Bethnal Green underground/6, 35, 55, 253 bus. **Open** *by prior arrangement* noon-6pm Wed-Sun (closed August). **Credit** £STC.
Run by the indomitable Maureen O' Paley from her tiny East End house, this gallery has a reputation for fascinating shows. The policy is to concentrate on changing exhibitions (mainly by young artists) and on theme shows rather than on building up a stable.
Export scheme. Wheelchair access to ground floor.

Lamont Gallery
65 Roman Road, E2 (081 981 6332). Bethnal Green underground. **Open** 11am-6pm Tue-Sat. **Credit** A, AmEx, £TC, V.
A small, two-tiered space, with no stable of artists, Lamont has changing exhibitions of smaller works by young artists. There's a good stock of prints at various prices plus hand-blown glass, ceramics, and graphics.
Delivery service. Export scheme. Framing service. Wheelchair access to ground floor

PORTOBELLO

The *Portobello Contemporary Art Festival* (mid-April) is the worst time to see the art at the area's 16 galleries. Crowds of artists, collectors, dealers and 'media types' create a festive mood, but block your view.

Anderson O'Day
255 Portobello Road, W11 (071 221 7592). Ladbroke Grove underground/7, 15, 52, 52A bus. **Open** 10am-5.30pm Tue-Sat (closed August). **Credit** A, £STC, V.
Anderson O'Day has quickly established a reputation for showing a stimulating and diverse range of contemporary painting and sculpture. Prices range from £300 to £8,000. Anderson O'Day also stocks a range of contemporary prints and incorporates an Art Consultancy based at Quintin Avenue.
Delivery service. Export scheme. Framing service. Wheelchair access.
Branch *5 St Quintin Avenue, London W10 (081 969 8085).*

Creaser Gallery
316 Portobello Road, W10 (081 960 4928/081 960 3415). Ladbroke Grove underground/7, 15, 52, 52A bus. **Open** 10.30am-5.30pm Tue-Sat. **Credit** A, AmEx, DC, V.
Creaser has a good selection of prints and paintings by young artists, whose images are strong, witty and colourful.
Export scheme. Delivery service. Framing service. Wheelchair access to ground floor.

Todd Gallery
326 Portobello Road, W10 (081 960 6209). Ladbroke Grove underground/7, 15, 52, 52A bus. **Open** 11am-5pm Tue-Fri; 10.30am-5.30pm Sat. **Credit** A, V.
This interesting space shows Alexis Hunter's images of women and demonic creatures, and Paul Furreaux's Jungian-influenced images.
Delivery service. Framing service.
Branch *Downstairs, 6 Meard Street, W1 (071 287 8195).*

Vanessa Devereux
11 Blenheim Crescent, W11 (071 221 6836). Ladbroke Grove or Notting Hill Gate underground/7, 15, 52, 52A bus. **Open** 10am-6pm

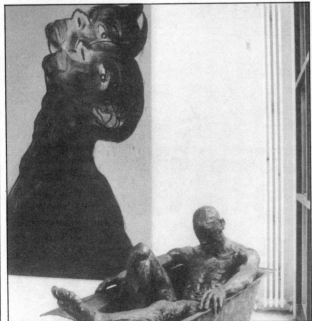

The dynamic Ingrid Raab of the **Raab Gallery** *(listed under* **Commercial Galleries***) also runs a successful gallery in Berlin, showing the best of Berlin's neue wilde artists, and a new space near the Tate Gallery. Raab stocks work by some extremely colourful artists, such as the Germans Rainer Fetting, Hermann Albert, Stephen Heidecker and Thomas Schindler. Some fine Scottish artists can also be seen here, including Ken Currie, famous for his Glasgow murals of working class life. There's plenty of work on sale for under £2,000.*

Tue-Fri; 11am-5pm Sat. **Credit** £STC.
A staunch supporter of young, individualists, such as the colourful painters Pete Nevin, Fred Pollock, Emma McClure.
Export scheme. Delivery service. Wheelchair access.
Branch: C20 Fine Art, 38 Powis Square, W11 (071 229 6063).

SOUTH WEST

Merz Contemporary Art
62 Kenway Road, SW5 (071 244 6008). Earl's Court underground. **Open** 10am-7pm Mon-Sat. **Credit** A, AmEx, £STC, V.
A new gallery showing figurative work over a broad spectrum of styles. Shows change every six weeks and feature established artists as well as newer names.
Wheelchair access to ground floor gallery.

SOUTH EAST

Pomeroy Purdy
At Jacob Street Film Studios, Mill Street, SE1 (071 237 6062). London Bridge or Tower Hill underground/BR/DLR. **Open** 11am-6.30pm Tue-Fri; 11am-4pm Sat. **No credit cards.**
A specialist in young artists, including Estelle Thompson and Rachel Budd. Work can be bought for under £200.
Catalogue. Mailing list.

NORTH

Boundary Gallery
98 Boundary Road, NW8 (071 624 1126). Swiss Cottage underground/159 bus. **Open** 11am-6pm Tue-Sat. **Credit** A, £STC, V.
A gallery near the Saatchi Collection that constantly surprises with fascinating, mainly figurative works by young Australian and British painters. Twice-yearly retrospectives.
Brochure. Export Scheme. Wheelchair access to ground floor gallery.

Lisson
67 Lisson Street, NW1 (071 724 2739). Edgware Road underground. **Open** 10am-6pm Mon-Fri; 10am-1pm Sat. **No credit cards.**
A very important promoter of new British sculptors, such as Anish Kapoor (representing Britain at 1990's Venice Biennale), Richard Deacon and Tony Cragg.
Delivery service. Wheelchair access.

FRINGE

Chisenhale Gallery
64-84 Chisenhale Road, E3 (081 981 4518). Bethnal Green or Mile End underground/D6, 8, 8A, 277 bus. **Open** 1-6pm Wed-Sun. **Credit** £STC.
This large, magnificent gallery space in a block of artists' studios is newly refurbished. Its brief is to show politically-oriented work by young artists rarely shown elsewhere.
Lectures. Guided tours. Wheelchair access. Workshops.

The Showroom
44 Bonner Road, E2 (081 980 6636). Bethnal Green underground. **Open** 11am-6pm Tue-Fri; 2-6pm Sat, Sun. **Closed** *1990* 19 Dec-8 Jan. *1991* phone for details. **No credit cards.**
An interesting non-commericial gallery showing installations, painting and sculpture. Stuart Brisley, Sharon Kivland and

Stelagh Wakeley have displayed here.
Lectures. Performance art. Wheelchair access. Workshops.

Young Unknowns Gallery
82 The Cut, SE1 (071 928 3415). Waterloo underground/BR. **Open** noon-6pm Mon-Sat. **No credit cards.**
Started by Peter Sylveire, who believes in de-mystifying art and selling it as cheaply as possible, the gallery is now run by a committee of artists who try to keep everything under £100 and concentrate on mixed and theme shows. Quality is varied.
Life class. Wheelchair access to ground floor.

PHOTOGRAPHY

Photographer's Gallery
5-8 Great Newport Street, WC2 (071 831 1772). Leicester Square underground. **Open** 11am-7pm Tue-Sat. **Credit** A, AmEx, DC, £STC, V.
As well as frequent exhibitions, often in new British colour works, the gallery has a good shop and a print room, where you can pick up a Victorian photograph from £10.
Bookshop. Café. Export scheme. Framing service. Mail order. Wheelchair access.

Portfolio
345 Portobello Road, W10 (081 969 0453). Ladbroke Grove underground/7, 15, 52, 52A

bus. **Open** 11am-6pm Tue-Thur; 9.30am-5.30pm Fri, Sat. **Credit** A, AmEx, DC, £TC, V.
An excellent place for exhibitions of work by young photographers. The old site at 105 Golborne Road, W10, is now a shop selling posters, postcards and framed photographs.
Export scheme. Framing service. Mail order. Wheelchair access.

Special Photographers Company
21 Kensington Park Road, W11 (071 221 3489). Ladbroke Grove or Notting Hill Gate underground/7, 15, 52, 52A bus. **Open** 10am-6.30pm Mon-Fri; 11am-5pm Sat. **Credit** A, £TC, V.
This fine gallery has about ten shows a year, from classical black-and-whites to fashionable art-manipulated prints. It holds work in stock and has lots of books on sale.
Delivery service. Export scheme. Wheelchair access to ground floor gallery.

Zelda Cheatle Gallery
8 Cecil Court, WC2 (071 836 0506). Leicester Square underground. **Open** 10am-6pm Mon-Sat. **Credit** A, AmEx, DC, £STC, V.
A well stocked, unintimidating place where you can buy works by Fay Godwin, Bill Brandt, Robert Doisneau, Helen Chadwick and young contemporary photographers.
Delivery service. Export scheme. Wheelchair access to ground floor gallery.

A branch of the renowned Edinburgh-based **Scottish Gallery** *(listed under* **Commercial Galleries***) was opened in Cork Street in 1988. It shows the wonderful variety of modern Scottish painters, such as William Gear, Alberto Morocco, Elizabeth Blackadder, William Crozier, Alan Davie and John Houston and also the best of work by younger Scottish painters such as National Portrait Gallery Award-winner Alison Watt. Look out for some vigorous work by Jock McFadyen representing life in the East End of London.*

Museums

London's museums are stuffed with the spoils of empire and collections by British eccentrics. We measure the pulse of old institutions and assess the new arrivals.

The British Empire lives on in London's museums. The great collections are veritable warehouses of imperial booty. Fanatical collectors of anything from stamps to entire temples, Britons have shown taste when raiding Greece, Egypt, India and the ex-colonies. Back home they stocked up the **British Museum** and the institutions down Exhibition Road – the **Natural History**, **Science** and **Victoria & Albert** Museums. (*see* **The Big Nine**; *see also chapter* **Victorian Times**.) Eccentrics and enthusiasts have added colour to the diversity with quirky exhibitions such as the **Vintage Wireless Museum** (*see* **Science**) and the brand new **Fan Museum** (*see* **Art & Design**).

At one time London's museums were famous for having no admission charges. But in recent years many have resorted to entrance fees. The current revolution in museum design is partly responsible. Flash, independent specialists – the **Design Museum** (*see* **Art & Design**), **MOMI** (*see* **The Big Nine**) – are thriving financially. Their state-of-the-art displays attract queues of visitors. Faced with an insatiable public demand for education to be entertaining, the venerable, more established institutions have collected what funds they could and set their designers to work.

EVOLUTION OF A GALLERY

Spiders, crabs and lice rarely excite public passions. This was what the **Natural History Museum** (*see* **The Big Nine**) discovered from the poor attendance at their old arthropod gallery. Rows of tiny dead insects, pinned to essay-like labels in a glass cabinet were dull. The designers were brought in and arthropods became creepy-crawlies. The new **Creepy-crawlies Gallery** is great fun. A cafeteria carousel shows you which insects eat what food and

interactive displays explain how a spider's eyesight works, even giving examples of human parasites. The exhibits are as much toys as they are museum displays and are presented with intelligence and wit. The **Imperial War Museum** (*see* **The Big Nine**) spent £17 on transforming itself into the best-looking museum in town. The multi-sensory Blitz Experience took four years to design and hit the news headlines when it opened. Ironically, the traditional show cabinets are the museum's greatest achievement. Everything is so well lit, mounted, labelled and arranged, that you hardly notice the design.

CASH CRISIS

The Imperial War Museum used to have a free admissions policy. But when it reopened in 1989 it introduced entry charges, although on Fridays it remains free. They are the latest museum in an ever-longer line to abolish the idea of wide and free public access to museums. When the Science Museum, V&A and Natural History Museum started charging for admission they lost nearly half of their visitors. Gradual improvement has followed and after five years of charges, the National Maritime Museum has made up much of its losses. Some museums suffer from leaky roofs, hazardous wiring, and insufficient insurance cover. It would need £50 million just to put that right.

The Government has shown little concern about the state of the museums and repeatedly cut state funding. Government policy appears to be that museums are leisure complexes rather than places of education. This hasn't been popular. There was international uproar in 1989 when the V&A sacked several of its world-class experts and brought in managers. Even government appointees to the boards of museums issued a public plea for more support.

GOING SHOPPING

If you're someone prepared to pay admission, the Science Museum and the V&A have discovered that you empty your wallet even more when tempted into their enormous shops. But new galleries can't be funded on sales of postcards. Sponsorship is the way round this. Companies have been supporting museums for years, but sponsorship opens up a whole can of dinosaurs. No matter what people claim, the commercial partner does influence what goes on show, particularly when the museum has no alternative. The new Sainsbury-sponsored nutrition gallery at the Science Museum, although needed, actually replaces the display on astronomy. During a relative boom-period, this trend may not be disastrous, but what happens when sponsors and the public are more hard-up? The museums we've taken for granted will be exposed to market forces and could be at mortal risk. So now you know; London's museums need you.

Bear in mind that although a museum might be open until 6pm, last tickets are usually issued half an hour before that. Most museums are closed on Christmas Eve, Christmas Day and Boxing Day (24-26 Dec); New Year's Day (1 Jan); the Easter Bank Holidays; and the May Day Bank Holiday. It's wise to phone before setting out. Unless otherwise stated, family tickets allow admission for two adults and up to four children.

THE BIG NINE

British Museum
Great Russell Street, WC1 (071 636 1555/recorded information 071 580 1788). Holborn, Russell Square or Tottenham Court Road underground/ 7, 8, 14, 19, 22, 24, 25, 29, 38, 55, 68, 73, 77, 77A, 134, 188.bus **Open** *10am-5pm Mon-Sat; 2.30-6pm Sun; 6-9pm first Tue every month.* **Admission** *free daily; £5 6-9pm first Tue every month; exhibitions: £2 adults; £1 children, OAPs, students, UB40s.* **Credit** *(shop only) A, AmEx, DC, £STC, USA currency, V.*
The world's greatest collection of antiquities – mostly spoils of Empire – is held in this handsome neo-classical building by Smirke. Behind a portico depicting the progress of civilization is a building so vast that weeks would be required to see everything. Highlights, among an embarrassment of riches, include the Rosetta Stone, Roman pavements, the Iron Age Battersea Shield, and Pete Marsh, the Lindow man found preserved in a Cheshire bog 2,000 years after being murdered. Rarely busy are the oriental galleries – with a new Isamic display – at the north end. The guided tours are not by

experts, but informatively delivered by entertaining actors; one woman gets applause after explaining the Sutton Hoo ship burial. The British Library, to the right of the main hall, is equally well endowed. Two of the four Magna Cartas (AD 1215) are here, along with the Lindisfarne Gospels and Shakespeare's first folio. The Reading Room, where Marx studied, is accessible by pass and tour only. Until December 1990 the Library will ask 'What Use is a Map?' in an exhibition exploring the weather, demography and orienteering varieties among others. If you are only going to see the mummies, use the north entrance of the museum, it's a short cut to the Egyptian Gallery. Although we recommend that you visit the museum, there are times to avoid it. At weekends it's not worthwhile struggling round, particularly in college vacations, when students are everywhere. Saturdays it's hogged by astonishing numbers of Jehovah's Witnesses here to see all the relics mentioned in the Bible. Go on Mondays and weekday mornings or get it all to yourself by paying £5 for the monthly late opening, when the Egyptian Gallery 25 is romantically lit up.

Café & licenced restaurant (10.30am-4.15pm Mon-Sat; 3-5.15pm Sun). Cassette tours of Library, Elgin marbles 60p. Lectures. Shop. Tour (105 mins; £5 inclusive). Toilets for the disabled. Wheelchair access by prior arrangement.

Geological Museum

Listed under Natural History Museum

Imperial War Museum

Lambeth Road, SE1 (071 735 8922). Elephant & Castle, Lambeth North underground or Waterloo underground/BR. **Open** 10am-6pm daily. **Admission** £2.50 adult; £1.25 children age 5-16, OAPs, students, UB40s; free under-fives Sat-Thur; free Fri. **Credit** (shop only) A, V.

Saddled with a name to ignite pacifist passion, this museum, completely redesigned at a cost of £17 million, is as much about the human side of war as it is about the mechanical and tactical paraphernalia. Illuminated by daylight, through the hi-tech atrium roof, large exhibits like tanks, submarines and dramatically suspended aircraft can be viewed from above and below. There are four spacious art galleries on the balconies of the museum, displaying adventurous, modern pieces along with classic works from the world war artists. Sound and film are used to show what an exhibit looked like and sounded like when it was in active service. The Home Front and the Far East displays are especially good. Information doesn't come from the clear labels only – you see the exhibits in action or hear them over the telephone: witnesses describe entering Auschwitz and the ruins of Hiroshima. The must-see exhibit is the Blitz Experience (£1 adults; 50p age 5-16s, OAPs, students, UB40s), the best multi-sensory display we've encountered. It's massively popular, so to avoid a 2-3-hour wait, go on Mondays or on afternoons in school term-time, not at weekends. A Trench Experience will open with the Great War

gallery in Spring 1990. The superb education and research programmes have improved facilites and the shop's stocked with imaginative souvenirs. Justin de Blanc has created yet another tasteful museum café with quality fare. For our money – and they now charge admission – this is the best specialist museum in London. *See chapter* **The World Wars.**

Films. Group discounts. Lectures. Library. Nursing mother facilities. Research facilities. Restaurant. Shop. Toilets for the disabled. Wheelchair access.

Museum of London

150 London Wall, EC2 (071 600 3699). Barbican, St Paul's underground or Moorgate underground/BR/4, 141, 279A, 502 bus. **Open** 10am-6pm Tue-Sat; 2-6pm Sun. **Admission** free. **Credit** (shop only) A, V.

The Museum of London's collection constitutes the city's biography from pre-history to the present. Established in 1976 and disguised as an office block, the museum has enviable facilites. The different ways things are displayed win prizes for being so imaginative, putting what you've seen outside in the city into historical perspective. Reconstructions include a Roman room, a seventeenth-century merchant's house, a Victorian grocer's shop and – in the refurbished Georgian Gallery – a pawn-broker's shop and gruesome Newgate Prison cell. A filmshow simulates the impact of the Great Fire that devastated the City in 1666. Some of the individual exhibits are remarkable, including the Lord Mayor's Coach of 1756. The Roman marble bust of Mithras is one of the treasures to come from archælogical digs overseen by the museum, which itself stands by excavations of the old City wall (*see chapter* **Roman & Saxon London**). The museum is busier in the summer and can get overrun with schoolchildren. However, there are plenty of well-placed seats for wilters. Exhibitions on less prominent subjects – such as contemporary illustrations of Brixton market and the docks – give the museum great credit.

Braille guide and taped commentary for the visually impaired. Lectures and films with induction loop for the hard of hearing in the-atre. Restaurant (10am-5pm Tue-Sat; noon-5pm Sun). Shop. Toilets for the disabled. Wheelchair access. Workshops.

Museum of Mankind

6 Burlington Gardens, W1 (071 437 2224/recorded information 071 580 1788). Green Park, Oxford Circus or Piccadilly underground/3, 6, 9, 12, 13, 14, 19, 22, 38, 53, 88, 159 bus. **Open** 10am-5pm Mon-Sat; 2.30-6pm Sun. **Admission** free. **Credit** (shop only) A, AmEx, DC, £STC, V, USA currency.

This is the Ethnographic Department of the British Museum and doesn't have a massive promotion budget, so it's blissfully quiet for visitors. Ethnography is the study of civilizations and the way in which people live their lives. The Museum of Mankind exhibits artefacts, clothing, even housing from areas in the Americas, Oceania and Africa. On show are Aztec turquoise mosaics, wonderfully gaudy rickshaw paintings from Bangladesh (until May 1991) and a Toraja Ricebarn Carving. Sulawesi craftsmen from Indonesia built the huge edifice in the museum, so you

The **Museum of the Moving Image** *(listed under* **The Big Nine***) has a fun way of explaining film and television. It's won awards for the way you can activate or play with the exhibits, but their big innovation is the use of actors as guides for a Victorian magic lantern show or a film set. Others help you to animate a cartoon or to read the uncrowded television news. It's less tiring in the uncrowded evenings. MOMI has balanced humour, activity and nostalgia trips with good technical information about the moving image's history from Chinese shadow theatre to satellites.*

can be sure it's the genuine article. A new display of Palestinian Costume will run beyond 1991. Over the years people have sent a Japanese execution sword and other cursed items to the museum in the belief that the good spirits here will counteract the evil. Also Californians have been spotted clutching crystals near the Mexican crystal skull in attempts to extract forces from it. The most enigmatic – and best loved – resident is the Easter Island statue in the foyer.

Education department. Films. Lectures. Library. Shop. Sketching boards and stools available from cloakroom. Wheelchair access by prior arrangement.

Museum of the Moving Image (MOMI)

South Bank, SE1 (081 928 3535/box office 081 928 3232/recorded information 081 401 2636). Embankment underground or Waterloo underground/BR/1, 5, 68, 70, 149, 171, 171A, 177, 188, 501, 502,, 507 bus. **Open** Jun-Sept: 10am-8pm Mon-Sat, 10am-8pm Sun; Oct-May: 10am-8pm Mon-Sat; 10am-6pm Sun. **Admission** £3.50 adult; £2.50 children age 5-16, disabled, OAPs, students, UB40s, ; free under-5s; £10 family (2 adults, 4 children). **Credit** A, V.
See picture and caption.
Cinema (integrated with National Film Theatre). Education department. Group discount. Restaurant and bar in NFT. Shop (noon-7pm Mon; 10.30am-8.45pm Tue-Sat; 10.30am-7pm Sun). Study rooms and workshops. Wheelchair access by prior arrangement.

National Maritime Museum

Romney Road, SE10 (071 858 4422). Greenwich or Maze Hill BR/1, 177, 188 bus/boat to Greenwich Pier Open Mar-Oct: 10am-6pm Mon-Sat, 2-6pm Sun; Nov-Feb: 10am-5pm Mon-Sat, 2-5pm Sun. **Admission** (includes entry to Old Royal Observatory) £3 adults; £1.50 children age 7-16, OAPs, UB40s, disabled, students; free under-7s. **Credit** A, AmEx, £TC, V.
Attracted by its glorious setting in Greenwich riverside buildings (designed by Wren and Inigo Jones), half a million people visit this museum every year. But we feel that to really love it you need to be obsessed with all things nautical. It can be boring if you're not that interested in boats. It's the world's most exhaustive collection of marine artefacts: paintings, barges, weapons and carved figureheads. In 1990 the Queen's House reopens and the navigator Captain Cook gets a special exhibition (30 Mar-30 Sept); a new gallery of model warships (1650-1810) testifies to their makers' skill and the beauty of the full-sized vessels. The Battle of Trafalgar display – including Admiral Nelson's bloodstained uniform – is popular, but the rows of cabinets become a blur after a while. A welcome break is Wren's quirky Old Royal Observatory up the hill, with its telescope dome and mark of the prime meridian. The information, with an exhibition on British astronomy, is more digestible and the walk in Greenwich Park is rejuvenating. *See chapter* **The River & Docklands.**
Educational department. Group discount. Library. Restaurant. Shop. Wheelchair access to ground floor only.

The **Natural History Museum** *(listed under* The Big Nine*) is being transformed with interactive displays. Typical of the trend are the Creepy-crawlies Gallery (above) and, opening in 1991, a huge multi-level gallery describing the environment. Inside Waterhouse's neo-Gothic building are 50 million exhibits on evolution, from the dinosaurs to human biology. Sadly, the former Geological Museum is now a mere department of this one. In it you can follow the story of the earth with superb models, mineral displays and special effects including an earthquake simulator.*

Natural History Museum (incorporating the Geological Museum)

Cromwell Road, SW7 (071 938 9123/recorded information 071 725 7866). South Kensington underground/4, 9, 30, 45, 74, 264 bus. **Open** 10am-6pm Mon-Sat; 1-6pm Sun. **Admission** £2.50 adults; £1.25 under-15s, OAPs, students, UB40s; £5 family (2 adults, 4 children); 4.30-6pm Mon-Fri; 5-6pm Sat, Sun, Bank Holidays. **Credit** (shop only) A, AmEx, £TC, V.
See picture and caption.
Café and restaurant. Discovery Room for children (Easter and summer holidays). Field excursions. Films. Lectures. Shop. Wheelchair access.

Science Museum

Exhibition Road, SW7 (071 938 8111/recorded information 071 938 8123). South Kensington underground/4, 9, 30, 45, 74, 264 bus. **Open** 10am-6pm Mon-Sat; 11am-6pm Sun. **Admission** £2 adult; £1 children, OAPs, students, UB40s; £12 family. **Credit** (shop only) A, £TC, V.
Renowned for the buttons and levers that work its exhibits, the Science Museum is having to work on its image; many of its rivals are installing similar interactive displays. There's a flash new look to some galleries and the museum remains an exciting place, especially for kids. The space gallery, Launch Pad, is a favourite. Take time out to measure your heartbeat, shake hands with yourself and star in your own special effects video. The holograms are popular but get a bit samey and are not explained very clearly. The permanent galleries cover every science and technology known, but in some the exhibits are a bit sparse: the textile, handmade tool and astronomy collections are now mostly in store. Replacing the stars is a major gallery on nutrition, Food For Thought. To avoid the school party hordes, go late afternoon on weekdays; avoid weekends.
Café (10.30am-5pm Mon-Sat). Dramatized gallery. Films by prior arrangement. Group discounts. Lectures by prior arrangement. Library. Dillons bookstore. Wheelchair access.

Victoria & Albert Museum

Cromwell Road, SW7. (071 938 8500/recorded information 071 938 8441/exhibitions 071 938 8349). South Kensington underground/4, 9, 30, 45, 74, 264 bus. **Open** 10am-5.50pm Mon-Sat; 2.30-5.50pm Sun. **Admission** free donation requested: £2 adult, £1 under-16s, OAPs, students, UB40s. **Credit** (shop only) A, AmEx, £TC, V.
The V&A, the world's greatest decorative arts museum, is relaxed and peaceful. Despite the gentle ambience, a million people visit the museum every year. Even at the busiest times (weekends and mid-day midweek) you're likely to find only the odd person sketching or gazing in the romantic galleries of Italian statuary that include full-sized plaster reproductions of Trajan's Column and Michelangelo's *David*. There are 7 miles/11 kilometres of galleries, full of designer-collectables for the rich and mighty, from ancient India to the matt

black eighties. Treasures include Rodin bronzes, Medieval and Byzantine art, an extraordinary hoard of decorative ironwork, a room of Raphaels, Gothic of every description (Italian, Northern, Spanish and neo- for starters), a glittering array of oriental carpets, Chinese thrones and samurai swords. The Dress Collection is a popular exhibit, recording the fickleness of fashion, as the recent show of Elton John memorabilia demonstrated. Fewer than half of the visitors pay the controversial 'voluntary' admission fee – and there are other – not all sad – signs of commericalism. 'An ace caff, with quite a nice museum attached,' runs a V&A advertising slogan, and the café is good, if over-priced. The shop is more like a branch of Liberty than a postcard stall. In a shedding of academic priorities, the evening lectures are becoming like college cheese and wine parties. Nice location, though.
Gallery talks (2.30pm daily). Lectures. Restaurant (10am-5pm Mon-Sat; 2.30-5.30pm Sun). Shop. Tour. Touch sessions for the visually impaired. Wheelchair access.

Guards Museum
Wellington Barracks, Birdcage Walk, SW1 (071 930 4466, ext 3271). St James's Park underground/10, 44, 76 bus. **Open** 10am-4pm Sat-Thur. **Admission** £2 adults; £1 under-16s, ex-guardsmen, OAPs, students; £4 family (2 adults, 3 children). **Credit** (shop only) A, V.
A military buff could while away ecstatic hours in this newish and impressively housed museum. Others might find it a touch boring. The exhibits trace the history of various Guards regiments (Grenadier, Coldstream, Scots, Irish and Welsh), from the English Civil War (1642-1648) to the recent Falklands debacle. Although the uniforms, weapons and documents have had a colourful existence, earnestly displayed behind glass they look static and dull.
Group discount. Shop. Tour by prior arrangement. Wheelchair access.

Museum of Artillery
The Rotunda, Repository Road, SE18 (081 316 5402). Woolwich Dockyard BR. **Open** Nov-Mar: noon-4pm Mon-Fri; 1-4pm Sat, Sun. Apr-Oct: noon-5pm Mon-Fri; 1-5pm Sat, Sun. **Admission** free. **No credit cards.**
The Rotunda is one of London's earliest purpose-built museums. The building is an architectural novelty; it was customized in 1822 by architect John Nash around an enormous tent. Encircled by large field-guns and armoured vehicles, the round building contains everything you need to know about the development of cannons and ammunition. A short film even shows you how a cannon is made. Fans of militaria will appreciate the detail, but some find more entertainment jumping over the cannonballs scattered about the floor. The often delicate craft involved in the weapons' manufacture – look out for the bronze Burmese cannon – contrasts with their brutal use in battle.
Shop. Wheelchair access.

National Army Museum
Royal Hospital Road, SW3 (071 730 0717). Sloane Square underground/39 ,11 bus. **Open** 10am-5.30pm Mon-Sat; 2-5.30pm Sun. **Admission** free. **No credit cards.**
No bombastic imperial house for this military museum: the building's as functional as a welfare office. This is wholly appropriate for the laudibly matter-of-fact way with which the history of the British Army is treated. There's no inappropriate patriotism here. Since Henry VIII formed the Yeomanry, and until the Falklands dust-up, the British land forces have notched-up plenty of victories and disasters. Relics include Marlborough's gold-embroidered saddle-cloth, a French standard captured at Waterloo in 1815 and the order responsible for the 1854 Charge of the Light Brigade. But you'll also learn that life for a seventeenth-century soldier and his family was nasty, brutish and short. A refreshing change from their stereotypical representation, soldiers are depicted as people with a natural curiosity and wide interests. But more on the contemporary social problems of army life would be welcome. There are staggering arrays of arms displayed here, from long-bow to Gatling gun to heat-seeking missile.
Café (10.30am-4.15pm Mon-Sat). Reading room. Shop. Tour by prior arrangement. Wheelchair access. Worksheets.

Royal Air Force Museum
Grahame Park Way, NW9 (081 205 2266/recorded information 081 205 9191). Colindale underground/Mill Hill Broadway

BR (Thamesline)/32, 226, 292 bus. **Open** 10am-6pm daily. **Admission** £3.30 adults; £1.65 under-15s, disabled, OAPs, students, UB40s. **Credit** (shop only) A, £TC, V.
See **picture and caption.**
See chapter **The World Wars.**
Classroom. Educational films. Restaurant (10am-5pm daily). Shop. Tour by prior arrangement. Wheelchair access. Worksheets.

Design Museum
Butlers Wharf, Shad Thames, SE1 (071 403 6933/recorded information 071 407 6261). Tower Hill underground/Tower Gateway DLR then riverboat shuttle/15, 42, 47, 70, 70A, 78 bus. **Open** 11.30am-6.30pm Tue-Sun, Mon Bank holidays; **Admission** £2 adult; £1 under-16s, OAPs, students, UB40s. **Credit** A, V.
See **picture and caption.**
Bar. Café. Restaurant. Cassette tour (free; £2 deposit). Education department. Films. Lectures. Reference library. Shop. Tour by prior arrangement. Toilets for the disabled. Wheelchair access.

Fan Museum
10-12 Crooms Hill, SE10 (081 305 1441). Greenwich or Maze Hill BR/boat to Greenwich Pier. **Open** *workshop* by appointment; *museum* from mid-1990: phone for details.

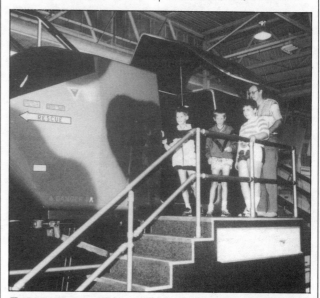

The **Royal Air Force Museum** *(listed under* **Armed Services***) has a special Battle of Britain display from Easter 1990. There are two hangars-full of historic flying machines. But it's like an aeroplane car park, so you only see them in close-up – and sadly none are suspended from the ceiling. The audio-visuals are comprehensive, but there are no seats to watch them from. Sitting down in the simulator – the most popular display – entails trial by vibration while piloting a low-flying Tornado.*

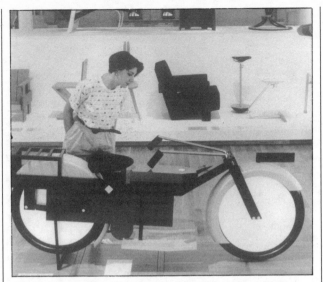

*The **Design Museum** (listed under **Art & Design**) is dedicated to mass-production's best moments. The Study Collection has themed displays on the office, kitchen and such like, plus computers on which you can design a tooth-brush. More ambitiously, the Boilerhouse has provocative exhibitions and the Design Review showcases contemporary products and projects. Unsurprisingly, the museum is a tasteful, clean-looking building, with banks of windows and balconies overlooking the river. A disappointingly small space in the bar has exhibitions of graphic works.*

See **picture and caption.**
Café. Shop. Tour by prior arrangement. Toilets for the disabled. Wheelchair access.

Geffrye Museum
Kingsland Road, E2 (071 739 9893/recorded information 071 739 8543). Old Street underground/Dalston Kingsland BR/22B, 48, 67, 149, 243 bus. **Open** 10am-5pm Tue-Sat, Bank holidays; 2-5pm Sun. **Admission** free. **No credit cards.**
Design buffs shouldn't miss this museum of the Great British front room. Housed in a terrace of former almshouses, the Geffrye contains room sets with furniture and fittings from Tudor times onwards. The craftsmanship of the exhibits (there's a Georgian workshop reconstruction) and the class of the people who owned them is clearly explained. Look out for the exhibition of pre-fabs, council houses and domestic life of the 1950's it's bound to supplant the 1930s sitting room in popularity, though the refurbished William and Mary parlour has its adherents. The archives are open by appointment and there are details of walking tours of the Shoreditch furniture industry and Spitalfields architecture.
Café (10am-12.30pm, 1.30-5pm). Education department (worksheets, workshops). Gardens. Library. Shop (closed 12.30-1.30pm). Wheelchair access to ground floor.

Percival David Foundation of Chinese Art
53 Gordon Square, WC1 (071 387 3909). Goodge Street, Euston Square, Russell Square underground or Euston underground/BR. **Open** 10.30am-5pm Mon-Fri. **Admission** free. Under-14s must be accompanied by an adult. **No credit cards.**
Chinese vases, pots and amphorae make up the collection at this quirky museum. The most famous exhibits are the tenth-century David vases. Bequeathed by the Chinese scholar Sir Percival David to the University of London, the collection is a ceramic document of Chinese court taste from the tenth to the eighteenth century. A number of pieces bear the imperial insignia of Chinese emperors. The exhibition room is rarely crowded.
Library (10.30am-1pm, 2-4.45pm, by written application). Shop. Wheelchair access by prior arrangement.

Thomas Coram Foundation for Children
40 Brunswick Square, WC1 (071 278 2424). Russell Square underground or King's Cross underground/BR/68, 77A, 170, 188 bus. **Open** 1am-4pm Mon-Fri. **Admission** 50p adult; 25p under-18s, OAP's, students. **No credit cards.**
William Hogarth, painter and governor of the eighteenth-century Coram's Foundling Hospital, asked his friends and fellow painters (including Gainsborough, Reynolds and Handel) to contribute works to attract funds. Today, only the art treasures remain because the hospital was demolished in 1926, but the Governor's Court Room and staircase have been reconstructed and there is a display of momentoes relating to the hospital. Look out for Benjamin West's *Suffer Little Children*, a Raphael cartoon, Hogarth's portrait of *Captain Thomas Coram* and *March of the Guards to Finchley* and a first draft of Handel's *Messiah*.

William Morris Gallery
Lloyd Park, Forest Road, E17 (081 527 3782 /081 527 5544 ext 4390). Walthamstow Central underground/BR/34, 48, 97, 123 bus. **Open** 10am-1pm, 2-5pm, Tue-Sat; 10am-noon, 2-5pm, first Sun every month. **Admission** free.
Poet, writer, textile and furniture designer, manuscript illuminator, printer, conservationist and socialist, William Morris was a seminal figure in the Arts and Crafts Movement. As an early modernist, he was lampooned by cartoonists and the leading writers of his day, but is now treated with respect. His boyhood home contains a wide-ranging tribute to his life and work: embroideries, carpets, tiles, stained glass, fabrics and wallpapers (many of which are still in production). In the gallery is a display on William Morris as Socialist. Other work of the period also shown includes paintings and drawings by Burne-Jones, pre-Raphaelite paintings and sculptures by Sickert, Rossetti and Rodin. The William Morris Society (081 741 3735) exhibit an original press and other items at his last town residence, Kelmscott House, 16 Upper Mall, W6 (free; 1.30-5.30pm Thur, Sat).
Guided tours by arrangement. Lectures. Mail order service. Reference library, by prior arrangement. Shop. Wheelchair access to ground floor only. Workshops .

BOTANICAL

Chelsea Physic Garden
66 Royal Hospital Road, SW3 (071 352 5646). Sloane Square underground/11, 39 bus. **Open** Apr-Oct: 2-5pm Wed, Sun. **Admission** £2 adults; £1 under-16s, students, UB40s. **No credit cards.**
A living museum, Chelsea Physic Garden was founded in 1673 by the Society of Apothecaries to grow plants for medicinal research. Lord of the Manor, Sir Hans Sloane, whose statue stands in the garden, saved it from financial ruin in the early eighteenth century. The garden has remained an important collection of species discovered in the New World and has a valuable collection of rare herbs. A walk around the garden reveals Europe's oldest rockery (with basaltic lava brought from Iceland by Joseph Banks and stone from the old Tower of London). Having recovered well from the 'hurricane' damage of 1987, this tranquil spot is worth a visit for both horticultural buffs and the city-weary.
Guided tours by appointment (£10 inclusive price, up to 25 people). Shop. Tea (3.15-4.45pm). Wheelchair access.

Museum of Garden History
St Mary-at-Lambeth, Lambeth Palace Road, SE1 (071 261 1891). Waterloo underground/BR/3, 159, 170, 507 buses. **Open** mid Mar-mid Dec: 11am-3pm Mon-Fri; 10.30am-5pm Sun. **Admission** free. **No credit cards.** See **picture and caption.**
Café. Tour by prior arrangement. Lectures. Shop. Wheelchair access.

CHILDHOOD

Baden-Powell House Museum

Queen's Gate SW7 (071 584 7030). South Kensington or Gloucester Road underground/74 bus. **Open** 7am-11pm daily (closed for two weeks over Christmas). **Admission** free. **Credit** A, V.

The toggles, tents and short trousers on display here will rekindle many a childhood trauma, if not a camp fire. The museum commemorates the Scout Movement's founder, Lord Baden-Powell; his famous hat and uniform are on display on the upper floor. Much is made of his Boer War years: there's a chocolate tin sent by Queen Victoria to his troops and a very stale loaf of bread that was baked at the seige of Mafeking in 1899. Baden-Powell's reaction to the Boer War was to found a pseudo-military organization for children. His aim was 'to promote good citizenship in the rising generation'. On leaving the museum, you hear a tape of the great Akela's last speech, rallying the young to carry on his ideals.
Accommodation bookable in the hostel for any scout or guide worldwide (Single £18; twin £14). Restaurant. Shop. Wheelchair access.

Bethnal Green Museum of Childhood

Cambridge Heath Road, E2 (081 980 3204/recorded information 081 980 2415). Bethnal Green underground/BR/8, 8A, 106, 253 bus. **Open** 10am-6pm Mon-Thur, Sat; 2.30-6pm Sun (closed Fri). **Admission** free. **No credit cards.**

This branch of the V&A has one of the world's greatest collections of toys, dolls and games, but the only sense of play comes courtesy of the schoolchildren running around. Nearly everything is frozen dead in a cabinet, inexpertly lit so the glass reflects, and badly labelled. Rare patience is demanded to learn about board games, model cars and arctophilia (love of teddy bears). However, the doll's houses (there's even a swish 1930s modernist one) are superb and conjure up a sense of social history. But there's no excuse for the dullness of the train set or the inaction of the puppets, and why aren't the soft toys ranged round a bed or at a picnic? A lot of good workshop education goes on here, but it's just as well kids come armed with more imagination than the museum designer.
Lectures by prior arrangement. Shop (10am-5.30pm Mon-Thur; 10.15am-1pm, 2-5.30pm Sat; 2.30-5.30pm Sun). Wheelchair access by prior arrangement. Workshops.

London Toy and Model Museum

21 Craven Hill, W2 (071 262 7905). Queensway underground or Paddington underground/BR/12, 88, 15 bus. **Open** 10am-5.30pm Tue-Sat; 11am-5.30pm Sun. **Admission** £2.20 adults; 80p age 6-15s; £1.20 OAPs, students, UB40s; £5 family (2 adults, 2 age 6-15s); under-fives free. **Credit** £TC.

Children of all ages get a lot of joy out of this museum. However, it's prone to marauding school parties, so it's best to visit out of term-time. Unfortunately, it seems to be the practice to shunt the girls into the impressive

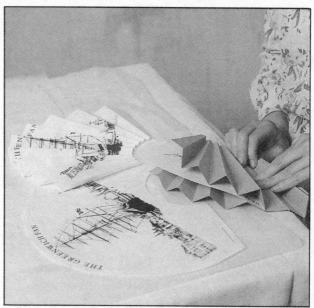

*Fans of fans will relish the **Fan Museum** (listed under **Art & Design**). Opening in mid-1990, the ground and first floor of two Georgian houses will hold exhibitions, changing every four months. There's no permanent collection since the delicate exhibits can't withstand prolonged exposure. In the basement workshop craftspeople repair and make both fans and lace. At demonstration sessions (phone for details) you can see the artisans at work.*

dolls' room and amuse the boys with model cars and tin soldiers. Paddington Bear gets good exposure, as do lesser-known oddities such as a German mechanical pool player. Disappointingly, there isn't a complete model railway inside the museum, but two scale miles/three scale kilometres of track circle the garden outside and a larger version takes children for a quick ride. A decorative carousel whirls the under-tens merrily round in circles for just 10p. Summer events include a model boat regatta and a teddy-bear's picnic, and you can even book-up birthday parties.
Activity room. Café. Group discount. Shop. Tour by prior arrangement. Videos. Worksheets. Workshop.

Pollock's Toy Museum

1 Scala Street, W1 (071 636 3452). Goodge Street underground/14, 24, 29, 73 bus. **Open** 10am-5pm Mon-Sat. **Admission** £1 adults; 50p age 4-18s, OAPs, students; free under-3s. **Credit** (shop only) A, AmEx, V.
See **picture and caption**.
Shop. Toy theatre (only during school holidays).

CLOCKS

Clockmakers' Company Museum and Library

The Clockroom, Guildhall Library, Aldermanbury, EC2 (071 606 3030 ext 1865). Bank, Mansion House, Moorgate or St Paul's underground. **Open** *museum:* 9.30am-4.45 pm Mon-Fri; *library:* 9.30am-5pm Mon-Sat). **Admission** free. **No credit cards.**

Exploding the myth that the Swiss had the monopoly on fine quality timepieces is the achievement of the Clockmaker's Company Museum. There are some exquisite British and international examples of astronomical clocks, early self-winding watches and elaborate long-case clocks collected by its members since the Company formed in 1631. Indeed, this is one of the few livery companies (*see chapter* **The City**) retaining a link to their origins as craftsmen. The pride of the collection are the pocket watches, with some superlative works by notable English artesans such as Harrison, Tompion, Quare and Arnold. Occupying rooms off the Guildhall Library foyer, and with a substantial library of its own, the museum is the chief British research base for antiquarian horology (clockmaking).
Library. Toilets for the disabled. Wheelchair access.

ETHNOGRAPHY

Commonwealth Institute

Kensington High Street, W8 (071 603 4535). High Street Kensington, Holland Park, Earl's Court or Olympia underground/9, 10, 27, 28, 31, 49 bus/701, 704 Green line coach.

Open 10am-5pm Mon-Sat; 2-5pm Sun. **Admission** free. **Credit** A, V.

Inside this oddly shaped building, there's a genuinely friendly mood, with children showing great interest in the diverse cultures of a quarter of the earth's population. The kids excitedly buzz around the three floors of circular galleries, themed by country or region, which overlook a central marble performance space, often the venue for music and dance. But it's a nightmare for people with push-chairs and wheelchairs. A lot of the displays are interactive and humorous. You can learn to play the sitar, sit astride a snowmobile and watch a bizarre model of a New Zealand cow's bodily functions, with bellow lungs, dripping udder and hind quarter joint of meat. The Institute has a hyperboloid (tent-shaped) roof and is one of the few sixties' buildings to be given listing protection. The displays on the 40-plus member nations are enlivened even more by a series of festivals held in the Institute. The national days of Commonwealth nations are celebrated with gusto in Kensington High Street. We recommend Commonwealth Day (second Monday in March), the Trinidad Carnival (February) and the Chinese New Year. A further taste of the Commonwealth can be experienced in the restaurant, where dishes from the different countries are served. The shop is something special, too, with imported craft work from musical instruments and antique Indian jewellery to inexpensive gifts for children. A wonderful place.

Activity room with induction loop for hearing aids. Concerts and performances. Conference

facilities. Educational programme. Festivals. Library. Restaurant. Shop. Wheelchair access..

Horniman Museum
London Road, SE23 (081 699 2339). Forest Hill BR. **Open** 10.30am-6pm Mon-Sat; 2-6pm Sun. **Admission** free. **No credit cards.**
See **picture and caption.**
Cassette tour for music section (£1). Education department. Gardens (animal enclosure, picnic area and nature trails). Information sheets and writing boards available. Lectures. Shop. Tea room (11am-4.30pm Mon-Fri; 11am-5.30pm Sat; 2.30-5.30pm Sun). Wheelchair access limited.

LITERARY

Carlyle's House
24 Cheyne Row, SW3 (071 352 7087). Sloane Square underground. **Open** *Easter-31 Oct:* 11am-5pm Wed-Sun, Bank Holidays. **Admission** £2 adult, £1 under-16s. **No credit cards.**

'The house itself is eminent antique,' wrote Thomas Carlyle of this red-brick Queen Anne building when, in 1834, he and his wife Jane moved in. The contents of the house are venerable and have remained largely untouched since the essayist's death in 1881. His hat is still on its peg. Carlyle penned his works *Frederick the Great*, *The French Revolution* and *Latter Day Pamphlets*

*The **Museum of Garden History** (listed under **Botanical**) has a grand name that belies the quirkiness of this little enterprise. The Tradescant Trust administer the gardens that are full of plants known in the seventeenth century and are presented in the fashion of that time. The first two John Tradescants were gardeners to Charles I and important plant collectors. The Trust has also preserved the church of St Mary at Lambeth and its churchyard, where the Tradescants and Captain Bligh, of Mutiny on the Bounty infamy, are buried.*

in the attic and many an intellectual point was argued when John Ruskin and the Charleses Dickens and Kingsley popped in for dinner. However, Mrs Carlyle had Lord Tennyson banished to the kitchen so he and Thomas could smoke into the chimney away from her more delicate lungs (what a sensible woman).
Guided tour on request.

Keats' House
Keats Grove, NW3 (071 435 2062). Hampstead underground/Hampstead Heath BR. **Open** *Apr-Oct:* 2-6pm Mon-Fri; 10am-1pm, 2-5pm Sat; 2-5pm Sun; *Nov-Mar:* 2-5pm Mon-Fri, Sun; 10am-1pm, 2-5pm Sat. **Admission** free. **No credit cards.**
See **picture and caption.**
Library by prior arrangement. Tour by prior arrangement. Shop.

LOCAL HISTORY

Bruce Castle Museum
Lordship Lane, N17 (081 808 8772). Seven Sisters or Tottenham Hale underground/BR/Bruce Grove BR/243 bus. **Open** 1-5pm daily; Regimental Museum (1st floor): 1-5pm Tue-Sat. **Admission** free. **No credit cards.**

Bruce Castle, a prominent Haringey landmark since 1514, houses one of London's best local museums. Its displays of photographs, old domestic appliances and some watercolours give an insight into what the area was once like. Upstairs a small exhibition, the Riches of the East, illustrates the effect that trading links with India and the Far East had on local society. The display features typical interiors of both Indian and English merchant homes. Named after Robert the Bruce, who owned part of the manor of Tottenham, the castle was the home of Rowland Hill, the man who introduced the Penny Black stamp. It now holds the Morten Bequest, an important exhibition on the history of the British postal system. Under the same roof is the Museum of the Middlesex Regiment, the 'Diehards', who saw action from the 1775 American War of Independence to 1950 Korea. Maori war clubs, Russian epaulettes and Zulu shields are the prize spoils.
Shop.

Church Farm House Museum
Greyhound Hill, NW4 (081 203 0130). Hendon Central underground/143, 183 ,113 bus. **Open** 10am-1pm, 2-5.30pm Wed-Mon, Bank Holidays; 10am-1pm Tue; 2-5.30pm Sun. **Admission** free.

Hendon isn't a pretty place, but this local museum is a haven of peace. Part of the old farmhouse dates from the mid-seventeenth century, with rooms left much as they were. Weight restrictions mean that no more than 15 people can enter any of the three quaint, first-floor rooms. The kitchen, the pièce de résistance, has a vast open hearth cluttered with kettles, girdles, pot hooks and wrought iron ratchet hangers.
Shop.

Crystal Palace Museum
*Anerley Hill, SE19 (081 676 0700 Sun).
Crystal Palace BR/2B, 3, 63, 108B, 122,
137, 157, 227, 249 bus.* **Open** 2-5pm Sun.
Admission free (donation requested). **No
credit cards.**
Unfortunately, the glorious glass and ironwork of the Crystal Palace was destroyed
by fire in 1936, but you can tour the
remains. The former Palace Engineering
School has been converted into a museum
devoted to Joseph Paxton's building, which
housed the Great Exhibition of 1851 before
being moved from Hyde Park and re-
erected in South London. Archive photographs depict the history of the glass fun-
park, but with more funds, a proper
museum will be developed here. The
Crystal Palace Foundation (081 778 2173)
can supply information during office hours.
The park includes bizarre plaster dinosaurs
and the national athletics stadium.
*Tour by prior arrangement and on the follow-
ing Sundays: 11 June, 9 July, 13 Aug, 10 Sept,
8 Oct, 12 Nov 1990 (2.30pm at Park gate by
Crystal Palace station. £1 adult; 50p children,
OAPs, students, UB40s). Shop.*

Forty Hall Museum
*Forty Hill, Enfield ,EN2 (081 363 8196).
Enfield Chase or Enfield Town BR/191, 231
buses.* **Open** *Easter-30 Sept:* 10am-6pm Tue-
Sun; *1 Oct-Easter:* 10am-5pm Tue-Sun.
Admission free. **No credit cards.**
Forty Hall is a magnificent Caroline mansion
built in 1629 and first owned by Sir Nicholas
Raynton, then Lord Mayor of London. The
ornately plaster-ceilinged ground floor has
displays of seventeenth and eighteenth century furniture. In the Raynton Room, there
are works by local artists and some
Victorian ceramics. Upstairs is devoted to a
small and unexciting exhibition of local geology. However, there's also a wonderfully
bizarre exhibition of the history of advertising and packaging. A childhood gallery, built
around the Victorian nursery, has become a
resident exhibition. The hall stands in an
attractive garden.
*Café (11am-5pm). Tour by prior arrange-
ment. Shop. Wheelchair access to ground floor.*

Gunnersbury Park Museum
*Gunnersbury Park, W3 (081 992 1612).
Acton Town underground. * **Open** *Mar-Oct: 1-
5pm,Mon-Fri Mon-Fri; 2-6pm Sat, Sun.Nov-
Feb:* 1-4pm Mon-Fri, 2-4pm Sat, Sun.
Admission free. **No credit cards.**
Like the fabric of so many British public
institutions, this Regency mansion – former home of the Rothchilds – is in need of
repair. Sadly, the superb gallery on the
social history of Ealing and Hounslow, and
artefacts in the main building, are off-
bounds until summer 1990 at least. This
progressive museum also tackles black
history, and, equally bravely, the up and
down story of Brentford Football Club.
The Victorian Kitchens, also used for temporary exhibitions, offer an intriguing, but
limited insight into regency life (open on
the last weekend of each month, May-
Sept). Gunnersbury Park boasts a
Victorian folly and the Small Mansion Arts
Centre. This spacious gallery has six resident artists exhibiting innovative work,
including sculptures, which are placed
throughout the park.
*Tour by prior arrangement. Shop.
Wheelchair access.*

Pollock's Toy Museum *(listed under* **Childhood***) is hidden above a shop
stocking traditional toys. In a succession of tiny, cluttered rooms is almost every
imaginable type of plaything, from Meccano to Sicilian puppets to teddy bears.
There's a recreation of an antique London toy shop, plus cabinets of educational toys, puppets, optical and constructional devices, jigsaws, dolls, model soldiers, and folk crafts from all parts of the world. Benjamin Pollock's toy theatres
were a Victorian institution and you can still see one working (check for times).*

Passmore Edwards Museum
*Romford Road, E15 (081 519 4296).
Stratford underground/BR/DLR.* **Open**
10am-5pm Mon-Fri; 2-5pm Sun, Bank
Holidays. **Admission** free.
The Passmore Edwards, dedicated to the
county of Essex, offers some gruesome
sights of wildlife preserved in jars, and if
you're interested in taxidermy you'll love
the stuffed animals – the hawks are particularly lifelike. The most impressive exhibits
are those related to Essex's archaeological
history, which are housed in a circular display above the main hall. There's plenty of
geological jargon, lots of jaw-bones and bits
of old pots, which are well laid out so you
don't need to be Indiana Jones to find something interesting.
Shop. Lectures by appointment.

Ragged School Museum
*46-48 Copperfield Road, E3 (081 980
6405). Mile End underground/D14 bus.*
Open early 1990. **Admission** free. **No
credit cards.**
The East End needed a decent museum
about its history and now it's got one. The
ragged schools were founded by Dr
Barnardo to educate and feed poor kids.
This former warehouse was once the
largest of the ragged schools and has
changed little, even retaining its rooftop
bell. There's a recreation of a Jewish
sewing workshop and of a 1890s lighter-
man's (men who ferried cargo round the
docks) parlour, furnished with retrieved
original items.
Café. Shop.

MUSIC

Musical Museum
*368 High Street, Brentford, Middlesex (081
560 8108). Gunnersbury underground/Kew
Bridge or Brentford Central BR/65, 237, 267
bus.* **Open** *April-Oct* guided tours only 2pm,
3.30pm Sat, Sun. **Admission** £2 adults; £1.50
under-16s, OAPs. **No credit cards.**
Slightly eccentric Frank Holland collected
more than 200 automatic musical instruments. The collection is housed in this converted church and is still growing, despite
Mr Holland's recent death. Perhaps not as
idiosyncratic as Frank, the able guides conduct an unusual 90-minute tour. You'll be furnished with details about the history and
workings of exhibits, such as automatic vio-
lins and the only self-playing Wurlitzer organ
in Europe. The noise they make can be
startling and you'd be ill-advised to bring
small, restless children. You may even be
encouraged to sing along.
Group discount. Shop. Wheelchair access.

POSTAL

National Postal Museum
*King Edward Building, King Edward
Street, EC1 (071 239 5420). Barbican or
St Paul's underground.* **Open** 9.30am-
4.30pm Mon-Thur; 9.30am-4pm Fri.
Admission free. **No credit cards.**

*The **Horniman Museum** (listed under **Ethnography**) started with tea merchant John Horniman opening his house to exhibit his collection of head-dresses, puppets and Egyptian mummies. The presentation is dated, but the funds are limited and this 'free museum' does valuable educational work. The 6,000-plus musical instruments – 100 of which you can hear on a cassette guide – include Peruvian whistling pots and an armadillo guitar. The natural history section is presided over by an enormous, 100-year-old stuffed walrus.*

Viewing the stamps in the National Postal Museum is a laborious business. It involves pulling the displays of stamps out of the glass-fronted drawers in which they are stored. Although not the rarest stamp here, the Penny Black is the one that visitors head for. An exhibition in 1990 will celebrate the Penny Black's 150th anniversary as the world's first adhesive stamp (*see also* **Bruce Castle Museum**, *listed under* **Local History**). The galleries are extremely cramped, particularly when a party of school kids descends. With the awkward bureaucracy so reminiscent of the Post Office, you have to book in advance to see the collection of postboxes. A philatelist's paradise, but of limited interest to plain letter writers.
Tour by prior arrangement. Shop. Wheelchair access by prior arrangement.

PUBLIC RECORDS

Public Records Office Museum
Chancery Lane, WC2 (071 876 3444). Chancery Lane underground. **Open** 9-30am-5pm Mon-Fri. **Admission** free. **No credit cards.**
Public records from the Norman invasion to the latest census are stored along with treaties, writs and state papers in this mock-Tudor building, The latter are usually made public after 30 years, except if they're embarrassing to the establishment or contain 'state secrets'. The museum's riches include the Domesday Book (1086), one of the four existing Magna Cartas (1215) and the log-book of *HMS Victory*, plus displays of glass and monuments from the medieval chapel which stood on the site of the PRO. Unfortunately, one of the most fascinating documents in British hands – Adolf Hitler's dental X-rays – are kept under lock and key at the PRO's office in Kew. If you want to trace your roots, you should go to St Katharine's House at 10 Kingsway, WC2 (071 242 0262). This is where the records of births, deaths and marriages are kept. Armed forces and government records, dating from the sixteenth century, are held at the Public Record Office, Ruskin Avenue, Kew (081 876 3444).
Shop.

RELIGIONS & SOCIETIES

Freemasons' Hall
Great Queen Street, WC2 (071 831 9811). Covent Garden or Holborn underground. **Open** 10am-5pm Mon-Fri; Sat by appointment. **Admission** free. **No credit cards.**
Funny handshakes are not compulsory at this temple to the history of freemasonry. However, most visitors are brethren (you can see them sign the guest book). To the uninitiated, it is still a revelatory experience.

Masonic history is explained on the free tour, but not all of your questions on the heavy symbolism, or the uses of the various artefacts, are answered. The collection of masonic regalia, medals, art and glassware is the largest in existence and is an impressive sight, as are the art deco ceremonial rooms and Grand Temple. But you'll glean little about its secrets or why grown men dress up in aprons to perform seemingly ridiculous rituals that bind the masons into unquestioning obedience. The power gained through masonic links with royalty, the police and business, is indignantly denied, but conspiracy theorists can have a field day. The building, built between 1927 and 1933, is a fine example of thirties' Art Deco architecture (although it was loathed by critics at the time).
Guided tours. Wheelchair access.

Jewish Museum
Woburn House, Tavistock Square, WC1 (071 388 4525). Euston Square or Russell Square underground/Euston underground/BR. **Open** *May-Sept:* 10am-4pm Tue-Fri, Sun; *Oct-Mar:* 10am-4pm Tue-Thur, Sun; 10am-12.45pm Fri; closed on Jewish festival days. **Admission** free (donation requested). **Credit** (Shop only) A, V.
A large, elaborately carved, sixteenth-century Venetian Ark steals the limelight in the Jewish Museum. It was found by a bookseller in Northumberland, where it had been used as a servant's wardrobe. The nucleus of this treasure trove, which concentrates on Anglo-Jewish life, history and tradition, was deposited on loan by the United Synagogue. It consists mainly of ritual objects from early London synagogues: a small Byzantine gold votive plaque embossed with Jewish symbols; illuminated marriage contracts; and enchanting eighteenth-century pieces, such as the Torah bells by silversmith Abraham Lopes de Oliveira. The belief that functional items should be so beautified is one that today's designers should note.
Shop (071 387 3081). Video programmes. Wheelchair access. Worksheets.

Museum of Methodism
Wesley Chapel, 49 City Road, EC1 (071 253 2262, ext 23). Old Street underground/BR. **Open** 10am-4pm Mon-Sat; 11am morning service, followed by lunch and guided tour on Sun. **Admission** *Museum or house:* 75p adults; 40p under-16s, OAPs, UB40s. *Museum and house:* £1.20 adults; 60p under-16s, OAPs, UB40s. **No credit cards.**
John Wesley's House, where he lived for the last 12 years of his life, contains a museum showing a selection of his belongings. These include examples of commemorative pottery, a gallon teapot given to him by Josiah Wedgwood and, most intriguing of all, an electric-shock machine used by Wesley to treat followers who came to him for medical advice. Next door is the chapel built by John Wesley in 1778, after he had split from the Church of England. It has pillars made from old warship masts donated by George III. Prime Minister Margaret Thatcher (née Roberts) was married here, before she left to join the Anglicans. Most of the fretwork on the oak pews is original, as is the 15-foot/4.5-metre high pulpit, and the font from Nathaniel Gilbert's house in Antigua (he is famous for his part in promoting Methodism abroad). Take the steps down to the crypt where a small museum of Methodism is

housed. It contains some amusing relics used by the early Methodist missionaries, including a portable writing desk used by a missionary on the move round North America and the West Indies and a pack of playing cards whose suits have been replaced by biblical texts and verses of hymns. Sunday services are followed by a meal, talk and guided tour.
Films. Shop. Tour by prior arrangement.

Museum of the Order of St John

St John's Gate, St John's Lane, EC1 (071 253 6644). Barbican underground or Farringdon underground/BR/5,55,243 buses. **Open** 10am-5pm Mon-Fri; 10am-4pm Sat. **Admission** free (£2 donation requested). **Credit** (Shop only) A, AmEx, DC, V.
Housed in the early sixteenth-century Gatehouse, the museum contains a comprehensive collection of items relating to the order of St John, including armour, weapons, ships' cannon and documents. Some of the documentation and manuscripts in the collection are magnificent and include early examples of printed books. Of particular interest are two panels of a Flemish triptych and the illuminated Rhodes Missal, presented to the Convent at Rhodes in 1504. Under the Grand Priory Church of the Order is a twelfth-century crypt, all that remains of the priory established here about 1140. The original mission of the medieval Knights of the Order of St John was to care for pilgrims and the sick. But boys being boys, they couldn't resist a bit of miltiary action and, under the guise of the Knights Hospitaller, were one of the principal defenders of the Christian kingdoms during the Crusades. They were a pretty bloody lot who controlled Rhodes and then Malta for more than 400 years. It is the peaceful arm of the society that continues to this day in the shape of the St John Ambulance Brigade. The church and gatehouse rooms are only viewable on the tour.
Guided tours (11am, 2.30pm Tues, Fri, Sat). Reference library by prior arrangement. Shop.

SCIENCE

Charles Darwin Memorial

Down House, Luxted Road, Downe, Orpington, Kent (0689 59119). Bromley South BR (from Victoria) then 146 bus.to Downe. **Open** 1-5.30pm Wed-Sun. **Admission** £1.50 adults; 50p under-15s; £1 OAPs, students. **No credit cards.**
Charles Darwin outraged the scientific and ecclesiastical worlds when he proposed his theory of evolution and radically altered the way we see the world. From 1842 to 1882, he lived at Down House, which has been restored as closely as possible to its state in Darwin's lifetime. There are collections of birds, butterflies, fossils and scientific instruments and original documentation of his theories. The pieces of period furniture include Wedgewood Plaques and a model of HMS Beagle, the ship in which he travelled the world. Ever practical, Darwin kept his snuff jar in the hall, so that he might stop himself from excessive use by having to fetch it.
Shop. Wheelchair access.

Florence Nightingale Museum

St Thomas' Hospital, 2 Lambeth Palace Road, SE1 (071 620 0374). Westminster underground or Waterloo underground/BR/12, 53, 77, 109, 170, 171, 171A, 184, 196, 507, C1 bus. **Open** 10am-4pm Tue-Sun. **Admission** £2 adults; £1 under-16s, OAPs, students, UB40s; £5 family (2 adults, 3 under-16s); **Credit** A, AmEx, V.
See **picture and caption.**
Film. Group discount. Lectures. Shop. Study and resource centre.

Freud's House

20 Maresfield Gardens, NW3 (071 435 2002). Finchley Road underground/Finchley Road and Frognal BR/2B, 13, 31, 46, 82, 113, C11 bus. **Open** noon-5pm Wed-Sun. **Admission** £2 adults; £1, OAPs, students, UB40s; under 12s free. **Credit** A, AmEx.
See **picture and caption.**
Tour by prior arrangement. Lectures. Seminars by prior arrangement. Shop. Video.

Kew Bridge Steam Museum

Green Dragon Lane, Brentford, Middlesex (081 568 4757). Gunnersbury underground/Kew Bridge BR/27,65,237,267 bus. **Open** 11am-5pm. **Admission** Mon-Fri: £1 adults; 50p under-16's, OAP's, students; Sat, Sun, Bank Holidays: £1.80 adults; 90p under-16s, OAPs, students; £5 family (2 adults, 3 children). **No credit cards.**
The museum appears to be wrapped around its inside, vast, solid-cast structures such as the rotative and bull engines that powered the Industrial Revolution. Before being replaced by electric pumps, these 150 tonne beasties from another age pumped 472 gallons per stroke into London's expectant plumbing. The museum is designed to give access to most of the working machinery and the exhibits are still put 'in steam' at varying times throughout the week. *See chapter* **Victorian Times.**
Group discount. Shop. Tour by prior arrangement. Wheelchair access is limited.

Vintage Wireless Museum

23 Rosendale Road, SE21 (081 670 3667). West Dulwich BR/2, 3 bus. **Open** by appointment only: 11am-7.30pm Mon-Sat. **Admission** free (donation requested). **No credit cards.**
Run by the tireless Gerry Wells, the Vintage Wireless Museum has over a thousand exhibits dating mostly from 1917 to 1946, all in perfect working order. If you have a broken wireless set, experts here will perform surgery upon it before your very eyes. This free service is very informative and has plenty of drama with the wireless owner liable to faint with concern or joy at any moment. After a compulsory cup of tea, you can explore the display rooms, which are reconstructions of storerooms and a 1936 wireless shop. Gerry not only collects and repairs radios, but makes his own replicas of individual parts using the original implements and techniques, right down to blowing the glass for his own glass valves. If you're fed up of watching repeats on television, avoid the original 1938 goggle-box, which is still broadcasting pre-war programmes. The museum has become the

A visit to **Keats' House** *(listed under* **Literary***) makes a rewarding end to a jaunt on Hampstead Heath. One of the poets who gave Romantic poetry its name, John Keats (1795-1821) wrote many of his greatest works – including 'Ode to a Nightingale' – at this unpretentious Regency house. The tranquil surroundings nurtured his courtship of the girl-next-door, Fanny Brawne. Their engagement was tragically cut short by his death, from consumption, in Rome. The two houses were later converted into one and now contain fascinating artefacts.*

The **Florence Nightingale Museum** *(listed under* **Science** *) shows why she deserves her portrait on the £10 note. Her famous lamp is here, with a reconstruction of the Crimean wards, where Florence showed the army how to care for its injured and founded modern nursing in the process. A witty before-and-after display dramatizes the awesome Nightingale effect: 'She found a pigsty – she left it a tidy airy room'. Queen Victoria remarked, 'I wish we had her at the War Office.'*

unofficial clubhouse for radio enthusiasts all over the world. All day, and often well into the night, you are likely to find enthusiasts with their noses inside sets, researching data in the library, or swapping yarns over endless cups of tea in the kitchen.
Lectures. No children. Restoration and repair service. Tea & biscuits on the hour. Wheelchair access.

SPORT

Cricket Memorial Gallery
Marylebone Cricket Club, Lord's Ground, NW8 (071 289 1611). St John's Wood underground. **Open** *by prior arrangement; match days:* 10.30am-5pm Mon-Sat. **Admission** £1 adults; 50p under-16s, OAPs. **Credit** (shop only) A, £TC, V.
Connoisseurs of the sport cannot possibly miss this museum. The noble game's origins are traced with the help of countless paintings, photos, old relics and battered bats. In 1936 a ball bowled here hit a sparrow, killing the poor bird instantly. The sparrow was stuffed, the ball kept, and the whole scene has been gorily recreated. The Ashes are also kept here. Any self-respecting Aussie or Pom will appreciate the importance of the little urn, the symbolic prize that England and Australia have played for, and cheated over, for over a century. (The ashes are, in fact, those of a bail from the second series of Tests held in 1882 between the two sides; in the first, England had been beaten, prompting an obituary in the sporting

press.). The guided tour lasts almost two hours and takes in other aspects of the grounds as well; there's a Real tennis court and someone is usually playing a game of Henry VIII's favourite sport, a cross between lawn tennis and squash. Then there's the Long Room, the holiest of cricketing shrines and strictly boys-only territory. Lord's is so stuffy and archaic that women are still banned from here on match-days. But if you're a cricket buff, the sense of occasion is enormous, treading the floor that Bradman, Botham and other hallowed icons crossed on their way to bat.
Guided tour. Shop. Wheelchair access to ground floor only.

Rugby Football Union Museum
Rugby Football Union Stadium, Rugby Road, Twickenham, Middlesex (081 892 8161, ext 246). Hounslow East underground/ Twickenham BR then 281 bus. **Open** 9.30am-1pm, 2.15-5pm Mon-Fri. **Admission** free. **Credit** A, V.
Ever since a naughty footballer at Rugby School picked up the ball and ran towards goal, grown men have knocked each other about doing the same thing, and even more have gone to watch them. Housed in the National Stadium, this museum covers the rise and not too infrequent falls of British Rugby Union Football. Exhibitions trace the history of the sport from its early nineteenth century public school origins, through the era of long shorts and waxed moustaches, to the internationals of the present day. Old kits, caps and photographs and a history of the

Calcutta Cup are haphazardly assembled behind heavy glass cabinets, but a film on the preparations for match days livens things up. The guided tour of the ground will take you through the official suites and sweaty changing rooms, with the famous double baths, but not onto the hallowed turf itself.
Reference library. Tour by prior arrangement. Shop (9am-5pm daily). Wheelchair access.

The Thomas-a-Becket Boxing Museum
320 Old Kent Road, SE1 (071 703 2644). Elephant & Castle underground. **Open** noon-3pm, 8pm-midnight Tue, Wed; noon-3pm, 8pm-1.30am Thur-Sat; noon-3pm, 7pm-12.30am Sun. **Admission** £3 Fri, Sat 8pm-1.30am; otherwise free. **No credit cards.**
The Thomas-à-Becket is a pub and not a museum in the real sense. But it's the nearest thing this country has to a boxing museum. For the price of a drink, you can study the mementoes of Britain's past boxing glories that adorn the pub's walls. There are posters, dating back to the thirties, which advertise the big fights of the day and some excellent photographs of memorable fighters such as 'Enry Cooper, Joe Bugner, Maurice Hope, and John Conteh. Cooper used to train in the gym upstairs, which is still regarded as a prestigious stable for young hopefuls.
Disco. Late licence. Pub food. Tour of gym by prior arrangement.

Wimbledon Lawn Tennis Museum
Church Road, SW19 (081 946 6131). Southfields underground/39,93,200 bus. **Open** 11am-5pm Tue-Sat; 2-5pm Sun. *During Championships (spectators only):* 11am-7pm daily. **Admission** £1.50 adults; 75p under-16s, OAPs. **Credit** (shop only) A, V.
If you want quirky facts about tennis, the Wimbledon Lawn Tennis Museum can provide plenty of them – like how many tonnes of strawberries are consumed during the championships. If you love the game of tennis, it will be a source of great delight. Tennis footwear seems to figure prominently: from John McEnroe's pungent trainers to equine overshoes for horse-drawn mowers. And you can trace the history of the ankle through to the skimpy skirts of today. The huge amount of information contained within the museum's small gallery may be a little overwhelming, but you can always escape to the Centre Court viewing gallery and dream of serving a succession of aces past a helpless Martina Navratilova or Boris Becker. A newly refurbished video theatre now offers any tournament match recorded on film, but a summary of highlights should satisfy most visitors. A special gallery has also been included to show exhibitions (May-Dec). Avoid visiting the museum during Championship Fortnight (see *chapter* **London by Season**).
Library open by prior arrangement. Shop. Wheelchair access.

THEATRE

Shakespeare Globe Museum
Bear Gardens, Bankside, SE1 (928 6342). Mansion House or London Bridge underground/BR. **Open** 10am-5pm Mon-Sat; 2-

5pm Sun. **Admission** £1 adults; 50p under-16s, OAPs, students, UB40s, Southwark residents. **No credit cards.**

The Globe Museum is not on the site of Shakespeare's theatre – that was built a 100 yards/33 metres away. The museum is actually on the site of the last bear-baiting ring on Bankside where such notable regulars as diarist Samuel Pepys and writer John Evelyn came for their 'nasty pleasures'. A working reconstruction of the theatre is being built, following the 1599 designs, plans of which can be seen in the museum. The foundations are underway and if you're lucky you may get to view craftsmen employing traditional skills and tools in site workshops. The Rose gallery has also been opened to the public, displaying material amassed in the recent excavation. The museum's academic emphasis makes Bankside's exotic history seem a little sterile, but model theatres and a seventeenth-century 'Swan' festival on the frozen Thames do capture the spirit. *See also chapter* **Tudors & Stuarts.**
Café. Lectures. Walks around local area. Workshops.

Theatre Museum
1E Tavistock Street,, WC2 (071 836 7891/recorded information 071 836 7624).
Covent Garden underground. **Open** 11am-7pm Tue-Sun. **Admission** £2.25 adults; £1.25 age 6-14s, OAPs, students, UB40s; free under-fives. **Credit** (shop and box office only) A, £TC, V.

The old flower market of Covent Garden is the home of the Theatre Museum – a branch of the Victoria & Albert Museum. The fascinating collection of stage models, costumes, prints, posters, puppets, props and a variety of memorabilia come from all the performing arts: ballet, opera, circus and even rock's more theatrical moments. Exhibits deserving encores are the models of Shakespeare's Globe, a Reformation theatre and an Equus set from the original National Theatre production. A golden angel from atop the Gaiety Theatre hoots its horn at the box office queue in the foyer, doubtless dispirited by the posters for classic productions they cannot buy tickets for. Exhibitions take place throughout the year in the Irving and Gielgud galleries
Café. Induction loop for hard of hearing. Lectures. Library (10.30am-1pm, 2-4.30pm Tue-Fri) and archives with a study room. Shop. Theatre Box Office. Wheelchair access.

TRANSPORT

Heritage Motor Museum
Syon Park, Brentford, Middlesex (081 560 1378). Syon Lane BR/237,267 bus. **Open** *Mar-Oct:* 10am-5.30pm daily; *Nov-Feb:* 10am-4pm daily. **Admission** £2 adults; £1.25 age 6-16, OAP's; under-fives free; £5-00 family. **No credit cards.**

Next-door to a Butterfly house and Syon House (*see chapter* **The River & Docklands**), the Heritage Motor Museum is a good element of a day out in Syon Park, but only motor enthusiasts should make a special trip. The gleaming crome and leather upholstry illustrates the ascent of the British motor industry from its eccentric infancy to the glory years of Jaguar and Austin. The odd, customized Metro represents its calamitous decline since the sixties. Annoyingly, the exhibits are obscured by each other as if in a carpark. There aren't many audio-visuals, but they are informative. The museum generally presumes an already developed interest in motorcars.
Café. Cassette tour. Group discount. Lectures by prior arrangement. Shop. Tour by prior arrangement. Wheelchair access.

London Transport Museum
39 Wellington Street, WC2 (071 379 6344). Covent Garden underground/6, 9, 11, 15 bus. **Open** 10am-6pm daily. **Admission** £2.60 adults; £1.20 under-16s, OAPs, students, UB40s; free under-5s; £6 family (2 adults, 2 under-16s). **Credit** (shop only) A, V.

For a place dedicated to transport, this museum is static, even dull. LT glamourizes its history with spotless exhibits, including omnibuses, horse-drawn trams and tube trains. But there's just too much of the same sort of thing in this small space. To cover the subject properly and satisfy transport connoisseurs, the museum needs larger premises and room to move the exhibits. People wandering in from Covent Garden (it's less crowded in the mornings) get frustrated because there's only one driver's seat to sit in. The simulation of a trip around the Circle line (seen from the driver's point of view) seems like a good idea to every visitor. Unfortunately it's black and uneventful; worse, the simulator takes two people only and queues develop while the 5-10 minute tape rewinds. London Transport is justly proud of its graphic art; not just the wonderful tube map, but also its Art Deco and 1980s posters. These are popular purchases from the shop.
Group discount. Lectures. Shop. Toilets for the disabled. Wheelchair access. Worksheets for children.

North Woolwich Old Station Museum
Pier Road, E16 (071 474 7244). North Woolwich BR/pedestrian tunnel/ferry from Woolwich BR. **Open** 10am-5pm Mon-Sat; 2-5pm Sun, Bank Holidays. **Admission** free. **No credit cards.**

People who like their trains to make choo-choo noises and cover everything in soot will love this museum. In the restored North Woolwich Old Station the history of the Great Eastern Railway and the docklands rail system is lovingly documented. One engine here is regularly in steam and you'll find the oldest GER loco, which has been dubbed the 'Coffee Pot'. The principles of steam locomotion and railway communications are explained in model demonstrations. The Victorian ticket office is faithfully reconstructed but does not dispense travelcards at nineteenth-century prices. The collection of models, photographs and other relics is from an era when the British railway system was something to be proud of. The Old Station is a branch of the Passmore Edwards Museum and shares its educational facilities.
Lectures by prior arrangement. Shop. Wheelchair access.

Freud's House (*listed under* **Science**) *feels like it's still lived in. Six rooms remain untouched since 1939 when Sigmund died. He decorated his home with the furniture he took with him when he fled from Nazi Vienna in 1938. The pruriently curious can see the couch on which Freud's patients relaxed while he interpreted their 'free association'. Much of the house's charm comes from Freud's important and beautiful collection of antiquities – many with graphically sexual themes – which spill out from every shelf.*

Children's London

London's a great old place for young people, _Sarah McAlister_ shows how to keep your kids occupied and entertained while still having a ball yourself.

The facilities for children and parents in London are far from ideal. But if you know where to look there are some wonderful places to occupy, entertain and feed London's youngest visitors.

GETTING AROUND

For children who've never seen the Underground, finding your way around on the tube and riding the longest escalators (at Leicester Square and Holborn) is half the fun of being in London. For seeing the sights, you can't beat riding on top of a double-decker bus – take the number 15 through the West End, all the way from Oxford Street (Marble Arch) to **St Paul's**, via **Piccadilly Circus** and Trafalgar Square with **Nelson's Column**. Or try one of the open-top bus tours – they take in all the main sights. (For details of all these, see chapter **Sightseeing**).

Even more exciting (and relaxing for parents) are river boats, canal trips and rides on the Docklands Light Railway (from Tower Gateway to Island Gardens, opposite Greenwich) for a traffic-free view of London. See chapter **The River & Docklands**.

Under-5s travel free on London Transport, and under-16s pay a child's fare until 10pm (after that children are charged at the adult rate). The child's one-day travel card costs 90p (which includes use of bus, tube and the Dockland's Light Railway). The one-week card costs £5.50 (all zones) but 14- and 15-year-olds must carry a Child Rate Photocard (free from underground stations and post offices, but you'll need a passport-size photo).

Unless you can't possibly avoid it, give the rush hour (8.30-9.30am and 4.30-6.30pm Monday to Friday) an exceptionally wide berth.

assortment of murderers and guillotined heads. For the real thing, you can't beat the **Tower of London**, although it's by no means as gory as the two establishments mentioned above. Here you can imagine headless ghosts roaming the ramparts, and see a small assortment of real torture instruments held in the Bowyer Tower.

Less blood-thirsty, but very spooky is a lamplight tour through the maze of chalk tunnels at **Chislehurst Caves**. Or visit one of London's peaceful cemeteries, at **Highgate** or **Kensal Green** (see chapter **Victorian Times**) where you can wander through a wilderness of tombs and angels, and discover many eminent names hidden under the ivy.

Chislehurst Caves
Old Hill, Chislehurst, Kent (081 467 3264). Chislehurst BR. **Open** *May-Sept* 10.30am-5pm daily; *Oct-Apr* 11am-5pm Sat, Sun, Bank Holidays. **Admission** £2 adults; £1 under-15s; free under-5s .
Take a spooky lamplight tour through this maze of chalk tunnels and caves, dug out and used by man since the stone age. Previous occupants include the druids, the Romans and war-time Londoners sheltering

from the air-raids. More recently it was used as a pirate radio station and sixties disco. The whole place is largely untouched and unspoilt and there are chilling stories of druid sacrifices and ghosts. Snacks are served in the small hut near the entrance.

London Dungeon
28-34 Tooley Street, SE1 (071 403 0606). London Bridge underground/BR/boat to London Bridge Pier. **Open** *Apr-Sept* 10am-5.30 daily; *Oct-Mar* 10am-4.30pm daily. **Admission** £4.50 adults; £2.50 under-16s, OAPs; free entry for the disabled in wheelchairs. **Credit** £TC.
Gruesome exhibits of blood-curdling moments from the seamy side of London's history – sacrifices, tortures, plagues, murders and executions. Give this a miss if your children are very young, sensitive or prone to nightmares. See chapter **Sightseeing**. *Café. Group discount. Wheelchair access.*

Madame Tussaud's
Marylebone Road, NW1 (071 935 6861). Baker Street underground. **Open** 10am-5.30pm Mon-Fri; 9.30am-5.30pm Sat, Sun. **Admission** £5.20 adults; £3.95 OAPs; £3.45 under-16s. *Combined ticket with Planetarium* £6.65 adults; £5.25 OAPs; £4.25 under-16s. **Credit** £STC.
Hundreds of life-size figures of the famous and the notorious are packed into Madame Tussaud's. Spot royalty, politicians, sports personalities and popstars. In the grisly Chamber of Horrors (not recommended for young children or anyone prone to nightmares) the spotlight is turned on murderers

and villains. Both Madame Tussaud's and the **Planetarium** (see chapter **Sightseeing**) are hot favourites for tourists, You can avoid the worst of the queues if you take a combined ticket and visit the Planetarium first. See chapter **Sightseeing**. *Café. Group discount. Wheelchair access by prior arrangement.*

Tower of London
Tower Hill, EC3 (071 709 0765). Tower Hill underground/Fenchurch Street BR/15, 42, 78 bus. **Open** *Mar-Oct* 9.30am-5pm Mon-Sat, 2-5pm Sun; *Nov-Feb* 9.30am-4pm Mon-Sat. **Admission** £4.80 adults; £3 OAPs, students, UB40s, disabled; £2 under-15s; free under-5s; £3 OAPs, students, UB40s, disabled; under-5s free. **Credit** (shop only) A, £TC, V.
Allow at least half a day to explore this fascinating place (at its gloomy best in winter, when it's also less crowded). Start with a free tour by one of the Beefeaters, then explore the ramparts and the amazing collection of armour in the White Tower. See the horrible instruments of torture in the Bowyer Tower, the Crown Jewels in their underground strongroom (closed February for cleaning), and the famous ravens on Tower Green (beware, they peck!) In summer, you can picnic by the riverside. See chapter **Sightseeing**. *Guided tours (free, every half hour for one hour). Restaurant. Shop. Wheelchair access with help (1 adult admitted free if assisting disabled person).*

PLACES TO VISIT

London's museums and exhibitions have changed dramatically over the last few years. The new look is lighter and brighter. At the **Natural History Museum** and **Imperial War Museum** (see chapter **Museums**) many of the old displays have been redesigned and have push-button machines, videos and all the latest 'interactive' techniques. Films, talks, quiz trails, workshops and special events are aimed at children and families. Enjoyable new arrivals are **MOMI** (see chapter **Museums**) and **Royal Britain** (see chapter **The City**), but old favourites – HMS Belfast, **London Planetarium** (for both see chapter **Sightseeing**) and the museums of childhood (see chapter **Museums**) – continue to be popular with kids.

Brass Rubbing Centre
St Martin-in the Fields, Trafalgar Square, WC2 (071 437 6023). Charing Cross underground. **Open** 10am-6pm Mon-Sat; noon-6pm Sun. **Admission** free. **Brass rubbings** according to size 50p-£10.50. **Credit** A, V.
See **picture and caption**. *Gift shop. Wheelchair access.*

Chessington World of Adventures
Leatherhead Road, Chessington Surrey (0372 727227). Chessington South BR/65 bus.

*The world-famous **London Zoo** (listed under **Meet the Animals**) holds over 8,000 mammals, birds, insects, reptiles and fish. Feeding time is always a popular attraction (check the Zoo's notice board for details). The Children's Zoo includes a farmyard and pet animals: demonstrations of milking are given at 3pm daily when a cow is in milk. The Moonlight House contains nocturnal animals and there's also an aquarium. In summer there are daily meet-the-animals sessions, an elephant's weigh-in and bath-time, plus camel and pony rides. Take a picnic as the zoo café is crowded and expensive.*

Open *Mar-Oct* 10am-5pm daily (all attractions); *late Oct-late Mar* 10am-4pm daily (zoo only). **Admission** £8.25 adults; £7.25 under-15s, OAPs. **Credit** A, V.
See **picture and caption**.
Group discount.

Horniman Museum
London Road, SE23 (081 699 2339). Forest Hill BR. **Open** 10.30am-6pm Mon-Sat; 2-6pm Sun. **Children's club** *term time* 10.30am-12.30pm Sat; *school holidays* 10.30am-12.30pm Mon-Sat. **Admission** free. **No credit cards.**
A fascinating collection of oddities is kept in this museum, including an observation beehive (complete with bees). You can also play recordings of all the weird and wonderful musical instruments on display. The Horniman is famous for its superb work with children

London Butterfly House
Syon Park, Brentford, Middlesex (081 560 7272). Gunnersbury underground then 237, 267 bus. **Open** 10am-3.30pm daily. **Admission** £1.90 adults; £1.10 under-15s; £5.50 family (2 adults, 4 children). **Credit** (shop only) A, V.
A greenhouse jungle with hundreds of exotic butterflies to spot, and Syon Park all around. Great to visit on a fine day, and take a picnic. A shop sells souvenirs with a butterfly theme. *Restaurant.*

Science Museum
Exhibition Road, SW7 (071 938 8000; recorded information 071 938 8123). South Kensington underground/4, 9, 30, 45, 74,

264 bus.. **Open** 10am-6pm Mon-Sat; 11am-6pm Sun. **Admission** £2 adult; £1 children, OAPs, students, UB40s; £12 family. **Credit** (shop only) A, V.
See **picture and caption**.
See chapter **Museums**.
Café (10.30am–5pm Mon-Sat). Dramatized gallery talks. Films by prior arrangement. Group discount. Lectures by prior arrangement. Library. Dillons bookstore. Wheelchair access.

BEHIND THE SCENES

It makes a change from sightseeing to take a look behind the scenes and see how things work.
It's not only football fans who enjoy a tour round **Wembley Stadium**, scene of many famous sporting events and pop concerts. Glass-blowing and silk block-printing are two of the many crafts you can still see being practised in London; also look out for Craft Fairs and Toy Fairs, listed in the Around Town section in *Time Out*.

David Evans Craft Centre of Silk
Bourne Road, Crayford, Kent, DA1 (0322 59401). **Open** 9.30am-5pm Mon-Fri; 9.30am-4pm Sat. **Tours** £1.25 adults; 75p children,

OAPs, students. **Credit** (shop only) A, V.
The last of the London silk printers give guided tours of their mill where you can see the printing and finishing in process. In the shop silk is sold by the metre at mill prices, and there are silk gifts and accessories. *Audio-visual presentation. Café.*

The Glass House
65 Long Acre, WC2 (071 836 9785). Covent Garden underground. **Open** 10am-6pm Mon-Fri; 11am-5pm Sat. **Credit** A, AmEx, DC, V.
Behind this small shop and gallery is a glass partition through which it's possible to watch the bulging cheeks of glass makers in action. The work displayed features four of Britain's best-known contemporary glass makers. Groups should book in advance, as the workshop is small.

Wembley Stadium Tours
Empire Way, Wembley, Middlesex (081 903 4864; recorded information 081 900 1234). Wembley Park tube/Wembley BR. **Tours** phone for details of times and prices.
Young football fans particularly enjoy a visit to this famous sports stadium. The new tour is due to open in April 1990 following major refurbishments. It will include an interactive display of the Stadium's history, visits to the dressing rooms, the Royal Box and the players' tunnel (where you can hear the roar of the crowd). No tours are run on days of major sporting events. *See also chapter* **Sport & Fitness**.

LETTING OFF STEAM

There are boats for hire on the lakes in Regent's Park and Hyde Park, swimming, ice-skating, riding, waterslides and even skiing within easy reach of central London; children are also well catered for at sports centres. **Skateboarding** is staging something of a revival (*see* **picture and caption**) and tennis courts can be hired in Regent's Park, NW1, and Battersea Park, SW11. We've recommended a few places below (*see chapter* **Sport & Fitness** for more details).

Broadgate Ice Rink
Eldon Street, EC2 (071 588 6565). Liverpool Street underground/BR. **Open** *Nov-Apr* **Sessions** 11am-3pm Mon; 11am-3pm, 5.15-8pm, Tue-Fri; 11am-2pm, 3-6pm, Sat, Sun. **Admission** £2.50 adults; £1.25 under-12s, OAPs.
A tiny, outdoor circular rink. The skates for hire are new and the changing rooms are comfortable. On a good day it's glorious. *See chapter* **Sport & Fitness**.

Fulham Baths
Normand Park, Lillie Road, SW6 (071 385 7628). West Brompton underground. **Open** noon-8pm Mon, Thur; noon-3.30pm, 5.15-8pm (adults only), Tue; noon-6pm Wed; noon-4.30pm, 6-8pm (women only), Fri; 9.30am-4pm Sat, Sun, Bank Holidays. **Admission** *Peak hours* £1.60 adult; 80p

The **Brass Rubbing Centre** (*listed under* **Places to Visit**) *is housed in one of London's most famous churches – St Martin-in-the-Fields, off Trafalgar Square. Children can rub replicas of medieval church brasses and so follow a tradition that has been popular in Britain for generations. Try to steer them towards the smaller exhibits; you pay according to size.*

under-16s; 55p OAPs. *Off-peak* noon-4pm 90p adults; 9.30am-noon 90p adults with toddlers, over50s.
Visit the latest swimming attraction – the Space Swirl – incorporating new gimmicks in water-chutes. The pool also has facilites for mothers with young children. Children under nine must be accompanied by an adult. *Café*.

The Serpentine
Maxwell's Boathouse, Hyde Park, W2 (071 262 3751). Knightsbridge or Hyde Park Corner underground. **Open** *summer* 9am-7pm daily; *winter* 9am-3.30pm daily.
Charges *rowing boat (holds 4 people)* £3.75 per hour; *motor boat trip (lasts 10 mins)* 85p per person; *pedal boat (holds 2 people)* £3.50 per hour; *canoes and kayaks (summer only)* £3.50 per hour.
Taking out a rowing boat on the Serpentine is an excellent way of either relaxing or letting off steam (depending on who is rowing). There is also a bathing area open during the summer.

Regent's Park Boating Lake
Maxwell's Boathouse, Regent's Park, NW1 (071 486 4759). Regent's Park underground. **Open** *Mar-Nov* 9am-7pm daily. **Charges** *rowing boat (holds 4 people)* £3.75 per hour; *pedal boat (holds 2 people)* £3.50 per hour; *canoes and kayaks (summer only)* £3.50 per hour.
There's both a large boating lake and small boating lake for children-only in the attractive setting of Regent's Park. Closed in winter.

Queens Ice Skating Club
17 Queensway, W2 (071 229 0172). Queensway or Bayswater underground. **Open** 11am–4.30pm, 7.30–10pm, Mon–Fri; 10am–noon, 2–5pm, 7–10.30pm, Sat; 10am–noon, 2–5pm, 7–10pm Sun. **Admission** £1.30–£3.60 adults; free OAP; £1.60–£2.70 under-15ss. **Skate hire** 90p. **Credit** (shop only) A.
Children's classes (5-6pm Thursdays and Fridays) cost £15 for a four-week course. Children's hours are 5-6pm Monday and Tuesday. *See chapter* **Sport & Fitness**.

Ross Nye Riding Stables
8 Bathurst Mews, W2 (071 262 3791). Lancaster Gate underground. **Open** 7am-4.30pm Tue-Sat; 10am-4.30pm Sun. **Lessons** £12 per hour groups; £16 private.
This riding school has 16 horses for hire. Riding takes place in Hyde Park. *See chapter* **Sport & Fitness**.

SHOPS & MARKETS

Children seem to have an insatiable appetite for delving in toyshops or hunting for bargains on market stalls. **Hamleys** is the perfect place for a rainy day. **Harrods** toy department on the fourth floor is another Aladdin's Cave (especially in late November and December when Father Christmas takes up residence). **Covent Garden Market** is an endless source of delight for chil-

dren. There's a variety of market stalls and small shops including the **Puffin Bookshop** (specially for children), the **Doll's House Shop**, **Eric Snook's Toyshop** and the **Cabaret Mechanical Theatre** (*see below* **Entertainment**) with its fabulous collection of comical automata. Not far from Covent Garden, hidden in the underground shopping arcade at Charing Cross station, is **Davenport's Magic Shop**, a favourite hunting ground for children who collect magical tricks and practical jokes. **Camden Lock Market** and **Carnaby Street** (for both, *see chapter* **To the Eighties**) are popular haunts for teenagers.

Davenport's Magic Shop
Charing Cross Underground Shopping Arcade, Strand, WC2 (071 836 0408). Embankment underground or Charing Cross underground/BR. **Open** 10.30am-5.30pm Mon; 9.30am-5.30pm Tue-Fri; 9.30am-4.30pm Sat. **No credit cards**.
London's oldest magic shop, stocking all the tricks for professional magicians and enthusiasts, plus masks and hundreds of practical jokes.

The Doll's House Shop
29 The Market, Covent Garden Piazza, WC2 (071 379 7243). Covent Garden underground. **Open** 10am-8pm Mon-Sat. **Credit** A, £$TC, V.

Traditional doll's houses are sold in this small shop. You can buy them in kit form or ready-made and there are also miniature furniture accessories.

Eric Snook's Toyshop
32 The Market, Covent Garden Piazza, WC2 (071 379 7681). Covent Garden underground. **Open** 10am-6pm Mon-Sat; 11am-6pm Sun. **Credit** A, AmEx, £TC, V.
You won't find any loud or vulgar toys in this smart and selective Covent Garden shop. Instead there are Beatrix Potter characters such as Jemima Puddleduck, and hand-made wooden soldiers sitting proudly in a carriage.

Hamleys
188 Regent Street, W1 (071 734 3161). Oxford Circus underground. **Open** 9.30am-6pm Mon-Wed, Fri; 9.30am-8pm Thur; 9.30am-6pm Sat. **Credit** A, AmEx, DC, £$TC, V.
See **picture and caption**.
See chapter **Shopping & Services**.
Baby-changing facilities. Restaurant.

Harrods
Knightsbridge, SW1 (071 730 1234). Knightsbridge underground. **Open** 9am-6pm Mon, Tue, Thur-Sat; 9.30am-7pm Wed. **Credit** A, A/c, DC, SC, £$TC, V; most foreign currencies.
The toy department, on the fourth floor of this famous store, is one of the best in town. On the first floor there's a great selection of British and European designer and traditional clothes for children. Good bargains in the January and July sales. *See chapter* **Shopping & Services**.

It's worth getting up early to go to **Chessington World of Adventure** *(listed under* **Places to Visit***). The number of people allowed into this 65-acre/26-hectare, Disney-style theme park is limited and in summer the gates are often closed before lunchtime. The latest attraction is a Transylvania vampire ride which is the first major suspended rollercoaster in Europe. The zoo has a fascinating collection of animals and birds, including gorillas, lions, polar bears and tigers; and there's also a circus. You can get a panoramic view of it all by jumping on board the safari Skyway monorail.*

The Launch Pad, on the first floor of **The Science Museum** *(listed under* **Places to Visit***) is more exciting than ever, with dozens of do-it-yourself experiments to engross children. The Museum fills five floors with scientific inventions and discoveries, from the first steam locomotive to space flights and computers.*

Puffin Bookshop
1 The Market, Covent Garden, WC2 (071 379 6465). Covent Garden underground. **Open** *10am-8pm Mon-Sat; noon-6pm Sun (phone for details).* **Credit** A, AmEx, DC, V.
All Puffin titles are stocked in this well laid-out book store. You will also find a great breadth of classics, fiction, non-fiction, poetry and picture books. They are open most Sundays.

ENTERTAINMENT

Circuses and funfairs (*see chapter* **London by Season**) frequently visit London's parks and open spaces; for details see the weekly **Children** listings in *Time Out* magazine. There's plenty of free entertainment to be found at **Covent Garden Market**, WC2; **Carnaby Street**, W1; and **St Martin-in-the-Fields** (off Trafalgar Square, WC2) with a variety of jugglers, musicians, and other buskers performing through the day.

There are three specialist children's theatres in London and children's shows at theatres such as **Battersea Arts Centre** (*see chapter* **Local London**) and **Riverside**

Studios (*see chapter* **Theatre**). Films for youngsters are shown regularly at Children's Cinema Clubs at the **Barbican Cinema**, **Everyman**, **ICA** and the **National Film Theatre** (*see chapter* **Film**).

In summer, look out for free children's shows in the parks, particularly at the children's playgrounds in Kensington Gardens and Regent's Park (*see chapter* **Sightseeing**). At Greenwich Park (*see chapter* **The River & Docklands**), SE10, there are free puppet shows (at 11am and 2.30pm) from Mondays to Saturdays through August. See *Time Out* magazine for details.

Cabaret Mechanical Theatre
33 The Market, Covent Garden Piazza, WC2 (071 379 7961). Covent Garden underground. **Open** *Easter-Sept* 10am-7pm daily; *Oct-Easter* noon-6.30pm Mon; 10am-6.30pm Tue-Sun. **Admission** £1.50 adults; 75p under-16s, OAPs, students; free under 5s; family ticket £3.50 (2 adults, 3 children), UB40s.**Credit** (shop only) A, AmEx, DC, £TC, V.
A unique collection of comical push-button machines and colourful automata are housed in these small premises. All the gadgets are made by contemporary craftsworkers and inventors. There's also a shop where you can buy some of these marvellous machines – at a price. *Group discount. Shop.*

Little Angel Marionette Theatre
14 Dagmar Passage, off Cross Street, N1 (071 226 1787). Highbury & Islington underground/BR. **Performances** 11am Sat (3-5s); 3pm Sat, Sun (over-6s); extra shows at half-term and school holidays, phone for details. **Admission** £3.50 adults; £2.50 under-17s. **No credit cards.**
The only permanent puppet theatre in London. Its a delightful place with seating for 110, and is hidden away in Islington. There are regular weekend and holiday performances and they usually book a visiting company for August.

Lyric Theatre Hammersmith
King Street, W6 (081 741 2311). Hammersmith underground. **Performance** 11am Sat; noon Sun. **Admission** £1.50. **Credit** A, AmEx, DC, V.
Children's entertainment, from plays and puppets to clowns and workshops, is put on every weekend.
Wheelchair access by prior arrangement.

Polka Children's Theatre
240 The Broadway, SW19 (081 543 0363/081 543 4888).Wimbledon South underground/Wimbledon BR. **Open** *box office* 9.30am-4.30pm Tue-Fri; 11am-5.30pm Sat. **Admission** £2-£5.30. **No credit cards.**
A purpose-built complex for the under-12s, with a 300-seat theatre, an adventure playground and exhibitions related to the performances. They stage colourful and imaginative productions of specially-commissioned children's plays and puppet shows.
Café. Induction loop for the hard of hearing. Wheelchair access.

Tricycle Theatre
269 Kilburn High Road, NW6 (boc office 071 328 1000/information 071 372 6611). Kilburn underground. **Performances** 11.30am, 2pm Sat; extra matinées during Christmas and Summer holidays. **Admission** *in advance* £1.50; *on the day* £2 . **Credit** A, AmEx, £TC, V.
After rebuilding following a fire, the Tricycle has continued with its superb children's shows and after-school and holiday workshops. On Saturdays, the café's children's menu is good value at £2.50.
Bar. Café. Wheelchair access.

Unicorn Theatre for Children
6 Great Newport Street, WC2 (071 836 3334). Leicester Square underground. **Open** *box office* 10am-8pm Mon-Sat. **Performances** *term time* 10.30am, 1.30pm Tue-Fri; 2.30pm Sat, Sun; *school holidays* 2.30pm Tue-Sun. **Admission** £3-£5.50, plus 10p temporary membership. **No credit cards.**
Founded in 1948, this is London's oldest professional children's theatre. It puts on an adventurous programme of specially commissioned plays and other entertainment (puppets, magic, music) for 4-12-year olds. The Children's Club organizes weekend and holiday workshops through the year.
Café.

EATING

These restaurants and cafés have been recommended to us by parents and children. It's always wise to check the arrangements and book in advance when going to a restaurant with children. This is especially the case for Sunday lunches.

The big problem is where to eat when you're in the middle of doing something else, like sightseeing or shopping, so we selected the following with this in mind. If you're stuck in Oxford Street, the restaurants in **Selfridges** and **Bhs** are reliable, with good value children's menus. Kew Gardens has the wonderful **Maids of Honour** café (*see chapter* **The River & Docklands**). Of course, for teenagers the **Hard Rock Café**, Piccadilly is a must-see. Convenient for Trafalgar Square is **Fields**, in St Martin-in-the-Fields crypt; for details of this and many other restaurants ,(*see chapter* **Eating& Drinking**).

Bhs
101-111 Kensington High Street, W8 (071 937 0919). High Street Kensington underground. **Open** *9am-6pm Mon-Sat.* **Average** *£5.50 adults, £1.55 under 12s.* **Credit** A, DC, £TC, V. The children's menu is good value, but is somewhat limited to the classic favourites: fish fingers, chips, ice-cream and jellies. *Baby changing facilities. Toilet for the disabled. Wheelchair access.*

Holland Park Café
Holland Park, W8 (071 602 2216). Kensington High Street or Holland Park underground. **Open** *Feb-Dec* 10am-30 mins before sunset. **Average** £3 adults, £1 children. **No credit cards**. This delightfully situated café has plenty of outside seating. Wholesome, home-made Italian food – soup, pizza, ice-cream – is on the menu. A child's portion of spaghetti costs just £1.

Legends Café
17-18 King William Walk, SE10 (081 858 0871). Greenwich BR/boat to Greenwich pier/Island Gardens DLR then foot tunnel to Greenwich. **Open** 11.30am-11pm daily.. **Average** £4.50 adults, £1.50 children.. **Credit** A, AmEx, DC, £TC, V. This family-owned restaurant by Greenwich Park is very convenient for all the sights nearby. The three-course set lunch is excellent value – and there are plenty of children's favourites; beefburger, egg, sausage and chips.

Marine Ices
8 Haverstock Hill, NW3 (071 485 3132). Chalk Farm underground. **Open** *Ice-cream parlour* 10.30am-10.15pm Mon-Sat; noon-8pm Sun. **Average** *Ice cream* £1 **No credit cards**. An Italian restaurant and ice-cream parlour. The fresh pastas and pizzas are delicious, but the ices and sorbets, made on the premises without additives, are the main attraction for kids.

Picnic
108 Seymour Place, W1 (071 723 2107). Baker Street underground. **Open** 8am-8pm Mon-Fri; 11am-3pm Sat. **Average** £7adults. **Credit** A, AmEx, DC, LV, £TC, V. A large, popular Jewish restaurant near Madame Tussaud's, the Planetarium and Regent's Park. Family favourites such as salt-beef, schnitzel, goulash, drumsticks, apfel-strudel and trifle are on the menu, all of which is kosher. There are reduced-price children's portions on request and a high chair for babies.

Smollensky's Balloon
1 Dover Street, W1 (071 491 1199). Green Park underground. **Open** noon-midnight Mon-Sat; noon-10.30pm Sun; *Family lunches* noon-3pm Sat, Sun. **Average** £15 adults, £6 children. **Credit** A, AmEx, DC, V. Highly recommended for family lunches at weekends. The children's menu has burgers, junior steaks, and mouth-watering desserts. There's also balloons, magic tricks at your table and a puppet show from 2.30 to 3pm. It's essential to book.

Texas Lone Star Saloon
154 Gloucester Road, SW7 (071 370 5625). Gloucester Road underground. **Open** noon-11.30pm Mon-Wed; noon-12.15am Thur-Sat; noon-11.15pm. **Average** £8 adults. **Credit** £TC. This Tex-Mex restaurant is done out like a saloon, complete with Wild West videos. It's a hit with kids,who also enjoy the ribs, burgers, pecan pie and ice-cream.

Tony Roma's
46 St Martin's Lane, WC2 (071 379 3300). Leicester Square underground. **Open** noon-2.30pm daily; children's menu 12.30-2.30pm Sun. **Average** £14 adults. **Credit** A, AmEx, DC, £TC, V. American-style chicken and ribs dishes, with children's portions on Sunday for £2.95, plus a magician at the tables 1.30-2.30pm. Book ahead.

Villa Estense
624 King's Road, SW6 (071 731 4247). Fulham Broadway or Sloane Square underground/11, 19, 22, 137, 219, C1 bus. **Lunch** 12.30-2.30am daily;. **Dinner** 7-11pm Mon-Sat. **Average** £15 adults. **Credit** A, AmEx, V. The family lunches on Saturdays and Sundays have a choice of pizza and pasta dishes from £2.50. There's a disco downstairs for 5-12-year-olds.

STAYING UP LATE

Parents may need some persuading but evenings are a great time for window shopping. **Covent Garden** stays lively in the evening and wandering around **Chinatown** is especially exciting. The brightly-lit restaurants and supermarkets, full of strange and exotic delicacies, don't close till late (for both *see chapter* **The West End**).

Some Sports Centres and

The South Bank, SE1 has become a favourite hang-out for **skateboarders** *(listed under* **Letting Off Steam***) and many skilful practitioners can be seen in action. The concrete dips and curves of the architecture make it an ideal place to swerve and turn. Another popular (and free) venue is around the Albert Memorial, Kensington Gardens. Quite what Prince Albert would have thought of this activity is a moot point.*

Swimming Pools also stay open on some evenings (*see chapter* **Sport & Fitness**). But if you're looking for entertainment, remember the **Guiness World of Records** and **Rock Circus** (*see chapter* **Sightseeing**) are usefully open every night until 10pm. Many museums have occasional early-evening sessions.

The month before Christmas is a great time to be in London after dark. **Selfridges** and **Hamleys** are famous for their window displays; there are Christmas lights and decorations through Oxford Street, Regent Street, Carnaby Street, Covent Garden Market, Piccadilly and Burlington Arcade; and a giant tree (London's annual Christmas present from Norway) in Trafalgar Square.

UNDER-FIVES

Pacifying an irritable toddler after dragging it round sightseeing is not impossible in London. **One O'Clock Clubs** are free, enclosed areas in parks exclusively for under-5s, who must be accompanied by an adult. Run by local councils, they provide indoor and outdoor play with sand, water, paints, wendy houses, books, climbing frames and push-along toys. If you take an under-five-year-old to a swimmming pool (*see above* and **Sport & Fitness**), the water temperature should be 82-84°F/28-29°C.

The Islands, Alexandra Park
The Grove, N22 (081 883 7173). Wood Green underground/Alexandra Palace BR/then W3 bus. **Open** 1-4pm Mon-Fri.

Barnard Park
Barnsbury Road, N1 (071 278 9494). Angel underground/Caledonian Road & Barnsbury BR. **Open** 9.30am-noon, 1-4pm Mon-Fri.

Battersea Park
Albert Bridge Road, SW11 (081 871 6349). Sloane Square underground/Battersea Park or Queenstown Road BR/ 19, 39, 44, 45, 49, 130, 137 or 170 bus. **Open** *office:* 9.30am-4pm.

Holland Park
Abbotsbury Road entrance, W8 (071 603 2838). Holland Park underground. **Open** 1-4pm Mon-Fri.

Hamleys *(listed under* **Shops & Markets***) is the most famous toy shop in the world. It's a paradise for children, with five floors filled with toys and games of every imaginable description – radio-controlled cars and planes, computer games, magic tricks, model kits, puzzles and puppets, miniature railways and sports equipment, dolls and (of course) plenty of teddy bears. There are dozens of working models and demonstrations, so the whole place is like a gigantic play-ground.*

TAKING A BREAK

There may be times when parents and children need a break from each other. Here are a few places where you can find a babysitter, or leave the kids to play.

Central YMCA
112 Great Russell Street, WC1 (071 637 8131). Tottenham Court Road underground. **Open** (Junior Programme) 10am-noon Sat. **Admission** 85p.
The junior programme on Saturday mornings welcomes 9- to 16-year olds, for two hours of activities. You can choose from art, pottery, basketball, climbing, gymnastics, table-tennis, trampolining and swimming, with excellent facilities and tuition. Bring sports clothes. *See also chapter* **Sport & Fitness**.

Childminders
9 Paddington Street, W1 (071 935 2049/071 935 9763). **Open** 9am-1pm Mon-Fri; 2-4.30pm Sat. **Rates** *day* £3.75 per hour; *evening* (from 6.30pm) £2.45 per hour Sun-Wed; £2.55 per hour, Thur, Fri; £3.25 per hour Sat. **Minimum** £4 plus fare. **No credit cards**.
A large agency with over 1,000 referred babysitters (mainly nurses and infant teachers) who live all over London and the suburbs.

Marshall Street Leisure Centre
Marshall Street, W1 (071 798 2007). Oxford Circus underground. **Open** 10am-1pm Sat. **Admission** £3 per child. **Credit** A
A useful 'drop and shop' session just near Oxford Circus. While parents shop in the West End, 6 to 13-year olds can be left to tire themselves out at the leisure centre. Activities include table tennis, short tennis, gymnastics, keep-fit, and a fun swim with inflatables.

Universal Aunts
250 King's Road, SW3 (071 351 5767). **Open** 9.30am-5.30pm Mon-Fri. **Booking fee** £3 (under 5 hours), £6 (over 5 hours). **Rates** *evening* (from 6pm) £2.50 per hour; *day* £4 per hour. **No credit cards**.
An old-established agency that can provide proxy parents to babysit or take children sight-seeing for the day.

INFORMATION

Circusline
(0522 681591). **Open** 24 hours daily.
Recorded information on circuses performing around Britain.

Kidsline
(071 222 8070). **Open** *term-time* 4-6pm Mon-Fri; *school holidays* 9am-4pm Mon-Fri. Information on children's clubs, classes, sports, holiday activities and entertainment all over London.

Sportsline
(071 222 8000). **Open** 10am-6pm Mon-Fri. Information about every sport in London, and details of your nearest club or class.

New Comedy

No other city in the world has as many comedy clubs as London. *Malcolm Hay* of *Time Out* chortles his way around the venues.

It all started back in 1979 with the **Comedy Store**, now situated in a Leicester Square basement. Since then, what became known as 'alternative cabaret', or more recently 'new comedy', has grown to the point where there are well over 50 different venues in London. And the number continues to multiply from month to month. For those who relish comedy, and for anyone in search of an exciting and relatively cheap night out, watching alternative cabaret can soon become a habit that is happily hard to break.

Stand-up comedians are the backbone of new comedy. They come in many different shapes and forms, ranging from those with radical views to the more surrealist types, from the reflective to the fiercely aggressive, as well as some who are just downright silly. But many clubs provide what is essentially variety entertainment: alongside the stand-ups are musicians, jugglers, magicians and acts that simply defy description.

Performers from the live cabaret circuit are now regularly appearing on TV, both in late-night comedy shows and in a host of advertisements (what's 'alternative' about that?, you may well ask). But the clubs are where they began their careers and where many of them still provide their most dynamic entertainment. The clubs are normally to be found in the back rooms of pubs or the studio spaces in fringe theatres. They vary greatly in size and in their suitability for live comedy. Ideal semi-circular spaces such as **Banana Cabaret**, which can hold about 200 people, are unfortunately the exception rather than the rule. But even the smaller venues with just a few tables can serve up cracking good performances. The most important factor, after all, is the quality of the acts. And the large pool of talent that London promoters can draw on is now a virtual insurance against finding any show completely disappointing, wherever you choose to go.

The cost for a night out generally ranges from £2 to £7 (the top price at top clubs like the **Comedy Store** and **Jongleurs**). But be warned: by its very nature, the cabaret circuit is not entirely predictable. Venues come and go and even long-established clubs suddenly bite the dust, when the premises are redeveloped or the pub is taken over by an unfriendly landlord. Bear in mind, too, that more than half the regular venues close down during late July and the whole of August, when many comedians head off to the **Edinburgh Festival** *(see chapter* **Trips Out of Town***)*. The list below gives a guide to the best of the current clubs. You'd be well advised, though, to check the weekly listings in *Time Out* before you risk a trek to NW6 or SW11, only to discover that the developers moved in the week before. But for every venue which sadly disappears, two or three are likely to spring up in the blinking of an eye. The true test of any form of entertainment is its capacity to continually renew itself.

CENTRAL

Alley Club
at The Horse & Groom, 128 Great Portland Street, W1 (information 081 646 1324). Great Portland Street or Oxford Circus underground. **Open** 8.15pm Sat **Performances** 9pm. **Admission** £3; £2.50 students, UB40s.
A pleasant, intimate atmosphere is created in this club, held in a small room above a pub. Stand-up comedy provides the entertainment.

Apples & Snakes
Covent Garden Community Centre, 46 Earlham Street, WC2 (information 081 690 9368). Covent Garden underground. **Performances** 8pm Fri. **Admission** £3.50; £2.50 students, UB40s.
This is London's only regular weekly cabaret devoted to performance poetry and comic poets. These are combined with music acts and, rarely, stand-up comedians.

Chuckle Club
15 Bressenden Place, SW1 (071 828 7827). Victoria underground/BR. **Open** 7.45pm Fri, Sat. **Performances** 8.30pm. **Admission** £3.50; £2.50 students, UB40s.
Resident host Eugene Cheese transforms a fairly unprepossessing room into a palace of delights through his silliness and sheer amiability. High quality acts are booked.

Comedy Store
28A Leicester Square, WC2 (071 839 6665). Leicester Square underground. **Open** 8pm Wed, Thur; 8pm, 11pm Fri, Sat; 7.30pm Sun. **Performances** 9pm Wed, Thur; 8pm, midnight Fri, Sat; 8.30pm Sun. **Admission** £5-£7.
The place where alternative comedy began is still the most famous comedy club in the country. The crowds queue for stand-up performances on Fridays and Saturdays, but there's a more relaxed combination of stand-up and music on Thursdays. The infinitely talented Comedy Store Players (*see* **picture and caption**) purvey improvised comedy on Wednesdays.

Guilty Pea
The Wheatsheaf, 25 Rathbone Place, WC1 (information 081 986 6881). Tottenham Court Road underground. **Open** 8pm Sat. **Performances** 8.30pm. **Admission** £3.50; £2.50 students, UB40s.
A small and intimate pub venue with comedy bills largely devoted to new acts.

Oranje Boom Boom
De Hems Dutch Coffee Bar, Macclesfield Street, W1 (071 701 6605/071 706 3531). Leicester Square or Piccadilly Circus underground. **Open** 8pm Wed. **Performances** 8.45pm. **Admission** £3.50; £2.50 students, UB40s.
One of the first coffee bars to be penetrated by cabaret (but alcohol is also sold). You're likely to see a fair number of newish acts, along with those who've already established a reputation.

Tattershall Castle
Victoria Embankment, SW1 (071 839 6548). Embankment underground or Charing Cross underground/BR/59 bus. **Open** 7.30pm Sun. **Performances** 8pm. **Admission** £3; £2.50 students, UB40s.
London's only floating cabaret: it's held on a paddle steamer moored on the Thames, opposite Embankment tube. The décor is pleasant and the swell from passing boats sets you rocking very gently as you watch the show. *See chapter* **Nightlife**.

WEST

Canal Café Theatre
The Bridge House, Delamere Terrace, W2 (071 289 6054). Warwick Avenue underground. **Performances** times vary. **Membership** 25p per year. **Admission** £2.50-£5.
Improvised comedy and scripted pieces are more usual than cabaret bills at this fringe theatre beside the canal in Little Venice. It's also the home of Newsrevue, a group which mounts revues based on topical events.

Ealing Comedy
The Queen Victoria, St Mary's Road, W5. South Ealing or Ealing Broadway underground. **Performances** 8pm Sun. **Admission** £3.50; £2.50 students, UB40s.
A combination of new and established acts elicit titters at this Ealing pub. The atmosphere is relaxed and amiable, despite the stern portrait of Queen Victoria hanging on a wall behind the stage.

Gate Theatre
The Prince Albert, 11 Pembridge Road, W11 (071 229 0706). Notting Hill Gate underground/3, 28, 52A bus. **Open** 10pm Thur, Fri. **Membership** £1 per year. **Admission** £4; £3 students, UB40s.

Imaginative programming at this fringe theatre combines plays with regular cabaret performances, a full season of comedy during August, and improvised comedy (now a very popular form) late-night at various points throughout the year. *See chapter* **Theatre**.

SOUTH WEST

Banana Cabaret
The Bedford, Bedford Hill, SW12 (081 673 8904). Balham underground/BR. **Open** 7.30pm Fri, Sat; 8pm Sun. **Performances** 9pm Fri, Sat; 8.30pm Sun. **Admission** £3.50; £2.50 students, UB40s.
One of the most enterprising and enjoyable clubs in London. Downstairs the large, circular domed room looks like a stage set. Upstairs a smaller space with wooden panels provides a cosier atmosphere. Promoter Andy Waring books excellent cabaret entertainment in both.

Battersea Arts Centre
Old Town Hall, Lavender Hill, SW11 (071 223 2223). Battersea Park or Clapham

The **Comedy Store Players** *(listed under* **Central: Comedy Store***) are renowned for the brilliance of their on-the-spot improvisations. They're part of the exciting increase in the number of groups performing improvised comedy. The attractions of impro are its unpredictability and spontaneity: comedy games, sketches, scenes, soap operas, even improvised plays are all based on suggestions made by the audience. Other skilled practitioners include the outfit headed by Peter Wear (which often appears at the* **Gate Theatre** *listed under* **West***) and the brash and boisterous London Theatresports group, whose performances resemble sporting contests, complete with referees.*

Junction BR. **Performances** 9.15pm Fri. **Membership** £1 for six months. **Admission** £3.50; £2.50 students, UB40s.
Two performance-spaces house theatre, dance, music and occasional cabaret shows. *See chapter* **Local London**.

Cartoon at Clapham
The Plough Inn, 196-198 Clapham High Street, SW4 (071 738 8763). Clapham Common underground. **Open** 8.30pm Fri, Sat. **Performances** 9pm. **Admission** £3-£3.50 Fri; £3 50-£4 Sat.
A large pub venue with plenty of tables. It's relatively comfortable and generally good value. The bar is open until midnight.

CAST New Variety
The Old White Horse, 261 Brixton Road, SW9 (071 487 3440). Brixton underground. **Performances** 9pm Fri. **Admission** £3.50.
The enterprising CAST organization, which also runs the Hackney Empire, books a bill of comedians and speciality acts to play on the site of a nineteenth-century music hall.

Jongleurs at The Cornet
49 Lavender Gardens, SW11 (081 780 1151). Clapham Common underground then 45 bus/Clapham Junction BR. **Open** 8pm Fri, Sat. **Performances** 9.30pm. **Membership** £2.50 per year. **Admission** £6; £4 students, UB40s.
One of the most popular clubs on the circuit – you're advised to book well in advance. Top acts appear every week, the food is reasonable, the bar is open until 1.30am, and the audience is often very lively indeed.

Jongleurs at the Wessex
1 St Johns Hill, SW11 (081 780 1151). Clapham Junction BR. **Open** 8.30pm Sat. **Performances** 10pm. **Admission** £6; £4 students, UB40s.
A second Jongleurs venue which opens on Saturday nights at peak periods in the year for cabaret (normally October to May). You'll find a similar high-quality bill to the sister venue (*see above*).

Screaming Blue Murder
The White Lion, 232-236 Streatham High Road, SW16 (081 543 6329). Streatham BR. **Open** 8pm Mon. **Performances** 8.30pm. **Admission** £3.50; £3 students, UB40s.
The room is far from prepossessing, but the line-ups offer a good, representative sample of the acts currently performing on the London circuit.

SOUTH EAST

Albany Empire
Douglas Way, SE8 (081 691 3333). New Cross underground/Deptford or New Cross BR. **Open** 7.30pm-midnight Sun. **Performances** 8pm. **Membership** £8 per year. **Admission** £4.50; £3.50 students, UB40s.
The Empire is like a cross between a huge circus tent and a planetarium, but it makes a splendid, enchanting performance-space. Occasional comedy shows and cabarets occur here throughout the year.

East Dulwich Cabaret
The East Dulwich Tavern, 1 Lordship Lane, SE22 (081 299 4138). East Dulwich BR. **Open** 9pm Fri, Sat. **Performances** 10pm. **Admission** £4; £3 students, UB40s.
A pub venue that has line-ups of reliable quality in an area of London which isn't blessed with many comedy clubs. The bar is open until midnight.

South of Deptford
The Tramshed, 51 Woolwich New Road, SE18 (081 317 8687). Woolwich Arsenal BR/51, 53, N77, N82, 99, 122, 180, 272, 469 bus. **Open** 7.30pm Sat. **Performances** 8.30pm. **Membership** £10 per year. **Admission** £2.50-£5; £2-£4.50 students, UB40s.
The Tramshed is less cramped than many clubs. Although it's quite a trek out of the centre of town, the trip is worth it. Acts are booked by enterprising promoter Addison Cresswell of Off the Kerb Productions. The bar is open until midnight.

EAST

Hackney Cabaret
Unity Club, 96 Dalston Lane, E8 (081 986 3485). Dalston Kingsland or Hackney Downs BR. **Open** 9pm Fri. **Performances** 9.30pm. **Membership** 50p (valid for 12 performances). **Admission** £3; £2 students, UB40s.

Resident host and promoter Ian Pilchard has recently moved his Hackney Cabaret to this venue. The blend of well-known and new acts gives a good idea of what the circuit has to offer.

Hackney Empire
291 Mare Street, E8 (081 985 2424).
Hackney Central or Hackney Downs BR/22,
35, 38, 55, 106, 253 bus. **Open** *Oct-Easter*
7pm Sat. **Performances** 8.30pm.
Admission £5-£10. **Credit** A, V.
One of London's famous old variety theatres is now a home for new comedy of every kind. The spectacular mock-Turkish interior is almost as beguiling as the shows, which range from star-studded cabaret bills to special solo performances by big names such as Joan Collins Fan Club and Harry Enfield. *See chapter* **Early Twentieth Century**.

NORTH
Black Cat Cabaret
The Rose & Crown, 199 Stoke Newington
Church Street, N16 (071 254 7497). Manor
House underground or Stoke Newington BR.

Performances 9pm Fri, Sat. **Admission** £3; £2.50 students, UB40s.
Resident compere and club organizer Piers Gladhill makes a point of giving new acts a platform to show their talent. The resulting performances might be variable in quality, but there is always something to enjoy. A good place to spot some of the stars of the future.

CAST New Variety
Wood Green TU Centre, Station Road, N22
(071 487 3440). Wood Green underground.
Open *Oct-Jun* 8pm Sun. **Performances**
8.45pm. **Admission** £4.
The New Variety Sunday date features bright new acts at the beginning of their careers. The venue is styled like a working men's club from the north of England, and makes for a great atmosphere.

Downstairs at The King's Head
2 Crouch End Hill, N8 (081 340 1028).
Finsbury Park underground/BR then W7 bus.
Open 8pm Sat; 7.45pm Sun. **Performances**
8.30pm. **Membership** 50p per year.
Admission £3; £2 students, UB40s.

Run by Peter Grahame, one of the most respected promoters, the club is well equipped and the audiences are remarkably genial and friendly. Highly recommended.

Meccano Club
The Market Tavern, 2 Essex Road, N1 (081
800 2236). Angel underground. **Open**
8.30pm Fri, Sat. **Performances** 9pm.
Admission £3.50; £3 students, UB40s.
There's a very low ceiling here and the intimacy often brings out the best from comedians.

Red Rose Cabaret
129 Seven Sisters Road, N7 (071 263 7265).
Finsbury Park or Holloway Road under-
ground. **Performances** 9.30pm Fri, Sat.
Membership 50p per year. **Admission**
£3.50; £2.50 students, UB40s.
See **picture and caption**.

T & C 2
20-22 Highbury Corner, N5 (071 700 5716).
Highbury & Islington underground. **Open**
7.30pm Sat. **Performances** 8.30pm.
Admission £5.
There's usually a good atmosphere in this large room with comfortable seating. Holders of tickets for the cabaret are entitled to attend the subsequent disco free. The bar is open until 2am and food is sold.

NORTH WEST
Delivery Room
La Folie Wine Bar, 53 Salusbury Road, NW6
(071 624 9153). Queen's Park underground.
Open 8pm Thur. **Performances** 8.30pm.
Admission £3.50; £2.50 students, UB40s.
One of the very few comedy clubs to set up shop in a wine bar. The place has a very pleasant feel and it's well worth a visit.

Punchline Comedy Club
The Railway, West End Lane, NW6 (081 969
8351). West Hampstead underground/BR.
Open 8pm Sat. **Performances** 8.30pm.
Admission £3.50; £2.50 students, UB40s.
A justifiably popular venue, so it's advisable to go early. The performances are mainly oriented towards stand-up comedy. The bar is licensed until midnight.

Town & Country Club
Uptown Bar, Town and Country Club, 9-17
Highgate Road, NW5 (071 485 5256).
Kentish Town underground. **Open** 10.30pm
Fri. **Admission** £5 (includes nightclub after the show).
A celebrated live music venue (*see chapter*
Music: Rock, Folk & Jazz) which has established Friday night comedy shows of good quality. The bar at the disco following the cabaret is open until 3am.

MIDDLESEX
Bearcat Club
The Turk's Head, Winchester Road, St
Margaret's, Twickenham, Middlesex (081
892 1972). St Margaret's BR, then 37 bus.
Performances 8pm alternate Mon.
Membership 50p for life. **Admission** £3.50;
£2.50 students, UB40s.
Probably the most reliable club on the outskirts of London – the organizers have a lot of experience in mounting alternative cabaret and the bills usually mix stand-up comedy with a wide range of different kinds of acts.

Comedian **Ivor Dembina** *has made* **Red Rose Cabaret** *(listed under* **North***) a club that rivals top venues for the quality of the entertainment on offer at half the admission price of the Comedy Store. His cheery style as resident host also gives the club a strong identity of its own. Sit at the long, raised table at one end of the room and you can imagine you're part of a tableau representing The Last Supper.*

Dance

Dance is one of London's most varied forms of live entertainment. *Allen Robertson, Time Out's Dance editor, takes us on a twirl round the hot spots.*

Dance can be many different things, catering for all types of audiences and budgets. Famous ballet companies from the Soviet Union and the US regularly visit London, but there's also plenty of physical activity from a plethora of troupes, both big and small, based in the capital. The diverse menu ranges from the greatest of classics, such as *Swan Lake* and *The Sleeping Beauty*, to contemporary masterpieces, world premières and radical experimentations that spotlight the latest ideas.

Surprisingly, dance in London is affordable and sometimes even ludicrously cheap. Although the best seats in the major theatres can cost from about £15 to £25, they are considerably less for fringe venues, where prices are usually about £5. And even at the large theatres, it's usually possible to get a cheap standby ticket – if you're prepared to queue. Having said that, it must be pointed out that for visiting companies such as the Bolshoi Ballet, a ticket can cost in excess of £50.

Here's a rundown of the major London venues, from the plush and grand expanses of the **Coliseum** to the intimate bonhomie of **The Place**.

MAJOR VENUES

ICA
The Mall, SW1 (071 930 3647; membership enquiries 071 930 0493; recorded information 071 930 6393). Piccadilly Circus underground or Charing Cross underground/BR. **Open** *box office noon-9.30pm daily.* **Tickets** *£6.60 adults; £5.60 OAPs, students.* **Credit** A, AmEx, DC, £TC, V.
Much of the dance presented at the ICA belongs to the genre known as performance art. Tending to be radical, eclectic and nonconformist, performance art breaks down conventional notions through an uninhibited mix of movement, music, text, mime and design. The result is a hybrid that often can't be confined within standard definitions of either dance or theatre. The Institute is a beehive of activity, with galleries, a cinema, an extensive video library, a bookshop, a bar and a restaurant. The ICA theatre has seating for approximately 200 people. *See also*

chapters **Art Galleries**, **Film** and **Theatre**. *Bar. Bookshop. Café. Group discount. Lectures. Workshops.*

The London Coliseum
St Martin's Lane, WC2 (071 836 3161; credit card 071 240 5258; recorded information 071 836 7666). Leicester Square underground or Charing Cross underground/BR. **Open** *box office 10am-9pm Mon-Sat.* **Tickets** *£3-£33.* **Credit** A, AmEx, DC, £STC, V.
This 2,530-seat theatre, London's biggest, is home to the English National Opera. During the summer months, while the opera is off, dance moves in. It's one of London's most spacious and attractive theatres and is the first choice of visiting foreign companies. The Bolshoi and Kirov Ballets have frequently been seen here. The Dance Theatre of Harlem and the National Ballet of Canada have also played the 'Collie'. Champagne and coffee bars are dotted around the theatre, but sandwiches and dessert goodies are on sale in the Edwardian ambience of the Dutch Bar, hidden away in the cellar. Stand-by tickets are sold at reduced prices on the day of performance. *See also chapter* **Music: Classical & Opera**.
Group & family discount (071 836 0111 ext 318). Shop (10am-7.30pm Mon-Sat). Toilets for the disabled. Wheelchair access.

The Place
17 Duke's Road, WC1 (071 387 0031). Euston underground/BR. **Open** *box office noon-6pm Mon-Fri; Sat, when there is a performance.* **Tickets** *£4-£7; concessionary rates for OAPs, students, UB40s, Camden residents.* **Credit** A, £TC, V.
Cheap ticket prices and an intimate performance space (it only seats 250) have helped keep The Place one of the most exciting dance spots in the country. The building is home to the London Contemporary Dance School, which explains the full-length mirrors in the foyer – it's a classroom by day. The programming over recent years has included regular seasons such as: *Spring Loaded* (new British dance); *April in Paris* (the best from France); *Indian Summer* (a variety of classical and folk dance from the Subcontinent); and **Dance Umbrella** (*see below* **Special Attractions**).
Wheelchair access.

Riverside Studios
Crisp Road, W6 (081 748 3354). Hammersmith underground. **Open** *box office noon-8pm daily.* **Tickets** *£7; £5 OAPs, students, UB40s.* **Credit** A, V.
Originally built as television studios for the BBC, this venue is now a busy arts complex with a gallery, an excellent buffet, a bar, a book-shop, workshops and two performance spaces of 375 and 240 seats respectively. *See also chapters* **Art Galleries** and **Theatre**.
Bar. Bookshop. Café. Restaurant. Wheelchair access.

Royal Opera House
Covent Garden, WC2 (071 240 1066). Covent Garden underground. **Open** *box office 10am-8pm Mon-Sat.* **Tickets** *£8.50-£82.* **Credit** A, AmEx, DC, V.
The queen of London's posh theatres, this handsome 2,000-seat house is regally decorated. It provides a home for both the Royal Ballet and the Royal Opera. There's a house policy that holds back 65 rear amphitheatre seats for sale that day only. When an event is sold out, there are also approximately 50 standing-room places available. Patient queuing, at the advance box office around the corner in Floral Street, is usually required. If the performance is a popular one, the line can start to form at the crack of dawn. Be warned, tickets are strictly limited to one per person. If you get into the theatre that evening, you can munch expensive sandwiches and rub elbows with lots of well-heeled champagne-guzzlers. A favourite interval pastime is spotting the celebrities who congregate in the upstairs bar. There's an extensive bookshop at the back of the building (on James Street) which stocks ballet and opera videos as well as books. *See also chapters* **Sightseeing** and **Music: Classical & opera**.
Opera and ballet education officers. Shop. Wheelchair access. Toilets for the disabled.

Sadler's Wells Theatre
Rosebery Avenue, EC1 (071 278 8916). Angel underground. **Open** *box office 10.30am-7.30pm Mon-Sat (till 6.30pm when there's no performance).* **Tickets** *Main theatre £4-£25; Lilian Baylis theatre £1-£7.* **Credit** A, AmEx, DC, £TC, V.
Sadler's Wells Royal Ballet moves its home to the Birmingham Hippodrome in Oct 1990 when it will be known as the Birmingham Royal Ballet. But this departure will not affect the theatre's diverse programming. This historic 1,500-seat theatre is the most popular dance venue in London. The stage isn't the world's largest, but sightlines are exceptionally good, particularly in the dress circle. Major dance companies from home and abroad all pay regular visits to the Wells: from flamenco and Lindsey Kemp, to the Northern Ballet Theatre and the Bolshoi Ballet of Byelorussia. Whirligig Theatre, Britain's leading company for children, performs a season every autumn. The de Valois wine bar serves meals both before and after performances. Drinks are sold in the three bars – all of which can be a tight squeeze when there's a full-house. The theatre has a policy of reserving 50 stalls tickets for sale on the day of performance only. They're sold from 10.30am at the advance box office, on the corner across the road. The Lilian Baylis Theatre (*see chapter* **Theatre**) is the latest addition to the Wells complex. Situated in Arlington Way, behind the main theatre, this studio opened in October 1988. It's named after the immortal Lilian – who saved the theatre from extinction in 1931 – and it holds just over 200 people. Tickets for Baylis performances are rock bottom in price for often experimental, small-scale dance, theatre, and music performances.
Restaurant. Toilets for the disabled. Wheelchair access to main theatre.

South Bank Centre
South Bank, Belvedere Road, SE1 (box office 071 928 8800; general information 071 928 3002; recorded information 071 633

0932).*Waterloo underground/BR/Riverbus.*
Open *box office* 10am-10pm daily. **Tickets**
£3-£50 **Credit** A, AmEx, DC, V.
This centrally-located riverside complex
includes three separate theatres which are
used for dance and music. The biggest theatre, the **Royal Festival Hall**, holds 3,000
people and offers excellent viewing no matter where you sit. It was built to commemorate the Festival of Britain in 1951 (*see chapter* **To the Eighties**) and was originally occupied by the London Festival Ballet, a company first formed for that occasion. In 1989
the troupe, under the direction of Danish-
born Peter Schaufuss, changed its name to
English National Ballet. Each year, ENB presents a month-long season of *The Nutcracker*,
which opens on Boxing Day. It also puts on a
summer season that lasts between three and
six weeks. The **Queen Elizabeth Hall** holds
1,000 people and is designed like a lecture
hall. However, the sightlines are good, even if
the atmosphere is somewhat impersonal.
The intimate **Purcell Room** – which shares
the same foyer as the Queen Elizabeth Hall –
holds just 375 people. The bustling South
Bank complex provides many amenities,
including buffets, cafeterias, bars, shops and
galleries. *See also chapters* **Music: Opera &
Classical.**
*Car Park. Free exhibitions. Front seats for the
partially sighted by prior arrangement.
Guided tours. Infra red audio for the hard of
hearing. Poetry library. Restaurants & cafés.
Shops for books, music and records. Toilets for
the disabled. Wheelchair access.*

SPECIAL ATTRACTIONS

Broadgate Arena
*Corner of Liverpool Street and Eldon Street,
EC2 (071 588 6565). Liverpool Street under-
ground/BR.* **Performances** *Apr-Nov*
12.30pm Mon-Fri. **Tickets** free.
This outdoor site in the middle of the massive
Broadgate complex becomes an amphitheatre
during the summer. Used mainly as a music
venue, it also presents some dance companies. The format includes free lunch-time performances that run for an hour. From
November to April the Broadgate Arena
becomes Britain's only open-air ice rink (*see
chapters* **Sport & Fitness** and **The City**.)
Toilets for the disabled. Wheelchair access.

Dance Books
*9 Cecil Court, WC2 (071 836 2314).
Leicester Square underground.* **Open** 11am-
7pm Mon-Sat. **Credit** A, £TC, V.
Stock of books and periodicals, plus videos,
records, photos, out-of-print volumes and
memorabilia, make this a well-known haven
for dance fans. Dance Books also publishes its
own, invariably handsome, books. This shop is
a must for any dance-minded visitor to London.

Dance Umbrella
*Riverside Studios, Crisp Road, W6 (081 741
9358). Hammersmith underground.* **Tickets**
£4-£16. **Credit** A, V.
Now in its second decade, Umbrella has
become recognized as one of the most
exciting showcases for new dance anywhere in the world. The autumn season
runs for approximately six weeks and takes
place in a variety of venues all over London,
including **The Place**, the **Riverside
Studios**, the **ICA**, the **South Bank Centre**
and **Sadler's Wells Theatre** (*see above for
all*). The programme is filled with premières of the best and most creative work
from young British choreographers,
together with productions by interesting
companies from around the globe. Dance
Umbrella, in association with *Time Out*,
also sponsors the annual **London Dance
and Performance Awards**, which honour
the exceptional creative talents working in
new dance and performance art.

Holland Park Theatre
*Holland Park, Kensington High Street, W8
(box office 071 602 7856; information 071
603 1123). High Street Kensington underground.* **Performances** 8pm, Jun-Aug.
Tickets £7; £3.50 OAPs, students, UB40s,
disabled. **Credit** A, £TC, V.
This 600-seat open-air theatre is in the middle of the Park's lush gardens, close to
woods, peacocks, and picnickers. Opera,
dance and theatre are performed through
the summer. A canopy stretches across the
audience and the stage, so you won't be
drenched if it rains.
Toilets for the disabled. Wheelchair access.

*Ballet has benefitted more from the end of the Cold War than any other art. Russia's Kirov and Bolshoi Ballet companies
now regularly make London one of their summer homes. In 1990 it will be the Leningrad-based* **Kirov Ballet** *which
returns for a six-week season (the troupes appear here on alternate years). Check* 20/20 *or* Time Out *magazines for dates
and venues. The Kirov company performs the great classics with unrivalled flair. The company is headed by some of the
world's most marvellous dancers, including the exotic Altyani Asylmuratova and her partner Faroukh Ruzimatov (above).*

Film

Where can you see Woody Allen's wit, Mel Gibson's muscles, Oliver Stone's Oscar-winner or a Warhol all-night bill? Read on for the pick of London's cinemas.

In an average year, over 250 new films are premièred in London. Of these, 60 per cent are from the USA, 30 per cent from Britain, and the final ten per cent from the rest of the world. You can see these films, together with myriad second-run and classic works, in anything from an eight-screen multiplex to a converted Victorian theatre. The **London Film Festival** grows in importance each year. Mainly based at the **National Film Theatre** (*see below* **Repertory**), it takes place in November.

After the doldrums of the sixties and seventies, when many picture houses were converted into bingo halls, cinema-going boomed in the eighties. The greatest innovation has been the building, by American companies, of new multiplex 10- and 12-screen cinemas around Britain. By paying more attention to audience comfort, these houses have found they can tempt people away from the TV and video. Contoured chairs, plus wine, coffee and ice-cream bars, are replacing steamy hot dog stands. Many independent cinemas thought of food long ago, of course, and great cinema snacks can be found at the **Ritzy** and **Scala** (*see below* **Repertory**).

The severe fright this has given the large companies that run the Cannons, Odeons and Empires, has forced even them to change their complacent ways, and many older houses are now introducing multiplex 10- and 12-screen cinemas around the UK. **UCI Whiteleys 8 Cinema** (*see below* **First-Run**) opened recently in Queensway; others are planned for Wembley and near the Brent Cross Shopping Centre. The newer cinemas also slope more, so if a seven foot tall basketball player sits in front of you (and he always does) you can still see the screen.

BLOOD & GORE

In 1989, the British Board of Film Censors introduced new age restrictions with the '12' certificate classification for films. There are now six different certificates: '**U**' (meaning universal) – suitable for all; '**PG**' (parental guidance) – children under 13 must be with an adult; no blood and gore is permitted but the occasional ten-second kiss or gun shot is allowed; the new '**12**' (anyone over 12) – a degree of violence and a hint of sex is acceptable; *Batman* was the first film to carry this certificate; '**15**' (anyone over 15) – these can be a little more explicit and can include swear words; '**18**' (adults only) – most horror movies are given this classification, and the language can be enlightening; '**R-18**' (anything goes, as long as it doesn't contravene the Obscene Publications Act) – these films can only be shown at licensed cinema clubs.

FIRST-RUN

West End cinemas are the best places to see mainstream movies. Latest releases are usually screened in 70mm and Dolby stereo, in a large and spacious auditorium. To prevent endless queues at some of the larger cinemas, you can book in advance by credit card over the phone. However, you often won't be able to pay by plastic on the door. For details of cinemas with late-night shows, *see chapter* **Late-Night London**. Consult *Time Out* magazine's 'Film' listings for current programmes in London.

Camden Parkway
14 Parkway, NW1 (071 267 7034). Camden Town underground. **Tickets** £3.50 adults; £1.50 children (till 6pm); 50p OAPs; £2 middle show daily. **No credit cards**.
Having been dark since 1987, the Parkway finally re-opened at the end of 1989. The two screens show first- and second-run movies, and there's an introduction before the evening screening.
Wheelchair access by prior arrangement.

Camden Plaza
211 Camden High Street, NW1 (071 485 2443). Camden Town underground. **Tickets** £4; £2.80 first show daily, Mon (except Bank Holidays); £1.70 OAPs, students, UB40s. **Credit** A, V.
Primarily a local cinema, with shabby décor, but a spacious auditorium and plenty of legroom. Foreign-language films and unusual British productions are screened, as well as Hollywood blockbusters.
Advance booking.

Cannon Haymarket
Haymarket, SW1 (071 839 1527). Piccadilly Circus underground. **Tickets** £4; £3 under-15s; £3 Mon. **Credit** £TC.
A three-screen, standard Cannon house, with small seats and a bold sixties-style interior. Lower prices than in some other West End cinemas.
Weekend late shows.

Cannon Shaftesbury Avenue
135 Shaftesbury Avenue, WC2 (071 836 8861; credit card 071 836 8606). Leicester Square or Tottenham Court Road underground. **Tickets** £4; £3 Mon. **Credit** A, V.
A comfortable two-screen cinema that's frequented by theatre trendies who come to see exclusive showings of critically-acclaimed English-language films.
Advance booking.

Cannon Tottenham Court Road
30 Tottenham Court Road, W1 (071 636 6148; enquiries 071 636 6749). Tottenham Court Road underground. **Tickets** £4; £3 under-15s; £3 Mon. **No credit cards**.
This small, three-screen theatre looks like a flea-pit outside, but has a surprisingly clean and modern interior. Hidden around the corner from the mainstream Cannon Oxford Street, it doesn't attract long queues. European and independent US and British films form the main programme.
Weekend late shows.

Chelsea Cinema
206 King's Road, SW3 (071 351 3742). Sloane Square underground. **Tickets** £4.50, £4; £3 Mon; first show Tue-Sun; £1.70 first show OAPs, students, UB40s daily.* **Credit** A, £TC, V.
High-class movies are shown in these high-class surroundings. The atmosphere can be forbidding, but there's a wine bar, attractive seating and an impressive foyer. It shows mainly prestige, art-house movies.
Advance booking.

Curzon Mayfair
Curzon Street, W1 (071 499 3737). Green Park underground. **Tickets** £6.50, £5.50. **Credit** A, AmEx, V.
Programming and prices at this plush, large-screened cinema reflect the Mayfair area where it's located: high-brow stuff, mainly prestige foreign-language films, provides the entertainment.
Advance booking.

Curzon Phoenix
110 Charing Cross Road, WC2 (071 240 9661). Leicester Square or Tottenham Court Road underground. **Tickets** £5. **Credit** A, AmEx, DC, £TC, V.
Admirable British and European pictures are shown at this luxury single-screen cinema hidden just off Charing Cross Road.
Advance booking.

Curzon West End
Shaftesbury Avenue, W1 (071 439 4805). Leicester Square or Piccadilly Circus underground. **Tickets** £6.50, £5.50. **Credit** A, AmEx, DC, £TC, V.

The third Curzon cinema, formerly the Première. The theatre offers similar comfort, elegance and programming to the **Phoenix** and **Mayfair** (*see above*). *Advance booking.*

Empire

Leicester Square, WC2 (081 200 0200; credit card 071 240 7200). Leicester Square underground. **Tickets** £6-£7.50; £4 first show daily, all screens. **Credit** A, AmEx, DC, V.
A luxury three-screen cinema with luxury prices. A coffee bar, an arcade and a video bar were added during the refurbishment in early 1989. Tacky laser shows are put on before each show. Major light-entertainment money-earners are shown, together with more surprising hits on a vast screen with amazing THX Lucasfilm sound.
Advance booking. Weekend late shows.

The Gate Cinema

87 Notting Hill Gate, W11 (071 727 4043). Notting Hill Gate underground. **Tickets** £4.25; £2.50 OAPs, students, UB40s; £3.50 first show Sun; £2.50 first show Mon-Fri (not Bank Holidays). **No credit cards.**
A wonderful cinema, where baskets of papier mâché fruit adorn the foyer. Unusual movies, mainstream blockbusters and independent films are screened throughout the week, but it's worth a visit for the Sunday matinée, single director's double-bills.
Advance booking. Weekend late shows. Wheelchair access.

Greenwich Cinema

180 Greenwich High Road, SE10 (box office 081 853 0053). Greenwich BR/177 bus.

Tickets £3.50; £2 Mon. **Credit** A, V.
A mainstream, three-screen cinema that opened in September 1989. The main foyer has exhibitions. The management aims to show blockbusters on Screens One and Two, plus an art-house film on Screen Three. On Wednesdays there are late-night shows and rerpertory matinées.

Lumière

42 St Martin's Lane, WC2 (071 836 0691; 071 379 3014). Leicester Square underground. **Tickets** £4.50; £3.30 Mon (not Bank Holidays), first show Tue-Sun; £2.20 OAPs, students, UB40s. **Credit** A, £TC, V.
The Lumière is renowned for showing critically-acclaimed works in luxurious surroundings. Critics have been known to rave about this relaxing and pleasant cinema. Major foreign-language films are an important part of the programme.
Advance booking. Weekend late shows. Wheelchair access.

Metro

11 Rupert Street, W1 (071 437 0757). Piccadilly Circus or Leicester Square underground. **Tickets** £4; £2.50 Mon, under-16s, nurses, OAPs, students, UB40s. **No credit cards.**
A two-screen cinema showing independent English-speaking films alongside Asian, Chinese and European successes. It's quite common to be the only person watching a film on a weekday. The cinema has a confusing layout, with long walkways, exhibiting photography, but which make it almost impossible to find Screen Two.
Advance booking.

Minema

45 Knightsbridge, SW1 (071 235 4225). Knightsbridge or Hyde Park Corner underground. **Tickets** £5; £2.50 first show; £2.50 OAPs, students, UB40s Mon-Fri. **Credit** £TC.
A small independent cinema specializing in quality films that have won the critics' praise.
Advance booking.

Odeon Haymarket

Haymarket, W1 (071 839 7697). Piccadilly Circus underground. **Tickets** £5.50, £5, £4.50. **Credit** A, V.
A pleasant single-screen cinema with a small bar. Some distributors insist on their films being shown here first, because of the cinema's reputation for screening more critically-acclaimed mainstream works.
Advance booking.

Odeon High Street Kensington

High Street Kensington, W8 (071 602 6644; credit card 071 602 5193). Kensington High Street. **Tickets** £4.50; £4; £2 under-16s, OAPs, UB40s (matinées only). **Credit** A, V.
There's not much in the way of refreshments at this four-screener. Hollywood hits are the order of the day, but films tend to stay for a longer run than in the West End. This means disasters outstay their welcome.
Advance booking. Weekend late shows. Wheelchair access to Screens 2, 3 and 4.

Odeon Leicester Square

Leicester Square, WC2 (071 930 6111). Leicester Square or Piccadilly Circus underground. **Tickets** £8, £7, £6; £1 discount under-16s (first two shows only). **Credit** A, AmEx, £TC, V.
Famed for its black art deco façade and tower, this is the largest cinema in London. The Royal Family come here to see films premiered. It's first choice for major Hollywood films.
Advance booking. Weekend late shows. Toilets for the disabled. Wheelchair access.

Odeon Marble Arch

10 Edgware Road, W2 (071 723 2011; credit card 071 723 8072). Marble Arch underground. **Tickets** £6, £5; £1 off under-16s. **Credit** A, V.
Battle through massive weekend queues to watch Hollywood blockbusters shown on a gigantic screen with great sound. The best views are from the balcony.
Advance booking.

Odeon West End

Leicester Square, WC2 (071 930 5252; credit card 071 930 7615). Leicester Square underground. **Tickets** £7, £6.50, £6, £5. **Credit** A, AmEx, £TC, V.
This one-screen movie house specializes in macho movies. It's very busy at the weekend. The auditorium is staggered, offering good views, and the sound is ear-shattering. It's not all muscle and brawn though: Annaud's *The Bear* was premiered here.
Advance booking. Weekend late shows.

Plaza

17-25 Lower Regent Street, SW1 (071 930 0144; credit card 071 240 7200). Piccadilly Circus underground. **Tickets** £6. **No credit cards.**
American and British money-makers are shown at this US-style, four-screen movie house. This is one of the few cinemas with a sufficient number of ticket booths. The facilities are similar to the **Empire** (*see above*).
Advance booking. Late weekend shows.

Since **Daniel Day Lewis** *played National Front supporter Johnny in* My Beautiful Laundrette *in 1985, he's continued to win praise for such diverse roles as the upper-crust suitor in* A Room With A View *and the sensual Czech doctor in* The Unbearable Lightness of Being. *After success at the National Theatre in Hamlet, he portrayed Christy Brown, a writer and artist who battled against cerebral palsy, in* My Left Foot. *His next cinematic role is the British/Argentinian movie,* EverSmile New Jersey.

Première

*Swiss Centre, 10 Wardour Street, WC2 (071
439 4470). Leicester Square or Piccadilly Circus
underground.* **Tickets** £4. **No credit cards.**
Deep inside the Swiss Centre, this movie-
house is well-kept and pleasing to look at.
Refreshingly, the diet at this four-screen
auditorium is mainly of French films.

Renoir

*Brunswick Centre, Brunswick Square, WC1
(071 837 8402). Russell Square underground.*
Tickets £4; £3 Mon (not Bank Holidays) and
first shows daily; £1.70 OAPs, students,
UB40s first show daily. **Credit** A, V.
Even though this cinema was built under a
housing estate, its off-beat British pictures and
critically-acclaimed foreign-language films draw
cinema-goers away from Leicester Square.
Advance booking.

Screen on Baker Street

*96 Baker Street, NW1 (071 935 2772).
Baker Street underground.* **Tickets** £4; £2.50
Mon (not Bank Holidays) and first show
Tue-Fri. **No credit cards.**
Best known for screening *The Rocky Horror
Picture Show* every Saturday night since
1984. Fans return to see it each week.
Quality independents and British movies are
shown during the day at this small, two-
screen theatre.
Advance booking. Weekend late shows.

Screen on the Green

*83 Upper Street, N1 (071 226 3520). Angel
underground.* **Tickets** £4; £2.50 Mon (not Bank
Holidays) and first show Tue-Fri. **Credit** £TC.
See **picture and caption.**
Advance booking. Weekend late shows.

Screen on the Hill

*203 Haverstock Hill, NW3 (071 435 3366).
Belsize Park underground.* **Tickets** £4; £2.50
Mon (not Bank Holidays) and first show
Tue-Fri. **Credit** A, V.
Mainly American and British releases of
artistic note are screened in this small but
comfortable, local cinema which has tasty
cakes and coffee.
*Advance booking. Weekend late shows.
Wheelchair access.*

UCI Whiteleys 8 Cinema

*Whiteleys of Bayswater, Queensway, W2 (box
office 071 792 3324; recorded information 071
792 3332). Bayswater or Queensway underground.* **Tickets** £4.75 adults; £2.50 under-14s;
£2.50 before 4pm daily. **Credit** A, £TC, V.
London's first multiplex cinema opened in
December 1989 with a Royal première of
Ghostbusters II. Expect a stream of blockbusters on each of the eight screens.
Copying US-style cinema-going, there are
two impressive foyers with sufficient numbers of ticket booths and concession stands
to prevent long queues. For those not content with Baskin-Robbins ice-cream and pop-
corn, all the cafés in the adjoining shopping
centre remain open until the last show. The
auditoriums have computer-designed sight-
lines, comfortable seats and Dolby Stereo
sound. The largest screen seats 330 and has
ear-shattering THX (Lucasfilm) sound.
*Advance booking. Toilets for the disabled.
Wheelchair access.*

Warner West End

*Leicester Square, WC2 (recorded informa-
tion 071 439 0791; credit card 071 494*

Emily Lloyd *was such a hit in the film* Wish You Were Here *that she's since
gone on to bigger and better things in the USA. She starred with Peter Falk in*
Cookie, *and won praise for her role as niece to Bruce Willis' Uncle Emmett in
the post-Vietnam movie* In Country. *Returning to the UK she shot* Chicago
Joe and the Showgirl, *based on the true story of a showgirl and a GI who
went on a murder spree in World War II.*

3001). Leicester Square underground.
Tickets £5, £4; £3 all day Mon and first
show Tue-Fri. **Credit** A, V.
The five auditoriums here are very wide, but
not deep, so the view doesn't vary much
from the front to the back. This five-screener
shows all the Warner multi-million-dollar
smashes, but unfortunately the foyer wasn't
built to hold the numbers that flock here, so
you'll have to queue outside until 15 minutes
before the programme starts.
Advance booking.

REPERTORY

Repertory cinemas screen a spectrum of new and vintage English
and foreign-language films, often
with programmes changing daily.
Watch out for seasons of films
(consult *Time Out* magazine).
Some repertory cinemas will only
admit members, but the fee is
often about 50p per year, payable
with your ticket.

Barbican Cinema

*Level 1, Barbican Centre, Silk Street, EC2
(071 638 8891). Barbican underground
(closed Sun) or Moorgate underground/BR.*
Tickets £4; £3 OAPs, student and UB40

standby. *Children's Cinema Club membership*
£2.50 per year, tickets £2 (£2.50 adults).
Credit A, AmEx, DC, £TC, V.
Part of the Barbican concrete jungle. Recent
productions have moved away from the foreign works that this modern two-screen cinema was known for, and veered towards the
mainstream. Films are often linked to
Barbican exhibitions.
*Advance booking. Car park. Restaurant &
cafés. Shops. Toilets for the disabled.
Wheelchair access.*

Centre Charles Péguy

*16 Leicester Square, WC2 (071 437 8339).
Leicester Square or Piccadilly Circus underground.* **Tickets** *members* 60p; *non-members* day-
membership £1, plus 60p ticket. **Credit** £TC.
A small cinema in a French cultural centre.
French-language films are screened, usually
without subtitles.

Everyman

*Hollybush Vale, NW3 (071 435 1525).
Hampstead underground.* **Membership**
50p per year. **Tickets** £3.50; £2 under-
15s; £2.50 nurses, OAPs, students,
UB40s. Mon-Fri and before 4.30pm Sat,
Sun; season tickets £25 for ten tickets.
No credit cards.
London's oldest repertory cinema, with
plush seating, good food and friendly
staff. European and English-language
favourites intermingle with cult films and
seasons of directors.
Toilets for the disabled. Wheelchair access.

French Institute
17 Queensberry Place, SW7 (071 589 6211). South Kensington underground. **Tickets** *members* free; *non-members* £2.50; £1.50 OAPs, students, UB40s. **No credit cards.**
French film culture is celebrated at the Institute, by the café-bar and exhibition area. Present-day and classic successes are shown on a large screen two or three times a week. Booking is recommended.

Goethe Institute
50 Princes Gate, Exhibition Road, SW7 (071 581 3344). South Kensington underground. **Tickets** £1. **No credit cards.**
German celluloid triumphs from as early as 1913 are shown twice weekly, often without subtitles. The occasional US classic has been known to sneak in.
Personal & postal bookings only.

ICA Cinema & Cinémathèque
Nash House, The Mall, SW1 (071 930 3647; 071 930 6393 recorded information). *Piccadilly Circus underground or Charing Cross underground/BR.* **Membership** £15 per year, £1 per day. **Tickets** *Cinema* £3.60; £2.60 OAPs, students, UB40s, first show daily; *Children's Cinema Club* membership £2.50 per year, seats £1.80 (adults £3.60). *Cinémathèque* £2.60; £2 Sun. **Credit** A, AmEx, DC, V.
Modern and archive work from the Soviet Union, Asia, Europe and America can be seen during the week, while cinematic treats for young children are shown at the weekend. The Cinémathèque is a small, but ambitious cinema which screens seasons of directors' work, together with horror, animated, video and political films. Day membership allows you to visit the exhibitions and café.
Advance booking. Bar. Bookshop. Café. Group discount. Lectures. Workshops.

National Film Theatre
South Bank, SE1 (071 928 3232). Waterloo underground/BR/. **Membership** £10.25 per year (student membership £7.50; daily membership 40p). **Tickets** £3.25; £2 disabled, OAPs, UB40s; £3 standby (tickets 30mins before each show). **Credit** A, £TC, V.
Widely varied programmes are shown at the three screens inside the NFT, plus the new one at **MOMI** (*see chapter* **Museums**). The NFT has a confusing layout and there's rarely someone around to give directions. Seasons dedicated to directors or to individual countries, genres or themes are featured alongside classics. The British Film Institute Awards are held here in October; the London Film Festival in November.
Advance booking. Bar, café and restaurant. Toilets for the disabled. Wheelchair access.

Phoenix
52 High Road, N2 (081 444 6789; recorded information 081 883 2233). East Finchley underground. **Tickets** £3; £1.50 under-15s, OAPs; £2 students, UB40s all shows except 6.30-11pm Fri-Sun. **No credit cards.**
European, American and Asian cinematic successes are shown in this comfortable, local old auditorium, often in double bills. The programme changes daily and there's a children's cinema club on Saturday mornings.
Advance booking. Saturday late show. Wheelchair access by prior arrangement.

Rio
107 Kingsland High Street, E8 (071 249 2722; recorded information 071 254 6677).

Dalston Kingsland BR/67, 76, 149, 236, 243 bus. **Tickets** £3; £2 under-15s, OAPs, UB40s; £2.50 adults Mon; £1.50 OAPs, students, UB40s Mon. *Children's Cinema Club* membership 50p, tickets £1 (£2 adults). **No credit cards.**
A decaying old theatre that's dilapidated enough to be charming. Everything from acclaimed European films to cult American pictures are shown as double-bills here, with a children's film club on Saturday mornings.
Toilets for the disabled. Weekend late shows. Wheelchair access.

Ritzy
Brixton Oval, Brixton Road, SW2 (071 737 2121). Brixton underground. **Membership** 50p per year. **Tickets** £3; £1 under-15s, OAPs; £2 students, UB40s all shows except Fri, Sat, Sun evenings. **No credit cards.**
Classics, mainstream films and documentaries from Europe, Hollywood and Australia are shown in double-bills. There are weekend late shows which have a reputation for being rowdy. The Ritzy is an impressive old building of character, but which desperately needs repainting.
Weekend late shows. Wheelchair access.

Riverside Studios
Crisp Road, W6 (081 748 3354). Hammersmith underground. **Tickets** £3; £2 under-16s, Equity, nurses, OAPs, students, UB40s, . **Credit** A, V.
A converted film studio that's hidden in an arts centre, it screens a surprising choice of films. Recent, prestige British work is shown alongside films like the US documentary *The Thin Blue Line*, the Canadian *Family Viewing* and the Fellini classic *La Dolce Vita*. *See also chapters* **Art Galleries**, **Dance** and **Theatre.** *Advance booking. Bar. Bookshop. Café. Restaurant. Wheelchair access.*

Scala
275-277 Pentonville Road, N1 (071 278 0051). King's Cross underground/BR. **Membership** 50p per year. **Tickets** £3.50; £2 under-16s, OAPs, students, UB40s Mon-Fri before 4.30pm only. **No credit cards.**
This cinema was originally a monkey house (no joke). The programmers like to get hold of controversial films: 'The day we show *Crocodile Dundee* we'll slash our wrists', they told us. A different double bill is shown each day, such as Arnold Schwarzenegger double-bills, where fans shout 'Arnie! Arnie!' in the fight scenes. As it's a licensed cinema club, so R-18 films may be shown.
Saturday all-night shows.

The name **Screen on the Green** (*listed under* **First-Run**) *is strikingly displayed in pink and green neon at the front of this distinctive cinema. It's reminiscent of a picture palace, with a bold white exterior, and pillars framing the entrance. The programmers pick films that will bring in the money, but redeem themselves by showing some impressive movies unlikely to be seen at other locals. Good snacks and coffee are sold.*

Lesbian & Gay

Lesbian and gay nightlife in the Big Smoke is unparalleled anywhere else in Britain. The hardest thing is choosing where to go.

London's lively lesbian and gay nightlife scene is fast-moving and ever-changing. Visitors might feel confused or even intimidated by the sheer volume of places to go, to say nothing of the variety on offer. While some of the venues cater exclusively for gay men or lesbians, others are both lesbian and gay, and recently there has been an upsurge of places that, though predominantly lesbian and gay oriented, have a sprinkling of sympathetic straights. There are many clubs and bars that cater for a specialist clientele and operate strict dress codes, or may have a gay or lesbian night just once a week. One of the main attractions of the London scene is that it's anything but predictable, and careful study of the information here should ensure that visitors will always know exactly what they're letting themselves in for.

NIGHTCLUBS

Though the details here are correct at time of going to press, the commercial lesbian and gay nightclub, bar and disco scene is constantly on the move. It's a wise precaution to phone and check before setting out – phone numbers are listed where possible – as well as looking in *Time Out* magazine for the latest details.

In the listings below (XM) *denotes men only;* (XW) *means women only.*

Apollo
11 Wardour Street, W1 (071 437 7301). Leicester Square and Piccadilly Circus underground. **Open** 8pm-3am Mon-Sat; 6.30-10pm Sun **Admission** £4 members; £5 non-members. **Credit** A, V.
Centrally located upstairs club on two floors, with early evening bar 'Franklins' 8-10pm, plus late discos (and occasional live entertainment). Generally a lively, young, mixed lesbian and gay crowd.

Club Copa's
180 Earl's Court Road, SW5 (071 373 3407). Earl's Court underground. **Open**
10.30pm-2am Mon-Sat. **Admission** £2.50 Mon-Thur; £3.50 Fri; £4.50 Sat. **No credit cards**.
An Earl's Court institution and one of the most consistently popular gay men's venues in town. This friendly club is a good place to conclude a night out in Earl's Court after moving on from the nearby Bromptons or The Colherne (*see below* **Pubs and Bar**).

Heaven
Underneath the Arches, Villiers Street, WC2 (071 839 3852). Embankment or Charing Cross underground/BR. **Open** 10.30pm-3am Tue, Fri, Sat (XM). **Admission** £2-£8.
Britains largest, busiest and most famous gay club is still buzzing after all these years. It features a cavernous central dancefloor, with impressive and exciting lights and lasers, a great sound system and a small stage with frequent live shows. Upstairs the 'Star Bar' is a marginally quieter video lounge with a small dancefloor, and the stylish 'Dakota Room' is for the dressier cocktail crowd. The labyrinthine complex also features a coat-check, snack bar and small shop selling cards, T-shirts, vests and condoms.

Madame Jo Jo
8-10 Brewer Street, W1 (071 734 2473). Piccadilly Circus underground. **Open** 10pm-3am Mon-Sat. **Admission** £6 Mon-Thur; £8 Fri-Sat. **Credit** A, AmEx, V.
Famous for its excellent live shows and gorgeous waiters, this small, plush, late-night cabaret club, bar and restaurant, situated in the heart of Soho, has a great atmosphere and, as an added bonus,features the delightful hostess Madame Jo Jo. It's very camp and theatrical with consistently wonderful live drag musical extravaganzas performed on the tiny stage. Usually full to bursting point, there's waiter service, a small dancefloor, plenty of tables – which can be reserved by phoning – and loads of fun.

Paradise
1 Parkfield Street, N1 (071 354 2590). Angel underground. **Open** 7.30pm-2.30am Mon-Sat; 5-11.30pm Sun. **Admission** £1-£4.
Islington's busiest late-night gay venue has three bars, two discos, a restaurant, pool-table and games room plus occasional live entertainment. A handy place to move onto after an early drink at *The Fallen Angel* (*see below* **Eating Out**).

Paris Metro
65 Old Kent Road, SE1 (071 237 2182). Elephant & Castle underground. **Open** 8.30pm-12.30am Tue, Wed; 8.30pm-12.30amThur (XW), 10pm-2.30am Fri, Sat; 8-11pm Sun. **Admission** free Sun, Tue, Wed; £3 Thur-Sat.

A south London lesbian and gay club with Italian marble bars and lots of deep crimson velvet and leather. It looks great. There is plenty of seating, including a large, yet cosy, champagne booth. The women's toilet is an annexe in itself with deep pile carpets and a large mirror. Though the area isn't salubrious, the club is protected by hefty security people and there's a nearby phone to call for taxis.

Spats
37 Oxford Street, W1 (071 437 7945). Tottenham Court Road underground. **Open** 10pm-3am Fri (XW) 7pm-1am Sun. **Admission** £4 Fri; £2,50 members, £3.50 non-members Sun. **No credit cards**.
An intimate central bar/club with dancefloor and lounge area, which is often packed with a generally young, non-stereotyped smartish crowd.

CLUBS: ONE NIGHTERS

A selection of the best and most established alternative and one-night clubs and discos around town.

Bang
at Busby's, 157 Charing Cross Road, WC2 (071 734 6963). Tottenham Court Road underground. **Open** 10.30pm-3am Mon, Sat. **Admission** £3.50; £2 students, UB40s Mon; £4; £3 students, UB40s Sat.
The legendary big, brash, bright and busy party nights with pure dance music. Occasional theme nights and live entertainment.

Below Stairs Disco
at London Lesbian & Gay Centre (Basement), 67-69 Cowcross Street, EC1 (071 608 1471). Farringdon underground/55, 63, 259, 277, N21, N83, N90 bus. **Open** 9pm-(no admission after 12.30am) Sat. **Admission** £3; £2.50 students, UB40s. (XW).
Atmospheric disco with a regular but varied mix of women.

The Daisy Chain
at The Fridge, Town Hall Parade, Brixton Hill, SW2 (071 326 5100). Brixton underground. **Open** 10pm-2.30am Tue. **Admission** £3 before 11pm, then £4.
Weekly camp and wacky lesbian and gay night in a cavernous setting with more than 100 video screens. There are live DJs and go-go dancers, plus frequent theme parties and live entertainment. It's wild, hedonistic and always full.

The 48 Club
at Reeves Private Hotel (Lower Ground Floor), 48 Shepherd's Bush Green, W12 (081 740 1158). Shepherd's Bush underground. **Open** Fri 8pm-1 am. **Admission** £3 8-9pm, £4 9pm-1pm. (XW).
Weekly disco night with smart, mature crowd of women and relaxed atmosphere. There's a variety of music – including requests – and cocktails with original and apposite names are served.

The Garage
at Zanadu's, 144 Upper Street, N1 (071 359 0154). Angel underground. **Open** 9pm-2am Wed. **Admission** £3.
Popular weekly women's club (gay men welcome as guests) catering for all music tastes.

Heds

at HQs, West Yard, Camden Lock, NW1 (071 485 6044). Camden Town underground. **Open** 9pm-1am (No entrance after midnight) Sun. **Admission** £3; £2 members, students, UB40s.

A weekly night for 'Les Girls' at this unique and beautiful canal-side venue with tables overlooking the Lock, two bars, videos and live DJs. The spacious dancefloor is quickly filled, so it's best to get there before 10.30pm. Though it's really a women's night, gay male guests are allowed with members.

Mania

at The Hippodrome, Charing Cross Road, WC2 (071 437 4311). Leicester Square underground. **Open** 9pm-3am Mon. **Admission** £6.

A smart, stylish mixed and gay night with spectacular lights and sound. There is a good, but expensive, restaurant upstairs.

Movements

at the Bell, 259 Pentonville Road, King's Cross, N1 (071 837 5617). King's Cross underground/BR. **Open** 8.30pm-midnight Sun, 9pm-2am Wed. **Admission** £1.40 Sun; £1 Wed.

Two popular dance nights with excellent DJs Martyn & Berni playing the sounds that have been pulling in the punters (on Sundays) for the past eight years.

Pyramid

at Heaven, underneath The Arches, Villiers Street, WC2 (071 839 3852). Embankment or Charing Cross underground/BR. **Open** 10pm-3amWed. **Admission** £2-£4.

Busy, hot and steamy alternative/trash night with dance music, videos and occasional live entertainment. Very popular with a party-loving crowd of young gay men and lesbians.

Singers

at Ivory's Bar, 12 Sutton Row, W1 (071 439 4655). Tottenham Court Road underground. **Open** 8pm-1am Sat, Mon. **Admission** £4.

Popular piano bar with live singers, some famous, some not, plus lots of audience participation.

Troll

at Sound Shaft, 180 Hungerford Lane, Craven Street, WC2 (071 839 4252/071 839 3852). Embankment or Charing Cross underground/BR. **Open** 10.30pm-3am Sat. **Admission** £5 (including use of Heaven £6.50).

Brilliant and busy deep house and dance crazy night in day-glo surroundings with gay, mixed, straight fun-loving crowd. Featuring sensational and spacey music. Always packed.

Venus in Progress

at The Fridge, Town Hall Parade, Brixton Hill, SW2 (071 326 5100). Brixton underground. **Open** 10pm-3am monthly Wed. **Admission** £3-£4.

Third-Wednesday-of-the-month, mainly women's club when women patrons may take along one male guest. (Positively no unaccompanied men admitted.) With live entertainment and great music.

Venus Rising

at The Fridge, Town Hall Parade, Brixton Hill, SW2 (071 326 5100). Brixton underground. **Open** 10pm-3am.monthly Wed. **Admission** £2-£3 . **(XW).**
See picture and caption.

Venus Rising *at The Fridge,* (listed under **Clubs: One Nighters***)is the largest regular women-only club in Europe. The hosts of this monthly extravaganza, have ensured that this is the place to be for women who like to do things on a grand scale. The vast auditorium of this Brixton venue achieves an intimate atmosphere with its warm black walls and black barrel seats dotted around the edge of the huge dancefloor. The DJs play constant dance music, mainly house, plus the odd blast from the past. There are live go-go dancers and cabaret.*

PUBS & BARS

The Attic Bar

at The Peacock (Upstairs) 13-14 Maiden Lane, Covent Garden, WC2 (071 836 8260). Covent Garden or Charing Cross underground/BR. **Open** 5.30-11pm Mon-Sat; noon-3pm, 7-10.30pm Sun. **No credit cards.**

A small and friendly bar with a theatrical atmosphere and luxurious furnishings. A handy place for an early evening drink before going on to Heaven.

The Bell

259 Pentonville Road, N1 (071 837 5617). King's Cross underground/BR. **Open** 8.30pm-midnight Sun-Tue; 9pm-1am Wed; 9.30-2am Thur; 9pm-2am Fri,Sat.

Large, comfortable and friendly King's Cross bar with excellent lights and sound and a different 'alternative' disco each night.

Brief Encounter

41 Street Martins Lane, WC2 (071 240 2221). Leicester Square and Charing Cross underground/BR. Open 11am-11pm Mon-Sat; 7-10.30pm Sun. **No credit cards.**
See picture and caption.

The Britannia

Chilton Street, off Bethnal Green Road, E2 (071 729 6502). Bethnal Green underground. **Open** 8pm-midnight Mon-Thur; 9pm-2am Fri, Sat; noon-3pm, 7.30-10.30pm Sun. **No credit cards.**

Intimate and friendly East End pub. Mon, Fri and Sat 'singles nights'. Men-only at weekends, women allowed as guests during the week.

Bromptons

Old Brompton Road, Earl's Court, SW5 (071 373 6559). Earl's Court underground. **Open** 8pm-12.30am Mon-Thur; 8pm-1am Fri; 8pm-1.30am Sat; 8-10.30pm Sun (no entrance Mon-Thur after 11.30pm, and Fri-Sat after 12.30am). **Admission** free 8-11pm daily; £2-£4 11pm-12.30am Mon-Thur; £2-£4 Fri, Sat.

Comfortable and established gay men's bar complex with live DJs, dancefloor, shop and food. A good place to start an evening before moving on to the nearby Copa (*see above* **Nightclubs**).

The City Apprentice

York Way King's Cross, N1 (071 278 8318). King's Cross underground/BR. **Open** 8pm-2am Mon, Thur, Sat; 8pm-midnight Sun. **Admission** £1 after 10.30pm.

Busy gay men's disco/bar on two floors, that caters for a macho gay crowd. Plus Sat, Sun and Mon 'The Block' (**XM**), brilliant downstairs leather, rubber and uniform club.

The Coleherne

Old Brompton Road, Earl's Court, SW5 (071 373 9859). Earl's Court underground. **Open** 11am-11pm Mon-Sat; noon-3pm, 7-10.30pm Sun. **Admission** £2 Sun.

A famous leather-scene institution that is usually packed every lunchtime and evening with gay men. They have a restaurant called 'Detour'.

Comptons of Soho

53 Old Compton Street, W1 (071 437 4445). Tottenham Court Road, Leicester Square and Piccadilly Circus underground. **Open** 11.30am-11pm Mon-Sat; 12.30-3pm , 7-10.30pm Sun. **No credit cards.**

Central gay men's bar with loud taped music, friendly staff and frenetic atmosphere. Very mixed clientele and quite touristy.

Drill Hall Women Only Bar
*16 Chenies Street, WC1 (071 631 1353).
Goodge Street underground.* **Open** 11.30am-
11pm Mon. **(XW)**. **No credit cards**.
Lively and informal central women-only weekly
bar, with friendly staff, a varied selection of
taped background music and low bar prices.
Creche for children under five.

King's Arms
*23 Poland Street, W1 (071 734 5907).
Oxford Circus and Tottenham Court Road
underground.* **Open** 11am-11pm Mon-Sat,
noon-3pm, 7-10.30pm Sun. **No credit cards**.
Set on two levels, this central gay men's pub
has comfortable décor and very friendly
staff. Food available. Downstairs is always
very busy with local Soho and media crowd,
upstairs is a cheap doubles bar with a quiet,
more relaxed feel.

King William IV
*77 Hampstead High Street, NW3 (071 435
5747). Hampstead underground.* **Open**
11am-11pm Mon-Sat, noon-3pm , 7-10.30pm
Sun. **Credit** A, V.
This small and cosy pub is situated in the
heart of Hampstead Village, and has a pretty
beer garden that is open in good weather.
The staff are very friendly, and the crowd,
though mixed at lunchtimes, is mainly gay
men in the evenings.

The Locomotion
*Upstairs at 18 Bear Street, Leicester Square,
WC2 (071 839 3252). Leicester Square
underground.* **Open** noon-11pm Mon-Sat;
noon-10.30pm Sun. **Credit** A,V.
Centrally located fifties American-style
mixed diner/bar/café has a spacious, cool
feel. Usually quite touristy and busy. 'Chaps',
the men-only bar, is upstairs.

Market Tavern
*'Market Towers', 1 Nine Elms Lane, Vauxhall,
SW8 (071 622 5655). Vauxhall underground.*
Open 9pm-2am Mon-Thur; 9pm-3am Fri;
9pm-3am Sat **(XM)**; 1pm-7pm (lunch available), 9pm-midnight Sun. **Admission** £2
Thur-Sun. **No credit cards**.
The most consistently brilliant gay men's
venue south of the River. The main bar has
a large dancefloor, a long bar and a small
coat-check and tiny Clone Zone shop. The
DJs play great dance music (very loud)
and there's a quieter back bar with pool
tables, fruit machines and plenty of seats.
The crowd is mainly denim and leather
wearers; the staff are particularly efficient
and welcoming.

Royal Vauxhall Tavern
*372 Kennington Lane, SE11 (071 582
0833). Vauxhall underground/BR.* **Open**
8pm-1am Mon; 8pm-midnight Tue-Wed;
8pm-2am Thur, Fri; noon-3pm, 8pm-2am Sat;
noon-3pm, 7-10.30pm Sun. **Admission** £1.50
Mon, Thur-Sat.
Situated just a short way from Vauxhall
underground via underpasses,this very, very
busy pub is a South London drag scene institution with live cabaret entertainment
nightly. The atmosphere is always congenial,
and the pub is popular with an established
and loyal crowd of regulars.

The Two Brewers
*114 Clapham High Street, SW4 (071 622
3621). Clapham Common underground.*
Open 6pm-1am Mon-Sat; noon-3pm, 7.30-
10.30pm Sun. **Admission** £1.50 Fri, Sat. **No
credit cards**.
One of South London's most popular gay
venues, split into two sections offering disco
or cabaret – and a great atmosphere in either.

Brief Encounter *(listed under* **Pubs and Bars***) is central London's
busiest gay men's bar. The main street-level bar is long, narrow and decorated
in various warm shades of beige, magnolia and mushroom. There's
comfortable, dark brown, alcove seating. The downstairs bar is marginally
quieter with more seats. There's also a piano downstairs that is often played
early evening. A varied and interesting mix of men here. Usually packed both
at lunchtimes and in the evenings.*

SHOPPING

Clone Zone
*1 Hogarth Road, SW5 (071 373 0598).
Earl's Court underground/31, 74 bus.* **Open**
10am-7pm Mon-Fri; 9.30am-8pm Sat; 1-7pm
Sun. **Credit** A, AmEx, DC, £TC, V.
Small, hi-tech, split-level shop (conveniently
situated just a short walk from Earl's Court
underground). The Leather Loft stocks
leather chaps, jackets, waistcoats, caps and
so on, while downstairs there's sportswear,
Levi's, T-shirts, sweatshirts, briefs and a
selection of cards and books.

Expectations
*at GHQ, 75 Great Eastern Street, EC2 (071
739 0292). Old Street underground).* **Open**
11am-6pm Mon-Thur; 11am-8pm Fri; 11am-
10.30pm Sat. **Credit** A, AmEx, V.
A comprehensive range of excellent leather,
rubber and leisure wear is to be found in this
spacious and atmospheric store. They sell
jackets, jeans, caps, waistcoats, belts, vests
and boots, a large selection of casual
clothing, plus loads of accoutrements, lubri-
cants and novelties
Branch: *176 Ifield Road, SW5
(071 244 6900).*

Gay's The Word Bookshop
*66 Marchmont Street, WC1 (071 278
7654). Russell Square underground.* **Open**
11am-7pm Mon-Sat; 2-6pm Sun. **Credit** A,
AmEx, DC, V.
Britain's best selection of lesbian and gay
books, both new and second-hand, British
and imported, plus magazines, greetings
cards, records and badges. This shop has a
community notice board and tea and coffee
is served; it doubles as a shopping and
meeting place.

Obsessions
*1B Coleherne Road, SW5 (071 244 8220).
Earl's Court underground.* **Open** noon-8pm
Tue-Sat. **Credit** A, AmEx, V.
A beautiful up-market shop, situated just
opposite The Coleherne, it's a haven of good
taste set on two floors and crammed full of
gorgeous 'obsessional' desirables.
Everything, from American motorcycle jackets and Tom of Finland prints, chrome, steel
and leather furniture, Corinthian columns,
leather-dressed teddy bears, luxurious
leather luggage and designer artefacts
through to the beautiful iridescent glassware, is top-quality.

Silver Moon Women's Bookshop
*68 Charing Cross Road, WC2 (071 836
7906). Leicester Square underground.*
Open 10.30am-6.30pm Mon-Sat. **Credit**
A, AmEx, V.
A large selection of books by and for
women. Stock includes work by black
women, a comprehensive lesbian section,
non-sexist children's books, cards, book
vouchers and small gifts including jewellery,
socks and gloves.

Zipper Store
*283 Camden High Street, NW1 (071 267
7665). Camden Town underground.* **Open**
10.30am-6.30pm Sat-Thur; 10.30am-7pm Fri.
Credit A, AmEx, V.

Lesbian and Gay Switchboard *(listed under* **Information***) is one of the best helplines around.. The volunteer staff have information on clubs, pubs, shops, festivals, events, flatshares and just about every facet of life in the big city. There's also a counselling service that will listen and advise on problems and crises. It's a popular service so the line is frequently engaged, but keep trying; it's worth it.*

London's only licensed gay men's sex store has a light and airy, hi-tech feel and, thanks to the clever design, manages to cram a surprisingly large variety of goods into a comparatively small space. These include sports, leisure and leather wear, plus cards, calendars, accoutrements, novelties, books and raunchy magazines.

EATING OUT

The Fallen Angel
65 Graham Street, N1 (071 253 3996). Angel underground. **Open** noon-midnight Wed-Sun; noon-midnight Tue **(XW)**. **No credit cards.**
Lesbian and gay bar/café with friendly staff and busy but relaxed atmosphere. Vegetarian and vegan meals, snacks, tea, coffee and cakes are available throughout the day. Unusual décor, frequent lesbian and gay art exhibitions, community notice board and meeting rooms (upstairs).

First Out Coffee Shop
52 Giles High Street, WC2 (071 240 8042). Tottenham Court Road underground. **Open** 11am-11.30pm Mon-Sat; 2-7pm Sun. **No credit cards.**
London's first lesbian and gay continental-style coffee house is situated on two floors. Its handy central location, just opposite Centre Point, means it's usually busy, especially at lunchtimes and pre-club hours. The cool, clean, décor matches generally style conscious staff and customers. Excellent hot and cold meals, teas, coffees, pastries and gateaux available. Licensed.

Reeves Hotel For Women
48 Shepherd's Bush Green, W12 (081 740 1158). Shepherd's Bush underground. **Open** 7-10.30pm Mon-Thur; 8.30-1pm Fri; 7-11pm Sat; noon-3.30pm Sun. **Credit** A, AmEx, V. **(XW).**
This women-only hotel has social evenings for residents and non-residents with 'The 48 Club' disco taking place every Friday in the basement,. There's a vegetarian buffet on Saturday nights and an informal brunch on Sundays. Meals, average price £8, are available in the restaurant all week but booking is necessary.

Roy's Restaurant
206 Fulham Road, SW10 (071 352 6828/071 351 0278). Earl's Court and South Kensington underground. **Open** 7.30pm-2am Mon-Sat; 1.30-3pm, 7.30-11pm Sun. **Credit** A, AmEx, £TC, V.
London's best known gay restaurant offers excellent service, frequent live entertainment and good Anglo/French food. Set menu, £12.50, includes starter and main course. Recommended.

Steph's
39 Dean Street, W1 (071 734 5976). Leicester Square , Piccadilly Circus and Tottenham Court Road underground. **Open** noon-3pm, 5.30-11.30pm Mon-Fri; 5.50pm-midnight Sat. **Credit** Airplus, AmEx, DC, JCB, V.
Charming, efficient (and camp) staff with wonderful and well presented food. Mainly gay customers, but there is a sprinkling of well-adjusted straights. Relaxed, unhurried atmosphere. Average price around £12 for three courses.

Women's Theatre Café
at Lauderdale House, Waterlow Park, Highgate Hill, N6 (081 348 8716). Archway underground. **Open** 7-10.30pm. **Admission** £3, £2 (£1.50 students, UB40s). **No credit cards.** **(XW).**
Regular women-only, second-Friday-of-the-month café with hot home-made meals, salads, snacks, tea, coffee, wine and lager plus live cabaret/theatre.

Power Station
533 King's Road (entrance in Lot's Road), SW10 (071 351 5718). Fulham Broadway underground. **Open** 11am-10pm Mon-Fri ; 11am-6pm Sat; noon-6pm Sun. **Credit** A, AmEx, £STC, V.
London's only Nautilus gym for men has been running now for more than six years. It offers tuition, free weights, Jacuzzi, sauna, bar plus snacks, solarium and more.

INFORMATION

Lesbian & Gay Switchboard
(071 837 7324)
see **picture and caption.**

GLLAD (Gay & Lesbian Legal Advice)
(071 253 2043). **Open** 7-10pm Tue-Fri.

Jewish Lesbian & Gay Helpline
(071 706 3123). **Open** 7-10pm Mon , Thur.

LGCM helpline(Lesbian & Gay Christian Movement)
(071 587 1235).
Counselling referral service.

Lesbian Line
(071 251 6911). **Open** 2-10pm Mon and Fri; 7-10pm Tue-Thur.
Help and advice.

London Friend
(071 837 3337). **Open** 7.30-10pm nightly.
Counselling and help for gay men and women.

London Friend Women's Line
(071 837 2782). **Open** 7.30-10pm Tue, Thur.
Advice for lesbians.

LL & GC (London Lesbian & Gay Centre)
67-69 Cowcross Street, EC1 (071 608 1471). Farringdon underground. **Open** mixed: 5.30-11pm Mon-Thur; noon-midnight Fri, Sat; noon-10.30pm Sun; women-only 'Orchid' bar: 7-11pm Tue-Thur; 7-midnight Fri, Sat; 1-6pm Sun **(XW).** **No credit cards.**
Social centre with discos, bars, workshops, restaurant and theatre as well as being the meeting place for numerous groups and societies.

Quest
(071 373 7819). **Open** 7-11pm Fri, Sat and Sun.
Advice and information for gay Catholics.

Survive The Streets
(0306 79633). **Open** 9am-9pm Mon-Fri.
Registration £5. Class fee £4.
Gay self-defence course details.

Terrence Higgins Trust
(071 242 1010). **Open** 3-10pm daily .
Advice and information on Aids.

Media

These are the heights and depths of British press and broadcasting.*Sid Smith* and *Alkarim Jivani* of *Time Out* tune in to the radio and TV airwaves.

When visiting this country, you'll probably hear the British assert that their television and radio are the best in the world. With market forces about to be unleashed on these hitherto sheltered media, all this looks set to change. Are they about to go the same way as our once proud, but now soiled, press? If you want to know what's happening back home, then consult *chapter* **Survival** for stockists of overseas newspapers and magazines.

NEWSPAPERS

At the quality end of the market, the press keeps a loyal readership with the occasional good story, job advertisements and cartoons. Towards the gutter, there are the vice-ful excesses of clerics, exaggerations of mammary glands and more cartoons.

Downmarket Tabloids
Rupert Murdoch's **Sun** is the best-selling paper with over four million readers. A tabloid of knee-jerk right-wing politics, its SHOCK HORROR headlines are mostly about soap opera characters. The *Sun* introduced the 'Page Three Girl', a larger-than-life model who appears in various degrees of undress throughout the tabloids. With good reason, the vast majority of the *Sun*'s readers don't believe much of what the paper prints. More left-of-centre is the **Daily Mirror**, with over three million readers. Once distinctive, it now differs from the *Sun* insofar as the Page Three Girl retains her bra, it's in colour and it frequently calls on the Government to resign. The **Daily Star**, selling about a million, was an attempt by the *Daily Express* Group to break into the sewers. Originally touted as an independent tabloid, it swiftly went the way of the rest.

Tabloids with Aspirations
The **Daily Express** and the **Daily Mail**, with a readership of one and a half million each, both support the Establishment, so long as it's conservative. This pair crusade against anything that doesn't fit their world view. **Today** was Britain's first colour daily. An aggressive bandwagon-jumper, it was accused by the *Daily Express* of being the jackdaw of Fleet Street, for 'borrowing' stories. *Today* responded with a magpie on its masthead and a new media correspondent, Jack Dawe.

Quality Broadsheets
The quality press expect a certain level of intelligence from their readers. Isolated on the soft-left is the **Guardian**. Look out for Andrew Rawnsley's excellent Parliamentary sketches and *Doonesbury* in the cartoons. The **Independent** proclaims that its name tells its politics, but is rightish at heart, and it can be stern with people who offend its sensibilities. The leader pages can be pithy, but the best writing is found in its Saturday editions. The voice of the establishment, **The Times** has lost its reputation as 'the Thunderer'. It's simply dull, now that it's just another paper under Murdoch's ownership. Until recently, the **Daily Telegraph** was getting old with its million readers; as they died off, so the paper's circulation declined. This trend has been reversed recently (*see* **picture and caption**). The **Financial Times** (not owned by Murdoch) dominates the world of money; when it quivers with rage at the defalcations of the stock market, even the government trembles. The *FT* also has remarkably good arts coverage.

Sunday Tabloids
The **News of the World** (five and a half million readers), **People** and **Sunday Mirror** are even more outraged and outrageous than their weekday counterparts, obsessed with footballers and bimbos, or vicars and choirboys. The **Sunday Sport**, appropriately owned by a porn publisher, is for you, if you really believe that Marilyn Monroe is alive and living with Elvis on the moon with a bust the size of Mars. The half million who buy it are people who move their lips when looking at pictures.

Respectable Sunday Tabloids
The **Mail on Sunday** and the **Sunday Express** are more populist on the day of rest than during the week. The good gossip columns are one of the main reasons they sell about two million each.

Quality Sunday Broadsheets
The quality Sundays aspire to serious investigative journalism and fairly good arts coverage. The **Sunday Times** has the thunderous impact of a falling tree and weighs almost as much. Its attempts to regain its investigative reputation have been hampered by the loss of its good reporters to rival papers. Oh that its million readers felt the same way. The **Observer** is leftish and dominated by a proprietor who's more interested in buying Harrods. It has some witty writers. The **Sunday Telegraph** is not as physically weighty as the opposition, but the writing is ponderous. The financial pages are good for those with money. The **Sunday Correspondent**, a newcomer in 1989, is progressive, but a touch bland. Its art coverage is refreshing and its news stories have a welcome international flavour. It faces stiff competition from the **Independent on Sunday**, launched in January 1990, which has attracted some excellent writers from other papers.

The weekday *Independent* has been a great success, so all of the Sunday broadsheets must be apprehensive about what the nineties will bring. Given that both the *Sunday Telegraph* and the *Sunday Times* have fundamentally loyal audiences, it's the *Sunday Correspondent* and the *Observer* that have most to fear.

MAGAZINES

The eighties saw a proliferation of magazines. Of course, you won't be going anywhere without your indispensable guide to what's on in London – **Time Out**. This is *the* weekly listings magazine on stage, screen and street. **20/20** is an arts-based, monthly review which scoops some of the best interviews.

Satirical magazines
The doings of the above papers, and of all public figures, are scathingly dissected in **Private Eye**. A bi-weekly satirical magazine, it attracts many libel suits, often exhorting its readers to contribute legal funds. Its chief rival, **Punch**, has been twitting the Establishment for over a century, and has a tradition of good cartoons. Now a bit flaccid, it can't decide whether it's an organ of parody (literally) or a lifestyle mag. The bi-monthly adult comic, **Viz**, has accelerated to a readership of a million by being as offensive as possible. With characters Sid the Sexist, the Fat Slags and the Pathetic Sharks, it parodies tabloid papers in the style of the *Beano*. More City businessmen read *Viz* than the *Financial Times*.

Lifestyle magazines
Blitz, **GQ**, **Arena** and **The Face** are all designed (a word not used lightly in these publications) for the man who has, thinks he has or wants to have it all. *Arena* is probably best read. **i-D** has referred to itself as the most pretentious magazine in the universe. It takes its street fashion seriously but is self-deprecating in its editorial and design.

Women's magazines
Best, **Bella**, **Options**, **Woman's Own**, **Prima**, **She**, **Marie Claire** and **Woman** specialize in knitting patterns, recipes and invented horoscopes. Collectively, they've done hideous damage to the feminist movement. **Cosmopolitan** claims to represent the modern woman's aspirations: no politics, snappy dressing and a career plan.

Serious magazines
The Economist is relentlessly humourless and market-minded in its good coverage of financial, political and foreign news. The **Spectator** promotes a crusty, old-fashioned conservatism, with entertaining columns by Taki and Jeffrey Bernard. It has in-depth arts reviews. The **New Statesman & Society** has a centre-left editorial policy, but it's righteous and a little dull. **Marxism Today** has recently been re-vamped as a Euro-style review, advertising that 'it's offensive'.

RADIO

British radio is undergoing its biggest-ever expansion. Hundreds of new stations will begin broadcasting in the next few years, and half a dozen of them should be on air in London by the time you read this. Many overseas visitors to London are astonished to discover that until recently Europe's biggest city was served by only nine stations, six of them provided by the BBC. Certainly, the BBC has been splendid in serving its chosen audience. Funded by a TV licence fee, the organisation is not only ad-free but also untrammeled by any commercial pressures to maximise its audience. The result is an expensive output of plays, documentaries and worldwide news.

Throughout the UK, new stations are being created for ethnic and specialist audiences. So far, only six of the new London licences have been handed out. One has gone to an all-jazz service, and another to a group with varied programming for several ethnic minorities. Four smaller stations will serve each of the four corners of London.

At the time of writing none of these have begun transmission. We're also listing a handful of the more reliable pirates – though these illegal stations are notoriously hard to pin down and a trawl up the FM waveband is the best way to keep up with their activities. For details of the new legal stations and for advance news of selected programmes, consult *Time Out* magazine.

The Daily Telegraph Building (*listed under* **Newspapers***) is where numerous hacks tap out the weird utterances of the* Telegraph *newspaper (and its Sunday version). A falling readership has been reversed by the new editor, Falklands War macho-man Max Hastings, aided by vigorous management from the Canadian proprietor, Conrad Black. The sports pages (which feature a great deal of American Football) are worth more than a cursory glance.*

MAJOR STATIONS

BBC Radio 1
275m/1089kHz and 285m/1053kHz (MW); 104.8mHz (FM).
Producers say that the most vital factor in making a hit is 'Radio 1 airplay'. Bland teen music rules in the daytime, but programming is more grown-up and varied after dark, when John Peel promotes new and independent bands.

BBC Radio 2
330m/909kHz and 433m/693kHz (MW); 89.1mHz (FM)
London's most listened-to station, Radio 2 aims middle-of-the-road music at the over-45s. But many younger listeners value it as a relief from the follies of daytime Radio 1. Its evening output is a strange and endearing sub-culture of quizes, comedies and affectionate shows of pre-Beatles music.

BBC Radio 3.
247m/1215kHz (MW); 90-92.5mHz (FM).
This classical music station has a tiny audience, a huge budget, and a chorus of critics of its non-populist approach. Yet, even listeners uninterested in classical music will find much to enjoy in its high-quality discussion and drama shows.

BBC Radio 4
500m/200kHz(LW); 417m/720kHz (MW); 92-95mHz (FM).
The BBC's main speech station is probably the quickest way for overseas visitors to discover the preoccupations of Britain's chattering classes. Plays, phone-ins, discussions, humour and news programmes follow each other seamlessly. Millions of Britons habitually wake up to the station's newsy breakfast show, *Today* (6.30am-8.45am Mon-Fri).

BBC Greater London Radio (GLR)
206m/1458kHz (MW); 94.9mHz (FM).
The BBC's local station for London, GLR serves 25 to 45 year olds with album-oriented rock. Some of the presenters are pretty inexperienced, but the two drive-time shows are a pleasing mix of news bites and ad-free music.

BBC World Service
463/648kHz (MW); 500m/200kHz(LW) at night.
Britain's equivalent of Radio Moscow or the Voice of America, is funded by the Foreign Office and is transmitted worldwide. Fortunately, it's little affected by its propaganda role and plays a weird mix of pop music, drama, comedy, features and inordinate quantities of news. It's prized for providing high quality speech throughout the night, when there's nothing else on but music and dismal phone-ins.

Capital FM
95.3mHz (FM).
A London-only commercial station which – with some specialist music shows and concerts – concentrates on perky presenters and current hits.

Capital Gold
194m/1548kHz
Exclusively hit records of the last 30 years, played by DJs so old they spun the discs when they were new.

LBC Crown FM
97.3mHz (FM).
The closest London has to a rolling news format, Crown enlivens a news-oriented output with phone-ins and – especially at the weekend – arts and leisure coverage.

LBC London Talkback
1152kHz (MW).
A 24-hour phone-in station.

PIRATE STATIONS

Supreme
94.8 (FM).
Professionally presented, smooth soul music.

Laser
94 (FM).
Reggae music.

London Arabic
89.7 (FM).
A very slick diet of Arabic music and prayers.

City
94.4 (FM).
Reggae music with slick presentation and a stereo signal. It's one of the best pirates.

Radio Free London
92.05 (FM).
London's only pure rock music station, but it only runs at weekends.

Sunrise
33.3 (FM).
House music.

T E L E V I S I O N

British television is experiencing its greatest series of changes since John Logie Baird invented the medium. With the arrival of satellite TV in 1989, the number of channels has more than doubled. This turmoil is likely to continue into the foreseeable future.

New laws are ushering in new channels and making fundamental changes to the way the industry is financed: the auctioning of franchises; the relaxation of quality standards. The British have long believed that they make the best TV programmes in the world – there's enormous anxiety that this will not be the case for long. Visitors don't come to London to watch television, but you owe it to yourself to watch a little bit and make up your own mind. And remember, if the pessimists are right, this will be regarded as the golden age of British television.

Below is a list of the four terrestrial channels and the satellite services. Each has its own distinct char-

acter which we delineate below. For detailed information, news and features, pick up a copy of *Time Out* magazine which provides a weekly selection. Happy viewing.

BBC1
The oldest channel in this country, BBC1 has long had a reputation for quintessential Britishness. The BBC channels are funded by a licence fee and therefore do not need to take commercials to pay their way. BBC1 provides a mass market mix of comedies, drama, soaps, game shows and current affairs. The main news broadcasts are at 1pm, 6pm and 9pm.

BBC2
This is the BBC's cultural channel and has a greater emphasis on arts, music and minority audiences. Music recitals and dance are regularly transmitted at prime time on Saturdays. This is also the channel which carries the classic drama serials for which the BBC is best known. Recently it's begun commissioning films for TV transmission and produced some gems. An impressive regular is *Newsnight* – a nightly news and current affairs compendium.

ITV
This is the main commercial channel and has long suffered from being regarded as a repository of unmitigated populism. The tag is not entirely deserved (there are some fine documentaries), although it does have more than its fair share of nudge-nudge comedies. In London, two channels share the same slot: Thames (which transmits from Monday to early Friday evening); and London Weekend Television (which takes over at the weekends). The main news bulletin of the day is broadcast at 10pm.

Channel 4
This, the youngest and most admired channel, was set up to provide programming for those viewers whose needs were not being met. This has produced a varied diet which caters to supposed minority interests – from mushroom-picking to black politics. The longest and most analytical news programme available on terrestrial TV is Channel 4 News (7pm on weekdays). Channel 4 also runs interesting, off-beat movies as well as commissioning its own films, including Peter Greenaway movies, *Mona Lisa* and *A Room With A View*.

SATELLITE TV

Satellite TV is taking its first tentative steps in Britain and – at time of writing – has not been the commercial success that many people expected (and feared). Britain began receiving satellite signals which could be picked up by small roof-top aerials in early 1989, when Rupert Murdoch, the US-Australian media magnate, launched a bundle of channels aimed at Britain. Another set of channels was due to be launched

in spring 1990 by British Satellite Broadcasting (BSB, the official British satellite TV project).

ASTRA

Sky One
A general entertainment channel, which kicks off with kids' programmes in the mornings and goes on to game shows and soaps – largely bought from America and Australia – plus TV movies.

Sky News
Britain's first 24-hour news channel which delivers bulletins every hour on the hour. The rest of the time is filled with documentaries and discussion programmes. Bear in mind that Murdoch is the owner of the right wing *Sun* and *Times* newspapers.

Sky Movies
Various first run and re-run movies till the early hours of the morning with the emphasis on mainstream blockbusters. During the morning this slot is occupied by the Satellite Shop – a visual version of a mail order catalogue.

Eurosport
Sporting events culled from European broadcasters – including the BBC – are transmitted with coverage of fixtures which often get squeezed on terrestrial TV.

Screensport
A slightly more off-beat sports channel which broadcasts every conceivable sporting activity.

Lifestyle
A daytime channel for people at home which devotes itself to cookery and magazine programmes, interspersed with soaps and game shows.

MTV
The original 24-hour music channel with wall to wall videos. Very much modelled on its American sister, although the European version is a little more adventurous.

BSB

Galaxy
This, the main entertainments channel, will start the day with children's programmes and go on to drama and light entertainment. At the time of writing, BSB was negotiating to have access to the BBC archives.

The Movie Channel
There are plans to show six movies a day, with the afternoon movies transmitted free of charge and a subscription charge for the blockbusters lined up for evening transmission.

The Sports Channel
Sports a go-go with the emphasis on the kind of fixtures British fans are keen on. The rights to English and Scottish Football Association have already been acquired.

Now
An informational channel which will provide documentaries on the environment, health, leisure pursuits, politics and so on.

The Power Station
A Channel aimed at teenagers and young adults with the emphasis on music-based programming.

Music: Classical & Opera

Do you ooze over opera and rhapsodize over rhapsodies? Or do your sympathies lie with symphonies? *Time Out's Martin Hoyle* **conducts you around London's classical venues.**

London has the highest standard of classical music of any western capital outside New York. Over-endowed with orchestras, London concert-goers are grateful for their multiplicity of choice, while harbouring a suspicion that if the best of the bands were combined, London would have a super-orchestra fit to beat Berlin or Vienna.

Some years ago, the worthies of the Arts' Council – that ill-defined body whose functions fall between the stools of artistic adviser, paymaster-general and government stooge – suggested that one of the big London bands should move into the provinces to establish a musical beach-head. Nobody would go. London is where the gossip is – and the session work: the moonlighting whereby the most professional and the worst paid of the world's musicians scrape a living. The Thatcher years will go down in our musical cultural history as philistine and repressive. The wonder is that music-making goes on at all. London's two opera houses manage on grants that are the laughing stock of the civilized world, yet they present more and better productions than you'll find in such culturally conscious capitals as Paris or Vienna. But then, Berlioz noted the same phenomenon nearly 150 years ago when he admired English musicians and deplored their working conditions.

Financial uncertainty has meant that opera houses are unable to plan ahead. Still, it's a safe bet that 1991 is to be dominated by a bicentenary: that of the death of Amade, as the Royal Opera insists on calling him – the child prodigy who grew into an adult genius: Mozart. At least the opera houses have stable orchestras. The symphony orchestras have long taken visiting conductors by surprise by presenting them with different line-ups for rehearsal and performance. Sound-track work, TV commercials, crossover and pop-

backing all help to pay the bills for London's desperately drudging, and indefatigably talented, players.

Nevertheless, on any one night, the musical visitor to London will be presented with a choice wider than anywhere else. Chances are that more than one of the Big League will be playing: the Philharmonia, the London Symphony Orchestra, the London Philharmonic, the Royal Philharmonic or the BBC Symphony, with its reputation for superbly-executed modern works. Chamber orchestras include the Academy of St Martin-in-the-Fields, the English Chamber Orchestra, the recently-revived London Mozart Players, and gifted ensembles specializing in modern and avant-garde work.

For detailed information of performances, times and places see *Time Out's* **Classical Music** listings.

MAJOR VENUES

Barbican Centre

Silk Street, EC2 (071 638 8891). Barbican underground (closed Sun) or Moorgate underground/BR. **Open** *box office* 9am-8pm daily. **Admission** £5-£20. **Credit** A, AmEx, DC, V. This grim cultural stalag was the City's gift to London's arts world. And London never stops grumbling about it. The Barbican concert hall is home to the London Symphony Orchestra and the English Chamber Orchestra – though both bodies hop across the river to the **South Bank** (*see below*), for large-scale choral and orchestral works that the Barbican's designers neglected to plan for. In 1990, the Barbican's programme will have an international emphasis: the Chamber Orchestra of Europe will give a series of concerts in April, and from November to December. In October, the LSO will feature the talents of Anne-Sophie Mutter, who combines the glamour of a Hollywood starlet with the musicianship of a young Heifitz. The Great Orchestras of the World series brings over the Bolshoi band in October, the great Leipzig Gewandhaus under Kurt Masur in November (joined in two of their three concerts by pianist Alfred Brendel) and the Orchestre de Paris under

Bychkov in December – let's see if French playing has improved from the decline it suffered a few years ago. March 1991 sees the arrival of the Vienna Symphony Orchestra (note, not the more famous Philharmonic) under Harnoncourt; 1991 also features the rather good Oslo Philharmonic under Maris Janssens (April); the Royal Concertgebouw under Riccardo Chailly (May); and the Czech Philharmonic for three concerts in September. One of the year's highlights will be the return of the Leningrad Philharmonic, conducted by Yuri Temirkanov, for two dates in November. By this time, of course, we're well into Mozart year. The English Chamber Orchestra has the fine idea of mounting a series of concerts, each devoted to a single year's output of the phenomenon who wrote his first symphony as an infant in Pimlico and died a pauper at 35. The calendar of genius is played out in two parts: from January to March and from September to December, with a host of guest artists. It all culminates on 5 December 1991, commemorating the last tragic year with the *Clarinet Concerto* and the *Requiem*. Daniel Barenboim conducts, Anne Sophie von Otter is among the soloists. This is all interspersed with the BBC's Henze Festival (January); the LSO's variations on the theme of childhood; plus a Rostropovich and Prokofiev Festival (November) honouring both the composer and the benign Slava himself. *See chapter* **Theatre**. *Car Park. Restaurant & cafés. Shops. Toilets for the disabled. Wheelchair access.*

The London Coliseum

St Martin's Lane, WC2 (box office 071 836 3161; credit card 071 240 5258; recorded information 071 836 7666). Leicester Square underground or Charing Cross underground/BR. **Open** *box office* 10am-9pm Mon-Sat. **Tickets** £3-£33. **Credit** A, AmEx, DC, £STC, V. After a distinguished and varied theatrical past, Matcham's lovely Edwardian auditorium rang to the sound of the Sadler's Wells Opera in 1968. The company stayed, and is now the English National Opera. Performances are in English, but the current directorate of Mark Elder (conductor) and David Pountney (producer) has nothing parochial about it. The company has toured abroad and its home-grown stars include Valerie Masterson (a success in French opera) and John Tomlinson (who has played Wotan at the Bayreuth Festival). Among the established stars is international Wagnerian Norman Bailey, to be seen in such unshowy roles as the American consul in *Madam Butterfly* or the father in *Hansel and Gretel*. Above all, ENO productions exist as theatre – sometimes controversial, sometimes outrageous, sometimes a brilliantly successful gamble. The opera boom in London owes more to the Coli than to the glossy, expense-account appeal of Covent Garden. Parents take children to their first opera here. Sandwiches and coffee in the Dutch Bar take the place of Covent Garden's champagne and smoked salmon. The nearby Coliseum shop has an excellent selection of records, videos, libretti, books and magazines. ENO has provided much of the most exciting theatre – musical or spoken – to be seen in the West End in recent years. They range through the repertoire, from Monteverdi to the moderns. Current enterprises include Berg's *Wozzeck*, *Peter Grimes* (following a successful *Billy Budd*) and Bartok's *Bluebeard's Castle*. *See also chapter* **Dance**.

Group & family discount (071 836 0111 ext 318). Shop (10am-7.30pm Mon-Sat). Toilets for the disabled. Wheelchair access.

Royal Albert Hall

Kensington Gore, SW7 (071 589 3203; credit card booking 071 589 9465). Knightsbridge or High Street Kensington underground/9, 73 bus. **Box office open** *10am-6pm Mon-Sat (also Sun if performance that day).* **Tickets** *£1.50-£33.* **Credit** *A, V.*
See **picture and caption.**
Guided tours (May-Oct). Toilets for the disabled. Wheelchair access by prior arrangement.

Royal Opera House

Covent Garden, WC2 (071 240 1066). Covent Garden underground. **Open** *box office 10am-8pm Mon-Sat.* **Tickets** *£8.50-£82.* **Credit** *A, AmEx, DC, V.*
See **picture and caption.**
Opera and ballet education officers. Shop. Toilets for the disabled. Wheelchair access.

St James's Church, Piccadilly

Piccadilly, W1 (071 734 4511). Piccadilly Circus underground. **Admission** *lunchtime free (donation appreciated); festivals £2-£6;* tickets available at the door 1 hour before performance starts. **No credit cards.**
Designed by Christopher Wren, St James's provides a peaceful oasis in the middle of London. Young musicians give lunchtime recitals during the week, and concerts are slotted in among such activities as talks, discussions and healing sessions. The past few years have seen the emergence of a good resident ensemble, the St James's Baroque Players. The Lufthansa Festival (a regular summer event) yields a feast of baroque music which attracts some of the best international performers of early music.

St John's Smith Square

Smith Square, SW1 (071 222 1061). Westminster underground. **Open** *box office 10am-5pm Mon-Fri; till start of concert on concert nights.* **Tickets** *£2.50-£15.* **Credit** *A, AmEx, £TC, V.*
Situated within belching distance of Conservative Party headquarters, St John's church is a happy example of conversion to other uses. The musical fare is similar to the Wigmore's *(see below)*, though slightly more space means that chamber orchestras figure more prominently here. BBC lunchtime concerts provide a frequent bargain. *Restaurant. Shop.*

South Bank Centre

South Bank, Belvedere Road, SE1 (box office 071 928 8800; general information 071 928 3002; recorded information 071 633 0932). Waterloo underground/BR/Riverbus. **Open** *box office 10am-10pm daily.* **Tickets** *£3-£50* **Credit** *A, AmEx, DC, V.*
The windy wastes of concrete detract from this fun-palace complex. The **Royal Festival Hall** is the largest concert hall on the South Bank, ideal for orchestral concerts and large-scale choral works. The **Queen Elizabeth Hall** is smaller – a good space for chamber orchestras – and is convertible into a temporary theatre for visiting opera productions. The smallest hall, the **Purcell Room**, hosts the debut recitals of many young artists. The South Bank Arts Centre has come to emphasise the 'theme' series as a way of beating the jaded palates of the musically over-fed or the lethargy of those timid souls who aren't too keen on trying something new. A season devoted to Szymanowski, following hard on the heels of Peter Maxwell-Davies, lasts until June 1990. Early summer sees performances of Mozart's operas, the early *Idomeneo* and the late *Clemenza di Tito*. Modernism takes over in the autumn, cheek by jowl with Early Music. Old and new come together in a joint Tippett/Beethoven Festival, also in the autumn, with such starry names as Esa-Pekka Salonen, Neville Marriner and Peter Donohoe. Opera is highlighted at the start of 1991: the City of Birmingham Touring Opera's pocket-sized staging of *The Ring*, no less, and the once iconoclastic Opera Factory's *Cosi fan tutte*. Spring 1991 sees a blockbuster series on Russia. The 'Russian/Soviet' festival, as it's cheerfully described, deals with Russian music before 1930 and in the 1980s. Muti conducts a Scriabin series, and Edward Downes conducts a Prokofiev cycle. Mozart's bicentenary celebration opera is *The Seraglio*, and a late summer 'Mozart Project' is designed to complement the other festive junketings for Salzburg's famous son. *See also chapters* **Dance** and **Theatre.**
Car Park. Free exhibitions. Front seats for the partially sighted by prior arrangement. Guided tours. Infra red audio for the hard of hearing. Poetry library. Restaurants & cafés. Shops for books, music and records. Toilets for the disabled. Wheelchair access.

Wigmore Hall

36 Wigmore Street, W1 (071 935 2141). Bond Street underground. **Open** *box office 10am-8.30pm Mon-Sat; Nov-Mar 10.30am, 3.15am Sun; Apr-Oct 10.30, 6.15pm Sun.* **Performances** *7.30pm Mon-Sat; Nov-Mar 11.30am, 4pm Sun; Apr-Oct 11.30am, 7.30pm Sun.* **Tickets** *£3-£15.* **Credit** *A, AmEx, DC, £TC, V.*
The intimate, friendly atmosphere adds to the pleasure of both hearing and making music here. Artists love the Wigmore for its consoling acoustics and immediate contact with the audience. The Hall is a favourite location for recitals and chamber music and offers the most civilized choice for Sunday morning (sex and papers notwithstanding) in its mid-morning concerts which include coffee or sherry. Evening concerts are held seven nights a week, apart from the summer closure, and include intimate music (chamber, instrumental, vocal) from every period in every style. Prices tend to be cheap, but popular concerts sell out fast.
Coffee bar. Wheelchair access.

The **Royal Albert Hall** *(listed under* **Major Venues***) is the major host of the best music festival in the world, the BBC Henry Wood Promenade Concerts. The Proms run from mid-July to mid-September and include a variety of orchestras, ensembles and performers from all over the world; tickets are at subsidized prices. The hall is rich in atmosphere and has been a well-loved venue for over a century. It's had its acoustical problems but there have been improvements in recent times. The old place comes into its own with massed choirs and big orchestral forces.*

The Royal Opera House *(listed under* **Major Venues***) is London's answer to La Scala, the Met, the Bastille, and the Vienna Staatsoper. This is where you might see Domingo and Pavarotti, if they bother to turn up. Government cuts have meant that seat prices have risen to levels previously unheard-of in London. The audience now has a high proportion of block business subscribers. Foreign-language performances are translated in sub-titles above the proscenium. Bar staff are still among the best in the world – fast, efficient and courteous.*

LUNCHTIME CONCERTS

One of the great pleasures of London's musical life is the tradition of performances in churches, not just as part of the service but in concert and recital, especially at lunchtime. Tired shoppers, workers enjoying their break, curious tourists and casual passers-by are all welcome. Concerts are usually free though donations are customary and sometimes collections are taken. Artists include young professionals, students and established musicians. Standards are usually high.

All Souls
Langham Place, W1 (071 580 3522). Oxford Circus underground.
All Souls is patronized by the BBC (aren't we all?). It specializes in organ music recitals and there's often an admission charge.

St Anne and St Agnes
Gresham Street, EC2 (071 373 5566). St Paul's underground.

St Anne and St Agnes not only puts on lunchtime concerts, but has performances of liturgical music in the church services. As a Lutheran church it excels in the music of Bach, performed as part of the Sunday service as originally intended.
Wheelchair access with assistance.

St Bartholomew-the-Great
West Smithfield, EC1 (071 606 5171). Farringdon underground/BR.
Regular lunchtime music, plus evening concerts with the resident choir are staged at this ancient church.

St Bride
Fleet Street, EC4 (071 353 1301). Blackfriars underground/BR.
Three lunchtime concerts are held here each week. Tuesdays and Fridays feature either professional musicians or senior students, and Wednesdays are generally reserved for organ recitals. Performances start at 1.15pm and last for 35 minutes. They stop during Lent and Advent.
Wheelchair access to ground floor only.

St Giles Cripplegate
Barbican, EC2 (071 606 3630). Barbican underground (closed Sun) or Moorgate underground.
St Giles Cripplegate stands across from the artificial lake of the Barbican and provides an atmospheric venue for lunchtime music.

The church is often used during Barbican 'theme' seasons or for performances by students of the adjacent Guildhall School of Music and Drama.
Wheelchair access.

St Katharine Cree Church
86 Leadenhall Street, EC3 (071 283 5733). Aldgate underground/Fenchurch Street BR.
One of the few pre-Wren churches in London. There's a lunchtime concert on the first Tuesday of each month, with some extra concerts during the summer.

St Lawrence Jewry
Guildhall, EC2 (071 600 9478). Bank or St Paul's underground.
A handsome Wren church (1678) which has a rather unusual Mander organ made out of parts saved during World War II. Lunchtime piano recitals are held on Mondays, and organ recitals on Tuesdays, both at 1pm.
Wheelchair access with assistance.

St Margaret
Lothbury, EC2 (071 606 8330). Bank underground.
Adjacent to the Bank of England, the church contains a recently restored English pipe organ of 1801, one of the finest in London. Frequent lunchtime recitals (usually on Wednesdays) feature guest organists as well as other vocal and instrumental combinations.

St Martin-in-the-Fields
Trafalgar Square, WC2 (071 930 0089). Charing Cross underground/BR.
St Martin-in-the-Fields has given its name to an excellent chamber orchestra. Young artists give two or three lunchtime recitals a week and there are occasional evening concerts.
Bookshop. Café. Toilets for the disabled. Wheelchair access.

St Martin-within-Ludgate
Ludgate Hill, EC4 (071 248 6054). St Paul's underground or Blackfriars underground/BR.
This striking church with a magnificent spire was completed by Wren in 1684. Despite a renovation programme scheduled throughout the summer of 1989, recitals are still given at lunchtime, and cover a wide spectrum, from classical to Palm Court.

St Mary-le-Bow Church
Cheapside, EC2 (071 248 5139). St Paul's underground.
This beautiful church provides a sympathetic environment for early, medieval and Renaissance music. Recitals are on Thursdays, starting at 1.05pm.

St Michael's
Cornhill, EC3 (071 626 8841). Bank underground.
St Michael's excellent series of Monday lunchtime organ recitals is now an integral part of the City's musical life.
Guided tours by arrangement.

St Olave's
Hart Street, EC3 (071 488 4318). Tower Hill underground/Fenchurch Street BR.
St Olave's lunchtime chamber music recitals, every Wednesday and Thursday at 1.05pm, feature a selection of solo, duo and trio instrumentalists.

St Sepulchre-without-Newgate

Holborn Viaduct, EC1 (071 248 1660). Chancery Lane or St Paul's underground/Holborn Viaduct BR.
St Sepulchre's is known as 'The Musicians' Church' – we're prepared to bet that it is the only church in the world where Mimi in *La Boheme* is depicted in a stained glass window. Sir Henry Wood, founder of the Proms, is also commemorated here.

AROUND & ABOUT

Almeida

Almeida Street, N1 (071 359 4404). Angel underground or Highbury & Islington underground/BR or Essex Road BR. **Open** *box office* 10am-6pm Mon-Sat. **Performances** 8pm Mon-Sat; *matinées* 4pm Sat. **Tickets** £6.50-£12.50. **Membership** £10 per year; £25 three yearly. **Credit** A, V.
This is perhaps the London venue most deserving of the adjectives 'avant garde' and 'international'. It has been condemned by its local authority for not being international enough. Such idiocies are the stuff of local arts commissars. In summer 1990 the Almeida is staging a festival of contemporary music. Through the year, drama alternates with occasional weekend concerts. *Restaurant. Toilets for the disabled. Wheelchair access.*

Blackheath Concert Halls

23 Lee Road, Blackheath, SE3 (081 318 9758 box office; 081 463 0100 information). Blackheath BR/54, 75, 89, 108 bus. **Open** box office 10am-6pm Mon-Fri; 10am-1pm Sat. **Tickets** £3-£15. **Credit** A, V.
A venue for high-powered series and cycles. International artists often perform here. See *Time Out* magazine's listings for details. *Educational projects. Shop (open for concert events only). Wheelchair access to ground floor only.*

British Music Information Centre

10 Stratford Place, W1 (071 499 8567). Bond Street underground. **Open** 10am-5pm Mon-Fri. **Recitals** 7.30pm Tue, Thur.
A unique collection of scores, taped music, records, compact discs and videos about composers are kept here. There's usually a free recital (predominantly new British music) on Tuesday and Thursday evenings – although not in August.

Burgh House

New End Square, NW3 (071 431 0144). Hampstead underground.
Regular concerts by local musicians are given in this museum venue. There's no set evening for music, so check *Time Out* magazine's listings for details. Tickets average £3. *See also chapter* **Local London.**

Crotchets Chamber Music

157 Denmark Hill, SE5 (071 737 4361). Denmark Hill BR/40, 68, 176, 184, 185 bus.
Ruth Franklin is a successful and respected piano teacher; her daughter Rachel is fast becoming recognized as one of the most talented of her generation. But apart from

music, this enterprising family has another passion: good food and wine. They have created a chamber music club in their home where members meet to enjoy a wonderful home-cooked three-course dinner on either Saturday evenings or Sunday lunch, which is followed by a recital by young musicians. If you would like to join their convivial company, ring the above number any time, and reserve a table. An evening costs between £15 and £18 plus wine.

Dulwich Picture Gallery

College Road, SE21 (081 693 5254). West Dulwich BR/P4, 12, 37, 78, 176 bus. **Open** 11am-5pm Tue-Sat; 2-5pm Sun. **Admission** *gallery* £1.50 adults; 50p OAPs, students, UB40s; *concerts* free-£5. **No credit cards.**
The oldest art gallery in England is also a venue for promenade concerts on one Saturday a month at 11.30am. Recitals are held in the evenings, also around once a month; phone for details. *See also chapter* **Art Galleries.**
Guided tours. Lectures. Wheelchair access.

Fenton House

Hampstead Grove, NW3 (071 435 3471). Hampstead underground. **Admission** £6; £12 for celebrity concerts.
Fenton House contains the treasured Benton Fletcher collection of early keyboard instruments. First-class musicians give recitals of baroque music on occasional Wednesday evenings between May and September.
Wheelchair access to ground floor only.

Kenwood Lakeside Concerts

Kenwood House, Hampstead Lane, NW3 (081 348 1286). Archway, Highgate or Hampstead underground. **Tickets** £3-£7.50; concessions for children, OAPs, students, UB40s. Book through Ticketmaster (*071 379 4444*) or on the night two hours before the concert begins. **Dates** Every Sat Jun-Aug. **Credit** A, AmEx, DC, V.
See picture and caption.
Wheelchair access.

Lauderdale House

Waterlow Park, Highgate Hill, N6 (081 348 8716). Archway underground. **Open** 11am-4pm Tue-Fri. **Tickets** £1-£4. **No credit cards.**
A family venue, you can treat children to a fair or a puppet show on Saturday morning and enjoy a recital in the evening, perhaps by a local professional trying out a programme before appearing at the Wigmore Hall. Saturdays and Sundays tend to be the music days, but phone for details.

National Sound Archive

29 Exhibition Road, SW7 (071 589 6603). South Kensington underground. **Open** 10am-5pm Mon-Wed, Fri; 10am-9pm Thur.
The proverbial Aladdin's Cave, housing millions of items of recorded sound from the 1890s to the present day, plus over 80,000 musical scores to use with recordings. If you want to hear Beatrice Harrison playing her cello to the nightingale in her garden, you must book in advance.

The **Kenwood Lakeside Concerts** *(listed under* **Around & About***) take place in a magical setting among the trees at the side of Kenwood lake. Take a picnic hamper, pray it doesn't rain, settle in a deckchair and let the classical melodies soothe away the city blues. The concerts tend towards safe, popular classics, but they're by top orchestras. A Russian night on 28 July 1990 marks 150 years since Tchaikovsky was born. Audibility is not first-rate, but never mind the music. The evening is finished off by a firework display.*

Music: Rock, Folk & Jazz

Over 600 bands, from pub rockers to stadium-fillers, play live in London each week. *Isabel Appio* of *Time Out* is your guide to the venues.

The London music scene may be accused of being transient and erratic, but it's never dull. From a Bros extravaganza at Wembley Arena (*see below* **Major Venues**), to the more modest, but no less entertaining, Iva Papasov and his Bulgarian Wedding Band at the **ICA** (*see chapter* **Theatre: Fringe**), there really is something for everyone. Fresh faces arrive on the scene as fast as unsuccessful bands disappear: it was in the **Africa Centre** (*see below* **Other Venues**) that Jazzie B and Soul II Soul first began playing; Texas took their first musical steps at the crowded **Borderline** basement (*see below* **Club Venues**); and Tanita Tikaram was first heard at the **Mean Fiddler** (*see below* **Pub/Wine Bar Venues**).

Music from right across the globe can be heard, with acts from Africa, Eastern Europe, the Far East and, most notably, South America, vying for performance space. In dance music, the definition between night clubs and live music venues is becoming blurred as DJs become performers, creating fresh sounds on the decks. Really, anything goes.

With most of these venues it's a good idea to book your tickets in advance from a booking agency – or even better, from the venue direct, avoiding the extra cost of a booking fee.

MAJOR VENUES

Academy Brixton
211 Stockwell Road, SW9 (071 326 1022). Brixton underground/BR/N2, N59, N78 bus. **Open** 7-11pm daily. **Music** 7.45pm. **Admission** £6-£12.50. **Credit** A, DC, V.
A majestic venue, and just a few minutes' walk from Brixton underground. In spite of its large capacity (roughly 4,000) there's usually a vibrant atmosphere, little problem reaching the bar and good sound. The sloping floor means you get a decent view, even from the back. Bands with a sense of adventure tend to play here. Watch out for over-zealous mounted police, especially at rap and reggae concerts.

Astoria
157 Charing Cross Road, WC2 (071 434 0403). Tottenham Court Road underground. **Open** 7.30pm-3.30am Mon-Thur; 10pm-3.30am Fri, Sat. **Music** times vary. **Admission** £4-£7.50. **Credit** A, AmEx, DC, V.
This capacious theatre, with a large dance floor and upstairs seating, doesn't take full advantage of its central location. Recently it's broadened its programming from straight R&B to indie and reggae music, but the sound is frequently muffled, the bar prices fluctuate with the interest rates, and you have to be careful not to miss your last train home after queueing for your coat. *See chapter* **Night Life**.

Dominion
Tottenham Court Road, W1 (071 580 9562). Tottenham Court Road underground. **Open** 7-11pm daily. **Music** 7.30pm daily. **Admission** £5.50-£15.50. **Credit** A, AmEx, V.
The conveniently placed Dominion is enjoying a healthy revival as a music venue. Although it's seating-only this theatre attracts raunchy rock acts such as the Mighty Lemon Drops, as well as cocktail crooners like Lou Rawls. A comfortable venue with few hassles.

Hackney Empire
291 Mare Street, E8 (081 985 2424). Hackney Central or Hackney Downs BR/22, 35, 38, 55, 106, 25, N11, N96 bus. **Open** 7.30-11pm various nights. **Admission** £3-£7. **Credit** A, V.
It may be far from the mainstream, but it's easy to reach by bus. This renovated music hall often hosts special benefit nights incorporating cabaret with live music. It's one of the few theatres in London with a bar and tables in the auditorium. *See chapters* **Early Twentieth Century** and **New Comedy**.

Hammersmith Odeon
Queen Caroline Street, W6 (081 748 4081). Hammersmith underground/N11, N93, N97. **Open** 7.30-10.30pm various nights. **Admission** £4-£7. **No credit cards.**
One of London's longest-established live music theatres, the Odeon attracts the full spectrum of mainstream bands. It's run in a conventional manner – crowded bars, dodgy hot dogs – and any movement from seats is discouraged by security (though Al Green managed to get the whole house dancing, including the bouncers). Good sound and good views.

London Arena
4 Limeharbour, E14 (071 538 1212). Crossharbour Street DLR/Riverbus to West India Pier. **Open** *box office* 10am-8pm Mon-Fri; 10am-4pm Sat. **Music** 7.30pm. **Admission** £10-£15. **Credit** A, AmEx, DC, V.

This new, custom-built venue with a 12,000 seating capacity was christened with a bang by Duranduran and continues to attract mainstream pop. Energetic movement from seats is discouraged and the local transport facilities are grim.

Marquee
105 Charing Cross Road, WC2 (071 437 6603). Leicester Square or Tottenham Court Road underground. **Open** 7-11pm daily. **Music** 8pm. **Admission** £3.50-£6. **No credit cards.**
In its sixties heyday most of the rock giants sweated in the Marquee (*see chapter* **To the Eighties**). Temporarily uprooted from its site in Wardour Street, the new Marquee, just a few streets away, is a little bigger – but still black, dingy and damp. It stages all types of indie, heavy metal and goth bands.

National Club
234 Kilburn High Road, NW6 (071 328 3141). Kilburn underground/N8, N94 bus. **Open** 9.30pm-1am Mon; 9.30pm-1.30am Fri; 9.30pm-1.45am Sat. **Music** 11pm Mon, Fri, Sat. **Admission** £4-£6. **No credit cards.**
An under-exposed venue – in the main it's the local Irish community which benefits from the splendid ballroom interior (*see chapter* **Ethnic London**).

Palladium
8 Argyll Street, W1 (071 437 7373). Oxford Circus underground. **Open** 6.45-10.30pm. **Music** 7.30pm. **Admission** £5-£25. **Credit** A, AmEx, V.
This sedate theatre, more often associated with tacky cabaret and pantomime, has recently started hosting acts like Elvis Costello and Lou Reed. Sit back and enjoy the intimate atmosphere. *See chapter* **Theatre**.

Town & Country Club
9-17 Highgate Road, NW5 (071 284 0303). Kentish Town underground/N2 bus. **Open** 7.30-11pm Mon-Thur, Sat; 7.30pm-2am Fri. **Music** 9pm. **Admission** £6-£10. **Credit** A, AmEx, DC, £TC, V.
See picture and caption.

T & C 2
20-22 Highbury Corner, N5 (071 700 5716/071 284 1221). Highbury & Islington underground/N92 bus. **Open** 7.30pm-2am daily. **Music** 9pm. **Admission** £4-£6. **Credit** A, AmEx, DC, £TC, V.
A small and intimate branch of the fine Town & Country Club. This one stages gentler rock, country and world music two nights a week, with cabaret on other nights.

Wembley Arena
Empire Way, Wembley, Middlesex (081 900 1234). Wembley Park underground or Wembley Central underground/BR/N18 bus. **Open** 6.30-11pm various nights. **Music** 7.30pm. **Admission** £9-£25. **Credit** A, AmEx, DC, V.
The largest indoor venue in London – and only for dedicated fans. Chances are that if you like the band, you'll overlook the venue's faults, such as the lack of atmosphere, the sound problems and the extortionately-priced merchandise and refreshments.

Wembley Stadium
Empire Way, Wembley, Middlesex (081 900 1234/081 902 8833). Wembley Park underground or Wembley Central underground/BR/N18 bus. **Open** 7.30-11pm various nights. **Admission** £14-£25. **Credit**

A, AmEx, DC, V.
Not even the video screens can make this mammoth 70,000-seater football stadium feel united; and no matter where you stand, the sound reaches you ten minutes after it left the artiste's mouth. Take your own sandwiches, arrive early to mark out your territory, and even if it's summer, take a large piece of plastic sheeting. If it's not raining, someone will be sure to shower you with beer.

PUBS & WINE BARS

Bull & Gate
389 Kentish Town Road, NW5 (071 485 5358). Kentish Town underground/N2 bus. **Open** 11am-3pm, 5.30-11pm, Mon-Fri; 11am-11pm Sat; noon-3pm, 7-10.30pm Sun. **Music** 8-11pm Mon-Sat. **Admission** £3; £2.50 students, UB40s; £2-£2.50 members.

Membership free. **No credit cards.**
At one time this was London's most notorious indie spawning-ground, but now there's a less adventurous management. You can still see up to five bands a night, although quality ranges from the inspired to the awful. The management has changed hands, but the vomit in the sinks remains.

Carnarvon Castle
7 Chalk Farm Road, NW1 (071 485 7858). Camden Town underground/N2, N29, N90, N93 bus. **Open** 11am-3pm, 5.30-11pm Mon; noon-3pm, 6.30pm-midnight Tue-Fri; noon-6pm, 7.30pm-midnight Sat; noon-4pm, 7-10.30pm Sun. **Music** 9.30pm Tue-Sat; noon-3pm, 7-10.30pm Sun. **Admission** £2-£3. **No credit cards.**
Regular standard R&B bands always ensure a hearty, if beer-drenched, night out. 'A good time' in its traditional pub form.

Cricketers
Kennington Oval, SE11 (071 735 3059). Oval underground/N59, N78, N79, N87 bus.

Open 8-11pm Mon-Sat; 8-10.30pm Sun. **Music** 9pm daily. **Admission** £2.50-£4. **No credit cards.**
This enterprising venue gives encouragement to fledgling indie bands, with an occasional world-music act thrown in. The management has an open-minded attitude.

Dover Street Wine Bar
8-9 Dover Street, W1 (071 629 9813). Green Park underground. **Open** noon-3.30pm, 5.30pm-3am Mon-Fri; 8pm-3am Sat. **Music** 10pm Mon-Sat. **Admission** £2-£6. **Credit** A, AmEx, DC, £TC, V.
A friendly, candle-lit basement brasserie, with seating for 200, featuring jazz, R&B, soul, blues and a small dance floor.

Dublin Castle
94 Parkway, NW1 (071 485 1773). Camden Town underground/N2, N29, N90, N93 bus. **Open** 11am-3pm, 5.30-11pm Mon-Sat; noon-3pm, 7-10.30pm Sun. **Music** 9pm Tue-Sun. **Admission** £2.50-£3.50. **No credit cards.**
A stage the size of a postage stamp. Favoured music is jump 'n' jive, rockabilly, cajun and freewheeling country.

Greyhound Fulham
175 Fulham Palace Road, W6 (071 385 0526). Hammersmith underground/N11, N93, N97 bus. **Open** 11am-11pm Mon-Sat; noon-3pm, 7-10pm Sun. **Music** 8pm Mon-Sat. **Admission** £2-£5. **No credit cards.**
A well-run venue with a solid reputation for putting on up-and-coming acts plus more established R&B. It's a spacious pub with a huge bar.

Half Moon
93 Lower Richmond Road, SW15 (081 788 2387). Putney Bridge underground/N14 bus. **Open** 11am-3pm, 5.30-11pm Mon-Thur; 11am-11pm Fri, Sat; noon-3pm, 7-10.30pm Sun. **Music** 8.30pm daily; 12.30pm Sun. **Admission** £2.50-£5. **No credit cards.**
The small stage of this pub is popular with ex-members of lesser-known R&B bands. Good-time boogieing is guaranteed most nights of the week in the packed back room.

King's Head
115 Upper Street, N1 (071 226 1916). Angel underground or Highbury & Islington underground/BR/N92 bus. **Open** 11am-11pm Mon-Wed; 11am-midnight Thur-Sat; noon-3pm, 7-10.30pm Sun. **Music** 9.30pm daily. **Admission** usually free. **No credit cards.**
A laid-back but crowded pub in the heart of Islington, this is a popular haunt for solo and acoustic duos. *See also chapter* **Theatre.**

Lennons
13-14 Upper St Martin's Lane, WC2 (071 836 4200). Leicester Square underground. **Open** noon-3am Mon-Sat. **Music** 11pm. **Admission** £5 after 11pm. **Credit** A, AmEx, DC, £TC, V.
A wine bar/restaurant which was set up by John Lennon's ex-wife Cynthia. You can be entertained by gentle rock duos while you eat unappetizing and expensive food.

Mean Fiddler
24-28A Harlesden High Street, NW10 (081 965 2487). Willesden Junction underground/BR/N18 bus. **Open** 8pm-2am Mon-Sat; noon-3pm, 8pm-1am Sun. **Music** 10pm. **Admission** £3-£6. **Credit** A, V.
See **picture and caption.**

The **Town & Country Club** *must be many people's favourite London venue, riding on a wave of success that's due to an active and open-minded booking policy. It's easy to get to and an ideal size: stand anywhere and you'll get good views and sound. There are two long, accessible and reasonably-priced bars, efficient cloakroom staff, plenty of loos, seating upstairs and loads of space for even the most energetic dancers. This is just as well: some of the most rocking bands in town perform here and many major acts use this stage as a warm-up to nationwide tours. It deserves an award.*

*The **Mean Fiddler** (listed under **Pub/Wine Bar Venues**) is going from strength to strength. Originally famous for staging country & western and folk music, the Fiddler is now a home for major indie rock bands. The main area has plenty of sitting and standing room, plus a high balcony and good spacious bars. In the smaller acoustic room (with poorer sound) you can see more folk-oriented acts. Fiddler regulars caught Tanita Tikaram warbling her first, nervous notes here.*

New Merlins Cave
Margery Street, WC1 (071 837 2097). King's Cross underground/BR. **Open** 11am-11pm Mon-Sat; noon-3pm, 7-10.30pm Sun. **Music** 9pm daily; 12.20pm Sun. **Admission** £2.50; £2 students, UB40s. **No credit cards.**
A large and adventurous venue for London's indie bands. There are usually two or three acts per night.

New Pegasus
109 Green Lanes, N16 (071 226 5930). Manor House underground/N21, N29, N90 bus. **Open** 11.30am-11.30pm Mon-Sat; noon-3pm, 7-10pm Sun. **Music** 9.30pm Wed-Sun. **Admission** £2.50-£3.
Mixed and lively music is put on every night of the week at this large venue, from indie to ska to goth.

Opera On The Green
127 The Precinct, Shepherd's Bush, W12 (081 749 5928). Shepherd's Bush underground/N11, N89. **Open** 7.30pm-1am Mon-Thur; 7.30pm-2am Fri, Sat. **Admission** from £3. **No credit cards.**
Nothing to do with classical music, this venue attracts indie, goth and psychedelic bands.

Plough Stockwell
90 Stockwell Road, SW9 (071 274 3879). Clapham North or Stockwell underground/N87 bus. **Open** 11am-3pm, 6.30pm-midnight Mon-Sat; noon-3pm, 7-10.30pm Sun. **Music** 9.30pm Tue-Sun; 12.30pm Sun. **Admission** £2-£3. **No credit cards.**
A very popular south London venue with rock residencies and standard R&B. It's open most nights of the week, and jazz bands play on Saturday nights (*see chapter* **Late Night London**).

Powerhaus
1 Liverpool Road, N1 (071 837 3218/credit card booking 081 963 0940). Angel underground/N92, N96 bus. **Open** 8pm-2am Mon-Sat; 7-10.30pm Sun. **Music** 9pm daily. **Admission** £3-£6. **Credit** A, V.
The former Pied Bull pub has had its public bar incorporated into the music venue. The stage and sound are good for a mix of lively folk and rock.

Sir George Robey
240 Seven Sisters Road, N4 (071 263 4581). Finsbury Park underground/BR/N21, N29, N90 bus. **Open** 8pm-2am Mon-Sat; 8-

10.30pm Sun. **Music** 9.30pm daily. **Admission** £2-£5. **No credit cards.**
A large, dark pub which is prone to all-day grebo grunges and goth thrash festivals. The organizers also promote squat rock, psychotrash and, in their own words, 'bands of varying degrees of proficiency'. Late opening hours and up to six bands a night.

Swan
1 Fulham Broadway, SW6 (071 385 1840). Fulham Broadway underground N11, N14 bus. **Open** noon-3pm, 5pm-midnight Mon-Sat; noon-3pm, 7-10.30pm Sun. **Music** 9pm daily. **Admission** £1.50-£2. **No credit cards.**
A traditional pub with traditional pub rock & roll from favoured regulars.

Station Tavern
41 Bramley Road, W11 (071 727 4053). Latimer Road underground. **Open** 11am-11pm Mon-Sat; noon-3pm, 7-10.30pm Sun. **Music** 9pm Mon-Sat; noon, 8.30pm Sun. **Admission** free.
A large pub where you can see British blues veterans for free.

CLUB VENUES

In many venues, the division between live music and pure dance clubs is no longer distinct. A word of warning: some trendier spots will be fussy about attire and may give problems on the door. Drinks tend to be more expensive than in pub venues and even in the freezing winter months bouncers like to develop a long queue, just because it looks good.

100 Club
100 Oxford Street, W1 (071 636 0933). Tottenham Court Road underground. **Open** 7.45pm-1am Mon-Sat; 7.45-11.30pm Sun. **Admission** £3-£6. **No credit cards.**
The Sex Pistols staged one of their first London gigs in this basement club in Oxford Street. Although it's hard to get a view of the stage, it's a fun place. These days you're more likely to hear trad and modern jazz, rockabilly, blues and swing.

Borderline
Orange Yard, Manette Street, WC2 (071 497 2261). Leicester Square or Tottenham Court Road underground. **Open** 8pm-3am Mon-Sat. **Admission** £5. **No credit cards.**
A basement venue in the centre of town which has become popular with record companies breaking in new acts. All sorts of pre-mega stardom bands play here, from Texas to Was Not (Was), (*see chapter* **Late Night London**).

JAZZ VENUES

Most of the places listed here are well-established haunts for jazzers but

there are many other restaurants and pubs that have trad jazz while you eat. Watch out for the distinction between trad jazz venues and places that stage more improvisational artists.

Bass Clef
35 Coronet Street, N1 (071 729 2476/071 729 2440). Old Street underground/N83 bus. **Open** 7.30pm-2am Tue-Sat; noon-3pm, 7.30-11.30pm Sun. **Music** 9pm. **Admission** £3.50-£7. **Credit** A, AmEx, DC, V.
A crowded and steaming basement club that's difficult to find in the backstreets of Hoxton. It plays host to well-known jazz and Latin artists from Britain and abroad. World music is also staged regularly. The capacity is limited: arrive early or book (*see chapter* **Late Night London**). *Restaurant*

Bulls Head
Barnes Bridge, SW13 (081 876 5241). Hammersmith underground, then 9 bus/Barnes BR/N93 bus. **Open** 11am-11pm Mon-Sat; noon-3pm, 7-10.30pm Sun. **Music** 8.30pm daily; 12.30pm Sun. **Admission** £3-£5. **Credit** A, AmEx, £TC, V.
A riverside pub which serves good food to go with traditional jazz. Every night you can witness some of the finest jazz musicians on the British circuit.

Duke of Wellington
119 Balls Pond Road, N1 (071 249 3729). Highbury & Islington underground/BR/Dalston Junction BR/N83, N93 bus. **Open** 5pm-midnight Mon-Fri; noon-midnight Sat; noon-3pm, 7-10.30pm Sun. **Music** times vary. **Admission** free-£4; £2 students, UB40s. **No credit cards.**
A pub venue with a respected reputation for staging adventurous contemporary jazz and free-improvisation combos. It's small and there's no booking, so arrive early.

Jazz Café
56 Newington Green Road, N16 (071 359 4936). Highbury & Islington underground/BR/Canonbury BR/N92, N96 bus. **Open** 6pm-12.30am Mon-Sat; 7-11pm Sun. **Music** 9pm Mon-Sat; 8.30pm Sun. **Admission** free-£3. **No credit cards.**
The best jazz venue in Islington: it's cheap, has charm and atmosphere. The café gets very packed so arrive early. Expect anything from contemporary fusion to experimental and Afro-jazz (*see chapter* **Late Night London**).

La Prison
79 Stoke Newington High Street, N16 (071 923 0775). Stoke Newington BR/67, 73, 76, 106, 243, N83 bus. **Open** 8.30pm-1am Mon, Wed, Thur; 10.30pm-3am Fri, Sat; 1-4pm, 9.30pm-2am Sun. **Music** from 9.30pm Wed, Thur. **Admission** free-£6. **No credit cards.**
A medium-sized and relatively new venue with a sporadic billing of young, usually British, jazz talents. Check *Time Out* for gig details.

Ronnie Scott's
47 Frith Street, W1 (071 439 0747). Leicester Square, Piccadilly Circus or Tottenham Court Road underground. **Open** 8.30pm-3am Mon-Sat. **Music** 9.30pm daily. **Admission** £10-£12; £4-£6 students. **Credit** A, AmEx, DC, £TC, V.
This legendary jazz venue in the heart of Soho still attracts all the major visiting jazz heroes. Book in advance, or arrive early (9.30pm), as there's usually a queue. The sound and atmosphere are excellent. Unfortunately the charges for food (tables are next to the stage) and drink are extortionate and the staff are often frosty. If you arrive early, you'll catch Ronnie's infamous warm-up jokes. Sunday nights are for rock/soul/world music bands (*see chapter* **Late-Night London**).

Palookaville
13A James Street, WC2 (071 240 5857). Covent Garden underground. **Open** noon-3.30pm, 5.30pm-1.30am Mon-Sat; 7pm-12.30am Sun. **Music** 8.45pm daily. **Admission** free. **Credit** A, AmEx, DC, V.
Admission is free to this cosy restaurant/wine bar which has mellow live jazz duos and quartets. There's a small dance floor if you feel like giving it a twirl (*see chapter* **Late Night London**).

Pizza Express
10 Dean Street, W1 (071 437 9595/439 8722).Tottenham Court Road underground. **Open** ; 8.30pm-1am Tue-Sun. **Music** 9.30pm Tue-Sun. **Admission** £4-£7. **Credit** A, AmEx, DC, V.
Well-known venue in the cellar of a pizza restaurant with its own resident band; popular mainstream combos also make an appearance. You have to eat, but the food is good (*see chapter* **Late Night London**).

Pizza On The Park
11 Knightsbridge, Hyde Park Corner, SW1 (071 235 5550). Hyde Park Corner underground. **Open** 7.30pm-2am daily. **Music** 9.15pm Tue-Sat. **Admission** £4-£10. **Credit** A, AmEx, DC, V.
An elegantly-designed restaurant. There are two jazz sets, one at around 9pm, the other at 11pm. Eat and be entertained by many popular names in mainstream and standard jazz (*see chapter* **Late Night London**).

Prince of Orange
118 Lower Road, SE16 (071 237 9181). Surrey Docks underground/47, 188, N47 bus. **Open** 7pm-midnight Mon-Sat; noon-3pm, 7-10.30pm Sun. **Music** 9pm Mon-Sat; 8.30pm Sun. **Admission** free. **Credit** V.
Mainstream and swing outfits play at this major south London jazz venue. It's busy, friendly, vibrant and free.

Vortex
Stoke Newington Church Street, N16 (071 254 6516). Stoke Newington BR/67, 73, 76, 106, 243, N83 bus. **Open** 11am-11pm Mon-Sat; noon-10.30pm Sun. **Music** 8.30pm daily. **Admission** £1-£4. **Credit** A, V.
An imaginatively-run north London venue which makes an effective contribution to the promotion of local jazz talent. Look out for their mini-festivals.

COUNTRY & FOLK VENUES

Cecil Sharpe House
2 Regent's Park Road, NW1 (071 485 2206). Camden Town underground/N2, N29, N90, N93. **Open** 9.30am-5.30pm Mon-Wed, Fri;

Is there life after acid house? But of course: there's techno-trance-soul-electro-industrial house or, more simply, Trance Dance, as expounded by **Electribe 1:01.** *'Talking with myself', their first single, featured the gut-grabbing vocals of Billy Ray Martin, a 29 year old German who's already talking ambitiously about a tour that's going to redefine the concept of live concerts. This we have to see.*

9.30am-5.30pm, 7.30-10pm Thur; 7.30-11pm Sat. **Music** 7.30pm Sat. **Admission** £2-£3.50. **No credit cards**.
A hub of folk activity, staging traditional dancing, fayres, regular singers' nights and special guest evenings. It's cheap, friendly and set in a canal-side building.

Cellar Upstairs
The Assembly House Pub, 292 Kentish Town Road, NW5 (071 485 2031). Kentish Town underground/N2 bus. **Open** 11am-11pm Mon-Sat; noon-3pm, 7-10.30pm Sun. **Music** 8.15-11pm Sat. **Admission** £2.50; £2 OAPs, UB40s. **No credit cards**.
A folk institution, held weekly in an upstairs room of a pub. It's a good place to see both familiar and fresh faces on the scene.

Halfway House
142 The Broadway, West Ealing, W13 (081 567 0236). Ealing Broadway underground/N50, N89. **Open** 11am-3pm, 5.30-11pm Mon-Thur; 11am-11pm Fri, Sat; noon-3pm, 7-10.30pm Sun. **Music** 9pm daily. **No credit cards**.
Specializing in Irish and country music, Halfway House has a resident roster that includes hot country through to cajun and blues.

Hare & Hounds
181 Upper Street, N1 (071 226 2992). Highbury & Islington underground/BR/N92 bus. **Open** 11am-midnight Mon, Thur-Sat; 11am-11pm Tue, Wed; noon-3pm, 7-10.30pm Sun. **Music** 9.15pm daily. **Admission** £2-£3. **No credit cards**.
A good place to see honky-tonk and country-rock foot-tapping bands.

Swan
215 Clapham Road, SW9 (071 274 1526). Stockwell underground/N87 bus. **Open** 11am-11pm daily. **Music** 9pm Thur-Sat. **Admission** free-£2.50. **No credit cards**.
Popular traditional Irish bands have made this Stockwell pub their base. A good drink and a good time.

OTHER VENUES

Check *Time Out* magazine for details of gigs. Universities and colleges are atmospheric, cheap venues.

Africa Centre
38 King Street, WC2 (071 836 1973). Covent Garden underground. **Open** 9pm-2am Thur; 9pm-3am Fri. **Music** 10.30pm Fri. **Admission** £4-£5. **No credit cards**.
The centre of arts, crafts and political activity for London's African community. Live music usually takes place in the large hall and you can expect a good African DJ. There's always a clear view to the stage and non-stop dancing (*see chapter* **Late-Night London**).

Albany Empire
Douglas Way, SE8 (081 691 3333). New Cross underground/BR/N47, N77 bus. **Open** 10am-6.30pm, 8-11pm Mon-Fri; 11am-3pm, 8-11pm Sat; 11am-3pm Sun. **Music** 8pm Wed-Sun. **Admission** £3-£6. **Credit** A, V.
This well-run, community-oriented venue in

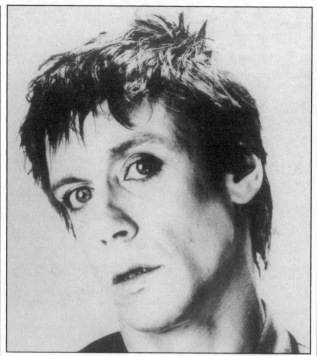

It was in 1988 that **Iggy Pop** *last came to town, upsetting many of his fans with some drug-free, heavy metal concerts based on his album,* Instinct. *Is the grandfather of punk losing his teeth? Or finding his lust for life?*

Deptford has a varied programming policy, incorporating hip hop, jazz and even some rock surprises. It's spacious, cheap and easy to get to (*see chapter* **Late-Night London**).

Electric Ballroom
184 Camden High Street, NW1 (071 485 9006). Camden Town underground/N2, N29, N90, N93 bus. **Open** 10.30pm-2am Fri, Sat. **Admission** £4-£5. **No credit cards**.
This under-used and run-down venue in Camden is the site for record fairs and an indoor market at weekends. Its medium-sized capacity is equally suited to jazz or new wave sounds (*see chapter* **Late-Night London**).

Fairfield Halls
Park Lane, Croydon, Surrey (081 688 9291/681 0821). East Croydon BR. **Open** 10am-8pm Mon-Sat. **Admission** £5-£20. **Credit** A, AmEx, DC, V.
This plush theatre is a popular stop-off point for mainstream popular acts (many of them has-beens). However, it's a reasonably-priced and relaxing.

South Bank Centre
South Bank, Belvedere Road, SE1 (box office 071 928 8800; general information 071 928 3002; recorded information 071 633 0932). Waterloo underground/BR/Riverbus. **Open** 7.45-10pm daily. **Music** 8pm daily. **Admission** free-£15. **Credit** A, AmEx, DC, V.
One of the major London venues, with three large, all-seating music theatres, it's the location for major jazz festivals (*see also chapters* **Dance**, **Music: Classical & Opera** and **Theatre**.

ROCK & ROLL TOURS

There are many facts (from the fascinating to the frankly tedious) that you can discover on a rock & roll tour of London. The **Rock Tour of London**'s double-decker bus leaves from Regent Street and trails around the capital's famous rock sites (*phone 071 734 0227 for details*). For more rock nostalgia, Madame Tussaud's has opened **Rock Circus** in the London Pavilion, Piccadilly Circus, W1 (*071 734 7203*) with waxworks of heroes and even animated life-sized models of The Beatles. If you feel like becoming a star yourself, go to **Star Trax** on the ground floor of the Trocadero, Piccadilly Circus, W1 where for £24.95, you can make your own rock video.

Night Life

Acid house and tabloid headlines! *Time Out's Dave Swindells* shows there's more to London's night-life than crazy clubbers on Ecstasy.

London's nightlife is arguably the most cosmopolitan to be found anywhere in the world, with venues to suit every taste in music, fashion and atmosphere. It was the proliferation of the one-nighter clubs during the eighties which stimulated this diversity.

New **one-nighter clubs** are continually opening up and closing down; each with their own sharply-defined profile. The first one nighters, at the beginning of the eighties, were exclusive parties hosted by flamboyant personalities for their friends and their particular trendy clique. Now, though, they are mainly inspired by the latest dance music and the DJ is the main attraction. While many last no more than a few weeks, others, like **Gaz's Rockin' Blues** (Thursday at Gossips) have become permanent fixtures on the clubland calender.

In 1988 London witnessed the growth of a musical phenomenon. A potent combination of 'House' disco music, originating in Chicago, and so-called 'Balearic Beats' (new European dance) created a dance-floor revolution, drawing huge crowds of energetic dancers. The music was played in a sweltering club atmosphere created by multiple lasers, lights and dry-ice. In 1989, in the 'second summer of love', the crowds grew too big for the clubs and people spilled over into huge all-night parties in the countryside around London. Luckily the weather was good. The authorities' ludicrous over-reaction to this comparatively trouble-free trend is so extreme that legislation is planned to stop people partying in large numbers at such original places.

The dance music scene is mainly of interest to the younger crowd, but there are plenty of more intimate (and sober) venues where it's possible to communicate without shouting. More mature clubbers (and tired dancers) may feel comfortable at some of the smarter, and more expensive, clubs in the West End, Mayfair, Kensington and Chelsea. Or they they may prefer one of the many new, smaller clubs, where singers and musicians perform classic songs or their own original material.

In London you can dance to anything from African to zydeco – if you know where to go. Find out in the Nightlife section of *Time Out* magazine, where you'll find listings of about 150 different clubs each week. In the meantime, you should bear in mind a number of suggestions to ensure that your night on the town lives up to expectations.

MEMBERSHIP

Venues are prohibited from selling alcohol after 11pm unless they have either a music-and-dance licence or a club licence. Most opt for the latter, since it gives them the freedom to pick and choose members. However, most clubs' membership regulations are quite flexible. Many venues include a membership fee as part of the the admission price, while most one-nighters only claim to be 'Members Only' if they don't think you would 'fit in'. If in doubt, phone and ask, but as a rough guide, the smarter the venue, the tighter the membership regulations.

DRESS CODE

Most nightspots have a vague 'smart but casual' dress code. Usually it's jeans, T-shirts and trainers (sneakers) that are frowned upon at the smarter venues, but at the end of the eighties these same clothes appeared to be the nightlife 'uniform'. Although fashion in clubs isn't as important as it used to be, it's worth bearing in mind that if a club has a reputation for a particular kind of music there's usually a style to go with it.

TRANSPORT

Clubs tend to close at around 3am, well over two hours after the underground network has ceased to operate. Taxis can be very hard to find at that time of the morning, so if at all possible it's worth arranging homeward transport in advance. Alternatively, you could take an unlicensed 'mini-cab' – although it would perhaps be unwise for a single woman to do so; reputable cab companies are listed in *chapter* **Travel**. Get to know the night bus system (*see chapters* **Late-Night London** and **Travel**), which may offer quite an entertaining ride home if you can stay awake.

The Astoria
157 Charing Cross Road, WC2 (071 434 0403). Tottenham Court Road underground. **Open** 7.30pm-3.30am Mon-Thur; 10pm-3.30am Fri, Sat. **Admission** £4-£7.50. **Credit** A, AmEx, DC, V.
Although it's never been properly adapted for nightlife use, this former theatre does have a huge balcony and an enormous dancefloor, which are always packed with a young, trendy crowd at the wildly-popular SIN on Saturdays. Various live concerts and one-nighters take place on other nights. *See chapter* **Music: Rock, Folk & Jazz**.

Bass Clef
35 Coronet Street, N1 (071 729 2476/071 729 2440). Old Street underground/BR/N83 bus. **Open** 7.30pm-2am Mon-Sat; 7.30pm-midnight Sun. **Admission** £3.50-£8 Mon-Sun; 25% discount students, UB40s, Musicians' Union. **Credit** A, AmEx, £TC, V.
This small, atmospheric club is one of London's best live jazz venues. It specializes in live jazz sessions (Tue-Thur), Latin jazz (Fri), African and 'tropical tunes' (Sat), and seventies funky tunes (Mon), with excellent and appropriate turntable sounds. Very popular, especially at weekends. *See chapters* **Late-Night London** and **Music: Rock, Folk & Jazz**.

The Borderline
Orange Yard, off Manette Street, WC2 (071 437 8595). Tottenham Court Road underground. **Open** 8pm-3am Mon-Sat. **Admission** £5-£7. **Credit** V.
A fairly basic bar-room venue (with Tex-Mex food available) for lively, unpretentious dance nights and live performance clubs. There are live band(s) at weekends.

Busby's
157 Charing Cross Road, WC2 (071 734 6963). Tottenham Court Road underground. **Open** 10.30pm-3am Mon-Sat; 8pm-midnight Sun. **Admission** £4-£7. **No credit cards.**
A large, mainstream disco which is popular as a result of its central location, rather than for its chrome and mirror styling. It's home to a variety of one-nighters including three gay club nights (Mon, Thur, Sat).

Café de Paris
3 Coventry Street, WC1 (071 437 2036). Leicester Square or Piccadilly Circus underground. **Open** 7.30pm-1am Mon, Thur; 10.30pm-3.30am Wed; 7.30pm-3am Fri, Sat; 7.30pm-midnight Sun. **Admission** £2-£7. **No credit cards.**
One of London's few elegant period-piece venues (dating from 1926) that plays host on Wednesdays to stylish clubbers, Sloane Rangers and Euro-trendies. On other nights a swing, jazz and retro dance band plays for older, dressed-up dancers to tango to. Meals are served on the balcony. Astonishingly, there is no preservation order on the building, so that the plans to knock it down and

redevelop the site in the early nineties may be impossible to stop. *See chapter* **Early Twentieth Century.**

Camden Palace
1 Camden Road, NW1 (071 387 0428). Mornington Crescent or Camden Town underground/N2, N29, N90, N93 bus. **Open** 9pm-2.30am Mon-Thur; 8pm-2.30am Fri; 9pm-2.30am Sat. **Admission** £5 Mon, Thur; £4 Tue, Wed; £8 before 9pm, £10 after 9pm, Fri; £6 before 10.30pm, £7 after, Sat. **Credit** A, AmEx, £TC, V.
This is one of the most popular tourist venues in town – and none the worse for that. A spacious dancefloor, lavish lights, a chunky sound system, a cocktail bar and a restaurant can all be discovered in the myriad different levels of this former music-hall theatre, although the club's disco design from 1980 is looking a bit tacky now. There's usually a commercial dance mix on most nights, except Tuesday's 'alternative' pop and rock night, *Feet First*, and the very lively sixties soul and pop session on Wednesdays. *Wheelchair access.*

Crazy Larry's
533 Kings Road, SW10 (071 376 5555). Fulham Broadway or Sloane Square underground/N11, N14 bus. **Open** 9pm-1am Mon-Wed; 9pm-2am Fri, Sat; 6pm-midnight Sun. **Admission** £5 Mon-Wed; £6 Thur-Sat; £3.50 Sun. **Credit** A, AmEx, £TC, V.
A comfortable, plush disco-cum-restaurant for a more civilized night out. Since it's in Chelsea, it's known as a Sloane Rangers'

haunt, but it also attracts a mixed crowd of trendies, buppies and hardcore dancers and features occasional one-nighters. *See chapter* **To The Eighties.**

Dingwalls
Camden Lock, Chalk Farm Road, NW1 (071 267 4967). Camden Town or Chalk Farm underground/Camden Road BR/N1, N29, N90, N93 bus. **Open** 8pm-2am Mon, Wed; 10pm-3am Tue, Thur-Sat; 9pm-1am Sun. **Admission** £1.50-£6. **No credit cards.** *See* **picture and caption.**
See also chapter **Music: Rock, Folk & Jazz.**

Electric Ballroom
184 Camden High Street, NW1 (071 485 9006). Camden Town underground/Camden Road BR/N2, N29, N90, N93 bus. **Open** 10pm-2am Thur; 10.30pm-2am Fri, Sat. **Admission** £5 Thur, Sat; £4 Fri. **No credit cards.**
A large basic two-tiered venue (with a huge dancefloor) that should have been refurbished long ago but which still draws crowds for their weekend dance sessions, where they'll mix anything from rock and glamour punk to trash disco and House dance. *Restricted wheelchair access.*

Empire Ballroom
Leicester Square, WC2 (071 437 1446). Leicester Square or Piccadilly Circus underground. **Open** 8.30pm-2am Mon-Wed; 8.30pm-3am Thur-Sat. **Admission** £5 before 10pm, £6 after 10pm, Mon-Thur; £6 before 10pm, £8 after 10pm, Fri, Sat. **Credit** A, AmEx, V.
If you like wild lightshows, lasers, video

screens, plush furnishings and a revolving stage for the in-house band at one of Europe's largest discos, then this is the club for you.

The Fridge
Town Hall Parade, Brixton Hill, SW2 (071 326 5100). Brixton underground/BR/N2, N78 bus. **Open** 10pm-3am Mon, Tue, Thur-Sat; first Wed each month. **Admission** £3 before 11pm, £5 after 11pm, Mon; £3 before 11pm, £4 after 11pm, Tue, Wed; £6 Thur-Sat. **No credit cards.**
See **picture and caption.**
Wheelchair access by arrangement. Restaurant.

Gossips
69 Dean Street, W1 (071 734 0201). Leicester Square or Tottenham Court Road underground. **Open** 10pm-3am Mon-Sat. **Admission** £4-£6.
The archetypal mid-eighties one-nighter venue: a dark cellar, home to all sorts of dance music, from psychedelia and heavy metal, to ska (at the long-running Gaz's Rockin' Blues on Thursdays), to black dance music and reggae.

Heaven
Underneath the Arches, Villiers Street, WC2 (071 839 3852). Embankment underground or Charing Cross underground/BR.. **Open** 10.30pm-3.30am Mon-Sat. **Admission** £3.50-£8. **Credit** A, AmEx, £TC, V.
London's major gay club (*see chapter* **Lesbian & Gay**) is also one of the best dance venues in town: a maze of bars, corridors and large dancefloors with excellent lasers, sound system and lightshows. On Mondays and Thursdays the club usually goes 'straight' for intense, high-powered dance clubs.

The Hippodrome
Cranbourn Street, WC2 (071 437 4311). Leicester Square underground/N89, N90 buses. **Open** 9pm-3am Mon-Sat. **Admission** £6 Mon, Wed; £8 Tue, Thur; £10 Fri; £12 Sat. **Credit** A, AmEx, DC, £STC, V.
This centrally-sited club has superb lighting and sound systems, but it's expensive and has the bizarre appearance of a chrome-clad disco dinosaur. The club usually offers a 'commercial' mix of dance music for a smartly-dressed crowd (and plenty of tourists), although there may be a heavy-rock night or avant-garde poseurs' parade, depending on your luck.

Legends
29 Old Burlington Street, W1 (071 437 9933). Green Park or Piccadilly Circus underground. **Open** 9.30pm-3am Mon-Thur; 9.30pm-4am Fri, Sat. **Admission** £5-£9. **Credit** A, AmEx, DC, £TC, V.
A sleek nightclub venue that's host to various very good one-nighters (especially at weekends) that attract a mixture of Mayfair trendies, smart Sloanes, wild dancers and snappy dressers.

Limelight
136 Shaftesbury Avenue, WC2 (071 434 0572). Leicester Square underground. **Open** 10pm-3am Mon-Sat; 7pm-2am Sun (licensed till midnight Sun). **Admission** £7 Mon-Thur, Sun; £10 Fri, Sat. **Credit** A, AmEx, DC, £TC, V.
Recently re-furbished in a style intended to emphasise the ecclesiastical and Baronial architectural features of this former church, the entrance now looks like the lobby of a

The transformation of **Dingwalls** *in the late eighties showed how much youth culture had changed during the decade. In danger of becoming a 'Live Music dinosaur' in an age when only dance-floor enthusiasts were regularly packing venues, the club metamorphosed into a serious dance venue that hasn't looked back. Its willingness to promote all kinds of dance music – from Acid Jazz and indie pop to sweet modern soul ballads and rootsy reggae – has made this one of the most popular venues around town.*

GOING GLOBAL

i-D

the magazine discovering
i-Deas for the '**90s**

i-Deas,

Fashion,

Clubs,

Music,

People,

Books,

Films

Subscriptions

(11 issues a year)

£20 UK. £24 Europe. £45
USA, Canada, South
America, Hong Kong,
Singapore, etc (airmail).
£48 Australia, New
Zealand, etc (airmail).
Cheques/postal orders
payable to Levelprint Ltd
in pounds sterling.

i-D magazine, 134/136 Curtain Rd, London EC2A 3AR.
Tel: 01 729 7305. Fax: 01 729 7266.

middle-of-the-range hotel. Although it can be a bit dull in the early part of the week, the sound system is excellent and it's worth a visit towards the weekend, especially if you like designer beers and vodka cocktails.

Maximus
14 Leicester Square, WC2 (071 734 4111). Leicester Square underground. **Open** 8pm-3am Tue-Sun. **Admission** £4-£7. **No credit cards.**
A comfortable mainstream disco with lots of alcoved seating areas and a small dance floor that attracts lots of passing tourists and people who still think cocktails are glamorous. Occasional interesting one-nighters redeem this classic example of mirror-tiled seventies disco kitsch.

Moonlighting
17 Greek Street, W1 (071 734 6308). Leicester Square or Tottenham Court Road underground. **Open** 9pm-3.30am Mon, Wed-Sat. **Admission** £5 Mon, Wed, Thur; £6 Fri; £8 Sat. **Credit** A, AmEx, £TC, V.
Once Le Beat Route, now a comfortable disco-venue that aims to attract a smarter, older crowd to slide on their (very slippery) dancefloor to a commercial dance mix,

Le Palais
242 Shepherd's Bush Road, W6 (081 748 2812). Hammersmith underground/N11, N93, N97 bus. **Open** 9pm-2am Wed, Thur; 9pm-3am Fri-Sat. **Admission** £7 Wed; £2 Thur; £4 before 10.30pm, £6 after 10.30pm, Fri; £5 before 10.30pm, £7 after 10.30pm, Sat. **Credit** A, AmEx, DC, £TC, V.
Redecorated in tacky, Art Deco revival style, West London's major disco comes complete with the requisite lightshow, lasers, video walls and a dance hall in an aircraft hangar. It still feels like a dance hall in an aircraft hangar. *Wheelchair access.*

Samantha's
3 New Burlington Street, W1 (071 734 6249). Oxford Circus or Piccadilly Circus underground. **Open** 9pm-3.30am Mon-Sat. **Admission** £6 Mon-Thur, Sat; £7 Fri. **Credit** £TC.
Another comfortable mainstream disco with lots of alcoved seating, two floors, two dancefloors, a fish pond and swing seats hanging on chains at the bar. Smart dress is expected, so it's probably one of the better discos for more mature ravers.

Shaftesbury's
24 Shaftesbury Avenue, W1 (071 734 2017). Leicester Square or Piccadilly Circus underground. **Open** 9pm-3am Tue-Thur; 9pm-3.30am Fri, Sat. **Admission** £5 Tue-Thur; £5-£7 Fri; £6-£8 Sat. **Credit** A, DC, V.
A lush, plush mainstream venue in the conventional mould. A venue for executives and smartly-dressed tourists, except for occasional one-nighters and Sunday's Confusion night – a hard-dancing session of Latino rhythms and deep House beats which should run and run.

Stringfellow's
16 Upper St Martin's Lane, WC2 (071 240 5534). Covent Garden or Leicester Square underground. **Open** 11.30pm-3.30am Mon-Sat. **Admission** £8 Mon-Thur; £12.50 Fri; £15 Sat. **Credit** A, AmEx, DC, £STC, V.
This is where the stars go, in theory. Well,

you may be lucky but you're more likely to see a dressed-up crowd trying to look elegant in glitzy surroundings. There's an à-la-carte restaurant. *Wheelchair access.*

Subterrania
12 Acklam Road, W10 (081 961 5490). Ladbroke Grove underground/N18, N50 bus. **Open** 8pm-2am Mon-Sat; 8pm-1am Sun. **Admission** £3-£6 Mon-Thur, Sun; £6 Fri; £7 Sat. **Credit** A, V.
Although it's hard to find and in an unlikely location, this is a state-of-the-art club that's a joy to behold. Opened in 1989, this is one of the very few clubs in London to have benefited from late eighties styling. The club has a European atmosphere, a great sound system and cold beer. *Wheelchair access.*

The Tattershall Castle
Victoria Embankment, King Street, SW1 (071 839 6548). Embankment underground. **Open** 8.30pm-2am Mon; 9pm-3am Fri, Sat. **Admission** £2.50 Mon; £6 Fri, Sat. **Credit** A, AmEx, DC, £TC, V.
You want novelty, we got it! How about a disco on a boat moored on the Thames? There's a mainstream mix of disco and pop rock, the boat won't rock too much and you're guaranteed fresh(er) air when you leave the confines of the dancefloor. *See chapter* **New Comedy.**

Tokyo Joe
85 Piccadilly, W1 (071 409 1832). Green Park underground. **Open** 8.30pm-3.30am Mon-Sat. **Admission** £10 Mon-Sat. **Credit** A, AmEx, DC, £STC, V.
A plush nightclub and restaurant with a full-à-la-carte menu. Non members can enter without being accompanied by members.

The Wag Club
35 Wardour Street, W1 (071 437 5534). Leicester Square or Piccadilly Circus underground. **Open** 10.30pm-4.30am Mon-Sat. **Admission** £5 Mon-Wed; £6 Thur; £8 Fri, Sat. **Credit** £STC.
For five years after it opened in the early eighties, the Wag was the place to be. Now the 'Wag crowd' has moved on and today the club responds to trends rather than creating them. Nonetheless, the dance crowd are young, trendy and friendly – unlike the bouncers, who can be unnecessarily choosy at the hugely popular weekend nights.

Wall Street
14 Bruton Place, W1 (071 493 0630). Bond Street or Green Park underground. **Open** 10.30pm-3.30am Mon-Sat. **Admission** £5 Mon, Tue, Thur; £6 Wed; £7 Fri, Sat. **Credit** A, AmEx, DC, £TC, V.
London nightlife's answer to Versailles, there's more gilt in here than in Zsa Zsa Gabor's jewellery box. Two floors of swirling rococo décor and florid styling attempt to bring style and exclusivity back to London's trendy nightlife – so dress up!

Always adventurous and interesting, **The Fridge** *is also the best large dance venue in town. It pioneered multi-media nightlife entertainment with superb décor, films and visuals, allied to live performance and go-go dancers. The club has a small, cheap-and-cheerful café where you can escape the sound of music and the baloney which gives an extra dimension to the club. It attracts a young, trendy crowd, which reflects Brixton's multi-racial culture. A rigorous security check at the door may come as a surprise at first, but on reflection is reassuring.*

Late-night London

If you're expecting the city to be buzzing after 11pm, think again; here we list the few hives of activity.

London is a city dedicated to the 9 to 5 way of life. We've largely got the draconian licensing laws to thank for this, since anywhere being used for public dancing, drinking or entertainment needs a licence. The rules have been tightening up and with each restaurant, club or bar that's refused a licence, the late-night void grows. Unless you're in the centre of town in the early hours you're unlikely to find much to do. The other centres of late-night action are around Queensway, Earl's Court and the Old Kent Road. Some of the places we've listed have been around for years, while others could well have shut since we went to press. If you're ever short of inspiration for a late-night excursion, hail a black cab and ask the driver to take you to where it's happening.

For a more in-depth look at the capital between 11pm and 6am, pick up a copy of the *Time Out Filofax Guide to Late & All Night London*. *See also chapters* **Shopping & Services; New Comedy; Film; Lesbian & Gay; Music: Rock, Folk & Jazz** and **Nightlife**.

COMEDY

The Comedy Store
28A Leicester Square, WC2 (071 839 6665). *Leicester Square underground.* **Open** 8pm, Wed, Thur; 7pm, 11pm Fri, Sat; 7.30pm Sun. **Performances** 9pm Wed, Thur; 8pm, midnight Fri, Sat; 8.30pm Sun. **Admission** £6.
Tickets on the door at this excellent alternative cabaret venue which has been the sounding board for countless numbers of British comedians. Doors open one hour before the show; start queuing early. *Bar till 3am. Food.*

Jongleurs at the Cornet
49 Lavender Gardens, SW11 (081 780 1151). Clapham Common underground then 45 bus/Clapham Junction BR/N68, N87 bus. **Open** 8pm Fri, Sat. **Licensed** to 1.30am. **Admission** £6; £4 students UB40s.
This hugely popular alternative comedy venue south of the river has often been used

for recording television entertainers. Light-hearted atmosphere; young upwardly mobiles meet lager louts and manage to remain dignified throughout.

DRINKING

There are relatively few places to drink after pub hours apart from nightclubs (where you have to pay an admission fee) or restaurants (where you have to eat a full meal). If the last orders bell is ringing around the capital and you're still parched, try one of the late-opening bars we've listed below.

CENTRAL

Café Pelican
45 St Martin's Lane, WC2 (071 379 0309). Leicester Square, Covent Garden underground or Charing Cross underground/BR. **Open** 11am-12.30am Mon-Sat; 11am-midnight Sun. **House wine** £6 bottle, £1.95 glass. Alcohol only served with food after 9.30 pm. **Credit** A, AmEx, DC, £TC, V.
A piece of the *Champs-Elysées* in the centre of London. Full meals, bar snacks, booze and coffee till the early hours.
Wheelchair access. Toilets for the disabled.

SOUTH WEST

The Pheasantry Cocktail Bar
152 King's Road, SW3 (071 351 3084). Sloane Square underground/N11 bus. **Open** 5.30pm-2am Mon-Sat; 7-10pm Sun. **Admission** free Mon-Thur, Sun; £5 Fri, Sat. **House wine** £6.95 bottle, £1.75 glass. **Credit** A, AmEx, DC, EC, £TC, V.
Popular pre-club haunt for lads and lasses before going on to a Leicester Square venue to dance round handbags. Tasteless décor, obnoxious cocktail list, very Club Tropicana.

SOUTH EAST

Gin Palace
205-209 Old Kent Road, SE1 (071 237 4911). Elephant & Castle underground/BR/53, 177, N77, N85 bus. **Open** 8pm-1am Mon-Wed; 8pm-2am Thur-Sat; 7pm-midnight Sun. **Admission** free Sun-Thur; £2 9-10.30pm, £3 after 10.30pm Fri, Sat. **Credit** £TC.
Sounds a bit glammy, but gin is not the only drink on sale. Punters knock back frightening amounts of intoxicating liquids before attempting to negotiate the dance floor.
Wheelchair access. Toilets for the disabled.

Frog & Nightgown
148 Old Kent Road, SE1 (071 701 1689). Elephant & Castle underground/BR/53, 177, N77, N85 bus. **Open** 7.30pm-2am Mon-Sat; 7.30pm-midnight Sun. **Admission** free Mon-Wed; £1 Thur, Sun; £3 Fri, Sat.
If conversation won't suffice, try this place which has the added distractions of laser shows and satellite TV.

Thomas-à-Beckett
320 Old Kent Road, SE1 (071 703 2644). Elephant & Castle underground/BR/53, 177, N77, N85 bus. **Open** 8pm-midnight Mon-Wed, Sun; 8pm-1am Thur-Sat. **Admission** £3 8pm-1.30am Fri, Sat; otherwise free.
The décor here mainly consists of photographs of famous boxers who trained at the gym upstairs. Typical of pubs in the area; a little intimidating to non-regulars. *See chapter* **Museums.**

EATING

One part of London's nightlife which isn't lacking in quantity, but sadly in variety. If you fancy something more substantial than a burger after 11pm, most parts of London have at least one restaurant which stays open late. For a more detailed look at London's restaurant selection see the latest edition of the *Time Out Guide to Eating Out in London*.

CENTRAL

Bill Stickers
18 Greek Street, W1 (071 437 0582). Tottenham Court Road underground. **Open** 5.30pm-3am Mon-Sat. **Admission** £3-£5 Fri, Sat. **Average** £12. **House wine** £6.50 bottle, £1.95 glass. **Service** 12½%. **Credit** A, AmEx, DC, £TC, V.
Last year Bill Stickers changed it's name to The Establishment, but it's now gone back to its former identity. There's a loud, garish décor; punters can even sit at Marilyn Monroe's dining table upstairs. Frequent club nights with dance floor downstairs, phone for details.

Canton
11 Newport Place, WC2 (071 437 6220). Leicester Square underground. **Open** 11am-1am Mon-Thur, Sun; 11am-2am Fri, Sat. **Licensed** till 11pm daily. **Average** £9. **House wine** £7.20 bottle. **Credit** AmEx, DC, £TC, V.
Service is brisk at this Cantonese café/restaurant on two floors. Passers-by always question how long the duck carcasses have been hanging in the window, but we've got no complaints about the freshness or quality of the food.

Costa Dorada
47 & 55 Hanway Street, W1 (071 636 7139). Tottenham Court Road underground. **Open** *tapas bar* noon-3am Mon-Fri; 8pm-3am Sat; 8pm-midnight Sun; *restaurant* 8pm-3am Mon-Sat; 8pm-midnight Sun. **Average** £15. **House wine** £7.75 bottle, £1.75 glass. **Credit** A, DC, £TC, V.
Why bother with the Costa Brava when you can find all the action, including flamenco dancing, at this restaurant off Tottenham Court Road. Good paella and tapas, with a lively atmosphere.

Ed's Easy Diner
*12 Moor Street, W1 (071 439 1955).
Leicester Square underground.* **Open**
11.30am-midnight Mon-Thur; 11.30am-1am
Fri, Sat; 11.30am-11pm Sun. **Licensed**
11.30am-midnight Mon-Sat; noon-11pm Sun
(beer licence only). **Average** £5. **Credit** £TC.
See **picture and caption**.

Harry's
*19 Kingly Street, W1 (071 434 8708). Oxford
Circus or Piccadilly Circus underground.*
Open 10pm-9am Mon-Fri; 10pm-6am Sat.
Average £6. **Service** 10%. **Credit** LV.
Favourite late-night haunt for nightclubbers.
The charismatic proprietor Harry serves up
generous hot breakfasts and delicious hot
drinks to two floors of lively punters.

Los Locos
*24-26 Russell Street, WC2 (071 379 0220).
Covent Garden underground.* **Open** 6pm-
3am Mon-Sat. **Average** £13. **House wine**
£6.80 bottle, £1.80 glass. **Service** 12**2**%.
Credit A, AmEx, DC, EC, £STC, V.
This rowdy Mexican place has a long cocktail list and vegetarian dishes. There's a
disco nightly at 11pm.
Branch *14 Soho Street, W1 (071 287 0005).*

Maharani
*77 Berwick Street, W1 (071 437 8568). Oxford
Circus, Piccadilly Circus, or Tottenham Court
Road underground.* **Open** noon-midnight
daily. **Average** £9. **House wine** £4.95 bottle,
£1.10 glass. **Credit** A, AmEx, DC, EC, £TC, V.
The food at this centrally-located Indian
restaurant is well above average, but the
place does fill up at weekends.
Wheelchair access.

Mr Kong
*21 Lisle Street, W1 (071 437 7341). Leicester
Square underground.* **Open** noon-2am daily.
Licensed noon-midnight Mon-Sat; noon-
10.30pm Sun. **Average** £13. **Minimum** £7.
House wine £5.40 bottle, £1.50 glass.
Service 10%. **Credit** A, AmEx, DC, £TC, V.
One of London's finest Cantonese restau-
rants, Mr Kong's is famous for its seafood
dishes and innovative set menus.

La Reash Cous-Cous House
*23-24 Greek Street, W1 (071 439 1063).
Leicester Square underground.* **Open** noon-
midnight daily. **Licensed** noon-midnight
daily. **Average** £15. **House wine** £6.50 bottle, £1.50 glass. **Credit** A, £TC, V.
Friendly service and atmosphere at this
Middle-Eastern restaurant. If you can't stomach cous-cous, English and French dishes
are also served.

WEST

Angelo's
*78 Westbourne Grove, W2 (071 229 0266).
Bayswater or Notting Hill Gate under-
ground/N50, N89 bus.* **Open** 7pm-3am Mon-
Sat. **Licensed** till 2.30am Mon-Sat. **House
wine** £7 bottle, £1.40 glass. **Average** £14.
Credit A, AmEx, DC, £STC, V.
Although this Greek restaurant with live
bouzouki music (Fri, Sat) is usually fairly
laid back, it occasionally gets lively with
dancing progressing into plate-smashing.

Rose
*13 Hammersmith Road, W14 (071 602
1549). High Street Kensington under-*
ground/N93 bus. **Open** noon-midnight Mon-
Thur, Sun; noon-4am Fri, Sat. **Licensed**
noon-11pm daily. **Average** £8. **House wine**
£7 bottle, £1.30 glass. **Credit** AmEx, £STC.
After 11pm on Friday and Saturday you can
bring-your-own bottle to this Persian restaurant with friendly service and atmosphere.

Tiroler Hut Restaurant
*27 Westbourne Grove, W2 (071 727 3981).
Bayswater or Queensway underground/N50,
N89 bus.* **Open** 6.30pm-12.30am Mon-Sat;
6.30-11.30pm Sun. **Average** £12. **House
wine** £11 carafe, £1.50 glass. **Credit** A,
AmEx, £STC, V.
Enjoy nightly yodelling and um-pah-pah in
real thigh-slapping fashion. Lots of *wurst* and
lager. Lederhosen optional.

SOUTH WEST

Villa dei Cesari
*135 Grosvenor Road, SW1 (071 834 9872).
Pimlico underground/N2 bus.* **Open** 7.30pm-
1.30am Tue-Fri, Sun; 7.30pm-3am Sat.
Licensed 7.30pm-1.30am Tue-Fri; 7.30pm-
2am Sat; 7.30pm-11.30pm Sun. **Average** £38.
Minimum £15.50. **Credit** A, AmEx,
DC, £STC, V.
The outward vulgarity of this expensive
Italian restaurant attracts a predominantly
nouvelle riche clientèle. Punters in white
evening wear and lots of ostentatious gold
jewellery come to dance the night away or
for a meal with riverside views.
Wheelchair access.

FILM

CENTRAL

Lumière
*42-49 St Martin's Lane, WC2 (071 836
0691/071 379 3014). Leicester Square
underground.* **Programme** 11.15pm Fri, Sat.
Admission £4.50. **Credit** A, £TC, V.
Comfy centrally-located cinema with a frequently changing programme. There's
integrity in their choice of films, which tend
to be arty classics like *Distant Voices, Still
Lives* and Peter Greenaway movies.

Screen on Baker Street
*96 Baker Street, W1 (071 935 2772). Baker
Street underground/N13, N56, N59 bus..*
Programme 11.15pm Fri, Sat. **Admission**
£4. **No credit cards.**
An independent cinema with two screens,
showing successful mainstream productions
and cult hits *The Blues Brothers* (11.15pm
every Fri) and *The Rocky Horror Picture
Show* (11.15pm every Sat).
Branches *Screen on the Green, 83 Upper
Street, N1 (071 226 3520); Screen on the Hill,
203 Haverstock Hill, NW3 (071 435 3366).*

WEST

Gate Cinema
*87 Notting Hill Gate, W11 (071 727 4043).
Notting Hill Gate underground/N89 bus.*
Programme 11.15pm Fri, Sat. **Admission**
£4.25. **No credit cards.**
A popular west London cinema, which at late
night usually repeats the film it has been
running for that week or the occasional off-
beat presentation.

The most lively part of the capital on any night is **Trafalgar Square** (*listed
under* **Transport**). *Night buses to all parts of town leave from here and it's also
quite a good place to catch a cab late at night. The square plays host to the capital's
biggest, but most primitive New Year's Eve celebrations (see chapter* **London by
Season**)*, when the fountains and base of Nelson's column are boarded up.*

Looking down Old Compton Street is Soho's latest success story, **Ed's Easy Diner** *(listed under* **Eating: Central**). *Decorated in a mock 1950s American diner style, complete with mini-juke boxes, the short menu of burgers and shakes should be enough to satisfy even the hugest appetites. Service is friendly without being obsequious and there's a healthy banter between the staff.*

SOUTH WEST

Ritzy Cinema Club
Brixton Oval, SW2 (071 737 2121). Brixton underground/N2, N60, N78 bus. **Programme** 11.15pm Fri, Sat. **Membership** 50p per year. **Admission** £4; £1 OAPs; £2 students, UB40s. **Credit** £TC.
An ever-changing programme of superb art, independent and minority movies. Very popular, especially for the frequent theme allnighters. Occasional women-only nights. *Wheelchair access.*

EAST

Rio Cinema Dalston
107 Kingsland High Street, E8 (071 249 2722). Dalston Kingsland BR/N83, N96 bus. **Programme** 11.15pm Sat. **Admission** £3; £2 OAPs, students, UB40s. **Credit** £TC.
Frequent themed all-nighters play at this independent cinema, specializing in kitsch and cult movies. Favoured by the lentil brigade with a smattering of local trendies.

NORTH

Scala Cinema Club
275-277 Pentonville Road, N1 (071 278 0051). King's Cross underground/BR/N21, N56, N90, N93, N96 bus. **Programme** 11.30pm Sat. **Membership** 50p per year. **Admission** £4.50. **No credit cards.**
Strong on cult, off-beat and kitsch movies, plus the occasional sneak preview of major releases. Popular themed all nighters, sometimes with dancing. Café stays open till 6am.

MUSIC

CENTRAL

100 Club
100 Oxford Street, W1 (071 636 0933). Tottenham Court Roads underground. **Open** 7.45pm-1am Mon-Sat; 7.45-11.30pm Sun. **Admission** £3-£6. **No credit cards.**
See **picture and caption.**

Astoria
157 Charing Cross Road, WC2 (071 434 0403). Tottenham Court Road underground. **Open** 7.30pm-3.30am Mon-Thur; 10pm-3.30am Fri, Sat. **Admission** £4-£7.50. **Credit** A, AmEx, DC, V.
Big-name bands, predominantly pop or hip-hop, play at this large music venue/nightclub with three bars, a balcony and a large stage.

Brahms & Liszt
19 Russell Street, WC2 (071 240 3661). Covent Garden underground. **Open** noon-1am Mon-Sat; noon-11pm Sun. **Admission** free Mon, Sun; £3-£5 Tue-Sat. **Credit** A, AmEx, DC, £TC, V.
Just off Covent Garden Piazza, this wine bar plays host to a lively selection of jazz, swing and R&B in the basement. The less rowdy can settle for a full meal in the ground floor restaurant.

Dover Street Wine Bar & Restaurant
8-9 Dover Street, W1 (071 629 9813/071 491 7509). Green Park underground. **Open**

5.30pm-3am Mon-Fri; 8pm-3am Sat. **Admission** £2-£6. **Average** £17. **House wine** £6.75 bottle, £1.80 glass. **Service** 12½%. **Credit** A, AmEx, DC, £STC, V.
An intimate and pleasant basement wine bar with nightly soul, blues or R 'n' B. Good food, with a few vegetarian dishes, but arrive early as the kitchen falls apart when busy. Have a dance from 10pm onwards. No jeans.

Palookaville
13A James Street, WC2 (071 240 5857). Covent Garden underground. **Open** 5.30pm-midnight Mon-Fri; 6pm-midnight Sat. **Admission** free Mon-Thur; free before 10pm Fri, Sat; £3 after 10pm Fri, Sat. **Average** £23. **House wine** £7.45 bottle, £1.80 glass. **Service** 12½%. **Credit** A, AmEx, DC, EC, £TC, V.
This basement restaurant has a largely ordinary European menu, nothing particularly ambitious. Jazz music nightly.

Pizza Express
10 Dean Street, W1 (071 437 9595/071 439 8722). Tottenham Court Road underground. **Open** 8.30pm-1am daily. **Admission** £5-£9. **Credit** A, AmEx, DC, £TC, V.
Good food, good jazz and a centrally-located venue. What more could any jazz buff wish for?

Rock Garden
6-7 The Piazza, Covent Garden Market, WC2 (071 240 3961). Covent Garden underground. **Open** 7.30pm-3am Mon-Sat; 7.30pm-midnight Sun. **Admission** £4-£7. **Credit** A, £TC, V.
Tourists, students and devotees of raw, young rock groups mingle in the basement of this good quality, but very over-priced burger bar. The bands will either return to obscurity or one day make it very big (U2 and Talking Heads played here).

Ronnie Scott's
47 Frith Street, W1 (071 439 0747). Leicester Square, Piccadilly Circus or Tottenham Court Road underground. **Open** 8.30pm-3am Mon-Sat; 8-11.30pm Sun. **Admission** £10 non-members Mon-Thur, Sun; £12 Fri, Sat. **Credit** A, AmEx, DC, £STC, V.
London's premier jazz venue may not have terribly interesting food but they do book among the best and most innovative acts in the country. Mellow, smoky and unmissable.

NORTH

Bass Clef
35 Coronet Street, N1 (071 729 2476/071 729 2440). Old Street underground/N83 bus. **Open** 7.30pm-2am Mon-Sat; 7.30pm-midnight Sun. **Admission** £3.50-£8 Mon-Sun; 25% discount students, UB40s, Musicians' Union. **Credit** A, AmEx, £TC, V.
The reputation of this north London jazz club is almost unrivalled; the weekend comprises Latin (Fri), African (Sat) and lunchtime jazz sessions (Sun noon-3pm). The food, although not obligatory, is above average for a music venue and there is a friendly, regular crowd.

Dingwalls
Camden Lock, Chalk Farm Road, NW1 (071 267 4967). Camden Town or Chalk Farm underground/N1, N29, N90, N93 bus. **Open** 8pm-2am Mon, Wed; 10pm-3am Tue, Thur-Sat; 9pm-1am Sun. **Admission** £1.50-£6. **No credit cards.**
Almost as legendary as the Marquee,

Dingwalls has seen debut performances by many of the capital's premier bands; funk, blues, rock and thrash metal are usually on the menu. The Sunday lunchtime club *Talking Loud, Saying Something*, plays Latin music and has already built up a loyal crowd of regulars. Ring to check for programme details.

Mean Fiddler
24-28 Harlesden High Street, NW10 (081 961 5490). Willesden Junction underground/BR/N18 bus. **Open** 8pm-2am Mon-Sat; 8pm-1am Sun. **Admission** £3-£8. **Credit** A, V.
The location – and a fair amount of the bands – may seem obscure, but it's well worth the trek to Harlesden. If you eat in the club's restaurant you might be able to get reduced price admission to the concert playing that night (depending on who is playing). Come here to see rock, country & western and folk bands.
Wheelchair access to ground floor.

Power Haus
1 Liverpool Road, N1 (071 837 3218). Angel underground/N92, N96 bus. **Open** 8pm-2am Mon-Sat; 7-10.30pm Sun. **Admission** £3-£8. **Credit** A, V.
An ex-pub (the Pied Bull) hosting a lively programme of folk and rock.
Wheelchair access.

Town & Country Club
9-17 Highgate Road, NW5 (071 284 0303). Kentish Town underground/N2 bus. **Open** 7.30-11pm Mon-Thur, Sat; 7.30pm-2am Fri. **Admission** £6-£10. **Credit** A, AmEx, DC, £TC, V.
Come here to see both major and totally irrelevant acts from all parts of Europe. You

may even catch a secret gig by a visiting rock legend. After 11pm on Friday Wendy May hosts the popular Locomotion club night.

TRANSPORT

Last trains from central London on the underground system are between midnight and 12.30am. London Regional Transport (LRT) operates a network of night buses until the tubes start again at about 6am (8-9am on Sunday). The focal point of this service is **Trafalgar Square** (*see* **picture and caption**); all night buses run to and from there. British Rail runs an irregular service of trains to commuter stations on the outskirts of London through the night from Euston, King's Cross (main line and Thameslink stations), Victoria and Waterloo. For further information on times for the tubes, night buses and overland trains call the LRT enquiry service on *071 222 1234* which is open round the clock, or *see* **Night Bus Map**.

You can catch a taxi or minicab any time, day or night. Try waiting outside big hotels or at cab ranks; *see chapter* **Travel**.

PHOTO PROCESSING

Most chemists can have your photographs developed and printed overnight while some specialist shops, including some branches of **Boots**, offer an express two-hour service. If you're in a bigger hurry, try the companies listed below.

Joe's Basement
89-91 Wardour Street, W1 (071 434 9313). Piccadilly Circus underground. **Open** 24 hours daily. **Credit** A, V.
Joe's Basement is a professional photographic laboratory, which can turn round a 35mm colour transparency film in two hours, and a black and white one in six hours; the cost is £3.50 plus VAT and £5 plus VAT respectively, for 36 exposures. All are done by hand, not machine. A 35mm colour print film can be processed in 24 hours and costs £4 plus VAT for 36 exposures. You can then decide which of your masterpieces you want printing.

Lancasters
23-25 Great Sutton Street, EC1 (071 250 1471). Farringdon underground/BR/N21, N83, N93, N96 bus. **Open** 24 hours Mon-Fri; 9am-5pm Fri, Sat. **Credit** £TC.
Lancasters process 35mm colour slide films in two hours; the cost is £3.60 plus VAT for 36 exposures. No prints.

SHOPPING

CENTRAL

Bliss
5 Marble Arch, W1 (071 723 6116). Marble Arch underground. **Open** 9am-midnight daily incl Bank Holidays and Christmas. **Credit** A, AmEx, DC, £TC, V.
See **picture and caption**.

Cheapo Cheapo Records
53 Rupert Street, W1 (071 437 8272). Piccadilly Circus underground. **Open** 11am-10pm Mon-Sat. **Credit** £STC, most foreign currencies.
Three floors of jazz, rock, classical and blues records.

Covent Garden General Store
105-111 Long Acre, WC2 (071 240 0331). Covent Garden underground. **Open** 10am-midnight Mon-Sat; 11am-7pm Sun. **Credit** A, AmEx, DC, EC, £TC, V.
An emporium of silly gifts such as novelty crockery, crossword toilet rolls and executive toys. A lot of goods that you hadn't realized you didn't want until you saw them, but useful for last minute presents when everywhere else is closed.

Goldrings of Holborn
2A Farringdon Road, EC1 (071 253 5488). Farringdon underground. **Open** 3.20am-4pm Mon-Fri. **No credit cards.**
A bakery and sandwich shop.

Disappearing into the basement of 100 Oxford Street, home of the **100 Club** *(listed under* **Music***) have been seen punters wearing anything from zoot suits to bondage gear. An ever-changing programme of new and established acts has been drawing in the crowds for decades. The atmosphere is smoky and the place gets packed, so arrive early.*

Harvest Food & Wine
178 Wardour Street, W1 (071 734 4845).
Oxford Circus or Tottenham Court Road
underground. **Open** 8.30am-11pm daily. **No**
credit cards.
A large grocery store, convenient for late-
night shopping in Soho.

Portlands of Charing Cross
75-77 Charing Cross Road, WC2 (071 734
5715). Leicester Square underground. **Open**
8am-11pm Mon-Fri; 9am-11pm Sat; 9am-
10.30pm Sun. **Credit** A, £TC, V.
Portlands used to be Hollywood Food &
Wine but has now been given a revamp
along with a new name. Still a good grocers
with a delicatessen, fresh vegetables, frozen
food, magazines and cigarettes.

Tower Records
1 Piccadilly Circus, W1 (071 439 2500).
Piccadilly Circus underground. **Open** 9am-
midnight Mon-Sat. **Credit** A, AmEx, V.
Megastore of music and video spread over
four floors, with particularly strong classical
and world music/jazz departments. Tower
also sells T-shirts and magazines.

WEST

Bestway
107 Edgware Road, W2 (071 723 6793).
Marble Arch or Edgware Road under-
ground/N18, N50, N56, N79, N94 bus.
Open 24 hours daily. **No credit cards.**
There's hardly room to walk around in this
supermarket, which has a variety of foods,
drinks and household goods overflowing
from the shelves.

7 Eleven
384 Edgware Road, W2 (071 723 2123).
Edgware Road underground/N94, N79 bus.
Open 24 hours daily. **No credit cards.**
An American chain of late-night supermarkets with frozen food, tins, alcohol,
cigarettes, papers and magazines. Also burgers, hot dogs and samosas with a microwave
for heating them up. Not cheap.

7 Eleven
134 King Street, W6 (081 846 9154).
Hammersmith underground/N11, N93, N97
bus. **Open** 24 hours daily. **No credit cards.**
See above.

Crispins
82 Holland Park Avenue, W11 (071 727
7332). Holland Park underground/N89 bus.
Open 8am-11pm daily. **No credit cards.**
A small grocer's and off-licence.

Ladbroke Supermarket
171 Ladbroke Grove, W10 (081 968 6760).
Ladbroke Grove underground/N18, N50 bus.
Open 8am-midnight daily. **No credit cards.**
Everything you'd expect to find in a supermar-
ket, plus a microwave to heat up its samosas.

Midnight Food Store
207 Sutherland Avenue, W9 (071 286 6084).
Warwick Avenue underground/N18 bus.
Open 7am-midnight daily. **No credit cards.**
Groceries, magazines, newspapers, cigarettes
and sweets.

Riteway
57 Edgware Road, W2 (071 402 5491).
Marble Arch underground/N18, N56, N59,

*Call in at **Bliss** chemist (listed under **Shopping: Central**), opposite Marble
Arch, if you find yourself in the centre of town and aren't feeling one hundred
per cent. The friendly staff should be able to oblige most requests, from a potion
to tackle a cold brought on by the British weather to prescriptions for trickier
ailments. For those not ailing but short of camera film or batteries, the shop
also has a limited selection of electrical and practical goods.*

N79, N94 bus. **Open** 24 hours daily.
No credit cards.
Groceries, magazines, newspapers, cigarettes
and sweets.

Waterstone's
193 Kensington High Street, W8 (071 937
8432). High Street Kensington underground.
Open 9.30am-10pm Mon-Fri; 9.30am-7pm
Sat; 11am-6pm Sun. **Credit** A, AmEx, £TC, V.
A late-opening branch of the excellent chain
of arts-oriented bookshops, with a strong
selection of fiction and travel-related titles.

SOUTH WEST

7 Eleven
119-121 Gloucester Road, SW7 (071 373
1440). Gloucester Road underground/N14,
N93, N97 bus. **Open** 24 hours daily.
No credit cards.
See above **Shopping: West**.

Cullens
182 Fulham Road, SW10 (071 352 7056).
Fulham Broadway or South Kensington
underground/14, 45, N11, N14 bus. **Open**
8am-midnight Mon-Sat; 8am-11pm Sun.
Credit A, £TC, V.
One of a chain of rather expensive supermarkets appealing to a predominantly middle class
local clientèle. A fair selection of fresh vegetables, magazines and a small delicatessen.

Midnight Shop
223 Brompton Road, SW3 (071 589 7788).
Knightsbridge or South Kensington under-
ground/N14, N97 bus. **Open** 9am-midnight
daily. **No credit cards.**
A friendly, small supermarket with a surprisingly large selection of fresh vegetables, groceries and frozen food.

Pan Bookshop
158 Fulham Road, SW10 (071 373 4997).
South Kensington underground/14, 45 bus.
Open 10am-10pm Mon-Sat; 1-9.30pm Sun.
Credit A, AmEx, £TC, V.
A paperback bookshop with a fair selection
of fiction, non-fiction and travel titles. Also a
few good quality greetings cards.

Perry's Bakery & Haminados Patisserie
151 Earl's Court Road, SW5 (071 370 4825).
Earl's Court underground/N56, N97 bus.
Open 6am-midnight daily. **No credit cards.**
An inviting patisserie with a few seats for eat-
in snacks. Good, fresh bread and cakes.

Star Delicatessen
176 Earl's Court Road, SW5 (071 244
7352). Earl's Court underground/N56, N97
bus. **Open** 9am-3am Mon-Thur, Sun; 9am-
4am Fri, Sat. **No credit cards.**
A general supermarket and delicatessen.

Sport & Fitness

Whether you want to watch the horses and hats at Royal Ascot or play baseball and golf in town, London's brimming over with sports facilities for people of all tastes and standards.

London is still the Big Smoke: land of drizzly rain and the shiny black cab. But gone are the days when every Londoner slouched home after work or left the office for the warm embrace of a pub. Today you're likely to see them jogging off to strut their stuff in a dance studio, gym or exercise class. London has a lot of public and private sporting facilities. Health clubs, gymnasiums, tennis courts, riding stables and pools abound. It doesn't matter where you live or where you're staying; it's easy to find and use London's sports facilities. For more detailed information buy the *Time Out Guide to Sport, Health & Fitness in London* (£4.95 from newsagents) or check *Time Out* magazine's Sport Pages. Alternatively, phone **Sportsline** (071 222 8000), a free sports information service.

OUT & ABOUT

It's not surprising that London is considered to be the greenest capital in Europe; there are 387 parks in the metropolis, all varying in size and style. Between them they cover more than 46,000 acres/18,615 hectares of the city. The variety of public sports facilities available is astounding, and they are often inexpensive to use. You can fight the flab by jogging in **Kensington Gardens, W8**, plunging into the open air ponds at **Hampstead Heath, NW3**, or, during winter, tobogganing down **Parliament Hill, NW5**. Also, you can ride, pole-vault, row or play softball in many of London's open spaces. There are **reservoirs** that are ideal for fishing or bird-watching and **rivers**, **canals** and **disused docks** that are excellent for all kinds of water

sports. If you want to fish, you'll need a **rod licence**, available from either angling shops or **The Water Authority (TWA)**, PO Box 214, Reading RG 8HQ (0734 593921). You will also have to buy a permit from the people who own the land; for example the Park Offices, in many parks, issue such permits. Below we give you a selection of sports venues where you can either participate or spectate.

PARKS & LAKES

Battersea Park
Queenstown Road, SW11 (081 871 7530 Park Office). Battersea Park BR/19, 39, 45, 137, 170 bus. **Open** dawn-dusk daily.
A popular park, situated by the Thames, where locals play tennis, football, rugby and hockey. It's well-known for the excellent athletics ground near Albert Bridge Road (admission cost 75p adult, 40p child; phone 081 871 7537). There's also the lake where visitors can hire boats or even fish (angling permits available from the Park Office).

Hampstead Heath
Hampstead Lane or Highgate Road, NW3 (071 485 4491). Hampstead underground, Gospel Oak or Hampstead Heath BR/53, 214, 268 bus. **Open** dawn-dusk daily.
Possibly one of the most beautiful parks in London; Hampstead Heath is full of sports facilities. The park is vast, hilly and, in parts, covered with woodland. It's perfect for jogging – there's a choice of tarmac or gravel paths – and open-air swimming. The mixed, men-only and women-only bathing ponds are a London institution. Parliament Hill Fields, on the south side of the park, has eight tennis courts, a bowling green, a superb athletics track (071 435 8998) near Highgate Road and angling ponds. Most casual passers-by climb to the top of Parliament Hill (319ft/99m) to admire the spectacular view of London and watch the kite-flying *aficionados* practising their loops and dives.

Hyde Park
W2 (071 262 5484). Hyde Park Corner, Lancaster Gate, Marble Arch or Queensway underground/2A, 2B, 6, 7, 8, 10, 12, 15, 16, 16A, 30, 36, 73, 74, 82, 88, 135, 503 bus. **Open** 5am-midnight daily.
This is Central London's largest park; it measures 340 acres/135 hectares. The orange-box orators at Speaker's Corner (Sunday mornings near Marble Arch) are

only one of the many attractions visitors can enjoy. The Serpentine has boating facilities as well as a bathing pond (open during the summer). You can also fish (angling permits available from the Park Office, or phone Colin Mellish, the water bailiff, on 081 673 8321 during reasonable hours) and ride along the bridleways (*see below* **Ross Nye** *under* **Sporting Venues: Horse Riding Schools**).

Regent's Canal
Information Centre, 289 Camden High Street, NW1 (071 482 0523). Camden Town underground/24, 27, 29, 31, 68, 74, 134, 135, 168, C2 bus. **Open** *Information Centre*: Apr-Oct 10am-4pm Mon-Fri; 10am-5pm Sat, Sun; *Canals & towpaths*: dawn-dusk daily.
See **picture and caption**.
See chapter **River & Docklands**.

Regent's Park
Outer Circle, NW1 (071 486 7905). Baker Street, Camden Town, Great Portland Street or Regent's Park underground/3, 13, 53, 74, 113 bus. **Open** *Park*: 5am-dusk daily; *Queen Mary's Rose Garden & tennis courts*: 5am-30 minutes before dusk daily; *playgrounds*: 10.30am-30 minutes before dusk daily.
A large park, once the hunting fields of Elizabeth I, that boasts a boating lake, a running track, a private tennis club and a golf coaching school (*see below* **Regent's Park Golf & Tennis School** *under* **Sporting Venues: Golf**). If you fancy a game of baseball or softball, visit the park at the weekend when London's amateur teams practise: newcomers who want to strike out are usually welcome, though you'll have to make your own introductions.

Richmond Park
Kingston Vale, SW15 (081 940 0654). Richmond underground/72, 264 bus. **Open** *Mar-Sept*: 7am-30 minutes before dusk daily; *Oct-Feb*: 7.30am-30 minutes before dusk daily.
More than 600 deer roam across the 2½ miles/4km of wild parkland that is Richmond Park. It's a wonderful place to ride as there are 14 miles of bridleways. There are also two busy public golf courses near Roehampton Gate that can be used by anyone (*see below* **Sporting Venues: Golf**), two pen ponds (enclosed areas of water) that are ideal for fishing, 24 football grounds and five cricket pitches.

RESERVOIRS

Although angling is permissible in many of London's lakes and ponds, such as the **Serpentine** (*see above* **Hyde Park**) or **Battersea Park Lake** (*see above* **Battersea Park**), try the reservoirs below for better quality fishing. In addition to angling, reservoirs are ideal for bird-watching and casual strolls. For fishing regulations *see above* **Out and About**.

Barn Elm Reservoirs
Merthyr Terrace (off Castelnau), SW13 (081 748 3423). Hammersmith underground/9, 33, 72 bus. **Open** *12 March-30 Nov* 7.30am-30 minutes after sunset daily.

Permits £10 per day; £7.50 half day. **Boat hire** £5 per day; £4 per half day.
A fantastic place to fish: there are four reservoirs stocked with game fish – mainly rainbow and brown trout – as well as salmon. Barn Elms is an important breeding ground for reed warblers and visiting place for coots, moorhens and great crested grebes. With the occasional appearance of goosanders, water rails and goldeneyes, this reservoir is an urban birdwatcher's paradise.

Walthamstow Reservoirs
Ferry Lane, N17 (081 808 1527).
Blackhorse Road or Tottenham Hale underground/BR/123, 230 bus. **Open** 7.30am-30 minutes after sunset. **Permits** *coarse:* £2-£2.50 per day; *game:* £5 per day, £3 per half day (surcharge at weekends and Bank Holidays 25p-£1).
The reservoirs at Walthamstow are teeming with so much wildlife that they have been designated a site of Special Scientific Interest. The reservoirs near the south end of the Lee Valley are the fifth largest heronry in Britain. Apart from spotting kingfishers, carrion crows and great crested grebes, the fishing is diverse enough for both coarse and game angling. The waters are stocked with bream, tench, roach and rainbow trout among other species. Permits and Thames Water Authority licences are available from the Gate House.

WATERSPORTS

There are a vast number of venues where Londoners mess about on and in the water. Seek out one of

Peter Chilvers Windsurfing Centre *(listed under* Watersports*) is an inner-city sport centre with a difference; miles of construction sites alongside post-modernist housing and cold, black water. Chilvers claims he invented the sport when he was 12 years old. He built the prototype by putting together a tent-fly, old plywood, a broom handle and a couple of curtain rings to hold the sail. Courses are well managed and cater for both beginners and advanced surfers. Worth visiting to experience an English and eccentric approach to sport.*

the centres and schools listed below if you want to try your hand at anything from sailing to sub-aqua. For information on swimming *see below under* **Sports Centres.**

Activ. London Windsurfing School
557-561 Battersea Park Road, SW11 (071 223 2590/071 228 0430). Clapham Junction BR/19, 39, 49 bus. **Open** 9.30am-6pm Tue, Wed, Fri; 10am-8pm Thur; 9.30am-5pm Sat. **Courses** £37.50 per day Mon-Fri; £47.50 per day Sat, Sun. **Credit** A, V.
Contact the staff at Activ. if you fancy a spot of windsurfing, canoeing or sailing on the lakes outside London. Courses in windsurfing are held at Longside Lake, Surrey, and Bray Lake, Windsor. Wetsuits and boards can be hired, along with canoes and dinghies.

The London Wet Bike School
King George V Dock, Woolwich Manor Way, E16 (071 511 5000). North Woolwich BR/East Ham underground then 101 bus. **Open** 10am-dusk Mon, Tue, Thur-Sun. **Credit** AmEx, V.
This is the only place in London where you can hire wet bikes or jet skis and zoom around to your heart's content, at a price. An introductory lesson to wet-biking costs £17.50; after that 30 minute sessions cost £15.95 each. These rates include use of wetsuits and club facilities.

Peter Chilvers Windsurfing Centre
Gate 6, Tidal Basin, west end of Royal Victoria Docks, E16 (071 474 2500). Canning Town underground/BR. **Open** Apr-

Oct: dawn-dusk Tue-Sun; *Nov-Mar:* dawn-dusk Sat, Sun. **Board hire** £4 per hour. **No Credit Cards.**
See **picture and caption.**

Princes Waterski and Windsurfing Club
Clockhouse Lane, Bedfont, Middlesex TW14 (07842 56153). Hatton Cross BR. **Open** 9am-dusk daily. **Credit** A, V.
A professionally run centre that offers waterskiing and windsurfing lessons; all equipment is provided. Waterskiing courses vary in length. Three ten-minute beginners' sessions cost £35; a day course is £65; a week's course (five tows per day and use of all club facilities) costs £225. Windsurfing for non-members costs £50 for eight hours, spread over two sessions.

Royal Yachting Association (RYA)
RYA House, Romsey Road, Eastleigh, Hampshire, SO5 (0703 629962). **Open** 9am-5pm Mon-Fri. **Membership** £12 per year adults; £4 per year under-16s.
This governing body for all aquatic endeavours (from sailing and canoeing to windsurfing and waterskiing) will answer questions about water sports. They can put you in touch with watersports centres in your area.

SPORTING VENUES

CYCLING

Cycling is an excellent way of getting around town. It's faster than going by car (motor traffic moves at a staggeringly slow 11 miles/17.7 kilometres an hour) and you don't have to rely on public transport. But there are drawbacks. Apart from inhaling car fumes, you're risking life and limb every time you swerve onto a roundabout. Assertive riding is the most important safety measure as well as reflective belts and armbands. Helmets are a good idea and only cost about £30. You can also stay clear of the more congested roads and take back routes and, in some cases, cycle lanes which have been purpose built. Below we list shops where you can buy, hire and repair bicycles.

FW Evans Cycles
77-79 The Cut, Waterloo, SE1 (071 928 4785). Waterloo underground/BR. **Open** 9.30am-5.30pm Mon-Fri; 9am-5pm Sat. **Credit** A, V.

Porchester Cycles
8 Porchester Place, W2 (071 723 9236). Edgware Road underground. **Open** 9.15am-6pm Mon-Fri. **Credit** A, V.

Portobello Cycles
69 Golborne Road, W10 (071 960 0444).
Ladbroke Grove or Westbourne Park under-
ground/7, 15, 52 bus. **Open** 10am-5pm
Mon-Sat. **Hire** £5 per day; £30 per week.
Deposit £50. **Credit** A, AmEx, V.

DANCE STUDIOS
Dance Attic
212-214 Putney Bridge Road, SW15 (081
785 2055). Putney Bridge
underground/Putney BR. **Open** 9am-10pm
Mon-Fri; 10am-5pm Sat, Sun. **Membership**
Dance: £30 per year, £20 per six months,
£1.50 per day adults; £20 per year, £15 per
six months, £1.50 per day Equity, nurses
and students. **Class fee** £2.50. **Classes**
10am, 1pm and 6pm. **Credit** A, £TC, V.
This popular Putney centre, with a gym and
a dance studio, is now in its eighth year.
Classes are held in ballet, jazz, contemporary, tap, belly-dancing, flamenco and fitness, aerobic and gymnastic lessons. The
standard of teaching is high. Classes are
scheduled on a daily basis in addition to the
fixed times listed. Phone for details.
Children under 15 pay a class fee (from £1)
but no membership.
Café. Crèche. Jacuzzi. Sauna. Shop. Sunbeds.

Danceworks
16 Balderton Street, W1 (071 629 6183).
Bond Street or Marble Arch underground.
Open *office:* 8am-10.30pm Mon-Fri; 9.30am-
6pm Sat, Sun. *Classes:* 8am (first class),
9.30pm (last class) Mon-Fri; 10am (first
class), 5pm (last class) Sat, Sun.
Membership £400 per year includes admission; £75 per year, £45 Thur-Sun only, £22
per month, £3 per day adults; £40 per year
£22 per month, £3 per day students and
nurses; £30 per year, £22 per month, £3 per
day Equity and UB40. **Admission** £3.50.
Credit A, V.
Danceworks has an impressive range of
dance classes at all levels in ballet, tap, various jazz forms, salsa, Dancersize, belly-
dancing and gypsy flamenco. Teachers are
excellent, for dance and fitness classes. No
membership for under-16s.
Alexander Institute. Café. Centre for comple-
mentary medicine. Massage. Pilates. Sauna.
Shop. Studio hire. Sunbeds.

Evening School at the Place
17 Duke's Road, WC1 (071 387 0152, ext.
243). Euston underground/BR. **Open** 6.30-
8pm Mon-Fri; 10-11.30am Sat. **Admission**
£3.50 per class. **No credit cards.**
The Place is the base for the London
Contemporary Dance School, which trains
some of Britain's finest contemporary
dancers. In the summer and during the
Easter holidays intensive courses are run.
The Young Place holds classes for children
and teenagers in classical ballet, contemporary dance and jazz. Discount is available
for repeat bookings in advance.
Bar. Café.

Pineapple Dance Centre
7 Langley Street, WC2 (071 836 4004).
Covent Garden underground. **Open** 10am-
8.30pm Mon-Fri; 10am-5pm Sat; 10am-
4.30pm Sun. **Classes** 10am (first class),
7pm (last class) Mon-Fri; 10am (first class)
4.30pm (last class) Sat; 10am (first class),
3pm (last class) Sun. **Membership** £55
per year, £18 per month, £10 per week, £3

per day adults; £37 per year Equity, £3 per
day; £33 per year student, UB40s and
under 15s; £3 per day students and UB40s
£1.50 per day under-15s. **Admission**
£3.50. **Credit** A, £TC, V.
This well-known dance studio is the setting
for classes in ballet, jazz, contemporary, tap,
Indian, flamenco and belly-dancing. The
Centre is professionally run and attracts
dancers who take the sport seriously.
Café. Hydra. Osteopath. Pilates. Massage.

GO-KARTS
Playscape
Old London Transport Bus Garage, Bohemia
Place, Mare Street, Hackney E8 (081 986
7116). Hackney Central BR. **Open** 9.30am-
10pm daily. **Admission** £34.50 per 4-hour
session. **Credit** A, V.
Go-karting is an exhilarating way of racing
in relative safety. Playscape is based in an
old, disused bus depot that even the
Princess of Wales has graced. Group bookings are the only bookings accepted during
weekdays; for individual karting at weekends phone in advance.

GOLF
Usually, private golf courses have
strict membership procedures that
might prevent casual golfers from
playing on a daily basis. If you have
difficulty teeing off at a private
course, try one of the public courses
that are open to everyone. Most
public courses hire out a half-set of
clubs for around £4 per round and
green fees cost, on average, £5. For
information on where to spectate,
see below **Golf Internationals.**

Coulsdon Court
Coulsdon Road, Surrey, CR3 (660 0468).
Coulsdon South BR then 409, 411 Green
Line bus, then long walk. **Open** 6.45am-dusk
daily. **Admission** £6.50 Mon-Fri, £9 Sat, Sun
adults; $2.70 Mon-Fri, £9 Sat, Sun OAPs;
Twilight tickets (9 holes) £3.25 weekdays,
£4.50 weekends **Season tickets** five-day
£150 and £1.50 per round, £3 per round Sat,
Sun adults; £60 and £1.50 per round. £3 per
round Mon-Fri OAP ; £50 and £1.50 per
round, £3 per round Sat, SunJunior. **No**
credit cards.
This picturesque 18-hole public course runs
along part of the North Downs; it has some
marvellous views and is well maintained.
Bar and restaurant. Conference facilities.
Equipment for hire. Shop.

Brent Valley
Church Road, Hanwell, W7 (081 567 1287).
Hanwell BR. **Open** 7.30am-dusk Mon-Fri;
6am-dusk Sat, Sun. **Green fees** £4.50 per
round Mon-Fri; £6.20 per round Sat, Sun.
Credit (shop only) A, GolfPlus, V.
An 18-hole public golf course with a putting
green on which beginners may practise.
Golf-pro Peter Bryan gives instruction at £8
for 40 minutes.
Bar. Equipment for hire. Shop.

Dulwich & Sydenham
Grange Lane, College Road, SE1 (081 693
3961). Sydenham Hill BR. **Open** 8am-dusk
daily (closed to non-members at weekends).
Membership £332 per year, plus £500 ini-
tial joining fee. **Green Fees** £18 per round
weekdays; £20 per round weekends. **No**
credit cards.
A quiet, private 18-hole course that allows
non-members to play (only during weekdays). It's sandwiched between Dulwich
village and Crystal Palace. Look closely at
the players and you may see Denis
Thatcher, consort to the Prime Minister,

Regent's Canal *(listed under* **Parks & Lakes***) is an unusual place to grab*
some exercise. The canal is an intriguing and often scenic network of waterways
over 54 miles/87km long that run through central London. Built at the
beginning of the eighteenth century, today's canal makes an ideal place for
walking, jogging or fishing. It's also possible to windsurf, sail or canoe. For
more information phone or drop into the Information Centre in Camden.

puttering around the course towards the nineteenth hole.
Bar and food. Equipment for hire. Shop.

Ealing
Perivale Lane, Greenford, Middlesex UB5(997 0937). Perivale underground. **Open** dawn-dusk daily. **Membership** £800-£900 per year. **Green fees** £20 per round. **No credit cards.**
An interesting and, at times, difficult private 18-hole golf course that runs through wooded parkland and has a river. The course contains some fairways that are only 20yd/18m wide. Non-members can try it out from Monday to Thursday only and should book in advance.
Bar and restaurant. Shop.

Regent's Park Golf & Tennis School
Outer Circle, Regent's Park, NW1 (071 724 0643). Baker Street or St John's Wood underground. **Open** 8am-9pm daily. **Credit** A, GolfPlus, V.
The ideal place to have your clubs and swing analyzed by computer. For £30, the in-house pro, Chris Meadows, will monitor the way you play, check the fit of your clubs and tell you how your game could be improved. The School offers personal coaching and organizes visits to golf courses around London.
Shop. Export scheme. Postal delivery.

Ruislip Golf Course
Ickenham Road, Ruislip, Middlesex HA4 (0895 638835/0895 638081). Ruislip underground. **Open** *course:* dawn-dusk daily; *club:* dawn-midnight daily. **Credit** (shop only) A, AmEx, V.
See **picture and caption.**
Bar and restaurant. Driving range. Equipment for hire. Buggies for the infirm. Shop.

Richmond Park
Richmond Park, Roehampton Gate, Priory Lane, SW15 (081 876 3205). Richmond underground or Barnes BR. **Open** 7.30am-30 minutes before dusk daily. **Green fees** £5 per round weekdays; £7.50 per round weekends. **Credit** (shop only) A, AmEx, GolfPlus, DC, V.
See **picture and caption.**
Equipment for hire. Shop.

HORSE RIDING SCHOOLS

Belmont Riding Centre
The Ridgeway, Mill Hill, NW7 (081 959 1588/081 906 1255). Mill Hill East underground. **Open** 9am-5.30pm, 7pm-9pm, Tue-Fri; 9am-5pm Sat, Sun. **Lessons** £8.50 per hour groups; £8.50 per half hour, £15.50 per hour private.
This north London school has some excellent riding horses. There's a viewing gallery from which you can observe the riders, a nifty cross-country course and an outdoor manège where you can ride and jump. Cross-country lessons are £17.50; show-jumping tuition £15. Book well ahead.

Ross Nye
8 Bathurst Mews, W2 (071 262 3791). Lancaster Gate underground. **Open** 7am-4.30pm Tue-Sat; 10am-4.30pm Sun. **Lessons** £12 per hour groups; £16 private.

This riding school has 16 horses for hire. Riding takes place in Hyde Park.

Suzanne's Riding School
Copse Farm, Brookshill Drive, Harrow Weald, Middlesex HA3 (081 954 3618). Harrow & Wealdstone BR, then 258 bus. **Open** 9.30am-8.30pm, 6.30-9.30pm, Tue-Sun; 9am-3.30pm Sat, Sun. **Lessons** £10-£11 per hour groups; £19 per hour private with senior instructor; £14 per hour private with assistant instructor.
Founded over 50 years ago, Suzanne's caters for all riders. They have leggy horses for the experienced rider, slower working ponies, 50 animals for show-jumping or cross-country hacking and lessons for the disabled. Book well ahead.

Wimbledon Village Stables
24A High Street, SW19 (081 946 8579). Wimbledon underground/93 or 80 bus. **Open** 8am-5pm daily. **Lessons** £16 per hour groups Mon-Fri; £17 per hour groups weekends.
Although costly, the horses at this stable are good for nervous beginners and the two-hour park rides, in Richmond Park and Wimbledon Common, are immensely popular. Serious tuition for dressage tests and jumping is available. Book in advance.

ICE RINKS

All the ice rinks listed below hire out skates (the hire cost is often included in the admission price or can be as little as 90p). Opening times vary from one season to another, so ring before setting off to make sure the session times haven't changed.

Broadgate Ice Rink
Eldon Street, EC2 (071 588 6565). Liverpool Street underground/BR. **Open** Nov-Apr. **Sessions** 11am-3pm Mon; 11am-3pm, 4-8pm, Tue-Fri; 11am-2pm, 3-6pm, Sat, Sun. **Admission** £2.50 adults; £1.25 under-12s, OAPs. **Credit** A, AmEx, V.
The newest and most pleasant ice rink in London; Broadgate is a tiny outdoor circle of ice open in winter only. The rink is encircled by spectacular, futuristic architecture.

Lee Valley Ice Centre
Lea Bridge Road, E10 (081 985 8865/081 533 3154). Blackhorse Road underground/BR or Leyton underground, then 38, 48, 55 bus. **Open** 10am-10.30pm daily (sessions vary, so please phone for exact times). **Admission** £2.50-£3.50 adults; £1-£2.50 under-16s; 70p under-fives. **Credit** A, V.
This huge rink has an extremely high standard of supervision on ice – troublemakers aren't tolerated. It's well worth a visit.

Queens Ice Skating Club
17 Queensway, W2 (071 229 0172). Queensway or Bayswater underground. **Open** 11am-4.30pm, 7.30-10pm, Mon-Fri; 10am-noon, 2-5pm, 7-10.30pm, Sat; 10am-noon, 2-5pm, 7-10pm Sun. **Admission** £1.30-£3.60 adults; free OAPs; £1.60-£2.70 under-15s. **Skate hire** 90p. **Credit** (shop only) A.
See **picture and caption.**

Wembley Stadium *(listed under* **General Stadia***) is a mega-venue for football cup finals as well as rock concerts that pull in the fans. It can hold a capacity crowd of 70,000 people and contains a 230-seater grandstand restaurant (something that has earned it a lot of brownie points with greyhound racing enthusiasts). Tickets for the soccer finals, the American football bowl each August, rugby internationals, greyhound races and hockey championships can be bought from the box office, or alternatively from booking agencies throughout London.*

PUBLIC TENNIS COURTS

As with other sporting facilities in London, there are both public and private tennis courts. Usually, **public tennis courts** are located in parks and cost about £2 per hour (*see also* **Parks & Lakes**). The quality of the courts can vary and booking isn't always possible.

Battersea Park

Battersea Park Road, SW11 (081 871 7542). Queenstown Road BR/19, 39, 44, 45, 49, 137, 170 bus.. **Open** 8am-9pm Mon-Fri; 8am-8pm Sat, Sun. **Registration** £3.75 per year. **Booking** three days in advance. **Court fee** £1.80 per hour.
There are 19 all-weather hard courts, of which nine are floodlit, in this riverside park. There's also a café and changing-rooms. *Wheelchair access. Toilets for the disabled..*

Highbury Fields

Highbury Place, N5 (071 226 2334). Highbury & Islington underground/BR/ 19, 30, 43, 271 bus. **Open** 8am-9pm Mon-Fri; 8am-dusk Sat, Sun (no floodlights at weekends). **Registration** £6 per year. **Booking** three days in advance **Court fee** £3 per hour adult; £1.50 per hour under-16s.
These 11 all-weather courts (three of which are floodlit) have good surfaces and have attractive surroundings. In addition to these facilities, there's an exceptionally good swimming pool nearby. *Wheelchair access. Toilets for the disabled.*

Holland Park

Kensington High Street, W8 (071 602 2226). High Street Kensington underground/9, 27, 31, 74 bus. **Open** 8am-dusk Mon-Sat; 9am-dusk Sun. **Registration** £5 per year for priority booking. **Court fee** £3 per hour adults, £1.10 under-18s. No advance booking.
Trendy public courts where Kensington residents love to be seen in order to pose in their latest tennis gear. There are six hard courts and a car park.
Wheelchair access. Toilets for the disabled.

Hyde Park

South side of park, off Exhibition Road, SW7 (071 262 5484 ext 34). South Kensington or Knightsbridge underground. **Open** 8am-dusk daily. **Court fee** £2.10 per hour.
Book in person at least two days in advance. There are four hard courts inside this grandiose park where you can also ride, fish and swim.

Lincoln's Inn Fields

WC2 (071 405 5194). Holborn underground/19, 38, 25, 171 bus. **Open** 8am-dusk daily. **Registration** £10 per year. **Booking** three days in advance. **Court fee** £2 per hour.
There are three hard courts (with showers and changing rooms) in this popular, small park situated behind the Law Courts. During the day the area is swarming with lawyers and accountants; at night the Fields become a refuge for many of London's tramps and homeless people. *Café. Wheelchair access.*

Parliament Hill

Highgate Road, NW5 (071 485 4491). Gospel Oak BR. **Open** 8am-dusk Mon-Sat; 9am-

Practice your swing at the impressive **Ruislip Golf Course** *(listed under* **Golf***). The 40-bay driving range is floodlit and there's an all-weather putting green for practice. The 18-hole public course forms part of a thriving leisure centre, with two bars and a restaurant open until 10pm. Book in advance to use the golf course at the weekends.*

dusk Sun, Bank Holidays. **Court fee** £1.40 per hour adults; 70p per hour under-16s, OAPs, UB40s (off-peak); **Registration** £2.75 per year. **Booking** three days in advance.
A popular haunt for amateur players. The ten hard courts here are next to a bowling green. Parliament Hill itself offers a superb view of London. Changing facilities for tennis players are pretty primitive and based in a wooden hut.

Regent's Park

York Bridge, NW1 (071 935 5729). St John's Wood underground. **Open** 8am-dusk daily. **Court fee** £2.60 per hour plus 20p advance booking fee. **Booking** two days in advance (no telephone booking).
Twelve all-weather hard courts that are allocated on a first come, first served basis at this large park.

PRIVATE TENNIS & SQUASH CLUBS

Private tennis and **squash clubs** are run for members only, although non-members can play either by invitation or on payment of a daily or guest fee.

Cannons Sports Club

Cousin Lane, EC4R (071 283 0101). Cannon Street underground/BR. **Open** 7am-10.30pm Mon-Fri; 10am-7pm Sat, Sun. **Membership** (14-week waiting list) £550 plus VAT per year. **Joining fee** £100. **Guest fee** £10. **Credit** A, AmEx, DC, V.
This health club is a favourite with City workers as many of them pay corporate membership fees with the rest of the amount being paid by the firms they work for. There are eight squash courts as well as a gym, a swimming pool and an aerobics studio.
Coaching (£6 for 30 minutes to £20 per hour). Women's nights. Racquet hire £1 + £10 deposit. Towel hire 50p + £5 deposit. Gym. Pool. Bar. Solarium.

Coolhurst Lawn Tennis & Squash Rackets Club

Courtside, Coolhurst Road, N8 (081 340 6611). Highgate underground. **Open** 7.30am-11pm Mon-Sat; 7.30am-9.30pm Sun. **Membership** £60 per year. **Joining fee** £50. **Guest fee** £1.50. **Court fee** £2.10 per hour. **No credit cards.**
An extensive range of facilities; four squash courts and 11 indoor tennis courts. Coolhurst is possibly the best tennis club in north London. The club runs regular in-house tournaments.
Bar. Pool.

The David Lloyd Slazenger Racquet Club

Southall Lane, Hounslow, Middlesex, TW5 (081 848 7556). Hayes & Harlington BR. **Open** 24 hours daily. **Membership** £135 per year. **Joining fee** £200. **Court fee** £6-£10. **No credit cards.**
This infamous, well-managed club (similar to the David Lloyd clubs in southern Portugal and Spain) has 15 indoor and nine

outdoor courts. There are eight professional coaches.

Dance. Pool. Bar. Snooker. Physiotherapist. Aerobics. Crèche. Pro Shop. Racket re-stringing.

Lamb's Squash Club
Lamb's Passage, Chiswell Street, EC1 (071 638 3811). Barbican underground or Moorgate underground/BR. **Open** 7am-11pm Mon-Fri; 10am-2pm Sat, Sun. **Membership** £377 per year. **Joining fee** £25. **Court fee** £2.50 per 30 minutes; £3.50 per 45 minutes. **Credit** A, AmEx, DC, V.
Lamb's has nine courts and offers coaching at £5 for 30 minutes. It's well-known for its other health club facilities (gym and aerobics studio) and is a favourite among City types.

Racquet hire £1.50 plus £5 deposit. Towel hire: 50p plus £5 deposit. Lounge area. Pro shop. Gym.

Queen's Club
Palliser Road, W14 (071 385 3421). Barons Court underground. **Open** 8am-10.30pm daily. **Membership** £168 per year under-28s; £335 over-28s. **Joining fee** £390. **Guest fee** £6. **Court fee** £6-£9 per hour. **Credit** A, AmEx, V.
Possibly the best tennis club in London with eight indoor and 27 outdoor courts. Unfortunately there's a five year waiting list for membership, although if you know a member you can play as a guest. There are also facilities for playing squash, Real tennis (an old form of tennis made popular in England by King Henry VIII) and racketball. Altogether an excellent club. (*See below* **Spectator Venues**).

Racquet re-stringing. Bar. Lounge area.

Vanderbilt Racquet Club
31 Sterne Street, W12 (081 743 9816/081 743 9822). Shepherd's Bush Central line

underground. **Open** 7am-11pm daily. **Membership** £590 per year. **Joining fee** £690. **Court fee** £12 per hour off-peak; £19 per hour peak. **No credit cards**.
The *cognoscenti* realize that the facilities here are extremely good. What everyone knows is that the fees are astronomical. There are three clay surface, two supreme (fast surface), three green set (artificial grass) and two short tennis courts. The club has 14 professional coaches; tuition is £10 for 50 minutes.

Bar. Lounge area.

Wimbledon Indoor Tennis Club
North Road, SW19 (081 542 9913). South Wimbledon underground/Wimbledon or Haydons Road BR.. **Open** 8am-11pm daily. **Membership** £150 per year adult; £115 per year under-18s. **Court fee** £10 per hour peak; £6 per hour off-peak. **Credit** A, V.
Non-members should book 48 hours in advance to play at this club. Members pay a reduced court fee. There are four indoor carpet courts. Coaching is either by group in training clinics or private (£10 per hour). Players can also take part in the short tennis clinics.

SPECTATOR VENUES

GENERAL STADIA

Crystal Palace National Sports Centre
Anerley Road, SW19 (081 778 0131). Crystal Palace BR. **Open** box office: 9.30am-5pm Mon-Fri.
This country's major athletics venue. Events

take place during the summer, mostly. The Peugeot Athletics Games and ASA swimming championships are held here in July each year.

Wembley Stadium
Stadium Way, Wembley, Middlesex, HA9 0DW (081 902 8833 admin/081 902 1234 box office). Wembley Park underground. **Open** box office: 9am-9pm Mon-Sat; 9am-7pm Sun
See **picture and caption**.

CRICKET

Lord's Cricket Ground
St John's Wood, NW8 (071 289 1611). St John's Wood underground. **Open** office 9.30am-5.30pm Mon-Fri. **Admission** *one-day finals:* £30-£34 grandstand, £27 grandstand balcony, tavern concourse, Mound stand, £22 G & H stands, £18 lower tier; *test matches:* £22-£25 grandstand; £21 grandstand balcony, tavern concourse, Mound stand, £18 G & H stands; £12 lower tier.
The home of world cricket, Lord's is an exceptionally beautiful, if at times stuck-up, venue. Famous features include the Pavilion, the Long Room and the Old Father Time weather vane. When cricket isn't being played, the museum is open to those who have booked (*see chapter* **Museums**). Get there very early if queuing for major matches. *See also chapter* **London By Season** for information on Test matches.
Bar and restaurant. Wheelchair access. Toilets for the disabled.

Oval Cricket Ground
The Oval Kennington, SE11 (071 582 6660). Kennington or Oval underground/Vauxhall BR. **Open** office: 9.30am-5pm Mon-Fri. **Admission** £13-£25.
Although this is an international ground (like Lords), the Oval isn't as attractive because it's dominated by gasometers. Those with poor eyesight might find the wicket a little too far from the seats, but the ground has a cosy charm and none of the pretensions of other Test Cricket grounds.

CROQUET & POLO

Hurlingham Club
Ranelagh Gardens, SW6 (071 736 3148). **Open** 8.30am-2pm Mon-Fri.
The famous Hurlingham Club, with its sweeping lawns and impeccable grounds is the home of croquet. Phone or write (enclosing a self addressed envelope) for information on dates of future fixtures. If you want to know more about polo, contact the Hurlingham Association on 07985 277, which is based at Ambersham Farm, Ambersham, Midhurst, West Sussex.

FOOTBALL

The football season lasts from August to May. In 1990 a new law will take effect that requires football spectators to have identity cards and club membership. As we go to press it seems likely that a London club will be one of those selected to test the scheme in the 1990-91 season. Read *Time Out* magazine's Sport pages for the latest news or

Queens *(listed under* **Ice Rinks***) is central London's most famous ice rink, used by serious skaters who want to practise figure-skating, as well as the Saturday night disco crowd. On weekdays you'll skate to synthesized music, while those taking a break will watch your antics from the bar overlooking the ice. There are 16 full-time instructors and personal tuition costs about £3.50 for 15 minutes.*

phone the club to check admission details. We advise any visitors embarking on their first visit to a professional football match to pay for seats, instead of joining the lads standing, jostling and shouting on the terraces. *See also chapter* **London By Season** for information on the summer FA Cup and American football.

Arsenal, Highbury Stadium
Avenell Road, N5 (071 226 0304). Arsenal underground. **Admission** £5 standing, £6-£12 seats.

Chelsea, Stamford Bridge
Fulham Road, SW6 (071 381 6221). Fulham Broadway underground. **Admission** £5 standing, £8-£12 seats.

Millwall, The Den
Cold Blow Lane, SE14 (071 639 3143). New Cross underground. **Admission** £5 standing, £8-£9.50 seats.

Queens Park Rangers, Loftus Road
South Africa Road, W12 (081 743 0262). White City underground. **Admission** £5 standing, £6-£12 seats.

Tottenham Hotspur, White Hart Lane
748 High Road, N17 (081 801 3323). Seven Sisters underground/White Hart Lane BR. **Admission** £4-£5 standing, £7-£14 seats.

West Ham United, Upton Park
Green Street, E13 (081 472 2740). Upton Park underground. **Admission** £4.50 standing, £6-£9 seats.

GOLF INTERNATIONALS

Moor Park Golf Club
Moor Park, Rickmansworth, Hertfordshire WD3 (0923 773146). Moor Park underground. **Open** 8am-dusk daily. **Admission** £4-£8.
This private club with two 18-hole courses plays host to the Four Star Golf Tournament. This is usually held at the beginning of June. The dates for 1990 are 7-10 June.

Sunningdale Golf Club
Ridgemount Road, Ascot, Berkshire SL5 (0990 21681). **Open** 8am-9pm daily. **Admission** announced in June.
The European Open Championships will be played here from 6-9 September 1990. Details and tickets can be obtained from the club. Non-members are welcome to play, Monday to Friday.

Wentworth Golf Club
Virginia Water, Surrey GU25 (09904 2201). Virginia Water BR. **Open** 7.30am-9.30pm daily. **Admission** £10.
This great golf course has recently been acquired by the Japanese. A bone of contention with old members is the fact that non-Japanese clientele are required to use different changing-rooms from those of their Japanese counterparts. The World

Matchplay Championship takes place here each October and one leg of the PGA European Tour is always played out in May. Spectator tickets are available from Keith Prowse ticket agencies and cost about £10.

GREYHOUND RACING

Catford Stadium
Ademore Road, SE26 (081 690 2261). Catford or Catford Bridge BR. **First race** 7.30pm Mon, Wed, Sat. **Admission** *restaurant area:* £3; *public area:* £2. **Credit** A, AmEx, V.
Catford is a smallish and slightly downmarket dog track, but it's easy to get to by public transport. There's a good view of the racing from the restaurant. Get there early to pick a seat.

Wembley Stadium
Stadium Way, Wembley HA9 (081 902 8833). Wembley Park underground. **First race** 7.30pm Mon, Wed, Fri. **Admission** £2-£3. **No credit cards.**
One side of the football stadium is cordoned off for the dog track on Mondays, Wednesdays and Fridays. It has a long finishing straight and a good view from the grandstand. There is a restaurant and bar on site.

HORSE RACING

A day at the races can be an exhilarating experience. Betting is done by either placing money on the TOTE (run by the State), which gives no odds until all the bets have been placed, or by putting your cash with one of the many bookies who stand on boxes and write the odds on small blackboards. Both are perfectly safe options – all you have to do is pick a winner.

Ascot Racecourse
Ascot, Berkshire SL5 (0990 22211). Ascot BR. **Open** *office:* 9am-5pm Mon-Fri. **Admission** £15 Grandstand, Paddock and Tattersalls; £3 Silver Ring; £1 Heath; *enclosure* by invitation only. **No credit cards.**
It's not always champagne, top hats and the latest fashion at Ascot; in fact there's racing all year round. But if you do go during June's Royal Ascot (particularly to the essentially snobby enclosure), you'll mix with the rich, the famous and all manner of gossip columnists. It's an impressive course, with crèche, bars and restaurants. You can buy a four-day pass to the big June Royal Meeting if you apply for tickets in advance. (*See also chapter* **London By Season: Summer**).

Epsom Race Course
The Paddock, Epsom, Surrey KT8 (03727 26311). Epsom BR. **Open** *office:* 9am-5pm Mon-Fri. **Admission** £5-£16. **No credit cards.**
Epsom is famous for the Derby, held in June, when the atmosphere is electric and the course becomes unbearably crowded. The club enclosure has some superior eating places; there are more bars and restaurants elsewhere in the course. (*See also chapter* **London By Season: Summer**).

The Racecourse Windsor
Windsor, Berkshire SL4 (0753 865234). Windsor Riverside or Windsor Central BR. **Open** *office:* 9.30am-5pm Mon-Fri. **Admission** £6 Tattersalls, Paddock; £3 Silver Ring. **No credit cards.**
This is one of the most beautiful courses near London; it's best enjoyed late on a summer's evening when the ambience becomes relaxed and people down the last of the Pimm's. The course is a lop-sided figure of eight and the view of the last five furlongs is head-on to the horses; this can be frustrating if you're trying to work out which horse is in the lead.

Richmond Park *(listed under* **Golf***), which was once a royal hunting forest, has two 18-hole courses that can get very busy. Considering that thousands of people wander round these attractive, undulating courses, it's amazing how well-kept the greens are. Phone reservations are taken with a registered player's card (costing £8). The new driving range can be booked for £3.50 per hour and a session in the computerized indoor teaching room costs £25.*

Sandown Park

Esher, Surrey (0372 63072). Esher BR.
Open *office:* 9am-5pm Mon-Fri. **Admission** £2-£12. **No credit cards.**
A favourite among punters who like the modern grandstand, Sandown has won the Racecourse of the Year award six times running. The oval-shaped course is set in an amphitheatre, so viewing facilities are wonderful.

MOTOR RACING

Brands Hatch

Fawkham, Dartford, Kent, DA3 (0474 872331). Swanley BR/A20 by car. **Open** *office:* 9am-5.30pm Mon-Fri. **Credit** A, AmEx, DC, V.
The big events in the summer can attract as many as 30,000 people, so be prepared for a crush. Races vary from Formula 3 championships and air displays to the World Sports Prototype Championships. Admission prices are £12 for adults and £2 for children for the big events; less for the smaller meets. Phone for information about forthcoming events.

Silverstone

Silverstone Circuit, Silverstone, near Towcester, Northamptonshire, NN12 (0327 857271). Milton Keynes or Northampton BR; by car, signposted from M1 motorway.. **Open** *office:* 9am-5pm Mon-Fri. **Credit** A, AmEx, V.
A circuit that hosts major racing events. When the Formula One Grand Prix is held here in July, it can attract up to 180,000 people over the three days (admission £33-£37). Other events include truck racing and saloon car events.

Wimbledon Stadium

Plough Lane, SW17 (office 081 946 5361/drivers 081 947 2394). Tooting Broadway and Wimbledon Park underground/Wimbledon and Earlsfield BR/ 44, 220 bus. **Open** *Aug-May:* 6-11pm on race day. **Admission** £5.50 adults; £2.50 under 16s. **Credit** A, AmEx, DC, £STC, V..
A great venue to watch that noisy, crash-prone, smoky sport called banger racing. If you've never been to this kind of event, it's worth the trek to Wimbledon to see what all the fuss is about. The Stadium also has superstock and hot-rod racing.
Wheelchair access. Facilities for the disabled.

TENNIS TOURNAMENTS

All England Lawn Tennis Club

Church Road, Wimbledon, SW19 (081 946 2244). Wimbledon underground. **Open** 9am-5pm daily, end of June-beginning July. **Admission** £5; £3 after 5pm. **Tickets** *Centre Court week one:* £10 Mon, Tue; £11 Wed-Fri; £15 Sat; *week two:* £14 Mon; £17 Tue, Wed; £21 Thur, Fri; £25 Sat, Sun; *No.1 Court week one:* £9 Mon, Tue; £11 Wed-Fri; £13 Sat; *week two:* £13 Mon; £16 Tue, Wed; £11 Thur; £7 Fri-Sun.
See **picture and caption.**

Queen's Club

Palliser Road, W14 (071 385 3421). Barons Court underground. **Open** 8am-10pm Mon-Fri, beginning of June.
Admission tickets from the club secretary. **Credit** A, AmEx, V.

One of the great championships in the world is held at the **All England Lawn Tennis Club** *(listed under* **Spectator Venues: Tennis***). You'll find the most expensive strawberries and cream in town at Wimbledon. Because tickets are issued by ballot months in advance, the only way to get tickets is to queue (and we mean queue), in some cases overnight. Another option is to approach a ticket tout, but be prepared to pay over the odds: some tickets go for £1,000.*

The club is best known for the Stella Artois Men's Tennis Tournament, which takes place a few weeks before Wimbledon.

SPORTS CENTRES

Central YMCA

112 Great Russell Street, WC1 (071 637 8131). Tottenham Court Road underground. **Open** 8am-10.30pm Mon-Fri; 10am-10pm Sat, Sun. **Membership** *full per year.* £206 over-26s; *full per week:* £22; phone for details of other memberships. **Admission** free to members; £2.70-£3.50 guests. **Classes** free-£4. **Credit** A,V.
A sports centre that offers the following: aerobics, keep fit, badminton, basketball, canoeing, climbing wall, cricket, dance classes, fencing, gymnastics, handball, sub-aqua, squash, swimming, table tennis, trampoline, volleyball, weight-training. There is also a sauna, a solarium, a physiotherapist, a chiropodist and a beautician. The place has a clean-cut, cosmopolitan atmosphere.

Chelsea Sports Centre

Chelsea Manor Street, SW3 (071 352 6985/071 352 0366). Sloane Square underground/11, 19, 22 bus. **Open** 7.30am-10pm Mon-Fri; 8am-6.30pm Sat; 8am-6.30pm Sun. **No membership fee.**
Classes 45p-£1.20.
This Chelsea sports complex and swimming pool has a number of activities including: aerobics, badminton, basketball, bowls, canoeing, dance, football, keep-fit, lacrosse, martial arts, netball, racketball, roller skating, squash, sub-aqua, swimming, tennis, volleyball, weight-training

and yoga. It also has a sauna, a solarium and spa baths. For those people who have over-indulged in fitness, there's a sports injury clinic.

Jubilee Hall Recreation Centre

Tavistock Street, WC2 (071 836 4835). Covent Garden underground. **Open** 7.30am-10pm Mon-Fri; 10am-5pm Sat, Sun. **Membership** £40 per year; free OAPs. **Admission** free to members; £1 non-members. **Classes** £3-£4. **Credit** A, V.
A centrally located sports complex frequented by trend-setters and street-wise athletes. On offer are aerobics, badminton, basketball, climbing, dance (contemporary, jazz, rock 'n' roll, football (five-a-side), gymnastics, hockey, 14 martial arts, keep fit, unihock, squash, trampoline, volleyball, weight-training. There's also a sauna, a solarium and a Jacuzzi. A sports injury clinic with practitioners of acupuncture, reflexology and the Alexander Technique is available.

Kensington Sports Centre

Walmer Road, W11 (071 727 9747). Latimer Road underground. **Open** 7.30am-10pm Mon-Fri; 8am-9.45pm Sat; 8am-6.30pm Sun. **Membership** *Borough residents:* £10 single, £15 family; *non-residents:* £16 single, £21 family. **Admission** 30p. **Charges** 65p-£5.
A west London sports centre that's crammed with classes and facilities for aerobics, athletics, badminton, basketball, bowls, cricket, football, gymnastics, hockey, judo, karate, netball, roller-skating, sub-aqua, squash, swimming, table tennis, tennis, trampoline, volleyball and weight-training. There's a sauna, a solarium and a Jacuzzi. Unusually, the centre provides a crèche for the kids while mum or dad work out.

Theatre

London is theatre land. *Jane Edwardes* **and** *Helen Rose* **of** *Time Out* **show you how to escape the Mousetrap, miss Saigon, and get on your bike to the Tricycle and the Fringe.**

Perhaps only the Russians are as enthusiastic about theatre as the British. This doesn't mean to say that everything on offer will be worth seeing, but with nearly 600 new productions opening a year, visitors can be confronted with a bewildering choice. The most important shows, though not necessarily the best, will play in the **West End**, the commercial theatre area surrounding Shaftesbury Avenue. That's where you'll discover the big musicals such as *Miss Saigon, Phantom of the Opera, Aspects of Love* and *Les Miserables*; the long-running farces, such as *Run for your Wife* (for those who share the British sense of humour); tired old thrillers, like *The Mousetrap,* which has, incredibly, been running since 1952; and the occasional interesting new play such as the intense, erotic *Les Liasons Dangereuses*.

Tourists are understandably drawn to the West End by the famous names, the historic theatres – many of them a joy to look at even if the facilities leave a lot to be desired – and the prolific publicity. However, don't forget the **Major Companies.** The **National Theatre** is worth visiting even if you're not seeing a play there; it boasts a wonderful view of the Thames, restaurants, a good bookshop and live music in the foyer. The three theatres – Olivier, Lyttelton and Cottesloe – attract many of the the most creative actors, designers and directors in the country, to present both classics and new plays.

The Barbican in the City is the London home of the **Royal Shakespeare Company (RSC)** – at least for the time being as the company is not happy with its mole-like existence here. Despite this, and financial troubles, the RSC still presents the most accomplished Shakespearean productions in the country.

The other major theatre in London is the **Royal Court** (the 'Writers' Theatre') where John Osborne's *Look Back in Anger* crashed through the french windows in 1956 and changed the course of British theatre. A little scruffy, the theatre's still a must for anybody interested in new writing, from Caryl Churchill to Timberlake Wertenbaker.

Beyond the West End and major subsidised theatres lies the **fringe,** the vast array of small theatres including the Theatre Royal Stratford East, E15, the Almeida, N1, the Tricycle, NW6, the Hampstead Theatre, NW3, and the Bush Theatre, W12. Many of these venues are outside the centre of town and attract a neighbourhood audience. Tickets are not usually available from agencies, nor are productions advertised in the daily newspapers, so the theatre listings in *Time Out* magazine are essential.

LIFT

The **London International Festival of Theatre** is a major biannual event, taking place throughout July 1991, and staged at various venues all over London *(enquiries 23 Neal Street, WC2, 071 240 2428).* In its sixth season, the LIFT will bring together the best of innovative contemporary theatre from around the world and will also treat the public to the best of new British work.

TICKETS

Ticket prices for West End musicals are the most expensive (£5-£25) and can be the most difficult to obtain. Beware of touts who'll try and rip you off by selling seats in the Upper Balcony for a vast sum. You may have to go to a ticket agency where a fee is charged on top of the ticket price.

Ten Tips for Cheap Theatre-going:
1. Go to the **SWET** ticket booth in Leicester Square (*see below*).
2. Go to a matinée, but be prepared for slightly lacklustre performances and understudies replacing the stars who are saving their voices for evening shows.
3. If you don't suffer from vertigo, sit in the 'gods' (the top of the theatre) and take opera glasses.
4. Take a risk and go to a preview before the critics have had a chance to deliver their verdict.
5. Go to the National Theatre early in the morning on the day of the show you want to see. A number of tickets are sold on the day, from 10am at the box office: 40 for the Olivier; 40 for the Lyttelton; and 20 for the Cottesloe.
6. Go to the Royal Court on a Monday night. All seats cost £4.
7. Go to any fringe theatre where ticket prices range from £2.50 to £10.
8. If visiting a West End theatre, check whether it operates a standby scheme (for student standbys identification is necessary).
9. When visiting a fringe theatre, find out if there are discounts for students, unwaged (UB40s), senior citizens, nurses or groups.
10. Look out for special offers in the back of *Time Out* magazine.

Society of West End Theatre (SWET) Ticket Booth
Ticket Booth: Leicester Square, WC2 (no phone). Leicester Square or Piccadilly Circus underground. **Open** *matinées* noon-30 mins before start of last matinée Mon-Sat; *evening shows* 2.30-6.30pm Mon-Sat. **Commission** £1 for tickets normally priced at £5 or below; £1.25 for tickets normally priced over £5. **No credit cards** (cash only).
The SWET ticket booth in Leicester Square has a limited number of tickets for some West End productions on the day of performance at half price (cash only). Tickets are restricted to four per person and you cannot return tickets to the booth, although the theatre might accept returns. The long queue at least isn't boring, since buskers enjoy playing to it. A list of theatres that operate the Society's standby scheme is available from *SWET, Bedford Chambers, The Piazza, Covent Garden, WC2 (071 836 0971);* open 10am-5.30pm Mon-Fri.

Artsline
5 Crowndale Road, NW1 (071 388 2227). Mornington Crescent or Camden town underground/Camden Road BR. **Open** 10am-4pm Mon-Fri.
A free advice and information service for disabled people on access to arts and entertainment in London. Ask them to send you the free monthly arts listings magazine, *Disability Arts in London. See also chapter* Survival.

WEST END

Compiled weekly, *Time Out* magazine's Theatre listings will provide full details of current London shows. Most theatres operate discount schemes on selected performances for students, the unwaged, senior citizens and large groups. Check before booking.

Adelphi

Strand, WC2 (071 836 7611; credit card 081 741 9999). Charing Cross underground/BR. **Open** *box office* 10am-8pm Mon-Sat. **Booking** four months in advance. **Performances** 7.30pm Mon-Fri; 8pm Sat; *matinées* 2.30pm Wed; 4.30pm Sat. **Tickets** £9-£21. **Credit** A, AmEx, DC, V.

Built by John Scott so he could put his daughter on the stage, the Sans Pareil theatre became the Adelphi in 1858. It was famous for its melodramas – not least the real-life incident when one unfortunate star was stabbed to death outside the stage door by a jealous colleague. Recently the theatre has built a reputation for colourful, mainstream musicals. At time of writing, *Me and My Girl,* the cockney rags-to-riches musical, featuring the famous 'Lambeth Walk', is still one of the best musicals in town.

Albery

St Martin's Lane, WC2 (081 867 1115; credit card 081 867 1111). Leicester Square underground. **Open** *box office* 10am-8pm Mon-Sat. **Performances** 7.45pm Mon-Sat; *matinées* 3pm Thur; 4pm Sat. **Tickets** £10-£22. **Credit** A, AmEx, DC, £TC, V.

During World War II the Albery was the home for the company of the Old Vic (*see below* **Major Comapnies**). It now stages a mixture of light comedy and mainstream theatre.

Aldwych

The Aldwych, WC2 (071 836 6404; credit card 071 379 6233). Covent Garden or Holborn underground. **Open** *box office* 10am-8pm Mon-Sat. **Booking** two weeks in advance. **Performances** 7.30pm Mon-Fri; 8pm Sat;

matinées 3pm Wed; 4pm Sat. **Tickets** £5.50-£16.50. **Credit** A, AmEx, DC, £TC, V.

Famous for its pre-war 'Aldwych farces', the theatre later became the home of the RSC between 1960 and 1982. Some of the better-quality West End shows are staged here.

Ambassadors

West Street, WC2 (071 836 6111; credit card 071 836 1171). Leicester Square underground. **Open** *box office* 10am-8pm Mon-Sat. **Performances** 7.30pm Mon-Fri; 8pm Sat; *matinées* 3pm Wed; 4pm Sat. **Tickets** £7.50-£15. **Credit** A, AmEx, DC, £TC, V.

One of the smallest theatres in the West End, the Ambassadors was the home of the marathon-running *The Mousetrap* for 21 years before it transferred to the St Martin's. The Ambassadors is ideally suited to more intimate dramas, such as *Les Liasons Dangereuses,* still packing them in as we went to press.

Apollo Shaftesbury Avenue

Shaftesbury Avenue, W1 (071 437 2663). Piccadilly Circus underground. **Open** *box office* 10am-8pm Mon-Sat. **Booking** one month in advance. **Performances** 8.30pm Mon-Fri; 8.45pm Sat; *matinées* 5.30pm Sat. **Tickets** £5-£15. **Credit** A, AmEx, £TC, V.

One of the four Victorian-Edwardian theatres in Shaftesbury Avenue, the Apollo is a small intimate theatre with a reputation for lightweight comedies.

Apollo Victoria

Wilton Road, SW1 (071 828 8665; credit card 071 630 6262/071 379 4444/071 240 7200). Victoria underground/BR. **Credit** A,

AmEx, DC, V.

Originally a 'Picture Palace' with elaborate art deco designs, the Apollo Victoria was dramatically transformed in 1981 for the staging of Andrew Lloyd-Webber's roller-skating extravaganza *Starlight Express,* which continues to roll up and around the auditorium. Sadly, only a few of the original art deco features still exist. Look out for the lovely bronze Egyptian mermaid above the gentlemen's toilets.

Cambridge

Earlham Street, WC2 (071 379 5299; credit card 071 379 4444). Covent Garden or Leicester Square underground. **Open** *box office* 10am-8pm Mon-Sat. **Booking** one week in advance. **Performances** 8pm Mon-Sat; *matinées* 3pm Sat. **Tickets** £7.50-£15.50. **Credit** A, AmEx, £TC, V.

This theatre has had a blighted history, as have the musicals staged here recently. Having undergone two major refurbishments since it opened in the thirties, it still falls dark for long periods.

Comedy

Panton Street, SW1 (071 930 2578; credit card 071 839 1438/071 240 7200). Piccadilly Circus underground. **Open** *box office* 10am-8pm Mon-Sat. **Booking** three weeks in advance. **Performances** 8pm Mon-Thur; 6pm, 8.45pm Fri, Sat. **Tickets** £4-£15.50. **Credit** A, AmEx, DC, £TC, V.

Built in 1881 and designed by the Victorian architect Thomas Verity, the theatre had its mainstay in comedies for several decades, but more recently has come to include serious drama. In the mid-fifties the theatre became a club to enable it to avoid the Lord Chamberlain's ancient censorship laws which forbade the staging of Miller's *View from the Bridge* and Williams' *Cat on a Hot Tin Roof.*

Dominion

Tottenham Court Road, W1 (071 580 9562; credit card 071 836 2428). Tottenham Court Road underground. **Open** *Box office* 10am-8pm Mon-Sat. **Performances** 7.30-8pm. **Tickets** £6.50-£33. **Credit** A, DC, AmEx, £TC, V.

The Dominion, opened in 1929 for the staging of lavish new musicals, became a cinema only three years later. It only reverts to its original function for Christmas pantos. *See also chapter* **Music: Rock, Folk & Jazz.**

Drury Lane Theatre Royal

Catherine Street, WC2 (071 836 8108). Covent Garden or Holborn underground or Charing Cross underground/BR. **Open** *box office* 10am-8pm Mon-Sat. **Performances** 7.45pm Mon-Sat; *matinées* 3pm Wed, Sat. **Tickets** £7-£22.50. **Credit** A, AmEx, £TC, V.

Built in 1812 on the site of the theatre in which Nell Gwynne made her stage debut, the Drury Lane has played host to some of Britain's greatest actors. David Garrick, the famous nineteenth century actor-manager, ran the theatre for 30 years. Since the 1950s, the theatre has been the British home of American musicals but, with the revival of the British musical, *Miss Saigon* (*see* **picture and caption**) looks set to outrun them all.

Duke of York's

St Martin's Lane, WC2 (071 836 5122; credit card 071 836 9837). Leicester Square underground or Charing Cross underground/BR. **Open** *box office* 10am-8pm

Miss Saigon *(listed under* **West End: Drury Lane Theatre Royal***), the new epic by the* Les Miserables *team of Alain Boubil and Claude-Michel Schonberg, scooped all the 1989 music awards. Set against the fall of Saigon, it reworks the* Madame Butterfly *story in depicting a romance between a Vietnamese bar girl and an American GI. The mixture of realism and melodrama can be intolerable, but there are some spectacular moments, including the landing of a helicopter on stage. Take Kleenex.*

daily. **Booking** two weeks in advance.
Performances 8pm Mon-Sat; *matinées* 3pm
Thur, 5pm Sat. **Tickets** £5-£14.50. **Credit** A,
AmEx, £TC, V.
The theatre is haunted by the grumpy ghost
of its first manager, Violette Melnotte,
although she has done little to scare away
the many stars who have appeared in the
theatre, including Ellen Terry, Isadora
Duncan, Charlie Chaplin, Orson Welles,
John Gielgud and Peggy Ashcroft.

Fortune
*Russell Street, WC2 (071 836 2238; credit
card 071 240 7200/081 741 9999) Covent
Garden underground or Charing Cross under-
ground/BR.* **Open** *box office* 10am-8pm Mon-
Sat. **Booking** three months in advance.
Performances 8pm Mon-Sat; *matinées* 3pm
Tue; 4pm Sat. **Tickets** £7.50-£15.50. **Credit**
A, AmEx, £TC, V.
This small theatre, opposite the stage door of
the impressive Drury Lane Theatre, became
the heart of Swinging Sixties London when it
staged the now famous Oxbridge revue,
Beyond the Fringe, which launched the
careers of Jonathan Miller, Peter Cook,
Dudley Moore and Alan Bennet. A good
venue for revues and West End transfers.

Garrick
*Charing Cross Road, WC2 (071 379 6107;
credit card 071 240 7200). Leicester Square
underground.* **Open** *box office* 10am-8pm
Mon-Sat. **Performances** 8pm Mon-Thur;
5pm, 8.15pm Fri, Sat. **Tickets** £7.50-£15.
Credit A, AmEx, £TC, V.
Built in 1889, the theatre was designed for
WS Gilbert (of Gilbert and Sullivan fame).
Arthur Bouchier was the ebullient manager
between 1900 and 1915, who refused entry
to the critic of *The Times*. Some say that his
ghost still haunts the staircase, although it
doesn't keep today's *Times'* critics away.

Globe
*Shaftesbury Avenue, W1 (071 437 3667;
credit card 081 741 9999). Piccadilly Circus
underground.* **Open** *box office* 10am-8pm
Mon-Sat. **Booking** one week in advance for
Fri, Sat. **Performances** 7.45pm Mon-Sat;
matinées 3pm Sat. **Tickets** £7.50-£15. **Credit**
A, AmEx, £TC, V.
Built in 1903 as the Hicks Theatre, it became
the Globe three years later. It boasts a lovely
Louis XVI interior with a beautiful oval gallery
and a twelve-arch bar. It flourishes on good
standard drama and comedy. Peter Shaffer's
award-winning comedy *Lettice and Lovage*
was still running at the time of writing.

Greenwich
*Crooms Hill, Greenwich, SE10 (081 858
7755). Greenwich BR/1, 177, 180 bus.* **Open**
box office 10am-8.30pm Mon-Sat. **Booking**
three days in advance. **Performances** 7.45pm
Mon-Sat; *Matinées* 2.30pm Sat. **Tickets** £5.50-
£9. **Credit** A, AmEx, DC, £TC, V.
A popular local theatre which has built up a
reputation for good quality plays which often
transfer to the West End. *See also chapter*
The River & Docklands.

Haymarket *The Haymarket, SW1
(071 930 9832). Piccadilly Circus underground.* **Open** *Box office* 10am-8pm Mon-
Sat. **Performances** 7.30pm Mon-Sat; *matinées* 3pm Thur. **Tickets** £6-£17. **Credit** A,
AmEx, DC, V.

For years we imagined that the audience at the **Open Air Theatre** *(listed under* **West End***) consisted almost entirely of tourists, but apparently it's young Londoners who relish the* al fresco *setting in the centre of the city. If this is true, it's about time that tourists did discover the famed production of* A Midsummer Night's Dream *in all its sylvan glory. Wait for the moment when, as daylight fades, the stage lights are gradually raised. Pure magic.*

This beautiful, authentic Georgian theatre,
graced with the stately elegance of John
Nash's design, has an impressive history.
Colourful characters associated with it
include the actor-manager Herbert
Beerbohm Tree, who staged Oscar Wilde's
A Woman of No Importance here, and the
famous actress and royal mistress Lily
Langtry, who made her stage début at the
Haymarket. The theatre's illustrious career
has continued to the present day; the solid
dramas and revivals frequently attracting the
very best British performers and directors.

Her Majesty's
*Haymarket, SW1 (071 839 2244). Piccadilly
Circus underground.* **Open** *box office* 10am-
8pm Mon-Sat. **Booking** eight months in
advance. **Performances** 7.45pm Mon-Sat;
matinées 3pm Wed, Sat. **Tickets** £8.50-£25.
Credit A, AmEx, V.
Built for Herbert Beerbohm Tree in 1897,
the magnificent French Renaissance-style
exterior is one of the most elegant in
London. Beerbohm Tree managed the theatre and founded a dramatic school attached
to it, which became the Royal Academy of
Dramatic Art (RADA). *The Phantom of the
Opera* (Lloyd-Webber's musical version)
seems to be residing here permanently.

London Palladium
*Argyll Street, W1 (071 437 7373). Oxford
Circus underground.* **Open** *box office* 10am-
8.30pm Mon-Sat. **Booking** three weeks in
advance. **Performances** variable. **Tickets**
variable. **Credit** A, AmEx, £TC, V.
A traditional home of pantomimes and vari-

ety, this former music hall is frequently dark
during the Summer. It's often the venue for
television specials and pop concerts (*see
chapter* **Music: Rock, Folk & Jazz**).

Lillian Baylis
*at Sadler's Wells Theatre, Rosebery Avenue,
EC1 (071 278 8916). Angel underground.*
Open *box office* 10.30am-7.30pm Mon-Sat
(till 6.30pm when there is no performance).
Performances 7.45pm Mon-Sat; 3pm Sat
matinées. **Tickets** £1-£7. **Credit** A, AmEx,
DC, £TC, V.
The Lilian Baylis Theatre is the latest addition to the Wells complex. Situated in
Arlington Way, behind the main theatre, this
studio opened in October 1988. It's named
after the immortal Lilian – who saved the
theatre from extinction in 1931 – and it holds
just over 200 people. Tickets for Baylis performances are rock bottom in price for often
experimental, small-scale dance, theatre, and
music performances.
Restaurant. Toilets for the disabled.

Lyric Hammersmith
*King Street, W6 (081 741 2311; credit card
071 836 3464). Hammersmith underground.*
Open *box office* 10am-8pm Mon-Sat;
11.30am-1pm Sun. **Booking** three days in
advance. **Performances** *main house* 7.45pm
Mon-Sat; *matinées* 2.30pm Wed; 4pm Sat;
studio 8pm Mon-Sat. **Tickets** *main house*
£7.50-£15; *studio* £6. **Membership** £3.50-
£6.50. **Credit** A, AmEx, DC, £TC, V.
Hammersmith once boasted one of the most
delightful Victorian playhouses. Amid much
controversy, it was demolished in 1972 to

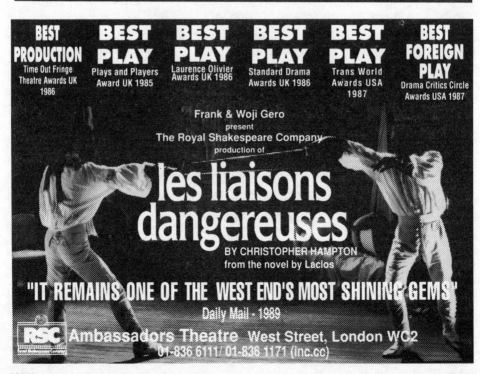

make room for a new shopping development, which includes a purpose-built theatre complex. But the delightful, original interior of the theatre has been maintained. There's a small Studio where visiting companies and more experimental work are found. The main theatre has a good reputation for all kinds of drama, especially international, and stages particularly good Christmas pantomimes.
Restaurant. Toilets for the disabled. Wheelchair access.

Lyric Shaftesbury Avenue
Shaftesbury Avenue, W1 (071 437 3686). Piccadilly Circus underground. **Open** *box office* 10am-8pm Mon-Sat. **Performances** 8pm Mon-Sat. **Tickets** £6.50-£25. **Credit** A, AmEx, £TC, V.
When this theatre opened in 1888 it specialized in comic operas, a tradition which continued into the twenties, augmented by productions of Shakespeare. The famous French actress, Sarah Bernhardt, performed here in 1898. It currently offers a good mix of straight theatre and some musicals.

Mermaid
Puddle Dock, EC4 (071 236 5568). Blackfriars underground/BR. **Open** *box office* 10am-7.30pm Mon-Sat. **Performances** 7.30pm Mon-Sat; *matinées* 2pm Wed; 2.30pm Sat. **Tickets** £6.50-£13.50. **Credit** A, £TC, V.
The spacious, raked auditorium of this modern theatre makes it one of the most comfortable around, with clear sight-lines. Its career in recent years has been chequered.

New London
Drury Lane, WC2 (071 405 0072). Covent Garden or Holborn underground. **Open** *box office* 10am-8pm Mon-Sat. **Performances** 7.30-8.15pm. **Tickets** £7-£25. **Credit** A, AmEx, DC, £TC, V.
With probably the most uninspiring exterior of all London's theatres, the New London, built on the site of the popular Elizabethan Winter Garden Theatre, currently houses the musical adaptation of TS Eliot's poems, *Cats*.
Wheelchair access by prior arrangement.

Open Air Theatre
Inner Circle, Regent's Park, NW1 (071 486 2431; credit card 071 486 1933). Baker Street underground. **Open** *box office* 10am-8pm Mon-Sat. **Performances** 7.45pm Mon-Sat; *matinées* 2.30pm Wed, Thur, Sat. **Tickets** £5-£12. **Credit** A, AmEx, V.
See **picture and caption**.
Restaurant. Group discount. Toilets for disabled people. Wheelchair access.

Palace
Shaftesbury Avenue, W1 (071 434 0909; credit card 071 379 4444). Leicester Square underground. **Open** 10am-7.30pm Mon-Sat. **Performances** 7.45pm. *matinées* 2.30pm. **Tickets** £5.50-£25. **Credit** A, AmEx, DC, V.
See **picture and caption**.

Phoenix
Charing Cross Road, WC2 (071 836 2294; credit card 071 240 7200). Leicester Square underground. **Open** *box office* 10am-8pm Mon-Sat. **Performances** 7.30pm Mon-Sat; *matinées* 2.30pm Thur, Sat. **Tickets** £12.50-£22.50. **Credit** A, AmEx, DC, £TC, V.
Built on the site of the old Alcazar music hall, the theatre opened with Gertrude Lawrence and Laurence Olivier in Noel Coward's *Private Lives*. It's recently been

graced by Kenneth Branagh – prematurely acclaimed by many as the new Olivier – and his all-star Renaissance Theatre Company.

Piccadilly
Denman Street, W1 (071 867 1118; credit card 071 867 1111). Piccadilly Circus underground. **Open** *box office* 10am-8pm Mon-Sat. **Booking** advisable two weeks in advance. **Performances** 7.45pm Mon-Sat; *matinées* 3pm Tue, Sat. **Tickets** £11-£21. **Credit** A, AmEx, £TC, V.
The Piccadilly was built in the twenties, was used briefly as a cinema, but now houses musicals. It's currently under threat from property developers.

Players
The Arches, Villiers Street, WC2 (071 839 1134). Embankment underground or Charing Cross underground/BR. **Open** *box office* 10am-5pm Mon; 10am-10pm Tue-Fri; 3.30-10pm Sat; 4.30-10pm Sun. **Performances** 8.15pm Tue-Sun. **Tickets** £12. **Credit** A, V.
A theatre club complete with restaurant and bar in keeping with the traditional Victorian music hall productions which are the hallmark of the Players theatre company. The ticket price gives temporary membership for one week.

Playhouse Theatre
Northumberland Avenue, WC2 (071 839 4401). Embankment underground or Charing Cross underground/BR. **Open** *box office* 10am-8pm Mon-Sat; *matinées* 3pm Sat. **Tickets** £6-£18. **Credit** A, AmEx, DC, £TC, V.
An elegant theatre which for several years was used as a BBC studio and has been recently refurbished. It's now owned by the best-selling novelist and playwright, Jeffrey Archer.

Prince Edward
Old Compton Street, W1 (071 734 8951; credit card 071 836 3464). Leicester Square or Tottenham Court Road underground. **Open** *box office* 10am-8pm Mon-Sat. **Performances** 7.30pm Mon-Sat; *matinées* 2.30pm Thur, Sat. **Tickets** £9-£22.50. **Credit** A, V.
This thirties-built theatre had a modest career as a musical/revue venue, before becoming the London Casino, a cabaret-restaurant with a dance floor. It declined in the sixties, and turned into a cinema, but was rescued by *Evita*, which ran for eight years. It's staged musicals ever since.
Wheelchair access.

Prince of Wales
Coventry Street, W1 (071 839 5972; credit card 071 836 3464/071 240 7200). Piccadilly Circus underground. **Open** *box office* 10am-6pm Mon-Sat. **Booking** five months in advance. **Performances** 7.45pm Mon-Sat; *matinées* 3pm Wed, Sat. **Tickets** £17.50-£25. **Credit** A, AmEx, £TC, V.
Formerly the Prince's, the theatre has a long-established tradition of presenting musical comedy, variety and American comedy. Lloyd-Webber's least gimmicky show yet, *Aspects of Love*, has been attracting unquestioning devotees by the coach-load.

Queen's
Shaftesbury Avenue, W1 (071 734 1166; credit card 071 836 2428). Piccadilly Circus underground. **Open** *box office* 10am-8pm Mon-Sat. **Performances** 8pm Mon-Sat; *matinées* 3pm Wed, Sat. **Tickets** £6.50-£15.50. **Credit** A, AmEx, £TC, V.
Despite its modernist frontage, dating from the fifties, the auditorium boasts an Edwardian elegance all of its own. Past productions have differed in quality.

The **Palace** *(listed under* **West End***) was praised by John Betjeman as the only theatre building of the last 60 years worth admiring. It's recently been magnificently refurbished by its owner, the ubiquitous Andrew Lloyd Webber. Even those who can't get to see* Les Miserables *can wander in during the daytime and enjoy lunch in the splendid surroundings.*

St Martin's

West Street, Cambridge Circus, WC2 (071 836 1443; credit card 071 379 4444). Leicester Square underground. **Open** *box office* 10am-8pm Mon-Sat. **Booking** two months in advance. **Tickets** £6-£14.50. **Performances** 8pm Mon-Sat; *matinées* 2.45pm Tue; 5pm Sat. **Credit** A, AmEx, V.
A companion to the Ambassadors, the solid-looking St Martin's, with its classic Ionic columns, is smaller than its rather grand exterior would suggest. The Agatha Christie whodunnit, *The Mousetrap*, began its long career next door at the Ambassadors on 25 November 1952, but transferred here in 1974 to continue its interminable run.

Savoy

Strand, WC2 (071 836 8888; credit card 071 379 6219). Charing Cross underground/BR. **Open** *box office* 10am-8pm Mon-Sat. **Booking** two weeks in advance. **Performances** 7.30pm Mon-Sat; *matinées* 2.30pm Wed, Sat. **Tickets** £7-£16. **Credit** A, AmEx, DC, £TC, V.
Adjacent to the grand Savoy Hotel, the theatre was designed for D'Oyly Carte to stage Gilbert and Sullivan operettas. Under Harley Granville-Barker's management it became renowned for Shakespeare revivals but more recently has gained a reputation for lightweight comedies.

Shaftesbury

Shaftesbury Avenue, WC2 (071 379 5399). Holborn or Tottenham Court Road underground. **Open** *box office* 10am-8pm Mon-Sat. **Performances** 8pm Mon-Thur; 8.15pm Fri, Sat; *matinées* 5pm Fri, Sat. **Tickets** £7.50-£16.50. **Credit** A, AmEx, DC, £TC, V.
Sited on the corner of Shaftesbury Avenue and High Holborn, the theatre opened in 1911 as the New Prince's theatre and only acquired its current name in 1963. It staged the controversial musical *Hair* in 1968, but was threatened with closure until campaigning made it a listed building. It now houses musicals, drama and comedies.
Wheelchair access by prior arrangement.

Strand

Aldwych, WC2 (071 836 2660; credit card 071 836 4143). Covent Garden or Holborn underground or Charing Cross underground/BR. **Open** *box office* 10am-8pm Mon-Sat. **Performances** 7.30pm Mon-Fri; 8pm Sat; *matinées* 3pm Thur; 4.30pm Sat. **Tickets** £8-£16.50. **Credit** A, AmEx, DC, £TC, V.
The Strand is adjacent to the Waldorf Hotel and was originally called the Waldorf. Despite being bombed during both wars, the show has always gone on. Many theatrical greats have appeared here from Beerbohm Tree and Henry Irving to Peggy Mount and Charles Laughton.

Vaudeville

The Strand, WC2 (071 836 9987). Charing Cross underground/BR. **Open** *box office* 10am-8pm Mon-Sat. **Performances** 8pm Mon-Sat; *matinées* 3pm Sat. **Tickets** £7.50-£15. **Credit** A, AmEx, DC, V.
This little theatre, true to its name, was once famous for its 'Charlot' music-hall revues and now offers a variety of light comedy and drama. *Group discount.*

Victoria Palace

Victoria Street, SW1 (071 834 1317). Victoria underground/BR. **Open** *box office* 10am-8pm Mon-Sat. **Performances** 8pm Mon-Thur; 8.30pm Fri, Sat; *matinées* 5.30pm Fri, Sat. **Tickets** £7-£18.50. **Credit** A, AmEx, £TC, V.
Originally a Music Hall, the theatre became the home of revues for several decades. The musical *Me and My Gal* was staged from 1937 to the outbreak of World War Two. It has also been the home of 'The Crazy Gang' and *The Black and White Minstrel Show*. It continues to stage mainly musicals. *Group discount. Wheelchair access.*

Whitehall

Whitehall, SW1 (071 867 1119; credit card 071 867 1111). Charing Cross underground/BR. **Open** *box office* 10am-8pm Mon-Sat. **Performances** 8pm Mon-Sat; *matinées* 2.30pm Thur; 5.30pm Sat. **Tickets** £5-£23. **Credit** A, AmEx, DC, £TC, V.
The home of farce and revue, the Whitehall was completely restored in 1985 to its former art deco splendour. Ray Cooney's farce, *Run for Your Wife*, just keeps on running.

Wyndhams

Charing Cross Road, WC2 (071 867 1116). Leicester Square underground or Charing Cross underground/BR. **Open** *box office* 10am-8pm Mon-Sat. **Performances** 8pm Mon-Sat; *matinées* 3pm Wed; 4pm Sat. **Tickets** £11-£16. **Credit** A, AmEx, DC, £TC, V.
Named after the actor-manager Charles Wyndham, this elegant Victorian playhouse is a centre for high quality, serious drama by the likes of Steven Berkoff.
Group discount. Infra red transmission for the hard of hearing.

MAJOR COMPANIES

National Theatre

South Bank Centre, South Bank, SE1 (box office 071 928 2252; credit card 240 7200) Waterloo underground/BR/Riverbus. **Open** *box office* 10am-8pm Mon-Sat. **Performances** 7-7.30pm. **Tickets** *Olivier and Lyttelton theatres* £2-£15.50. *Cottesloe theatre* £5-£8.50. **Credit** A, AmEx, DC, V.
The home of the National Theatre (now the Royal National Theatre) since 1976, this imposing concrete complex houses three theatres: the Olivier (a large open-platform stage); the Lyttelton (a proscenium arch); and the small, more flexible studio space of the Cottesloe. In the early evening, the main foyer offers free music recitals, from jazz and classical to guitar and harp. There are exhibition spaces, a bookshop, several small snack bars serving hot and cold food, and a restaurant. Regular lectures and talks are held in the early evenings, and occasionally the NT hold 'Celebriteas', where well-known theatrical personalities informally discuss their careers over afternoon tea and scones. As each theatre generally has three plays in repertory, there's a fair selection of work on offer at any one time. *See also chapter* **Music: Classical & Opera.** *Bookshop. Car Park. Group discount (071 620 0741). Front seats for the partially sighted by prior arrangement. Infra red audio*

Somehow, the **Royal Shakespeare Company at the Barbican** *(listed under* **Major** Companies*) manages to perform some great work in the uncreative environment of the concrete Barbican Centre (see chapter* **The** City*). The RSC is often knocked, perhaps because so much is expected, and always in dire financial trouble, but there are usually a couple of productions in their repertoire that will illuminate Shakespeare as never before.*

*The scene of a grisly murder in the fifties, the atmospheric **Almeida** (listed under **Fringe Theatre**) is always a great favourite with companies and audiences. A new artistic team of Ian McDiarmid and Jonathan Kent has planned an exciting programme of classics and new plays. The annual Festival of Contemporary Music is held here from mid-June to mid-July.*

for the hard of hearing. Restaurants & cafés.
Tour by prior arrangement (071 633 0880).
Toilets for the disabled. Wheelchair access.

Old Vic
Waterloo Road, SE1 (071 928 7616; recorded information 071 928 7618). Waterloo underground/BR. **Open** box office 10am-8pm Mon-Sat. **Booking** three months in advance.
Performances 7.30pm Mon-Fri; 7.45pm Sat; matinées 2.30pm Wed; 4pm Sat. **Tickets** £4-£16. **Credit** A, AmEx, DC, £TC, V.
Known as the Royal Coburg Theatre when it opened in 1818, it became the Royal Victoria Theatre in 1833 in honour of the young princess. But it was under the eccentric Lilian Bayliss that the Old Vic really took off with hugely popular seasons of Shakespeare. From 1963 to 1976 it was the home of the National Theatre led by Laurence Olivier. Today it is owned by 'Honest' Ed Mirvish who has restored its elegant splendour and installed Jonathan Miller as Artistic Director. Eclectic seasons of little-known classics and revivals are now produced.
Group discount.

Royal Court
Sloane Square, SW1 (071 730 1745; credit card 071 836 2428). Sloane Square underground. **Open** box office 10am-8pm Mon-Sat. **Tickets** £4-£15. **Credit** A, AmEx, DC, £STC, V.
The Royal Court opened in 1888 and, under Harley Granville-Barker's management from 1904 to 1907, enjoyed a success which established it as one of the most important centres for new drama. Many of GB Shaw's plays were premiered here, under his direc-

tion. In 1934 it became a cinema and in 1940 was bombed. Rebuilt in 1952, its modern career began under the direction of George Devine who founded the English Stage Company. It continues to be an important centre for adventurous, experimental drama, particuarly in the **Theatre Upstairs** (see below **Fringe**).
Educational workshop by prior arrangement (081 960 4041). Group discount (071 240 7941). Tour by prior arrangement (071 328 7558). Induction loop. Disabled facilities. Wheelchair access.

RSC Barbican
Barbican Centre, Silk Street, EC2 (071 638 8891). Barbican underground (closed Sun) or Moorgate underground/BR. **Open** box office 9am-8pm daily. **Performances** 7-7.30pm Mon-Sat; matinées 2pm Thur, Sat. **Tickets** £5-£20. **Credit** A, AmEx, DC, £TC, V.
See picture and caption.
Car Park. Restaurants & cafés. Shops. Toilets for the disabled. Wheelchair access.

FRINGE THEATRE

Almeida
Almeida Street, N1 (071 359 4404). Angel underground or Highbury & Islington underground/BR. **Open** box office 10am-6pm Mon-Sat; matinées 4pm Sat. **Tickets** £6.50-£12.50. **Membership** £10 per year; £25 three-

yearly. **Credit** A, V.
See picture and caption.
Restaurant. Toilets for the disabled. Wheelchair access.

Bush
Shepherds Bush Green, W12 (081 743 3388). Goldhawk Road or Shepherd's Bush underground. **Open** box office 10am-10pm daily. **Performances** 8pm Tue-Sun. **Tickets** £3-£6. **Membership** 50p. **No credit cards.**
The tiny theatre above the Bush pub has a firm commitment to discovering and nurturing new writers. The productions are marked by imaginative set designs and high-quality staging.

Drill Hall
16 Chenies Street, WC1 (071 637 8270). Goodge Street underground/14, 24, 29, 73, 134, 253 bus. **Open** box office 10am-6pm Mon; 10am-11pm Tue-Fri; noon-8pm Sat. **Performances** 8pm Tue-Sat. **Tickets** £3-£6. **Membership** free. **No credit cards.**
The Drill Hall favours work by and for the lesbian and gay community, feminist work and politically- and socially-oriented theatre. There's a vegetarian restaurant in the basement, a bar, and on Friday and Saturday evenings, a free crèche for under-fives. The theatre closes during August.
Crèche (6.30-10.45pm Mon, Fri, Sat). Group discount. Toilets for disabled people. Wheelchair access. Workshop.

Gate Notting Hill
The Prince Albert, 11 Pembridge Road, W11 (071 229 0706). Notting Hill Gate underground. **Open** box office 11am-6pm Mon-Fri; 2-6pm Sat. **Performances** 7.30pm daily; Late at the Gate 10.15pm Thur-Sat. **Tickets** £3-£5. **Membership** £1 per year. **No credit cards.**
This small pub theatre has a reputation for excellent revivals of little-known European classics, contemporary South American plays and new writing. The space is cramped but productions are generally of a high standard.

Half Moon
213 Mile End Road, E1 (071 791 1141; recorded information 071 790 4000). Stepney Green underground/10, 25, 225 bus. **Open** box office 10am-6pm Mon-Sat. **Performances** 7.30pm Mon-Sat; matinées 2.30pm Sat. **Tickets** £1-£6.50. **Credit** A, V.
In the heart of the East End this energetically-run theatre caters to a loyal local audience with a lively mix of plays, which includes a good selection for the Black and Asian communities. It also has a strong youth theatre group and invariably produces a good Christmas panto.
Group discount. Toilets for disabled people. Wheelchair access.

Hampstead
Swiss Cottage Centre, Avenue Road, NW3 (071 722 9301). Swiss Cottage underground. **Open** box office 10am-8pm Mon-Sat. **Performances** 8pm Mon-Sat; matinées 4pm Sat. **Tickets** £3.50-£8. **Membership** £2.50 per year. **No credit cards.**
The Hampstead Theatre (in fact in Swiss Cottage) offers a solid mix of new plays, contemporary revivals and American drama. It has attracted some very starry names over the years and has enjoyed several West End transfers. A recent and very welcome addi-

tion to its cramped foyer bar has been the rather elegant and airy conservatory. *Toilets for the disabled. Wheelchair access.*

ICA Theatre
The Mall, W1 (071 930 3647). Piccadilly Circus underground or Charing Cross underground/BR. **Open** *box office* noon-8pm daily. **Performances** 8pm daily. **Tickets** £4.60-£5.60. **Credit** A, AmEx, DC, V.
The Institute for Contemporary Arts is *the* place for new experimental work in London. The Centre has a large gallery space, a state-of-the-art bar and a vegetarian restaurant. It represents an important body of innovative, exploratory theatre. *See also chapters* **Art Galleries, Dance** *and* **Film.** *Bar. Bookshop. Café. Group discount. Lectures. Workshops.*

King's Head
115 Upper Street, N1 (071 226 8561; recorded information 071 226 1916). Angel underground or Highbury & Islington underground/BR. **Open** *box office* 10am-6pm Mon-Fri; 10am-8pm Sat; 10am-4pm Sun. **Performances** 1.15pm, 7pm Mon-Fri; 1.15pm, 3.30pm, 7pm Sat; 3pm, 8pm Sun. **Tickets** £4-£7. **Membership** *Associate* 50p per year; *Full* £5 per year. **Credit** £TC.
The King's Head is the oldest pub theatre in

London. Undaunted by the tiny stage, the King's Head presents an ambitious selection of works, specialising in musical revivals, some of which have gone on to successful West End runs. There's a three course pre-theatre dinner and you can stay at your table for coffee and the performance. *See also chapter* **Local London.** *Group discount. Toilets for disabled people. Wheelchair access.*

Man in the Moon
392 Kings Road, SW3 (071 351 2876). Sloane Square or South Kensington underground. **Open** *box office* 6.30pm Tue-Sun. **Performances** from 7pm Tue-Sun. **Tickets** £3.50-£5. **Membership** 40p per year. **No credit cards.**
This small pub theatre hosts productions from visiting companies, often running two shows a night. The productions are variable but the general artistic policy ensures a reasonably high standard is maintained.

Riverside Studios
Crisp Road, W6 (081 748 3354; credit card 071 563 0331). Hammersmith underground. **Open** 10am-8pm Mon-Sat. **Performance** 7.30pm Mon-Sat. **Admission** £5-£7. **Credit** A, V.
Two large studio spaces are used for experimental work, foreign visiting companies and

new plays. A lively and friendly atmosphere is the norm. There's a restaurant, a cinema, a gallery and a bookshop. *See also chapters* **Art Galleries, Dance** *and* **Film.** *Bar. Bookshop. Café. Restaurant. Wheelchair access.*

Soho Poly Theatre
16 Riding House Street, W1 (071 636 9050). Oxford Circus underground. **Open** *box office* 10am-5.30pm Mon-Sat. **Performances** 8pm Mon-Sat. **Tickets** £4-£6. **Credit** A, V.
This tiny basement theatre encourages play-wrights through workshops and an annual playwriting competition. Productions are always of a very high standard and programming is imaginative and adventurous. *Café. Group discount.*

Theatre Royal Stratford East
Gerry Raffles Square, E15 (081 534 0310). Stratford underground/BR. **Open** *box office* 10am-7pm Mon-Sat. **Performances** 8pm Mon-Sat. **Tickets** £2.50-£10. **Credit** A, V.
Out East, the crumbling splendour of this old Victorian theatre stands alone in an unsightly new shopping centre. The theatre took off in the sixties under Joan Littlewood's innovative management and its reputation for high quality new and popular drama continues today – still managing to cater to both a local and London-wide audience. *Group discount. Wheelchair access.*

Theatre Upstairs
Royal Court, Sloane Square, SW1 (071 730 1754; credit card 071 836 2428). Sloane Square underground. **Open** *box office* 10am-8pm Mon-Sat. **Performances** 7.30pm Mon-Sat; *matinées* 3.30pm Sat. **Tickets** £3-£6. **Credit** A, AmEx, DC, £TC, V.
This studio space above the Royal Court Theatre (*see above* **Major Comapnies**) has been an invaluable source of new writing; launching many playwrights on their careers. It stages the annual Young Writers Festival and successful plays often transfer downstairs to the main stage. *Educational workshop by prior arrangement (081 960 4041). Tour by prior arrangemen.t (071 328 7558). Induction loop for the hard of hearing. Disabled facilities.*

Tricycle
269 Kilburn High Road, NW6 (071 328 1000). Kilburn underground. **Open** *box office* 10am-8pm Mon-Sat. **Performances** 8pm Mon-Sat; *matinées* 4pm Sat. **Tickets** £1.50-£6.50 Mon-Sat. **Credit** A, AmEx, V. *See* **picture and caption.** *See also chapter* **Children's London.**

Young Vic
66 The Cut, SE1 (071 928 6363). Waterloo underground/BR. **Open** *box office* 10am-6pm. **Booking** two days in advance. **Performances** 7.30pm Mon-Sat. **Tickets** £4-£8. **Credit** A, V.
Despite an unprepossessing exterior, the Young Vic (a converted butcher's shop) offers seating in the round, which gives the large stage space an intimate feel. Although the theatre's Shakespeare productions attract school audiences, their classics are some of

The Tricycle *(listed under* **Fringe Theatre**) *is one of the liveliest and most comfortable of the fringe theatres with an eclectic programme that reflects the cultural diversity of London's inhabitants. After a devastating fire and two years' rebuilding, the theatre is now looking brighter and more welcoming than ever. Its programming of black theatre and children's shows is widely acclaimed.*

the best in town, and performers such as Vanessa Redgrave, Billie Whitelaw and Ian McKellen have graced the stage here. The small studio space is used by visiting companies and productions there can be variable. *Café. Group discount. Wheechair access.*

Trips Out Of Town

There's more to Britain than just London. This is your guide to the best of the provinces.

London is the hub of the nation's transport system, so it's easy to escape from. In the time it takes a bus to cross the West End in the rush hour, a train can whisk you to the lush countryside of the Home Counties (the counties around London), and it doesn't take much longer to reach historic southern cities such as Canterbury and Bath. Even the north of England, with its entirely different atmosphere, is only a couple of hours away.

From the jagged coast of Cornwall to the rolling Downs, from the prettiness of the Cotswolds to the bleak and beautiful Yorkshire moors, every county has something different to offer.

The history of Britain unfolds in its architecture. An ancient town may be built on a river and have foundations put down by the Romans, Britain's first major developers. The town is likely to be centred on a magnificent medieval cathedral or church, either a round-arched one thrown up by the Normans, post-1066, or a pointy-arched Gothic edifice built a few centuries later. Nearby may be a ruined abbey, laid waste by Henry VIII's Dissolution of the monasteries, and an equally ravaged castle, probably knocked around in the Civil War, a mere 350 years ago. Huddled around the medieval market square you'll find sturdy stone or black-and-white timbered Tudor and Jacobean houses. Farther out there are usually elegant eighteenth-century Georgian terraces, and yet farther down the high (main) street will be brash Victorian civic buildings, monuments to the British Empire.

GETTING STARTED

The best place to start your journey is at the **British Travel Centre** (*see below*). Here you can get guide books, free leaflets and advice on any

destination, you can book rail, bus, air or car travel, reserve sightseeing tours, theatre tickets and accommodation, and there's even a bureau de change. The queues tend to be long in summer, but it's worth the wait.

The **Scottish, Wales and Northern Ireland Tourist Boards** provide a similar but more detailed service for their own countries. When you get to your destination, head for the local **Tourist Information Centre**, where you can find out what's on and pick up a useful map-cum-guide (often free). Always check opening times beforehand if you're going to see a specific sight: most things are shut on Sundays, Christmas and New Year Bank Holidays, some on Easter and May Day Bank Holidays, and many museums are closed all winter.

British Travel Centre
4-12 Lower Regent Street, SW1 (071 730 3400). Piccadilly Circus underground. **Open** 9am-6.30pm Mon-Fri; *May-Sept* 9am-5pm Sat, 10am-4pm Sun; *Oct-Apr* 10am-4pm Sat, Sun. **Credit** A, AmEx, V.

Northern Ireland Tourist Board
4-12 Lower Regent Street, W1 (071 839 8416; enquiries 071 493 0601). Piccadilly Circus underground. **Open** 9am-6.30pm Mon-Fri; *May-Sept* 9am-5pm Sat, 10am-4pm Sun; *Oct-Apr* 10am-4pm Sat, Sun. **Credit** A, AmEx, V.

Scottish Tourist Board
19 Cockspur Street, SW1 (071 930 8661). Piccadilly Circus or Charing Cross underground. **Open** *May-Sept* 9am-6pm Mon-Fri; *Oct-Apr* 9.30am-5.30pm Mon-Fri. **Credit** A, V.

Wales Tourist Board
34 Piccadilly, W1 (071 409 0969). Piccadilly Circus underground. **Open** *May-Sept* 9.15am-5.30pm Mon-Fri; *Oct-Apr* 9am-5pm Mon-Fri. **Credit** A, AmEx, V.

RAIL TRAVEL

The railways are the best way to get around, and travel on the high-speed

Inter-City trains is much quicker than going by road. Do avoid rush hours when trains get very full.

TRAIN INFORMATION

King's Cross
(071 278 2477, 7am-11pm) for West Yorkshire, the North East and eastern Scotland.

Euston or St Pancras
(071 387 7070, 24 hours daily) for the Midlands, North Wales, the North West and western Scotland.

Paddington
(071 262 6767, 24 hours daily) for the West Country, West Midlands and South Wales.

Charing Cross, Waterloo, Victoria and Liverpool Street
(071 928 5100, 24 hours daily) for the South East, Essex and East Anglia.

RAIL TRAVEL CENTRES

Rail Travel Centres offer information on train services and local facilities; you can also book train tickets there. The main-line stations listed (*see above* **Train Information**) all have Travel Centres, and there are other offices dotted around London. Personal callers only (no telephone enquiries). All accept Access, American Express and Visa.

Heathrow Airport
Arrivals terminals **Open** 7.45am-9pm daily.

Gatwick Airport
Main concourse **Open** 7am-10pm daily.

W1
407 Oxford Street, Tottenham Court Road underground. **Open** 9am-5pm Mon-Sat.

SW1
14 Kingsgate Parade, Victoria Street. Victoria underground/BR. **Open** 7.15am-9.15pm daily.

EC4
87 King William Street. Bank or Monument underground. **Open** 9am-5pm Mon-Fri.

FARES & TICKETS

Rail tickets can be bought right up until the moment of departure, but for InterCity routes it's wise to reserve a seat at least two hours in advance — otherwise you may end up standing all the way. Reservations can be made when buying the ticket, and cost £1 extra. Tickets can be bought from stations and Rail Travel Centres (*see above* **Rail Travel Centres**) or by phone with Access, AmEx and Visa from the relevant terminus. The fare structure breaks down thus: full-price **Standard Returns** can be used at any time of day; most people buy off-peak **Saver Returns**, which have certain restrictions but are almost half the price. **Blue Savers** are best value, but for Friday travel you'll need a **White Saver**, which is up to £10 more expensive; both are valid for return within one month. For journeys under 50 miles/80 kilometres **Cheap Day Returns**, valid for one day only, are best value. **First Class** is so expensive you might as well go by plane. Finally, avoid the Friday exodus at all costs and don't travel on a Sunday – because of Sabbath engineering works even InterCity services are appalling and can take hours longer.

BUS TRAVEL

Bus travel is incredibly cheap and there's a comprehensive network, but it can be hair-raising on the motorways and buses take much longer than trains. However, many long-distance routes offer 'luxury' services with videos and refreshments for a few pounds more. **National Express** *(071 730 0202)*

have routes to all parts of the country, buses departing from Victoria Coach Station, Buckingham Palace Road, SW1, five minutes walk from Victoria railway station. **Green Line Buses** *(071 668 7261)* have routes within Greater London: their major departure point is from Eccleston Bridge, off Buckingham Palace Road, SW1, behind Victoria railway station. In these days of cut-throat competition in bus travel there may well be competing services to your destination. National Express offer Rover Tickets which can make travel even cheaper.

FINDING ACCOMMODATION

If you want to be sure to avoid spending a night in a railway station it's advisable to book a room in advance, at least for the first day. The **British Travel Centre** *(see above* **Getting Started)** has a **Room Centre** which, for a small booking fee and a deposit, reserves appropriate accommodation anywhere in

Britain. The Scottish, Welsh and Northern Ireland Tourist Boards do the same within their respective countries. If you do turn up somewhere without a room, make for the local **Tourist Information Centre**, which will reserve a bed in the area to suit your taste (and pocket). Most also provide a 'Book-a-Bed-Ahead' service, which means you can book the next night's hotel in another area. All these services are available to personal callers only.

SCENIC RAIL TRIPS

The railway network is still an excellent way to explore the country, with many little-known local lines branching off from the main InterCity routes. Many of these pass through areas of spectacular beauty, often where no roads exist (especially in Scotland), and cross breathtaking Victorian viaducts. British Rail has produced a series of excellent free colour leaflets on the subject, available from the **British Travel Centre**, Regent Street *(see above* **Getting Started)**, and major stations.

DAY TRIPS

Whichever way you end up heading you're bound to find somewhere that excites your curiosity. We list some of the more interesting, and some of the ones you'll want to be able to say you've seen. These excursions are close enough to London to be an easy day out, but in case you prefer to make the most of your journey by staying overnight, we've added a few hotel suggestions.

BATH

Bath is a mandatory visit on every whistlestop tour of the country, but don't let that put you off. The reason everybody goes there is that it really is worth seeing. Avoid peak season weekends – if possible, go out of season or on a weekday.

Bath owes its existence to a hot spring. The Romans, being fond of a dip, were the first to make use of the quarter of a million gallons of steaming water produced daily, and the **Roman Baths and Museum**,

The **Royal Crescent** *(listed under* **Day Trips: Bath***) comprises 30 magnificent Georgian houses and a total of 114 Ionic columns. Number One has been restored and refurbished to its original glory just as Jane Austen knew it. Once occupied by the Grand Old Duke of York (who had ten thousand men) it was scandalously allowed to deteriorate into a near slum until Bath Preservation Trust rescued it in the 1960s. There is a splendid kitchen museum in the basement where you can see what really went on downstairs in a classy Georgian residence.*

Stall Street, are unmissable – fascinating underground remains with huge pools still filled with bubbling hot spring water. The adjoining **Pump Room**, fashionable in Georgian times and immortalized in Jane Austen's *Northanger Abbey*, is still a civilized place for tea. Facing it is the magnificent **Bath Abbey**, dating back to the sixteenth century, and nearby in North Parade Passage is **Sally Lunn's**, reputedly Bath's oldest house, and now an over-subscribed tearoom with a tiny cellar museum.

The **Guildhall Banqueting Room**, High Street, boasts a fine eighteenth-century interior. Sadly, the equally fine **Assembly Rooms**, Bennett Street, which house the **Museum of Costume**, are closed until 1992. Console yourself with a visit to the excellent **Museum of English Naive Art** in the Countess of Huntingdon Chapel, The Vineyard/Paragon. Interesting streets include **Royal Crescent**, the wonderful Georgian crescent, where No 1 has been restored and is now a museum; **Camden Crescent** and **Lansdown Crescent**, steep climbs but a wonderful view; picturesque **Pulteney Bridge** which is walled with tiny shops; and **Riverside Walk**, below the bridge – see the city from Roman level, and enjoy a beautiful vista of **Pulteney Weir**. There are daily walking and bus tours and personal guides are available – details from the Information Centre.

History apart, Bath is a major shopping centre. Head for the area between Cheap Street and George Street, full of interesting little clothes and gift shops – some very exclusive and expensive – and try Northumberland Place and the little roads running off Old Bond Street. Antique emporia – a Bath speciality, naturally – congregate round Margaret's Buildings, Quiet Street, Queen Street and up Lansdown Road. There's an antique market in Guinea Lane every Wednesday, and the Antique Centre, Bartlett Street, has many vendors under one roof.

Getting there *by train* from Paddington 80 minutes (longer on Sun); *by bus* National Express from Victoria, 3 hours; *by car* M4 to exit 18; *local buses* Badger Line (0225 462831). **Tourist Information Centre** *Abbey Church Yard, Bath, Avon (0225 462831).* **Open** *May-Oct* 9.30am-8pm Mon-Sat, 10am-6pm Sun; *Nov-Apr* 9.30am-5pm Mon-Sat, 10am-4pm Sun. **Eating and drinking** *Pump Room* and

The **Royal Pavilion** *(listed under* **Day Trips: Brighton***) was built by the celebrated Regency architect, John Nash, for his patron, the Prince Regent, later George IV, in 1823. A hybrid of Indian, Chinese, various Oriental and even Gothic styles, the overall result is a grand almost Disney-like extravaganza, capturing the spirit of the Regency at play. Queen Victoria however was not amused with such frippery and sold the Pavilion to the town council in 1845. The rooms have been refurbished with many splendid pieces of Regency design and the Chinese décor is well worth seeing.*

Sally Lunn's apart, you can barely move for **tearooms and restaurants**. *Rossiters*, Broad Street (second floor of the shop), is excellent for tea and a bite. *The Moon And Sixpence*, Broad Street, is a popular bistro with a courtyard, conservatory and fountain; a more expensive alternative is *Woods*, Alfred Street. *Supannahong*, John Street, is an enjoyable Thai café. Vegetarians go to *Huckleberry's*, Broad Street. For a really posh meal book at the *Hole in the Wall*, George Street (0225 25242) or *Clos Du Roy*, George Street (0225 64356). **Pubs**; the *Volunteer Rifleman's Arms*, New Bond Street Place, and *Coeur de Lion*, Northumberland Place, vie to be 'Bath's smallest pub' (the latter is cosier); the *Grapes*, Westgate Street, is a bustling, ancient wine bar with a Jacobean beamed ceiling. In summer, drink on the riverside at the *Boater*, Argyle Street. **Events** *Badminton Horse Trials* 4-7 May; *Bath International Festival* a major musical event, 26 May-11 Jun; *Royal Bath & West Show* 4-day agricultural show, 31 May-3 Jun; *Toyota Royal Polo Challenge* 3 Aug. **If you want to stay** you can book a room above the *Hole in the Wall* (0225 25242). Good for bed and breakfast are *Haydon House* (0225 27351), *Paradise House* (0225 317723), or *Somerset House* (0225 66451). If you want to indulge yourself in real luxury, *Lucknam Park* (0225 742777) is the place.

BRIGHTON

Brighton used to be known as 'London by the sea', but whether that was because it was just as lively,

just as dirty, or just as packed with Londoners is hard to say. At first glance it's hard to see the attraction. The beach is all pebbles and tar, and the sea's filthy and freezing – there's even a nudist cove for the truly foolhardy. Forget swimming, though, and soak in Brighton's real asset – its atmosphere.

The most famous area is **The Lanes**, quaint, twisty alleys between North Street and the seafront, packed with antiques, jewellery and clothes shops. However, these are often stuffy and over-priced, and the centre of fashion has shifted to **The North Lanes**, a nineteenth-century conservation area bounded by North Road and the seafront, where you'll find yet more, but cheaper, antique shops. Brighton is a junk-collector's paradise (especially the flea-markets at Upper Gardner Street on Saturday, and behind the station on Sunday).

One sight that must be seen is the many-domed **Royal Pavilion**, a fantastic, pseudo-oriental summer palace built in 1823 for the Prince Regent and recently restored to its original splendour. **Brighton Art**

Gallery and Museum, Church Street, is good for fashion and Arts Nouveaux and Deco, and there's a dolphinarium at the **Brighton Aquarium**, Madeira Drive. Walk along the sweeping iron-fenced Prom all the way from the Marina to the depths of Hove, Brighton's sister town, or for a shorter journey, take Britain's first public electric railway, **Volks Seafront Railway**, from the Marina to the wonderfully tawdry Palace Pier.

Getting there *by train* from Victoria, 55 minutes; *by car* A23, M23, A23; *local buses* Brighton and Hove Bus Co (0273 206666). **Tourist Information Centre** *Marlborough House, 54 Old Steine, Brighton, East Sussex (0273 23755); or* **Hove Information Centre**, *(0273 775400)*. **Open** *Easter-May* 9am-5pm Mon-Fri, 9am-6pm Sat, 10am-6pm Sun. *Jun-Sept* 9am-6pm Mon-Sat, 10am-6pm Sun. *Jul-Aug* 9am-6.30pm Mon-Fri, 9am-6pm Sat, 10am-6pm Sun. *Oct-Easter* 9am-5pm Mon-Sat, 10am-4pm Sun.
Eating and drinking. The Lanes is brilliant for, **pubs, restaurants** (especially seafood places) **and teashops**, but one of the best places for your afternoon cuppa is the *Mock Turtle*, Pool Valley. *Food For Friends*, Prince Albert Street, sells above-average vegetarian fare. *Al Duomos*, Pavilion Gardens, is a cheap Italian place popular with locals. Preston Street is full of restaurants, but most are horrid tourist-traps. For a reliable meal, try the *French Cellar*, New England Road (0273 603643). Good **pubs** include the *Frock and Jacket*, Prince Albert Street, a trendy cocktails and beer joint in The Lanes. *The Great Eastern*, Trafalgar Street, is small, sweet and book-lined. *The Belvedere*, in a seafront arch between the piers, sells good beer. Further along at Marine Parade are Brighton's trendiest **clubs**; the *Escape* and the *Zap*; more sedate is the *Catfish*, Ship Street, a small classic jazz club.
Events *Brighton Festival* 3 weeks of cultural events, 4-27 May; *London to Brighton Bike Ride* Jun; *London to Brighton Veteran Car Run*, 5 Nov. Also see *The Punter*, a free magazine available in many shops and pubs, for listings of local happenings.
If you want to stay In Brighton and Hove every other house seems to be a hotel or bed and breakfast. *The Adelaide* (0273 205286) is old, four-star and mid-priced; the *Hotel Brunswick* (0273 733326) enables you to enjoy a Regency building for the same price; both the *Ramada Renaissance* (0273 206700) and the *Norfolk* (0273 821752) are in the expensive range; the no less comfortable *Marina House* (0273 605349) offers bed and breakfast from around £15, or if you prefer the country try *St Mary Farmhouse* (0273 692455).

CAMBRIDGE

Cambridge is famous for its **university**, and it's the colleges which make the town worth visiting. The grounds of these magnificent colleges are generally open to the public and they are empty of students in summer.

The oldest and most attractive colleges are all near the centre: **Trinity** is the largest and richest; second biggest is **St John's**, with its pseudo-Venetian enclosed Bridge of Sighs; **Emmanuel** has a Wren chapel. Others worth seeing are **Queens'** and **Jesus** and most awe-inspiring of all is **King's College Chapel**, one of the world's Gothic masterpieces. The best way to see the colleges is to do 'The Backs'; that is, meander through the serene lawns and riverside walks that run behind the colleges.

The town centres on the ancient streets round Market Square. The thing to buy here is **books** of course – there are scores of new and second-hand bookshops, stocking everything from the latest bestseller to the most obscure of tomes. **Museums** include the **Fitzwilliam**, Trumpington Street, for classical antiquities and old masters; the **Folk Museum**, Castle Hill, for local history; **Kettle's Yard**, Castle Street, holds a wonderful collection of modern art in the former home of an art curator.

Getting there *by train* from Liverpool Street or King's Cross; *by car* on M11, exit 11; *local buses* Camber (0223 355554).
Tourist Information Centre *Wheeler Street, Cambridge, Cambridgeshire (0223 322640)*. **Open** *Nov-Mar* 9am-5.30 Mon-Fri, 9am-5pm Sat. *Apr-Jun, Sept-Oct* 9am-6pm Mon-Fri, 9am-5pm Sat, 10.30am-3.30pm Sun. *Jul-Aug* 9am-7pm Mon-Fri, 9am-5pm Sat, 10.30am-3.30pm Sun.
Eating and drinking *The Old Spring* pub, Chesterton Road, serves superb traditional home-made pies at lunch-time; local colour – drunken students – can be found at the *Baron of Beef*, Bridge Street. *The Free Press*, Prospect Row, is run by an ex-rower, registered as a boat club and frequented by raucous boat crews; the *Fort St George*, Midsummer Common, is a part-Tudor pub on the riverside. For posher **food** try *Midsummer House*, Midsummer Common (0223 69299), or *Twenty Two*, Chesterton Road (0223 351880), in a terraced house: both serve excellent (and expensive) British cuisine. More interesting is *Upstairs*, Castle Street (0223 312569), which specializes in Middle-Eastern dishes.
Events *May Week* two weeks of boat races, balls and other social events, 4-18 Jun; *Footlights Revue* future-famous entertainers make their debut, 6-17 Jun; *Cambridge Festival* arts events, 15-30 Jul; *Cambridge Folk Festival* 28-30 Jul; *Cambridge Autumn Regatta* 10 Sept.
If you want to stay Sampling the real life of Cambridge involves staying at the moder-

The peaceful university town of **Cambridge** *(listed under* **Day Trips: Cambridge***), takes its name from the Romans who bridged the river Cam and built the first proper settlement, Camboritum, as an inland port. The town became a thriving market centre and in the thirteenth century, just as colleges were springing up all over Europe, learned men and students founded the first teaching institutions here. The colleges spread as far afield as Girton, some fifteen miles away. The oldest is Peterhouse, founded in 1284, followed by Clare, 1326, and Pembroke, 1347.*

'Will no-one rid me of this turbulent priest?' Thomas's tomb has been a site of pilgrimage ever since. **Trinity Chapel** contains the site of the original shrine, plus the tombs of Henry IV and the Black Prince.

Getting there *by train* from Victoria, 1 hour 20 minutes; *by bus* National Express, 2 hours; *by car* on A2 direct, or on M2 to exit 7 then A2; *local buses* East Kent Bus Co (0227 472082). **Tourist Information Centre**, *34 St Margaret's Street, Canterbury, Kent (0227 766567)*. **Open** *Easter-Sept* 10am-6pm daily; *Oct-Easter* 10am-5pm Mon-Sat. **Eating and drinking** *Restaurant Seventy Four*, Windcheap (0227 67411) serves good British food, as does *Waterfields*, Best Lane (0227 450276), which is in a converted forge. The specialty of *Tuo e Mio*, The Borough (0227 61471) is fresh pasta. All three are somewhat pricey, but do good-value set lunches. Try also *George's Brasserie* which is open all day serving French-style food. **Pubs** include the *Falstaff*, West Gate, very English with good food; the traditional *Three Tuns*, Watling Street; the *Seven Stars*, Orange Street, and the dark, student-frequented *Bell & Crown*, Palace Street. **Events** *Chaucer Heritage Pilgrimage* one week trek from London, including costume cavalcades en route, Apr; *Chaucer Festival* Apr; *Canterbury Festival*, three weeks of cultural events, 1-21 Oct. **If you want to stay** there's a good range of moderately priced accommodation here: try *Pointers Hotel* (0227 4568460); the *Millers Arms Inn* (0227 456057) for a traditional beer and breakfast; the *Thanington Hotel* (0227 453227); a little cheaper are the *London Guest House* (0227 65860) and *Broad Street Lodge* (0227 470185); in the expensive range is *County*, High Street (0227 66266).

*The **Cotswolds** (listed under* **Day Trips: Cotswolds***) abound with beautiful villages but the twin attractions of Upper and Lower Slaughter take some beating in the picture-postcard league. The two villages, adjacent to Bourton on the Water, and divided by the sleepy river Eye, do not take their name from being a scene of medieval carnage, as is often incorrectly surmised; slohtre is an old Anglo-Saxon word meaning muddy place. Upper Slaughter, pictured here, is almost the village the twentieth century forgot as the last house built here was in 1904. Most of the other honey-coloured stone dwellings here pre-date this by at least 150 years.*

ately priced *Parkside Guest House* (0223 311212); *St Mark's Vicarage* (0223 63339) will lend you a bike; you'd need one if you decide on the *Old Rectory* at Swaffham Bulbeck (0223 811986), 6 miles/9 kilometres from the city centre; at *Number 11* (0223 311890) you can stay in a reasonably priced hundred-year-old house; for downhome bed and breakfast, try *Mrs Hofford* at Girton (0223 276097) or the *Willows* (0223 860332), the latter is a Georgian house set in rolling fields; if you prefer a real hotel try *Cambridge Lodge* (0223 352833).

CANTERBURY

Long stretches of the **medieval walls** survive in Canterbury, one of Britain's oldest centres of habitation. It became the cradle of English Christianity: a new **Canterbury Cathedral** was built shortly after the Norman Conquest, and today it's the Mother Church of Anglicans world-wide.

The city centre is pretty, but very crowded and not notable for specialized shopping; it's much more interesting to go sight-seeing. **Eastbridge (St Thomas's) Hospital**, High Street, dates from the twelfth century and contains a medieval mural, sundry treasures and a crypt; there's the remains of a Roman town house and mosaic floor at **Roman Pavement**, Butchery Lane; and the **Royal Museum**, The Beaney, High Street, covers the history of the area. **King's School** is where Elizabethan playwright Christopher Marlowe, author of *Dr Faustus*, was educated. **Canterbury Heritage**, at the medieval Poor Priest's Hospital, is a walk through the city's past; **Canterbury Pilgrim's Way**, St Margaret's Street, is an animated interpretation of Chaucer's *Canterbury Tales*; **St Augustine's Abbey** is an important ecclesiastical site, but there's little left to see.

The city's only remaining gate, West Gate, now houses the **Museum of Arms and Armour**. Ancient houses overhang the lanes leading to Christ Church Gate, the cathedral's main entrance. There's a plaque before the altar where Thomas-à-Becket was murdered in 1170 by four over-zealous knights who'd heard Henry II moaning,

COTSWOLDS

Most places in Britain have at least one or two historic buildings dating back to Tudor times or even earlier, but in the Cotswolds you'll find whole towns and villages full of **Tudor** and **Jacobean architecture**. The buildings are constructed in **Cotswold stone**, quarried in Gloucestershire and Oxfordshire for centuries. There are public gardens at **Kiftsgate Court**, near the fine wool town of **Chipping Campden**, and at nearby **Hidcote Manor**, where Major Lawrence Johnston created one of the finest gardens in Britain. Also not to be missed is **Barnsley House**, a few miles north of Cirencester, with a garden restored by the writer Rosemary Verey.

Other places to be seen include **Broadway** with its twelfth-century church and sixteenth-century houses; **Stow on the Wold**, surrounded by little Cotswold villages and with a fine market place and ancient grammar school; **Bourton**, which really is **on the water** as the River Windrush winds through its main street. **Moreton in the Marsh** has yet more attractive buildings.

Take the children to the **Cotswold Wild Life Park** at Burford, or visit **Blenheim Palace**, birthplace of Winston Churchill, and **Sudeley Castle**, where Henry VIII's last wife Catherine Parr is buried. On the edges of the Cotswolds are the cities of **Gloucester**, where you can visit the cathedral and Roman ruins, and **Cheltenham**, a fine Regency town with a famous race course.

Getting there *by train* from Paddington to Moreton in the Marsh or Evesham; *local bus* Swanbrook Co., based in Cheltenham, but operating all over Cotswolds (0242 574444). To tour this area properly you need a car, which can be hired in London or Oxford (*see chapter* Travelling around London). **Tourist Information Centres** *Woolstaplers Hall, High Street, Chipping Campden (0386 840289)*. **Open** *Easter-Oct* 11am-6pm daily; *The Almonry Museum, Vine Street, Merstow Green, Evesham (0386 446944)*. **Open** 10am-5pm Mon-Sat; 2-5pm Sun. **Eating and drinking** *The White Hart, High Street, Moreton in the Marsh (0608 50731)*, serves English cuisine; in the same street, you'll find the expensive *Sheridans (0608 50251)*, which has a reputation for rich and

tasty dishes. In Broadway's High Street is *Hunters Lodge (0386 853247)*, a restaurant with a personal touch and quality cooking. Every village has a gem of a **pub**; in Bretforton near Evesham, try the *Fleece Inn*, which is owned by the National Trust and is strong on atmosphere.

If you want to stay and are feeling flush then the 600-year-old *Lygon Arms (0386 852255)* at Broadway may be a pleasant surprise; bed and breakfast at *The Orchard (0386 852534)* is a little cheaper, and only just down the road; the *Old Rectory (0386 853729)*, also at Broadway, is the sort of place where you forget that it's an hotel. Two bed-and-breakfasts worth mentioning at Moreton in the Marsh are *The Cottage (0608 50370)*, Oxford Street, and *New Farm (0608 50782)*, Dorn.

OXFORD

No-one knows when the great **university** at Oxford was established, but students started congregating here in the twelfth century. The city grew up in the Middle Ages around the shrine of **Frideswide**, a royal nun. It centres on Carfax, where you can ascend **Carfax Tower** for a commanding view; other vantage points are **St Mary the Virgin**, High Street, and the roof of Wren's neo-classical **Sheldonian Theatre**, Broad Street. Browse around the

immense **Blackwell's bookshop**, Broad Street; **Alice's Shop**, St Aldates, is where Alice bought barley-sugar in *Through the Looking Glass* and now sells Wonderland memorabilia.

Most visitors, however, head straight for the **colleges**; of the 30 or so, almost all are worth visiting (they are usually open to the public). **Christ Church** is the grandest, with its vast Quad; **Magdalen** (pronounced Maudlin) is considered the most beautiful; **St John's**, **New College**, **Trinity**, **Worcester** and **Wadham** have lovely gardens. Other temples of knowledge are the **Ashmolean Museum**, Beaumont Street, Britain's oldest, featuring mainly art and archaeology; the **Bodleian Library**, stunning medieval buildings containing one of the world's most important collections of books and ancient manuscripts; nearby **Radcliffe Camera**, an elegant circular reading room; the **Museum of Modern Art**, Pembroke Street; and for the area's history, the **Museum of Oxford**, St Aldates.

When you want to escape academia, stroll by the two rivers – the Cherwell (pronounced Charwell) and the Thames, known here as the Isis (from the Roman Thamesis). **Punts and rowing boats** can be hired from Folly Bridge, Magdalen Bridge and Cherwell Boathouse, off Bardwell Road. **Port Meadow** is a semi-wilderness mentioned in the *Domesday Book*, and the **university parks** are particularly peaceful.

Getting there *by train* from Paddington, 1 hour; *by bus* Oxford Citylink (0865 772250) or Oxford Tube (0865 772250) from Grosvenor Gardens Victoria, 1 - 2 hours; *by car* on M40, A40 A420 (or travel the pretty route via Windsor and Henley A423); *local buses* Oxford Tube (0865 772250). **Tourist Information Centre** *St Aldates, Oxford, Oxfordshire (0865 726871)*. **Open** *May-Sept* 9.30am-5pm Mon-Sat; 10.30am-1pm, 1.30-4pm, Sun, Bank Holidays; *Oct-Apr* 9.30am-5pm Mon-Sat. Closed Good Friday, Easter Sunday, Christmas and New Year. **Eating and drinking** The ancient *Turf Tavern*, Bath Place, is Oxford's most distinctive **pub**; the *Bear*, Alfred Street, its oldest; the *Perch*, Binsey Lane, is a thatched riverside pub. *Munchy Munchy*, Park End Street (0865 245710), sells great Malaysian fast **food**; *Browns*, Woodstock Road (0865 511995), serves reliable and generous meals at a reasonable price, and at the *Cherwell Boathouse*, Bardwell Road (0865 52746), you can sit outside and eat simple but delicious food. Raymond Blanc's internationally renowned *Le Manoir Aux Quat' Saisons*

Oxford *(listed under **Day Trips: Oxford**) was established late in the Saxon period as a fortified market town and flourished as a centre of the wool trade (records of this period, dating back to 1147, can be seen in the town hall). At some indeterminate time in the twelfth century it became a scholars' forum, possibly formed by a group of English students, expelled from the University of Paris in 1167. Whatever, by the end of the century Oxford was firmly established as the first university town in England. The earliest colleges founded were; University College, 1249; Balliol, 1263; Merton, 1264.*

(08446 8881) is at near-by Great Milton – dinner costs a fearsome £60 or so per person.
Events *Torpids* spring rowing races, Feb; *Eights Week* the great summer rowing races, end of May; *Encaenia* honorary degree awards, first Wed of Trinity term (May or Jun); *Oxford Regatta* Aug; *St Giles Fair* funfair, 4-5 Sept.
If you want to stay the *Turf* has rooms which are best described as quaint. In the luxury class is the *Randolph*, Beaumont Street (0865 247481). *Oxford Moat House*, Godstow Road (0865 59933) is comfortable, while the *River*, Botley Street (0865 243475) is an efficient bed and breakfast. Outside, the *City Hill Farm* (086 77 3944) offers bed and breakfast in more rural surroundings and *Two Chimneys* (0865 739144) allows you to stay under a thatched roof.

SALISBURY & STONEHENGE

Legend has it that an arrow was fired randomly and **Salisbury Cathedral** was built where it fell. However, the thirteenth century cathedral is carefully placed, soaring from a plain at the junction of five rivers. Its spire is the highest in England and its coffers contain one of the three original copies of the Magna Carta.

Most visitors come to Salisbury en route to Stonehenge, but the city is worth seeing in its own right. Because of its settled and prosperous history, Salisbury (officially New Sarum) has a wealth of interesting architecture – medieval gabled houses and narrow alleys abound. Cathedral Close has the best buildings, including the **Bishop's Palace**, the Old Deanery and the Tudor **King's House**, where Richard III and James I both stayed, now housing the local museum, which is strong on prehistoric remains. Also see superb **Mompesson House**, once a wealthy Georgian merchant's abode. There are more quaint streets round the market square, dominated by **Poultry Cross**, a 600-year-old Gothic monstrosity.

Walk across the meadows to the River Avon and medieval Harnham Bridge; nearby is an old watermill. In the other direction, it's possible to follow the river to Old Sarum.

Stonehenge is 10 miles/16 kilometres away, near Amesbury. It's ringed by a perimeter fence, but you can still get a good view (entrance costs £1.30 adults, 65p under 16s, £1 OAPs). It was built between 1900 BC and 1300 BC. Buses (usually route 3) run from the bus station, Endless

Street, and are supposed to connect at the railway station with incoming London trains. Alternatively go to Amesbury and get a 1, 5, 6 or 7 bus, or walk (check with the Information Centre for details). It can be seen by car from the A303.

Getting there *by train* from Waterloo, 1 hour 35 minutes; *by car* on M3, A303, A343 or A30; *local buses* Wilts & Dorset Bus Co (0722 336855).
Tourist Information Centre *Fish Row, Salisbury, Wiltshire* (0722 334956). **Open** *Oct-May* 9am-5pm Mon-Sat, *May* 11am-4pm Sun; *Jun, Sept* 9pm-6pm Mon-Sat, 11am-4pm Sun; *Jul-Aug* 9am-7pm Mon-Sat, 11am-5pm Sun.
Stonehenge *(0980 623108)*. **Open** *24 Mar-15 Oct* 9.30am-6.30pm daily (last admission 6pm); *16 Oct-23 Mar* 9.30am-4pm daily. **Admission** £1.60 adults; £1.20 OAPs, students, UB40s; 80p under-16s; **group discounts**.
Eating and drinking The *Old George* is an ancient inn; the *Haunch of Venison*, Minster Street, is the city's oldest **pub**, displaying a mummified hand clutching playing cards; the *King's Arms*, St John Street, is creakily Tudor; the *Red Lion*, Milford Street is a renovated coaching inn. *Harpers*, Ox Row (0722 333118), is a **restaurant** which serves robust

traditional fare and overlooks the vast market square. Also worth trying is *Crustaceans*, Ivy Street (0722 333948), which, as its name suggest, concentrates on seafood.
Events *Salisbury Festival* 3-17 Sept; *Salisbury Charter Fair* funfair celebrating ancient servants' charter, 17-19 Oct; *From Darkness To Light* candle-lit Advent procession, 26-27 Nov.
If you want to stay *Stratford Lodge* is an inexpensive haven of peace (0722 27844). *The Rose & Crown*, Harnham Road (0722 27908) is more expensive, and sits in the shadow of the cathedral; in the same price range is the *White Hart*, St John Street (0722 27476). The *Red Lion*, Milford Street (0722 23334) is more basic.

STRATFORD-UPON-AVON

It must be difficult being a resident of Stratford: Shakespeare's face beams down from every available surface, and the town is crowded all year round. Yet despite the inevitable commercialization it's still a very attractive place, and the sights are remarkably unspoilt.

There's been a settlement at Stratford-upon-Avon since the Bronze Age, and by William

Stonehenge *(listed under* **Day Trips: Stonehenge***) is the best British example of groups of ancient stone circles known as Druids' Circles, although the name derives from their custom of worship here, rather than as builders. This is certainly one of the most remarkable works of prehistoric architecture in the world and it is estimated that it took a mind-blowing 30 million man-years to erect. The earliest stage of its construction dates back to 2,800 BC but whether it was a lunar calendar, a temple, an eclipse-predictor, or whatever, is still a mystery.*

Shakespeare's time it was already an important market town. The surrounding countryside is glorious, especially on a late summer afternoon, when the herby fragrance of Elizabethan gardens fills the air

The main **Shakespeare** properties are: The **Birthplace Museum**, Henley Street; **Hall's Croft**, Old Town, where daughter Susannah lived; **New Place**, Chapel Street, the foundations of the Bard's last home (demolished in 1759 because the owner was fed up with visitors), set in an Elizabethan knot garden; **Mary Arden's House**, Wilmcote (three miles/five kilometres away), the farmhouse where his mother grew up; and the picturesque **Anne Hathaway's Cottage**, Shottery, his wife's lovely thatched home. The late medieval **Grammar School** where the Bard studied is still standing, as is riverside **Holy Trinity Church** where he and his family are buried.

Book well in advance to see a Shakespeare play at the modern **Royal Shakespeare Theatre** (booking information *0789 69191*); the Royal Shakespeare Company stages classics and modern works at three theatres. There's a walk along the **River Avon** from scenic Stratford Canal Basin, and **boat trips** in summer.

Guide Friday *(0789 294466)* does open-topped bus tours, and trips to near-by **Warwick Castle** (also reached by buses 518 and X16).

Getting there *by train* from Paddington; one through train every morning *(see above* **Train Information***);* alternatively, Shakespeare Connection rail/bus link from Euston via Coventry, various return times including an after-theatre service, 2 hours; *by bus* National Express, 3 hours 40 minutes; *by car* Oxford on M40 then north on A34; *local buses* Midland Red South, contact Stratford Travel Shop (0789 293127).
Tourist Information Centre *Judith Shakespeare's House, 1 High Street, Stratford-upon-Avon, Warwickshire (0789 293127)*.
Open *Apr-Oct* 9am-5.30pm Mon-Sat, 2-5pm Sun. *Nov-Mar* 10.30am-4.30pm Mon-Sat.
Eating and drinking The riverside **pub** the *Black Swan*, known locally as the Dirty Duck, is popular with actors; other theatrical hang-outs are the *Garrick*, High Street and the *White Swan*, Rother Street, where William himself probably drank. The *River Terrace* sells light refreshments all day; *Shepherd's*, Sheep Street (0789 68233), is probably the best bet for good English **food** although it's pricey; or try *Bunbury's Eating House*, Greenhill Street (0789 293563). *Sir Toby's*, Church Street, serves healthy café food, and *Giovanni's*, Ely Street (0789 297999), is a pretty good Italian place.
Events *Shakespeare's Birthday Celebrations*

Windsor *(listed under* **Day Trips: Windsor***) has been a royal town since medieval times. Edward the Confessor was a resident as far back as the mid-eleventh century but it was William the Conqueror who first realized the military importance of this town on the hill overlooking the Thames and had a fortress constructed. Some of the more spectacular building work still intact is due to Edward III, who built the the great Round Tower and the Norman gateway, Edward IV who began St George's Chapel and Henry VIII who built the castle gateway. The rotund tyrant also provided the castle with a major tourist attraction by being buried here.*

Jun; *Stratford-upon-Avon Festival* 11-30 Jul.
If you want to stay *Charlecote Pheasant Country Hotel* (0789 840200) is a converted eighteenth-century farmhouse, 4 miles/6.4 kilometres from the town. For something more central, try the *White Swan Hotel*, Rother Street (0789 297022). Bed and breakfasts abound: you'll get a good breakfast at *7 Broad Walk* (0789 298449), and plenty of attention at the one-bedroom *211 Evesham Road* (0789 299659).

WINDSOR

Windsor is a town made for tourism. On sunny summer days the town does get packed but it's surrounded by lovely countryside, so you can always take a stroll by the river if the crowds get too much.

Windsor Castle was built by William the Conqueror, but received substantial alterations during the reign of George IV. The **State Apartments** are open to the public when the Queen is not in residence, and not to be missed is the finest dolls' house in the world, designed by the architect Edwin Lutyens for Queen Mary, wife of

George V. Take a very close look at the books, the paintings and even the plumbing system. All are real, even though they are miniature. **St George's Chapel** is where Henry VIII is buried. There are other royal tombs – as well as the most beautiful roof you are likely to see, and Evensong is splendid too. By the way, if you missed the **Changing of the Guard** in London you can catch it here at 10.25 in the morning.

Down by the river is **Eton College**, whose buildings, some dating from the fifteenth century, are open in the afternoons, and where the schoolboys still wear tailcoats. You can walk in the Great Park or by the Thames to Runnymede or Cliveden House. You can even see Queen Victoria arriving in Windsor for her Diamond Jubilee at the local branch of **Madame Tussaud's** in the former Windsor and Eton Central Railway Station (where the time is always 11.32am on 19 Jun 1897, the exact time of Victoria's arrival).

If you get fed up with all the royal lions, you can see the real thing at **Windsor Safari Park** *(0753 869841)*, a short walk from the town centre. They throw in a few giraffes and rhinos as well.

Getting there *by train* from Paddington to Windsor and Eton Central (change at Slough) 35 minutes, or from Waterloo to Windsor and Eton Riverside; *by bus* Green Line 1 hour; *by car* on M25, exit 13, then A308; *local buses* Beeline Buses (0344 424938).
Tourist Information Centre *Windsor and Eton Central Station, Windsor (0753 852010)*. **Open** *Apr-Oct* 9.30am-6.30pm Mon-Sat, 10am-6.30pm Sun; *Nov-Mar* 9.30am-5pm Mon-Sat, 10am-4pm Sun.
Eating and drinking the *Taverna*, River Street, has reasonable pasta, or there is a hot pub lunch at the *Christopher Wren*.
If you want to stay the *Oakley Court Hotel*, Windsor Road (0628 74141), has grounds that slope down to the River Thames, or for something more homely *Mrs Pliszka* at 64 Bolton Road (0753 860789) has a friendly bed and breakfast.

FURTHER AFIELD

Accommodation price classification: **Budget** under £12; **Cheap** £12-£20; **Mid-price** £20-£40; **Upper bracket** over £40; all prices are minimum per person for one night's bed and breakfast. (*See above* **Finding Accommodation**.)

EDINBURGH

Edinburgh is world-famous for its Festival, usually held in the last three weeks of August and the first week of September, when for once the grim weather turns fine and the city hosts the world's greatest cultural beano. There's the official festival, major events in big venues; but far more stimulating is the unofficial Fringe. At this time of year Edinburgh's population doubles, the pubs open till around 3am and the streets are thronged day and night.

Rearing up on one side of the city is the dark, barbaric **Old Town**, a huge volcanic plug topped by the castle and terraced with crazily descending stone-slabbed tenements, packed incredibly tightly. A tangle of steps and alleys careers wildly up and down between them, necessitating doors at many different street levels. Below, the land plummets into a yawning gulf – once the stinking swamp of Nor'Loch, now luxuriant **Princes Street Gardens** – beyond which

slopes away the elegant Georgian New Town. To see the Old Town's history, simply walk down the **Royal Mile** from the castle to Holyrood House. Down the hill is spiky-crowned **St Giles's Cathedral**, Scotland's High Kirk (church); **Parliament House**; **John Knox's House**, one of Edinburgh's oldest; and **White Horse Close** and its restored seventeenth-century inn. At the bottom of the hill in rolling parkland lies the graceful **Palace of Holyrood House**, home of Mary Queen of Scots and, briefly, Bonnie Prince Charlie. Behind it looms **Arthur's Seat**, an extinct volcano which, if the climb doesn't kill you, affords exhilarating views.

The **New Town** is as much a shopping centre – stores line Princes Street, and behind it Rose Street harbours more individualistic shops – as a desirable place to live. Venture just a little further, though, and you'll come across the squares, circuses and crescents of the residential Georgian district. At the east end of Princes Street, facing

Arthur's Seat, rises **Calton Hill**, topped by what looks like a Greek ruin; it's actually the **National Monument**.

Edinburgh has loads of museums and galleries, mostly free – some of the best are: the **Royal Museum of Scotland**, Chambers Street, an extraordinary Victorian glass-roofed hall containing everything but the kitchen sink; **Huntly House Museum**, Canongate, a sixteenth-century house; **Museum of Childhood**, High Street, quite enchanting; **National Gallery of Modern Art**, Belford Road, a brilliant collection, lovely grounds and a most civilized café; **National Gallery of Scotland**, The Mound, a neo-classical temple packed with old masters; **City Art Centre**, Market Street, an adventurous municipal gallery with a good café; opposite is the **Fruit Market Gallery**, with changing contemporary exhibitions.

Getting there *by train* from King's Cross, about 5 hours – night-time sleepers (reservations only) are quite luxurious. Nightriders (sitting up all night) are cheap but an ordeal. *By bus* from Stagecoach Ltd (071 930 5781),

Princes Street Gardens, Edinburgh *(listed under* **Further Afield: Edinburgh***) was formed by glacial action and once held a great loch. Now it is home to Edinburgh's main British Rail station (Waverley) and is a splendid green swathe below the ominously looming castle. In the eastern end of the gardens is a memorial to the great Scottish explorer, David Livingstone, and at the western end stands an American Memorial to the Scottish soldiers who fell in World War One. Princes Street itself is the throbbing centre of the city; on the Gardens side, a pleasant verdant promenade, on the opposite side a row of predictable High Street shopping.*

8 hours. *By car* on A1/A1(M) direct or A1/A1(M) to Scotch Corner, then A68 (a far prettier route and as fast). *By air* from Heathrow, regular shuttle flights on British Airways (081 897 4000), 1 hour. *Local buses* Lothian Regional Transport (031 226 5087), Eastern Scottish (031 558 1616).
Tourist Information Centre *3 Princes Street, Edinburgh (031 557 2727).* **Open** *May, Jun, Sept* 8.30am-8pm Mon-Sat. *Jul-Aug* 8.30am-9pm daily. *Oct-Apr* 9am-6pm Mon-Fri, 9am-1pm Sat.
Entertainment For up-to-date information buy *The List* (50p), Scotland's version of *Time Out.*
Eating and drinking Pubs are open all day, usually till midnight. The Grassmarket and Stockbridge are full of decent pubs, but avoid the shoddy Lothian Road. The *Shore Bar,* The Shore, Leith, is a good **wine bar** with excellent seafood. For **lunch** try *Bagguley's,* Deanhaugh Street, steak 'n' Guinness pies; the *Edinburgh Bookshop,* George Street, serves **tea** and fruit scones in faded surroundings or the *Fruit Market Gallery,* Market Street, for honest vegetarian food. Open for **dinner** are the *Café Royal Oyster Bar,* West Register Street (031 556 4124), for superb seafood; The *City Café,* Blair Street (031 220 0125) is the place to be seen; *Howtowdie,* Stafford Street (031 225 6291), expensive but interesting; *Handsel's,* Stafford Street (031 225 5521), imaginative, expensive and outstanding; *Martins,* Rose Street (031 225 3106), modern and expensive; *Le Sept,* Old Fishmarket Close (031 225 5428), reasonably priced French cuisine and *Queen's Hall Café,* Clerk Street (031 668 3456), excellent jazz venue with decent suppers.
Where to stay Edinburgh has hundreds of hotels of all descriptions, but at Festival time it's packed solid. Visit the **Scottish Tourist Board** (*see above* **Tourist Information Centre**). For on-the-spot booking (not advisable in summer), there's an **On The Spot Reservation Service** kiosk at Edinburgh's Waverley Station, or go to the **Tourist Information Centre.** Here is a selection of what's available: guest houses; outer Edinburgh; **cheap** *Balfour House Hotel,* Pilrig Street (031 554 2106); *Merlin Guest House,* Hartlington Place (031 229 3864); central Edinburgh; **cheap** *Beresford Hotel,* Coates Gardens (031 337 0850); *Café Royal,* West Register Street (031 556 6894); New Town Georgian houses, **mid-range** *Osbourne Hotel,* York Place (031 556 2345); *Loch Ewe,* Royal Terrace (031 556 6749); *Barclays Hotel,* Royal Circus (031 225 5332); traditional hotels by the castle; **luxury** *Old Waverley,* Princes Street (031 556 4648); *Royal British,* Princes Street (031 556 4901); *Caledonian,* Princes Street – Edinburgh's finest (031 225 2433).
Events *International Folk Festival* Easter; *Royal Highland Show* agricultural show, 19-22 Jun; *Edinburgh Military Tattoo* 12 Aug-3 Sept; *Edinburgh International Festival* 14 Aug-3 Sept.

THE LAKE DISTRICT

The Lake District is widely regarded as one of the most beautiful parts of England, full of lofty fells, lake-lapped valleys, snow-capped peaks, mountain streams and waterfalls (and a great deal of rain).

All the top sights in the Lake District are best seen on foot, hence the area's popularity with walkers. **Windermere** is the principal tourist centre: it gets horribly crowded, but is a useful base. It's on the edge of Lake Windermere, England's largest; Bowness Bay Boating Co *(09662 3360)* does **boat trips** all year round, and there's a ferry to **Hawkshead**, on the opposite bank. From Windermere Station an easy path zig-zags up to **Orrest Head**, giving a panoramic view of the whole area. Lakeland's most famous resident was poet **William Wordsworth**. His home at Dove Cottage, Grasmere, is now a **museum**.

Other towns in the area are **Ambleside**, at the northern end of Windermere, favoured by hikers and rock-climbers; **Coniston**, at the base of towering 'Old Man' crag; Hawkshead, where Wordsworth's name is carved on a school-desk; Beatrix Potter wrote her much-loved tales at nearby **Sawrey**; **Keswick**, on Derwentwater, once home of Samuel Taylor Coleridge; and **Kendal**, gateway to the Lakes, a market town with a ruined castle.

Getting there *by train* from Euston to Oxenholme, 3 hours, then a branch line train to Windermere (20 mins). *By bus* National Express, to Kendal, 7 hours, then a Ribble or Lancaster City bus to Windermere. *By car* on M1, M6, exit 34, then A591 to Windermere.
Tourist Information Centres *Victoria Street, Windermere, Cumbria (09662 6499).* **Open** 9am-9pm daily. *Town Hall, Highgate, Kendal (0539 25758).* **Open** 9am-6pm Mon-Sat; 9am-1pm, 2-6pm, Sun. *Red Bank Road, Grasmere (09665 245)* **Open** *May-Oct* 9.30am-6.30pm daily; *Nov-Apr* 10am-4pm Sat, Sun; *'Gateway to Cumbria' Tourist Information Centre at the M6 Service Area, Forton, between junctions 32 and 33 (0524 792181).* **Open** 10am-6pm daily.
Eating and drinking. Local treats are **Kendal Mint Cake**, a hard, sugary slab of fell-walkers' sustenance; **Grasmere gingerbread**; large, spicy **Cumberland sausage**; and **char**, a trout-like Lake Windermere fish sometimes served in local **restaurants**: try the excellent *Roger's,* Windermere High Street (09662 4954); more expensive are *Sharrow Bay,* Howtown Road, in nearby Ullswater (085 36301), and *Miller Howe,* Rayrigg Road (09662 2536), two restaurants

Lake Windermere (listed under **Further Afield: The Lake District**), *over ten miles/sixteen kilometers long, is the biggest lake in England. Its surface in summer is crowded with pleasure craft dodging around its fourteen islands but for serious water activities go to Waterhead at the north shore where you can water-ski and sail. The National Park Centre at Brockhole on the shores of the lake, is a fine wisteria-covered mansion with an excellent information centre. Audio-visual shows will fill you in on the history, geology and folk-customs of the Lake District.*

where you can enjoy some of Britain's best food. *Sheila's Cottage*, The Slack, Ambleside is good for **afternoon tea**; *The Moon*, Highgate, Kendal, is a cosy vegetarian-ish bistro. Sir Walter Scott used to drink at the *Swan*, Grasmere, which has tasty home-made food. The *Globe* is one of Kendal's few decent **pubs**; the *George*, Keswick, is all Elizabethan beams and real ale; the beautiful *King's Arms*, Hawkshead, has white walls, roses, and benches outside.

Entertainment The Lake District isn't the place to come for flashy night-life – a night at the pub is by far the best way to relax after a hard day's exploring.

Where to stay There are loads of hotels, self-catering cottages and camp-sites in the area. The local **Tourist Information** office will have a list of accommodation in all price ranges. Here are a few: **budget** *Lakeside YMCA National Centre*, Ulverston (05395 31758); small guest houses; **cheap** *The Paddock*, Wordsworth Street, Keswick (07687 72510) and *Archway Guest House*, College Road, Windermere (09662 5613); good views; **mid price** *Low Spring Wood Hotel*, Thornbarrow Road, Windermere (09662 6383) and *Lindeth Fell Country House Hotel*, Windermere (09662 3286); country house; **upper bracket** *Langdale Chase Hotel*, Windermere (05394 32201).

Events *Coniston Water Festival* spectacular water event, 28 May-5 Jun; *Ambleside Rushbearing Festival* traditional village custom, 2 Jul; *Lake Windermere Festival* 2-10 Jul; *Lake District Summer Music Festival* 6-20 Aug; *Kendal Folk Festival* 27-29 Aug; *Windermere Waterspeed Record Attempts* 10-14 Oct.

YORK

York is unique among British cities in still having its entire **medieval walls** intact, and the best way to see the city's past is to trudge along the high walls (hair-raising on a windy day as there are few railings). There are four interesting 'bars' (gates): **Monk, Bootham, Walmgate** and **Micklegate**, where traitors' heads were once impaled.

The Romans first formed a base here, then the Vikings moved in and developed Jorvik, as they called it, into a major trading centre. Most street names end in 'gate' – the Viking word for road. A re-creation of Viking life at a genuine under-ground archaelogical site can be seen at the **Jorvic Centre**, Coppergate; it's a marvellous expe-rience, but the queues are long (up to four hours), it's expensive, and over far too quickly.

If you're keen to keep away from the hurly-burly you'd better take only a quick peek at **The Shambles**, a tiny street of over-hanging half-timbered houses, once butcher's shops.

For peace head for **York Minster**,

the Archbishop of York's seat and second in importance only to Canterbury Cathedral. The old area round the Minster has a genuine serenity, especially at dusk.

Other interesting places are medieval **Stonegate**, full of designer gift shops but still quaint; **Lady's Row**, Goodramgate, with some of York's oldest houses; narrow, crooked **High** and **Low Petergate**, full of interesting **shops** and **restau-rants**; Foss Street with its **antique** and **book shops**; and Micklegate, predominantly Georgian, with quirky collectors' shops.

Getting there *by train* from King's Cross, 2 hours; *by car* M1 to Leeds then A64, or take the slower but less suicidal A1 or A1(M) past Leeds, then the A64. *Local buses* York City and District Bus Co (0904 624161).
Tourist Information Centre *De Grey Rooms, Exhibition Square, York, North Yorkshire (0904 621756).* **Open** Jun-Sept 9am-8pm Mon-Sat, 2-5pm Sun. Oct-May 9am-5pm Mon-Sat.
Eating and drinking The *Black Swan* pub, Peasholme Green, is a Tudor landmark; *Ye Olde Starre Inne*, Stonegate, is very olde indeed, with good grub; the ancient *King's Arms*, King's Staithe, gets flooded some-times; the *York Arms*, High Petergate, is liked by the gay fraternity. For **snacks** or **lunch**, try *Jane's Place*, York Arts Centre, Micklegate; *Wheelers*, Fossgate; *Bootham Bistro*, Bootham, big and friendly; *St Williams Restaurant*, College Street, right beneath the Minster. The *Bonding Restaurant*, Skeldergate Bridge, a ware-house by the river serves good English food. For **dinner** try *Lew's Place*, King's Staith (0904 628167), a busy English bistro on the riverfront; *Kites*, Grape Lane (0904 641750), unusual and traditional dishes; *Oat Cuisine*, Ousegate (0904 627929), an upmarket, 'mould-breaking' vegetarian place. In the upper bracket are *The Judges Lodging*, Lendal (0904 38733), an historic building serving candlelit dinners at great expense (although you can get cheaper bar food in its eighteenth-century wine cellars); and the renowned *Middlethorpe Hall*, Bishopthorpe Road (0904 641241), serves modern cuisine in a grand 1699 mansion.
Entertainment For forthcoming events see the *Yorkshire Post*, daily except Sun, and *York: What's On*, a free weekly guide.
Where to stay There are plenty of hotels in York, especially along the main roads lead-ing away from the city gates, outside the walls – Bootham, Marygate, Fishergate and Tadcaster Road. The following are a selec-tion: **budget** *Youth Hotel*, Bishophill Senior (0904 625904) and *International Hostel*, Bootham, (0904 622874); guest houses; **cheap** *Abcombe Road Guest House*, Abcombe Road, (0904 792321) and *River View Hotel*, Marlborough Grove (0904 626826); central; **mid-range** *Galtres Lodge Hotel*, Lower Petergate (0904 622478) and *Bootham Bar Hotel*, High Petergate (0904 658516); lovely houses; **upper bracket** *Mount Royale Hotel*, The Mount (0904 628856) and *The Judges Lodgings*, Lendal (0904 38733).

York Minster *(listed under* **Further Afield: York***) is the biggest medieval cathedral in northern Europe. It was struck by lightning in 1984, and the roof of the south transept caught fire shortly after the present Bishop of Durham, of the Archdiocese of York, had shocked many clerics by publicly casting doubts on the reality of biblical miracles. Divine wrath or just plain meteorological misfortune? The perfectly restored roof and gleaming stonework has probably not looked this good for centuries. The Minster's greatest glory is its stained glass, second only to that in Chartres Cathedral, France.*

Business

Visiting London on business? Save yourself some time by using our essential guide to London's business services.

London is one of the great business capitals of the world. And just because you don't speak the language, it doesn't mean you can't do big business as a visitor. Before you start, buy the *Financial Times*, the best newspaper for an update on facts and figures in the City and all over the world. We've listed below everything else a business person may require on a visit to London, from translators to typewriters, fax machines to business libraries.

BANKING

Arrange banking facilities with your own bank before leaving home: the chances are, it'll have a reciprocal arrangement with a British bank, and you may need to obtain references. The head offices of the 'big four' commercial banks are listed below. Banks charge a commission of one to two per cent on foreign exchange transactions; bureaux de change charge slightly more. See *chapter* **Essential Information** for opening hours and further information.

Barclays Bank
54 Lombard Street, EC3 (071 626 1567). Bank underground.

Lloyds Bank
71 Lombard Street, EC3 (071 626 1500). Bank underground.

Midland Bank
Poultry, EC2 (071 260 8000). Bank underground.

National Westminster Bank
41 Lothbury, EC2 (071 726 1000). Bank underground.

COMMUNICATIONS & COPYING

British Monomarks
Monomarks House, 27 Old Gloucester Street, WC1 (071 405 4442/071 404 501; fax 071 831 9489). Holborn underground. **Open** 9.30am-5.30pm Mon-Fri; *telex bureau* 8am-8pm Mon-Fri; 8am-1pm Sat. **Credit** A, £STC, V.

Here you can use a telex or fax machine, or arrange to use the 24-hour telephone answering service. Leave a deposit to be able to telephone in your telex messages, 24 hours a day.

Copyfax Southern Services
3 Station Parade, W5 (081 993 7543; fax 081 992 8963). Ealing Common underground. **Open** 9am-6pm Mon-Fri. **No credit cards.**
CS rents and sells photocopiers and facsimile machines. Prices start at £36 per month for photocopiers.

Dictators
203 High Street, SE13 (081 318 1235; fax 081 318 1439). Lewisham BR. **Open** 8.30am-8.30pm Mon-Fri; 8.30am-5pm Sat; 8.30am-1pm Sun. **Credit** A, A/c, AmEx, DC, V.
Dictators are better known as Dictate-A-Fax: you can dictate a message over the phone and they'll fax or telex it for you anywhere in the world. Their telephone answering service is competitively priced at £10 per minute

COURIERS

A-Z
(071 251 4444; fax 071 253 8128). **Open** 24 hours Mon-Fri; 9am-6pm Sat; by prior arrangement Sun. **Credit** A, AmEx, DC, V.
Charges vary according to postal district; a journey from the West End (W1) to the City (EC2) for example would cost £6 and there's a minimum charge of £5.

Datapost
Head Office: 33 Grosvenor Place, SW1 (Freephone Datapost 0800 88 4422; fax 071 250 2938). Hyde Park Corner underground or Victoria underground/BR. **Open** 8am-6pm Mon-Fri. **Credit** A, V.
Datapost is a Post Office parcel service. Use it to send packages anywhere in Britain; next-day delivery is guaranteed. There's also an international service. Parcels are accepted at any main post office.

Harley Street Runners
65 Great Portland Street, W1 (071 323 5595; fax 071 323 5867). Oxford Circus underground. **Open** 8am-7pm Mon-Fri. **Credit** £STC.
A van, cycle, motorbike and foot messenger service. The couriers will go anywhere in mainland Britain for a fixed amount. The company can also organize direct mailing, removals, Datapost and foreign deliveries.

EQUIPMENT HIRE

ABC Business Machines
59 Chiltern Street, W1 (071 486 5634; fax 071 486 2634). Baker Street underground.

Open 9am-5.30pm Mon-Fri; 9.30am-12.30pm Sat. **Credit** A, £STC, V.
Answerphones, calculators and audio equipment are just some of the things you can hire from ABC. An electronic typewriter costs £34.50 a month and a Betacom Fax machine is only £85 for the same time period.
Branch *20 Holborn Viaduct, EC1 (071 329 4884).*

Network Office Equipment
63 Lupus Street, SW1 (071 821 8186; fax 071 630 5160). Pimlico underground. **Open** 8.30am-6pm Mon-Fri. **Credit** £TC.
All types of office electrical equipment can be bought or hired from Network. Short-term rental charges (per month) start from £45 for electronic typewriters; £120 for basic Rank Xerox 7010 A4 Fax machines; and £120 for twin-disc MS-DOS word-processors with Wordcraft printers.

Padhanis Computer Center International
70 High Street, Edgware, Middlesex, HA8 (081 952 2051; fax 081 951 5091). Edgware underground. **Open** 9am-6pm Mon-Fri; 10am-2pm Sat. **Credit** A, AmEx, DC, V.
Not are only are computers available for hire from this company but also electric typewriters from £15 per month, photo-copiers from £20 per month and basic A4 Fax machines from £40 per month. The wide range of computers begins with IBM-compatible 640K models from £40 per month.

SECRETARIAL

More typing services are advertised on bookshop noticeboards and in *Time Out* magazine's classified ads section.

Reed Employment, Staff Agency
181 Victoria Street, SW1 (071 828 2401; fax 071 821 5598). Victoria underground/BR. **Open** 8.45am-5.30pm Mon-Fri.
Reed supplies secretarial, computing, accountancy and technical services to registered companies.

Typing Overload
67 Chancery Lane, WC2 (071 404 5464; fax 071 831 0878). Chancery Lane underground. **Open** 9am-6pm Mon-Fri. **Credit** A, AmEx, DC, V.
Come here for a speedy and professional typing service for any job that can be done on a word-processor.
Branch *170 Sloane Street, SW1 (071 235 6855).*

TRANSLATION

AA Technical & Export Translation
The London International Press Centre, 76 Shoe Lane, Fleet Street, EC4 (071 583 8690; fax 071 353 3133). Chancery Lane underground or Blackfriar's underground/BR. **Open** 10am-6pm Mon-Fri. **No credit cards.**
AA provides native speakers of most languages; there are 612 translators speaking

Bicycle couriers *(listed under* **Couriers***) are a common sight in central London and the City and an essential part of business life. You'll see them wending their way through the traffic-clogged streets, fluorescent bicycle bags over their shoulders, ferrying important documents and parcels all over town.*

50 languages on the books. Translation rates vary from £6 to £18 per 100 words depending on the language and complexity of the text. Interpreters cost between £150 and £450 per day. AA is a member of the Association of Translation Companies and holder of the International Export Association Seal of Approval.

Interlingua
Rothschild House, Whitgift Centre, Croydon, CR9 (071 240 5361; fax 071 240 5364). Croydon BR. **Open** 9am-5.30pm Mon-Fri.
Credit A, AmEx, DC, V.
Interlingua is the largest translation company in the world. The 4,400 full-time and freelance staff translate an average of 12,000,000 words in 80 languages each month. Costs vary widely. Interlingua is a member of the Association of Translation Companies.

Oriental Languages (Contemporary Translations)
Berkeley Square House, Berkeley Square, W1 (071 409 0953; fax 071 409 0809; telex 266815). Green Park underground. **Open** 9.30am-6pm Mon-Fri. **No credit cards.**
This company specializes in Middle and Far Eastern languages, including Arabic, Farsi, Turkish, Chinese Japanese, Malay, Indonesian and Korean, as well as all the Indian and South

Asian languages. Rates for translations vary between £60 and £150 per 1,000 words: interpreters cost from £100 per day.

INFORMATION

Business Design Centre
52 Upper Street, N1 (071 359 3535; 071 226 0590). Angel underground. **Open** 9am-5.30pm Mon-Fri.
See **picture and caption**

Chamber of Commerce and Industry
69 Cannon Street, EC4 (071 248 4444; fax 071 489 0391). Cannon Street underground. **Open** 9am-5.30pm Mon-Fri (closed 12.30-1.30pm). **Reference library** 9.15am-4.45pm Mon-Fri.
The largest Chamber of Commerce in the world is open to members and overseas visitors only. Its **Voice of Business** service represents business interests to local and national government and to the EEC; **Market Information** can provide information on legislation, tariff regulation and commercial development; **Training Programme** fixes business training and also language

courses; and **Export Documentation** is the major supplier of carnets and certificates of origin for export consignments.

Companies House
55-71 City Road, EC1 (071 253 9393). Old Street underground. **Open** 9.30am-4pm Mon-Fri (last company search 3pm).
In order to export goods from Britain, register as a UK company (for taxation purposes) at Companies House. You can also gain access to information on companies, British and foreign (if registered here).

Design Centre
28 Haymarket, SW1 (071 839 8000; 071 925 2130). Piccadilly Circus underground. **Open** 10am-6pm Mon, Tue; 10am-8pm Wed-Sat; 1-6pm Sun.
Visit the Design Centre for full details of product, graphic and interior designers in Britain.

Extel Financial
Fitzroy House, 13-17 Epworth Street, EC2 (071 253 3400). Liverpool Street underground/BR or Moorgate underground/BR or Old Street underground/BR. **Open** *enquiries* 9am-5pm Mon-Fri; *help desk and computer desk* 24 hours daily.
Extel publishes financial data on easy-to-read cards about more than 7,000 British and foreign businesses. It costs £14 to take one of these cards away. The firm also does British and overseas company searches, as well as dealing with all kinds of corporate financial queries and problems.

Financial Times Cityline
(recorded information 0898 123456; list of all lines 0898 123099). **Open** 24 hours daily.
There are 28 FT Cityline recorded information services, updated constantly with news from the financial markets.

Jordan & Sons Company Information UK and Overseas
Jordan House, 47 Brunswick Place, N1 (071 253 3030; fax 071 251 0825). Old Street underground/BR. **Open** 9am-5pm Mon-Fri.
A full company search costs £24.92, which takes 48 hours. Jordans also organizes company formations (Britain and overseas), phone for a quote.

REFERENCE LIBRARIES

General reference libraries are listed in *chapter* **Survival**.

City Business Library
106 Fenchurch Street, EC3 (071 638 8215). Aldgate underground. **Open** 9.30am-5pm Mon-Fri.
The City Library has an excellent range of business reference works, including newspaper cuttings, Extel cards and world directories.

Chamber of Commerce & Industry Reference Library
69 Cannon Street, EC4 (071 248 4444; fax 071 489 0391). Cannon Street underground. **Open** 9.15am-5.15pm Mon-Fri.

A comprehensive library open to members and overseas visitors. You'll find general commercial information and detailed information on export and international trade.

Export Market Information Centre
Department of Trade and Industry, 1 Victoria Street, SW1 (071 215 5444; business statistics 0633 812973; fax 071 215 4231). St James's Park underground. **Open** *9.30am-5.00pm Mon-Fri.*
If you're a visiting exporter, make sure you visit the Centre, where you'll find everything you could possibly want to know about exporting. Its own database – the British Overseas Trade Information System – provides information on products, markets, overseas agents and export opportunities.

CONVENTIONS

London Tourist Board
26 Grosvenor Gardens, SW1 (071 730 3488; fax 071 730 9367). Victoria underground/BR. **Open** *Apr-Oct 9am-8.30pm daily; Nov-Mar 9am-7pm Mon-Sat; 9am-5pm Sun.*

The board will assist with the organization of conventions or exhibitions. Ask for the convention bureau or write or telephone for its free guide *Convention and Exhibition London*, which lists hotels and centres which host events, together with their facilities.

Queen Elizabeth II Conference Centre
Broad Sanctuary, SW1 (071 222 5000; 071 798 4200). St James's Park or Westminster underground. **Open** *8am-6pm Mon-Fri.* **Credit** *AmEx.*
This modern centre has some of the best conference facilities in London. There's a choice of rooms with capacities from 12 to 1,000; all fitted with the latest in security and communication equipment There are also four television studios.

IMPORT & EXPORT

Within EEC countries, import licences are needed only for raw steel and restricted items (for exam-

ple, firearms). Importers from outside the EEC need licences for a wide variety of goods, including clothing and shoes, textiles, agricultural goods, foodstuffs, and ceramics. An application must be made for each product to be imported and takes from three to five days to clear. Licences are valid from three months to a year.

Commercial goods must always be declared on arrival, and a SAD document completed. But for merchandise carried as baggage (valued under £600) a customs declaration may not be needed. There's a standard rate of 15 per cent value-added-tax (VAT) on most imported goods, based on the value of the goods plus the duty payable.

The exporting of certain goods – such as arms, electronic equipment, and chemical equipment – requires licences issued by the **Department of Trade & Industry** (*see below*).

British Overseas Trade Board
1 Victoria Street, SW1 (071 215 5000; 5.30pm-9am 071 215 4657). **Open** *9am-5pm Mon-Fri.*
If you're planning to export anything anywhere in the world, the BOTB will provide information and advice on tariffs, local conditions, and so on.

Customs and Excise
New King's Beam House, 22 Upper Ground, SE1 (071 620 1313, ext 3997; fax 071 865 5625). Waterloo underground/BR. **Open** *9am-5pm Mon-Fri.*
The official information source on VAT matters and import duty and licences. The staff also deal with enquiries on restricted goods and documentation.

Department of Trade & Industry
Export Licensing Unit Kingsgate House, 66-74 Victoria Street, SW1 (071 215 8070; fax 071 215 8202). Victoria underground/BR. **Open** *10am-4pm Mon-Fri.*
The Export Licensing Unit deals with any enquiries on export controls and licences.

Department of Trade & Industry
Import Licensing Branch, Dean Bradley House, 52 Horseferry Road, SW1 (071 276 2580). Victoria underground/BR. **Open** *9.30am-3.30pm Mon-Fri.*
For enquiries about, or applications for, import licences.

Institute of Freight Forwarders
Redfern House, Browells Lane, Feltham, Middlesex, TW13 (081 844 2266; fax 081 890 5546) Hatton Cross underground or Feltham BR. **Open** *9am-5pm Mon-Fri.*
The IFF gives information about sending freight and baggage, and puts callers in touch with reputable companies who handle air and sea freight. Ask for the Air or Sea division.

The **Business Design Centre** *in Islington (listed under* **Information***) opened in 1986 in what was the Royal Agricultural Halls. A trade centre for commercial interior design, this impressive building contains showrooms, an exhibition centre and a conference centre. The exhibitions display products used in commercial design, and usually change weekly.*

Survival

Dealing with a crisis, from a lost passport to health problems to a wheel clamp on your car, can spoil your visit to London. Don't despair, survival is possible.

Whatever your need – a chemist at midnight, a church to pray in or a public toilet – you'll find the answer below.

Health
Communications
Lost property
Public toilets
Security
Help and information
Disabled
Lesbian & Gay
Women
Travel
Work & Study
Religion
Embassies

HEALTH

Free medical treatment is available under the National Health Service to British citizens, people who are working in Britain, refugees and students studying on courses of six months or more.

EEC Nationals Citizens of Belgium, Denmark, France, Federal Republic of Germany, Greece, Italy, Irish Republic, Luxembourg, the Netherlands, Portugal and Spain are also entitled to free National Health treatment while they are staying in Britain.

Reciprocal arrangements with the following countries entitle their citizens to free medical treatment and subsidized dental care while in Britain, on production of a passport: Anguilla, Australia, Austria, British Virgin Islands, Bulgaria, the Channel Islands, Czechoslovakia, the Falkland Islands, Finland, German Democratic Republic, Gibraltar, Hong Kong, Hungary, Iceland, the Isle of Man, Malta, Montserrat, New Zealand, Norway, Poland, Romania, St Helena, Sweden, the Turks and Caicos Islands, USSR, Yugoslavia.

All other foreign visitors have to pay for any medical treatment they receive while in Britain.

AMBULANCES

Dial 999 for the ambulance service if there's an accident or someone is seriously ill.

CASUALTIES: NHS

Casualty departments will treat injuries and sudden illness if you cannot wait to see a doctor. There are 24-hour walk-in casualty departments at:

WC1: University College Hospital
Gower Street (entrance Grafton Way), W1 (081 387 9300). Euston Square or Warren Street underground.

W6: Charing Cross Hospital
Fulham Palace Road (entrance St Dunstan's Road), W6 (081 846 1234). Baron's Court or Hammersmith underground.

W12: Hammersmith Hospital
Du Cane Road, W12 (081 743 2030). East Acton underground.

SW1: Westminster Hospital
Dean Ryle Street, Horseferry Road, SW1 (081 828 9811). Pimlico underground. **Adults only.**

SW17: St George's Hospital
Blackshaw Road, SW17 (081 672 1255). Tooting Broadway underground.

SE1: Guy's Hospital
St Thomas Street (entrance in Weston Street), SE1 (071 407 7600). London Bridge underground/BR.

SE1: St Thomas's Hospital
Lambeth Palace Road, SE1 (071 928 9292). Waterloo underground/BR.

SE5: King's College Hospital
Denmark Hill, (entrance in Bessemer Road), SE5 (071 274 6222). Denmark Hill BR.

SE10: Greenwich District Hospital
Vanbrugh Hill, SE10 (081 858 8141). Maze Hill BR.

SE13: Lewisham Hospital
Lewisham High Street, SE13 (081 690 4311). Ladywell BR.

E1: London Hospital (Whitechapel)
Whitechapel Road, E1 (071 377 7000). Whitechapel underground.

E9: Hackney and Homerton Hospital
Homerton Row, E9 (081 985 5555). Hackney Central BR.

EC1: St Bartholomew's Hospital
West Smithfield (entrance Giltspur Street), EC1 (071 601 8888). Barbican or St Paul's underground.

N18: North Middlesex Hospital
Stirling Way, Edmonton, N18 (081 807 3071). Silver Street BR.

N19: Whittington Hospital
St Mary's Wing, Highgate Hill, N19 (071 272 3070). Archway underground.

NW3: Royal Free Hospital
Pond Street, NW3 (071 794 0500). Belsize Park underground/Hampstead Heath BR.

NW10: Central Middlesex Hospital
Acton Lane, NW10 (081 965 5733). North Acton underground.

CASUALTIES: PRIVATE

Medical Express
Chapel Place, W1 (071 499 1991). Oxford Circus underground. **Open** 9am-7pm Mon-Fri; 10am-5pm Sat.
A private walk-in casualty clinic. Treatment guaranteed within 30 minutes. A consultation costs £50, tests are carried out in the clinic and are extra.

CHEMISTS: LATE-OPENING

If you have a prescription you need made up outside normal shopping hours, all is not lost. Head for one of the following chemists:

W1: Bliss Chemist
5 Marble Arch, W1 (071 723 6116). Marble Arch underground. **Open** 9am-midnight daily. **Credit** A, AmEx, DC, £TC, V.

W1: Boots
44 Piccadilly Circus, W1 (081 734 6126). Piccadilly Circus underground. **Open** 8.30am-8pm Mon-Fri; 9am-8pm Sat. **Credit** A, AmEx, V. *Wheelchair access.*

W2: Boots
75 Queensway, W2 (071 229 9266). Bayswater underground. **Open** 9am-10pm Mon-Sat. **Credit** A, AmEx, V.

DENTAL SERVICES

Dental care is only free to British citizens receiving supplementary benefit. So whether you go with the National Health Service (NHS) or privately, you will have to pay. To find a dentist, get in touch with the local Family Practitioner Committee (*see below* **Doctors**). Prices vary enormously, starting at about £14 for a filling on the NHS. Private dentists can charge whatever they like, there are no set charges. We list emergency services below.

Dental Emergency Care Service

(071 400 0400/081 677 6363/081 677 8383,credit card registration/071 589 0107/081 993 5058). **Open** 24 hours daily. Callers are referred to a surgery of any sort open for treatment, whether private or National Health Service.

Eastman Dental Hospital

256 Gray's Inn Road, WC1 (071 837 3646). Chancery Lane or King's Cross underground/BR. **Open** 9am-noon, 1.30-4pm, Mon-Fri. A walk-in emergency dental hospital for anyone without a dentist in London. No appointment needed.

Guy's Hospital Dental School

St Thomas' Street, SE1 (071 407 7600). London Bridge underground/BR. **Open** 9am-4pm Mon-Fri; 9.30am-9.30pm Sat-Sun. A walk-in dental emergency service. Free treatment, except on Saturday and Sunday.

DOCTORS

If you're a British citizen visiting London or working in the city temporarily, you can go to any general practitioner (GP). You will most likely have to show your medical card or fill in a 'Lost Medical Card' form. Overseas students can register with an NHS doctor. Embassies and consulates may be able to recommend private doctors.

Great Chapel Street Medical Centre

13 Great Chapel Street, W1 (071 437 9360/071 434 2731). Tottenham Court Road underground. **Open** 12.45-4pm Mon-Fri. A walk-in NHS surgery for anyone with no doctor. As well as doctors, they have a psychiatrist and a chiropodist visiting from Monday to Thursday, and access to sick-bay facilities.

Family Practitioner Committees

The various London boroughs provide lists of GPs, chemists, opticians and dentists. The telephone number of the borough Committee and lists of local NHS doctors are available in libraries and post offices.

EMERGENCY MEDICAL SERVICES

See above **Casualties**.

MEDICAL INFORMATION

Healthline

(081 681 3311). **Open** 4-8pm Mon-Fri. 24-hour services are located at Hull *(0482 29933)* and Exeter *(0392 59191).* A free telephone information service (except for the cost of the call). Phone and ask to listen to any of the 300 plus tapes on health topics which give details of symptoms and contact names of groups involved with treatment or support for sufferers.

Medical Advisory Service

10 Barley Mow Passage, W4 (081 994 9874). **Open** 10am-10pm daily. Advice over the phone on anything from lumps to drugs.

MEDICATION

Many drugs cannot be bought over the counter in Britain. A pharmacist will dispense medicines on receipt of a prescription from a doctor. An NHS prescription costs £2.80 at present. If you are not eligible to see an NHS doctor you will be charged cost price for all medicines prescribed by a private doctor.

MEDICINE: ALTERNATIVE

The Acupuncture Association and Register

34 Alderney Street, SW1 (071 834 1012). Victoria underground/BR. **Open** 9am-5.30pm Mon-Sat. Phone for your local registered specialist. The Association will provide lists of practitioners. A list and handbook are also available, price £1.50 plus p&p.

British Homoeopathic Association

27A Devonshire Street, W1 (071 935 2163). Baker Street or Great Portland Street underground. **Open** 9.30am-4.30pm Mon-Fri. The Association will give you the address of your nearest homoeopathic chemist and doctor (send a stamped addressed envelope for a list). The Association also provides a booklist of helpful information.

British Society of Medical and Dental Hypnosis

42 Links Road, Ashtead, Surrey (0372 273522). **Open** 9.30am-5.30pm Mon-Fri. If you want to see a doctor or dentist who practises hypnotherapy, ring or write to (with a stamped addressed envelope) this organization.

Institute of Complementary Medicine

21 Portland Place, W1 (071 636 9543). Regent's Park underground. **Open** 9.30am-5pm. For information about practitioners and centres of complementary medicine, write enclosing a stamped addressed envelope, and state the therapy in which you are interested. The Institute also has lists of qualified herbalists.

MENTAL/EMOTIONAL HEALTH

Just Ask

YMCA 112 Great Russell Street, WC1 (entrance beside the door of the Y hostel) (071 636 4308/071 637 1333 ext 4241). Tottenham Court Road underground. **Open** 2-8pm Mon-Thur; 1-5pm Fri. Answerphone service in the morning for practical advice. Make an appointment either by calling in or phoning. Trained counsellors help people with personal problems. If necessary you'll be sent to a specialized agency.

Mind

22 Harley Street, W1 (071 637 0741). Oxford Circus underground. **Open** 9.15am-5.15pm Mon-Fri. A useful starting point for anyone with general enquiries regarding mental health. Callers will be referred to one of 34 London groups. The legal service advises on maltreatment, wrongful detention and sectioning (involuntary hospitalisation). Phone for details.

National Association of Victims Support Schemes

Cranmer House, 39 Brixton Road, SW9 (071 735 9166 answering machine out of office hours). Oval underground. **Open** 9am-5pm Mon-Fri. The Association helps victims of crime. Callers are put in touch with a volunteer who visits as soon as possible after the event to provide emotional and practical support. Guides on the social services and compensation are also provided.

Samaritans

(24-hour helpline 071 439 2224). The Samaritans will listen to anyone with emotional problems. It's a popular service and you may have to phone several times before you get through. There are several branches across London, so ring Directory Enquiries to find the nearest branch.

OPTICIANS

Eye Care Information Bureau

(071 928 9435). **Open** 9am-5pm Mon-Fri. This service gives you information on the different kinds of eye-care specialists, and which type is best suited to your needs.

PHARMACISTS

See above **Chemists: Late-Opening**.

PHYSIOTHERAPY

Chartered Society of Physiotherapy

14 Bedford Row, WC1 (071 242 1941). Chancery Lane or Holborn underground. **Open** 9am-5pm Mon-Fri. This is the professional body of physiotherapists. The Society can check whether any practitioner is a qualified member, and can also put patients in touch with practitioners.

SEX/CONTRACEPTION/ ABORTION

Family Planning advice, contraceptive supplies and abortions are free to British citizens on the National Health Service. This also applies to EEC residents and foreign nationals living, working and studying in Britain. According to the 1967 Abortion Act, two doctors must agree to a woman having an abortion, whether on the NHS or not. If you decide to go private, contact one of the organizations listed below.

Seek advice quickly. An abortion may take some time to arrange and the later it is carried out, the greater are the risks of both physical and psychological complications.

General practioners (GPs) advise on and prescribe contraceptives, give counselling for sexual problems, and refer patients for abortion.

British Pregnancy Advisory Service
7 Belgrave Road, SW1 (071 222 0985/071 931 7058 for emergency calls after 5pm). Victoria underground/BR. **Open** 9am-5pm Mon-Fri.
Contraception advice, contraceptives and the morning after pill are available here. The service carries out pregnancy tests and makes referrals to BPAS nursing homes for private abortions.

Brook Advisory Centres
233 Tottenham Court Road, W1 (071 323 1522). Tottenham Court Road underground. **Open** office 9am-5pm Mon-Fri.
There are 13 Brook Advisory family planning clinics in London. Call the office to find your nearest one. Advice is given on contraception, sexual problems and abortion with referral to NHS or a private clinic. There is a counsellor as well as medical staff.

Family Planning Association
27-35 Mortimer Street, W1 (071 636 7866). Oxford Circus underground. **Open** 9am-5pm Mon-Thur; 9am-4.30pm Fri.
There are more than 1,800 NHS-run Family Planning Clinics in Britain. Phone the FPA to find your nearest one or drop in to pick up free leaflets on family planning.

Marie Stopes Clinics
Family Planning Clinic *108 Whitfield Street, W1 (071 388 0662/071 388 2585 for Family Planning/071 388 5554 for sterilization).* **Pregnancy Clinic** *114 Whitfield Street, W1 (071 388 4843). For both clinics, Warren Street underground.* **Open** *Family Planning Clinic* 9am-8pm Mon-Wed; 9am-5pm Thur-Fri; 9.30am-1pm Sat; *Pregnancy Clinic* 9am-5pm Mon-Fri.
The clinics provide contraceptives, treatment, and advice for gynaecological complaints, counselling for sexual problems and referral for abortion. Fees are £17 for consultation plus costs of tests and medication. Vasectomies and female sterilization are performed.

Pregnancy Advisory Service
11-13 Charlotte Street, W1 (071 637 8962). Tottenham Court Road underground. **Open** 9.30am-5.30pm Mon-Wed, Fri; 9.30am-8pm Thur; 9.30am-12.30pm Sat. (Appointments are necessary except in an emergency.)
Pregnancy counselling; pregnancy tests; abortion advice and help; artificial insemination by donor; morning-after contraception; sterilization, cervical smears. A non-profit-making registered charity, also at 17 Rosslyn Road, East Twickenham, Middlesex (081 891 6833).

SEXUALLY-TRANSMITTED DISEASES (VD)

The following NHS Special Clinics are affiliated to major hospitals. They specialize in genito-urinary conditions, treating sexually-transmitted diseases and non sex-related ones such as thrush and cystitis.

WC1: University College Hospital Special Clinic
Gower Street, WC1 (071 388 9625). Euston Square underground. **Open** 9am-11.30am, 1-5pm Mon-Fri.
Appointment needed, except in an emergency.

W2: St Mary's Hospital Special Clinic
Praed Street, W2 (071 725 1697). Paddington underground/BR. **Open** 9am-6pm Mon, Tue, Thur, Fri; 10am-6pm Wed (new patients should arrive before 5.30pm on all days).
No appointment necessary.

W6: West London Hospital Special Clinic
Bute Gardens, W6 (081 846 7834/6). Hammersmith underground. **Open** 9.30am-noon, 2-5pm, Mon-Fri.
No appointment necessary. The clinic will be moving premises to Charing Cross Hospital (081 846 1234) in Feb 1990, so phone first.

AIDS/HIV POSITIVE

A confidential blood test for AIDS is available at any of the London Special Clinics (*see above* **Sexually-Transmitted Diseases**). The Government pamphlet *AIDS: What Everybody Needs to Know* is available from clinics and with a stamped addressed envelope by post from: Health Education Authority, Hamilton House, Mabledon Place, WC1. Enquiries about AIDS may also be addressed to:

AIDS Telephone Helpline
(0800 567 123). **Open** 24 hrs daily.
A free and confidential help and information service for anybody worried or concerned about HIV/AIDS and safer sex.

Body Positive
51B Philbeach Gardens, SW5 (071 835 1045/071 835 1046). Earl's Court underground. **Open** 11am-5pm Mon-Fri.
Run by and for people who are HIV positive, this is a drop-in centre for the public which also offers a *Helpline service (071 373 9124)* between 7pm and 10pm daily.

Health Line
(081 681 3311). **Open** 4-8pm Mon-Fri. 24hr service *(0392 59151/0482 29933).*
Phone and ask to hear one of the 16 tapes on AIDS. These are on all different aspects and give contact names of groups involved with treatment or support for sufferers. There are also more than 300 tapes on other illnesses.

Terence Higgins Trust
52-54 Gray's Inn Road, WC1 (Helpline 071 242 1010/Legal line 071 405 2381, 7-10pm Wed). **Open** 3-10pm daily for *general advice* on HIV/AIDS and safer sex.
The Trust advises and counsels those with HIV/AIDS, their relatives, lovers and friends. Send a stamped addressed envelope for free leaflets about AIDS, hepatitis B and VD. The Trust also gives advice about safe sex. Lines are constantly busy, so keep trying.

COMMUNICATIONS

TELEPHONES

Information on how to use the two telephone systems, British Telecom and Mercury, is given in *chapter* **Essential Information.**

OPERATOR SERVICES

Directory Enquiries
Dial **142** to find London numbers, **192** for all other numbers in Britain.

International Directory Enquiries
Dial **153** if you've left your address book at home.

International Operator
Dial **155** to use the international operator for collect calls or if you can't dial direct, but it is very expensive. Dial direct if you can. The international operator will tell you the code.

Operator
Call **100** for the operator when: you have difficulty in dialling; for an early-morning alarm call; to make a credit card call; for information about the cost of a call; to reverse charges for a call (call collect) and for international person-to-person calls.

International Telegrams
There is still a service for overseas telegrams. Call **193** if you urgently need to contact someone abroad or just like doing things in style.

Telemessage
The traditional telegram, sadly, no longer exists in Britain; instead by calling **190** you phone in your message and the next day it is delivered by post.

Telephone Directories
There are three telephone directories for London, two for private numbers, divided into alphabetical sections A-K and L-Z, and one listing companies. These are available at post offices and some call boxes have copies. All hotels and guest houses have them and they are issued free to all residents with telephones, as is the *Yellow Pages* directory, which lists commercial establishments and services under category headings such as 'Boat Hire' and 'Minicabs'. *Thomson Local Directory* is a similar directory. These are also available at post offices and are free to telephone subscribers.

POST OFFICES

Post office opening hours are normally 9am-5.30pm Mon-Fri; 9am-noon Sat, although they do vary occasionally; we list one office that opens late.

If you're travelling around Britain, you can ask friends from home to write to you care of a post office for up to one month. Your name and **Poste Restante, London** must be clearly marked on the letter: they are sent to the London Chief Post Office, King Edward Street, EC1. Bring your passport or ID card to collect your mail.

WC2: Trafalgar Square Post Office
24 William IV Street, WC2 (071 930 9580). Charing Cross underground/BR. **Open** 8am-8pm Mon-Sat.

NEWSPAPERS: HOME AND ABROAD

Books Nippon
64-66 St Paul's Churchyard, EC4 (071 248 4956). St Paul's underground. **Open** 10am-7pm Mon-Fri; 10am-6pm Sat. **Credit** A, AmEx, DC, £TC, V.
A Japanese book and magazine importer and retailer offering popular Japanese dailies such as *Asahi*, weeklies such as *Shonen-Jump* and *Newsweek* in Japanese. They also offer Japanese CDs, videos, cassettes and gifts.

Collet's International Bookshop
129 Charing Cross Road, WC2 (071 734 0782). Tottenham Court Road underground. **Open** 10am-6.30pm Mon-Fri; 10am-6pm Sat. **Credit** A, V.
Not all bookshops sell newspapers, but at Collet's you'll find many publications, from places as diverse as Central America, the Far East, and the Eastern Bloc.

Eman's
123 Queensway, W2 (071 727 6122). Bayswater underground. **Open** 7am-11pm daily. **No credit cards.**
Although there has recently been a change of ownership, there's still a large collection of Middle Eastern newspapers and magazines at the shop.

Gray's Inn News
50 Theobald's Road, WC1 (071 405 5241). Chancery Lane or Holborn underground. **Open** 4am-5.30pm Mon-Fri. **No credit cards.**
The stock is varied, ranging from the English edition of *Pravda* to titles from the USA and Europe. There's a good stock of local London newspapers and the specialities are finance, sport and leisure.

John Menzies
104-106 Long Acre, WC2 (071 240 7645). Covent Garden underground. **Open** 8am-8pm Mon-Fri; 8.30am-8pm Sat; 10.30am-8pm Sun. **Credit** A, £TC, V.
This spacious shop stocks newspapers from Europe and the USA, as well as a reasonable selection of American magazines such as *New Yorker* and *Vanity Fair.*

A Moroni & Son
68 Old Compton Street, W1 (071 437 2847). Piccadilly Circus or Leicester Square underground. **Open** 7am-7.15pm Mon-Sat; 7am-1pm Sun.
See **picture and caption.**

DS Radford
145 Fleet Street, EC4 (071 353 3700). Blackfriars underground/BR. **Open** 8am-6.30pm Mon-Fri; 7am-1pm Sat. **No credit cards.**
If you're looking for European fashion maga-

A Moroni & Son *(listed under* **Communications: Newspapers: Home and Abroad***) is a tiny shop, which celebrated its 100th anniversary in 1989. It stocks a superlative selection of foreign newspapers and magazines, but browsing is frowned upon.*

zines, this is the place to head for. DS Radford sells consumer magazines from the USA, as well as European newspapers.

LOST PROPERTY

Always inform the police if you lose anything (to validate any insurance claim). Go to the nearest police station or dial 142 and ask the operator for the telephone number. Only dial the emergency number (999) if violence has occurred. A lost passport should be reported to the police for security reasons, and to your embassy.

AIRPORTS

Gatwick Airport
(0293 28822). **Open** 8.30am-6pm daily.
The Lost Property Office is located

below the Service Air check-in desk at the south terminal on the lower level. It's for property lost in the airport only. For property lost on the plane, contact the airline or handling agents dealing with your flight.

Heathrow Airport
(081 759 4329). **Open** 9am-4pm daily.
The Lost Property Office is situated on the ground floor of Terminal 2 car park. It's for property lost in the airport only. For property lost on the plane, contact the airline by using the above number.

London City Airport
(071 474 5555). **Open** 6am-10pm daily.
The Lost Property Office is situated at the Information Desk for property lost in the airport only. For property lost on the plane, contact the airline on the same number.

Luton Airport.
(0582 405100). **Open** 24 hours daily.
Report to the Airport Duty Manager's Office (directions from the Information Desk) for property lost in the airport only. For property lost on the plane, contact the airline on the same number.

BRITISH RAIL

Charing Cross Station
(071 922 6061). **Open** 6.45am-10.30pm daily.
Lost property is deposited in the Information
Office after which it goes to Waterloo Lost
Property *(see below)*.

Euston Station
(071 922 6477). **Open** 7am-9.30pm daily.

King's Cross Station
(071 922 9081). **Open** 9.15am-4.15pm Mon;
9.15am-5.15pm Tue-Fri. **Closed** weekends.

Liverpool Street Station
(071 922 9189). **Open** 6.30am Mon-11pm
Sat; 7.30am-11pm Sun.

Marylebone Station
(071 922 4038). **Open** 8am-6pm Mon-Fri;
6.30am-2pm Sat.

Paddington Station
(071 922 6773). **Open** 7am-9pm daily.

St Pancras Station
(071 922 6478). **Open** 7am-10.30pm daily.

Victoria Station
(071 922 6216). **Open** 9am-5pm Mon-Sat;
8am-4pm Sun.

Waterloo Station
(071 922 6135 answerphone). **Open** 24
hours daily. If you leave your address they
will write to you if your property is found.
Personal calls can be made to the office
below the station 8.15am-6.45pm Mon-Fri.

BUS & UNDERGROUND

London Regional Transport
*Lost Property Office, 200 Baker Street, NW1 (071
486 2496 recorded information). Baker Street
underground.* **Open** 9.30am-2pm Mon-Fri.
Allow two days from the time of loss. If you
lose something on a bus, and can remember
which number or route it was, phone *071
222 1234* and ask for the phone numbers of
the depots at either end of the route.

TAXIS

Taxi Lost Property
*15 Penton Street, N1 (071 833 0996). Angel
underground.* **Open** 9am-4pm Mon-Fri.
Things left in taxis work their way back to
this central office, but it deals only with property found in registered black cabs. For
property lost in a minicab you will have to
call the office you hired the car from.

LOST CREDIT CARDS

Report lost or stolen credit cards to
the police and the 24-hour services
listed below. Inform your bank by
phone and in writing.

Access
(0702 352255/0702 352211).

American Express
(0273 696933).

Barclaycard/Trustcard/Visa
(0604 230230).

Diners Club/Diners Club International
(0252 516 261/0252 513 500).

MasterCard/Eurocard
(0702 352211/0702 362525).

Midland Gold MasterCard
(0702 339741).

Bank of Scotland Visa
(0383 738866).

PUBLIC TOILETS

You will find toilets signposted near
all the major sight-seeing attractions, in the museums, libraries,
parks, all railway and coach termini
and many underground stations.
You may duck into the toilet in any
pub, whether you're drinking or not.
The large department stores generally have clean loos. Few public toilets are open 24 hours a day, except
for the new, unisex, automatic types.
If you come from France you'll recognize these beige, corrugated life-
savers. Here's a list of public toilets
in the London parks:

Battersea Park
Open 7.30am-dusk daily.
There are three: in the middle near the
Pagoda; by the adventure playground; and
by the south-east entrance, at Queen's
Circus (the junction of Queenstown Road
and Prince of Wales Drive).

Green Park
Open 7.30am-11pm daily.
There are no toilets in the park but you'll find
some in Green Park underground subway.

Greenwich Park
Open *Summer* 7am-9.30pm daily; *Winter*
7am-6pm daily.
There are toilets in the Avenue and in
the rockery.
Wheelchair access.

Holland Park
Open *Summer* 8am-8pm daily; *Winter*
8am-5pm daily .
By Ilchester Place Gate, near the Orangery.
Wheelchair access.

Hyde Park
Open *Summer* 7.30am-8pm daily; *Winter*
7.30am-6pm daily.
There are three: in the centre near the
Serpentine; in the south-east corner near
Hyde Park Corner underground; and oppo-
site the bandstand in the south-east corner.
Wheelchair access.

Kensington Gardens
Open 5am-dusk daily throughout the year.
There are four: opposite Lancaster Gate
underground; by the Serpentine Gallery,

near the Royal Albert Hall; in the south-west
corner, the Kensington High Street
entrance; and by the children's playground
which is in the north-west corner.
Wheelchair access.

Regent's Park
Open *Summer* 7am-7.30pm daily; *Winter*
7am-4pm daily.
There are five: in Queen Mary's Gardens, in
the middle; by York Gate which is by the tennis courts near Madame Tussaud's; by the
boat-house near the boating lakes; on the
north end of the Broad Walk by the Zoo; and
at the junction of Chester Road and the
Broad Walk, east of Queen Mary's Gardens.
Wheelchair access to the York Gate toilets.

St James's Park
Open *Summer* 8am-9pm daily; *Spring and
autumn* 8am-7pm daily ; *Winter* 8am-6pm daily.
There are four: two by Marlborough Gate just
off Pall Mall and two on Horse Guards Road
opposite Horse Guards Parade. There is disabled access to the Marlborough Gate toilets
and a children's toilet at the playground.

The following are **automatic public
conveniences.** Admission is 10p
and they are open 24 hours daily.
See picture and caption.

Adelaide Street *off The Strand, WC2.*
Balderton Street *opposite Selfridges, just off
Oxford Street, W1. The only APC with
wheelchair access.*
Bressenden Place *at the junction with
Victoria Street, SW1.*
Cambridge Circus *by the junction of
Charing Cross road and Moor Street, WC2.*
Leicester Square *there are two APCs in the
south-east corner. WC2.*
Lumley Street *opposite Selfridges, just off
Oxford Street, W1.*
Hyde Park Corner *on the west side by Pizza
on the Park, Knightsbridge, SW3.*
Marylebone Road *opposite Madame
Tussaud's, near Baker Street underground.*
Soho Square *on the north side of the Square, W1.*
Victoria Embankment *in the Gardens
beside Hungerford Bridge, WC2.*

Here's a list of **old-fashioned
public toilets** that can be found
in the West End. Opening times
are 7.30am-11pm daily unless
otherwise stated. Most are free,
and those with wheelchair access
are indicated.

Bayswater Road *opposite Queensway, W2.*
Broad Sanctuary *by Westminster Abbey, SW1.*
Covent Garden *by the Piazza, WC2.*
Embankment *by Embankment under-
ground, WC2.*
Wheelchair access.
Great Marlborough Street *near
Carnaby Street, W1.*
Marble Arch *in the subway by the fountains, W1.*
Wheelchair access.
Oxford Circus *on the north side, W1.*
Parliament Street *by Parliament Square in
the subway, SW1.*
Piccadilly Circus *in the subway, W1.
Admission 10p.*
The Strand *opposite the Law Courts, at the top
of Fleet Street, WC2.* **Open** 10am-6pm daily.
Trafalgar Square *on the south side in*

Cockspur Street subway, SW1. **Admission** 10p. **Westminster Bridge** *by Westminster Pier, SW1. Wheelchair access.*

WASH & BRUSH UP

Many public swimming pools have individual bathrooms for hire, together with soap and a towel. If you need to clean up in transit, try a swimming pool or visit one of the major BR stations.

SECURITY

You can feel relatively safe in London, but it's unwise to take any risks, especially as robbery and mugging (robbery with violence) are currently increasing, and thieves and pickpockets lurk in crowded places. Follow these basic rules:

Keep your wallet and purse out of sight. Do not wear a wrist wallet (they are very easily snatched). Keep your handbag securely closed.
Don't leave a handbag, briefcase, bag or coat unattended, especially in pubs, cinemas, department stores or fast-food shops, on public transport, at railway stations and airports, or in crowds.
Don't leave your bag or coat beside, under or on the back of your chair. Hook the handle of your bag around the leg of the chair on which you're sitting.
Don't put your bag on the floor near the door of a public toilet.
Don't wear expensive jewellery or watches that can be easily snatched.
Late at night, travel in groups of three or more. Avoid parks and commons after dark.
Don't put your purse down on the table in a restaurant or on a shop counter while you scrutinize the bill.
Don't carry a wallet in the back pocket of your trousers.
Don't flash your money or credit cards around.

POLICE

Practically the only public service that hasn't been drained of resources during the Thatcher years is the police force. It's still fairly uncommon to encounter 'your friendly local bobby' patrolling his or her beat; more often they're roaring around in patrol cars, making high-speed arrests. Nevertheless, the police are a good source of information about the locality and are used to helping visitors find their way. If you've been robbed, assaulted or involved in an infringement of the law, look under 'Police' in the telephone directory for the nearest police station or call directory enquiries on 142. In an emergency, if you are in danger or threatened in any way, dial 999.

If you have a complaint to make about the police, then there are several things you can do. Always make sure that you take the offending police officer's identifying number, which should be prominently displayed on his or her shoulder lapel. You can then register a complaint with the **Police Complaints Authority**, 10 Great George Street, SW1 (071 273 6450). Alternatively, contact any police station or, if you'd rather not deal directly with the police, visit a solicitor or a law centre (phone directory enquiries on 142 for the nearest).

LEFT LUGGAGE

There are left luggage offices at Gatwick, London City and Heathrow airports and at all the main railway stations. Some places have left luggage lockers as well, or instead; these are often cheaper, but your possessions may not be as secure. Opening hours for and charges vary.

Gatwick Airport
(081 668 4211). **Office open** 24 hours daily. **Rates** Up to 6 hours, 55p per item; up to 12 hours, £1.10 per item; up to 24 hours, £1.70 per item; £2.50 per day thereafter.

Heathrow Airport
(081 759 4321). **Office open** *Terminals 1-2* 6.15am-11pm daily; *Terminal 3* 6am-10.15pm daily; *Terminal 4* 5.30am-10.30pm daily. **Rates** £1.50 per item for first 24 hours, £2.15 for each subsequent day. Luggage accepted up to 25kg.

London City Airport
(071 474 5555). **Office open** 6am-8.30pm Mon-Fri; 7.30am-1pm Sat; 2.30-10pm Sun. **Rates** Up to 6 hours, 50p per item; up to 24 hours, £1 per item; £1 for each subsequent day.

Charing Cross Station
(071 922 6061). **Office open** 6.30am-10.30pm daily. **Rates** £1.50 small, £2 large, till midnight on the day you deposit your luggage, thereafter the same rate per day. It is the same for all BR stations. **Lockers open** 24 hours daily. Rates £2 small, £2.50 medium, £4 large, up to 24 hours.

Euston Station
(071 928 5151, ext 40528). **Office open** 24 hours daily. **Rates** £1.20 small, £1.80 large per day.

King's Cross Station
(071 922 9081). **Office open** 7.30am-10.30pm daily. **Rates** £1 small, £1.50 large per day. **Lockers open** 24 hours daily. **Rates** £2.

Liverpool Street Station
(071 922 9189). **Lockers open** 24 hours daily. **Rates** £1.50 small, £2 medium, £3 large per day.

Marylebone Station
(071 922 4038). **Lockers open** 24 hours daily. **Rates** £1 small, £2 large per day.

Paddington Station
(071 928 6773). **Office open** 7am-midnight daily (no deposit after 10pm). **Rates** 80p small, £1 large per day.

St Pancras Station
(071 922 6478). **Office open** 7am-10.30pm daily. **Rates** £1 small, £1.50 large per day.

Victoria Station
(071 928 5151, ext 27514). **Office open** 7.15am-10.30pm Mon-Sat; 7.30am-10.30pm Sun. **Rates** £2.50 per day. **Lockers open** 24 hours daily. **Rates** £2 small, £2.50 medium, £4 large per day.

Waterloo Station
(071 928 5151, ext 22833). **Office open** 6.15am-11pm Mon-Sat; 6.30am-10pm Sun. **Rates** £1 small, £1.50 large per day.

LOCKSMITHS

If you get locked out of your car or house, or your flat is burgled, contact one of the following locksmiths. They charge a minimum of £16 to £30 and all run a 24-hour service.

W2: Barry Bros
121-123 Praed Street, W2 (071 734 1001/071 262 9009). **Open** 24 hours daily. Barry Bros will repair broken locks and doors, but the minimum price increases after 6pm to £40, and after midnight to £60.

SW1: Victoria Lock & Safe
4 Denbigh Street, SW1 (071 630 6500/071 630 0917 24 hour emergency service). **Open** 24 hours daily.
The call-out charge depends on the area and the work to be done. The minimum charge is £28.75 before 5.30pm; up to midnight it is £40 and after midnight £60.

N4: North London Locksmiths
79 Grand Parade, Green Lanes, N4 (081 800 6041). **Open** 24 hours. **Credit** A, V.
This firm operates an emergency service. After 5pm the call-out fee for local (anywhere with a North London post-code) calls is £30, after midnight it goes up to £40, plus parts.

HELP & INFORMATION

Citizens Advice Bureaux
Greater London Office, 136-144 City Road, EC1 (071 251 2000). **Open**

9.30am-5pm Mon-Fri.
Citizens Advice Bureaux are run by local councils and offer free advice on legal, financial and personal matters. The above address is the head office; call and ask where the nearest branch is situated. Alternatively, look in the phone book or ring the local Town Hall.

International Traveller's Aid
Portacabin, Platform 15, Victoria Station, SW1 (071 834 3925/071 834 3901). Victoria underground/BR. **Open** daily.
This is a voluntary body connected with the YWCA, which helps foreign nationals arriving in London. Advice is given on accommodation and a multitude of other things.

FINANCIAL ADVICE

For visitors from abroad who run into financial difficulties, embassies are the best places to contact for help. But people on long-term stays who need counselling or advice can go to Citizens Advice Bureaux *(see above* **Help & Information**) or to the **Mary Ward Centre**. Both places have qualified counsellors who can advise you free of charge on the options open to you and the best course of action to take.

Mary Ward Centre
42 Queen's Square, WC1 (071 831 7009 legal enquiries/071 831 7079 financial enquiries). Holborn or Russell Square underground. **Open** 9.30am-5.30pm Mon-Fri for telephone enquiries; 6-7.30pm Mon, Wed for financial counselling. Phone for an appointment.

LEGAL ADVICE

You never know when you're going to need a lawyer or a solicitor (hopefully not at all). If you are unfortunate enough to get involved in serious accidents, loss of life, crime or arrest, contact your embassy, go to a **Citizens Advice Bureau (CAB)** *(see above* **Help & Information**) or get in touch with one of the organizations listed below. Some people are eligible for Legal Aid. For a leaflet explaining how the system works write to **Legal Aid** *(see below)* or pick one up at a Citizens Advice Bureau.

Amnesty International
British Section, 99-119 Rosebery Avenue, EC1 (071 278 6000). Farringdon or Angel underground. **Open** 9am-6.30 pm Mon-Fri.
No introduction needed. Amnesty assists people held by immigration, finds organizations to fight cases and even enlists the help of MPs to delay deportation. All support is free. There are about 40 groups in the London area. For their London research office, phone *071 357 7421.*

Law Centres Federation
(071 387 8570). **Open** 10am-6pm Mon-Fri.
There are about 30 Law Centres in

London and this organization will put you in touch with your nearest office. Centres can give free help with all aspects of the law to people who cannot afford to pay for legal advice.

The Law Society
The Law Society's Hall, 113 Chancery Lane, WC2 (071 242 1222). Chancery Lane or Temple underground. **Open** 9.15am-5.15pm Mon-Fri.
The Law Society can give advice, though they prefer requests for information in writing, and will put you in touch with associations well-placed to deal with any query. Complaints against solicitors are dealt with by the society.

Legal Aid
Newspaper House, 8-16 Great News Street, EC4 (071 353 7411). Chancery Lane underground. **Open** 9am-5pm Mon-Fri.
Apply to the head office of Legal Aid for the names and addresses of solicitors who act within the Legal Aid scheme. Staff at the office will listen to your problems and advise you on how to proceed.

Release
169 Commercial Street, E1 (071 377 5905). Aldgate East or Liverpool Street underground/BR. **Open** 10am-6pm Mon-Fri.
This organization runs a 24-hour telephone helpline on *071 603 8654* for emergencies. During office hours contact the daytime number for free legal advice for anyone who has been arrested. Release is particularly helpful in cases involving drugs, and gives confidential drugs counselling and referrals.

CONSUMER PROBLEMS

Statutory rights protect the consumer, and when you buy a large or expensive piece of equipment you should be provided with a guarantee by the vendor. Many department stores, such as John Lewis, have a good reputation for their service to customers after a purchase has been made, so it often works out cheaper to buy a hi-fi, for instance, from a reputable shop rather than pay less in a street market. **The Office of Fair Trading** *(see below)* publishes free leaflets on all aspects of consumer purchase covering goods and services. You can also obtain their leaflets at **Citizens Advice Bureaus** *(see above* **Help & Information**). The Consumer's Association publishes *Which* magazine, *Which Car* etc – well worth reading before a purchase is made, and available from most newsagents.

Office of Fair Trading
Field House 15-25 Bream's Buildings, EC4 (071 242 2858). **Open** 8.30am-5.30pm Mon-Fri.

PHONELINES
Capital Helpline
(071 388 7575). **Open** 9.30am-5.30pm Mon, Tue, Wed, Fri; 9.30am-9pm Thur.
Run in conjunction with Capital Radio, this helpline tackles queries about anything. If the staff can't answer your query themselves, they'll put you in touch with someone who can help. The line is always busy, so keep trying. They have an answerphone after the lines close and will call you back.

London Regional Transport Travel Information Service
(071 222 1234). **Open** 24 hours daily.
Phone for information about travel by underground, bus and British Rail in Greater London, fares, how to get from A to B and timetable information.

Sportsline
(071 222 8000). **Open** 10am-6pm Mon-Fri.
Information on where to watch, play or train in any sport and where to buy the equipment.

Timeline
(123). Phone this number to find out the time.

TVTS (Transvestite and Transsexual Helpline)
2 French Place, off Batemans Row, E1 (071 729 1466). **Open** 2-6pm Tue; 8-10pm Fri-Sun.
If you feel a need to talk personally to someone about these subjects, phone the above number. Social groups are also organized on open nights (7.30pm-1am Fri, Sat; and 7.30pm-midnight Sun).

Weathercall
(London area 0898 500401).
Up-to-the-minute information on when to expect the next downpour.

REFERENCE LIBRARIES

Most of London's libraries are free and are an abundant source of information. Both local public libraries and the central London libraries are ideal places to sit, read and escape the bustle of the city. Here we list the main reference libraries:

Guildhall Reference Library
Aldermanbury, EC2 (071 606 3030). Bank, Mansion House, St Paul's or Moorgate underground/8, 25, 35, 76 bus. **Open** 9.30am-5pm Mon-Sat. **Admission** free.
Most of the material kept here deals with the history of London. On the ground floor are printed books and on the first floor is a collection of maps, prints and manuscripts. *Wheelchair access limited.*

Westminster Central Reference Library
St Martin's Street, WC2 (071 798 2034). Leicester Square, Piccadilly Circus or Charing Cross underground/24, 29 bus. **Open** 10am-7pm Mon-Fri; 10am-5pm Sat. **Admission** free.
A public reference library, with international telephone directories from most countries on the ground floor, a large collection of information on performing arts on the first floor and a register of companies trading in Britain and an arts library on the second floor.

DISABLED

Things are improving (slowly) for disabled visitors to London. Many tourist venues now have wheelchair access; some councils are doing their best to improve the situation farther. There are books and organizations which give useful information specifically for disabled people. The **London Tourist Board** publishes *London Made Easy*, costing £2.25 and available from **Tourist Information Centres** (*see chapter* **Essential Information**). For information about travelling on public transport, get a copy of *Access to the Underground* (£1; *see chapter* **Travelling Around London**). Write to London Regional Transport Unit for Disabled Passengers, 55 Broadway, SW1 (071 227 3312). *Access in London* is a booklet compiled by researchers with disabilities which covers tourist spots, shopping, pubs, theatres and much more. It costs £2.25 from good newsagents; or write to 39 Bradley Gardens, West Ealing, London W13.

Artsline
5 Crowndale Road, NW1 (071 388 2227). Mornington Crescent underground/24, 29, 68, 253 bus. **Open** 10am-5.30pm Mon-Fri.
This organization for the disabled gives free information on arts and entertainment events in London and on disabled facilities at venues such as cinemas, art galleries and theatres.

British Sports Association for the Disabled
34 Osnaburgh Street, NW1 (071 383 7229 24-hour answerphone). **Open** 9am-5.30pm Mon-Fri.
See **picture and caption.**

Greater London Association for Disabled People (GLAD)
336 Brixton Road, SW9 (071 274 0107). Brixton underground. **Open** 9am-5pm Mon-Fri.
GLAD is a good source of information through which you can be put in touch with disability associations within local boroughs and other helpful organizations.

Handicapped Helpline
c/o Community Links, 81 High Street South, E6 (081 472 6652). **Open** 11am-3.30pm Tue-Fri for visits. Legal advice is given on the 1st and 3rd Tuesday of every month, 6.30-7.30pm.
This organization is run by and for disabled people to give information and advice on a variety of subjects and counselling on careers. It can put you in touch with other organizations or specific associations and offers a drop-in service.

Royal Association For Disability and Rehabilitation (RADAR)
25 Mortimer Street, W1 (071 637 5400). **Open** 9am-5pm Mon-Thur; 9am-4.30pm Fri.
This is the central organization for disabled voluntary groups. Through it you can get advice on virtually any aspect of life. The Association publishes *Contact*, a quarterly magazine which has features on disabled issues, and *Bulletin*, a monthly newsletter, which has articles on more news-orientated subjects such as housing, education and Acts of Parliament.

LESBIAN & GAY

London has a varied and interesting gay scene if you know where to look. There are many lesbian and gay nightclubs, social meeting places and organizations. However, there's still a lot of prejudice against gays and lesbians, and violent attacks are on the increase. Be careful when leaving a gay or lesbian nightclub on your own. Some of the better-known lesbian and gay publications in London are: *Gay Times*, *The Pink Paper*, *Square Peg*, *HIM* and *Capital Gay*, available from gay bookshops and some newsagents. For more detailed information *see* chapter **Lesbian & Gay**, and for weekly events look in *Time Out* magazine's Gay columns.

WOMEN

Sexual harassment is not as great a problem in Britain as it is in some other countries. In cafés and restaurants a woman alone won't really get bothered, but you may feel uncomfortable in pubs and nightclubs as men often assume that any unaccompanied woman is looking for male companionship, and it can be a nightmare trying to get rid of their unwanted attentions. *Spare Rib* is a

Disabled people interested in watching or participating in sports can contact the **British Sport Association for the Disabled** *(listed under* **Disabled***), a national organization which can put people in touch with local sports groups and centres. The address is that of the Greater London regional office: there are regional branches throughout the country.*

monthly feminist magazine available from newsagents. In it are listed women's centres and women's groups; and the classified section has accommodation, events and job advertisements.

Feminist Library
Hungerford House, Victoria Embankment, WC2 (071 930 0715). Embankment underground. **Open** 11am-8pm Tue; 2-5pm Sat, Sun. London's main women's lending library, it stocks a wide range of feminist fiction and non-fiction, and a research index.

London Rape Crisis Centre
PO Box 69, WC1 (office 071 278 3956/24 hour phoneline 071 837 1600). **Open** 10am-12.30pm, 2.30-6pm Mon, Wed, Fri; 10am-1pm, 2-6pm Tue, Thur.
Run by women, Rape Crisis offers confidential advice and support for women who have been raped or sexually assaulted.

Women's Aid
(071 251 6537). **Open** 24 hours daily.
This organization will help you in an emergency, refer you to your nearest refuge, and provide advice and counselling.

TRAVEL

Orientation, fares and so on are covered in *chapter* **Travel**. If you're thinking of travelling outside London look at *chapter* **Trips out of Town**.

DISCOUNTS

The Young Person's Railcard
This can be held by anyone under 24 years old or those in full-time education. It costs £15 for one year, and entitles holders to a discount (usually a third off the off-peak standard fare, but more during special offer periods). They're available from main British Rail stations. You'll need identification and a couple of passport-sized photographs.

The Student Coach Card
Costing £4.25, this is for students only; it gives a 33 per cent discount on fares and is valid for a year. The form is available from Victoria Bus Station, and needs to be stamped by your college.

The Inter-Rail Card
Suitable for all those aged under 26 who are planning a trip to Europe. For £145, the pass (available from British Rail stations) entitles holders to unlimited train travel in 21 countries for one month. You can buy more than one and there's a small refund on return of your correctly filled-in card.

STA Travel
74 & 86 Old Brompton Road, SW7 (071 937 9962 Intercontinental/071 937 9921 European). South Kensington underground. **Open** 9am-6pm Mon-Fri; 10am-4pm Sat.
A wide range of low-cost fares across all five continents are offered here, with special rates for students, young people and academics. They also have offices at 117 Euston Road, NW1, **ULU Travel at the University of London** and many other colleges throughout London.

HIRED TRANSPORT

If public transport is getting you down and you dare to tackle London's hellish road system, here's how to get about. Cycling has become more popular in London, but tracks are still rare. A cycle path map is available from good bookshops. *See chapter* **Sport and fitness** for bicycle hire shops. Car hire firms are listed under *chapter* **Travel**. The following is a reputable motorcycle hire company:

Scootabout
59 Albert Embankment, SE1 (071 582 0055). Vauxhall underground/BR. **Open** 9am-6pm Mon-Fri; 9am-2pm Sat. **Credit** A, AmEx, DC, £TC, V.
Any driver's licence, British or foreign, qualifies you to drive a 50cc moped. The hire charge goes from £12.95 per day including unlimited mileage and helmet, and from £64.50 per week plus £100 returnable deposit. Motorcycles 125-1000cc cost from £14.95 per day and from £74.50 per week including helmet and unlimited mileage (you pay for the fuel). The deposit is from £100, and VAT at 15% is added on top.

PARKING

If you've heard that driving in Central London is difficult, just wait till you try to find somewhere to park. Car parks are very expensive but are still the best places to put your vehicle. **National Car Parks** produce a free guide called *London Parking Guide* that lists its car parks with maps showing places of interest and theatres. You can get it from NCP Offices at 21 Bryanston Street, W1 (071 499 7050), Marble Arch underground. Below we list a selection of central London's 24-hour car parks.

If you park illegally (check the regulations in the *Highway Code*, 60p from newsagents), you'll probably get a £12 **parking ticket** (London's traffic wardens are famed for their diligence). If you park illegally in central London your car will probably be immobilized by a yellow triangular wheel-clamp (*see below* **De-Clamping**). Vehicles may also be towed away and impounded. To retrieve your vehicle you have to go to a **Payment Centre** and pay £25 for **clamping**, £75 tow-away fee, a £12 parking fine and £10 storage for each day your car has been kept in the pound. Take the bus.

24-HOUR CAR PARKS

W1: Arlington Street
(071 499 3312). **Open** 24 hrs daily. **Rates** £6 for 3 hours; £12 for 6 hours; £20 for 12 hours.

W1: Audley Square
(071 499 3265). **Open** 24 hrs daily. **Rates** £2.80 for 2 hours; £8.40 for 6 hours; £4 night rate.

W1: Brewer Street
(071 734 9497). **Open** 24 hours daily. **Rates** £3.80 for 2hours; £7.60 for 4 hours; £17 for 8 hours; £8 night rate.

W1: Denman Street
(071 734 5760). **Open** 24 hours daily. **Rates** £3.80 for 2 hours; £11.50 for 6 hours; £8 night rate.

W1: Park Lane
(071 262 1814). **Open** 24 hours daily. **Rates** £1.90 for 2 hours; £5.70 for 6 hours; £12 for 24 hours.

W8: Royal Garden Hotel
Kensington High Street (071 937 8000, ext 851). **Open** 24 hours daily. **Rates** £4.75 for 4 hours; £6.75 for 6 hours; £6 night rate.

W8: Young Street
(071 937 7420). **Open** 24 hours daily. **Rates** £2.20 for 2 hours; £9.90 for 6 hours; £1.05 night rate.

WC2: Bedfordbury
(071 240 0397). **Open** 7am-midnight Sat. **Rates** £3.50 for 2 hours; £10.50 for 6 hours; £15.50 for 12 hours.

WC2: Cambridge Circus
(071 434 1896). **Open** 24 hours daily. **Rates** £6 for 4 hours; £9 for 6 hours; £3 night rate.

WC2: Upper St Martin's Lane
(071 836 7451). **Open** 24 hours Mon-Sat. **Rates** £6 for 4 hours; £14 for 9 hours; £18.50 24 hours; £5.80 night rate.

SW1: Abingdon Street
(071 222 8621). **Open** 24 hours daily. **Rates** £3.80 for 4 hours; £6 for 6 hours; £2.30 night rate.

SW1: Cadogan Place
(071 235 5106). **Open** 24 hours daily. **Rates** £2.80 for 2 hours; £8.40 for 6 hours; £12 for 9 hours; £2.20 night rate.

SW1: Dolphin Square Garage
Grosvenor Road (071 834 1077). **Open** 24 hours daily. **Rates** 55p for 1 hr; £1.85 for 4 hours; £2.70 for 6 hours.

SW1: Park Tower Hotel
(071 235 0733). **Open** 24 hours daily. **Rates** £4 for 4 hours, £6 for 6 hours; £4 night rate.

SW1: Rochester Row
(071 828 4298). **Open** 7am-midnight daily. **Rates** £5 for 4 hours; £7.50 for 6 hours; £11 for 24 hours.

SW1: Semley Place
(071 730 7905). **Open** 24 hours daily. **Rates** £1.90 for 2 hours; £5.70 for 6 hours; £1.70 night rate.

Call home with your news from London.

Whilst you're staying in London, remember that your family and friends at home would love to hear about what you've seen and done during your visit. That's where British Telecom can help, with services to suit your every need.

If you want to call home without paying in the UK, you should make a Collect call or use your telephone credit card by dialling 155 for the UK International Operator, who will be happy to connect your call.

Alternatively, if you prefer to pay as you call, you can always use British Telecom's International Direct Dialling service by simply dialling 010 and your country code, followed by your area code and local number.

Both of these services are available from most British Telecom payphones. The easiest way to make an International Direct Dialled call is by using a Phonecard payphone – you'll need a pre-paid green Phonecard for this, which you can buy at any Post Office.

You'll find British Telecom payphones and Phonecard payphones all over the UK, making it even easier to get in touch with family and friends at home.

For full information on these and other services, ask for our leaflet 'How to call home from the UK' at any tourist information centre.

British
TELECOM

SW3: Pavilion Road
(071 589 0401). **Open** 24 hours daily. **Rates** £3.20 for 2 hours; £6.50 for 4 hours; £9.80 for 6 hours; £2.60 night rate.

SW5: Swallow International Hotel
Cromwell Road (071 370 4200). **Open** 24 hours daily. **Rates** £3 for 4 hours; £4 for 6 hours; £6.75 for 9hours; £10 for 24 hours.

DE-CLAMPING

For years motorists ignored the thousands of tickets slapped onto their cars by traffic wardens and continued to park illegally, so the dreaded **wheel clamp** was introduced. However, it not only ruins your day, but also guarantees the road will remain blocked until the offending car is freed. If you've been clamped there will be a label attached to the car telling you which of the **Payment Centres** *(listed below)* to visit. When you get there you'll have to pay £25 on the spot for de-clamping and have 28 days in which to pay a £12 parking fine. Now the real fun starts. They promise to de-clamp your car within the next one to four hours but can't tell you exactly when. You are also warned that if you don't remove your car within one hour of its being de-clamped they will clamp it again. This means that you have to spend several hours, if not all day, waiting by your car.

Hyde Park Police Car Pound and Payment Centre
Located in the NCP Car Park, Park Lane, W1 (071 252 2222 ask for the Hyde Park Car Pound). Marble Arch underground. **Open** 24 hours daily.

Warwick Road Police Car Pound and Payment Centre
245 Warwick Road, SW5 (071 252 2222 ask for the Kensington Car Pound). Earl's Court underground. **Open** 8am-Midnight Mon-Sat.

Camden Police Car Pound and Payment Centre
Oval Road, NW1 (071 252 2222 ask for the Camden Car Pound). Camden Town underground. **Open** 8am-midnight Mon-Sat; 9am-6pm Sun.

Car Clamp Recovery Club
20 Newman Street, W1 (071 235 9901). **Open** 9am-midnight Mon-Fri; 10am-8pm Sat. **Membership** £25. **Credit** A, AmEx, DC, V.
If you're too busy to go through the de-clamp process yourself and want to have the car delivered to your door, you pay a total of £70.25 incl VAT: £30 goes to the police for the de-clamping plus £17.25 for the service of the company and £23 delivery fee. You'll have to pay the £12 parking fine yourself.

24-HOUR PETROL STATIONS

If you're driving late and are low on petrol don't panic, there are over 100 24-hour petrol stations throughout Greater London, so you're never far from help. They're also ideal for cigarettes and chocolate at three in the morning. Listed below are a selection of the town's finest.

WC1 Texaco *71 King's Cross Road.* **Shop** open *24 hours.*
W1 Mobil *83 Park Lane.*
W2 Shell *104-105 Bayswater Road.*
W3 Texaco *48 Horn Lane.* **Shop** open till 9pm.
W5 BP *119 Gunnersbury Avenue.* **Shop** open 24 hours.
W6 Mobil *161 Talgarth Road.*
W10 Texaco *235 A Scrubs Lane.*
W11 Texaco *7 Pembridge Villas.* **Shop** open 24 hours.
W12 Esso *87 Goldhawk Road.*
W14 BP *112 North End Road.*

SW1 City *132 Grosvenor Road.*
SW2 BP *47-51 Acre Lane.*
SW3 BP *Sloane Avenue.*
SW4 BP *33 Clapham High Street.*
SW6 Shell *8 Townmead Road.*
SW8 BP *366-370 Wandsworth Road*
SW9 Burmah *330 Brixton Road.*
SW11 Esso *635 Wansworth Road.*
SW12 Shell *67 Balham Hill.*
SW13 Heron *Loampit Vale.*
SW15 Texaco *29 Roehampton Vale.*
SW16 Texaco *275 Streatham Common.*
SW17 Mobil *260 Balham High Street.*
SW20 Mobil *314 Kingston Road.*

SE1 Shell *430-432 Old Kent Road.*
SE5 BP *90-110 Camberwell Road.*
SE6 Mobil *163 Bromley Road.*
SE7 BP *451-473 Woolwich Road.*
SE9 BP *21 Mottingham Road.*
SE10 Shell *25 Greenwich High Road.*
SE11 BP *238 Kennington Lane.*
SE12 BP *12 Burnt Ash Road.*
SE15 BP *95 Peckham Road.*
SE18 Shell *125 Woolwich High Street.*
SE21 BP *17 Thurlow Park Road.*

EC1 Texaco *309 City Road.* **Shop** open 24 hours.
E1 BP *261-267 Commercial Road.*
E2 Texaco *Hackney Road, Hackney.*
E3 City *24 Bow Road, Bow.*
E4. Mobil *Walthamstow Ave.*
E8 BP *139 Mare Street.*
E10 Mobil *666 Leyton High Road.*
E11 Hills *588 High Road, Leytonstone.*
E15 Shell *176 Romford Road.*
E17 Texaco *544 Forest Road.* **Shop** open 24 hours.

N1 BP *176-178 York Way.*
N2 Texaco *178 High Road.* **Shop** open 24 hours.
N4 Mobil *390 Green Lane.*
N7 BP *465-467 Holloway Road.*
N8 Texaco *Tottenham Lane.* **Shop** open 24 hours.
N10 Shell *Pages Lane.*
N14 Mobil *99 Chase Side.*
N16 BP *144-150 Stoke Newington Road.*
N17 Mobil *Ferry Lane.*
N19 Heron *Hornsey Rise.*

N20 Mobil *1,412 High Road.*
N22 Texaco *573 Lordship Lane.*
NW1 Mobil *142 Hampstead Road.*
NW3 BP *104A Finchley Road.*
NW6 Texaco *63 Fortune Green Road.*
NW8 Texaco *129 Park Road.*
NW9 BP *2-12 Blackbird Hill.*
NW10 Texaco *244 North Circular Road.*
NW11 Texaco *872 Finchley Road.* **Shop** open 24 hours.

CAR BREAKDOWN

The well-prepared visitor never travels without his/her membership card of a motoring organization. But if you're not organized and disaster strikes, contact the following:

AA (Automobile Association)
Fanum House, 5 New Coventry Street, W1 (information 081 954 9599; freefone breakdown service 0800 887766). Piccadilly Circus underground. **Open** office 9am-5pm Mon-Fri; 9am-12.30pm Sat. **Breakdown service** 24 hours daily. **Credit** A, V.
You can call the AA out if your car breaks down. Become a member on the spot: it will cost you £7.50 to join, £26.50 for the first year's membership, plus £30 surcharge for the mechanic to come to your car.

National Breakdown
(Head Office 0532 393434/Breakdown 0800 400 600/Membership 0532 3936661). **Open** 24 hours daily.
A non-member calling National Breakdown pays £19.50 call-out fee, mileage of 60p per mile plus labour and parts. To become a member, phone for details; degrees of cover vary from total protection (£39.50) to recovery (£19).

Olympic Breakdown Service
(West London 071 286 8282; East London 081 533 2911). **Open** 24 hours daily. **Credit** A, AmEx, V.
This company is AA- and RAC-approved and operates a 24 hour London-wide recovery and roadside repair service. It will cost £24 plus VAT call-out charge, plus the price of any new parts. To be towed away costs £30 plus VAT within a five mile radius and then £1 per mile, so call the right number. If you do need to be towed away you don't pay the call-out fee, only the tow charge.

RAC (Royal Automobile Club)
49 Pall Mall, SW1 (office 071 839 7050; 24hr national breakdown line 0800 828 282; enquiries 0293 333543/081 452 8000; membership 0272 232340). Charing Cross underground/BR. **Open** office 9am-5.30pm Mon-Fri; 9am-12.30pm Sat. **Breakdown service** 24 hours daily. **Credit** A, AmEx, DC, V.
Ring the appropriate number and ask for the Rescue Service. Membership costs £37.50 plus a £25 surcharge. Describe your mechanical failure to the controller and he'll send out an engineer to repair your car on the roadside or, if necessary, tow it away.

SPARE PARTS

Barnet Brake And Clutch Services
120 Myddleton Road, N22 (081 881 0847). Bounds Green and Wood Green underground/N21, N2 Night Bus. **Open** 24 hours

daily. **Credit** A, V.
If you know what the problem is and just need parts, this is a 24-hour car spare parts shop.

WORK & STUDY

Finding a summer job, or temporary work if you're on a working holiday, is a full-time job in itself. However, this is a busy capital and there's always work around. Some helpful books are listed under the **Central Bureau for Educational Visits and Exchanges** (*see below* **Useful Addresses**), while another useful read is *Summer Jobs in Britain* published by *Vacation Work, 9 Park End Street, Oxford*, available from good bookshops.

WORK PERMITS

EEC nationals (except from Spain and Portugal), residents of Gibraltar and some categories of overseas visitors don't need a work permit. All other visitors cannot work here legally without one. There are three government departments dealing with work permits. Try any **Jobcentre**, where you can get an application form, before going to the more bureaucratic **Department of Employment** or the **Home Office** (*see below* **Useful Addresses**). Basically, you need a British employer to apply on your behalf and he/she must prove that no UK resident can do the work better. However, there is a 'training and work experience' scheme operated by the Department of Employment for 18 to 35 year olds. This enables you to gain work experience or training in a certain field for a specific, limited period of time. A permit must be obtained by a British employer on your behalf before you enter the country.

Citizens of Commonwealth countries aged between 17 and 27 years can get a passport stamp as a 'Working Holiday Maker' which allows you to do part-time work without a work permit for up to two years. Contact the British High Commission or Consulate in your country to obtain the stamp before entering this country. If applying for a visa extension while in Britain, you might convince the Home Office Immigration department or the Overseas Labour Section at the Department of Employment that you need part-time work and are not looking for full time employment.

Visiting **students from the USA** can get a blue card enabling them to work for a maximum of six months. This is not difficult to obtain, but you must get it before entering the country. Contact the Work in Britain department of the **Council on International Educational Exchange** *205 East 42nd Street, New York, NY 10017 (0101 212 661 1414)* for details.

TYPES OF WORK

You should be able to get work doing catering jobs, labouring, bar/pub work or shop work; graduates with either English or a foreign language degree could try teaching. Temporary (temp) work is always available through agencies (*see below* **Useful Addresses**). Other alternatives are: despatch riding (bike messengers need their own bike and a courageous disposition), distributing free magazines or work in a betting shop. Also try summer work in tourist spots; local councils sometimes take on summer staff, such as playgroup leaders, assistants in homes for the elderly or swimming pool attendants.

To find work look in the *Evening Standard*, local and national newspapers, local newsagents' window cards or Jobcentres. For **temping**, sign on with temp agencies; there are branches all over the place (and listed in the phone book). It's wise to join several to widen your chances; there's no charge for registering and it's the employer who pays the agency if a deal is struck. If you have good shorthand, typing (40 words per minute upwards) or word processing (WP) skills - sometimes these are not necessary - and are well presesented, they can find you well-paid and sometimes glamorous office work. If you're desperate, try a fast food chain. You'll probably have to wear a hideous uniform and endure hyped-up competition to see who is the fastest burger-maker, and don a badge if you are, but they're always looking for staff (and no wonder).

WORK FOR FOREIGN VISITORS

London isn't the world's most friendly city and it's not easy meeting people here. So one of the advantages of working in London (apart from the money) is that you get to meet and share life with the city's natives. From joining the living dead on the tube every morning to finding people to go shopping, clubbing and eating with, this has to be a good thing. It is essential that you can speak English of a communicable standard. Visitors from abroad can try catering — there is a **Jobcentre** at *3 Denmark Street, W1 (071 831 5041)* dealing specifically in hotel and catering work. For office work you need a very high standard of English and office skills.

Au-pair work is another possibility. Try an au-pair agency in your own country or look in the Yellow Pages under employment agencies. Also look in *The Lady* magazine, which advertises au-pair and nanny jobs. The best thing about au-pairing is that you get free accommodation, although the wages are often low as a result. Voluntary work in youth hostels will usually pay board and lodging and some pocket money, but there is a great demand. Voluntary work on social and community projects won't pay, but you would gain an insight to local life. Contact local councils, you'll find them in telephone directories. Work can also be found in shops, pubs and bars (*see above* **Types of Work** for where to look).

USEFUL ADDRESSES

Central Bureau for Educational Visits & Exchanges
Seymour Mews House, Seymour Mews, W1 (071 486 5101). Marble Arch or Bond Street underground. **Open** 9.30am-5.30pm Mon-Fri. Funded by the Department of Education and Science, this office deals mainly with organizing visits ouside the UK. Contact them anyway, to get your mitts on their extemely useful books; *Working Holidays 1989* at £7.80, *Volunteer Work* at £3.50, *Home from Home* at £3.95 and *Study Holidays* at £6.20, available from bookshops and the Bureau itself (although only by post). The reception area stocks a selection of leaflets and booklets detailing their work.

Department of Employment
Caxton House, Tothill Street, SW1 (071 273 3000). St James's Park underground. **Open** 9am-5pm Mon-Fri.
The government department dealing with all aspects of employment. The Overseas

Labour Section can help with work permit enquiries *(071 273 5336)*, but apply early as applications may take up to three months.

Home Office
Immigration and Nationality Department, Lunar House, Wellesley Road, Croydon, CR2 (081 686 0688). East Croydon BR. **Open** 8.30am-4pm Mon-Fri.
The Immigration department of the Home Office deals with queries about immigration matters, visas and work permits.

Jobcentre
195 Wardour Street, W1 (071 439 4541). Tottenham Court Road underground. **Open** 9am-5pm Mon-Thur; 10am-5pm Fri.
Run by the Department of Employment. Employers advertise job vacancies on notice boards, and there's often temporary and unskilled work available. There are loads of Jobcentres throughout London - they're painted bright orange so you can't miss them - and they're listed under Manpower Services Commission in the telephone directory. The West End offices at *33 Mortimer Street, W1 (071 836 6622)* and *3 Denmark Street, W1 (071 836 6622)* both deal with catering vacancies only.

LANGUAGE SCHOOLS
These have mushroomed all over London, offering expensive and intensive courses in English as a foreign language. Be warned though; they are not all reputable educational establishments, so don't just walk into the first one you come across. Always check that the school you choose is recognised by the **British Council**, or is a member of **ARELS-FELCO** (*see below*). The good ones have teachers with teaching certificates either from the Royal Society of Art (RSA) or International House (ITTI), run classes of a maximum of 15 students and usually use high quality text books such as the *Cambridge* or *Meaning Into Words* series.

ARELS-FELCO
2 Pontypool Place, SE1 (071 242 3136). Waterloo underground/BR. **Open** 9.50am-5.30pm Mon-Thur; 9.30am-5pm Fri.
ARELS-FELCO, the Association for Recognized English Language Teaching Establishments in Britain, is the professional body for language schools. It publishes *Learn English in Britain*, a booklet listing its members and schools approved by the British Council.

British Council
10 Spring Gardens, SW1 (071 930 8466). Charing Cross underground/BR. **Open** 10am-4pm (personal calls); 9.30am-5pm phone Mon-Fri.
The British Council is the governing body covering language schools. The schools they approve after regular assessment and inspection are in *Learn English in Britain*, available from the Education Information Service Department *(071 389 4383/071 389 4391).*

Eurocentres
36 Honor Oak Road, SE23 (081 699 1174). Forest Hill BR/185 Bus. **Open** 9am-5pm Mon-Fri. **Credit** £TC.
Recognized by the British Council and a member of ARELS-FELCO, with three schools in London and affiliated ones throughout the continent, Eurocentres offer a range of classes all year round. The summer intensive courses offer 25 hours study a week, for three to four weeks, with morning and afternoon classes, and costs £109 per week. All classes have a maximum of 16 pupils and they can help find accommodation. **Other branches:** *21 Meadow Court, SE3 (081 318 5633); Davis's School of English, 56 Eccleston Square, SW1 (071 834 4155).*

International House
106 Piccadilly, W1 (071 491 2598). Piccadilly underground. **Open** 9am-8.30pm Mon-Fri. **Credit** £TC.
Not merely an institute for English language teachers, International House has been running English language courses for 36 years. It's recognized by the British Council and ARELS-FELCO and has affiliated schools in 18 countries worldwide. Open all year round, an intensive summer course in August lasts four weeks, 25 hours per week, and costs £455. There's a maximum of 15 pupils per class but the average is ten. International House also does a two-week summer intensive course for mature students, with a maximum of six to a group, for 30 hours a week, costing £699.

Marble Arch Intensive English
21 Star Street, W2 (071 402 9273). Edgware Road and Paddington underground. **Open** 9am-6.30pm Mon-Fri. **Credit** £TC.
General English courses last a minimum of two weeks, in groups of no more than 14. On average a short course of half days will cost £55 per week, but the rate gets cheaper the longer the course. Full-day courses are also available. The full range of courses includes teacher training, tourism and commercial English. This ARELS-FELCO recognized centre also boasts a restaurant, language library, social programme and accommodation service, placing students in college halls or with families.

STUDENTS
An **ISIC (International Student Identity Card)** is a useful asset in London. Many theatres, cinemas and galleries will give student discounts if you produce an ISIC card. It's always worth asking. If you've come without a student card, go to the **University of London Union** office or **STA Travel** (*see above* **Travel**), with your student and personal identification, and ask for one.

University of London Union
Malet Street, WC1 (071 580 9551/071 580 9552/071 580 9553). Goodge Street underground. **Open** 9.30am-11pm Mon-Sat; 9.30am-10.30pm Sun. **Closed** Aug.
University Travel Centre (071 636 0271). Open 9.30am-6pm Mon-Fri; 10.30am-4pm Sat. ULU has some of the best sports and social

facilities in town, with sunbeds, a swimming pool, a Jacuzzi and the flash Palms wine bar and Mergers bar. As long as you have a valid union card and your college is a reciprocal member, you can use as many of the facilities as you like.

RELIGION

Several churches of different denominations are listed in *chapters* **London By Area** and **Old London.**

BAPTIST
Bloomsbury Central Baptist Church
235 Shaftesbury Avenue, WC2 (071 836 6843/071 240 0544). Tottenham Court Road underground. **Open** *Office* 9am-6.30pm daily; *Friendship Centre* 11.30am-2.30pm Tue; 6-8.30pm Wed; 10.30am-8.30pm Sun. **Services** 11am, 6pm Sun.
This is one of central London's most famous Baptist churches. It's open during the week by request only.
Organ recitals, phone for details.

London Baptist Association
1 Merchant Street, E3 (081 980 6818). Mile End or Bow Road underground. **Open** 9am-5pm Mon-Fri.
The organization offers information on all Baptist churches throughout London.

Westminster Baptist Church
Horseferry Road, SW1 (071 821 1519). Pimlico or St James's Park underground. **Open** 10am-4pm Mon-Fri (Fri 7.30-10pm social evenings); 10am-noon Sat; 11am-1.30pm, 6-8.30pm Sun. **Services** 7pm Wed; 1-1.30pm Thur; 11am, 6.30pm Sun.
The oldest Baptist church in London; it celebrates its 183rd birthday in 1990.

BUDDHIST
Buddhapadipa Temple
14 Calonne Road, SW19 (081 946 1357). Wimbledon Park underground. **Open** 9am-5pm daily.
This Thai temple is used for meditation and the practice of basic Buddhism. Sundays are set aside for Thai students.

The Buddhist Society
58 Eccleston Square, SW1 (071 834 5858). Victoria underground. **Open** 2-6pm Mon-Fri; 2-5pm Sat.
The aim of the society is to make known the three schools of Buddhism; Theravada, Tibetan and Zen. Meditations, lectures and discussions are held here and the society has a large reference and lending library.

London Buddhist Centre
51 Roman Road, E2 (081 981 1225). Bethnal Green underground. **Open** 10.15am-5pm Mon-Wed; 11am-5pm Thur; 10.15am-5pm Fri.
This East End meditation and Buddhist teaching centre has introductory classes (£3 or £2 concessions) in meditation on Wednesday evenings at 7pm. There are free introductory classes on Tuesday, Wednesday and Thursday at 1pm.

CATHOLIC

Brompton Oratory
*Brompton Road, SW7 (071 589 4811
enquiries). South Kensington underground.*
Open 6.30am-8pm daily. **Services** 7am,
7.30am, 8am, 10am, 12.30am, 6pm Mon-Fri;
7am, 7.30am, 8am, 10am, 6pm Sat; 7am,
8am, 9am, 10am, 11am (sung Latin),
12.30pm, 4.30pm, 7pm Sun.
One of the best known Catholic churches in
London. Built in Baroque style, it was completed in 1884.

Church of Our Lady of Victories
*235A Kensington High Street, W8 (071 937
4778). High Street Kensington underground.*
Open *Apr-Oct* 7am-6pm daily; *Nov-Sept*
7am-7pm. **Services** 10am, 12.30pm, 6pm
Mon-Fri; 10am, 12.30pm, 6.30pm Sat;
8.30am, 10am, 11.15am High mass (in
Latin), 12.30pm, 6.30pm, benediction &
prayer 5pm Sun.
A modern, Gothic-style church designed by
Adrian Gilbert Scott, with a good choir.

Church of the Immaculate Conception
*Farm Street, W1 (071 493 7811). Bond
Street or Green Park underground.* **Open**
7am-7pm. daily. **Services** 7.30am, 8.30am,
12.05pm, 1.05pm, 6pm Mon-Fri; 6pm Sat;
7.30am, 8.30am, 10am, 11am (sung in Latin),
12.15pm, 4.15pm, 6.15pm Sun.
Catholic church run by the Jesuits.

St Mary's Church
*Cadogan Street, SW3 (071 589 5487).
Sloane Square underground.* **Open** 7.30am-
7.30pm Mon-Fri; 9am-7.30pm Sat; 8am-
1.30pm, 5.30-7.30pm Sun. **Services** 8am,
4.15pm, 6.30pm Mon-Fri; 10am, 6.30pm
Sat; 8.30am, 10am, 11am (sung mass),
12.15pm, 6.30pm Sun.
Founded in 1792, this central London
church serves the residents of Belgravia
and Chelsea.

Westminster Cathedral
*Victoria Street, SW1 (071 834 7452).
Victoria underground.* **Open** 7am-8pm daily.
Services Seven daily masses Mon-Sat; 7am,
8am, 9am, 10.30am, noon, 5.30pm, 7pm Sun.
The headquarters of the English Catholic
church.

CHRISTIAN SCIENTIST

Christian Science Committee on Publication
*108 Palace Gardens Terrace, W8 (071 221
5650). Notting Hill Gate underground.* **Open**
9am-5.30pm Mon-Fri.
The committee has details of churches
in London.

Eleventh Church of Christ Scientist
*1 Nutford Place, W1 (071 723 4572).
Marble Arch underground.* **Open** for ser-
vices only. **Services** 11am, 7pm Sun.
Testimony meetings 7pm Wed. Public
Reading Room *80 Baker Street, W1 (071
486 0759). Baker Street underground.* **Open**
9.30am-7.30pm Mon-Sat, 9.30am-6.30pm
Wed, 2.30pm-6.30pm Sun.
One of the largest of London's Christian
Science churches.

CHURCH OF ENGLAND

Paul's Cathedral
EC4 (071 248 2705). St Paul's underground.
Open Doors open 7.30am-6pm daily.
Services 8am, 12.30pm (not Friday), 5pm
(evensong) Mon-Fri; 8am, 10am (choral),
12.30pm, 5pm (choral) Sat; 8am, 10.30am
(choral), 11.30am (choral), 3.15pm (evensong) Sun. Times vary because of special
events, phone first to check.
Enjoy the spectacularly beautiful organ
recitals at Sir Christopher Wren's magnificent Cathedral at 12.30pm on Fridays (none
in Aug; at 6pm Thur in Oct). Evensong is
one of the best in the capital.

Westminster Abbey
*Dean's Yard, SW1 (071 222 5152). St
James's Park or Westminster underground.*
Open *Royal Chapels* 9am-4.45pm Mon, Tue,
Thur, Fri; 9am-7.45pm Wed; 9am-2.40pm,
3.45-5.45pm Sat. *Chapter House, Pyx
Chamber, Abbey Museum* 10am-4pm daily.
Brass Rubbing Centre (071 222 2085) 9am-
5pm Mon-Sat. **Admission** *Royal Chapels* £2
adults; 50p under-16s; £1 students, OAPs.
No Credit Cards. Services 8am, 10am,
11.15am, 3pm (evensong), 5.45pm (organ
recital), 6.30pm Sun.
The great medieval abbey is a wonderful
place to attend a service.

DANISH CHURCH

Danish Church
*5 St Katherine's Precinct, Regent's Park, NW1
(071 935 7584). Camden Town or Great
Portland Street underground/C2 Hoppa bus.*
Open 6.30am-10.30pm Tue-Fri; 10am-
10.30pm Sun. **Service** 11am Sun.
All the services are in Danish. The Church
was completed in 1827 by Ambrose Pointer,
one of John Nash's pupils.

EVANGELICAL

Evangelical Alliance
*Whitefield House, 186 Kennington Park Road,
SE11 (071 582 0228). Kennington under-
ground.* **Open** 9am-5pm Mon-Fri.
The organization will put you in touch with
your nearest Evangelical church.

All Souls Church
*Langham Place, 2 All Souls Place, London
W1. (071 580 4357/071 580 6029). Oxford
Circus underground.* **Open** 9am-8pm Mon-
Fri; 9am-9pm Sun. **Services** 9.30am Holy
Communion, 11am, 6.30pm Sun.
Designed by John Nash as part of his
Regent Street plan, the bizarre curved por-
tico turns an awkward corner in his grand
design. All Souls has an international reputa-
tion for its preaching and worship.

JEWISH

Liberal Jewish Synagogue
*152 Loudoun Road, NW8 (071 722 8872).
Swiss Cottage underground.* **Open** enquiries
9am-5pm Mon-Thur; 9am-4.30pm Fri.
Services 8pm Fri; 11am Sat.
The synagogue has a full range of social,
educational and youth programmes. Visitors
are welcome.

United Synagogue
*(Executive Offices) Woburn House,
Tavistock Square, WC1 (071 387 4300).*

Euston Square underground. **Open**
Summer 9am-5.30pm Mon-Thur; 9.30am-
4.30pm Fri; *Winter* 9am-5.30pm Mon-Thur;
9.30am-1.30pm Fri.
The offices will give you information about
orthodox synagogues and facilities. Inside
you'll find the treasure trove of the **Jewish
Museum** (*see chapter* **Museums**).

West Central Liberal Synagogue
*109 Whitfield Street, SW1 (071 636 7627).
Warren Street underground.* **Open** 10am-5pm
Mon-Thur; 10am-2pm Fri; 3pm Sat service.
The Union of Liberal and Progressive
Synagogues *(071 580 1663)* has offices
beside the synagogue.

METHODIST

Central Church of World Methodism
*Westminster Central Hall, Storeys Gate, SW1
(071 222 8010). St James's Park under-
ground.* **Open** *Chapel* 9am-5pm Mon-Fri.
Services 11am, 6.30pm Sun.
The foundation stone of the Chapel was laid
by John Wesley (*see chapters* **Museums** and
Georgian London) in 1777.

MORMONS

Church of Jesus Christ of Latter-day Saints
*64-68 Exhibition Road, SW7 (071 584
8868). South Kensington underground.* **Open**
Visitors' Centre & Church 9am-9pm daily.
Services 11.50am, 4.50pm Sun.
There's a Visitors' Centre attached to the
church which provides information on The
Church of Jesus Christ of Latter-day Saints.
There's also a *Family History Research
Library* where you can trace your family
records. Non-members are welcome. **Open**
9am-9pm Mon-Fri; 9am-3pm Sat.

MOSLEM

London Central Mosque
*146 Park Road, NW8 (071 724 3363).
Baker Street underground/74 bus.* **Open**
5.30am-8pm daily. **Services** 5.30am,
12.50pm, 3.40pm, 6.10pm, 7.50pm (times
vary by a few minutes every day, so
phone to confirm).

East London Mosque
*84-98 Whitechapel Road, E1 (071 247
1357). Aldgate East or Whitechapel underground.* **Open** 9am-9pm daily. **Service**
Friday prayer 1.25pm.
This modern mosque is one of the biggest in
the capital. More than 3,000 people turn up
for Friday prayer.

PENTECOSTAL

Assemblies of God, Pentecostal Church
*141 Harrow Road, W2 (071 286 9261).
Edgware Road underground.* **Open** for services only. **Services** prayer meetings and
bible study 7.30pm Wed; Young People's
Service 6pm Sat; 11am, 6.30pm Sun.
Formerly a pub, in 1935 this small mission
hall became one of the first Pentecostal
churches to open in West London.

Batman or Babette's Feast? Brighton Rock or Rambo 3? It'll put you in the picture.

THE Time Out FILM GUIDE

The definitive, up-to-the-minute A-Z directory of 9,000 films.

9,000 films reviewed and assessed in the definitive new film directory.

Over 750 pages

PRESBYTERIAN CHURCH OF SCOTLAND

St Columba's Church of Scotland
Pont Street, SW1 (071 584 2321).
Knightsbridge or Sloane Square underground.
Open 9am-5pm Mon-Fri; 9am-10pm Sun.
Services 11am, 6.30pm Sun.

Crown Court Church of Scotland
Russell Street, WC2 (071 836 5643). Covent Garden underground. **Open** to visitors 11.30am-2.30pm Tue-Thur. **Services** 1-1.30pm Thur; 11.15am, 6.30pm Sun.
There has been a church on this site since 1718. The present building is simple and very beautiful, built around 1909.

QUAKERS

Religious Society of Friends (Quakers)
Friends House, Euston Road, NW1 (071 387 3601). Euston underground/BR. **Open** 9am-5pm Mon-Fri. **Service** Meeting 11am Sun.
This is the London Headquarters of the Religious Society of Friends.
Bookshop.

SALVATION ARMY

Salvation Army
PO Box 249, 101 Queen Victoria Street, EC4 (071 236 5222). Blackfriars underground/BR.
Open 8.45am-4.30pm Mon-Fri.
The International HQ of the Salvation Army deals with more than 90 countries around the world. It provides information on Christian churches and Salvation Army Citadels in London.

Regent Hall Corps of the Salvation Army
275 Oxford Street, W1 (071 629 5424). Oxford Circus underground. **Open** Advice Bureau 10am-3pm Tue-Fri. **Services** 11am, 3pm (musical with choir & bands), 6.30pm Sun.

SWEDISH CHURCH

Swedish Church
6 Harcourt Street, W1 (071 723 5681). Edgware Road underground. **Open** *Office* 10am-1pm, 2-4pm Mon-Fri; *Reading room* 10am-9pm Mon-Fri. **Services** 8pm Wed; 11am Sun.
All services are in Swedish.

SWISS CHURCH

Swiss Church
79 Endell Street, WC2 (081 340 9740). Covent Garden or Tottenham Court Road underground. **Open** for services only.
Services 10.30am or 11am Sun.
The 225-year-old protestant church for the Swiss community holds three services each month (except August) in German, French and English.

UNITARIAN CHURCH

Essex Unitarian Church
112 Palace Gardens Terrace, W8 (071 221 6514).Notting Hill Gate underground. **Open** for services and on request. **Services** 7.30pm Wed; 11am Sun.

The Unitarian church is a liberal religious group welcoming people from different backgrounds. This modern church is the descendant of the founding congregation which started in 1774 at Essex Street, WC2.

Rosslyn Hill Unitarian Church
Rosslyn Hill, NW3 (071 435 3506). Hampstead underground. **Open** for services only. **Service** 11am Sun.
Toilets for the disabled. Wheelchair access.

UNITED REFORMED CHURCH

United Reformed Church
Central office, 86 Tavistock Place, WC1 (071 837 7661). Russell Square underground or King's Cross underground/BR. **Open** 9am-5pm Mon-Fri.
All English Presbyterian and most Congregational churches amalgamated in 1972 to form the United Reformed Church. This is the national office.

The City Temple
Holborn Viaduct, EC1 (071 583 5532). Chancery Lane or St Paul's underground. **Open** 7am-5pm Mon-Fri. Services 1.15pm Thur; 11am, 6.30pm (music group) Sun.

EMBASSIES

Embassies, consulates and High Commissions are listed in the telephone directory under their respective countries and in Yellow Pages under 'Embassies'. You can also dial directory enquiries on 142 and ask for the telephone number of your embassy or consulate. Most close on British public holidays and those of their own countries.

American Embassy
24 Grosvenor Square, W1 (071 499 9000/071 499 7010 Visa enquiries). Bond Street or Marble Arch underground. **Open** 9am-6pm Mon-Fri; *Visa section* 8.30am-noon Mon-Fri; *US citizens services* 8.30am-noon, 2-4pm, Mon-Fri. Seven-day, 24-hour phone line for emergency help.

Argentine Consulate
111 Cadogan Gardens, SW3 (071 730 4388/visa information 071 730 7173). Sloane Square underground. **Open** 10am-3pm Mon-Fri; *Visa section* 10am-1pm Mon-Fri.

Australian High Commission
Australia House, The Strand, WC2 (071 379 4334/visa information 071 836 3500). Temple underground or Charing Cross underground/BR. **Open** 10am-4pm Mon-Fri; *Visa section* 9am-1pm, 4-5pm, Mon-Fri.

Belgian Embassy
103 Eaton Square, SW1 (071 235 5422). Sloane Square or Victoria underground/BR. **Open** 9.30am-12.30pm, 2.30-4.30pm, Mon-Fri; *Visa section* 8.30am-noon Mon-Fri.

Brazilian Embassy
32 Green Street, W1 (071 499 0877). Marble Arch underground. **Open** 10am-1pm, 3-6pm, Mon-Fri. **Consulate** *Visa section 6 St Albans Street, SW1 (071 930 9055). Piccadilly Circus underground.* **Open** 10am-4pm Mon-Fri.

Canadian High Commission
Haut Commissariat du Canada, Macdonald House, 1 Grosvenor Square, W1 (071 629 9492 24-hour). Bond Street underground. **Open** 9am-5pm Mon-Fri.

Chilean Embassy & Consulate
12 Devonshire Street, W1 (071 580 6392/visa information 071 580 1023). Regent's Park or Great Portland Street underground. **Open** 9am-5.30pm Mon-Fri; *Visa section* 9.30am-12.30pm Mon-Tue, Thur-Fri.

Chinese Embassy
49-61 Portland Place, W1 (071 636 5197). Regent's Park or Oxford Circus underground. **Open** 9am-noon, 2-5pm, Mon-Fri. *Visa section 31 Portland Place, W1 (071 636 1835). Regent's Park or Oxford Circus underground.* **Open** 9am-noon Mon-Fri.

Colombian Embassy
3 Hans Crescent, SW1 (071 589 9177). Knightsbridge underground. **Open** 10am-5pm Mon-Fri. **Consulate** *Visa section Suite No 10, 140 Park Lane, W1 (071 493 4565). Marble Arch underground.* **Open** 24 hours daily. **Open** 10am-3pm Mon-Fri.

Danish Embassy
65 Sloane Street, SW1 (071 235 1255/visa information 071 235 5076). Sloane Square or Knightsbridge underground. **Open** 9.15am-5pm Mon-Thur; 9.15am-4pm Fri; *Visa section* 10am-1pm Mon-Fri.

French Embassy
58 Knightsbridge, SW1 (071 235 8080). Knightsbridge underground. **Open** 9.30am-1pm, 2.30-6pm Mon-Fri. **Consulate General** *21 Cromwell Road, SW7 (071 581 5292). South Kensington underground.* **Open** 9am-12.30pm Mon-Fri, 9am-4pm Wed. *Visa section 6A Cromwell Place, SW7 (071 823 9555).* **Open** 9-11.30am Mon-Fri; collection of visas 3.30-4.30pm Mon-Fri.

German Embassy
23 Belgrave Square, SW1 (071 235 5033). Hyde Park Corner or Knightsbridge underground. **Open** 9am-5pm Mon-Fri; *Visa section* 9am-noon.

Ghana High Commission
13 Belgrave Square, SW1 (071 235 4142). Hyde Park Corner or Knightsbridge underground. **Open** 9.30am-1pm, 2-5.30pm, Mon-Fri. *Visa section 38 Queens Gate, SW7 (071 584 6311). Gloucester Road underground.* **Open** 9.30am-1pm, 2-5.30pm Mon-Fri.

Greek Embassy & Consulate
1A Holland Park, W11 (071 727 8040). Holland Park underground. **Open** *embassy* 9am-4pm Mon-Fri; *consulate visa section* 9am-1.30pm Mon-Fri.

High Commission of India
India House, Aldwych, WC2 (071 836 8484). Holborn or Charing Cross underground/BR. **Open** 9.30am-5.45pm Mon-Fri.

Irish Embassy
17 Grosvenor Place, SW1 (071 235 2171/passports 071 245 9033). Hyde Park Corner underground. **Open** *9.30am-5pm Mon-Fri.*

Italian Embassy
14 Three Kings Yard, W1 (071 629 8200). Bond Street underground. **Open** *9.30am-1pm, 2.30-5.30pm Mon-Fri.* **Consulate** *Visa section 38 Eaton Place, SW1 (071 235 9371). Sloane Square underground.* **Open** *9am-noon Mon-Fri.*

Jamaican High Commission
1-2 Prince Consort Road, SW7 (071 823 9911). South Kensington underground. **Open** *9.30am-5.30pm Mon-Fri; Visa section 10am-3.30pm Mon-Fri.*

Japanese Embassy
101-4 Piccadilly, W1 (081 465 6500). Piccadilly Circus underground. **Open** *9.30am-12.30pm, 2.30-4.30pm Mon-Fri.*

Kenyan High Commission
45 Portland Place, W1 (071 636 2371/071 636 2375). Great Portland Street, Bond Street or Regent's Park underground. **Open** *9am-5pm Mon-Fri; Visa section 9.30am-12.30pm, 2-3.30pm Mon-Fri.*

Luxembourg Embassy
27 Wilton Crescent, SW1 (071 235 6961). Hyde Park Corner underground. **Open** *10.30am-12.30pm, 2.30-4.30pm; Visa section 10am-noon Mon-Fri.*

The Royal Netherlands Embassy
38 Hyde Park Gate, SW7 (071 584 5040, 24 hours). Gloucester Road or High Street Kensington underground. **Open** *9am-5.30pm Mon-Fri; Visa section 10am-1.30pm Mon-Fri.*

New Zealand High Commission
New Zealand House, 80 Haymarket, SW1 (071 930 8422). Piccadilly Circus underground. **Open** *9am-5pm Mon-Fri; Visa section 9.30am-4pm Mon-Fri.*

Nigeria High Commission
Nigeria House, 9 Northumberland Avenue, WC2 (071 839 1244). Embankment or Charing Cross underground/BR. **Open** *9am-5pm Mon-Fri.* **Visa section** *56-57 Fleet Street, EC4 (071 353 3776). Blackfriars, Chancery Lane underground or Temple underground.* **Open** *9.30am-1pm Mon-Fri.*

Pakistan Embassy
34-35 Lowndes Square, SW1 (071 235 2044). Knightsbridge underground. **Open** *9.30am-5.30pm Mon-Fri; Visa section 10am-1pm Mon-Fri.*

Portugese Embassy
11 Belgrave Square, SW1 (071 235 5331). Hyde Park Corner underground. **Open** *10am-1pm, 3-6pm, Mon-Fri.* **Consulate** *Silver City House, 62 Brompton Road, SW3 (071 581 8722/071 581 8723/071 581 8724). Knightsbridge underground.* **Open** *9am-1.30pm Mon-Fri.*

Royal Embassy & Consulate of Saudi Arabia
30 Belgrave Square, SW1 (071 235 0831/visa information 071 235 0303). Hyde Park Corner underground. **Open** *9am-3pm Mon-Fri; Visa section 9am-12.30pm Mon-Fri.*

Soviet Embassy
13 Kensington Palace Gardens, W8 (071 229 3628 24-hours). High Street Kensington or Notting Hill Gate underground. **Open** *9am-6pm Mon-Fri.* **Consulate** *5 Kensington Palace Gardens, W8 (071 229 3215/071 229 8027). High Street Kensington or Notting Hill Gate underground.* **Open** *10am-12.30pm, 2-6pm, Mon-Fri.*

Spanish Embassy
24 Belgrave Square, SW1 (071 235 5555). Knightsbridge underground. **Open** *9.30am-1pm, 2.30-5pm, Mon-Fri.* **Consulate** *Visa section, 20 Draycott Place, SW3 (071 581 5921). Sloane Square underground.* **Open** *9.30am-noon Mon-Fri; Spanish nationals only 9.30am-2.30pm Mon-Fri, 10am-noon Sat.*

Swedish Embassy
11 Montagu Place, W1 (071 724 2101/visa information 071 724 678, 2-4pm). Baker Street underground. **Open** *8.30am-5pm Mon-Fri; Visa section 9am-12.30pm.*

Turkish Embassy
43 Belgrave Square, SW1 (071 235 5252). Hyde Park Corner underground. **Open** *9.30am-1pm, 2.30-6pm, Mon-Fri.* **Consulate General** *Visa section Rutland Lodge, Rutland Gardens, SW7 (071 589 0360/071 589 0949). Knightsbridge underground.* **Open** *Visa section 9.30am-noon Mon-Fri; business 2.30-4pm Mon-Fri.*

Uganda High Commission
58-59 Trafalgar Square, WC2 (071 839 5783). Charing Cross underground/BR. **Open** *9.30am-5.30pm Mon-Fri.*

Zambian High Commission
2 Palace Gate, W8 (071 589 6655). Gloucester Road or High Street Kensington underground. **Open** *9.30am-5pm Mon-Fri.*

Zimbabwe High Commission
429 The Strand, WC2 (071 836 7755). Charing Cross underground/BR. **Open** *9am-1pm, 2-5pm, Mon-Fri.*

The American Embassy *(listed under* **Embassies***) in Grosvenor Square will provide you with all the necessary documentation, even the elusive Green Card, for a visit to the land of milk and money. There's a 24-hour emergency phone line if you get a sudden urge to seek asylum.*

CLASSIFIED ADS

1	**Accommodation**	**4**	**Museums/Art Galleries**	**7**	**Therapy/Growth**
2	**Car Hire**	**5**	**Food and Drink**	**8**	**Shopping**
3	**Motorcycle Hire**	**6**	**Entertainment**	**9**	**Tours**

1 ACCOMMODATION

FREE LETTING
Services to tenants, flats, houses.
DEREK COLLINS LTD
Panton House,
25 Haymarket,
London SW1
Tel: 930 7986

NO FEES TO TENANTS
JENNY JONES AGENCY
40 South Molton St
London W1
Tel: 493 4801

A1 ACCOMMODATION
Budget hotel in Central London near Earls Court Station

Clean, smart rooms, some with own bathroom, friendly relaxed atmosphere. From £11 per night including Breakfast.
Telephone: 370 3991

LUXURY SERVICED APARTMENTS

Spacious, newly refurbished, tastefully decorated. Fully furnished + equipped — lift, colour TV, intercom telephone and maid service. Conveniently situated near shops, restaurants, Portobello Antique Market, Marble Arch and parks.
22 Pembridge Crescent, London W11 3DS.
Tel: 01-221 5759
Fax: 01-961 9386

CENTRAL HOTEL
Hoop Lane,
Golders Green, NW1
Easy access to West End and M1.
Modern family hotel with private bathrooms, central heating, refreshments, parking and TV.
Tel: 01-458 5636
Fax: 01-455 4792

ELIZABETH HOTEL
37 Eccleston Square,
VICTORIA
London SW1V 1PB
Telephone 01-828 6812
Intimate, friendly, private hotel in ideal, central, quiet location overlooking lovely gardens of stately residential square. Comfortable single/double/twin/family rooms. Good ENGLISH BREAKFAST. MODERATE PRICES. *Free Colour Brochure.*

Camelot Hotel

'Affordable English Elegance'
(Just right for Mater and Pater)
Please do call us for information and brochure.

 Tel: 01-723 9118 or 01-262 1980 (Telex 268312)
45-47 Norfolk Square, London W2 1RX
(near Hyde Park and Oxford Street)

 I offer high quality Bed and Breakfast in beautifully renovated detached Victorian home. Spacious rooms, central heating, double glazed TV lounge, tea/coffee making facilities. Full English breakfast. Showers. Children welcome, sorry no pets. 3 mins from tube, easy access A4, M4, M40, Central London museums, theatres, Tower of London, Heathrow Airport, Hampton Court, Kew Gardens, Windsor and River Thameside walks.
Minimum stay two nights.
Reservations accepted by telephone or post.
Mrs J. A. Clements, 17 Madeley Road, London W5 2LA
01-998 5222. Telex: 933859. Fax: 01-994 9144

WINDSOR
House Hotel
12 Penywern Rd, Earls Court, SW5
01-373 9087

BEST VALUE HOTEL

Doubles from £17 per person
Singles from £24 per person
Groups £15 per person

★ Comfortable, clean ★ Colour TV
& community kitchen ★ Constant
hot water ★ Near Earls Court
underground ★

Recommended by English Tourist Board.

CENTRAL LONDON HOLIDAY APARTMENTS
English Tourist Board Approved
Self-contained apartments in various locations.
Details: 43 Whistlers Avenue,
London SW11 3TS.
Tel: 01-228 7158

TRAVELWISE RENT-A-CAR

Daily, weekly and monthly you would be hard pressed to find a better buy. The more you judge choice, reliability, turnout and helpfulness, the better Travelwise looks.

Unlimited mileage over one day. 100's of cars, most makes, estates, automatics and vans.

Also special all inclusive weekend rates.

City and West End Office, Vauxhall: 01-582 1769
South Lambeth Place, SW8. (next door to tube, Victoria Line & BR)

TRAVELWISE CHAUFFEUR

Prestigious Mercedes, Jaguars and Limousines driven by professional chauffeurs. All vehicles with telephones and air-conditioning.

01-582 1822 (24 hours)

3 MOTORCYCLE HIRE

The finest way to see the UK. Enjoy independence and freedom on two wheels, city mopeds to motorway tourers. An exciting range of new Hondas available from 50-1000cc.
Economical inclusive prices.
● Unlimited mileage ● Insurance
● AA cover ● Helmets ●
Luggage carriers ● and more ●
Foreign licences welcome.

**SCOOTABOUT
MOTORCYCLE CENTRE**

**59 Albert Embankment,
London SE1 7TP
Telephone 01-582 0055**

4 MUSEUMS/ART GALLERIES

**Grange Museum of
Community History**
(On the Neasden Roundabout)
**Neasden Lane, NW10 1QB
Telephone 01-908 7432**
Bizarrely located on a traffic roundabout in a picturesque eighteenth-century house. Brent's Grange Museum presents a lively programme of art, craft and history exhibitions, period room settings and permanent displays. Recently opened new conservatory cafe and refurbished museum shop.

**Why Not Visit
THE GEFFRYE MUSEUM
Kingsland Rd, E2**
*'One of London's most delightful
small museums — not to be missed'*
— The Times 1987
Tues-Sat, 10-5. Sun 2-5. Admission Free.
Tubes: Old St, Liverpool St. Buses: 22B, 48, 67, 149 & 243.

SPAIN & HISPANIC STUDIES

Old books, maps and prints.
Paul Orssich, 117 Munster Rd, London SW6 6DH.
Telephone 736 3869.

THE DICKENS HOUSE MUSEUM
48 Doughty St, WC1. 405 2127
Where Charles Dickens worked on *Pickwick Papers, Oliver Twist* and *Nicholas Nickleby*. 1000 to 1700, Monday to Saturday. Adults £1.50, Students £1.00, Children under sixteen 75p, Families £3.00.

ZELLA 9 ART GALLERY

Limited edition prints and watercolours. Largest and nicest selection of excellent coloured etchings, lithographs and screenprints by mainly British artists. Many internationally known names and younger lesser known artists.
£10-£500
seven days a week, 10-9 inc.
**2 Park Walk (off Fulham Rd)
London SW10
Tel: 351 0588**

5 FOOD AND DRINK

**THOMAS WHETHERET PUB
33-39 Rosomar Street,
London EC1
Telephone: 278 9983**
The country pub comes to town. Real ales, good food, fine wines, restaurant, real ale bar. Two comfortable lounges. Open fires. Weddings, birthdays, office parties our speciality

NAZARIO PASTA BAR
(opposite Highgate tube station)
For the best taste in homemade pizza and pasta.
Dining for two — with wine — approx £20.
Large selection of vegetarian dishes.
299 Archway Rd, Highgate N6
Telephone 346 2580

BAEDECKERS RESTAURANT & BAR
**Open Mon-Fri 12-2.45/
6-11.30
Fri-Sat 6-12pm**
International menu with a wide selection of dishes.
Cocktail bar serving the best Bloody Marys with a good selection of wines and beers. The atmosphere is lively, decor stylish, and don't forget Sunday brunch 11.30-4pm.
**50 Clapham High Street,
London SW4
Tel: 01-622 0070**

TYCOON CHINESE RESTAURANT
**143 St John's Hill, Battersea
SW11
01-228 3043**
Open Lunch Tue-Sat 12.00-2.30pm
Dinner Mon-Sat 6pm-11.30pm
An elegant restaurant offering excellent variety of dishes from Northern and inland China. Parties welcome. Bookings recommended.

GAYLORD RESTAURANT
The original people of India are offering the true taste of Indian cuisine. Authentic Tandoori and Indian specialities. (The only branch in London of this world famous Indian restaurant)
**79-81 Mortimer St
London W1
Tel: 01-580 3615
or 01-636 0808**

MANNA VEGETARIAN
Established in 1968, Manna is Europe's oldest vegetarian restaurant . Dubbed 'a sophisticate' by TIME OUT, the food is consistently mouth-watering, even to confirmed non-veggies. Open every evening from 6.30 to 12.30, last orders 11pm. Fully licensed.
Chalk Farm tube.
4 Erskine Rd (off Regents Park Rd), London NW3
Telephone 01-722 8028.

MARTIN'S BIJOU
Restaurant-Bar
Cuisine Francaise

3 COURSE MEAL WITH CHOICE — £10.50
also a la carte and French wines

TEL: 01-436 9231

38 Bloomsbury Street, London WC1B 3QJ
Fax: 01-436 6341. Telex: 945138

FERNDALES WINE BAR
A small and lively bar with a continental feel, that sells good value food and wines from around the world. Has also some of the best music around!

**118 Ferndale Road
Clapham
London SW4
01-733 9264**

---

6   ENTERTAINMENT

STATION TAVERN
41 Bramley Rd, W10
— opposite Latimer Rd tube —
Home of the blues — Live Blues
Every Night — and it's free —
727 4053

GEORGE & DRAGON
183 High St, Acton, W3
— Traditional Irish Music Fri to
Sun — **992 1932**

*London
Ticket
Bureau*

**THEATRE TICKETS
& SPORTING EVENTS**
Members of
London Tourist Board

Credit Cards Accepted

**Telephone 01-706 2211
Fax: 01-224 8800
Telex: 264 544**

---

8   SHOPPING

**LOON FUNG
SUPERMARKET LTD**

*Direct importers from
the Far East of*

Foods and Wines
Hardware
Craft Goods
Fancy Goods

SUPERMARKET
42/44 Gerrard Street
London W1V 7LP
Tel: 01-437 7332

CRAFT SHOP
31 Gerrard Street
London W1V 7LD
Tel: 01-437 1922

EXCITING GUIDED WALKS
The only way to see London!
Tours include City history, Charles
Dickens, Ghostly Encounters,
Royal Mayfair, Jack the Ripper,
Legal Heritage and Sherlock
Holmes. Also Picturesque
Hampstead Village every Sunday
morning meeting at Hampstead
Underground Station 11.00am.
Each walk takes about 1½ hours
and costs £3.50.

**All enquiries:
S J Harris (Guided Tours),
PO Box 1734,
London NW6 4SF
Telephone: 624 9981**

YORK

PERSONALLY YOURS

GUIDED TOURS

Packages available, can include:
travel, accommodation, museum
visits, shopping, boat trips,
walks . . .

Phone (0904) 412089
for details

---

7   THERAPY/GROWTH

**THE HEALING VOICE
WORKSHOPS**
with
JILL PURCE
Magical voice techniques,
Mongolian and Tibetan overtone
chanting, mantra and sonic
meditations.
Introductory weekends: week
intensives: voice of Shamanism.

**Info: G McGregor, Garden
Flat, 9 Yonge Pk, London N4
3NU. Telephone 607 5819.**

Mysteries

MYSTERIES
LONDON'S PSYCHIC SHOP
AND NEW AGE CENTRE

BOOKS AND MAGAZINES
All Mystical, Spiritual and New
Age Subjects covered.
New section devoted entirely to all
aspects of Alternative Medicine
and Holistic Living.

**EQUIPMENT AND
PARAPHERNALIA**
Pendulums, Healing Crystals,
Tarot, Games, Posters, Ionisers,
Massage Equipment, Jewellery,
Rainbow Crystals, Chimes, Oils,
Incense, Candles, Greetings Cards,
Runes, etc etc . . .

**NEW!!! AUDIO-VISUAL
DEPARTMENT**
The largest selection of NEW AGE
Music Tapes and LPs in Britain.
Also hundreds of subliminal self-
hypnosis and instructional tapes.
CDs and Videos available.

PSYCHIC READINGS
Available every day with
experienced Clairvoyant
Consultants in our new rooms
upstairs. Tarot, Palmistry,
Astrology, Graphology, Crystal
Ball. Counselling etc. Prices are
from £15.

Please send an A4 sized sae + 34p
stamp for new 60-page catalogue.

**MYSTERIES
9/11 Monmouth Street,
Covent Garden,
London WC2 9DA
Tel: 01-836 4679/240 3688
Open Mon-Sat 10am-6pm**

Index

Where multiple entries are not entirely in page number order, the first number given is the principal entry.

Written, edited and designed by Time Out Publications Limited, Curtain House, 134-146 Curtain Road, London EC2A 3AR (071 729 5959/Fax 071 729 7266).

Editorial
Managing Editor Hayden Williams
Associate Editors Peter Fiennes, Paul Murphy
Deputy Series Editor Katja Faber
Assistant Editor Philip Cornwel-Smith
Listings Editor Shane Michael Roe
Production Manager Su Small
Sub-Editors Philip Harriss, Grace Packman
Indexer Nick Rider
Editorial Assistant Joanne Reed
Listings Assistant Edoardo Albert

Design
Art Director Paul Carpenter
Art Editors Ashleigh Vinall, Annie Carpenter
Design Assistants Nancy Flint, Asim Syed, David Pinto
Picture Editor Lynda Marshall

Advertising
Sales Director Mark Phillips
Group Advertising Director Lesley Gill
Advertising Sales Nana Ocran, Clare Snow, Nigel Tradewell
Advertising Assistant Philip Haworth
Advertising Make-up Graham Keen

Administration
Publisher Tony Elliott
Managing Director Adele Carmichael
Financial Director Kevin Ellis
Company Accountant Suzanne Doyle

Cover Illustration Lo Cole

Features in this Guide were researched and written by:**Sightseeing** Philip Cornwel-Smith, Myra Hope Bobbitt. **London by Season** Philip Cornwel-Smith, Joanne Reed, Ruman Chaudhury, Stephanie Hannerley, Albert Harwood, Simon Key. **Essential Information** Julie Emery. **Travel** Julie Emery. **Accommodation** John Bell, Peter Fiennes, Grant Palmer. **The West End** Sue Moore. **The City** Katja Faber. **The River & Docklands** Philip Cornwel-Smith, David Eimer, Katja Faber, Conor McCutcheon, Troy. **Ethnic London** Edoardo Albert, Ian Crawshaw, Steafan Hannigan, Simon Key, Mewe Olugbo, Kam Patel, Simmy Richman. **Roman & Saxon London** Conor McCutcheon. **The Middle Ages** Joanne Reed. **Tudors & Stuarts** Yossie Brain. **Georgian London** Rick Jones. **Victorian Times** James Christopher. **Early Twentieth Century** Philip Cornwel-Smith. **The World Wars** Philip Cornwel-Smith. **To The Eighties** Philip Cornwel-Smith. **Eating & Drinking** Laurence Earle, Paul Lyons. **Shopping & Services** Natalia Marshall, Dee Nkagbu. **Art Galleries** Heather Waddell. **Museums** Philip Cornwel-Smith, Conor McCutcheon. **Children's London** Sarah McAlister. **New Comedy** Malcolm Hay. **Dance** Allen Robertson. **Film** Joanna Berry. **Lesbian & Gay** Michael Griffiths. **Media: Press** Hayden Williams; **Radio** Sid Smith; **TV** Alkarim Jivani. **Music: Classical & Opera** Martin Hoyle. **Music: Rock, Folk & Jazz** Isabel Appio. **Nightlife** David Swindells. **Late-Night London** Troy. **Sport & Fitness** Katja Faber. **Theatre** Jane Edwardes, Helen Rose. **Trips Out of Town** Grace Packman, Stephanie Hannerly, Grant Palmer. **Business** Julie Emery. **Survival** Steafan Hannigan, Conor McCutcheon.

The Editors would like to thank the following

Key to Bus Route Map

How to use this map Route numbers are shown in circles at places where routes cross. Locate where you are going and follow the route circles back towards your starting point. This will show if and where you need to change and the route number(s) for your journey.

KEY

⊖ Underground station
🛈 Travel Information Centre
⇄ British Rail Station
🚌 Bus routes

Departure point for the Original
London Transport Sightseeing Tour
One way only
Docklands Light Railway
© London Buses Ltd.

people and organizations for help and information:
The London Tourist Board (with special thanks to Gerald Parsons); Stuart Barnard and London Buses Ltd; Paul Castle and London Underground Ltd; Chris Tigg and FWT Cartography; Harry Boggis-Rolfe.

Picture credits:Allsport pages 228, 232; **David Crosswaite** page 236; **The Entertainment Group** page 191; **Geoff Franklin/Network** page 185; **Michael le Poer French** page 234; **Charles Friend** page 63; **Kim Furrokh** pages 10, 15, 17, 19, 21, 22, 24, 26, 41, 42, 44, 45, 49, 50, 51, 59, 60, 64, 65, 70, 73, 75, 76, 84, 86, 90, 91, 95, 96, 101, 106, 109, 110, 111, 112, 113, 117, 122, 125, 131, 138, 147, 149, 150, 153, 154, 155, 156, 171, 175, 179, 188, 195, 198, 201, 224, 227, 230, 239, 244, 245, 246, 253, 262; **S Galloway** page 243; **Richard Gillard** pages 92, 104, 132, 157, 158; **Susan Griggs** pages ,5, 13, 20, 46, 47, 48, 52, 53, 55, 56, 61, 63, 66, 68, 72, 87, 99, 102, 181, 204, 242, 245, 247, 248, 250, 251, 272; **Madelaine Harmsworth** page 93; **Beverley Harper** pages 10, 15, 17, 19, 21, 22, 24, 26, 41, 42, 44, 45, 49, 50, 51, 59, 60, 64, 65, 70, 73, 75, 76, 89, 98, 109, 110,

111, 112, 150, 171, 175, 179,188, 195, 198, 201, 224, 227, 230, 239, 244, 245, 246, 253, 262; **Julian Haynes** pages 12, 67, 82, 85; **London Photographic Library** (*see also* **Richard Gillard** *above*) pagesv, 3, 5, 7, 16, 92, 104, 132, 157, 206, 221; **John Marmaris/Susan Griggs** page 54; **Anthony Marsland** pages 29, 43, 77, 115, 121, 123, 126, 129, 130, 133, 135, 137, 139, 141, 142, 143, 145, 146, 148, 186, 205, 222, 226, 229, 231, 258; **Robert McFarlane/Susan Griggs** pages 52, 66; **David Morley** page 169; **Alistair Muir** page 235; **Museum of London** page 79; **Julien Nieman/Susan Griggs** pages 13, 102, 272; **Photo-Reportage** page 177; **Prudence Cunning Association** page 165; **Raob Gallery** page 163; **Miriam Reik** page 127; **Benjamin Rhodes Gallery** page 162; **RSC** page 238; **Savoy Press Office** page 118; **Leon Schadberg/Susan Griggs** page 99; **Science Museum** page 184; **Juliet Sensicle** page 197; **South Bank Centre** page 108; **Steve Stephens** page 240; **Nicola Suton** page 199; **Dave Swindells** page 217; **Heather Waddell** pages 159, 161; **Woodmansterne** page 81; **Adam Woolfit/Susan Griggs** pages 4, 20, 48, 55, 56, 61, 68, 72, 87, 97, 181, 204, 242, 247, 248.

Key to Street Map

Places of Entertainment
Places marked with * and the same number are too close to be separated.

1. Adelphi Theatre
2. Albery Theatre
3. Aldwych Theatre
4. Ambassadors Theatre
5. Apollo Theatre
6. Arts Theatre
7. *Astoria
8. Bill Stickers
9. Boulevard Theatre
7. *Busby's
10. Café de Paris
11. Café Theatre Upstairs
12. Cambridge Theatre
13. Cannon Haymarket Cinema
14. Cannon Oxford Street Cinema
15. Cannon Panton Street Cinema
16. Cannon Piccadilly Cinema
17. Cannon Shaftesbury Avenue Cinema
18. Cannon Tottenham Court Road Cinema
19. London Coliseum
20. Comedy Store
21. Comedy Theatre
22. Criterion Theatre
23. *Curzon Phoenix Cinema
24. Curzon West End Cinema
25. Dominion Theatre
26. Donmar Warehouse Theatre
27. Drury Lane Theatre Royal
28. Duchess Theatre
29. Duke of York's Theatre
30. *Empire Discotheque
30. *Empire Leicester Square Cinema
31. Fortune Theatre
32. Garrick Theatre
33. Globe Theatre

34. Gossips
35. Haymarket Theatre
36. Heaven
37. Her Majesty's Theatre
38. Hippodrome
39. ICA Cinema, Gallery & Theatre
40. Limelight
41. Lumière Cinema
42. Lyric Theatre Shaftesbury Avenue
43. Marquee
44. Metro Cinema
45. New London Theatre
46. Odeon Haymarket
47. Odeon Leicester Square
48. Odeon West End
49. Palace Theatre
23. *Phoenix Theatre
50. Piccadilly Theatre
51. Players Theatre
52. Playhouse Theatre
53. Plaza Cinema
54. Première Cinema
55. Prince Charles Cinema
56. Prince Edward Theatre
57. Prince of Wales Theatre
58. Queen's Theatre
59. Rock Garden
60. Ronnie Scott's
61. Royalty Theatre
62. St Martin's Theatre
63. Savoy Theatre
64. Shaftesbury Theatre
65. Strand Theatre
66. Stringfellows
67. Vaudeville Theatre
68. Wag Club
69. Warner West End Cinema
70. Whitehall Theatre
71. Wyndhams Theatre

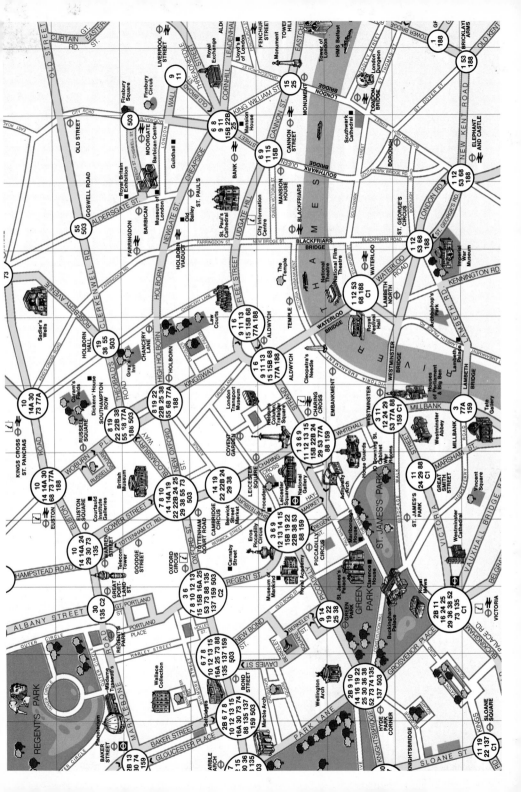

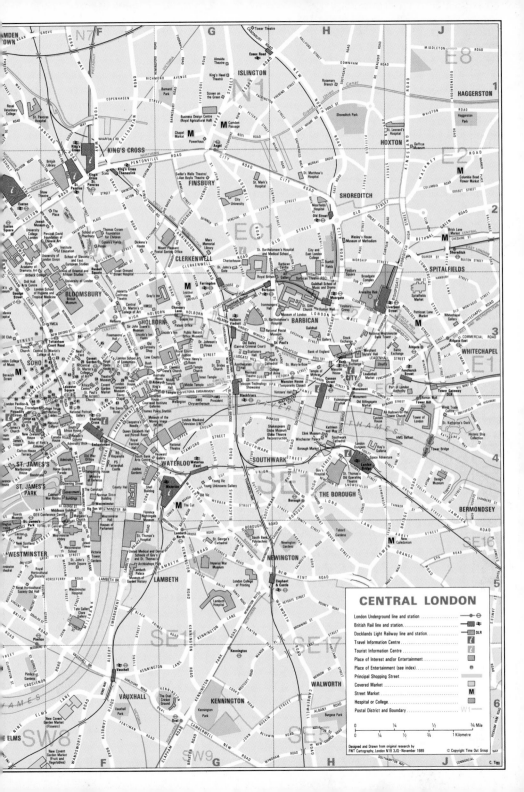

CENTRAL LONDON

London Underground line and station ....
British Rail line and station ....
Docklands Light Railway line and station .... DLR
Travel Information Centre ....
Tourist Information Centre ....
Place of Interest and/or Entertainment ....
Place of Entertainment (see index) ....
Principal Shopping Street ....
Covered Market ....
Street Market .... M
Hospital or College ....
Postal District and Boundary W1

0   ¼   ½   ¾ Mile
|___|___|___|___|___|___|___|___|
0   ¼   ½   ¾   1 Kilometre

Designed and Drawn from original research by
FWT Cartography, London N19 3JG · November 1989
© Copyright Time Out Group

London's Underground

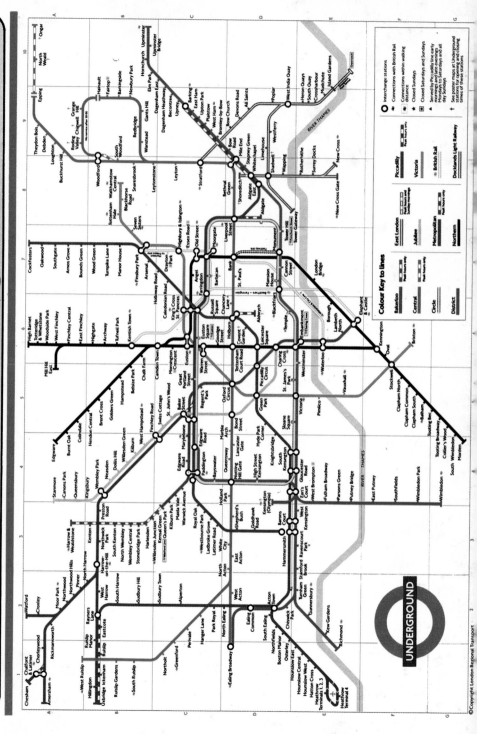

UNDERGROUND

© Copyright London Regional Transport